READINGS IN
THE DEVELOPMENT OF BEHAVIOR

READINGS IN

THE DEVELOPMENT OF BEHAVIOR

VICTOR H. DENENBERG, Editor
Departments of Biobehavioral Science and Psychology
The University of Connecticut

SINAUER ASSOCIATES INC. • PUBLISHERS
STAMFORD, CONNECTICUT

Readings in The Development of Behavior
© 1972 by Sinauer Associates, Inc.
20 Second Street
Stamford, Conn. 06905

Library of Congress Catalog Card No. 78-181-990

ISBN: 0-87893-151-1

PREFACE

As with most other sciences, there are two basic approaches to the understanding of development. One is by observation and, when possible, capitalizing upon observations of "natural experiments." The other is by experimenting with an isolated subject that is exposed to certain stimuli under rigorously controlled conditions. Each method has advantages and shortcomings: naturalistic observation does not allow us to get at cause-effect relationships, and the experimental approach isolates the subject from his natural environment. These two routes to the study of development are complementary to each other, and both are necessary.

From the research literature one would infer that the experimental approach is more common among those working with animals, and the naturalistic approach is more likely among the researchers studying infants and older children. Of course there are exceptions. Quite often those studying animals do not keep up with the human literature, and *vice versa*, but in many cases the results are similar.

The purpose of this book is to present a broader perspective on the development of behavior by uniting within each chapter readings from the literature involving both animals and humans. Each chapter has a common theme, and each paper views that theme from a different perspective, illuminating a basic principle.

I believe that the development of behavior is an exciting research area, and that notable advances will be made in this field within the next decade.

I am also convinced that advances depend on more two-way conversations between the animal researchers and those who work with the human child. We now have sufficient convergence of research findings between animal and human studies to support my conviction, as I hope this book of readings will demonstrate.

Several people helped with this book by suggesting readings, criticising drafts of the various chapters, and arguing with me. They include Robert T. Brown, Benson E. Ginsburg, Evelyn B. Thoman, Sheldon H. White, and Sam L. Witryol.

Victor H. Denenberg

CONTENTS

Chapter One

THE BIOBEHAVIORAL BASES OF DEVELOPMENT

How does the environment influence the behavioral and biological development of a newborn infant? All of us have ideas about this question, though often these ideas are based on incomplete or fragmentary information. Only recently have we obtained sufficient scientific information to give us a clearer picture of what takes place during development. Originally we thought "the environment" performed only a passive role during early life, supporting and nurturing an organism that was genetically pre-programmed to develop, mature, and express itself in a predictable fashion. Now we know that this environment has many dynamic properties that interact with genetic potential to contribute significantly in specifying the ultimate characteristics and capabilities of a developing organism. Some of these environmental forces are so powerful that they influence the individual throughout his lifetime and may also affect his unborn children and grandchildren. Such findings have begun to change our thinking about the manner in which the newborn infant grows and develops.

What are some of these findings? Consider the following examples: a program of environmental enrichment during early development will improve problem-solving and learning performance; an organism will have fewer brain cells if malnourished during prenatal or early postnatal life; mildly stressful stimulation during the neonatal period will cause reduced emotionality in adulthood and better physiological adaptation; sex hormones during critical periods in early life determine whether the organism behaves in a masculine or feminine fashion; the mother's behavior toward her young influences their later aggressive tendencies; social restriction in early development may result in sexual incompetence in adulthood; the pregnant female's experiences during the prenatal period may affect the future emotional behavior of her offspring; genetic resistance to the lethal effects of radiation is influenced by the environment surrounding the genes; the newborn perceives his world in an orderly manner and is capable of low-level information processing within a few hours after birth.

These examples are taken from the readings in this text. Some are from experiments with animals, others from human studies. These readings have been assembled and organized so that one can derive from them broad principles which apply in the general case to animals and humans alike. In order to do this it is necessary to assume continuity between animals and humans for both biological and behavioral factors — this is what is meant by a "biobehavioral" approach to development. Man and other animals are viewed as biological organisms with evolutionary histories and genetic legacies, who are capable of adapting to the many complex facets of their physical and social environments. This viewpoint emphasizes that the relationship between man and other animals is one of continuity through evolution, similarity through common biological and behavioral structures and functions, and distinctiveness through different modes of adaptation and adjustment.

Both similarities and differences between man and animal must be studied to aid in the understanding of man.

It is only proper that we turn to animal research to further our understanding of ourselves, since man is fundamentally a biological organism and has been subjected to many of the same sorts of selection pressures as other organisms during his long evolutionary history. Because man is a product of evolutionary forces, his behavior cannot be understood without some knowledge of the underlying biology which is the base upon which his behavior is built. Comprehension of the dynamics underlying social forces, cultural pressures, and environmental contingencies also requires information concerning the biology of man, since man's reactions to such forces are intimately related to his biological heritage.

In the areas of early development and early experiences, much of our new knowledge has come from research with animals, primarily mammals. In a number of instances supporting or confirming studies have been done with human infants. In many cases the human research has followed from the animal experimentation, although in several notable areas, e.g., learning and perception, research on human subjects has led to experimentation with animals.

Cross-Species Comparisons

How can one make valid generalizations from animal research to the human condition? There are two general approaches to this problem. One is by a series of *comparative studies*; the other, by use of *animal models*. Within each of these two major approaches generalizations may be based upon *common structures* or *common functions*.

Comparative Studies

The researcher who undertakes a comparative study works with different species ordered along a phylogenetic scale, performs the same or similar experiments with each, and compares the results. If he finds the same general phenomenon in all species studied, it is highly likely that the finding may be generalized to man.

The basic assumption here is that if the same phenomenon is obtained at different species levels, the underlying principle probably has survival value in an evolutionary framework and can therefore be expected to be present in other species as well, including the human. Note that it is not necessary to repeat the experiment in man, though obviously this should be done if possible.

A good example of the comparative approach in psychology is in the area of "learning sets" (Harlow, 1949), in which the capability of various species to solve two-choice discrimination problems has been investigated. The general finding has been that the higher the species on the phylogenetic scale, the more rapidly and effectively it forms learning sets. As expected, the human does best of all species on this type of task.

In actual practice, a full-fledged comparative approach involving a large number of species is rarely used because of limitations on the number of organisms which can be maintained in one laboratory and on the amount of time available for research. Thus, instead of a comparative series, researchers often select one or a few species to work with as animal models for their studies.

Animal Models

Animal models have been employed in two ways: (1) as a special case of the more general comparative approach and (2) as a source for generating hypotheses.

A special case of the comparative method. The researcher using this approach studies one, or at most a few, species with the hope that results will generalize to the human. A large number of different animals have been used in this fashion; probably the rat, the mouse, and the nonhuman primate are the most common. The obvious disadvantage of this approach, which is avoided by the comparative study, is the lack of a test of phylogenetic continuity. In a comparative study of several species, it is possible to determine whether the same principle occurs in a variety of animals, thus establishing continuity. When only one species is studied, there is always the likelihood that a principle uncovered is unique to that organism and does not have continuity in phylogeny. By adding one more species to his study, the researcher markedly increases the likelihood that the assumption of continuity holds. This is best done by using a second animal from a different order. For example, finding the same principle in two rodents, the rat and the mouse, allows the researcher to make a broad statement, but he can make a more powerful generalization by showing that the same principle obtains in the rat and the rhesus monkey.

An outstanding example of the use of the animal model as a special case of the comparative study is the recent work in molecular biology, where genetic principles and the nature of the DNA molecule have been worked out with bacteria and viruses and are assumed to apply to all living matter. In fact, comparative studies are not done in genetics, presumably because the principles of genetic inheritance have been so clearly shown to apply at all levels that species comparisons are no longer necessary and the more efficient animal model approach can be used.

A source for generating hypotheses. The use of animal models described above is based on the principle of phylogenetic continuity. Another approach disregards the continuity principle and looks for suggestions from animal findings which may be tested on human populations. In this context an animal model performs the same function for the researcher as does a mathematical model. Given a logically consistent system (whether animal or mathematical model), one can make predictions and test hypotheses. Whether the hypotheses and principles found within these systems apply to the "real world" (in this case the human situation) is a matter for empirical testing. Within the field of psychology the use of the rat in deriving learning principles is probably the best known example of this use of animal models.

In the area of developmental research, an example is the ethological investigation of imprinting in birds, which has been a direct stimulus to studies on attachment behavior in hu-

mans (e.g., Ainsworth and Bell, 1969). The ethologist studying imprinting works with a newly hatched precocial bird that is able to walk effectively shortly after birth (for a review of this field, see Hinde, 1970). This animal model is a far cry from the human infant, who is not precocious at birth, who was born rather than hatched, and who has virtually no locomotor skills until several months after birth. These two species differ too much to be viewed within a comparative framework; yet the research on imprinting suggests the general principle that attachments may be formed very early in life and that such attachments are particularly enduring ones. This general principle can be, and has been, tested in humans.

Whether the researcher uses a comparative series or an animal model approach, the strength of his generalizations is in part determined by the nature of the dependent variable, or endpoint, involved. This endpoint may be based upon common structures or common functions.

Common Structures

The researcher has the strongest basis for generalizing from animal studies to the human situation when he is investigating some structural characteristic common to all species studied. "Structure" here is used in a broad sense to indicate an anatomical, chemical, or physiological similarity. As an example, consider the field of endocrinology and the thyroid gland. This gland is morphologically similar in all animals and is located in the same region of the body. The hormone thyroxine is secreted from this gland in both animal and man and influences metabolic processes and growth in all species studied. Thus, the thyroid gland is anatomically, regionally, chemically, and physiologically similar in all species. Given this strong relationship between the thyroid gland in animals and in man, the researcher can study this gland in an animal and feel confident that the principles derived will enhance understanding of thyroid activity in the human. However, even with this degree of relationship, he should not assume that working with any one animal model will yield maximum information about thyroid activity in the human. Each species has its own unique constellation of behavioral and physiological patterns, as well as patterns that resemble those of other species. By studying several species the investigator will learn more about human thyroid activity than if he studies only one animal model.

In the area of developmental research a good example of common structure is physical growth. Height and weight curves in a variety of species follow the same general form as a function of age, and independent variables which affect physical growth in animals are also likely to affect physical growth in humans. For example, malnutrition stunts the growth of animals and humans alike.

The reason we have high confidence in generalizing from one species to another regarding the results of studying a common structure is that the shared structure is probably *homologous* (i.e., derived through evolution from some remote common ancestor) and therefore controlled in all species by similar underlying biological processes (mechanisms). As an example, protein is necessary for physical growth in all species. Thus, a researcher who can demonstrate structural similarity among species can take as a working hypothesis that the mechanisms uncovered by intensively analyzing one species apply to other species, albeit with appropriate adjustments and modifications caused by species differences.

To summarize, structural comparisons can be made across species levels whenever similarity can be shown among any of a number of physical components including anatomy, chemistry, or physiology. Since we know from evolutionary theory and from previous research that similar mechanisms are highly likely to obtain among species, intensive research with one or a few animal models is often the most efficient way to attack a problem.

Common Functions

Virtually all structures subserve some meaningful biological function (a few — like the appendix — do not appear to have any function). As indicated in the prior section, similarity in structure often implies homology and this

may carry over to the functional level. For example, one function of the gonads is to secrete certain chemicals (hormones) which influence the organization of the brain during development (see Chapter Five) and influence sexual physiology and behavior as well. Here we can trace the chain of events from structure to function, including functional behavior.

When we start with structure, we may be able to follow a pathway to determine function, but it is exceedingly difficult to start with function and work backward up this path to uncover the determining structure. This is particularly true when the endpoint is behavioral. Here the validity of our generalizations from one species to another is less certain because we cannot be as confident that the behaviors observed or the mechanisms underlying them are the same. When we deal with function we usually lack the kinds of benchmarks which aid us in analyzing structure, and rather than homologues, we are likely to be dealing with *analogues*, i.e., behaviors which appear similar but which are not derived through a common evolutionary pathway and are thus unlikely to be based on the same mechanisms in different species.

However, there is one general class of behavioral events which may be treated in the same manner as we treat structural events. These are *species-specific behaviors*, which are to be distinguished from *psychological behaviors*.

Species-specific behaviors. The concept of species-specific behavior is one of the noteworthy contributions of the European ethologists (for a good review, see Hinde, 1970). This concept refers to behavior patterns which occur naturally in the wild animal and are common to all members of the species. Some behaviors in this category include courtship, mating, establishment of dominance, aggression, and maternal behavior. Consider two behavior patterns as divergent as maternal care by a bird and by a mammal. Superficially they are very different, and yet they have the same function — to care for and maintain a newborn until it is capable of surviving by itself in nature. Regardless of the particular behaviors involved, and whether they are similar or different from other behaviors by other animals, anyone knowing the natural history of a species would have no difficulty in describing "maternal behavior." Thus, this complex of events may be taken as a natural unit for comparative analyses across phyla in the same sense as the thyroid gland was used in a previous example. This argument appears to hold well within the animal kingdom, but the generalization to the human level is questionable and requires empirical justification.

With our endpoint now securely anchored, we can proceed in our experimentation as with a structural phenomenon (at least up to the level of man) and study independent variables which affect our criterion. When this is done, cross-species generalizations can often be made. For example, the hormones estrogen, progesterone, and prolactin affect maternal behavior in many organisms (Zarrow et al., 1971).

An interesting aside is that the ethologists, as a group, have little or no interest in generalizing their findings to other animals or to the human. They study animal behavior for its own sake. Yet their concept of species-specific behavior is one of the most powerful tools for making cross-species comparisons at a behavioral level.

A cautionary note should be injected here. All species-specific behaviors are *patterns* of behavior involving a number of component acts. Thus, for example, one does not study "maternal behavior" as such, but studies nest building, retrieval, nursing, or some other aspect of this behavioral complex. Likewise, one does not study "the brain" or "the pituitary gland" as such, but rather highly specified portions of each.

The hallmark of species-specific behaviors is their occurrence naturally in the wild. They are to be distinguished from other behaviors usually studied by psychologists in the laboratory.

Psychological behaviors. Included within this category are such classes of behavior as learning, perception, memory, emotions, and other psychological phenomena. As indicated earlier, with these behaviors there is greater uncertainty concerning the validity of our generalizations from animals to humans because there are serious questions whether we are dealing with homologues or analogues. Because the same semantic label is assigned to similar behaviors in different species does not mean that the same mechanisms are involved. For a thoughtful discussion of the conceptual and empirical difficulties involved in the area of comparative psychology, the reader is referred to Lockard (1971).

A major methodological problem in this area is finding equivalent psychological tasks (akin to equivalent measures of maternal behavior at the species-specific level). Consider the area of learning. A common task for the rat is to learn to run down a straight alleyway to escape electric shock. What is the equivalent task for the human? There is none. Even for a mouse, which is another rodent, the task is probably not equivalent because while the rat characteristically runs when shocked, the mouse jumps, and this natural difference in behavior must be taken into account in designing test apparatus.

Then why not use tasks which have equivalent experimental operations, as in certain classical or instrumental conditioning procedures? The answer is that even though the operations are the same with different species, the impact of these operations upon the nervous systems of the various animals is not necessarily equivalent. Take the classical paradigm of conditioning a dog to salivate when a bell is rung and followed by presentation of food. To do a comparative study with another species it is necessary (1) to equate the two species for degree of hunger and (2) to equate the reinforcing value of the food in the two species. We can deprive both species of food for 23 hours, but this does not ensure that they are both equally hungry at the end of that time. We can give both animals their standard laboratory diet, but this does not mean that they "enjoy" their food equally.

We come, then, to a paradox. We know that all animals learn in order to adapt to their environment and to survive, so learning is as "species-specific" as maternal behavior. Then why can we not find a set of equivalent tasks to compare learning in different species in the same manner as we found a set of procedures to allow us to compare maternal behavior? The answer is that maternal behavior (or courtship, or aggression, or any other species-specific behavior) is a natural unit which occurs under highly specific conditions, involves particular forms of behavior, and has the same biological function. But we do not have a natural unit for learning; the animal does not display a particular behavior pattern when it learns; and there are many reasons why an animal learns. Psychological variables, including learning, may be thought of as higher-order variables which allow the animal to adapt to more abstract or generalized conditions of his environment, while species-specific behaviors are related to particular environmental characteristics (e.g., care of young, defense of territory, wooing of mate). Thus, if we wish to study a more abstract set of variables, we must give up the convenience of working with species-specific behaviors.

But the problem is not insoluble. There are several ways to approach cross-species comparisons when studying psychological variables. One approach is simply to assume that principles from one species level will generalize to other levels. This is the route taken by learning psychologists who study the laboratory rat and make generalizations to humans. It is apparent that it takes considerable courage (or arrogance) to follow this course. Empirically, this approach has been useful and has yielded some valuable generalizations concerning learning (e.g., reinforcement principles, temporal parameters, the shapes of curves). However, these generalizations are usually descriptive in nature and do not define mechanisms.

A second approach attempts to attack the problem at the level of mechanism. The argument goes as follows. Learning, no matter what kind, involves the central nervous system. Thus, we arbitrarily choose a learning task and then perform experiments on the central nervous system (e.g., lesions, ablations, electrical stimulation) to see how task performance is affected. If we find that the same area of the brain affects the performance of similar tasks in different species, we can draw the general conclusion that the brain area studied is probably critically involved in processing this kind of learning material. This is a fruitful approach,

though it does not distinguish whether the brain area localized is involved in "learning," "motivation," "reinforcement," or some other parameter. Also, since the learning task is arbitrarily chosen, two other difficulties arise: (1) within a species the brain area found to be critical for one type of learning task may not be involved in a different type of learning task, so that the true role of that brain area is still in doubt; and (2) between species, the same brain area may not have equivalent effects, so that no definite conclusion can be drawn about the comparative functions of this brain area.

A third method involves an even higher level of abstraction. Harlow's (1949) learning sets exemplify this approach. Even though one cannot equate different species on task parameters involved in two-choice discrimination learning — and thus cannot make direct cross-species comparisons — one can ask how many problems an animal must be exposed to in order to solve the general class of two-choice problems. As indicated earlier, the more advanced the animal phylogenetically the more quickly he reaches the general solution. This technique has the greatest promise of allowing us to derive a psychological scale which has validity across species. When combined with the second approach described in the previous paragraph, it should allow us to make major advances in understanding brain-behavior relationships phylogenetically.

To summarize, functional comparisons may be made among species with fair confidence, at least up to the human level, when we are dealing with species-specific behaviors; generalizations to the human level need empirical verification and should be made with caution. When we are working with psychological variables, the base for generalizing is even narrower, and we are much more dependent on empirical results to allow us to forge the missing links between species.

Research Designs for Developmental Studies

We now have a general idea of how animal and human research studies are fitted together in a comparative or animal model framework. We next turn our attention directly to developmental research. The usual strategy in scientific investigations is to narrow the research procedure to obtain as simple and pure a situation as possible. In this manner the researcher is generally better able to understand the mechanisms underlying the phenomena investigated. The simplest situation in developmental research is probably a descriptive age norm study. For example, at different chronological ages, subjects are observed, their behaviors are recorded (e.g., sitting up, creeping, crawling, babbling), and developmental norms are derived from the observations. This kind of study may be done *longitudinally*, in which case the same subjects are followed over a period of time and observed repeatedly, or *cross-sectionally*, in which case different-aged subjects, drawn at random from the same population, are observed once.

If the investigator now introduces a research variable into his experimental design, he at least doubles the number of groups needed in his study. The research variable may be a natural one (e.g., genetic differences or number of siblings in the family) or an experimental one (e.g., stress in infancy or injection of a hormone). Generally researchers involved in human studies manipulate natural variables while those who work with animals use experimental variables.

Regardless of whether the investigator is working with humans or animals, manipulating natural or experimental variables, the objective is the same: to evaluate the effects, across time, of the variable under investigation. Consider the magnitude of that task. The use of an immature organism — a necessary condition — imposes a number of demands, or challenges, upon the researcher. Even when he is engaged in the simplest task of observing the developing subject, the intrinsic changes occurring as a function of growth and maturational processes mean (1) that the same behavior may have to be interpreted differently at different times in development (a babbling teenager is not just an older version of a babbling baby); (2) that the same stimulus input has different meanings as the organism grows (the identical electric shock to an infant and an adult rat has markedly different consequences); (3) that motivational

control and the incentive value of reinforcers may change rapidly during development (many adults are indifferent to candy, but youngsters love it). Many parameters of the environment that are considered *constants* in the usual experiment are *variables* in the developmental research experiment.

If the researcher now imposes a set of experimental manipulations upon his immature and rapidly developing subject, he adds further complications. We know that we can affect neuronal growth, rate of maturation, and a host of behavioral and physiological characteristics by our interventions. The task of the developmental researcher is to devise studies — including appropriate controls — that will enable him to gain further insight into the basic processes affecting the organism and how these processes are changed by various forms of intervention.

Chronological and Ontogenetic Age

We see, then, that the key to the understanding of ontogeny is through the time dimension. In the context of developmental research we speak not of time but of *age*.

Chronological Age

The usual way of measuring age is along the chronological time scale of seconds, minutes, days, weeks, months, or years. Such a scale is highly accurate and convenient to use. It is also deceptive, since its simple quantitative nature may lure us into categorical thinking. Thus, we talk about "5-year-olds" or "the 100-day-old rat" as though all 5-year-old children or all 100-day-old rats belong in the same category. At times it may be useful, even necessary, to do this, but we should always be aware that individuals grouped on the basis of age usually differ on other dimensions. Often these differences are more crucial than the fact that the individuals have been alive for the same length of time.

In a real sense time is a biologically and behaviorally meaningless dimension. What matters are the events which take place in time. Consider an important biological event — puberty. When we say that the rat's estrous cycle begins at 42 days, we do not mean that time has "caused" this. We realize that a number of morphological, biochemical, and physiological changes have occurred in the rat, culminating in a set of biological and behavioral events which we call puberty. The timing of these events is such that they occur, on the average, at about 42 days of life. Our interest is in these underlying events or mechanisms, not in the animal's chronological age.

A parallel phenomenon is present at the behavioral level. For example, 100-day-old rats are frequently used in learning studies. Obviously, they learn well at this age not just because they are 100 days old, but because they have had certain experiences prior to this time which enable them to learn. If they lack these experiences, their learning may be poor.

We need, then, an age construct which focuses upon the organism's biological and behavioral characteristics and emphasizes that his current performance is in part a function of the historical accumulation of experiences over time. Such a scale would be related to the animal's chronology, yet would allow us to distinguish among organisms which are chronologically identical but which have had different biological or behavioral experiences in their pasts. We will call this scale ontogenetic age.

Ontogenetic Age

One way to describe an animal's age is in terms of the length of time it has been alive (chronological age). Another way is in terms of key biobehavioral and psychological markers of development (ontogenetic age).

Some of the biobehavioral benchmarks include conception, birth, play weaning, puberty, courtship, sexual behavior, pregnancy, parturition, maternal care, aggression, senescence, and death. As the animal grows and develops, its biobehavioral capabilities change qualitatively — sometimes quite remarkably. The sequencing of these biobehavioral events is generally immutable, and a change, once it happens, is usually irreversible.

A number of the biobehavioral markers listed above are called maturational events, a term which implies that they are under the control of endogenous biological processes and thus not subject to modification. However, we now know that at least some of these markers can be modified by experience.

At the biological level we know that various indices of maturational growth can be affected by prior experiences. For example, the rat's adrenal gland matures earlier and the animal has earlier onset of puberty if exposed to extra stimulation in infancy (Papers 1 and 48), or the rate of development can be retarded by malnutrition or by lack of proper experience (Papers 21 and 40).

Similar phenomena are seen when we examine behavioral endpoints along the ontogenetic scale. Sexual behavior can be prevented or reversed by the injection of sex hormones during very early development (Papers 16 and 17) or by means of social isolation (Papers 38 and 57). Species-specific aggression in the mouse has been increased by Southwick (Paper 55) through a change in the maternal environment, while both Kuo and Myer (Papers 61 and 62) were able to reduce aggression toward prey by early social interactions.

The biobehavioral markers listed at the beginning of this section are all species-specific and are sufficiently predictable in their initial occurrence to be used as developmental indicators. There is evidence from studies with animals that some psychological variables too can be used as developmental indicators (e.g., see Campbell, 1967), though the data are not nearly as extensive as for species-specific behaviors. At the human level, of course, we can find many examples of developmental phenomena tied to psychological states rather than to chronological age, including such concepts as reading readiness, mental age, developmental quotient, age-normed tests, and birth order (see Olson and Hughes, 1943). Thus, in theory, the construct of ontogenetic age encompasses psychological as well as species-specific behaviors.

There is now massive evidence from animal and human research alike that psychological behaviors are affected by early life experiences. For example, emotional reactivity and exploratory behavior are changed by infantile stimulation (Papers 49 and 50); problem solving in the rat may be improved or depressed as a function of early environmental enrichment or restriction (Paper 7); the intelligence test scores of disadvantaged preschoolers may be improved by a tutorial language program (Paper 47).

Genes and Ontogeny: A General Model of Development

The concept of ontogenetic age uses behavioral and maturational indices of development, in combination with information concerning the individual's past history, as a way of describing the person's biobehavioral characteristics. An important part of one's past history is his genetic legacy. An equally important part is his experience. Our task now is to relate genetic and ontogenetic factors in a general model of development.

First, a few comments about genes. The gene is the basic biological unit responsible for transmitting phylogenetic information from one generation to another and is available to the species as a whole. The information transmitted has been selected over eons of time through evolutionary mechanisms and often (though not always) serves an adaptive function of better enabling the species to survive. We now know that the specific information within the gene is coded in a DNA molecule. However, the information transmitted by the gene is not absolute, but is partly dependent upon other factors. For example, genes interact among themselves so that the information transmitted by one gene may be affected and modified by characteristics of neighboring genes. This principle is illustrated in Paper 6. The principle extends beyond gene-gene interaction and involves gene-environment interaction as well; the expression of a gene is in part determined by the surrounding environment, a principle illustrated in Paper 7.

Thus, our ancestral heritage is not a genetic straitjacket which restricts our potential, but a remarkably malleable organic entity which is responsive to environmental inputs. There are obvious limits to this plasticity (for example, it is virtually impossible to conceive of any non-human primate using language in the complex symbolic manner of the human), but these limits are much broader than was formerly thought. This point is best documented by the readings in Chapter Five, which show that an individual's sexual capabilities, as determined by the genes at the moment of conception, may be drastically modified by hormones during early life, to the extreme that a genetic female may have a "male brain" and vice versa.

A limiting factor on genetic flexibility is age. For example, in order to reverse genetic sex as described above, it is necessary to introduce the hormones during certain critical or sensitive periods in development. If the hormone is introduced either too early or too late, no sex change occurs. The matter of critical and sensitive periods is discussed in Chapter Two. For purposes of this discussion the principle to remember is that environmental inputs are likely to be maximally effective when they occur at the appropriate time in ontogeny. It is necessary to keep in mind that the ontogenetic age appropriate for one kind of environmental input may not be appropriate for a different form of stimulation.

How can we account for these age differences? A hint comes from another field where age is critical — embryology. If an embryologist wishes to affect a given organ system, he must intervene *while* that system is developing. Intervention before differentiation has started or after the system is complete does not affect that organ, though other systems in the process of developing may be affected. Thus, by analogy we may conclude that various behavioral systems are affected at different times in ontogeny because components of the basic biological substrates required for the system to function are undergoing differentiation and development.

Two examples should clarify this point. Handling, a form of stimulation widely used in experiments with rodents, is maximally effective during the period of infancy, i.e., between birth and weaning (see Chapter Eleven). Handling changes the animal's later affective behaviors and a number of physiological states related to homeostatic adaptation (Levine, 1962). Since the animal, at the time of birth, must have many of his physiological systems functioning in order to survive, it is reasonable to find that experimental intervention during this very early interval affects these systems and related behaviors as well. Now consider a different system – one that involves problem-solving behavior, presumably mediated through higher cortical centers. An experimental technique which improves rats' problem-solving ability is to rear them in enriched environments (Chapter Ten). This procedure is most effective if the rat receives the enriched experience after weaning. This makes sense since (1) the rat's eyes and ears are not open and functional until late in the preweaning period and these sensory avenues are necessary for conveyance of information to the brain, and (2) the higher cortical centers are more fully developed at weaning than at birth.

We may now put these various points together into a general model. We start out with the individual's genetic potential. It is important to remember that this potential is present for all the individual's lifetime and that some genes may not express themselves until quite late (e.g., baldness). As the genes are expressed during ontogeny, and as their substrates grow and develop, these processes interact with ongoing experiences (which may be behavioral or biological) to influence each other and affect the animal's future behavior and biology. The nature of the stimulation and the animal's ontogenetic age jointly determine the systems to be affected.

What are these ongoing experiences which affect later behavior and biology? The research to date allows us to group a number of these into classes, as follows: sex hormones, nutrition, learning, perception, environmental deprivation, environmental enrichment, infantile stimulation, maternal influences, and social factors. These nine classes are the headings for the last nine chapters of this book, ordered roughly on a continuum from biological determinants to social determinants. These chapters are preceded by three others which are concerned with various aspects of development. Thus, the organization of this book constitutes an outline of the determinants of development:

Embryonic and temporal determinants
   Critical and sensitive periods
   Genetics and behavior
   Prenatal effects
Biological and physiological determinants
   Sex hormones
   Nutrition
Process variables
   Learning
   Perception
Environmental determinants
   Environmental deprivation
   Environmental enrichment
   Infantile stimulation
Social determinants
   Maternal influences
   Social factors

A few paragraphs about each of these sections will serve to give the reader an overview of the book.

An Overview of the Book

Embryonic and Temporal Determinants

One of the most impressive phenomena in development is the exquisite timing of events as a fertilized ovum grows into a mature adult. Embryologists have been particularly concerned with timing mechanisms and the impact of various forms of "insult" via teratogenic agents upon growth processes. Their general approach is to introduce an insult such as a virus or a chemical at a specific time during prenatal development and later to remove the embryo and look for morphological damage. From this work has come the concept of critical periods in embryological development.

At the behavioral level also there is a critical period hypothesis analogous to the embryological concept. In the study of behavioral critical periods the organism is exposed to or deprived of stimulation, usually during early postnatal life (e.g., exposed to handling or electric shock, deprived of social interaction). Later the animal is tested to detect any changes in his behavior or physiology that might result from this experience. In some cases definite evidence of critical periods has been found. More often, however, the all-or-none characteristics of embryological critical periods are not seen. For this reason some researchers have suggested that the term "sensitive" period may be more accurate than critical period. Thus, the critical period concept is controversial, though it has been of considerable heuristic value. The papers in Chapter Two are concerned with behavioral critical periods and with some of the complexities involved in trying to use this conceptual scheme to account for developmental processes.

Chapter Three discusses genes and behavior. The way in which genetic factors come to influence behavior is one of the least understood areas of growth and development. All sorts of extreme positions have been proclaimed *ex cathedra*, ranging from the idea that environment determines everything ("Give me a dozen healthy infants, well-formed, and my own specified world to bring them up in and I'll guarantee to take any one at random and train him to become any type of specialist I might select"; Watson, 1924) to the notion that genetic factors explicitly govern behavior ("He acts just like his father"). Coupled with the latter position are some vague ideas concerning genetics and instinct and a notion that genetic factors are little influenced by environmental events. In this area one most clearly sees a scientific knowledge gap, but this gap is between disciplines within science rather than between scientists and nonscientists. A number of behavioral and social scientists have given bad genetic interpretations to behavioral data because of misunderstanding of modern genetic concepts. The readings in Chapter Three should help to correct this misunderstanding by demonstrating that the manner in which genes express themselves is a function of the environment in which they exist. The term "environment" is broadly defined here to include other genes as well as prenatal and postnatal experiences.

The purpose of Chapter Four is to show that the experiences of the mother during her pregnancy may have subtle but measurable effects upon the offspring's future behavior and biolo-gy. The notion that nature has designed the perfect support system in the mammalian uterus and that nothing can be done to improve upon this system is one of our major medical myths. We know that medical intervention during intrauterine development can correct certain abnormalities in the growing fetus (e.g., the distress of the "blue baby" whose Rh-factor-containing blood is incompatible with its mother's blood, which lacks the Rh factor), but virtually nothing has been done to try to improve the lot of the normal fetus. The readings in Chapter Four suggest that some prenatal experiences may be beneficial to the organism.

Biological and Physiological Determinants

Chapter Five discusses the role of the sex hormones normally present in the fetus and newborn in organizing the developing brain. The presence or absence of certain sex hormones (androgen for the male and estrogen for the female) can determine whether an organism will behave in a male-like or a female-like fashion. This is true regardless of the subject's genetic sex. In other words, the presence of a certain type of hormone at a certain stage in very early development is sufficient to override the sexual characteristics determined by the genes at the moment of conception.

The impact of malnutrition is documented in Chapter Six. The profound effects of these deficits have been widely publicized in recent years. If the mother is malnourished during pregnancy or if the young organism receives inadequate nutrition during its growth and development, the infant's brain contains less protein and less DNA. When tested in later life such an individual is markedly deficient in performing various tasks requiring the ability to learn and to solve problems. Can these deficiencies be overcome by appropriate diet and training later on? At present the data are insufficient for conclusions to be drawn, but they suggest a pessimistic interpretation if remediation is introduced too late. This emphasizes the need for careful control of the diets of pregnant women and young infants to prevent nutritional deficiencies.

Process Variables

Chapters Seven and Eight are concerned with how much and how well the newborn can perceive and learn from his environment; they reveal part of the foundation upon which behavioral development is built. Though developmental studies. in learning and perception go back over 50 years, research on infant organisms is of relatively recent origin. One reason is that newborn infants did not seem to show systematic behavior that could be called learning or perception; another reason is the difficulty of finding an appropriate response indicator by which the newborn could express evidence of learning or perception. Within recent years researchers have developed appropriate response measures and have set about enthusiastically studying both learning and perceptual processes. Two of the surprising and exciting findings are that the newborn is capable of learning very shortly after birth and that he perceives his world in a structured and orderly fashion. Moreover, the neonate has certain perceptual preferences that can appear within about 6 hours after birth. These findings compel us to rethink our concept of the newborn infant as merely a biological system that develops under the control of a set of internal maturational processes until its central nervous system is mature enough to be affected by the environment.

Environmental Determinants

Chapters Nine, Ten, and Eleven concern environmental deprivation, environmental enrichment, and infantile stimulation. These topics have received extensive research attention, in part because variables such as deprivation, enrichment, and stimulation are relatively easy to control experimentally, compared, for example, with the difficulties of controlling social interactions or of eliminating the confounding features of studies on malnutrition.

The research on environmental deprivation yields the general principle that behavioral and physiological deficits result from long isolation. Two of the most startling findings are that rearing animals in isolation (1) can reduce their ability to foresee and react appropriately to painful stimuli and (2) can cause them to be sexually incompetent. Since both these behaviors presumably have a strong genetic base, these findings reinforce the principle that the rearing environment critically shapes the behavioral potential of the developing organism.

The research on environmental enrichment demonstrates a complementary principle — that enriched experience often results in improved perceptual and cognitive capabilities in later life. This principle is the basis for various Federal intervention programs, such as Head Start, which attempt to upgrade the intellectual capacities of culturally deprived children.

Chapter Eleven is concerned with the effects of brief exposures to physical manipulations during the period between birth and weaning, including such events as handling, electric shock, and exposure to cold. These brief experiences elicit a stress reaction from the young organism, the consequence of which is to change the animal's biobehavioral capabilities in adulthood. Some of these consequences are more rapid maturation, reduced emotional reactivity, greater curiosity, reduced responsiveness of the adrenal cortex, greater capability of withstanding stress, and more rapid learning in simple situations.

The discovery that stressful or traumatic experiences in infancy can have beneficial effects contradicts our "common-sense theory" of development. Many of us construct hypotheses from our own experiences and feeling states to account for psychological phenomena. Because we know from experience that traumatic events are unpleasant and may be harmful to the adult, we hypothesize (assuming that what is bad for an adult must also be bad for a baby) that trauma is harmful and unpleasant to the infant. This process of attributing adult feeling states and thinking processes to the infant ("adultomorphism") is based upon the concept of the infant as a "miniature adult" without the adult's backlog of experiences. This approach is now obsolete. We know (1) that the brain of the newborn infant is not a miniature version of the adult brain but a radically different organ, (2) that the physiology of the newborn infant differs drastically from the physiology of the adult, and (3) that the hormones present at birth are not in the same ratios and do not have the same functions as the hormones in adulthood. It is clear that we cannot look to the adult human being as an appropriate model of the developing infant. To understand how a newborn organism develops, it is necessary to study the development of newborn organisms, both human and animal.

Social Determinants

The unique characteristic of all mammals is that the newborn are nursed by the mother; thus the biological importance of the bond between mother and young is immediately apparent. How influential the mother is in affecting her offspring's future behavior was largely unknown until quite recently when a number of researchers began to investigate the effects of the mother's behavior upon her offspring. Even the most fervent champion of motherhood would probably not have anticipated the powerful influence of the mother. For example, aggressive behavior, emotional reactivity, sexual activity, maternal behavior, and the physiological reaction of the adrenal cortex are shaped by the mother's behavior toward her young during early life.

The biobehavioral basis of mother-young interactions is apparent because we are aware of hormonal and nervous system changes which occur in the female with parturition and which result in the complex of events called maternal behavior. Because many of the biological changes which we see in animals also occur in the human, we are probably willing to agree that the principles derived from research with subhuman organisms on maternal behavior may generalize to the human situation. However, we are less likely to agree that findings on social behavior with animals tell us much about human social behavior.

Why do we have different attitudes about these two types of social interaction? Two reasons suggest themselves: (1) there are obvious biological determinants affecting pregnancy, parturition, and maternal behavior, but no similar set of determinants for other forms of social behavior; and (2) psychologists and sociologists have generally given human-centered interpretations of social behavior and have ignored the findings from animal research. Yet, as we examine each of these reasons closely, we see that they are flawed. There are biological determinants of social behavior in animal groups, though these are more subtle than the major changes of pregnancy, parturition, and maternal behavior. The social behaviors which the ethologists call species-specific (including courtship, aggression, social dominance, and communications) have adaptive value for the survival of the species and have been selected through evolutionary mechanisms. Thus, the biological basis of these social behaviors resides in the genes of the species. Since man engages in many social behaviors which are similar in form to social behaviors seen in lower animals (including courtship, aggression, social dominance, and communication), it seems reasonable to suppose that an understanding of the factors which affect and control these behaviors in animals may provide insight into the factors influencing our own social behavior.

Organization of the Chapters

The purpose of this text is to present a number of principles underlying development and early experiences which apply in the general case to animals and humans alike. Each chapter consists of a group of papers, reporting both animal and human studies, concerned with the chapter topic. Juxtaposition of experiments involving animals and humans enables the reader to appreciate the continuity which exists in nature and which has been exposed by experimentation. In each chapter, the papers reporting on human experiments were chosen to illustrate the same principles demonstrated in the papers on animal studies. This was easy to do in many instances: Some of the human research shows direct continuity with the animal work, and indeed, at times the human research suggested the animal studies. For example, studies on learning and perception in the human infant influenced animal research in these areas, and psychoanalytical theory initiated some of the research on infantile stimulation and deprivation.

In other instances papers on appropriate human studies were hard to find because medical or moral sanctions forbid certain kinds of experimentation on humans. In these cases, reports on "natural experiments" with humans have been substituted (e.g., Papers 19 and 20).

In natural experiments and even in "controlled" experiments on infants and young children, strict experimental control is not attainable. It is impossible to utilize the classical experimental technique of randomly assigning subjects to treatment conditions, which is the *sine qua non* for eliminating correlated or potentially biasing variables. It is this use of randomization which allows the experimental researcher to conclude that his independent variable is the causal agent of the change in his endpoint or dependent variable. Thus it is always easy to criticize human studies. One can often find some uncontrolled variable or some source of contamination that allows an alternative interpretation of the data. However, unequivocal experimental data are not necessary to establish a principle in science. If the animal experiments, based upon a variety of species with appropriate experimental controls, and the human studies, even with possible sources of contamination, both lead to the same over-all conclusion, the principle observed in animal experiments may be generalized to the human. In other words, any set of research findings

with one species must be considered within the broader context of findings with other species in a comparative framework.

Six mammalian species are represented in the readings: mouse, rat, cat, dog, monkey, and human. Of the 65 readings, 23 report rat studies and 21 human studies; the rest report approximately equally on the four remaining species. This "bimodal" distribution is fairly representative of the research in development — the rat and the human are most often investigated. There are wide differences in developmental times for these six species, and Table 1 presents some of the important age parameters for comparative purposes.

In selecting the readings for this book I have often chosen an earlier rather than a more recent publication to give the reader some feeling for the historical development of the various research areas within this field. A few notable pioneers were carrying out excellent experiments on early experiences and development a number of decades ago and should be recognized. Five represented in this book are Dennis, Kuo, Sontag, Wolf, and Young.

I have also tried, when possible, to select short articles. The style in which most research papers are written is not likely to generate enthusiasm in the reader. But be aware that behind that very impersonal and dull statement "it was found that . . . " may lie profound insights and discoveries about the way a baby develops and how behavior is structured.

Table 1. Some Developmental Parameters for Six Species of Mammals

Species	Gestation time	Weaning age	Age of onset of puberty in female
Mouse (house)	19-20 days	21-30 days	37-54 days
Rat	21-23 days	21-30 days	38-46 days
Cat	56-65 days	28-56 days	7-12 months
Dog	58-63 days	42-70 days	7-12 months
Monkey (Macaque)	156-172 days	6-12 months	2-4 years
Human	271-289 days	1-3 years	11-14 years

References

Ainsworth, M. D. S., and Bell, S. M. Some contemporary patterns of mother-infant interaction in the feeding situation. In A. Ambrose (Ed.). *Stimulation in Early Infancy.* New York: Academic Press, 1969, pp. 133-163.

Campbell, B. A. Developmental studies of learning and motivation in infraprimate mammals. In H. W. Stevenson, E. H. Hess, and H. L. Rheingold (Eds.). *Early Behavior.* New York: Wiley, 1967, pp. 43-71.

Harlow, H. F. The formation of learning sets. *Psychol. Rev.,* 1949, 56, 51-65.

Hinde, R. A. *Animal Behavior.* New York: McGraw-Hill, 1970.

Levine, S. Psychophysiological effects of infantile stimulation. In E. L. Bliss (Ed.). *Roots of Behavior.* New York: Harper & Row, 1962, pp. 246-253.

Lockard, R. B. Reflections on the fall of comparative psychology: Is there a message for us all? *Amer. Psychol.,* 1971, 26, 168-179.

Olson, W. C., and Hughes, B.O. Growth of the child as a whole. In R. G. Barker, J. S. Kounin, and H. F. Wright (Eds.). *Child Behavior and Development.* New York: McGraw-Hill, 1943, pp. 199-208.

Watson, J. B. *Behaviorism.* New York: Norton, 1924.

Zarrow, M. X., Denenberg, V. H., and Sachs, B. D. Hormones and maternal behavior in mammals. In S. Levine (Ed.). *Hormones and Behavior.* New York: Academic Press, 1971. In press.

EMBRYONIC AND TEMPORAL DETERMINANTS

*These additional readings refer to other papers which appear in different sections of this book. They are cross-listed here because they also contribute to the topic of this chapter.

Chapter Three GENETICS AND BEHAVIOR

Chapter Four PRENATAL EFFECTS

Chapter Two

CRITICAL AND SENSITIVE PERIODS

When we talk about development, we are talking about events and processes which change with time. Certain activities disappear as the organism grows (e.g., some reflexes seen only in the newborn human infant). Other activities emerge as a function of maturation and experience (e.g., the acquisition and articulation of a language).

Time — which is a convenient quantitative dimension — is a meaningless concept by itself. It is the underlying biological factors coupled with the organism's accumulation of experiences throughout its life that are the keys to our understanding of growth, development, and behavioral change.

In the study of developmental phenomena the major temporal variable is the organism's *age.* We know that the same experiences at different ages can have different effects. A simple, yet dramatic, example of this is seen in language acquisition. Virtually every human being learns a language — which may well be the most complex learning he ever does — in an untutored, unschooled situation called "the family" before he has even reached nursery school age. An equivalent investment in time at the high school or college level, where we systematically attempt to teach the young person a language, yields results which are grossly inferior to the learning which the infant and young child exhibit. Since a dull normal child of French parentage will learn the French language better than an intensely motivated near-genius college student who is receiving special instruction, it seems reasonable to conclude that a critical reason for these differences lies in the state of the central nervous system of the young child as compared with that of the college student.

Observations and conclusions such as the above are the stuff of which theories are made, and the theory derived from these findings is that experiences in early life affect a variety of behaviors. However, we also know that our theoretical predilections are affected by selective perception. Other researchers look at other commonly occurring events, such as the appearance of baldness in the male in adulthood, the development of secondary sexual characteristics, and the emergence of locomotor skills, and they emphasize the unchanging nature of certain developmental processes which they relate to genetic factors coupled with maturation.

Thus, we have "learning-experience" theories of development and "genetic-maturational" theories of development. We are now at a level of knowledge and sophistication where we realize that these are not mutually exclusive positions and that both can enhance our understanding of development. However, neither position alone is sufficient to account for the myriad complex characteristics involved in the growth and development of even the simplest of living organisms.

The two theoretical approaches described above have generally used postnatal physiological or behavioral evidence to support their viewpoints. A somewhat different concept concerning developmental events has come from embryologists, who study the organism during its prenatal life. Their research has revealed the precision timing of developmental processes, and one of the derivatives of their findings has been the concept of "critical periods." In embryology, the term critical period refers to the time when a particular organ (e.g., heart, spinal cord, palate) is developing during embryogenesis. If, during this interval, there occurs a biological "insult" (e.g., the intrusion of a foreign chemical or biological event such as thalidomide or German measles), the normal development of that organ will be upset, and abnormalities are likely to occur. The more rapidly the organ is growing, the more sensitive and vulnerable it is to interference. However, if the insult occurs either before the organ starts to develop or after development is complete, there is little, if any, damage to that particular system. Thus, the time when the organ is developing is a "critical period" with respect to the future potential of that organ.

This concept of a critical period in the embryological sense has been adopted by Scott in his theoretical formulations concerning postnatal development (Scott, 1962; Scott and Marston, 1950). He has postulated that critical periods occur after birth which are analogous to those found during embryological development. Indeed, he has stated that there are three major kinds of postnatal critical period phenomena. The first is concerned with critical periods for the formation of basic social relationships; the second has to do with optimal periods for learning; and the third involves the effects of early stimulation. Much current research data support Scott's ideas concerning a critical period for socialization; there are not sufficient data to allow adequate evaluation of his idea of a critical period for early learning; and there are sufficient data to raise considerable doubt concerning the validity of the notion of a critical period for early stimulation (see Denenberg, 1968).

It is apparent that this is a controversial field; even some ethologists have questioned whether the term "critical periods" should remain in the literature. Ethologists also study developmental phenomena and temporal factors, and one of their research topics is imprinting — the phenomenon in which newly hatched precocial birds follow the first moving object they see. At first imprinting was thought to be rapidly acquired and highly irreversible, but further investigations have shown this not to be the case. Thus, instead of critical periods in development, the ethologists prefer to talk about "sensitive periods," thus avoiding the connotations of finality and irreversibility inherent in the embryological meaning of the critical period concept.

The following readings have been chosen to give the student some feeling for results as well as controversy in this area.

Paper 1, by Levine and Lewis, describes one of the simplest and cleanest demonstrations of a critical period in development. These researchers had previously found that rats stimulated in infancy by a procedure called "handling" (see Chapter Eleven for a discussion of handling) matured faster than nonhandled controls as measured by their ability to respond to a cold stress by depletion of ascorbic acid from the adrenal gland. This reaction typically does not occur in the normally developing rat until 16 days of age but may occur at 14 days if the animal has received handling stimulation for the first 13 days of life. Levine and Lewis asked whether stimulation was necessary on all 13 days to hasten maturation or whether stimulation for a briefer interval would have the same effects. Therefore, they stimulated their animals at ages 2 through 5 days, 6 through 9 days, 10 through 13 days, and 2 through 13 days. They found that handling on Days 2 through 5 had the same effect as handling on Days 2 through 13.

Paper 2 adds several layers of complexity to the critical period concept. Henry investigated audiogenic seizures — a form of wild running and convulsion induced in some animals by exposure to intense noise (as from a doorbell). Henry was interested in seeing how audiogenic seizures in mice were affected by prior auditory stimulation and by the animal's age at time of testing (in the Levine and Lewis experiment all animals were tested at 14 days). Henry found relatively smooth continuous developmental curves, showing that stimulation at certain ages predisposed the mouse to a seizure later on, but the shape of the curves and the age of maximum response varied as a function of the test age. Thus, the stimulation period which was "critical" for one test age was not critical in animals tested at a different time in development.

A set of experimental data which strongly refutes Scott's concept of a critical period for early stimulation is presented in Paper 3. Rats received handling experience for different 3-day or 5-day intervals during early life and were later evaluated with respect to their weaning weight, avoidance learning ability, adult weight, and survival capability. So many "critical periods" were found that the concept became useless as an explanatory or integrative device. In that paper Denenberg then reexamined his findings from the point of view of number of days of stimulation, rather than age at stimulation, and found a consistent pattern relating a variety of performance indices to amount of stimulation (see also Denenberg, 1964).

Although there does not seem to be a critical period for early stimulation, there is evidence for an early socialization critical period. Paper 4 supports this concept. Pfaffenberger and Scott were able to show a strong relationship between the age at which young German shepherd dogs were taken from the kennel and placed into a home to be socialized and the later capability of the animals to be trained as guide dogs for the blind. Animals placed into private homes at 12 weeks of age were most likely to be successful. The longer they were kept in the kennel after this time, the less likely they were to become acceptable guide dogs, presumably because of a disruption of social adaptation during early development.

At the human level, it is difficult to find a good research example of a critical period in the embryological sense or of a sensitive period in the ethological sense. At the present time there is insufficient evidence concerning the human to make any strong scientific statement, though it is intuitively obvious that at least sensitive periods must exist (as the example of language acquisition demonstrates).

Paper 5 points toward a critical period type of phenomenon. Ack *et al.* examined the effects of diabetes mellitus upon the intelligence of children who acquired this disease before the age of 5 years or after that age. They had two reasons for selecting 5 years as a separation point, and both reasons have a critical period philosophy underlying them. The first reason was that "experience in the treatment of emotionally disturbed children has demonstrated that traumatic experiences such as hospitalizations, surgical procedures, separations, etc., before the age of 5 are infinitely more significant for future development than are the same experiences after this age." The second reason was "that the most striking structural maturational changes in the infantile brain are largely completed during the first 5 postnatal years." The IQ of each diabetic child was compared with that of a randomly selected sibling – a very nice control procedure. No difference was found in the average IQ scores between diabetic children and their sibling controls when the diabetics had acquired the disease after age 5. However, the average IQ score of children who had become diabetic before the age of 5 was 10 points lower than that of their siblings.

As computer techniques are increasingly applied to the study of medical records, it should be possible to carry out statistical analyses on large numbers of subjects to determine whether there are certain critical ages at which diseases or injuries are likely to have a greater or more widespread effect than at other ages. However, whether the research concerns animals or humans, the investigator must keep in mind that the isolation of a critical or sensitive period is really the beginning of a research program, not the end of one. Having isolated a time when biobehavioral events imposed upon the organism have drastic effects upon the subsequent biology or behavior of that organism, the researcher must inquire into the biological and behavioral factors involved and their mechanisms of action. These are the crucial questions for those concerned with the study of critical or sensitive periods in development.

References

Denenberg, V. H. Critical periods, stimulus input, and emotional reactivity: A theory of infantile stimulation. *Psychol. Rev.,* 1964, 71, 335-351.

Denenberg, V. H. A consideration of the usefulness of the critical period hypothesis as applied to the stimulation of rodents in infancy. In G. Newton and S. Levin (Eds.). *Early Experience and Behavior.* Springfield, Ill.: Thomas, 1968, pp. 142-167.

Scott, J. P. Critical periods in behavioral development. *Science,* 1962, 138, 949-958.

Scott, J. P., and Marston, M. V. Critical period affecting the development of normal and maladjusted social behavior in puppies. *J. Genet. Psychol.,* 1950, 77, 25-60.

SEYMOUR LEVINE & GEORGE W. LEWIS

1 Critical Period for Effects of Infantile Experience on Maturation of Stress Response

Abstract. Manipulated infant rats respond to cold with depletion of adrenal ascorbic acid (AAA) significantly earlier than nonmanipulated infants. The study discussed in this report examined the critical period for infantile manipulation on the depletion of AAA. It was found that infant rats manipulated immediately following birth exhibited significant AAA depletion, whereas infants manipulated later did not exhibit depletion.

Recently it has been reported (*1*) that infant rats which had been manipulated (handled) once daily from birth responded to cold stress with a significant depletion of adrenal ascorbic acid as early as 12 days of age, whereas nonmanipulated infant rats did not show significant AAA depletion until 16 days of age. One question which arose from this study was whether the age at which the experimental treatment of manipulation was initiated is a significant factor in the accelerated maturation of the systems which result in AAA depletion with stress.

The experiment discussed in this report (*2*) was directed, therefore, toward answering the question of whether there exists a critical period in the development of the organism during which manipulation has its greatest effect on the AAA depletion response to stress. The

existence of such a period seemed likely, since critical periods have been documented for many other aspects of development (*3*).

Seventy-six infant Sprague-Dawley albino rats were used as subjects. The subjects were assigned at birth to one of four groups. For the infants in group I (*N* = 20), the treatment was initiated on the second day following birth and continued through day 5. The treatment was started on day 6 and was continued through day 9 for group II infants (N = 20). The treatment for the group III subjects (N = 20) was given from day 10 through day 13. The last group, group IV, received the treatment from day 2 through day 13. The experimental treatment was identical to that previously described (*1*) and consisted of removing the pup from the nest, placing it in a 2.5- by 3.5- by 6-in. compartment for 3 minutes, and then returning it to the nest. This procedure was followed once daily during the period assigned to the subject. At 14 days of age, approximately half the pups within each group were randomly assigned to either the stress or control condition to test for AAA depletion with stress.

The stress conditions and method of analysis for AAA are fully described in previous reports (*1*) and, therefore, will be only briefly described here. The nonstressed subjects within each group were killed by cervical spinal separation and weighed. The adrenals were removed, weighed, and assayed for AAA by the modified method of Glick *et al.* The stressed infants were subjected to a cold stress of 5°C for 90 minutes before removal of the adrenals and determination of AAA.

The results of this experiment are shown in Fig. 1 and are expressed in terms of milligrams percent change in AAA level. Change in AAA level was determined by subtracting the AAA present in the stressed animals from the mean for the nonstressed subjects.

The data clearly indicate that the age during which the infant rat is manipulated is a major variable in the effect described in this report. Only the animals in groups I and IV showed significant AAA depletion. In terms of percentage, the group I subjects showed a 25-percent depletion and the group IV subjects showed a 32-percent depletion. The depletion in AAA in the group II

and group III animals (9 percent and 0 percent, respectively) did not differ significantly from that in the respective controls. Thus, in the groups (I and IV) which had been manipulated during the period directly following birth, a significant depletion in AAA is evidenced in response to cold stress at 14 days of age, whereas the groups manipulated later in infancy do not show significant AAA depletion.

Recent evidence has indicated that the early postnatal period is also critical for behavioral changes during adulthood. Schaefer (4) found that handling during the first 7 days produced the greatest reduction in adult emotionality measured in terms of behavior in an open field situation. Denenberg (5) reports that handling during the first 10 days of life resulted in avoidance learning superior to that found when handling was initiated later. In both of these studies, the period during which the treatment was initiated includes the critical period found in the experiment discussed in this

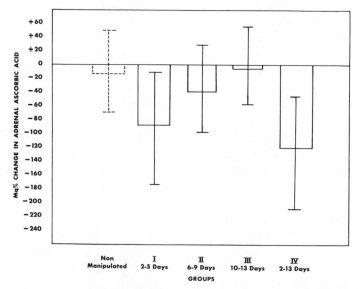

Fig. 1. Comparison of depletion in AAA in the various groups of infant albino rats of the study. The bar represents the mean depletion; the lines, the range. The dotted bar and dotted line represent untreated animals that had previously been tested.

report. Whether behavioral difference can be detected in experiments with such restricted age groups as were tested in this experiment remains to be determined.

References and Notes

1. S. Levine, M. Alpert, G. W. Lewis, *J. Comp. Physiol. Psychol.*, in press.

2. This investigation was supported by research grant PHS M-1630 from the National Institute of Mental Health of the National Institutes of Health, U.S. Public Health Service.

3. J. P. Scott, *Psychosom. Med.* 20, 42 (1957).

4. T. Schaefer, Ph.D. dissertation, University of Chicago (1957).

5. V. Denenberg, paper presented at the 1958 meeting of the American Psychological Association.

KENNETH R. HENRY

2 Audiogenic Seizure Susceptibility Induced in C57BL/6J Mice by Prior Auditory Exposure

Abstract. *Pronounced susceptibility to audiogenic seizures was produced in highly resistant C57B1/6J mice after earlier exposure to a loud electric bell. There is a critical period between initial acoustic presentation and subsequent testing for susceptibility; this suggests a minimum age and a minimum lapse of time during which this "priming" is effective.*

Many studies of audiogenic seizures with inbred strains of mice have attributed differences in susceptibility to specifically defined genetic backgrounds. Mice of the C57B1/6J strain are highly resistant to sound-induced convulsions, and those of the DBA/2J strain are extremely susceptible to them *(1)*. This behavior has been ascribed to differences between these two strains in (i) oxidative phosphorylation and adenosine triphosphatase which are involved in energy metabolism *(2);* (ii) concentration in the brain of norepinephrine and serotonin, which have been proposed as neural transmitter hormones *(3);* and (iii) phenylalanine hydroxylase activity, the liver enzyme that degrades the amino acid phenylalanine *(4)*. Simple treatments (prior to exposure to a loud noise) which make C57B1/6J mice nearly as susceptible as their DBA/2J cousins should be of importance

Reprinted from *Science* 158:938–940, 1967. Copyright 1967 by the American Association for the Advancement of Science.

for two reasons. (i) Any early behavioral condition of such a transient nature that yields so dramatic an aftereffect as a severe convulsion followed by death may be useful in the analysis of normal neural-behavioral development and of the pathology of seizure. (ii) The physiological correlates which used the C57B1/6J strain as a nonsusceptible standard should be reevaluated. There have been reports of these procedures *(5)*.

The C57B1/6J-strain inbred mice, offspring of parents obtained from the Jackson Laboratory, were tested for audiogenic seizures when either 21 or 28 days old. The age groups contained 255 and 355 mice, respectively. They were placed individually in a glass chromatography jar (45 cm high and 30 cm wide) and exposed for 30 seconds to an electric bell (103 decibels relative to 2×10^{-4} dyne/cm^2) mounted directly overhead. Occurrence of the successive stages of the audiogenic seizure syndrome (wild running, myoclonic convulsion, myotonic convulsion, and death) was recorded for each animal. All animals were kept under conditions of 12 hours of light followed by 12 hours of darkness and were weaned at age 21 days into separate cages in groups of five. All subjects were tested between the 4th and 6th hour of the daily 12-hour light cycle, in view of the circadian nature of audiogenic seizures. The mice were tested under either an X-21 or an

X-28 schedule, the X designating the age in days at which they were initially exposed to the bell for 30 seconds (constituting the priming condition) and the second number designating the age in days at which their response to auditory stimulus was observed. Of the 580 mice tested, only 27 exhibited wild running during the initial exposure, mostly at ages 14 and 15 days, and none exhibited clonic convulsions, tonic convulsions, or deaths. This supports the conclusions of earlier reports which describe this strain as nonsusceptible. The results (Table 1) show that this technique is differentially effective, depending upon the ages at which both priming and testing occur; the age of 19 days is optimum for priming mice to be tested at 28 days of age, whereas the age of 16 days is most effective for priming mice to be tested at 21 days. Acoustic priming appears to be ineffective before the age of 14 days, corresponding to the normal onset of hearing in mice (6). To be effective, priming requires a minimum number of days; this period is shorter in the 21- than in the 28-day-old mice. An orthogonal polynomial analysis (7) of the severity scores in Fig. 1 showed that the quadratic component accounted for 76.2 percent of the treatment sum of squares [ratio of variances (F) = 190, degrees of freedom (df) = 1, 154] for the X-21 schedule, and 56.4 percent of the treatment sum of squares $(F = 232, df = 1, 238)$ for the X-28 schedule. The same analysis of only those data that show a treatment effect (from 13 to 20 days for priming 21-day-old mice, and from 13 to 25 days for priming 28-day-old mice) showed that the quadratic term accounted for 99.01 and 82.14 percent of the treatment effect for the X-21 and X-28 schedules, respectively. Figure 1 also shows the least-squares quadratics (8) superimposed over the severity scores. These statistical results indicate that the quadratic curve best describes, for this experiment, the ages at which acoustic priming is most effective. Further support is obtained from a study in which 11 strains of mice were tested at 21 days of age and tested again later (9). The four "least susceptible" strains, including the C57B1/6J strain, did not show seizure at the initial acoustic presentation but did so when tested again 7

		Mice (%) exhibiting four components of audiogenic seizure:		
Priming age (days)	Wild running	Convulsions		Death
		Myoclonic	Myotonic	
X-21 Schedule				
21	0	0	0	0
20	7	0	0	0
19	87	20	20	20
18	87	80	67	33
17	93	80	80	47
16	100	80	80	60
15	80	80	80	47
14	60	40	40	33
13	0	0	0	0
12	0	0	0	0
X-28 Schedule				
28	7	0	0	0
27	0	0	0	0
26	0	0	0	0
25	0	0	0	0
24	20	0	0	0
23	73	13	0	0
22	67	7	0	0
21	80	47	13	0
20	100	40	27	13
19	100	73	53	47
18	100	100	20	13
17	93	80	13	13
16	87	73	7	0
15	67	53	7	0
14	20	0	0	0
13	7	0	0	0
12	7	0	0	0

Table 1. Audiogenic seizure profile for mice (of the C57B1/6J strain) primed and tested at various ages. On the X-21 schedule the age at the second acoustic presentation was 21 days; on the X-28 schedule, this age was 28 days. Priming age, age in days at initial acoustic presentation. Fifteen mice were used for each priming age.

days later. Fuller and Sjursen noted this in their tables but did not discuss it in the text.

These data indicate that this is not a transient sensitization effect; instead, it involves a longer-term neural change — perhaps an increase in auditory sensitivity or a decrease of neural inhibition. Acoustic priming can occur during wakefulness or under anesthesia by ether or sodium pentobarbital (Table 2); this suggests that neither the brainstem reticulum nor a conscious mechanism is involved. Because the C57B1/6J strain is homozygous nondilute (its

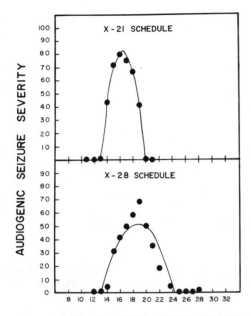

Fig. 1. Severity of audiogenic seizure for various priming and testing ages. This represents an average of the scores for wild running, clonic seizure, tonic seizure, and death.

Treat-ment	Seizure behavior (%)			
	Wild run-ning	Clonic seizure	Tonic seizure	Death
Nembutal	0	0	0	0
Ether	0	0	0	0
None	0	0	0	0
Nembutal plus bell	93	87	87	53
Ether plus bell	100	100	100	67
Bell only	100	80	80	60

Table 2. Effects of different treatments (at 16 days of age) on audiogenic seizures of 21-day-old mice of the C57B1/6J strain. Doses of Nembutal (sodium pentobarbital) for 30 mice were 12.5 mg per 10 g of body weight; acoustic priming for 15 of these animals occurred 10 minutes after injection. The 30 mice anesthetized with ether were exposed for 30 seconds to atmosphere containing 5 ml of ether per 1 liter of air; half of these were acoustically primed 10 seconds later. Fifteen mice were used for each priming age.

chromosomes do not carry the mutant genes responsible for a lighter coat pigmentation and reduced liver phenylalanine activity; the dilute condition has been used by some as an analog of the human phenylketonuric mental deficient condition), its susceptibility to audiogenic seizure rules out the dilute genetic locus as a necessary condition for seizures, as some have suggested (10). The priming technique may provide a more useful means of analyzing audiogenic seizures than comparison of strains that differ at many loci does, in that it permits an experimental rather than a correlative approach. Biochemical examinations of primed and nonprimed mice may reveal whether differences in oxidative phosphorylation, concentration of norepinephrine and serotonin in the brain, or liver phenylalanine hydroxylase activity are associated with changes in audiogenic seizure susceptibility. Whether audiotory priming affects other behaviors — chemoconvulsive and electroshock seizures, learning, and emotionality — is still unknown. The phenomenon in this study is analogous in some respects to Lorenz' descriptions of imprinting; both

have a critical period early in life during which a relatively brief stimulus can exert a profound, long-lasting effect on later behavior (although acoustic priming may not constitute as natural a situation as that which occurs when a duckling imprints its behavior to the first moving object it sees, accepts it as its mother, and models later behavior after this relationship). This technique may be useful in the investigation of behavioral development and of musicogenic seizures in humans.

References and Notes

1. C. S. Hall, *J. Hered.* 38, 2 (1947); G. M. Witt and C. S. Hall, *J. Comp. Physiol. Psychol.* 42, 58 (1949); J. L. Fuller and W. R. Thompson, *Behavior Genetics* (Wiley, New York, 1960), pp. 154-156.
2. L. G. Abood and R. W. Gerard, in *Biochemistry of the Developing Nervous System*, H. Waelsch, Ed. (Academic Press, New York, 1955), p. 467.
3. K. Schlesinger *et al.*, *Life Sci.* 4, 2345 (1965).
4. D. L. Coleman, *Arch. Biochem. Biophys.* 91, 300 (1960); S. D. Huff and J. L. Fuller, *Science* 144, 304 (1964).
5. K. R. Henry, unpublished thesis, Univ. of North Carolina, Wilson Round Library (1966); W. B. Iturrian and G. B. Fink, *Fed. Proc.* 26, 736 (1967).
6. B. R. Alford and R. J. Ruben, *Ann. Otol. Rhinol. Laryngol,* 72, 237 (1963).
7. R. A. Fisher and F. Yates, *Statistical Tables* (Hafner, New York, 1953).
8. G. W. Snedecor, *Statistical Methods* (Iowa State Univ. Press, Ames, 1956).
9. J. L. Fuller and F. H. Sjursen, Jr., *J. Hered.* 58, 135 (1967).

10. S. D. Huff and R. L. Huff, *Science* 136, 318 (1962); D. L. Coleman and K. Schlesinger, *Proc. Soc. Exp. Biol. Med.* 119, 264 (1965).
11. I thank R. E. Bowman and F. E. Harding for their
assistance. Supported by grant FR-0167 from NIH to the Wisconsin Regional Primate Research Center.

VICTOR H. DENENBERG

3   An Attempt To Isolate Critical Periods of Development in the Rat

An examination of the critical-period literature shows that two related but different approaches have been followed by researchers. One approach is to ask whether the same stimulation at different ages in early life has the same effect; if not, this has been considered proof that there are critical periods in development. The other approach is to try to find certain limited periods in development during which a particular stimulus will have rather profound effects. This approach stems directly from the embryological meaning of critical periods, and it is in this context that Scott (1958; Williams & Scott, 1953) has used the term.

A number of studies have shown that the same stimulation at different ages will have different effects in adulthood (e.g., Denenberg & Bell, 1960; Denenberg & Karas, 1960, 1961). There have been fewer studies which have been able to demonstrate the second meaning of critical periods (Levine & Lewis, 1959). The purpose of this experiment was to stimulate Ss for brief intervals during the first 10 days of life to see whether evidence supporting either or both concepts of critical periods could be found. The first 10 days was chosen for investigation since prior work has shown that stimulation throughout this interval had significant effects upon avoidance learning, body weight, and survival time (Denenberg &

Reprinted from *Journal of Comparative and Physiological Psychology* 55:913–815, 1962. Copyright 1962 by the American Psychological Association and reproduced by permission.

This investigation was supported in part by Research Grant M-1753 from the National Institute of Mental Health of the National Institutes of Health, United States Public Health Service.

Karas, 1960, 1961), the variables in this experiment.

METHOD

The procedures followed were identical in all respects to those of Denenberg and Karas (1960, Experiment III; 1961) and may be briefly summarized.

Subjects

Sixty-nine Harvard Wistar rats from 12 litters were used. They were born in cages measuring 9 in. by 9 in. by 15 in. Litters were reduced to eight pups as soon as discovered. No litter containing less than four pups was used. After a litter was born, the shavings in the cages were never changed.

Infantile Experience

Two litters were randomly assigned to each of the following experimental treatments: handling on Days 1 to 3, 3 to 5, 1 to 5, 6 to 8, 8 to 10, or 6 to 10. Handling consisted of removing the young from the cage once daily, placing each S individually into a 1-gal. tin can partially filled with shavings, leaving the Ss in the cans for 3 min., and then returning them to the cages. At 21 days the Ss were weaned, earpunched, sexed, weighed to the nearest .1 gm., and placed in small cages with like-sexed litter mates. Food and water were always present until the terminal phase of the experiment.

Adult Testing

The avoidance learning apparatus consisted of an interchangeable start box and escape box, and a center chamber. A constant-current shock unit, set at .8 ma., was used. The current was randomly distributed over the bars of the grid by means of a scrambler.

Starting at 60 days the Ss were habituated to the apparatus for 2 days, followed by 8 days of avoidance training with five trials per day. The S was placed in the starting chamber at the beginning of each trial. At the same time that the door in front of the start box opened, an auditory CS began and a Standard Electric timer started. The CS terminated 4 sec. later and shock began. Entrance into the escape chamber turned off the timer. If S entered the escape chamber within 4 sec., both the CS and timer were terminated, and this was scored as an avoidance response.

At 69 days after the last set of learning trials the Ss were weighed and placed on terminal food and water deprivation. Hours until death occurred were recorded.

RESULTS AND DISCUSSION

The data consist of the body weights at 21 and 69 days, number of avoidance responses, and survival time for the six groups. Data for Ss which received no handling in infancy and for Ss which were handled for the first 10 days of life are also presented as reference values. These values were obtained from other experiments by Denenberg and Karas (1960, Experiments II and III; 1961) in which the identical procedure was followed and which overlapped the present experiment in time. Table 1 summarizes the pertinent statistics.

TABLE 1

MEANS AND N FOR THE SIX EXPERIMENTAL GROUPS AND THE TWO REFERENCE GROUPS ON THE FOUR VARIABLES

Group	N	21-Day Wt. (gm.)	Avoidance Learning	69-Day Wt. (gm.)[a]	Hours Survival
1–3	10	41.35	8.50	170.84	265.40
3–5	13	38.81	8.62	199.27	344.92
1–5	12	37.81	8.50	193.24	393.58
6–8	11	35.61	13.45	185.78	256.78[b]
8–10	12	39.52	11.17	198.30	311.67
6–10	11	36.85	20.91	202.14	316.64
Control[c]		37.50 (46)	13.85 (18)	176.64 (24)	175.79 (24)
1–10[c]		38.63 (50)	18.85 (18)	205.10 (25)	255.52 (25)

a Means equally weighted for sex.
b $N = 9$ for survival time; 2 Ss escaped.
c Ns given in parentheses; from Denenberg & Karas (1960, 1961).

Day 21 Weight

The analysis of variance of these data found no significant differences among the six experimental groups. This is consistent with the previous finding (Denenberg & Karas, 1961) that the control group and Group 1–10 did not differ significantly.

Avoidance Learning

The analysis of variance of number of avoidance responses yielded an overall F ratio of 3.97, $p < .01$. Further analyses determined that Group 6–10 was significantly superior in avoidance learning to all other experimental groups; the remaining five groups did not differ among themselves. When compared with

the two reference groups, Group 6–10 was significantly better than the control group ($p < .05$) and did not differ from Group 1–10. The difference between Group 1–5 and the control group approached significance ($p < .08$).

Day 69 Weight

The body weights were subjected to an analysis of variance after classification by experimental groups and sex. The six groups differed significantly among themselves and sex was significant as well (both beyond the .01 level), but the interaction between sex and experimental groups was not significant. The 69-day-weight means in Table 1 are equally weighted for sex.

Further analyses of the significant treatment difference revealed that Group 1–3 weighed significantly less than all other groups. In addition, Group 6–10 was heavier than Group 6–8 ($p < .05$) but did not differ from the remaining four groups. Comparisons of these six means with those of the reference groups showed that Group 1–3 had essentially the same mean weight as Ss which received no stimulation in infancy while the means of the other groups were similar to the Group 1–10 mean.

Survival Time

The analysis of these data yielded an F of 5.67 ($p < .01$). Group 1–5 survived significantly longer than all other groups except Group 3–5. Comparisons within the first 5 days of life indicated that Group 3–5 survived longer than Group 1–3 ($p < .01$), but there were no significant differences within the second 5 days. All six experimental groups survived significantly longer than the control Ss. Four groups were found to survive significantly longer than Group 1–10: Groups 3–5, 1–5, 6–10, and 8–10.

Number of Days of Handling and Performance

Another way to analyze these data is to examine the relationship between number of days of handling and performance, disregarding when S was stimulated. Since the experimental conditions were the same, the present results were combined with the previous work of Denenberg and Karas (1960, Experiments II and III; 1961) yielding five durations of stimulation: 0 (controls), 3, 5, 10,

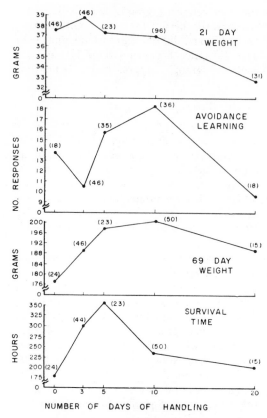

GRAMS

NO. RESPONSES

GRAMS

HOURS

21 DAY
WEIGHT

AVOIDANCE
LEARNING

69 DAY
WEIGHT

SURVIVAL
TIME

NUMBER OF DAYS OF HANDLING

FIG. 1. Weight at 21 days, avoidance learning, weight at 69 days, and survival time as a function of number of days of handling in infancy. (Numbers in parentheses indicate the *N* for each point.)

and 20 days. Figure 1 presents curves relating 21- and 69-day body weight, avoidance learning, and survival time to number of days of handling. With the possible exception of the 21-day weight curve, the general function of these data may be described by an inverted **U** curve (Denenberg, 1959).

The data amply demonstrate that both *S*s' age when handled and the number of days of handling are significant parameters affecting later behavior. If one considers the demonstration of an age effect in early life to be proof of critical periods, then these data support the critical-period hypothesis. However, the data do not support the concept of critical periods if one thinks of this term in a manner analogous to its use in embryology, namely, that only during certain limited periods of development will a particular stimulus have an effect. The finding that handling on Days 6 to 10 was sufficient to improve

learning scores while 3 days of stimulation was not sufficient may be considered to be a demonstration of the second use of this concept. However, more recent research (Denenberg & Kline, unpublished) has found that this "critical period" is strictly a function of intensity of stimulation; when *S*s are shocked rather than handled, the critical period disappears. The present data, in combination with other research (Denenberg & Bell, 1960; Denenberg & Karas, 1960, 1961), strongly indicate that, for the rat and mouse at least, there may be as many critical periods as there are combinations of independent-variable parameters and dependent-variable measures. It appears to be more fruitful to study the functional relationships among these variables than to try to isolate specific critical periods in development.

SUMMARY

In an attempt to isolate critical periods in development, infant rats were handled on Days 1–3, 3–5, 1–5, 6–8, 8–10, or 6–10. They were weighed at 21 days, received avoidance training from 60 to 69 days, were weighed at 69 days, and were then placed on a terminal deprivation schedule until death occurred. Significant differences among the groups were obtained on all measures except 21-day body weight. It was concluded that both *S*s' age and the number of days of handling are critical parameters affecting later behavior.

REFERENCES

DENENBERG, V.H. The interactive effects of infantile and adult shock levels upon adult learning. *Psychol Rep.*, 1959, **5**, 357–364.
DENENBERG, V. H., & BELL, R. W. Critical periods for the effects of infantile experience on adult learning. *Science*, 1960, **131**, 227–228.
DENENBERG, V. H., & KARAS, G. G. Interactive effects of age and duration of infantile experience on adult learning. *Psychol. Rep.*, 1960, **7**, 313–322.
DENENBERG, V. H., & KARAS, G. G. Interactive effects of infantile and adult experiences upon weight gain and mortality in the rat. *J. comp. physiol. Psychol.*, 1961, **54**, 685–689.
LEVINE, S., & LEWIS, G. W. Critical period for effects of infantile experience on maturation of stress response. *Science*, 1959, **129**, 42–43.
SCOTT, J. P. Critical periods in the development of social behavior in puppies. *Psychosom. Med.*, 1958, **20**, 42–54.
WILLIAMS, E., & SCOTT, J. P. The development of social behavior patterns in the mouse, in relation to natural periods. *Behaviour*, 1953, **6**, 35–64.

C. J. PFAFFENBERGER & J. P. SCOTT

4 The Relationship Between Delayed Socialization and Trainability in Guide Dogs

A. INTRODUCTION

The senior author since 1945 has been Chairman of the Puppy Testing Committee of a project for selecting puppies to be raised and trained as guide dogs for the blind. At the time this project was first set up barely 25 per cent of dogs trained could pass the final tests, and a great many failed because of "inability to take responsibility." This meant that the dogs were not able to exercise independent judgment in meeting unusual situations, even when related situations had been covered by the training procedure. Such dogs would react well in training, but lost confidence and became confused when required to lead a trainer who was actually blindfolded.

In an effort to remedy this situation a program of puppy testing and selection was set up in consultation with staff members of the Division of Behavior Studies at the Jackson Laboratory and Dr. C. S. Hall, then at Western Reserve University. This program was put into effect and careful records were kept of the performance of the animals.

When we analyzed these data we found that an experimental environmental variable had been accidentally introduced and that it was producing important effects on the results of training. The puppies which were kept in the kennels after the early testing program showed a much higher percentage of failures than those removed to homes immediately. This result has considerable bearing on the studies of the effects of early socialization. The results of the selection program will be discussed in another paper.

B. SUBJECTS

As shown in Table 1, the puppies used were predominantly from the German Shepherd breed. There was a considerable rate of attrition between puppyhood and the time of training at one year of age. Of 185 puppies which passed the puppy tests only 124, or 67 per cent, were given guide dog training. Those eliminated were divided into three approximately equal categories: died, unsuitable size, or retained for breeding. None of these factors involved are related to the early environment of the subjects. Of 64 puppies which failed the test, 30 were selected as controls to test the efficiency of the puppy testing program. The subjects thus comprise two groups, selected respectively for

Reprinted from *The Journal of Genetic Psychology* 95:145–155, 1959.

Data for this work was collected at Guide Dogs for the Blind, Inc., San Rafael, California, and analyzed while the senior author was a Guggenheim Fellow at the Roscoe B. Jackson Memorial Laboratory, Bar Harbor, Maine.

probable proficiency and lack of proficiency in the training program. The results for each population are analyzed separately.

TABLE 1
BREED OF ANIMALS GIVEN GUIDE DOG TRAINING

Breed	Passed tests Became guide dogs	Failed	Failed tests Became guide dogs	Failed	Total
German Shepherd	61	42	5	25	133
Labrador Retrievers	12	2			14
Boxers	5				5
German Short Hair	1	1			2
Total	79	45	5	25	154

C. METHODS

1. *Birth to Eight Weeks*

The standard type of training and environment can be briefly described as follows: from birth to five weeks of age the puppies are confined to the 24 x 40 inch whelping box and to the puppy room where they are born. There is an access door to the kennel run, but usually only the mother uses this as the threshold is 14 inches high. At about five weeks of age the puppies and mother are moved to the puppy kennel, where the exit is more convenient for the puppies to go in and out. They start playing in their runs, which have a concrete floor enclosed by a chainlink fence and are approximately 7 feet wide and 22 feet long. All kennels are radiant heated in winter and air conditioned in summer. At night the puppies are confined to the kennel, which is 8 feet long by 6½ feet wide. While the walls of each compartment or puppy room do not reach the ceiling, they are 4½ feet high and thus prevent the puppies from seeing anything that is going on outside of their own compartment until after they start playing in their runs. In the runs they see other puppies in adjoining runs and the mothers which still have unweaned litters. Thus they have an environment rich in dogs but meager in human contacts.

The kennel manager (female) cleans the kennel rooms daily, keeping the floor covered with torn newspaper for bedding. The runs are scrubbed down each morning before the puppies are released from the compartment. The door from the run to the compartment is closed after the puppies are let out to play in runs, keeping puppies out while the compartment is cleaned. After that, puppies may enter and leave freely during the day. These runs are concealed from other human activities by walls on four sides, except for an access sidewalk.

The kennel manager feeds each bitch in the compartment with the puppies. As soon as the puppies are old enough to start trying to eat, food is put in for them, usually about a week or 10 days before they are weaned. Except for such medication as may be needed, their feeding, and the cleaning of the kennels, the puppies have no contact with people until they start playing in the runs, and then only incidentally as staff members or puppy testers pass their pens while going about their work on the access walk. This leads only to the runs and the incinerator, and so has a minimum amount of use.

At seven, nine, and eleven weeks of age the puppies receive their inoculations against hepatitis and distemper. During this procedure the puppy is handled and has more extensive contact than usual.

2. *Eight to Twelve Weeks*

Beginning on the first Thursday after the eighth week birthday the puppies are given the simple training and testing program summarized in Table 2.

TABLE 2
PUPPY TESTING PROGRAM*

		Age in weeks				
Name of test		8	9	10	11	12
Weighing, observe sense organs, teeth		x	x	x	x	x
Physical Measurement		x	x	x	x	x
Trainability:	come	x	x	x	x	x
	sit	x	x	x	x	x
	fetch	x	x	x	x	x
	heel	x	x	x	x	x
Responses to novel or frightening situations through stimulation of:	ear	x	x	x	x	
	body	x	x	x	x	
	eye					x

* In addition pups were rated as to intelligent response, willing temperament.

This requires about 30 minutes each week, and during this time the puppy comes into contact with several testers, mostly women.

During the tests the puppies are taken out of the kennel runs for the first time. They are first taken to a weighing room, and then to a testing room where they are given simplified dog training: learning to come when called, sit on command, walk on a leash, and to retrieve a ball.

The puppy is then placed in a small pen outside the kennel and tested for his reactions to sound and touch. On the final week the puppy is taken out into a simulated city block area and exposed to moving objects and obstacles similar to those it may meet later as a guide dog. This test most closely simulates its later experience as a guide dog.

Each puppy is rated by two observers on its performance, and in addition is given a general rating on "intelligent response" and "willing temperament."

In general, this experience briefly introduces the puppy to a new and much more complex social and physical environment. The puppy meets this experience alone, unsupported by its familiar social group, and outside its accustomed locality.

3. *Twelve to 52 Weeks*

Time of removal to private homes. This is the experimental variable. Puppies on schedule were promptly removed at 12 weeks. However, some were left in the kennels for periods varying from one to 11 weeks afterward, depending on whether homes were immediately available. As it happened, exactly 50 per cent of the puppies which passed the tests were kept in the kennels more than two weeks, while 73 per cent of the control group were kept longer (see Table 3).

TABLE 3
EFFECT OF HOLDING PUPPIES IN KENNEL BEYOND 12 WEEKS OF AGE

Weeks in kennel	Passed tests Became guide dogs	Failed	Failed tests Became guide dogs	Failed	Total Became guide dogs	Failed
0–1	36	4	1	5	37	9
1–2	19	3	0	2	19	5
2–3	11	8	4	5	15	13
3 or more	13	30	0	13	13	43
Total	79	45	5	25	84	70

The puppies are individually raised in private homes by 4-H Club members. Instructions are given on how to care for the dogs and how to give them simple training. The home environments are not identical, but the dogs are sent out to them by random choice, and supervision is exercised so that only homes are used which provide good environment for the animals. In the home environment a puppy is isolated from other dogs, has close contact with several people but particularly with the one child who cares for it, and has a rich physical environment closely related to the environment where it will eventually live.

4. *Fifty-Two Weeks*

The dog is returned to the kennels and is given an intensive training as guide dog over a period of 12 weeks. The animal may be discarded at any time during this period if it does not respond adequately to training. The dog is scored by the trainers on a series of tests. The reasons for failure are summarized in Table 4.

D. RESULTS

When the number of failures in training is analyzed according to the time at which the puppy is placed in the foster home (see Table 3 and Figure 1), it is seen that the record of dogs which passed the original tests and were placed immediately after 12 weeks is excellent, with approximately 90 per cent of success. The record of those placed in the second week is slightly poorer, but not significantly so, while those which have been retained in the kennel more than two weeks show a highly significant increase in the number

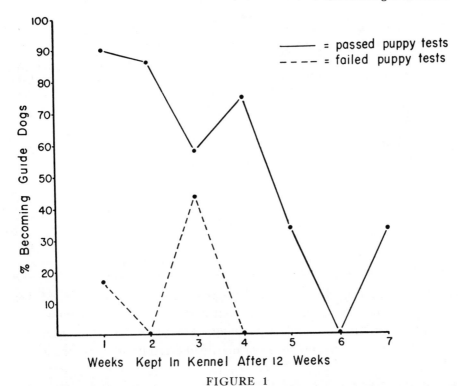

FIGURE 1

Puppies retained in the kennel more than two weeks after the conclusion of testing at 12 weeks of age show a markedly poorer performance as guide dogs. Puppies which failed the original tests are even poorer. Fluctuations in the curves are probably caused by small numbers.

of failures. A comparison of the puppies left in the kennels more than two weeks with those removed sooner, using the Chi-square test, gives a probability of obtaining such a result by accident of random sampling of less than .001.

The record of puppies which failed as puppies and were used as controls for the predictive value of the puppy tests is, as expected, much poorer in both early and late groups than the record of puppies which passed the tests. However, no statistical comparison is possible between early and late groups, since only eight out of 30 pups were removed from the kennel within two weeks after completion of the tests. Within this small sample there was actually a greater proportion of failures among puppies removed early. Adding all puppies together gives almost exactly the same Chi-square value for the effects of early and late removal from the kennels as was obtained with the "passed" group alone. It may be concluded that leaving the puppies in the kennels for more than two weeks has an important effect on their later trainability, at least in animals which pass the puppy tests.

Detailed causes of failure are shown in Table 4. Those animals which failed the puppy tests show a different distribution of reasons for failure as

TABLE 4

REASONS FOR FAILURE OF GUIDE DOG TRAINING

Reasons for Failure	Passed tests		Failed tests	
	Out before 2 weeks	Out after 2 weeks	Out before 2 weeks	Out after 2 weeks
Refuses to take responsibility	3	16		2
Will not train		3	4	7
Frightened of people, awnings, obstacles	2	11	3	7
Flighty, unstable	1	1		
Sharp (bites, aggressive)	1	3		
Car sick		1		1
Nervous wetting or defecation		3		
Too soft (over reacts to correction)				1
	7	38	7	18

guide dogs, indicating that the tests have separated two genetically different populations. The tests evidently select out a large proportion of dogs which are timid or will not respond to training. On the other hand, refusal to "take responsibility" appears to be primarily the result of being retained in the kennels.

Among puppies which passed the tests, the rate of failure for each cause is increased approximately five times as the result of retention in the kennel. It is suggestive that the last three items on the list, including nervous wetting, are found only in dogs retained in the kennels, but the numbers are too small to be significant.

E. DISCUSSION

1. *Relation to Primary Socialization*

In previous studies it has been shown that the puppy normally begins the process of primary socialization at approximately three weeks, and that if human contact is completely prevented the process becomes noticeably difficult by seven to eight weeks of age (4, 5, 6). By 12 weeks of age primary socialization to human beings becomes so difficult that it is almost impossible to train a dog so that it is closely attached to human beings. This process of forming a close social relationship with human beings involves taking the puppy from the mother and litter during the period of socialization and making it entirely dependent upon the human handler.

The dogs in the present experiment were not entirely deprived of human contact during the first eight weeks, but neither were they given any experiences which would make them completely dependent on human handlers. Dogs reared in this fashion till later life tend to become increasingly timid toward human beings, particularly toward strangers. During this period they are usually strongly interested in the food brought by the caretaker, and show no excessive fear or attraction.

From eight to 12 weeks puppies are given an opportunity for closer contact with human beings. This means that the development of a deeper social relationship is begun only at the very end of the period of primary socialization. Furthermore, this training is carried on for a period of only one half hour per week. It is surprising that this amount of contact will produce a normal dog. Whether it would be sufficient if continued into adult life is not answered by the data.

Under the regular system, intensive socialization is delayed until 12 weeks of age, when the puppies are placed in homes. So far, the amount given appears to be sufficient for success in guide-dog training, at least for the selected group of puppies which pass the tests.

The puppy which is retained in the kennels two weeks longer suffers in two ways. The moderate degree of socialization experience involved in the testing procedure is broken off, and intensive socialization is delayed still farther beyond the end of the natural period. It is not clear whether age is the factor involved, or the breaking off of the early relationship. At any rate, the increase in the failures due to refusal to take responsibility indicates a disturbance of social relationships.

2. *Effect of Poor and Rich Environment*

The fact that many of the pups fail because of fearful reactions, in addition to the lack of confidence alluded to above, raises the possibility that the pups may not have had a sufficient variety of early experience in order to develop familiarity and confidence in new situations.

Hebb (2), Melzack and Scott (3), and Thompson and Heron (7) have offered data showing that animals reared in barren environments are unable to deal effectively with the problems of life in a rich adult environment. The environments in the experiments described by these authors are barren both in a physical and a social sense. By contrast, puppies reared as guide dogs have for the first eight weeks a barren physical environment, a relatively barren one regarding human contacts, and a rich one in respect to other dogs. From eight to 12 weeks they are taken out for brief weekly periods into an environment rich in physical contacts and human social contacts. The life in the foster home is similarly a rich one in these respects. If we assume that the poor results with animals kept in the kennels is due to a barren physical and human environment, we must conclude that there is a critical period during which an animal must make contact with a rich environment if it is to have a permanent effect. This explanation is closely related to the next.

3. *Critical Periods of Learning*

Thorpe (8) has found that in the life of song birds there is a critical period in which the song can be learned from the adults, and that this cannot be done earlier or later. Tinbergen (9) observed that Eskimo dogs in Greenland learned territorial boundaries within a week of the time of sexual maturity. This, however, occurs much later in life than the phenomenon found in guide dogs.

It is possible that there is a critical period at approximately 12 weeks for learning and adjusting to a new physical environment. This is suggested by some of our observations of puppies reared in large fields. These animals tend to stay close to the nest box until approximately 12 weeks of age, and then begin to wander farther away.

4. *Break in Socialization*

The senior author of this paper is inclined to believe that the phenomenon produced here is the result of a break in the process of socialization. During the testing period the puppies are being given only a minimum amount of socialization each week and, if this is discontinued for two weeks or longer, the animal may forget its early training in this respect and be unable to relate it to later experience. With this in mind, puppies which now must be left in the kennels beyond 12 weeks are being given the regular tests each week, thus providing human contacts and socialization. The results should decide between the hypothesis of a break in socialization and those hypotheses which depend on maturation.

In conclusion, we can say that the experiment definitely demonstrates an effect of delay of normal early social experience on later behavior. It does not provide a clear-cut differentiation between various theoretical explanations which might be responsible for it.

The phenomenon itself is an interesting one, not only because of its practical use in the rearing of guide dogs, but because of its implications for human behavior. The "taking of responsibility" required of the guide dog is essentially similar to one kind of social relationship which is demanded of adult human beings. The guide dogs which fail for this reason tend to be (in human terms) somewhat socially immature and overdependent.

The dog's experience may be compared to that of a child in an orphanage, well cared for but having no special contacts with adults except for a group of visitors who come once per week and take him for a short excursion into the outside world. In one case they finally take him away permanently to a new home outside. In the other, they forget to come for several weeks, but finally come again and suddenly take him to a new home.

The studies of Bowlby (1) on the effects of deprivation of maternal care on children raised in normal homes indicate that serious emotional disturbances result. In the above case, where the relationship set up is a more superficial one, we would expect a less drastic effect. Puppies treated in this fashion appear to get along fairly well in their foster homes, and it is only when they face the strain and responsibility of guide-dog training (which involves adjusting to still another group of people and new circumstances) that they fail.

F. Summary

1. Dogs trained as guide dogs for the blind frequently fail in training at one year of age. The most frequent cause of failure is failure to take responsibility for the blind person in situations requiring independent judgment.

2. This paper describes an experiment in which factors of heredity and early experience were varied.

3. Two hundred forty-nine puppies, predominantly of the German Shepherd breed, were given a series of aptitude tests at eight weeks and continuing through 12 weeks of age. Of these, 185 passed and 64 failed. One hundred twenty-four of the first group and 30 of the second were given guide dog training at one year of age.

4. Performance as a guide dog involves the development of a close social relationship with a human being. The development of this relationship occurs as follows: (a) 0–8 weeks—kennel rearing; casual contact with caretaker during cleaning and feeding; (b) 8–12 weeks—kennel rearing; one-half hour weekly periods of intensive socialization as puppies are tested; contact with several persons; (c) 12–52 weeks—home rearing; intensive socialization with a child and its family; (d) 52 weeks—return to kennel; intensive training in the guide dog relationship with a trainer; transferral of this relationship to the blind owner.

The development of this relationship may be compared to that of a child reared in an orphanage, removed to a foster home, and finally leaving home as an adult.

5. An environmental variable is introduced when dogs are left in the kennel beyond the age of 12 weeks. Since training is discontinued during this time two factors may affect these dogs: (a) age at which adjustment is made to the foster home, (b) a break in the developing relationship with human beings.

6. Puppies which passed the aptitude tests are significantly different from those which failed, both in the number of failures as guide dogs and the reasons for failure. This supports the validity of the original tests.

7. Of the group which passed, 50 per cent were kept in the kennels two weeks or more beyond the age of 12 weeks. Those kept longer than two weeks show a highly significant increase in failures as guide dogs, all causes of failure being multiplied about five times. Numbers in the "failed" group were not sufficiently large to make a statistical comparison, but these additions to the total do not change the result.

8. It is concluded that failure to develop a satisfactory relationship as a guide dog is produced both by the factor of heredity and that of early experience.

9. Two hypothetical explanations are offered for the effect of early experience: (*a*) a break in the development of a social relationship with consequent emotional disturbance, (*b*) a critical period for learning the adult social environment (or for adjusting from a "poor" to a "rich" social environment). Either one or both factors may be involved.

10. The result can be compared to the development of social relationships as experienced by children reared in orphanages.

REFERENCES

1. BOWLBY, J. Maternal Care and Mental Health. Geneva: World Health Organization, 1951.
2. HEBB, D. O. The effects of early experience on problem solving at maturity. *Amer. Psychol.*, 1947, **2**, 306-307.
3. MELZACK, R., & SCOTT, T. H. The effects of early experience on the response to pain. *J. Comp. & Physiol. Psychol.*, 1957, **50**, 155-161.
4. SCOTT, J. P. The process of socialization in higher animals. In: *Interrelations between the Social Environment and Psychiatric Disorders*. New York: Milbank Memorial Fund, 1953.
5. ————. Critical periods in the development of social behavior in puppies. *Psychosom. Med.*, 1958, **20**, 42-54.
6. SCOTT, J. P., FREDERICSON, E., & FULLER, J. L. Experimental exploration of the critical period hypothesis. *Personality*, 1951, **1**, 162-183.
7. THOMPSON, W. R., & HERON, W. The effects of early restriction on activity in dogs. *J. Comp. & Physiol. Psychol.*, 1954, **47**, 77-82.
8. THORPE, W. H. Learning and Instinct in Animals. London: Methuen, 1956.
9. TINBERGEN, N. The Study of Instinct. Oxford: Clarendon Press, 1951.

MARVIN ACK, IRVING MILLER, & WILLIAM B. WEIL, JR.

5   Intelligence of Children with Diabetes Mellitus

IT IS WIDELY RECOGNIZED that an understanding of the intelligence and the intellectual functioning of patients with chronic diseases plays a critical role in the management of such illnesses as diabetes mellitus. The life expectancy for children with diabetes is lengthening, so their future as adults must be thoughtfully considered. Their productivity as adult members of society is contingent upon the enlightened management of all aspects of their disease, and in particular the physician needs to understand the effect of diabetes on intellectual functioning and intellectual potential.

Reprinted from *Pediatrics* 28:764–770, 1961.

This study was supported in part by the National Institute of Arthritis and Metabolic Diseases, Public Health Service (Grant A-1317), the Foundation for the Study of Diabetes and Related Metabolic Disorders, the Cleveland Diabetes Fund, and the Lorain (Ohio) United Health Foundation.

Although the need has long been recognized as crucial and the problem of the intellectual functioning of persons with diabetes mellitus has been under investigation since 1922, nonetheless our knowledge of the intelligence of persons with diabetes is extremely sketchy. Results of previous investigations are contradictory. Many of the studies have been based on groups of patients in which unrecognized bias occurred as a result of the method of patient selection. The present communication is intended to indicate some of the inconsistencies and misconceptions that exist.

The study reported here is part of a longitudinal study of diabetes mellitus in children designed to investigate the relationship between the duration of the disease process and the intellectual functioning of these children during a period of 10 to 15 years. The results reported here represent findings of the initial phase of the larger investigation. In this initial phase, the authors were primarily interested in whether certain factors could possibly affect the level of intellectual functioning of children with diabetes as measured by I.Q. tests. These factors are age of onset of the illness, duration of the illness at the time of examination, and the number of episodes of hypoglycemia and acidosis.

PROCEDURE

The subjects were 38 children with diabetes mellitus receiving their total medical care at University Hospitals of Cleveland. The age range of these children was from 3 years 1 month to 18 years 6 months, with a mean age of 10 years. The group of children being followed is comprised of those children ordinarily followed in a University Hospitals Outpatient Department plus all the diabetics referred as private patients to one of us (W.B.W.). Thus a wide range of socioeconomic levels is represented. In an attempt to control factors such as environmental background, educational opportuni-

ties and geographic location, one sibling from each family was randomly selected and tested.* The age range of the siblings was from 3 years 1 month to 17 years 3 months, with a mean of 9 years 4 months.

The Stanford-Binet Intelligence Scale, Form M, was administered individually to each child. The variable used in testing all hypotheses was the difference in I.Q. score between a diabetic and his sibling (diabetic I.Q. minus sibling I.Q.). If a specific factor has no effect upon the intellectual functioning of children with diabetes, then the differences, when classified according to that factor, would tend to have an average value of zero throughout, rather than a trend with changing values of the factor.

With regard to age at onset, the I.Q. differences were divided into two groups: those for diabetics whose disease was diagnosed before the age of 5 years and those for diabetics who became ill at or after the age of 5. A mean difference was computed for each group and compared. Age 5 was selected as a point of division for two reasons. Experience in the treatment of emotionally disturbed children has demonstrated that traumatic experiences such as hospitalizations, surgical procedures, separations, *etc.*, before the age of 5 are infinitely more significant for future development than are the same experiences after this age. It is known that children under 5 years have only limited personality resources available for the handling of such disturbing events, and therefore the possibility of pathologic sequelae is greatly enhanced. The second reason that led the authors to choose this age is that the most striking structural maturational changes in the infantile brain are largely completed

* The only factors not controlled by this population were age and sex. Previous investigations on intellectual functioning indicate that there is no significant difference in intelligence between sexes. To have used a population which would have controlled for the age factor would have meant sacrificing other variables inherently controlled by the use of siblings.

during the first 5 postnatal years, and if any disturbance in carbohydrate metabolism occurs while the maturational process is going on, the likelihood of irreversible organic damage occurring is increased.

Other factors were investigated as explained under the sections entitled "Results" and "Discussion". The number of episodes of hypoglycemia and acidosis were obtained and quantified as follows. The only hypoglycemic episodes enumerated were those in which convulsions occurred or those in which the child was seen in a hospital emergency ward or was admitted to a hospital for this complaint. The episodes of acidosis that were counted were limited to those in which the child was

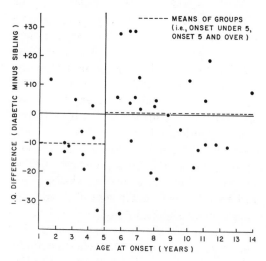

FIG. 1. I.Q. differences according to age at onset of diabetes.

admitted to the hospital and analytic documentation of the disturbance was confirmed.

RESULTS

Effect of Age at Onset

Detailed data on effect of age at onset of diabetes are plotted in Figure 1, and are summarized in Table I.

A t test on the differences shown in Table I gave t=2.13, or a p value slightly less

than 0.05, indicating that age at onset does have an effect on the intellectual functioning of children with diabetes.

It is also interesting to note that separate

TABLE I

MEANS OF PAIRED I.Q. DIFFERENCES BY AGE AT ONSET OF DIABETES

	Age at Onset	
	< 5 yr	>5 yr
Number of pairs of siblings	13	25
Average difference in I.Q.	− 10.15	+ 0.720
Sample variance*	145.5	261.5

* Sample variance was calculated as:

$$S^2 = \frac{\sum\limits_{i=1}^{m} (X_i - \overline{X})^2}{m-1}$$

t tests indicate that the mean I.Q. difference for the group with age of onset under 5 years is significantly different from zero (p <0.02), and that for the other group is not. Therefore, it appears that children who become diabetic before the age of 5 years suffer some intellectual impairment, and those who become diabetic after this age show no such decrement.

Effect of Length of Illness

It is apparent that age of onset and duration of disease at time of testing could be related.* Accordingly, a more meaningful test of the effect of length of illness would be one in which the sample was controlled on age of onset. In order to do this a so-called nonparametric technique[1] was used. The I.Q. difference for those with a total duration of less than $2\frac{3}{12}$ years and those with duration of more than $2\frac{2}{12}$ years in each age group was compared with the

* Patients with early onset (roughly before 7 years of age) tended to have a higher average duration of illness and a much wider range of duration than patients with late onset, but these points were not subjected to statistical test.

medians for the two age groups as to whether they were above (+) or below (−) the median. The data were then examined, as shown in Table II. It is apparent without a formal test that length of illness does not affect the I.Q. differences.

Effect of Episodes of Hypoglycemia and Acidosis

The data indicated a negative relationship between I.Q. difference and the total number of both types of episodes only for patients in whom the onset occurred before 5 years of age (Fig. 2). The number of episodes of each type were generally too few or too concentrated around a few values to permit meaningful separate analysis. Episodes occurring both before and after the age of 5 were counted. Although the data are suggestive, it turns out that the negative linear regression coefficient (onset before 5 years) of I.Q. difference on number

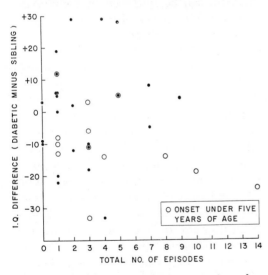

FIG. 2. I.Q. differences according to total number of episodes of hypoglycemia and acidosis.

of episodes is not significantly different from zero (p >0.10).

Because siblings were used as controls, age, of course, could not be controlled. In order to ascertain whether diabetic-sibling age differences were affecting I.Q. differ-

ences, an analysis using the same method as in Table II was undertaken.

It is apparent, without a formal test, that diabetic-sibling age difference does not affect I.Q. difference.

TABLE II

EFFECT OF LENGTH OF ILLNESS ON I.Q. DIFFERENCE,* WITH AGE OF ONSET CONTROLLED

Length of Illness at Time of Examination	Age at Onset†		
	< 5 yr	>5	Totals
<2 yr 2 mo	3+ (2.3) 2−	7+ (6.7) 7−	10+ (9) 9−
>2 yr 2 mo	3+ (3.7) 5−	5+ (5.3) 6−	8+ (9) 11−
Total	13	25	38

* I.Q. differences are compared with medians for each age group (+ indicating above and −, below). Figures in parentheses indicate expected number of observations above medians if length of illness had no relationship to I.Q. difference.

† Equal groups of 19 each.

COMMENT

As has been stated, though much attention has been given to the problem of intellectual functioning of diabetic children, previously reported research presents evidence to support contrary views. A review of these studies indicates that there have been three implicit hypothesis underlying a majority of these studies. The first assumes that children with diabetes are probably of lower than average intellectual ability.[2-5] Teagarden[2] summarized the reasoning for this position by stating:

There are reasons for thinking that neurological and psychological functions may be impaired by diabetes and that insulin shock may produce neurological damage. Therefore, it seems unlikely that diabetic children as a group will be superior intellectually. There is no biological reason why they should be superior.

The second hypothesis assumes that diabetic children possess higher than average

TABLE III

EFFECT OF DIABETIC-SIBLING AGE DIFFERENCE ON I.Q. DIFFERENCE, WITH
AGE AT ONSET CONTROLLED

	Age at Onset*		
	<5 yr	>5	Total
Sibling older than diabetic	4+ (4.2)	5+ (4.3)	9+ (8.5)
	5−	4−	9−
Sibling younger than diabetic	2+ (1.8)	7+ (7.7)	9+ (9.5)
	2	9−	11−
Total	13	25	38

* Expected values are given in parentheses.

intelligence.[6-8] The underlying assumption is that because of the physical limitations often imposed upon these children, they compensate for this by excessive emphasis upon intellectual activities.

By far the largest group of investigators[9-14] suggest that the intelligence of children with diabetes is normally distributed and does not differ significantly, in either direction, from that of the total population.

When one reviews the previous work accomplished in this area it is clear that many of the factors known to affect intelligence were not sufficiently controlled to rule out the possibility of bias. The major factor ignored in almost all of the investigations reported was socioeconomic standing. It is a well-established fact that socioeconomic background is positively correlated with level of intelligence as measured by standard I.Q. tests. Yet of all the studies quoted, only one[9] achieved any measure of control over this very important variable. Those studies in which lower I.Q.'s were found among diabetics, when compared with national norms, were based on samples drawn from clinic populations and therefore from lower socioeconomic backgrounds.[1, 4, 10] Those investigations indicating that diabetic children are of higher than average intelligence were based on samples from private patients of higher socioeconomic levels.[2, 7, 8]

Because the number of diabetic patients available to any one clinical investigator is limited, it is nearly impossible to select a sample that faithfully reflects the socioeconomic distribution of the population and other possibly important variables. It is extremely doubtful, therefore, if the understanding of the intelligence of children with diabetes can be furthered by simply comparing the mean I.Q. of randomly acquired patients with published national norms. As a result of this limitation, it becomes necessary to select a control group matched for all—or as many as is possible—of the variables known to affect the measurement of intelligence. Unless one uses such a control group and attempts to equalize the effects of socioeconomic background, age, educational opportunities and sex, little can be scientifically stated from the mere testing of children with juvenile diabetes. Only Brown and Thompson[9] used an adequate control group. In 28 of their cases the next oldest sibling was also tested. White[6] used a control group matched for age, but the control of just this one variable is not sufficient. In the present study, the use of siblings as control subjects served to take into account socioeconomic, ethnic, geographic and environmental factors that could affect I.Q.

Another serious limitation of the previous studies is the lack of any systematic attempt to assess the relative importance of factors such as age of onset, the duration of illness at the time of examination and the number of episodes of hypoglycemia and/or keto-acidosis. In light of the first hypothesis, which assumes that diabetes has a degenerative effect upon intelligence, it is unusual that more longitudinal studies involving follow-up investigations and retesting were not attempted. Fischer and Dolger,[11] who also deplore the lack of long-term investigations, did retest 10 patients; but this, of course, is an extremely small sample.

Although the studies mentioned were concerned with the I.Q. status of diabetics in general in relation to the total population, in view of the finding that age at onset may have some bearing on I.Q., the usefulness and validity of such an over-all verdict is questionable. Such a verdict from the present sample, for purposes of comparison, could be done only if it is reasonable to assume that this sample reflects the general population of child diabetics by age at onset. We have little evidence to make this assumption, but if made, our sample indicates an over-all judgment that there is no I.Q. difference between diabetics and their nondiseased siblings. A comparison of the over-all mean I.Q. difference of our sample with zero produced a t value of −1.18, which is not significant.

The preponderance of children with onset after 5 years of age in our sample obscured the importance of age of onset when an over-all judgment was made. If the importance of age at onset is borne out by additional studies or by extension of our own series, it would seem imperative to determine the etiology of this I.Q. loss.

The data on episodes of severe hypoglycemia and acidosis as related to loss of intellectual capacity in the young diabetic indicate that either or both of these metabolic disturbances could be important. It is intriguing that the one child with three episodes of loss of diabetic control, and whose I.Q. is 33 points below that of her sibling (Fig. 2), has an I.Q. of 109; the sibling has an I.Q. of 142; another sibling (not

the randomly selected one) has an I.Q. of 129. Furthermore, the child had a peculiar episode of apnea at age 2 years (prior to diabetes) in which mouth-to-mouth resuscitation was required, and normal respiration did not return for a period of about 30 minutes. If this value were not included, the slope would be significant, with a p value between 0.02 and 0.05. However, we feel that we have no firm basis for excluding this observation. The apneic episode was discovered accidentally, and there was no systematic search for events of this type prior to the onset of diabetes. While the present data do not implicate hypoglycemia and acidosis as possible causes of loss of intellectual functioning, the final resolution of this question must await a larger sample and/or the development of a more precise method of counting episodes.

Prolonged hypoglycemia has been related to mental deterioration, and whether the relatively brief periods observed in diabetes is important remains to be determined. The work of Kety et al.[15] on the correlation of decrease in cerebral oxygen uptake with increase of ketones in serum in diabetic acidosis would indicate that episodes of acidosis could be a rational etiologic agent in the decreased I.Q. of the preschool diabetic as well.

It would have been more desirable to test each of these types of metabolic disturbances separately and to limit the episodes to those that occurred prior to 5 years of age, but the relative infrequency of these severe aberrations in control and the small size of the group made this impossible.

The amount of hypoglycemia and acidosis occurring after 5 years of age does not appear to affect I.Q. in this group of patients. The data indicate no relationship whatever between the diabetic-sibling I.Q. differences and the number of episodes of acidosis and hypoglycemia for the group with onset after 5 years of age.

Other metabolic abnormalities are known that lead to mental deterioration in the early years of life but do not have such an effect in older children. Galactosemia and phenylketonuria do not produce continuing loss of mental functioning after the infancy period. Hypothyroidism is not associated with permanent cerebral damage when the onset is in later childhood, in contrast to the retardation associated with cretinism. Severe jaundice is not a factor in the production of mental deficiency in older individuals, but it certainly has an effect on the newborn. Thus it does not seem unreasonable that the young diabetic may have some loss of I.Q. as a result of early metabolic disturbances that do not produce damage in later childhood.

An alternate hypothesis has already been suggested, namely, that the impact of a chronic illness on a child under 5 years results in some degree of intellectual loss. The critical factor appears to be the immaturity of the personality. By the time the average child reaches 5 years of age he has matured sufficiently to handle successfully many events that might have been upsetting at an earlier age. This fact has been recognized for years by educators, who have established the age of 5 years as the critical age for the beginning of school. The child under 5, however, does not have the resources available to his older counterpart and is much more vulnerable to environmental stress. Therefore, the onset of diabetes with all of its ramifications tends to overwhelm the younger child. Much of his mental energy that would normally be used for sublimated intellectual activity remains bound by the illness and unavailable for such pursuits.

The specific dynamics involved in the intellectual loss are not known, but two possibilities have suggested themselves to the authors during the course of this investigation. Because the child under 5 has only an incomplete picture of himself, the onset of diabetes has an especially disrupting effect on this development. The child tends to feel himself damaged, different and worthless, and this attitude becomes translated into feelings of inadequacy in intellectual endeavors. It also seems that diabetes disrupts the normal growth of independence, both mental and physical, so that the child does not feel capable of adequate, independent functioning.

Because of the small size of the present sample, the findings must be considered tentative. However, because of the importance of this finding, the authors hope other investigators of childhood diabetes will consider the collection of similarly controlled data, so that the numbers of cases could be expanded in an attempt to settle this important question. For our part, we intend to retest the diabetics and their siblings regularly to determine if the above difference persists, and to expand the study to include children with other chronic illnesses.

SUMMARY

I.Q. tests were administered to 38 pairs of diabetic and nondiabetic children. In each family the nondiabetic child was a randomly selected sibling of the diabetic child. No relation was found between I.Q. difference (diabetic I.Q. − sibling I.Q.) and duration of illness. Children in whom diabetes began before the age of 5 years had significantly lower I.Q.'s than their nondiabetic siblings. There was no statistical difference between the diabetic and his sibling when the disease began after 5 years of age. A suggestive relationship (but not statistically significant) was found between the number of episodes of hypoglycemia and acidosis and the magnitude of the I.Q. difference between diabetics and siblings for those with onset of disease before 5 years of age.

REFERENCES

1. Mood, A. M.: Introduction to the Theory of Statistics. New York, McGraw-Hill, 1950, Chapt. 10.
2. Teagarden, F. M.: The intelligence of diabetic children with some case reports. J. Appl. Psychol., **23**:337, 1939.

3. Miles, P., and Root, H. F.: Psychologic tests applied to diabetic patients. Arch. Intern. Med., **30**:767, 1922.

4. Dashiell, J. F.: Variations in psychomotor efficiency in a diabetic with changes in blood sugar level. J. Comp. Psychol., **10**:187, 1930.

5. Shirley, H. F., and Greer, I. M.: Environmental and personality problems in the treatment of diabetic children. J. Pediat., **16**:775, 1940.

6. White, P.: Diabetes in Childhood and Adolescence. New York, Lea, 1952.

7. West, H., Richey, A., and Eyre, M.: Study of the intelligence of juvenile diabetics (Abstract). Psychiat Bull., Claremont College, **31**:598, 1934.

8. Grishaw, W. H., West, H. F., and Smith, B.: Juvenile diabetes mellitus. Arch. Intern. Med., **64**:787, 1939.

9. Brown, G. D., and Thompson, W. H.: The diabetic child: an analytic study of his

10. development. Amer. J. Dis. Child., **59**:238. 1940.

10. McGavin, A., *et al.*: The physical growth, the degree of intelligence and the personality adjustment of a group of diabetic children. New Engl. J. Med., **223**:119, 1940.

11. Fischer, A. E., and Dolger, H.: Behavior and psychologic problems of young diabetic patients: 10-20 year survey. Arch. Intern. Med., **78**:711, 1946.

12. Lisansky, E. S.: Convulsive disorders and personality. J. Abnorm. Soc. Psychol., **43**:29, 1948.

13. Johannsen, D. E., and Bennett, E. N.: The psychodynamics of the diabetic child. Psychol. Monogr., **68**:11, 1954.

14. Kubany, A. J., Danowski, T. S., and Moses, C.: The personality and intelligence of diabetics. Diabetes, **5**:462, 1956.

15. Kety, S. S., *et al.*: The blood flow and oxygen consumption of the human brain in diabetic acidosis and coma. J. Clin. Invest., **27**:500, 1948.

Chapter Three

GENETICS AND BEHAVIOR

There has been much naivete in the literature concerning how genes influence development and behavior. Virtually all this literature has been written by people with no formal education in modern genetics and, indeed, virtually no background in either biology or zoology. The knowledge explosion of the past 17 years in genetics has passed them by.

Why do nongeneticists use genetic interpretations of their data? One reason is the study of "individual differences" in human populations. The measurement of individual differences by the psychometrician in both psychology and education has a long and rich tradition, and the contribution these researchers have made to the measurement and prediction of a vast variety of psychological and behavioral characteristics has been of considerable importance. As long as this research was pragmatic in nature and empirical in content (so-called "dustbowl empiricism"), there was no controversy. However, as soon as researchers began to attribute causal mechanisms to their findings of statistically reliable individual differences, controversy was upon us. The two most obvious sets of causal determinants (only slightly updated from the days of Darwin and Galton) were (1) genetic factors and (2) early environmental experiences. For some reason, no one took the obvious next step of concluding that *both* genetic factors and experience were jointly important in determining any behavioral characteristic. There was some lip service to the idea, but no one thought about it seriously enough to build it into a research design. An illustration is provided by the work on the Intelligence Quotient and the argument about whether a person's IQ was genetically determined and immutable or could be raised by appropriate environmental experiences. A more sophisticated question, equally empty and based on a misconception regarding the meaning of "heritability" statistics, was what proportion of a person's intelligence was genetically determined and what proportion attributable to environmental factors.

This controversy is still with us and will continue to interfere with our research and logical thinking until we can span the conceptual generation gap that separates modern biologists, with their updated understanding of genetic determinism, from the behavioral and social scientists whose model of genetic thought more nearly resembles the Model A than the model based upon DNA.

(The fact that many workers in the behavioral and social sciences misunderstand genetic concepts and employ them erroneously in interpreting their data should not be considered an asymmetrical arrangement. Zoologists and geneticists are often guilty of equally naive errors when they attempt behavioral interpretations of some of their data.)

One of the important conceptual errors that has persisted for years is the belief that behavior is genetically determined. This is typified in such statements as, "the IQ is inherited." If one thinks about this situation, it becomes apparent that any behavioral characteristic is complexly determined by the individual's genetic background, the nutritional status and general health of the mother during pregnancy and while nursing her young, the nature of the postnatal physical environment, the family interactions with the baby, the social relations of the child with its peers, and so on. Thus, to state that a particular characteristic is genetically determined is essentially to ignore everything we know about factors which influence growth and development. Ginsburg (1958) has expressed this position exceptionally well in his statement that "all aspects of an organism may be thought of as 100 per cent genetic but not 100 per cent determined." The reason for the lack of determinism is "environmental influences which, in the extremes, determine whether the processes can continue and produce an organism and — within the most reasonable boundaries — provide substance, energy, and milieu for the unfolding of the potentialities already represented in the fertilized egg." Ginsburg is a geneticist who has been investigating genetic-behavior interactions from a gene-action approach. The reader is referred to his 1958 paper for a literate and well-articulated discussion of how genetics may be used as a tool in the study of behavior, as well as to a more recent review and summary of his research (Ginsburg, 1967).

Though one cannot ask whether behavior is inherited, one can ask the important experimental question: Are behavioral *differences* genetically based? Animal populations (e.g., highly inbred fruit flies or mice) in which genetic differences are known to exist among strains can be reared under identical environmental conditions so that the only difference between groups is that brought about by genetic factors. One may then measure any of a variety of phenotypes (i.e., dependent variables) to determine whether there is a significant difference among the groups. If there is, this difference may be attributed to the difference in the genetic make-up of the animals tested. Note the great distinction between the erroneous statement that a certain behavioral characteristic is genetically determined and the correct statement that the behavioral difference between two strains of animals is genetically based. This method of conceptualizing the relationships between genetic factors and behavioral characteristics has been discussed by

Hinde and Tinbergen (1958), two zoologists who have specialized in ethology. The reader is referred to their article for a thoughtful discussion of this concept.

A more up-to-date version of the question, Is this behavior inherited? is the question, What proportion of this behavior is attributable to genetics? Continuing with our analogy of the Intelligence Quotient, the question posed is: What proportion of a person's IQ is due to hereditary factors, and what proportion is due to environmental influence? Again, upon careful consideration, it is apparent that this question cannot be answered for the general case because of all the intricate interactions across time involving genetic and nongenetic factors. For example, one group of individuals may manifest a certain behavior which is different from that of another group of individuals; these two groups may also differ on several genetic factors. However, these two groups in all likelihood differ on a number of environmental dimensions as well, including such things as maternal nutrition, diet during infancy, and nature of the rearing environment. Thus, to try to determine the proportion of the behavior attributable to genetic as compared with nongenetic factors becomes a logical impossibility.

The difficulty, of course, is that genetic and nongenetic factors *interact* with one another instead of behaving in an *additive* manner. For a simple analogy consider the area of a rectangle. If we ask the question, What proportion of the area of the rectangle is due to its length and what proportion is due to its width? we immediately see the fallacy of such thinking. The length and width multiply against each other rather than adding together, and it is because of the nature of multiplicative (or interactive) functions that we cannot talk meaningfully about the proportion due to genetic factors and proportion due to nongenetic factors. However, the student who thinks in an analytical fashion immediately realizes that we can attack this question by the experimental procedure of holding one variable constant while allowing the other one to vary systematically. Thus, with the rectangle, we can keep the length constant and vary the width, or vice versa. And, of course, by doing so, we can readily demonstrate that the area of the rectangle was "caused" by the variable of length, or we can equally well demonstrate that the area of the rectangle was "caused" by the variable of width. The analogy breaks down at this point because the rectangle, entirely determined by two dimensions, is too simple a model to represent genetic-environmental interactions. One principle, however, emerges from this discussion: *the manner in which genetic factors express themselves is a complex function of the environment in which those genes exist.* The readings in this chapter have been chosen to demonstrate that principle.

Paper 6 has nothing to do with behavior. It is concerned with the effects of a single gene upon the resistance of mice to the lethal effects of radiation. The paper was chosen because it illustrates some of the exquisite techniques that geneticists have for manipulating genetic materials, because it demonstrates that a single gene can have powerful effects upon an organism, and because it shows that the nature of the genetic effect is dependent upon the surrounding genetic material (i.e., the "environment"). Though Doolittle discusses the effects of radiation upon five different strains of mice, the reader should pay particular attention to the two strains designated as SEA/Gn and SEC/1Gn. In these two strains there is a recessive mutation called the short-ear gene which is designated by the symbol *se*. The normal dominant gene is designated by the symbol *Se*. The presence of a pair of short-ear genes in an animal (i.e., *sese*) results in an animal which has a very small ear. If an animal is fully dominant for these genes (i.e., *SeSe*) or is a mixture of one dominant and one recessive gene (i.e., *Sese*), the animal will have normal length ears. It is important to emphasize that this same mutation is present in both the SEA/Gn strain and the SEC/1Gn strain, so that the effects of this single gene upon two different genetic backgrounds can be determined. Using animals which are genetically identical except for a single gene mutation enables the investigator to study the effects of that specific gene, and its

mutation, upon phenotypic expression, with the remaining genes and the environmental conditions held constant. This is a powerful tool for genetic research.

One other genetic phenomenon should be noted here. Genes often have multiple effects. This is called *pleiotropy*. Thus the short-ear gene, in addition to reducing the amount of cartilage around the animal's ears, also modifies its susceptibility to radiation.

Though Doolittle's entire paper should be examined, the reader's attention should be focused upon Table 2 and the two columns which summarize the data for the SEA/Gn strain and the SEC/1Gn strain. The figures in that table indicate the average number of days that the animals survived following irradiation. In the column labeled "Gene dose" the numbers 0, 1, and 2 refer to the number of recessive *se* genes present. Thus, 0 indicates the *SeSe* genotype, 1 refers to the *Sese* genotype, and 2 refers to the *sese* genotype. The first important set of findings for the principle of concern to us is found under Test (B), where the males and the females of strain SEA/Gn are compared. Males with one recessive gene lived an average of 16.1 days, while males with two recessive genes lived 14.8 days, a significant difference. On the other hand, females with one recessive gene lived 14.8 days, while those with two recessive genes lived 16.6 days. Therefore, the addition of a second recessive gene can either significantly increase or decrease survival time following irradiation depending upon the sex of the animal involved.

Turning now to Test (C), fully dominant males (i.e., *SeSe*) lived 24.2 days. The addition of a single recessive gene had no effect (these males lived 24.3 days), while the presence of two recessive genes markedly reduced survival time to 17.3 days. The females, however, show an increase in survival time as a function of the number of recessive genes. Fully dominant females lived 17.3 days, those with one recessive gene lived 19.8 days, while those with two recessive genes lived 23.9 days.

Now look what happens when the identical genes are placed on a different genetic background. Consider the Test (C) males for the

SEC/1Gn strain. Those with no or one recessive gene lived 19.2 days, while those with two recessive genes lived 21.4 days. This is opposite from the finding for the SEA/Gn strain. This paper therefore demonstrates that a single gene can affect an important biological process, namely, survival time following irradiation. It demonstrates that a gene's effects are dependent upon the surrounding "environment" of the other genes, since survival time varies as a function of differences in genetic background of the strains involved. This is an example of the subtlety and complexity of modern genetic research and it makes clear that questions such as, What proportion of this variable is due to heredity? are nothing but pseudoquestions in this context.

Paper 7 also illustrates that the manner in which genes express themselves is a function of the environment in which the genes exist. Here we return to the behavioral level. Previous research had shown that animals whose early environment was enriched, performed markedly better in problem-solving behavior (see Chapter Ten). This was known to be the case for animals whose genetic endowment made them "average" in learning ability. Cooper and Zubek's objective was to determine the effects of environmental enrichment or restriction upon animals of known superior and inferior genetic endowment with respect to problem-solving behavior. They were able to demonstrate that genetically "dull" rats reared in an enriched environment were as competent in problem solving as were the far better endowed "bright" rats. Likewise, the bright and the dull group were equally poor in solving problems if they were both reared in restricted environments. The only instance in which the genetic difference between the two groups expressed itself was when the animals were reared under normal laboratory environmental conditions. In other words, the problem-solving capabilities of these animals were jointly determined by their genetic background and the environment in which they grew and developed.

The dog is an excellent animal for studying genetic-environmental interactions because of the variety of breeds available with different behavior patterns, physical characteristics, and temperaments. This rich research potential was used by Freedman (Paper 8), who took four different breeds and reared them in early life under conditions of indulgence or discipline. His critical test was to observe the reactions of the dog to a bowl of food after it had been punished for eating from the bowl. With two of the breeds Freedman found that the manner of rearing was without effect, but that the breed characteristic (i.e., genetic nature) was important. However, with two other breeds, Freedman was able to demonstrate that the animals reared under indulgent conditions were less likely to eat than were those reared under disciplined conditions.

At the human level there are a number of genetic anomalies which result in physiological and behavioral pathology. One of these is phenylketonuria, a disease caused by a single recessive gene. An individual with a pair of these recessive genes is unable to metabolize phenylalanine, an amino acid which occurs naturally in the body. Phenylalanine is necessary for a number of bodily functions, and the organism cannot live in its absence. Unfortunately, when this amino acid is not properly metabolized and excreted from the body, waste products accumulate and affect brain tissue, and this results in mental retardation. However, the situation is not hopeless because the expression of the recessive gene can be modified by changing the environment in which that gene acts. This is done by feeding the baby or child a low-phenylalanine diet — one which gives the body enough phenylalanine to function normally but not so much that there is an accumulation of waste products. Paper 9 reports the intelligence test scores of phenylketonuric children who were started on such a special diet at different ages in early development. Scores were obtained both before and after the diet was started. As controls there were two reference groups. One consisted of siblings of these treated children who did not have phenylketonuria; thus their intelligence test scores give an indication of what the phenylketonuric children would have been like if they had not had the disease. The second reference group consisted of children who received no dietary treatment; they reveal the long-term consequences of this disturbance. These researchers found that the mental deterioration brought about by the biochemical consequences of the recessive gene could be arrested and reversed somewhat by keeping the children on the low-phenylalanine diet. All treated groups had an increase in intelligence scores following dietary therapy, while the scores of the untreated children progressively decreased. Another finding of importance was that the longer the delay in introducing dietary treatment, the greater was the intelligence loss. Even the children who received treatment before the age of 4 months were markedly lower in intelligence than controls. This may indicate that the recessive gene is always associated with some mental retarda-

tion regardless of age at treatment, or it may indicate that therapeutic intervention must start at birth or even in utero if the negative expression of this gene is to be reduced still further.

References

Ginsburg, B. E. Genetics as a tool in the study of behavior. *Perspect. Biol. Med.,* 1958, 1, 397-424.

Ginsburg, B. E. Genetic parameters in behavioral research. In J. Hirsch (Ed.). *Behavior-Genetic Analysis.* New York: McGraw-Hill, 1967, pp. 135-153.

Hinde, R. A., and Tinbergen, N. The comparative study of species-specific behavior. In A. Roe and G. G. Simpson (Eds.). *Behavior and Evolution.* New Haven: Yale University Press, 1958, pp. 251-268.

DONALD P. DOOLITTLE

6 The Effect of Single Gene Substitutions on Resistance to Radiation in Mice

STRAIN differences, indicating differences in genetic factors, in response to radiation damage were first reported by HENSHAW (1944), who found that more radiation was required to produce a given effect in LAF$_1$ hybrid mice than to produce the same effect in inbred C3H mice. The effects he studied included the lethal dose, hematology, and the histopathology of the lymphoid organs, bone marrow, and testes. Since then, numerous workers have demonstrated strain differences in various responses to radiation (RUGH 1953).

GRAHN and HAMILTON (1957) found differences in the median lethal dose (LD$_{50}$) of four strains of mice. GRAHN (1958) crossed the least and most resistant of the four strains and estimated the heritability of the LD$_{50}$ from data on F$_1$, F$_2$, and a few F$_3$ offspring. The estimate, approximately 50 percent, indicated that the difference between the strains crossed was genetic.

From these studies we may conclude that genetic differences at many loci, collectively, can cause differences in radioresistance. The question remains whether single loci can influence resistance sufficiently to be important. HANCE (1928) reported that if mice heterozygous for the albino gene, *c*, were exposed to X-rays with partial body shielding, the unshielded portions grew white hairs, while mice homozygous for the color gene, *C*, did not show this effect. CHASE

Reprinted from *Genetics* 46:1501–1509, 1961.

This investigation was supported in part by contract AT(30-1)-1979 of the United States Atomic Energy Commission and by grant CRT-5013 of the National Institutes of Health.

(1949) could not show any increased effect in six *BbCc* mice he irradiated. STORER (unpublished) compared normal heterozygotes (*SeSe*) and short ear homozygotes (*sese*) in the strain SEC/1Gn, and found that, under daily doses of 100 roentgens of X-rays, the two genotypes of each sex survived for different periods. GRAHN (1958) thought that the albino segregants from his outcrosses of F₁ females to A/Jax males were less resistant than their colored littermates. Neither of these investigators tested sufficient numbers of mice for an adequate experiment.

The purpose of this paper is to report the results of comparing mice differing at a single loci with respect to their resistance to radiation. Five inbred strains, each segregating at single loci, were used for this purpose. Mice of each of the three genotypes at the segregating locus were compared in each stock. The criterion of radioresistance was the survival time under daily doses of X-rays.

MATERIALS AND METHODS

Five inbred stocks of mice, each segregating for two alleles at a single locus, were used in this study. Table 1 shows the strains used in this study. The "number of generations inbred" represents the number of generations of brother-sister mating with heterozygosity forced on the segregating locus by backcrossing, except in the case of strain C57BL/6J-*a^t*. The latter strain was maintained by repeated backcrossing of *a^t a* individuals to *aa* individuals from the inbred strain C57BL/6J.

In strains SEA/Gn and SEC/1Gn, the short ear locus was segregating for the normal (*Se*) and short ear (*se*) alleles. *SeSe* and *Sese* animals are normal in phenotype; *sese* individuals are distinguished by the reduced size of the external ear (LYNCH 1921) due to a severe reduction in the cartilage of the ear. GREEN (1951) reviewed the known pleiotropic expressions of the *se* gene, including many skeletal and cartilaginous defects, as well as some other anatomical abnormalities and reduced body size, and showed that most of these can be related to a single primary effect of the gene in reducing the growth rate of cartilage in the *sese* embryo. Embryonic mortality seems to be greater among *sese* embryos than among their normal littermates, and while *sese* individuals may survive as well as *SeSe* or *Sese* under favorable environmental conditions, *sese* animals succumb more readily to stress (SNELL 1931).

Strain C57BL/6J-*a^t* carried two alleles at the agouti locus, black-and-tan, *a^t*, and nonagouti black, *a*. DUNN (1928) first described the action of the *a^t* gene; *a^t a^t* and *a^t a* mice are black dorsally, with orange or yellow ventral fur, while *aa*

TABLE 1

Strains and segregating loci

Strain	Segregating locus	Number of generations inbred
SEA/Gn	*Se/se*	50
SEC/1Gn	*Se/se*	50
C57BL/6J-*a^t*	*a^t/a*	12 (BC)
HRS/Ls	*Hr/hr*	15
129/J	*c^{ch}/c*	21

mice are black on back and belly. No pleiotropic action of these genes is known. It should be noted that since this strain was maintained by backcrossing a^ta individuals to the inbred strain C57BL/6J, which is homozygous aa, the a gene in this strain occurs on a genetic background that has been adapted to it by the process of selection in the formation of the inbred strain. The a^t allele is foreign to the background on which it appears in this strain.

The HRS strain was segregating at the hairless locus for the normal (Hr) and hairless (hr) alleles. $HrHr$ and $Hrhr$ animals are normal in phenotype; $hrhr$ animals appear normal until the age of about 10–14 days, at which time they begin to lose their hair. By the age of 20–24 days, $hrhr$ mice are completely naked. At about six weeks of age, an abortive regeneration of the hair may take place, after which the mouse remains hairless until death (BROOKE 1926). Hairless mice eat voraciously. In older mice, the skin tends to thicken and wrinkle. The eyes and teeth are weak and the nails tend to be abnormal (DAVID 1930). Prenatal and early postnatal viability of $hrhr$ individuals is apparently normal, but after the loss of hair, the hairless mouse is less viable than normal; as might be expected, they are especially susceptible to low temperatures. CREW and MIRSKAIA (1931) noted that since the establishment of their colony in 1925, selection and outcrossing had improved the viability of the hairless mice. About 50 percent of their hairless females proved infertile, and those that were fertile could not suckle their young, for the mammary glands were abnormal. In our HRS strain, however, as in the hairless mice studied by STEINBERG and FRASER (1946), hairless females seemed normally fertile, and were usually successful in suckling their young. It would appear that this pleiotropic effect of the hr gene has also been altered by selection.

The 129/J strain carried two alleles at the albino locus, chinchilla, c^{ch} and albino, c. The chinchilla gene, described by FELDMAN (1922), dilutes yellow pigment to a faint cream or ivory, but does not affect black pigment. In this strain, which was homozygous for pink-eyed dilution (pp) and white-bellied agouti (A^wA^w), $c^{ch}c^{ch}$ animals were a light orange-brown on the dorsal side with white bellies. Heterozygous $c^{ch}c$ animals were cream or ivory colored dorsally; their bellies also were white. Animals homozygous for the albino gene (cc) were, of course, pure white albinos. No information exists on the relative vigor of these three genotypes; in our strain, none of the three appeared to have an obvious advantage in vigor.

In each strain except 129/J, one or two pairs of heterozygous sibs were obtained from the generation indicated in Table 1 and mated together. Offspring of the dominant genotype were test-mated to homozygous recessive sibs. Production of seven mice, all of dominant phenotype, from such a cross was considered sufficient grounds to conclude that the animal under test was homozygous dominant.

One homozygous dominant male was then mated to two homozygous dominant and one homozygous recessive females. Simultaneously, one homozygous recessive male was mated to one homozygous dominant and two homozygous recessive females. In this way, approximately equal numbers of mice of each genotype, homozygous dominant, heterozygous, and homozygous recessive, were produced. The eight animals required for each set of six matings as described above were as closely related as possible. In most cases, all were full sibs; in a few cases one animal was a double first cousin of the rest.

In the 129/J strain the testing procedure was unnecessary since the three genotypes $c^{ch}c^{ch}$, $c^{ch}c$, and cc were distinguishable. Several pairs of sibs were obtained; one of each pair was of the genotype $c^{ch}c$, the other cc. Matings within these sib pairs gave $c^{ch}c$ individuals which were mated together to produce all three genotypes for testing.

The offspring of the genotype test matings made in each strain, except 129/J, were irradiated beginning at an age of 33 days. Tests on these mice will be referred to as tests A. Mice from the sets of six matings were also exposed at the age of 33 days; tests on these mice will be referred to as tests B. Other mice from these same matings, or from the $c^{ch}c \times c^{ch}c$ matings in strain 129/J, were exposed beginning at an age of 120 days; these are the tests C. In each strain and test group, approximately ten animals of each sex and genotype were used.

The source of radiation was a General Electric Maxitron 250 deep therapy X-ray machine, run at 250 kvp, 20 ma. The mice were exposed in plastic centrifuge tubes on a rotating table 24 inches from the X-ray tube. A filter of 1.0 mm Al, 0.5 mm Cu was used. Each mouse was exposed to 70r daily from the beginning of exposure until it died. The number of days till death was used as the criterion of radiation resistance.

Daily readings of the dosage rate were made with a thimble chamber exposed on the rotating table on every day when mice were exposed. Due to variability of the power source, the average dosage rate received by different mice varied from 0.9r per second to 1.4r per second, although each mouse received a standard 70r per day, within the two percent error of the dosimeter. The average dosage rate received by a mouse was negatively correlated with the survival time. A covariance analysis was used to remove effects of the dosage rate both within and between groups. The results in the tables of the following section are, therefore, adjusted for the regression of survival time on average dosage rate.

RESULTS

The results of the tests are summarized in Tables 2 and 3. Table 2 gives means and standard errors of survival times in days, adjusted for regression on the

TABLE 2

Mean survival times and standard errors of the means

Test	Sex	Gene dose*	SEA/Gn Se/se	SEC/1Gn Se/se	C57BL/6J-a^t a^t/a	HRS/Ls Hr/hr	129/J c^{ch}/c
(A)	Male	1	19.7 ± 0.76	18.0 ± 0.88	24.8 ± 1.22	20.5 ± 1.00	....
		2	18.6 ± 0.72	17.2 ± 1.05	21.7 ± 2.17	20.3 ± 1.17	....
	Female	1	20.7 ± 0.69	16.4 ± 1.23	22.9 ± 1.26	20.3 ± 0.80	....
		2	19.5 ± 0.89	17.1 ± 0.46	22.2 ± 1.46	23.6 ± 0.75	....
(B)	Male	0	....	12.0 ± 0.63	....	16.1 ± 0.77	....
		1	16.1 ± 0.67	13.5 ± 0.16	....	....	....
		2	14.8 ± 0.85	13.8 ± 0.23	....	15.2 ± 1.08	....
	Female	0	....	13.1 ± 0.26	....	16.2 ± 0.50	....
		1	14.8 ± 0.41	13.4 ± 0.34	....	....	....
		2	16.6 ± 0.95	13.8 ± 0.21	....	15.5 ± 0.56	....
(C)	Male	0	24.2 ± 1.00	19.2 ± 1.40	37.4 ± 0.57	23.5 ± 1.84	29.2 ± 2.79
		1	24.3 ± 1.40	19.2 ± 0.40	24.1 ± 1.07	20.6 ± 2.44	36.1 ± 3.51
		2	17.3 ± 1.16	21.4 ± 1.71	39.9 ± 1.10	26.8 ± 1.78	36.0 ± 3.03
	Female	0	17.3 ± 0.89	18.6 ± 1.03	31.3 ± 1.00	17.5 ± 0.61	34.3 ± 2.53
		1	19.8 ± 0.92	18.8 ± 0.87	18.9 ± 0.61	19.9 ± 1.00	36.9 ± 3.04
		2	23.9 ± 1.23	18.2 ± 0.77	32.5 ± 1.10	18.3 ± 0.93	38.2 ± 1.13

* Gene dose refers to the number of recessive genes, or of c genes in strain 129/J.

average dose rate, for each genotype-sex combination in each of the three groups. In Table 3, the analyses of variance for each test group are summarized.

TABLE 3
Results of variance analysis

Test group	Source of variation	d.f.	SEA/Gn MS	F	d.f.	SEC/1Gn MS	F	d.f.	C57BL/6J-a† MS	F	d.f.	HRS MS	F	d.f.	129/J MS	F
(A)	Genotypes	1	14.05	2.23	1	0.87	<1	1	39.14	<1	1	28.74	2.89	1	⋮	⋮
	G × S Interaction	1	0.01	<1	1	6.68	<1	1	13.33	<1	1	33.87	3.00	1	⋮	⋮
	Error	34	6.31		42	13.46**		31	29.28		36	9.93		36	⋮	⋮
(B)	Genotypes	1	0.30	<1	2	3.96	1.97	⋮	⋮	⋮	1	3.31	<1	⋮	⋮	⋮
	G × S Interaction	1	15.64	4.60*	2	0.07	<1	⋮	⋮	⋮	1	0.15	<1	⋮	⋮	⋮
	Error	22	3.40		134	2.01**		⋮	⋮		24	3.93		⋮	⋮	⋮
(C)	Genotypes (linear)	1	0.23	<1	1	87.16	7.42*	1	102.49	11.64*	1	15.64	<1	1	1.10	<1
	Genotypes (nonlinear)	1	22.89	1.11	1	78.57	6.69*	1	1031.22	117.05*	1	5.45	<1	1	2.36	<1
	G (linear) × S	1	279.58	13.51*	1	96.57	8.22*	1	4.99	<1	1	1.32	<1	1	145.83	1.36
	G (nonlinear) × S	1	43.24	2.09	1	84.15	7.16*	1	4.16	<1	1	99.20	4.36*	1	19.43	<1
	Error	48	20.70**		48	11.75**		48	8.81		36	22.73**		60	107.38**	

* F test significant at the 0.05 level.
** Within subclass error variances nonhomogeneous.

SEA/Gn: In this strain, no *SeSe* animals were available for test B, so that in both test A and test B, the comparison was between *Sese* and *sese* animals, only. No differences were observed in test A. In test B, however, *Sese* males were more resistant than *sese*, while *Sese* females were less resistant than *sese*. In the mature mice in test C, where all three genotypes were compared, male *SeSe* and *Sese* were about equally resistant, and both were more resistant than *sese*. In females, on the other hand, resistance increased in the order *SeSe*, *Sese*, and *sese*; the increase in resistance was almost linear with increasing dosage of the *se* gene. These effects appear to be real, despite the nonhomogeneity of the subclass error variances, which throws some doubt on the validity of the F test.

It is not too surprising to find that an effect dependent on sexual differentiation appears in animals 120 days old, and not in animals 33 days old. More surprising is the fact that the effect does appear in one set of animals 33 days old (test B). A new and presumably more adequate ration was introduced between tests A and B. Body weights taken prior to the first exposure to radiation reveal that test A animals weighed less than those of test B, and were gaining weight more rapidly. These observations suggest that, although the animals of test A and of test B were chronologically the same age, the test B animals were developmentally more mature, perhaps due to the improved nutrition. This hypothesis, if true, would suggest a simple explanation of the greater resemblance of test B animals to the adult animals of test C.

SEC/1Gn: In this strain, the segregation of the genes *Se* and *se* apparently did not affect the radioresistance of test A or B animals. In test C, *SeSe* and *Sese* males were approximately equal in resistance, while *sese* males were more resistant. *SeSe* and *Sese* females were of approximately the same resistance, but *sese* females were less resistant. Nonhomogeneity of the subclass error variances was noted in all three test groups.

Thus, in both strains segregating at the short-ear locus, differences between the genotypes were found in mature animals. However, the differences were diametrically opposed in the two strains. In SEA/Gn, *se* increased the resistance of females, and decreased that of males. In SEC/1Gn, *se* decreased the resistance of females and increased that of males.

C57BL/6J-a^t: In this strain, there were no animals available for test B, so that only tests A and C were run. In test A, no differences were found. In test C, however, *aa* animals were more resistant than $a^t a^t$. Heterozygous $a^t a$ animals were much less resistant than either homozygote.

The difference in resistance between the homozygotes might be interpreted as an adaptation effect; the gene *a* is native to the rest of the genotype, while a^t is not. There is, however, no apparent general effect on vigor, since the body weights of the two homozygous genotypes, taken before radiation, did not differ.

The low resistance of the heterozygous $a^t a$ animals appears to be an example of negative heterosis. It should be noted, however, that the three genotypes were not compared contemporaneously. Most of the homozygous animals were tested before any heterozygotes were available for testing. Some of the apparent reduced resistance in the heterozygote may therefore be due to temporal environmental changes. Again, the factors affecting resistance do not seem to have general effects on vigor, for heterozygotes weighed more than either homozygous genotype.

HRS/Ls: In this strain, no heterozygous (*Hrhr*) animals were available for test B; therefore, in this test, the two homozygous genotypes were compared. Tests A and B revealed no differences between genotypes. In test C, heterozygous males were less resistant than either homozygote, while heterozygous females were more resistant than either homozygous female genotype. Again, the within subclass error variances were nonhomogeneous. In this case, the males varied more within subclass than did the females. Testing the two sexes separately, the genotypic differences within sex were not significant in either sex. The validity of the F test in the combined analysis is called in question by the nonhomogeneity of error variances; in the separate analyses, since this is a result-guided analysis, the F test is again not valid. The possible difference in radiation sensitivity due to the *hr*-locus should be tested further.

129/J: Since no test matings were made in this strain, there was no test A. The strain was slow in breeding, and it was not possible to obtain enough animals for test B. Therefore, only test C was run on this stock. No differences between genotypes could be shown.

DISCUSSION

The results indicate that a single gene locus, marked by its effects on color or body conformation of the mouse, may also affect resistance to radiation. The effect may take the form of an interaction between sex and genotype, the difference between genotypes in males being different from that in females. A gene recessive in its effect on the visible phenotype may be recessive or partially dominant in its effect on resistance. The type of gene action may also differ in the two sexes. The effect of these genes on radioresistance does not seem to be mediated via general effects on vigor; in general, differences in resistance do not seem to be related to differences in body weight.

This finding has potential value in the evaluation of mechanisms of radiation damage. The correlation of resistance effects of a given gene and other known effects of that gene may yield important clues to mechanisms affording protection from radiation damage. Means of preventing or curing somatic radiation damage in animals or in man might be suggested by such correlations.

Differences between genotypes are likely to be greater in mature mice than in weanlings. As a result, despite the fact that within-class error variances are likely to be nonhomogeneous in mature mice, these seem to be preferable in attempting to assess differences between genotypes. This fact is obviously related to the fact that many of the differences observed are dependent on sex differences.

These results may also throw some light on the question of which sex is more resistant to radiation. ABRAMS (1951) reported no sexual difference in mice less than 90 days old. In our work, sexual differences did not appear in 33 day old mice, but did in mice 120 days old. It may be that ABRAMS found no sexual difference because his mice were too young.

ELLINGER (1950) reported that testosterone decreased the resistance of male mice to X-rays. PATT, SWIFT, STRAUBE, TYREE and SMITH (1949) reported increased resistance in mice given estradiol benzoate. CHAPMAN (1955) found that males were less resistant than females. RUGH and CLUGSTON (1955) also found females more resistant than males, and presented evidence that resistance varied cyclically in females with changes in the level of estrogen production during the estrus cycle.

On the other hand, GRAHN, SACHER and HAMILTON (1954) found females less resistant than males in three strains of mice with different average resistances.

Our results also indicate a general superiority of males in this respect. However, in two cases a single gene change was sufficient to alter the rank of the sexes. It is not hard to imagine that the rank of the sexes may differ between strains differing at many loci if a change at a single locus can affect this character. The irradiation schedule may also be involved. GRAHN, SACHER and HAMILTON used a repetitive periodic exposure schedule; our studies were carried out with a similar schedule. The investigators reporting that females were superior to males used a single exposure, either to determine an LD_{50} or to compare time of survival and percent survival after the single dose of irradiation.

SUMMARY

The results of irradiating animals differing at a single locus in each of five inbred strains are presented. Substituting the short ear gene (se) for its normal allele (Se) in two strains affected radiation resistance, the nature of the effect depending on sex and on the genetic background. Radiation resistance was also affected when the black-and-tan gene (a^t) was substituted for its nonagouti allele (a) in the C57BL/6J genotype. When the hairless gene (hr) was substituted for its normal allele (Hr) the results were not clear, but this substitution may have an effect. There was no indication of an effect from substituting the chinchilla gene (c^{ch}) for the albino gene (c).

The radiation resistance effects were obtained in adults; in general, younger mice did not show any effect. Sex is important in determining the effect of a given substitution on radiation resistance.

ACKNOWLEDGMENTS

The author wishes to express his appreciation to the staff of the Jackson Laboratory for their assistance in carrying out this research.

LITERATURE CITED

ABRAMS, H. L., 1951   Influence of age, body weight, and sex on susceptibility of mice to the lethal effects of X-irradiation. Proc. Soc. Exptl. Biol. Med. **76**: 729–732.

BROOKE, H. C., 1926   Hairless mice. J. Hereditary **17**: 173–174.

CHAPMAN, W. H., 1955   The weight and mortality response of male and female mice in the lethal X-ray dose range. Radiation Research **2**: 502–511.

CHASE, H. B., 1949   Greying of hair. I. Effects produced by single doses of X-rays on mice. J. Morphol. **84**: 57–80.

CREW, F. A. E., and L. MIRSKAIA, 1931   The character "hairless" in the mouse. J. Genet. **25**: 17–24.

DAVID, L. T., 1930   Comparative histologic studies on hairless mammals, with some genetic notes. Univ. Pittsburgh Bull. **27**: 1–27.

DUNN, L. C., 1928   A fifth allelomorph in the agouti series of the house mouse. Proc. Natl. Acad. Sci. U.S. **14**: 816–819.

ELLINGER, F., 1950   Some effects of testosterone propionate on mice irradiated with X-rays. Proc. Soc. Exptl. Biol. Med. **74**: 616–619.

FELDMAN, H. W., 1922   A fourth allelomorph in the albino series in mice. Am. Naturalist **56**: 573–574.

GRAHN, D., 1958 Acute radiation response of mice from a cross between radiosensitive and radio-resistant strains. Genetics **43**: 835–843.

GRAHN, D., and KATHERINE F. HAMILTON, 1957 Genetic variation in the acute lethal response of four inbred mouse strains to whole-body X-irradiation. Genetics **42**: 189–198.

GRAHN, D., G. A. SACHER, and KATHERINE F. HAMILTON, 1954 Genetic and nongenetic factors in the response of mice to periodic subacute doses of X-rays. Radiation Research **1**: 497.

GREEN, MARGARET C., 1951 Further morphological effects of the short ear gene in the house mouse. J. Morphol. **88**: 1–22.

HANCE, R. T., 1928 Detection of heterozygotes with X-rays. J. Heredity **19**: 480–485.

HENSHAW, P. S., 1944 Experimental roentgen injury. II. Changes produced with intermediate range doses and a comparison of the relative susceptibility of different kinds of animals. J. Natl. Cancer Inst. **4**: 485–501.

LYNCH, CLARA J., 1921 Short ears, an autosomal mutation in the house mouse. Am. Naturalist **55**: 421–426.

PATT, H. M., MARGUERITE N. SWIFT, R. L. STRAUBE, ELLA B. TYREE, and D. E. SMITH, 1949 Influence of a conditioning injection of estrogen on the hematologic and organ weight response to X-irradiation. Federation Proc. **8**: 124.

RUGH, R., 1953 Radiobiology; irradiation lethality and protection, Military Surgeon **112**: 395–413.

RUGH, R., and HELEN CLUGSTON, 1955 Radiosensitivity with respect to the estrous cycle in mice. Radiation Research **2**: 227–236.

SNELL, G. D., 1931 Inheritance in the house mouse; the linkage relations of short-ear, hairless, and naked. Genetics **16**: 42–74.

STEINBERG, A. G., and F. C. FRASER, 1946 The expression and interaction of hereditary factors affecting hair growth in mice: external observations. Can. J. Research **24(D)**: 1–9.

R. M. COOPER & JOHN P. ZUBEK

7 Effects of Enriched and Restricted Early Environments on the Learning Ability of Bright and Dull Rats

SEVERAL RECENT SURVEYS of the literature (2, 3, 4, 9) reflect the increased emphasis being placed upon study of the relationship between early environment and later behaviour in animals. Learning ability has received particular attention, and several studies have shown that the learning ability of adult animals is affected by the quality of their infant environment. More specifically, they indicate that animals raised in "enriched" or "stimulating" environments are superior in adult learning ability to animals raised in "restricted" or "unstimulating" environments.

These results were obtained with animals possessing a *normal* heritage

Reprinted from *Canadian Journal of Psychology* 12:159–164, 1958.

This research was supported by a grant in aid from the Associate Committee on Applied Psychology of the National Research Council of Canada. The writers wish to acknowledge their indebtedness to Dr. D. O. Hebb for his critical reading of the manuscript.

of learning ability; hence there remains the possibility of differential effects for animals of superior or inferior endowment. The present study was designed to explore this possibility. Its specific object was to test for possible differential effects of enriched and restricted early environments on the problem-solving ability of bright and of dull rats.

Method

Subjects

Forty-three rats of the McGill bright and dull strains (F_{13}) served as subjects. They were divided into 4 experimental groups: a bright-enriched group containing 12 rats (6 males, 6 females); a dull-enriched group containing 9 rats (4 males, 5 females); a bright-restricted group containing 13 rats (6 males, 7 females); and a dull-restricted group containing 9 rats (4 males, 5 females). Normally reared rats served as controls.

Environments

The 4 groups of experimental animals were placed in 4 cages which occupied a grey painted room 12′ × 6′ × 8′. At one end of the room a window allowed diffuse light to pass through. A large rectangular partition, suspended from the ceiling, divided the room lengthways. The two restricted cages were placed on one side of the partition, the two enriched cages on the other side. The side of the partition facing the restricted cages was grey, matching the colour of the room. The side of the partition facing the enriched cages was white with "modernistic" designs painted upon it in black and luminous paint. The partition was so placed that animals in the restricted environment were unable to see the enriched cages.

The 4 cages, each measuring 40″ × 25″ × 13″, were covered with ½-inch wire mesh. Each of the enriched cages contained the following objects: ramps, mirrors, swings, polished balls, marbles, barriers, slides, tunnels, bells, teeter-totters, and springboards, in addition to food boxes and water pans. Some of the objects were painted black and white, and all were constructed so that they could easily be shifted to new positions in the cage. The restricted cages were identical with the enriched ones in size and mesh coverings, but contained only a food box and a water pan.

Test Apparatus

The 12 problems of the Hebb-Williams closed field maze were administered in the manner described by Rabinovitch and Rosvold (8).

Procedure

The 4 groups of animals were kept in their respective environments from the time of weaning at 25 days of age until the age of 65 days, when testing on the Hebb-Williams maze was begun. They were also kept there throughout the testing period.

Since one of the restricted and one of the enriched cages received more light than the others did from the window, the animals were shifted every three days to equate for this difference. In addition, the objects in each of the enriched cages were moved about at random every three or four days. During these moving periods and while the cages were being cleaned all animals were given the same amount of handling.

RESULTS

For purposes of statistical analysis and interpretation of the data the performances of the enriched and restricted animals were compared with the performances of 11 bright and 11 dull animals raised in a "normal" laboratory environment. These were the animals that formed two control groups in an experiment by Hughes and Zubek (6).

Effect of the Enriched Environment

In Table I are recorded the mean error scores for the bright-enriched group, the dull-enriched group, and the bright and dull animals raised in a normal environment. It can be seen that the average number of errors

TABLE I

MEAN ERROR SCORES FOR BRIGHT AND DULL ANIMALS REARED IN
ENRICHED AND NORMAL ENVIRONMENTS

	Enriched environment	Normal environment
Bright	111.2	117.0
Dull	119.7	164.0

made by the bright animals in the enriched environment is only slightly below that of the bright animals raised under normal conditions (111.2 *vs.* 117.0). This difference is not statistically significant ($t = 0.715$, $p > .4$). On the other hand, the error scores of the dull animals raised in an enriched environment are considerably below those of dull animals reared in a normal environment (119.7 *vs.* 164.0). This difference of 44.3 errors is significant ($t = 2.52$, $p > .02 < .05$). The results indicate, therefore, that an enriched early environment can improve considerably the learning ability of dull animals, while having little or no effect on that of bright animals.

Effect of the Restricted Environment

Table II shows the mean error scores of the bright-restricted group, the dull-restricted group, and the bright and dull animals raised in a normal environment. It is seen that the bright-restricted group made many more

TABLE II

MEAN ERROR SCORES FOR BRIGHT AND DULL ANIMALS REARED IN
RESTRICTED AND NORMAL ENVIRONMENTS

	Restricted environment	Normal environment
Bright	169.7	117.0
Dull	169.5	164.0

errors than the normally raised bright animals. The difference of 52.7 errors is statistically significant ($t = 4.06$, $p < .001$). On the other hand there is no significant difference between the dull-restricted group and the normally raised dull animals ($t = 0.280$, $p > .7$). Thus the dull animals were not affected by their restricted early experience while the bright animals were significantly impaired in learning ability.

Comparative Effects of Enriched and Restricted Environments

Tables I and II also indicate the degree of improvement produced in the dull animals by their period of enriched experience, and the degree of retardation which the bright animals suffered because of their impoverished experience. Although the dull-enriched group averaged 8.5 more errors than did the bright-enriched, this difference is not significant ($t = .819$, $p > .5$). In other words, after undergoing a period of enriched experience the dull animals became equal in learning ability to the bright animals. The difference between the bright- and dull-restricted groups in Table II is also obviously insignificant; thus, the bright animals, after a period of early impoverished experience, showed no better learning ability than did the dull animals.

DISCUSSION

The results clearly show that both enriched and restricted early environments have differential effects on the learning abilities of bright and of dull rats. A period of early enriched experience produces little or no improvement in the learning ability of bright animals, whereas dull animals are so benefited by it that they become equal to bright animals. On the other hand, dull animals raised in a restricted environment suffer no deleterious effects, while bright animals are retarded to the level of the dulls in learning ability.

Although it had been anticipated that the two extremes of environment would have differential effects on the bright and dull animals, the bright-enriched animals were still expected to perform better than the dull-enriched animals. Bright animals, with their presumably better cerebral functioning, would be expected to make better use of the extra experience afforded by an enriched environment than would dull animals, with their presumably inferior cerebral functioning. The bright-enriched group did in fact make fewer errors, and the difference, though not statistically significant, suggests the possibility of a real difference in learning ability which the twelve problems of the Hebb-Williams test failed to reveal. The ceiling of the test may have been too low to differentiate the animals, that is, the problems may not have been sufficiently difficult to tax the ability of the bright rats. This has happened with tests of human intelligence such as the Stanford-Binet (1), on which adults of varying ability may achieve similar I.Q. scores although more difficult tests reveal clear differences between them. It might also be suggested that it is relatively more difficult for the bright animals to reduce their error scores, say from 120 to 100, than for the dull animals to reduce theirs from 160 to 140.

In spite of these possible qualifications of the present results for the enriched environment, it seems reasonable to accept them pending future experimentation.

The effects of the restricted environment are not so difficult to accept. Under such conditions the bright animals, even with their superior learning capacity, would be expected to show an inferior performance. Learning is a function of experience as well as of capacity, and hence, under conditions that severely limit experience, the superior capacity of the bright animals is never fully utilized and they perform far below their potential level. On the other hand, not much decrement would be expected in the dull animals, since they are already functioning at a low level of intellectual capacity.

What physiological mechanism or mechanisms underlie these changes in learning ability? Several theories have attempted to explain the relationship between sensory stimulation and learning behaviour, perhaps the most systematic being that of Hebb (5). Hebb has suggested that neural patterns or "cell assemblies," which he regards as the physiological basis of learned behaviour, are built up over a period of time through varied stimulation coming through specific sensory pathways. This stimulation is especially effective if it occurs during infancy. Others (7, 9) also believe that varied stimulation coming through non-specific projection pathways (e.g., the thalamic-reticular system) aids in the learning process by keeping the brain in an alert state. Thus at the neurophysiological level varied stimulation seems to play a dual role in the learning process; it may act directly on cerebral cells to form cell assemblies, and may also aid learning by keeping the brain "primed" or alert.

If, then, varied stimulation has such an important role in establishing the physiological components (e.g., cell assemblies) underlying learned behaviour, it seems reasonable to assume that a certain level of varied stimulation is necessary if learning (i.e., establishment of cell assemblies) is to occur with maximum efficiency. It may also be assumed that the initial difference in learning ability between the bright and dull rats in some way reflects an underlying neurophysiological difference in their capacity to "utilize" such stimulation. On the basis of these assumptions the present findings might be explained as follows.

In a *normal* environment the level of stimulation is sufficient to permit the building up of cell assemblies (or some other neurophysiological unit underlying learned behaviour) in the superior brains of the bright animals. It is not sufficient, however, to permit them to be readily built up in the inferior brains of the dull animals. In a *restricted* environment the level of stimulation is so low that it is inadequate for the building up of cell assemblies even with the superior cerebral apparatus of the bright rats, who therefore show a retardation in learning ability. The dulls, however, are not retarded further, since the level of stimulation provided by the normal environment was already below their threshold for the establishment of cell assemblies. In the *enriched* environment the level of stimulation is above the higher threshold of the dull animals, who consequently show improvement in learning ability. The brights show little or no improvement because the extra stimulation is largely superfluous, that provided by a normal environment being adequate for the building up of cell assemblies.

Such an interpretation is open to several criticisms. For instance, the assumption that bright and dull rats differ in their inherited capacity to utilize stimulation is open to question. Furthermore, as pointed out above, possible inadequacies of the Hebb-Williams test may throw doubt on the findings for the bright-enriched rats. Nonetheless, although this theoretical interpretation obviously needs a more adequate foundation, it seems best fitted to account for the experimental data in the light of present neurophysiological knowledge.

SUMMARY

Forty-three rats of the McGill bright and dull strains were used as experimental subjects in an investigation of possible differential effects of enriched and restricted early environments on learning ability.

At 25 days of age, 12 bright rats and 9 dull rats were placed in enriched environments, and 13 brights and 9 dulls were placed in restricted environments. At 65 days of age all animals were introduced to the training and testing procedures of the Hebb-Williams maze, their performances being compared with those of normally reared bright and dull controls.

The bright animals reared in enriched environments showed no improvement in learning ability over bright controls reared under normal laboratory conditions. The dull animals, on the other hand, benefited greatly from the enriched experience and attained a level of performance equal to that of the bright animals. Rearing in restricted environments had converse effects. The dull animals suffered no impairment as compared with dull controls, while the bright animals were retarded to the level of the dulls in learning performance.

Possible neurophysiological explanations are suggested.

REFERENCES

1. ANASTASI, ANNE. *Psychological testing.* New York: Macmillan, 1954.
2. BEACH, F. A., & JAYNES, J. Effects of early experience upon the behavior of animals. *Psychol. Bull.*, 1954, **51**, 239–263.

3. BINDRA, D. Comparative psychology. In *Ann. Rev. Psychol.* Palo Alto, Calif.: Annual Reviews Inc., 1957, **8**, 399–414.

4. DREVER, J. The concept of early learning. *Trans. New York Acad. Sci.*, 1955, **17**, 463–469.

5. HEBB, D. O. *The organization of behavior.* New York: Wiley, 1949.

6. HUGHES, K. R., & ZUBEK, J. P. Effect of glutamic acid on the learning ability of bright and dull rats. I. Administration during infancy. *Canad. J. Psychol.*, 1956, **10**, 132–138.

7. MILNER, P. M. The cell assembly: Mark II. *Psychol. Rev.*, 1957, **64**, 242–252.

8. RABINOVITCH, M. S., & ROSVOLD, H. E. A closed field intelligence test for rats. *Canad. J. Psychol.*, 1951, **5**, 122–128.

9. THOMPSON, W. R. Early environment—its importance for later behaviour. Chap. 8 in P. H. HOCH, & J. ZUBIN (Eds.), *Psychopathology of children.* New York: Grune & Stratton, 1955.

D. G. FREEDMAN

8 Constitutional and Environmental Interactions in Rearing of Four Breeds of Dogs

The initial intention of the present study was to determine the relative effects of "indulgent" and "disciplinary" modes of rearing in dogs, with particular emphasis on how each method affects the obedience of the animal at maturity. The work derived from the extensive observations of children made by D. M. Levy (*1*), who has shown that overindulgent rearing may lead to psychopathy, a syndrome which involves an abnormal inability to inhibit one's impulses. The study described in this report was an attempt to deal experimentally with Levy's concept. As will be seen, the results are of interest aside from their reflection on this initial hypothesis.

Eight litters of four pups each were used. These included two litters each of Shetland sheep dogs, basenjis, wirehaired fox terriers, and beagles. Following weaning at 3 weeks of age, each litter of four was divided into two pairs

equated as closely as possible on the basis of sex, weight, activity, vocalizations, maturation of eyes and ears, and reactivity to a startling stimulus. Each member of one pair was thereafter indulged, and each member of the other pair was disciplined, during two daily 15-minute periods from their third to their eighth week of age.

Indulgence consisted of encouraging a pup in any activity it initiated, such as play, aggression, and climbing on the supine handler. These pups were never punished. By contrast, the disciplined pups were at first restrained in the experimenter's lap and were later taught to sit, to stay, and to come upon command. When still older they were trained to follow on a leash. The pups were handled and tested individually by a single experimenter throughout the study. They lived in pairs in isolation boxes the remainder of the time, where members of indulged and disciplined pairs received identical treatment. The results were as follows.

At 8 weeks of age each pup was subjected to the following test: Each time a pup ate meat from a bowl placed in the center of a room, he was punished with a swat on the rump and a shout of "no!" After three minutes the experimenter left the room and, observing through a one-way glass, recorded the time that elapsed before the pup again ate. The results over 8 days of testing are summarized in Fig. 1. Basenjis tended to eat soon after the experimenter left, the method of rearing having no statistically significant effect. Shetland sheep dogs tended to refuse the food over the entire 8 days of testing. Again, the fashion of rearing had no significant effect. Beagles and wire-haired fox terriers, however, differentiated into two significantly disparate groups, depending on the condition of rearing. The Friedman nonparametric analysis of variance (2) indicates that the indulged pups took significantly longer to return to the food than did the disciplined pups ($p = 0.001$). Thus, as measured in this test, essentially the same differences in treatment had a decisive effect upon only two breeds.

Can characteristics of the breeds explain the differences in performance on this test? It was clear that, during training, beagles and wire-haired terriers were strongly oriented to the experimenter and sought contact with him continuously. Basenjis, by contrast, were interested in all phases of the environment and often ignored the experimenter in favor of inanimate objects. Shetland sheep dogs showed yet another pattern; all became fearful of physical contact with the experimenter and tended to maintain distance from him. We see, then, that the two breeds that were highly attracted to the experimenter differentiated as a result of the mode of rearing, whereas the breeds that exhibited aloofness (basenjis) and excessive timidity (Shetland sheep dogs) did not. Apparently it was the strong (constitutional) attraction in interaction with indulgent treatment that enhanced the effectiveness of later punishment. It should be noted that basenjis and Shetland sheep dogs were not entirely unaffected by the differential treatment. The scores of *all* indulged animals were significantly different from those of their disciplined counterparts on five of ten tests administered. In general, these tests indicated that the indulged pups were more active, more vocal, less timid (although more easily inhibited with punishment) than the disciplined pups.

A test of individual reactions to veterinary treatment based on vocalizations and the degree of activity during routine injections indicates that indulged pups were more vocal and active than disciplined pups in their protest ($p = 0.02$, Mann-Whitney) and that basenjis were more vocal and active than the other three breeds ($p = 0.01$, Friedman analysis of variance). It has been found at our laboratory that basenjis generally gain higher scores on this test than other breeds; hence these data suggest that similar behavior may be due in one instance to constitution (as in the basenjis) and in other instances to the conditions of rearing.

A test of the level of activity, in which the pups were observed from a hidden vantage point for 10 minutes, was administered. The testing area was 10 by 20 ft and was demarcated into eight squares of 5 by 5 ft each. In this setting, *disciplined* Shetland sheep dogs showed significantly less activity than any other animals ($p = 0.001$, Friedman analysis of variance). In another test the experimenter sat silently in a room for 10 minutes and recorded the amount of time the pups spent in contact with him.

In this test the *indulged* Shetland sheep dogs differed significantly from all other

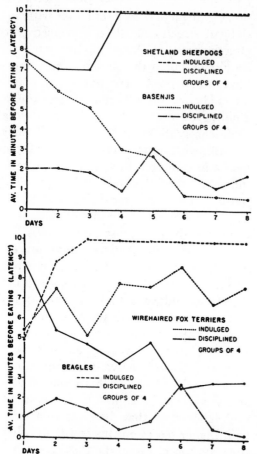

Fig. 1. Performance of 8-week-old puppies on the "inhibition-to-eating" test (see text for details of procedure).

dogs in that they rarely approached the experimenter ($p = 0.001$, Friedman analysis of variance). From these results it is clear that a specific test for a specific breed may facilitate expression of the effects of early rearing.

The conditions of rearing were continued over a second period, when the pups were 11 to 15 weeks of age, and all tests were readministered, with essentially the same results.

In the follow-up observations and tests, the indulged beagles, in contrast to all other animals, underwent dramatic changes, in time, although all animals were maintained under standard conditions. On a weekly test in which the time taken to catch each animal was recorded, these animals became exceedingly shy and wary of being caught when approached by various human beings, including the experimenter ($p = 0.05$, t test). Thus, it appears that changes in the behavior of certain animals may occur that are seemingly independent of the current environment and belatedly dependent, instead, upon the mediation of past experiences.

References and Note

1. D. M. Levy, *Maternal Overprotection*. (Columbia Univ. Press, New York, 1943).
2. S. Siegel, *Non-parametric Statistics*. (McGraw-Hill, New York, 1956).

PHYLLIS W. BERMAN, HARRY A. WAISMAN, & FRANCES K. GRAHAM

9 Intelligence in Treated Phenylketonuric Children: A Developmental Study

Changes in intelligence of 22 diet-treated phenylketonuric children, and of their 6 untreated and 44 unaffected siblings, were studied for an average of 27 months. On both the first and the last intelligence testings, treated children, including those treated from early infancy, had significantly lower

Reprinted from *Child Development* 37:731–747, 1966. © 1966 by the Society for Research in Child Development, Inc.

scores than their unaffected siblings. However, those treated before 2 years were more intelligent than later-treated children. During the study treated children developed more rapidly than they had before treatment but at a significantly slower rate than that of their unaffected siblings. Age at the beginning of treatment was significantly related to initial IQ, but not to rate of development during treatment. The untreated phenylketonuric group tended to show a decline in intelligence.

Phenylketonuria, a disease associated with an inborn error metabolism, has usually been accompanied by severe mental retardation which increases with age, at least up to year 8 (Bickel & Gruter, 1963). During the last decade, however, treatment with a low-phenylalanine diet has prevented severe retardation in many cases. It appears that the age of initiating treatment is important in determining the eventual intellectual attainment, but there is disagreement as to whether treatment is ever completely effective in preventing impairment, even when begun in early infancy. It is also uncertain whether the effect of the age of beginning treatment is due to impairment occurring prior to treatment or to age differences in the capacity to respond to treatment. To the extent that the former is true, intelligence at the onset of treatment should be negatively correlated with age. If there are age differences in capacity to respond, the rate of intellectual growth during treatment should be expected to vary with age.

Several investigators (Bickel & Gruter, 1963; Knox, 1960) believe that little or no deterioration in intellectual potential results when the disease is untreated for the first 6 months of life, but that rapid loss follows thereafter. In contrast, others (Berman, Graham, Eichman, & Waisman, 1961; Centerwall, Centerwall, Acosta, Chinnock, Armon, & Mann, 1961; Woolf, Griffiths, Moncrieff, Coates, & Dillistone, 1958) have found that despite early treatment children with phenylketonuria are less intelligent than their own siblings who are not affected by the disease. In the study by Berman et al. (1961), eight treated children were compared with their untreated phenylketonuric siblings and with siblings who were unaffected by the disease.

This study was supported by the Wisconsin Alumni Research Foundation and by research grants B1550, M2730, M3699, HD-00341, and 5-K3-Mh-21762 from the Public Health Service, National Institutes of Health. During the preparation of the manuscript, the first author was supported by P.H.S. postdoctoral grant 5 F2 MH-25, 137-02. We are indebted to Nancy Rane and Kenneth Kosier for their indispensable help with many phases of the research, and to the parents of the children studied, who so often sacrificed their time and convenience to cooperate with the study. The authors wish to thank Ellen Bahow, Robert Birch, Elizabeth Fisher, Mary Lindquist, Joan Marshall, Don Pearson, Edward Rosenbaum, Laila Salamao, and Richard Whitehill of the University of Wisconsin for their assistance with psychological testing. We also thank Kenneth Blessing of Wisconsin Bureau for Handicapped Children, Karol Fishler of Children's Hospital of Los Angeles, Mary Reidy of Georgetown University, Ronald Todd of Cairo State Hospital, C. Maves of Northern Wisconsin Colony, Gerald Bensberg and Daniel Ringenheim of Southern Wisconsin Colony, and the staffs of the foregoing institutions for making available the results of intelligence tests.

Five of the eight treated children had begun diet therapy before 3 months of age. While the children treated in early infancy were significantly more intelligent than their untreated siblings, they had significantly lower intelligence test scores than those siblings who were unaffected by phenylketonuria. Unaffected siblings were used as a comparison group so that environmental variables and those genetic factors not related to phenylketonuria might be held as constant as possible. Sibling performance was assumed to represent the best estimate of what the performance of phenylketonuric children might have been if the children had not been affected by the disease. Although early-treated children were less intelligent than their siblings without the disease, it was not possible to conclude from the available data whether the decrement was due to loss which had taken place in the period before treatment was initiated or to a slower than normal rate of development during the course of treatment.

The present paper reports results of repeated intelligence tests for an enlarged group of treated phenylketonuric children and for their untreated and their unaffected siblings. Twenty-two children have been treated for an average of 33 months and studied for an average of 27 months. The first children admitted to the sample have been followed for more than four years. It is now possible, not only to compare intellectual status of treated children with that of their unaffected siblings, but also to compare the rates of development of the two groups of children. The additional comparison of treated and untreated phenylketonuric siblings is complicated by the effects of institutionalization on some of the untreated group.

METHOD

Subjects

Subjects were 22 treated children from 19 families and all of their 50 full siblings. The sample included every child receiving treatment for phenylketonuria from the outpatient clinic of the Department of Pediatrics of the University of Wisconsin Medical Center during the period July, 1957, to April, 1964, with the exception of one infant who could not be tested because of blindness. Ten of the treated children (A4, D3, J2, L2, M2, N8, O3, Q5, R4, and S1) had originally been tested for phenylketonuria because of mental retardation. In four cases (B3, G1, H2, and I1), phenylketonuria was detected by routine medical screening. Eight children (A6, C5, D4, E3, F1, J4, K3, and P2) were tested for the disease when it was discovered that a sibling or cousin was affected by phenylketonuria.

Serum phenylalanine levels of all siblings were determined, and on this basis six children who had not been treated were identified as phenylketonuric. The remaining siblings were found to be unaffected by the disease. Treated, untreated, and unaffected subjects are listed by group in Table 1. Family membership is designated by letter, and birth order by number. Subjects included in the earlier report (Berman et al., 1961) are designated by the letter and number previously used.

Treated children were living at home at the time they were admitted to the sample, as were unaffected siblings with two exceptions: Subjects N1 and N2 were working or attending school in cities away from the family home. They were not followed beyond an initial test session.

Of the six untreated phenylketonuric children, three (C1, C3, and P1) were in institutions at the time that their treated siblings were admitted to the sample; E1 and Q4 were living at home but were later institutionalized; N5 remained at home. Untreated children were tested regularly while they lived at home, and after institutionalization all possible data were gathered relating to their development.

During the course of the study, treated subjects L2 and Q5 were institutionalized, but diet therapy was continued. Since scores of institutionalized children were not considered to be comparable to those of children living at home, they and their siblings were dropped from the regular sample at the time of institutionalization, although testing of the treated children was continued in an attempt to assess the effects of institutionalization.

Diet therapy of Subject D3 was terminated at age 6 after 4 years of treatment. Only results of examinations during the treatment period will be reported here.

The 19 families studied represented a somewhat higher than average socioeconomic sample. Four of the fathers were professionals, three owned small businesses, and ten were engaged in clerical, sales, farm, semiskilled, or unskilled work. In two familes the mother was either divorced or widowed and received state aid.

Pediatric Procedure

On his first visit to the clinic, each newly diagnosed child was evaluated by a physical examination after a complete medical and genetic history was obtained from the parents. The pediatrician discussed with both parents the genetic aspects, prognosis, and course of treatment of the disease. The program of dietary control was explained to the parents by the research dietician, and printed information concerning the phenylalanine content of foods and methods for formulation of the low-phenylalanine milk was provided.

During the first year, monthly visits were scheduled for each family, but it was later possible to lengthen the intervals between appointments to 3 months. The parents were seen by the dietician at each visit. Most of the parents were able to follow the diet with little difficulty. When problems were encountered, more frequent visits to the clinic were scheduled, and greater attention was paid to these problems during the visits.

On each visit, the treated child's progress was evaluated by a physical examination, by fasting plasma phenylalanine levels, and sometimes by additional blood samples taken after the child had eaten his usual meal. These phenylalanine levels provided the most objective available checks on the child's response to the diet (Bickel & Gruter, 1963). Care was taken not to restrict phenylalanine to such a severe degree that it interfered with

TABLE 1
First and Last IQ Test Scores[a] of Treated and Untreated Phenylketonuric Children and Unaffected Siblings and Developmental Rates of Treated and Unaffected Children

SUBJECT	FIRST TEST Age (Year)	Deviation IQ or DQ	LAST TEST Age (Year)	Deviation IQ or DQ	DEVELOPMENTAL RATE
Unaffected Subjects:					
A1	9	110	12 11/12	101	0.81
A2	6 9/12	122	10 7/12	133	1.87
A3	5	121	9	132	1.50
A5	2 3/12	91	6 3/12	99	1.04
B1	4 7/12	124	8 5/12	129	1.28
B2	2 8/12	105	6 6/12	111	1.11
C2	8 6/12	153	12 7/12	149	1.65
C4	4 8/12	126	8 11/12	122	1.22
D1	6 7/12	98	10 6/12	87	0.66
D2	5 9/12	120	9 7/12	116	1.17
D5	9/12	101	1 3/12	110	...
D6	4/12	99	4/12	99	...
E2	4 1/12	115	8 11/12	111	1.05
F2	6/12	117	2 7/12	117	1.23
G2	4/12	88	4/12	88	...
H1	4 2/12	101	5 2/12	91	0.58
H3	4/12	115	1 1/12	99	...
I2	5/12	108	5/12	108	...
J1	5 11/12	111	6 5/12	104	...
J3	3 2/12	83	3 2/12	83	...
K1	7 3/12	123	8 4/12	124	1.58
K2	4 8/12	114	5 7/12	129	1.58
L1	2 3/12	108	3 4/12	116	1.38
M1	3 4/12	116	4 4/12	126	1.58
M3	4/12	110	4/12	110	...
N1	19 2/12	126	19 2/12	126	...
N2	17 9/12	82	17 9/12	82	...
N3	16 8/12	109	17 9/12	106	...
N4	13 3/12	99	14 3/12	89	...
N6	8 3/12	115	9 4/12	113	1.08
N7	4	127	4 6/12	118	...
N9	4/12	110	4/12	110	...
O1	6 9/12	130	9 10/12	160	2.54
O2	4 1/12	139	7	163	1.77
P3	2	127	3	128	1.50
P4	1 1/12	120	1 7/12	121	...
Q2[b]	15 2/12	124	16 3/12	123	...
Q3	10 6/12	108	11 7/12	111	1.38
R1	8 5/12	99	9 11/12	95	0.72
R2	7 7/12	90	9 1/12	88	0.72
R3	6	116	7 6/12	103	0.56
S2	2 2/12	90	3 2/12	88	0.75
S3	1 7/12	106	2 7/12	97	0.82
S4	1 11/12	95	2 6/12	106	...
Treated Subjects[c]:					
A6 (3)	4/12	84	2 11/12	92	0.93
G1 (3)	4/12	82	1 4/12	100	1.03
B3 (4)	5/12	87	4 4/12	60	0.57
C5 (5)	1	80	5 1/12	87	0.91
D4 (6)	1 8/12	72	5 7/12	82	0.89
H2 (8)	6/12	90	1 6/12	101	1.05

TABLE 1 (Continued)

SUBJECT	FIRST TEST Age (Year)	Deviation IQ or DQ	LAST TEST Age (Year)	Deviation IQ or DQ	DEVELOP-MENTAL RATE
E3 (10).........	2 4/12	91	7 1/12	115	1.25
I1 (15).........	4/12	84	1 1/12	67	0.57
J4 (25).........	6/12	62	1 4/12	58	0.56
K3 (30).........	11/12	78	2 2/12	86	0.93
L2 (39).........	9/12	36	2	54	0.65
M2 (43)........	1 3/12	63	2 9/12	73	0.78
F1 (51).........	2 8/12	83	6 8/12	81	0.81
N8 (74).........	1 8/12	48	3 2/12	83	1.20
03 (78).........	1 6/12	35	4 8/12	47	0.54
P2 (95).........	1 10/12	98	4 3/12	109	1.21
D3 (104)........	4 4/12	46	5 10/12	43	0.50
A4 (118)........	3 4/12	45	7 2/12	59	0.76
Q5 (145)........	2 9/12	27	4 2/12	47	0.86
R4 (147)........	2 11/12	52	4 5/12	53	0.53
S1 (163)........	3 1/12	24	4 6/12	33	0.78
J2 (186)........	4	48	4 6/12	50	...
Untreated Subjects:					
C1..............	7	[18]d	12 3/12	[7]	...
C3..............	11/12	29	8 6/12	[6]	...
E1..............	2	39	7	15	...
N5..............	5 6/12	40	12 9/12	57	...
P1e.............	...	...	...	...	...
Q4..............	8 11/12	54	11	60	...

aThe conventional Binet IQ scores reported in an earlier paper (Berman et al.) have been adjusted for age differences in the means and standard deviations of the 1937 standardization group.
bThe first-born child of family Q is deceased.
cFigures in parentheses indicate the age, in weeks, at which treatment began.
dScores in brackets were from tests administered to untreated subjects after a period of institutionalization.
eNo intelligence test has been given to untreated Subject P1. His score on the Vineland Social Maturity Scale at 2 7/12 years was 27.

normal metabolism, since undue restriction would lead to the breakdown of the patient's own tissue protein, thus contributing to elevated phenylalanine levels. Generally the serum phenylalanine level was allowed to rise 1 mg/100 ml. for each year of life up to age 5, but at no time was it allowed to remain above 6 mg/100 ml. in a fasting state. In those instances when the level did exceed the desired level, diet was modified within 1 week.

Psychological Procedure

Depending on mental age, the Stanford Binet Intelligence Scale and/or the Cattell Infant Intelligence Scale (a downward extension of the Binet) were administered individually at regular intervals. Forms L and M of the 1937 Binet were used on consecutive test sessions, except that on three occasions several children from families A and N were tested with the 1960 L-M form. To achieve comparability at different ages, scores were corrected for age differences in the means and standard deviations of the 1937 normative group. Such corrected IQ scores are commonly called "deviation IQ's."

When the study began, six subjects (A4, C5, D3, D4, E3, F1) had already been treated for periods of 11–28 months, and nine children (A6, B3, G1, H2, J2, K3, M2, N8, P2) from 2 to 4½ months. Seven children (I1, J4, L2, O3, Q5, R4, S1) were tested at the onset of diet therapy and retested 3–4 months later. The same test-retest time schedule was followed for each treated child and for all of his siblings living at home after the child's first postdiet test. Two 6-month retests were administered, followed by yearly retests. A departure was made from this schedule in the case of three families (E, M, and R) who were unable to bring their children for one of the 6-month retests, but the same schedule of testing was followed with treated, untreated, and unaffected children within these families. Nine children missed one or more of their tests: A5, B1, B2, and C2 each missed one test; A1, A2, D1, and D2 missed two tests; A3 missed three tests.

Care was taken to establish good rapport before testing and to maintain the interest and attention of each child throughout the test procedure. However, extreme shyness, irritability, or negativism interfered with the test procedure in one or two of the test sessions of nine of the younger children from both the treated and unaffected groups (A5, A6, I2, J3, K3, M1, P4, S2, S3). In these instances, a reliable score could not be derived.

Testing was carried out by trained psychologists; 182 of the 204 regular tests were administered by one of two examiners. The 22 additional tests were administered by nine different psychologists. Additional tests had been given to eight of the children by psychologists at other institutions.[1]

RESULTS

Corrected intelligence test scores on the first and last examination are summarized in Figure 1, with scores for the treated group subclassified ac-

---

[1] On one occasion, treated subject E3 and unaffected sibling E2 were tested by a psychologist at another institution when they were unable to visit the clinic for a regular retest.

Treated subject P2 was referred by another hospital where he had first received diet treatment. A prediet Gesell Developmental Schedule, a later Gesell, and a form L-M Binet had been administered there.

Before untreated subjects E1 and N5 entered the sample, an early Cattell test had been given to E1, and three Binet tests had been given to N5. Both children were living at home at the time of testing.

Institutionalized untreated subjects C1 and C3 were tested by one of our examiners with the Cattell test when they were 12 years and 3 months, and 8 years and 6 months, respectively. Both of the children had been given earlier tests by institution psychologists. Subject C3 had been given a Cattell at the time of institutionalization, and C1 had been given a Kuhlman Binet test 2 years and 5 months after admission to the institution.

Untreated subjects E1 and Q4 were institutionalized after they had been followed for several years. The latest test scores reported for these children are from tests administered by the institutions at the time of admission. Form L-M of the Binet was used to test Q4, and E1 was tested with the Kuhlman Binet.

cording to the age at which treatment was instituted. Scores of individual children are listed in Table 1. At the time of the initial test, the mean score of the subgroup treated in earliest infancy was 27.5 IQ points below that of the unaffected siblings. Subgroups of children treated at successively later ages had increasingly lower mean IQ scores. Initially, the subgroup first treated after age 2 was only slightly more intelligent than untreated phenylketonuric children, but by the time of the last test the late-treated sub-

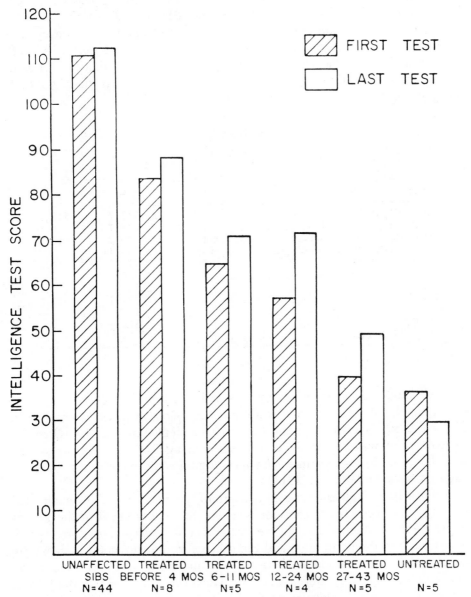

Fig. 1.—Mean intelligence test scores of groups of phenylketonuric children with treatment begun at different ages, and of their untreated phenylketonuric and unaffected siblings.

group had surpassed the untreated group by 19.4 IQ points. Except for the untreated children, every group made IQ gains between the first and the last tests, with the smallest gain accrued by the unaffected siblings.

Differences between treated phenylketonuric children and their unaffected siblings were highly significant on both the first and last examination, even when treatment started before 4 months. This was true, not only when the total unaffected group was compared with each of the treatment subgroups, but also when each of the treatment subgroups was compared with its own unaffected siblings. All t ratios exceeded $p = .01$ levels.

Treatment did improve the scores of treated children, however. An analysis of the variance in first and last test scores of the 35 unaffected and 22 treated children who were tested at least twice showed that the IQ gain among treated children was significant, while there was no significant change in IQ of the unaffected children (Table 2).

TABLE 2

ANALYSIS OF VARIANCE IN CORRECTED IQ SCORES ON FIRST AND LAST TESTING OF TREATED PHENYLKETONURIC AND UNAFFECTED CHILDREN

Source	df	MS	F
Treated vs. unaffected.................	1	57,212.7	118.8**
First vs. last test (treated)............	1	618.7	9.6**
First vs. last test (unaffected).........	1	30.2	<1.0
Among treated age groups............	(3)	(3,708.4)	7.3**
Below vs. above 1 yr...............	1	7,277.9	14.2**
Below vs. above 6 mos.............	1	1,746.8	3.4
Second vs. third yr.................	1	2,100.5	4.1*
Ages × testings....................	3	44.4	<1.0
Error:			
Ss/groups........................	52	511.6	...
Residual.........................	52	64.5	...

*$p < .05$.
**$p < .01$.

Although earlier-treated subgroups had significantly higher scores than later-treated, this was not due to differential response to treatment but to differences in IQ existing at the time of treatment onset. Initial IQ in the treated group was negatively correlated with age ($r = -.72$, $df = 20$, $p < .01$), but during treatment the age subgroups did *not* differ in IQ gains (ages × testing interaction, Table 2).

Since treated children were, as a group, younger than their unaffected siblings, it is necessary to consider whether differences between the groups might be an artifact of age differences. Binet IQ scores were corrected to remove any relation with age, and the success of the correction is shown by an essentially zero correlation between age and initial test score within the unaffected group ($r = .003$, $df = 42$). However, below MA 2, the Cattell Infant Intelligence Scale was used. While this scale was constructed as a downward extension of the Binet, there are insufficient data concerning its standardization to permit age correction of scores or to insure its comparability to the Binet. To determine whether use of the Cattell introduced any systematic bias, initial scores of unaffected children tested before and after age 2 were compared.

There were 11 unaffected children below age 2, with a mean IQ of 106.3; and 33 unaffected children 2 and above, with a mean IQ of 112.8. The difference of 6.5 points was not significant but might be related to slightly lower intelligence among unaffected children of all ages in those families in the sample who continued to have children after an older child was treated for phenylketonuria. Therefore, a comparison was also made of younger and older children from the same families. Eight children tested before age 2 had a mean score of 107.0, and their 12 siblings tested after 2 had a mean of 109.2 ($t < 1.0$).

While age was not related to differences in corrected IQ scores, a systematic relation does exist between age and the amount of IQ change. Since IQ is a ratio score, if MA changes during any specific interval of time, the magnitude of the related change in IQ will depend upon the magnitude of the CA. The older the child, the smaller the IQ change will be, whether MA increases or decreases. A child with an MA of 1 year and an IQ of 100 at age 1 would, for example, gain 50 IQ points if he gained 2 years in MA during a 1-year interval. In contrast, a 4-year-old with an MA of 4 years and an IQ of 100 would gain only 20 points if he also gained 2 years in MA over a 1-year interval. Scores are slightly altered when corrected scores are used, but the relations among CA, MA, and IQ remain essentially the same.

Therefore, to determine whether there were group differences in development during the period of study, an age-independent measure is required. Mental age gain is such a measure and, if converted to a per month rate of gain, is also independent of the length of time that children are studied. These *developmental rate* scores were computed for the 27 unaffected and 21 treated children who were under 13 years and had been followed for at least 8 months (Table 1). Children over 13 were excluded, since the Stanford Binet was so standardized that, beyond age 13, the average child gains less than 1 month MA for each chronological month. To remove other age-associated irregularities in MA scores, Pinneau's tables (1961) were used to obtain corrected MA scores, similar to the corrected IQ scores. A correlation of .05 between age and developmental rate, within the unaffected group, indicated that the rate measure was, in fact, unrelated to age.

Table 3 shows mean developmental rates during the period of study and also the mean developmental rate during the life span prior to study, that is, the initial mean IQ expressed as a rate. Although unaffected children had not shown a gain in IQ, while treated children had, it is clear that unaffected children developed more rapidly during the period of study than did their treated phenylketonuric siblings. An analysis of the variance in developmental rates during study (Table 4) revealed that the difference between unaffected and treated children was highly significant but that no significant difference existed among subgroups of treated children or between individual subgroups forming orthogonal comparisons.

TABLE 3

MEAN DEVELOPMENTAL RATES BEFORE AND DURING STUDY

Group	N	Rate before Study	Rate during Study
Unaffected...............	27	1.14	1.23
Treated..................	21	0.65	0.82
Before 4 mos............	8	0.84	0.90
6–11 mos...............	5	0.64	0.75
12–24 mos..............	4	0.57	0.86
25–43 mos..............	4	0.37	0.73

When developmental rates during study were compared with developmental rates for the life span preceding study (Table 4), findings paralleled those of the IQ analysis. Unaffected children showed more rapid rates of development overall than treated children, but the treated children increased their developmental rates significantly under treatment, while unaffected children did not change significantly during the same period of time. Since both groups were followed for equal periods of time (unaffected mean time = 29.8 mos., treated mean time = 27.2 mos.; $t < 1.0$), differential increase in rates of the two groups was not confounded with differential practice.

TABLE 4

ANALYSIS OF VARIANCE IN DEVELOPMENTAL RATES DURING STUDY AND IN DEVELOPMENTAL RATES DURING AND PRECEDING STUDY

SOURCE	df	DURING STUDY MS	DURING STUDY F	DURING AND PRECEDING STUDY MS	DURING AND PRECEDING STUDY F
Treated vs. unaffected......	1	19,160.9	12.6**	47,207.1	38.6**
Among treated age groups...	(3)	(386.8)	<1.0	(1,917.5)	3.3*
Below vs. above 1 yr.....	1	92.7	<1.0	2,822.1	4.8*
Below vs. above 6 mos....	1	729.7	1.2	1,857.8	3.2
Second vs. third yr.......	1	333.0	<1.0	1,072.6	1.8
During vs. preceding (treated)...............	1	...	...	3,154.7	11.7**
During vs. preceding (Unaffected)............	1	...	...	971.1	1.4
Differential change among age groups.............	(3)	...	...	(543.4)	2.0
Below vs. above 1 yr.....	1	...	...	1,560.7	5.8*
Below vs. above 6 mos....	1	...	...	24.0	<1.0
Second vs. third yr.......	1	...	...	45.6	<1.0
Error: Ss/groups...............	(43)	(1,523.0)	...	(1,223.2)	...
Treated...............	17	584.7	...	581.9	...
Unaffected............	26	2,136.5	...	1,642.5	...
Residual................	(43)	...	...	(536.0)	...
Treated...............	17	...	...	269.2	...
Unaffected............	26	...	...	710.4	...

*p < .05.
**p < .01.

The analysis also showed that, while all treated subgroups developed equally rapidly during treatment, the late-treated groups (those treated after 1 year) made significantly greater gains over their relatively slower rates preceding treatment than earlier-treated children who had faster rates preceding treatment.

In both analyses of the developmental rates, error terms of the treated and unaffected groups differed significantly. Consequently, when treated subgroup comparisons were made, error terms for the treated group were used rather than pooled error terms.

Within the sample there appeared to be no relation between developmental rate and the adequacy of diet control. The percentage of all phenylalanine blood levels taken which were above 10 mg/100 ml. was used as a measure of deviation from control for each child. The correlation between this measure and developmental rate during treatment was .057.

Figure 2 graphs all of the consecutive IQ scores for individual treated and untreated phenylketonuric children. Most treated children did not develop at a steady rate, or with a regular increase or decrease in rate. Rather, like most normal children (Sontag, Baker, & Nelson, 1958), they developed with sporadic gains and plateaus. Most of the children who were treated late proceeded at an increased rate after treatment began, but increases in rate and in IQ were not always immediate or regular.

DISCUSSION

An earlier paper (Berman et al., 1961) reported the results of examinations of a group of treated phenylketonuric children and their siblings. Five children treated from early infancy were intellectually superior to their late-treated and untreated siblings but significantly less intelligent than siblings who were not affected by the disease. Since the earlier report, three additional early-treated children have been studied. The entire group of eight children earned a mean score of 84 on the initial test given, compared with a mean of 83 for the smaller group reported earlier. There was little variability of scores on the initial test, and the children, who were all treated before 4 months of age, scored almost 28 points lower than their unaffected siblings. During the 12–57 months of study, the early-treated children made a mean gain of 4 IQ points, a somewhat greater gain than that of their siblings, and they became more variable in intelligence than they had been initially. The majority of the early-treated children had been tested before 6 months age and, as noted above, the decrement in intelligence was evident at that time. The low scores cannot be attributed to characteristics of the infant test. Unaffected siblings who were tested in early infancy did not have uniformly low scores similar to those of the treated phenylketonuric infants.

Although early IQ's (or Developmental Quotients) may not predict later intelligence test scores of individual children well, they do provide an accurate appraisal of the developmental lag of the treated group. The lag

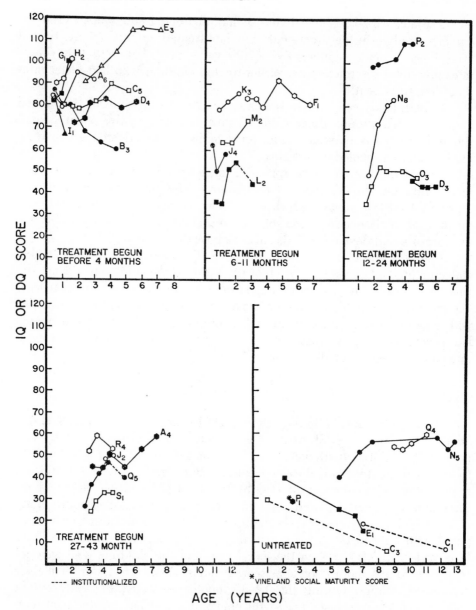

Fig. 2.—Consecutive intelligence test scores of treated and untreated phenyl-ketonuric children.

has persisted for the group as a whole despite the fact that, after several years of diet therapy, some of the treated children have caught up with their unaffected siblings in intellectual development. During the years we have studied them, the children treated from earliest infancy have developed, as a group, at a rate which is only 90 per cent as rapid as the developmental rate of the normative population, while their siblings have developed more rapidly than the norm. Two early-treated children surpassed their siblings in intelligence, but two children, treated at 4 and 15 weeks, respectively, have developed very slowly. The earliest developmental test scores could not allow us to predict which of the children would make gains and which would lag behind in development while under treatment. Dietary control was relatively stringent for the entire treated group, and there was no significant relation between adequacy of diet control and rate of development during treatment.

Several investigators have concluded that there is no appreciable loss of intellectual potential when treatment is begun in the first few months of life (Bickel & Gruter, 1963; Knox, 1960). It is remarkable that this view persists despite the consistency of evidence to the contrary. When standardized infant tests have been used, quotients for early-treated groups have generally fallen between 80 and 90.

In 1961, a survey of the literature yielded 13 cases treated before 6 months for whom psychometric test scores were reported. The mean quotient was 85.9 (Berman et al., 1961). Bickel and Gruter made a similar survey in 1963 (see their Table 18) and found 11 children with scores averaging 88.3. Four of the same children were included in both Bickel and Gruter's and Berman's group. Centerwall et al. (1961) reported a mean of 90.5 for four children treated before 2 months age, and Hsia, Rowley, and Raskin (1962), a mean of 80.2 for five children treated before 6 months. An occasional early-treated child does poorly, with scores in the 40's, 50's, or 60's (Case 24, Coates, 1961; Case 5, Hsia et al., 1962; Case 3, Partington, 1962; Subjects B3 and I1, reported here). Although early diet treatment has not completely prevented retardation in the foregoing cases, it is possible that the intellectual status of these children might have been even more impaired if treatment had been delayed or not given at all. Some children treated early reach a level at or above that of the normal population, with test scores of 100 or above (Subjects B1 and B2, Centerwall et al., 1961; Case 2, Horner & Streamer, 1959; Cases 1 and 3, Koch, Fishler, Schield, & Ragsdale, 1964; Subjects E3, G1, and H2, reported in the present study), but, on the average, early-treated children fall within the dull-normal range and are generally slower than their siblings who do not have the disease (Centerwall et al., 1961; Kleinman, 1964; Woolf et al., 1958).

Centerwall comments that, although mental retardation can be prevented by early diet treatment, "the diet may not afford complete protection." As noted earlier, severe restriction of phenylalanine by diet is not considered desirable since other nutritional damage might result. Anderson (1965) has also emphasized that diet cannot maintain blood levels which are as low as those of normal children and suggests that further diet modification may be needed to better meet the nutritional needs of individual children. He has further noted the possibility of intrauterine damage and of significant damage in the first few weeks of life before an accurate diagnosis is made.

In contrast with the children treated earlier, the five children treated after age 2 initially had an average IQ score only a few points above that of the untreated children. The late-treated group responded well to treatment, increasing its score, while the untreated group suffered a decline in mean score. The decline of the untreated group, besides reflecting the effects of untreated phenylketonuria, probably shows the effect of institutionalization on two of the group, Subjects C1 and C3. Unfortunately, these variables are confounded, since children who are more deteriorated are institutionalized earlier. Two children of the treated group, L2 and Q5, lost 10 and 7 points, respectively, on the first tests administered after institutionalization, although treatment was continued. One of the untreated children, E1, remained at home until age 7 and showed a steady decline in IQ. On the other hand, Subjects N5 and Q4 made some gains while at home.

There is little information about the course of untreated phenylketonuria in patients who are not hospitalized, but there is no reason to expect spontaneous improvement in intelligence comparable to the improvement of the late-treated group. Moreover, the decline in prediet IQ generally found with increased age at start of treatment, would lead one to expect decline in the intelligence of untreated phenylketonurics with time. Bickel and Gruter (Table 14, 1963) made a survey of the data for untreated phenylketonurics with repeated psychometric tests and found decline, rather than spontaneous improvement, during the first 8 years of life. The patients included some who were institutionalized and some who had remained at home.

Most studies have noted the great variability of intellectual response to treatment when it is begun after early infancy (Bickel & Gruter, 1963; Coates, 1961; Kleinman, 1964). Similar variability occurred in the present study, not only in the later-treated groups, but also in the group treated in earliest infancy. It was illustrated by the differences between early-treated Subjects B3 and I1, with developmental rates under .60, and E3, G1, and H2, with rates over 1.00 and, in the later-treated groups, by rates varying from .50 to 1.21. Subjects N8 and O3, for example, had scores of 48 and 43, respectively, on their first postdiet tests at approximately 18 months (Fig. 2). During treatment, Subject N8 increased her developmental rate to 1.20, a rate which is comparable to that of the unaffected sibling group, whereas the developmental rate of Subject O3 rose only to .54 during treatment. Both children suffered heavy losses before treatment. The loss of Subject O3 has been, for the most part, irreversible. That is, with treatment, a further decline in intelligence was prevented, and she was able to make a modest improvement in IQ, but her rate of development was far from what it might have been had she not had the disease. The outlook for Subject N8 is brighter. Since treatment was initiated, her developmental rate has been normal, and, although it is possible that she may not be able to maintain this rate, from the progress she has made to date there is no reason to suspect that irreversible damage has occurred.

While phenylketonuric children showed significant gains in developmental rate and IQ during dietary treatment, the fact that they did *not* attain rates as high as their unaffected siblings suggests that some of the effects of phenylketonuria continue to be operative even when blood phenylalanine levels are controlled. Apparently the response to treatment does not depend upon age, at least within the age range studied. Children treated early attained higher intelligence levels than children treated later, but this was because they had, in general, suffered less impairment at the time treatment was instituted. Treatment, once begun, permitted more rapid rates of development, but the rates were not higher for earlier-treated than for later-treated groups. However, an upper limit on the effects of diet treatment is suggested by the lack of improvement in patients first treated in adulthood (Hsia, Knox, Quinn, & Paine, 1958) or even between the ages of 10 and 20 (Garfield & Carver, 1960).

Woolf, Griffiths, and Moncreiff (1955) used "progress rate" (developmental rate × 100) to predict tentatively later IQ for two treated children. Coates (1961) subsequently stated that the progress rate does not stay constant enough for a particular child to predict the final intelligence level. Studies of IQ changes of normal children (Pinneau, 1961; Sontag et al., 1958) suggest that the changes are quite irregular, but that some predictions may be made. While the data which we now have permit no more than the most gross predictions for individuals in terms of later intellectual achievement, the concept of developmental rate does permit more adequate description of the course of phenylketonuria and the accompanying IQ changes with treatment at various ages. Efforts to relate variability in intellectual change to personality and environmental interactions might permit better prediction for individuals; the effects of institutionalization seem especially worthy of further investigation.

REFERENCES

Anderson, V. E. Genetics and behavior in mental retardation. Paper read at Amer. Ass. Advancm. Sci., Berkeley, Calif., December, 1965.

Berman, P. W., Graham, F. K., Eichman, P. L., & Waisman, H. A. Psychologic and neurologic status of diet-treated phenylketonuric children and their siblings. *Pediatrics*, 1961, **28**, 924–934.

Bickel, H., & Gruter, W. Management of phenylketonuria. In F. L. Lyman (Ed.), *Phenylketonuria*. Springfield, Ill.: Charles C Thomas, 1963. Pp. 136–172.

Cattell, Psyche. *The measurement of intelligence in infants and young children.* New York: Psychol. Corp., 1947.

Centerwall, W. R., Centerwall, S. A., Acosta, P. B., Chinnock, R. F., Armon, V., & Mann, L. B. Phenylketonuria: II. Results of treatment of infants and young children. *J. Pediatr.*, 1961, **59**, 102–118.

Coates, S. Results of treatment in phenylketonuria. *Brit. med. J.*, 1961, **1**, 767–771.

Garfield, S. L., & Carver, M. J. Phenylketonuria: a further study. *J. nerv. ment. Dis.*, 1960, **130**, 120–124.

Horner, F. A., & Streamer, C. W. Phenylketonuria treated from earliest infancy; report of three cases. *A.M.A. Amer. J. dis. Child.*, 1959, **97**, 345–347.

Hsia, D. Y., Knox, W. E., Quinn, K. V., & Paine, R. S. A one-year controlled study of the effect of low-phenylalanine diet on phenylketonuria. *Pediatrics*, 1958, **21**, 178–202.

Hsia, D. Y., Rowley, W., & Raskin, N. J. Clinical management of phenylketonuria. *Quart. Bull. Northwestern Univer. Med. Sch.*, 1962, **36**, 1–8.

Kleinman, D. S. Phenylketonuria: a review of some deficits in our information. *Pediatrics*, 1964, **33**, 123–133.

Knox, W. E. An evaluation of the treatment of phenylketonuria with diets low in phenylalanine. *Pediatrics*, 1960, **26**, 1–11.

Koch, R., Fishler, K., Schild, S., & Ragsdale, N. Clinical aspects of phenylketonuria. *Amer. J. ment. Def.*, 1964, **69**, 47–54.

Partington, M. W. Variations in intelligence in phenylketonuria. *Canad. Med. Ass. J.*, 1962, **86**, 736–743.

Pinneau, S. R. *Changes in intelligence quotient: infancy to maturity.* Boston: Houghton Mifflin, 1961.

Sontag, L. W., Baker, C. T., & Nelson, V. L. Mental growth and personality development: a longitudinal study. *Monogr. Soc. Res. Child Develpm.*, 1958, **23**, No. 2 (Whole No. 68).

Woolf, L. I., Griffiths, R., & Moncrieff, A. Treatment of phenylketonuria with a diet low in phenylalanine. *Brit. med. J.*, 1955, **1**, 57–64.

Woolf, L. I., Griffiths, R., Moncrieff, A., Coates, S., & Dillistone, F. The dietary treatment of phenylketonuria. *Arch. Dis. Childh.*, 1958, **33**, 31–45.

Chapter Four

PRENATAL EFFECTS

Research in the area of prenatal determinants of development has classically involved the field of embryology. The concern has been with cellular growth and differentiation, morphological development, timing, and the myriad other factors involved when a fertilized egg develops into a complex living organism. In general, embryology is concerned with the immediate consequences of growth and development rather than with their effects in postnatal life. One of the major techniques used by the embryologist is experimental intervention with the developing embryo or fetus. The usual result of this intervention is disruption of development, and some abnormality often results from the experimental "insult" or teratogenic agent. The inadvertent production of abnormal children because of a biochemical insult during early embryological development is well known in medical practice. German measles (rubella) and thalidomide are two familiar causal agents.

Perhaps it is because experimental intervention during embryogenesis has generally resulted in the creation of abnormal organisms that many people think nature's design and construction of the mammalian uterus and its physiological support systems are the best possible. The implication is that any form of intervention will be deleterious. However, when we examine the behavioral consequences in later life of certain subtle forms of prenatal stimulation, we do not necessarily find abnormal behavior patterns, but instead, changes which might be beneficial to the organism. It must be noted, however, that the behavioral effect of prenatal stimulation is the least investigated of any of the areas involved in the biobehavioral

basis of development, and any generalization must be held as highly tentative. For a good review of the literature in this field see Joffe (1969).

The papers in this chapter serve to establish the principle that prenatal manipulations involving psychological and behavioral variables (as contrasted with explicit biochemical intervention procedures) affect the behavior of the offspring after birth. The distinction drawn in the previous sentence between psychological or behavioral variables and biochemical ones is for convenience of classification and does not necessarily imply different types of causation. Any psychological or behavioral modification of the pregnant female must produce changes in her central nervous system, physiology, biochemistry, etc., and it is these changes which must ultimately act to influence the developing embryo and fetus.

Thompson (Paper 10) was the first to document clearly that "anxiety" in a pregnant rat could modify the emotionality of her offspring. He used the nice procedure of training female rats *before* pregnancy to associate the sound of a buzzer with the pain of electric shock. *After* pregnancy the females were exposed only to the buzzer which, because of its prior associations, engendered a state of "anxiety." Thus, Thompson was able to create a psychological state of upset during gestation without resorting to the use of any distinctly noxious stimulus, such as shock. Thompson found that the induction of anxiety resulted in greater emotional upset of the pups. This finding can be interpreted as evidence of behavioral abnormality, and therefore consistent with the findings of embryologists that intervention during prenatal development has deleterious consequences. However, Paper 11 indicates that rat offspring are less emotional if their mothers are handled during pregnancy. Thus, increase or decrease of emotional reactivity appears to be a function of the kinds of manipulations to which the female is exposed while pregnant.

Papers 12 and 13 establish that the effects of prenatal stimulation can be extraordinarily subtle and can reach across one or two generations to affect descendents. In the experiment reported in Paper 12, two populations of rat mothers were generated by handling one group of females during their infancy while a second group was left undisturbed. This procedure of handling animals in infancy has been shown to bring about a marked reduction in emotional behavior in later life (see Chapter Eleven). When adult, these two groups of females were mated, and at birth the young were cross-fostered. Examination of body weight and behavioral scores of the offspring revealed that the females' experiences during their infancy had affected their offspring's subsequent weight and behavior.

This phenomenon was extended yet another generation by Denenberg and Rosenberg (Paper 13) who found that the experiences which female rats received in infancy coupled with the experiences of their offspring affected their grandpups' behavior. The results of these two experiments indicate that there is a form of communication between generations which is not based upon a genetic or a learning mechanism and which probably serves some sort of adaptive function for the developing embryo-fetus and neonate.

Because of the obvious difficulties involved, research on prenatal determinants of development in humans has not been extensive. One of the pioneers in this field is Sontag, and the work reported in Paper 14 demonstrates that the human fetus is responsive to such a mild auditory stimulus as music. Though no postnatal behavioral follow-up was made of these subjects, this paper is important because it shows the responsiveness of the fetus to fairly neutral external environmental stimuli. For a brief review of research with humans in this area see Sontag (1966).

Paper 15 does relate postnatal behavior of the infant to prenatal and/or genetic factors. Ottinger and Simmons sorted a group of pregnant women into high- or low-anxiety groups by means of a personality test administered three times during gestation. The experimenters then measured the crying behavior of the newborn infants on the second through the fourth days of life and found that those mothers who had been classified as highly anxious had infants who cried significantly more prior to their feeding. The increase in crying could be due to a prenatal mechanism, since the neural and hormonal states of the anxious mother would differ from those of the nonanxious mother and could be communicated to the fetus (compare this interpretation with the findings of Thompson concerning prenatal maternal anxiety in the rat). Since Sontag has shown that music can affect the fetus, it is quite reasonable to expect that the mother's internal physiological and neurological states can also affect the developing organism in utero.

Even though this is a reasonable interpretation, its validity is not established. An alternative hypothesis, also reasonable, is that a genetic mechanism is responsible for both the mother's anxiety and the baby's crying. That is, certain women are more anxious because of a genetic predisposition. When they become pregnant, the genes involved are passed on to their offspring, who express their own anxiety by crying. Even though this latter interpretation may not, intuitively, appear as likely as the former, it cannot be dismissed, but must be given serious consideration. It is apparent that the investigator can never distinguish between these alternative hypotheses, regardless of the kind or amount of data obtained, as long as he restricts his research to humans. He must use an animal in which he can separate genetic factors from prenatal effects in order to determine whether either or both mechanisms are at work. From our knowledge of the literature we can safely predict that both mechanisms would be involved in the transmission of anxiety states.

This can be seen by a rereading of Papers 8 and 10. (For the interested student three methods for separating genetic and prenatal effects are (1) by a genetic backcross experiment, (2) by transplanting fertilized ova from one maternal host to another, and (3) by transplanting an ovary from one female to another. However, a discussion of these procedures is beyond the scope of this book.)

The complementarity of animal and human research in attacking a general problem is nicely illustrated by the history of the Ottinger and Simmons paper. Ottinger, Denenberg, and Stephens had previously carried out a set of experiments with rats showing that multiple mothering resulted in an increase in the offspring's emotionality (this is Paper 54). As part of the design of one of the experiments animals were cross-fostered at birth to separate the genetic-prenatal factors from the postnatal maternal influence. Both factors were found to have important effects. The finding of the prenatal-genetic effect relating maternal emotionality to offspring emotionality in the rat suggested to Ottinger and Simmons that this principle might also appear at the human level, and they tested the principle by studying the relationship between maternal anxiety and infant crying.

References

Joffe, J. F. *Prenatal Determinants of Behaviour.* New York: Pergamon Press, 1969.

Sontag, L. W. Implications of fetal behavior and environment for adult personalities. *Ann. N.Y. Acad. Sci.,* 1966, 134, 782-786.

WILLIAM R. THOMPSON

10 Influence of Prenatal Maternal Anxiety on Emotionality in Young Rats

The purpose of the observations reported in this article (*1*) was to test the hypothesis that emotional trauma undergone by female rats during pregnancy can affect the emotional characteristics of the offspring. By now, a good deal of evidence favoring this possibility has accumulated from diverse sources, including teratology (*2*), pediatrics (*3*), experimental psychology (*4*), and population biology (*5*). While none of the studies done has directly confirmed this hypothesis, many of them indicate that such hormones as cortisone, adrenalin, and adrenocorticotropic hormone, injected into the mother during pregnancy, have drastic effects on the fetus

Reprinted from *Science* 125:698–699, 1957. Copyright 1957 by the American Association for the Advancement of Science.

via the maternal-fetal blood exchange. Since strong emotion may release such substances into the mother's blood stream, there are grounds for supposing that it may have an important influence on fetal behavioral development. This experiment was the first in a projected series designed to examine this question in detail.

The rationale of the procedure was to create a situation which would predictably arouse strong anxiety in female rats, and to provide them with a standard means of reducing this anxiety; then to expose them to the anxiety-arousing situation during pregnancy, but block the accustomed means of escaping it. The assumption was that strong, free-floating anxiety would be generated in the pregnant females, and that any endocrine changes resulting would be transmitted through the maternal-fetal blood exchange to the fetus. The experiment was done by training five randomly chosen female hooded rats in a double compartment shuttlebox, first to expect strong shock at the sound of a buzzer, and then to avoid the shock by opening a door between the compartments and running through to the safe side. When the rats had learned this, the five experimentals, together with five control females, were mated to five randomly chosen males in a large cage. As soon as the experimentals were found to be pregnant (by vaginal smears), they were exposed to the buzzer three times every day in the shock side of the shuttlebox, but with the shock turned off and the door to the safe side locked. This procedure was terminated by the birth of a litter. The controls were placed in breeding cages during the same time.

Possible postnatal influences were controlled by cross-fostering in such a way as to yield a design with six cells, each containing ten offspring with two main variables—namely, prenatal and postnatal treatment. The data obtained from tests given to the young were examined by means of analysis of variance. In all tests of significance, three error estimates were used: the within-cell variance, the within-plus-interaction variances, and the within-plus-interaction plus between-postnatal-treatment variances. Thus, as shown in Table 1, all tests of significance reported involve three F values.

The emotional characteristics of the 30 control and 30 experimental offspring were compared by two tests given at 30 to 40 and 130 to 140 days of age. In test A, measures of amount and latency of activity in an open field were taken in three daily sessions of 10 min-

utes each. In test B, emotionality was measured by latency of leaving the home cage, and latency of reaching food at the end of an alley way leading out from the cage after 24 hours' food deprivation. In the second test, the maximum time allowed an animal to reach food was 30 minutes. In the measures used, low activity and high latency were taken as indices of high emotionality.

The results are summarized in Table 1. On test A, striking differences between experimentals and controls were obtained in amount of activity, both at 30 to 40 days and at 130 to 140 days. On the first testing, a significant interaction was obtained which probably represents genetic variation. On the second measure, experimental animals showed a much higher latency of activity than controls at both ages of testing. In neither of these activity measures were there any significant differences due to postnatal treatment or interaction besides the one mentioned.

In test B, experimental animals were slower to leave the home cage than controls at the first age of testing. There was no significant difference between groups in this measure, however, at 130 to 140 days of age. Similarly, experimentals showed a much higher latency than controls in getting to food at the end of the alley way at the first age of testing. The difference was less at the later age of testing. At both ages, significant interaction variances were found. As before, both may well be due to genetic variation. On neither of the measures used in test B were any significant differences found between methods of postnatal treatment.

It is clear from this analysis that the experimental and control animals differ strikingly on the measures of emotionality used, and that these differences persist to a great extent into adulthood.

Table 1. Comparison of experimental and control animals on two tests of emotionality.

Item	Test A		Test B	
	Amount of activity (distance)	Latency of activity (seconds)	Latency to leave cage (minutes)	Latency to food (minutes)
	Tests given at age 30 to 40 days			
Experimentals	86.0	146.3	14.9	23.7
Controls	134.5	56.8	5.2	11.8
F values	(15.79, 14.21, 13.57)	(8.51, 7.91, 8.07)	(16.13, 16.46, 15.62)	(31.73, 25.66 25.87)
p	< .001	< .01	< .001	< .001
	Tests given at age 130 to 140 days			
Experimentals	114.5	71.5	4.8	11.6
Controls	162.3	26.8	2.1	6.2
F values	(9.77, 9.12 8.76)	(4.95, 4.79, 4.57)	(2.39)	(4.48)
p	< .01	< .05	> .05	< .05

While there is no question about the reliability of these differences, there is some ambiguity regarding their cause. Thus, we do not know exactly how the stress used had effects. It is possible that the buzzer was strong enough to act on the fetuses directly rather than indirectly by causing release of hormones in the mother. Only a more careful repetition of the experiment will throw light on this problem.

A more serious objection than this is that, besides the main factor of prenatal stress, genetic variation could also have been responsible for the offspring differences if there had been inadvertent selection of nonemotional mothers for the control group and emotional mothers for the experimental group. However, several points argue against this possibility. Choice of female animals for the two groups was carried out randomly, and at least some of the genetic variance was included in the error estimates used to test the main effects. Further, an examination of scores within and between individual litters indicates that interlit-ter variances tend to be smaller than intralitter differences. This means that, in the population used, genetic variation was relatively slight compared with environmental variation. Consequently, it is improbable that even if accidental selection had occurred it could have resulted in an experimental group genetically very different from the control group.

Accordingly, we may state that there are some grounds for supposing that prenatal maternal anxiety does actually increase the emotionality of offspring. This conclusion is offered tentatively until further experimentation has been completed.

References and Notes

1. This research was done at Queens University, Kingston, Ontario, and supported by grants from the Queens Science Research Council and the National Science Foundation. Grateful acknowledgment is made to C. H. Hockman for his invaluable aid in helping to build the apparatus and to test the animals.

2. F. C. Fraser and T. D. Fainstat, *Am. J. Diseases Children* **82**, 593 (1951).

3. L. W. Sontag, *Am. J. Obstet. Gynecol.* 42, 996 (1941).
4. W. D. Thompson and L. W. Sontag, *J. Comp. and Physiol. Psychol.* 49, 454 (1956).

5. D. Chitty, "Adverse effects of population density upon the viability of later generations," in *The Numbers of Man and Animals,* (Oliver and Boyd, London, 1955).

ROBERT ADER & PETER M. CONKLIN

11   Handling of Pregnant Rats: Effects on Emotionality of Their Offspring

Abstract. *Pregnant rats were either unmanipulated or were handled for 10 minutes three times daily throughout pregnancy. Offspring remained with their natural mothers or were cross-fostered within and between experimental and control groups. When tested at 45 and 100 days of age, the offspring of handled mothers were found to be generally less emotional than the controls.*

By using conditioning techniques, it has been shown that prenatal maternal "anxiety" increases offspring emotionality in the rat (*1, 2*). The effects which might obtain from other types of behavioral treatment of a pregnant animal are not known. Various manipulations, notably "handling," decrease emotionality in the rat when administered postnatally. The present study, then, was designed to determine the effects of prenatal handling, that is, handling of the pregnant animal, on emotionality of the offspring.

Data were obtained from a total of 138 offspring of primiparous Sprague-Dawley rats. These females were placed with males each evening and

Reprinted from *Science 142*:411–412, 1963. Copyright 1963 by the American Association for the Advancement of Science.

pregnancy was determined by vaginal smears taken the following morning. By random selection, half the pregnant animals remained unmanipulated and half were handled for 10 minutes three times daily (once each morning, afternoon, and evening) throughout the period of gestation. Pregnant animals were group-housed until approximately 1 week before delivery when they were individually placed into nesting cages. Handling consisted of picking up the animal and holding it loosely in one hand.

Litters were culled to seven or eight pups within 48 hours of birth and cross-fostering was also accomplished within this time. An equal number of litters remained with their natural mothers, were cross-fostered to mothers of that same group, or were cross-fostered to mothers of the opposing group. After this time the nesting cages in which the animals were housed were not cleaned and the pups were not manipulated in any way until weaning at 21 days. After weaning, animals were segregated by sex and treatment, and group-housed in standard laboratory cages. Food and water were available at all times.

Approximately half the animals were tested for emotionality at 45 days and

120 animals were tested at 100 days in an open-field situation. The field was 5 ft (1.5 m) in diameter and marked off into 7.5-inch (19-cm) squares and four concentric circles. Behaviors recorded were squares traversed and entries into the inner concentric circles (inversely related to emotionality), and defecation (directly related to emotionality). At 100 days all animals were also observed in an emergence-from-cage test in which the time required by animals to emerge from their open home cage (directly related to emotionality or "timidity") was recorded up to a maximum of 900 seconds.

Beginning at weaning a biweekly record of body weight was kept for 13 weeks. These data indicated no difference in the absolute weight or rate of growth between the prenatally handled and control animals.

Taken together, the emotionality data did not reveal any consistent tendency for animals fostered to handled mothers to differ from those fostered to control mothers. The data obtained from the open-field are given in Table 1. An analysis of variance applied to squares traversed revealed no differences as a function of group, sex, fostering, previous experience in the field, or any interaction of these. Inspection of the data on the percentage of animals entering inner circles did not suggest the presence of any interactions within either the 45- or 100-day tests. Chi-square analyses indicated that a somewhat larger percentage of the combined offspring of handled mothers approached the center of the field at 100 days, but not on the earlier test.

Defecation in the open-field also showed no interaction effects. Within each subgroup of handled and con-

Table 1. Open-field behavior in prenatally handled (H) and control (C) offspring.

Group	Squares traversed (mean No.)	Animals entering inner circles (%)	Animals defecating (%)
Test age 45 days			
H (N = 28)	25.6	14.3	17.9
C (N = 30)	29.5	16.7	63.3
p	> .10	> .10	< .01
Test age 100 days			
H (N = 59)	25.2	45.8	20.3
C (N = 61)	23.2	27.9	45.9
p	> .10	< .10	< .01

trol offspring at both 45 and 100 days, an equal or greater number of control offspring relative to handled offspring defecated. Chi-square analyses indicated that the number of prenatally handled animals defecating in the field was significantly lower than the number of control offspring on both tests ($\chi^2 = 10.54$; $\chi^2 = 7.71$).

The *F* test showed a significant Group × Fostering interaction on the emergence-from-cage test. Among males there was no difference between the non-cross-fostered handled (N = 7) and control (N = 10) groups, whereas both cross-fostered groups of prenatally handled animals (N = 11 and 20) emerged significantly sooner than controls (N = 10 and 12). Among females it was the cross-fostered groups (N = 13 and 11 for handled and 10 and 9 for control animals) which did not differ significantly, but the non-cross-fostered offspring of handled mothers (N = 12) emerged significantly sooner than controls (N = 13). These data are presented in Fig. 1.

In contrast to the greater offspring emotionality effected by prenatal maternal "anxiety," prenatally handled

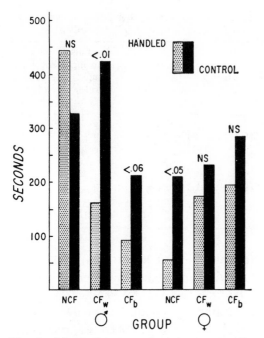

Fig. 1. Mean time required by prenatally handled and control offspring to emerge from their home cage (NCF = non-cross-fostered; CF_w = cross-fostered within group; CF_b = cross-fostered between groups).

prenatal maternal manipulations are brought about by the hormonal changes which occur in the mother in response to the anxiety-provoking stimulation. Presumably, these changes are transmitted to the fetus via the maternal-fetal blood exchange. If such are the mediating mechanisms, it would follow from the present data that the response of the pregnant (or for that matter, the nonpregnant) animal to handling is qualitatively and/or quantitatively different from the response to some if not all other forms of "stressful" stimulation of the kind commonly used in studies of environmental influences on behavior. Such a hypothesis has implications for the design of research on the effects of "early" as well as prenatal experiences since it would appear that one cannot necessarily generalize from the effects of one type of manipulation to another. Unfortunately, little is known at this time about the psychophysiological responses concomitant with handling or other behavioral manipulations (3).

animals appear to be less emotional than controls. To the extent that high emotionality may be considered maladaptive, such results serve to contradict any orientation or expectation that only deleterious effects can result from prenatal manipulation.

It has been hypothesized by Thompson (1) that the behavioral effects of

References and Notes

1. W. R. Thompson, *Science* **125**, 698 (1957).
2. R. Ader and M. L. Belfer, *Psychol. Rept.* **10**, 711 (1962); G. Doyle and E. P. Yule, *Animal Behav.* **7**, 18 (1959); C. H. Hockman, *J. Comp. Physiol. Psychol.* **54**, 679 (1961).
3. Supported by grant MH 03655 from the National Institute of Mental Health.

VICTOR H. DENENBERG & ARTHUR E. WHIMBEY

12　Behavior of Adult Rats Is Modified by the Experiences Their Mothers Had as Infants

Abstract. *Some rat pups were handled for 20 days in infancy, while others were not. When the rats reached adulthood the females were bred. Some of the offspring were left with their natural mothers, others were fostered to mothers*

Reprinted from *Science* 142:1192–1193, 1963. Copyright 1963 by the American Association for the Advancement of Science.

of the same background (handled/nonhandled) as that of their natural mothers, while still others were fostered to mothers with a different background from that of their natural mothers. The offspring were weaned and weighed at 21 days; at 50 days, activity and defecation scores were obtained in the open field. The weights at weaning and the defecation scores at 50 days were significantly influenced by the experience in infancy of the "postnatal" mother, whether she was the natural mother or a foster mother. The natural mother and the foster mother jointly affected the open-field activity of the offspring.

Handling rats in infancy has marked effects upon their subsequent behavioral and physiological processes (*1*). To date no one has investigated whether the handling of female rats in infancy affects their offspring. Modifications of the offspring's characteristics could occur during their fetal period, as a result of physiological changes induced in the mother by the handling she had received in infancy, or they could occur after birth as a result of either physiological changes (which could, for example, modify milk supply) or behavioral changes induced in the mother by the handling she had received in infancy. We now report results of such an investigation (*2*).

About 45 litters of Purdue-Wistar rats were handled in infancy. Handling consisted of removing a complete litter from the home cage (leaving the mother in the cage), placing the pups on shavings in a can for 3 minutes, and then returning the pups to their home cage. This was done once a day from day 1 through day 20 of life. About 45 other litters were not disturbed during this time. Once these litters were born the shavings in their cages were never changed; food and water were supplied without opening the cages.

At 21 days the handled and nonhandled litters were weaned, and the females were placed in specially designated cages. When mature, the females were bred to a random sample of colony males; the males were systematically moved from one cage to another and were exposed equally often to handled and nonhandled females.

When pregnant, the females were placed in stainless-steel maternity cages. The day after birth all litters were sexed, and those containing more than eight pups were reduced to four of each sex when possible, but never to less than two of one sex. No litter containing less than seven pups was used. The litters were then returned to their natural mothers. At this time (i) some litters were left with their natural mothers, (ii) other litters were fostered to mothers that had had the same experience (handled or not handled) in infancy as the natural mothers, and (iii) still other litters were fostered to mothers that in infancy had received the treatment opposite to that of the natural mothers. Fostering was done by moving the mothers from one cage to another, leaving the pups in the cage in which they had been born. In most instances fostering took place between litters born on the same day; in six cases the foster mother had given birth 1 day earlier than the natural mother, and in one case the foster mother had given birth 3 days earlier than the natural mother. Except for fostering, the litters were not disturbed. At 21 days the pups from 55 litters were weaned, weighed, sexed, earpunched, and placed in laboratory cages with littermates of the same sex.

Starting at 50 days of age, the animals were given 4 days of open-field testing. The field was 45 inches (115 cm) square, painted flat black, with walls 18 inches (46 cm) high. The floor was marked off in 9-inch (23-cm) squares by thin white lines. A rat was placed in one corner of the field, and its behavior was observed for 3 minutes. Total numbers of squares entered and boluses defecated were recorded. Two males and two females from each of 47 litters were tested in the open field. Testing was completed at 53 days, at which time the animals were again weighed.

The body weights at 21 days are summarized in Table 1. The weights of all animals within a litter were averaged to give one mean litter weight, thus yielding a Between Litter Error Mean Square based upon 49 degrees of freedom. To determine whether fostering had any effect, the two nonfostered groups (A and D) were compared with the two groups in which litters were fostered to mothers with the same infantile experiences as the natural mothers (groups B and E). No significant effects were found. Therefore, the fostering variable was ignored in assessing the prenatal and postnatal contributions of the mothers toward the body weight of the offspring. The analysis of these data found that the postnatal factor was significant ($F = 5.08$, $p < .05$). Young reared by mothers that had been handled in infancy (groups C, D, and E) weighed significantly more than pups reared by mothers that had not been handled in infancy (groups A, B, and F). The

only significant difference among the body weights in adulthood was between males and females.

The data for open-field behavior are summarized in Table 1. In the analysis of variance the scores of the 4 animals within each litter were combined to give one litter score, thus yielding a Between Litter Error Mean Square based upon 41 degrees of freedom. To evaluate the sex variable and all interactions with this variable, the male and female means were obtained separately for each litter, and the Between Litter × Sex Error Mean Square (df $\doteq$ 41) was used in the denominator of these F tests.

When the two nonfostered groups (A and D) were compared with the two groups in which fostering was done between mothers with the same experience in infancy (B and E), a significant interaction ($F = 4.58$, $p < .05$) was obtained between the presence or absence of fostering and the mother's experience in infancy; those young which were born of and reared by nonhandled mothers and which were not fostered (group A), were significantly more active than the other three groups. Therefore, the four fostered groups were used to evaluate the prenatal and postnatal contributions of the mothers toward the activity pattern of the offspring. A significant interaction ($F = 4.81$, $p < .05$) was found between the prenatal and postnatal mothers. Young born of mothers that had not been handled in infancy, and fostered to handled mothers (group C), were significantly more active than young from the other three groups (B, E, and F); the next most active group was the complement of this—rats born of handled mothers and reared by non-

Table 1. Mean body weight, in grams, at 21 days, mean number of squares entered, and mean number of boluses defecated during 4 days of open-field testing. The *N* per mean is given in parentheses.

Group	Experience of natural mothers in infancy	Postnatal fostering of pups	21-days body wt.	Squares entered		Boluses	
				Male	Female	Male	Female
A	Not handled	Not fostered	35.87 (69)	75.69 (16)	118.62 (16)	7.12 (16)	4.19 (16)
B	Not handled	Fostered to nonhandled mother	36.93 (62)	47.00 (16)	67.94 (16)	6.37 (16)	4.37 (16)
C	Not handled	Fostered to handled mother	41.29 (62)	90.56 (16)	97.75 (16)	12.31 (16)	5.56 (16)
D	Handled	Not fostered	40.81 (70)	53.06 (16)	58.69 (16)	10.87 (16)	7.81 (16)
E	Handled	Fostered to handled mother	38.87 (56)	50.64 (14)	70.93 (14)	10.50 (14)	12.21 (14)
F	Handled	Fostered to nonhandled mother	38.24 (101)	53.69 (16)	85.94 (16)	6.87 (16)	5.37 (16)

handled mothers (group F). The sex variable was significant ($F = 6.87$, $p < .05$) but did not interact significantly with any of the maternal variables.

The test evaluating the fostering effect found that offspring born of and raised by mothers that had been handled in infancy (groups D and E) defecated significantly more ($F = 7.69$, $p < .01$) than offspring born of and raised by nonhandled control mothers (groups A and B); the procedure of fostering did not have any significant effect. The test separating the prenatal and the postnatal factors found that the postnatal mother was the significant contributor: young raised by mothers that had been handled in infancy (groups C, D, and E) defecated more ($F = 6.62$, $p < .05$) than young raised by mothers that had not been handled in infancy (A, B, and F). Again the sex factor was significant ($F = 9.15$, $p < .01$). Though sex did not interact significantly with any of the maternal variables, the Sex × Prenatal Mother interaction approached significance ($F = 3.49$, $p < .07$).

The results clearly establish that the experiences which the mother received while an infant were profound enough to modify her offsprings' body weight at weaning and open-field behavior in adulthood. These modifications were mediated through both the prenatal mother-fetus relationship and the postnatal mother-young interaction. The generality of this phenomenon has been confirmed by Grota (3), who extra-uterized fetuses (that is, removed the fetuses from the uterus but left them in the body cavity) of rat mothers which had been handled or not handled in infancy. Grota found that, for handled mothers, fetuses reared in the uterus had a higher survival rate between birth (by means of cesarean delivery) and weaning than those reared in the body cavity; extra-uterization of fetuses in nonhandled mothers did not affect postnatal survival rate. In addition,

Grota found that both the prenatal and postnatal mother contributed significantly to the weaning weights of pups delivered by cesarean section.

References and Notes

1. V. H. Denenberg, *J. Comp. Physiol. Psychol.* **55**, 813 (1962); ——— and G. G. Karas, *Psychol. Rept.* **7**, 313 (1960); *J. Comp. Physiol. Psychol.* **54**, 685 (1961); S. Levine, *J. Personality* **25**, 70 (1956); *Science* **135**, 795 (1962); J. R. C. Morton, V. H. Denenberg, M. X. Zarrow, *Endocrinology* **72**, 439 (1963); J. T. Tapp and H. Markowitz, *Science* **140**, 486 (1963). For a general review of much of this work, see V. H. Denenberg, in *The Behaviour of Domestic Animals*, E. S. E. Hafez, Ed. (Bailliere, Tindall and Cox, London, 1962), pp. 109–138.
2. Research was supported in part by a grant from the National Science Foundation.
3. L. J. Grota, thesis, Purdue University (1963).

VICTOR H. DENENBERG & KENNETH M. ROSENBERG

13 Nongenetic Transmission of Information

The handling of female rats in infancy has been shown to affect the activity and weaning weight of their grandchildren.

We have shown that one significant determinant of the rat's behaviour is the handling experience of the mother while she was an infant.[1] This experience was profound enough to modify her offspring's weaning weight and open field performance in adulthood. Thus the experience of one generation was visited on the next generation. Such a finding would appear to have broad implications for the evolution of behaviour. In this context a relevant question is: How far into the future can such effects extend? We have investigated this question by determining whether the experiences of female rats during their infancy would significantly affect the behaviour of their grandpups.

Again within an evolutionary framework, the habitat in which the animal is born and reared is known to affect profoundly his subsequent performance. We have shown that rats which are born and reared in a complex free environment between birth and weaning, or which are given free environment experience

Reprinted from *Nature 216*:549–550, 1967.

This work was supported, in part, by grants from the National Institute of Child Health and Human Development and the National Institute of Mental Health, U.S. Public Health Service.

after weaning, differ along a number of behavioural dimensions from rats which are reared in standard cages during infancy and after weaning.[2-5] Thus for the laboratory rat, cages and free environments may be thought of as two different habitats. We investigated the effects of these habitats on the offspring's behaviour in this experiment.

The grandmothers' experience was as follows. At birth, litters of Purdue-Wistar rats were reduced to eight pups. Whole litters were randomly assigned to groups to be handled or not handled. Handling consisted of removing the pups from the maternity cage, leaving the mother in the cage, and placing each one in a tin can partially filled with shavings. The pups remained in the cans for 3 min. and were then returned to their home cage. This procedure was followed once a day from day 1 until day 20. Non-handled controls were not disturbed between day 1 and 21, when all litters were weaned. The handled and non-handled females from these litters were the grandmothers of the animals used in this study. They were bred when about 100 days old. When pregnant, the females were assigned randomly to one of two housing conditions, to be described later.

The mothers' experiences were as follows. The females were placed either into stainless steel maternity cages (15 in. × 10 in. × 7.5 in.) or into free environment boxes. These boxes were triangular compartments formed by placing a diagonal insert into a 34 in.[2] box. Food was scattered on the floor, water was supplied by an externally mounted bottle, and "toys" (wooden block, can, ramp, running disk) were placed into each environment. At birth, litters were cut back to eight subjects consisting of four to six females.

When weaned on day 21, the females from each litter were randomly split into two groups, one going into a stainless steel laboratory cage (11 in. × 8.25 in. × 7.5 in.), and the other into a free environment. The free environments were the same as previously described except that the diagonal partition was removed. Two or three females were placed in each laboratory cage, while ten to twelve pups shared each free environment. On day 50 the females from the free environment were placed in the same type of laboratory cages as those described above.

These females were the parents of the animals used in this study. When approximately 150 days old, one female from each litter was bred to a randomly chosen colony male. All pregnant animals were placed in stainless steel maternity cages. At birth, litters were reduced to eight pups consisting, when possible, of four males and four females. No litter contained less than four pups. The pups remained undisturbed until they were 21 days old. At this time they were placed into a 32 in.[2] open field consisting of sixty-four squares. An activity count was recorded each time a pup made contact with a different square. Each pup was given one 3 min. test, and after this was weighed.

Table 1 presents the experimental design, the mean activity score, the mean body weight, the number of pups and the number of litters for each of the eight treatment combinations. In the statistical analysis of these data the litter was used as the unit of measurement with a sub-classification for the sex of the pup. For example, the activity scores of all males within a litter were combined and a mean was obtained; the same procedure was applied to the females. These litter sex scores were subjected to a split plot unweighted means analysis of variance.[6] All F tests were based on 1/47 degrees of freedom.

Table 1. SUMMARY OF MEANS FOR ALL EXPERIMENTAL CONDITIONS

Handling experience of grandmothers of experimental subjects	Preweaning housing of mothers of experimental subjects	Postweaning housing of mothers of experimental subjects	No. of litters	No. of subjects	Open-field activity		Weaning weight (g)	
					Male	Female	Male	Female
Non-handled	Maternity cage	Laboratory cage	17	123	17.00	15.02	50.00	47.05
		Free environment	17	133	23.60	20.70	48.43	46.26
	Free environment	Laboratory cage	11	82	13.08	9.31	51.45	50.32
		Free environment	11	85	15.48	11.58	45.63	44.29
Handled	Maternity cage	Laboratory cage	12	90	11.39	18.30	49.73	48.35
		Free environment	12	86	16.32	19.17	47.07	44.76
	Free environment	Laboratory cage	11	84	25.56	24.29	44.76	42.93
		Free environment	11	86	11.35	17.46	48.76	46.91

Activity

The interaction of grandmother handing $\times$ mother preweaning housing was significant at the 0.01 level (F, 7.68): descendants of non-handled grandmothers were more active than descendants of handled grandmothers if their mothers had been reared in a maternity cage between birth and weaning. Exactly the opposite pattern was obtained if their mothers had been reared in a free environment during infancy. The grandmother handling $\times$ mother postweaning housing interaction was significant (F, 5.04; $P < 0.05$): the pattern was just the opposite to that described for the previous interaction. In addition, the preweaning housing $\times$ postweaning housing interaction was significant at the 0.05 level (F, 5.77). Offspring of mothers reared in two different environments during early life (that is, cage and free environment, or free environment and cage) were more active than the offspring of mothers which had been reared only in cages or only in free environments for the first 50 days of life.

The grandmother handling $\times$ sex interaction was significant at the 0.01 level (F, 21.44). Male weanlings were only slightly affected by the handling experience their grandmothers had received, while the females were markedly affected, with grandpups of handled females being significantly more active than grandpups of non-handled females. Finally, the preweaning housing $\times$ postweaning $\times$ sex interaction was significant at the 0.05 level (F,4.55).

Weaning Weight

The two main effects of grandmother handling and mother postweaning housing were both significant at the 0.05 level (Fs of 4.55 and 5.20, respectively), while the interaction of these two factors was significant at the 0.01 level (F, 8.49). All three of these effects were brought about by one cell: those weanlings whose grandmothers were not handled in infancy and whose mothers were reared in laboratory cages after weaning weighed significantly more than the other three groups making up this interaction. Such groups did not differ among themselves. In addition, the grandmother handling $\times$ preweaning housing $\times$ postweaning housing interaction was significant (F,

18.80; $P < 0.01$), and sex was significant (F, 87.99; $P < 0.01$) with male weanlings weighing more than females.

These data for activity and weaning weight reveal that handling females in infancy can have an effect two generations further on; that the nature of the mother's living quarters during her early life will affect her offspring, and that these variables act in a non-additive interactive manner. The interactive nature of the variables should be emphasized: if we had merely taken the female offspring of handled and non-handled grandmothers and maintained them in standard laboratory caging conditions from birth until adulthood (first and fifth groups listed in Table 1) most of the significant findings would have disappeared. Thus the occurrence of free environment experience some time during the mother's early ontogeny was necessary for the effects of the grandmother's handling experience to express itself in the grandpups.

Others have reported findings extending into the next generation. Ginsburg and Hovda[7] reduced the incidence of death from audiogenic seizures in *dba* mice by transplanting fertilized *dba* eggs into *C57Bl* foster mothers shortly after fertilization, and Ressler[8] has shown that the strain of foster grandparent rearing young mice will influence the operant response rate of the offspring of those mice. As far as we know, the present experiment is the first documentation that the experiences which an animal has in early life will influence her unborn descendants two generations away by nongenetic mechanisms.

The nature of the mechanisms underlying these effects is not known. Both handling and free environment experience have behavioural and biological effects on the stimulated organisms.[2-5, 9-12] These effects could act through changes in grandmaternal or maternal behaviour or through physiological changes which would affect the developing foetus or modify the milk supply of the grandmother or mother.

References

1. Denenberg, V. H. and Whimboy, A. E., *Science* 142, 1192 (1963).

2. Denenberg, V. H., and Morton, J. R. C., *J. Comp. Physiol. Psychol.*, 55, 242 (1962).
3. Denenberg, V. H., and Morton, J. R.C., *Anim. Behav.*, 12, 11 (1964).
4. Denenberg, V. H., Morton, J. R. C., and Haltmeyer, G. F., *Anim. Behav.*, 12, 205 (1964).
5. Whimbey, A. E., and Denenberg, V.H., *Multivar. Behav. Res., 1, 279 (1966)*.
6. Winer, B. J., *Statistical Principles in Experimental Design* (McGraw-Hill, New York, 1962).
7. Ginsburg, B. E., and Hovda, R. B., *Anal. Rec.*, 99, 621 (1947).
8. Ressler, R. H., *J. Comp. Physiol. Psychol.*, 61, 264 (1966).
9. Denenberg, V.H., Brumaghim, J.T., Haltmeyer, G. C., and Zarrow, M. X., *Endocrinology* (in the press, 1967).
10. Levine, S., Haltmeyer, G. C., Karas, G. G., and Denenberg, V. H., *Physiol. Behav.*, 2, 55 (1967).
11. Krech, D., Rosenzweig, M. R., and Bennett, E. L., *J. Comp. Physiol. Psychol.*, 53, 509 (1966).
12. Rosenzweig, M. R., *Amer. Psychol.*, 21, 321 (1966).

L. W. SONTAG, W. G. STEELE, & M. LEWIS

14   The Fetal and Maternal Cardiac Response to Environmental Stress

Although emotional states in postnatal life are recognized as affecting physiological-endocrinological state, as for example the effect of anxiety on the thyroid function and blood sugar levels, there has been in the past little general recognition of the fact that such psychosomatic relationships and others might, through placental interchange, constitute powerful changes in fetal physiology—and perhaps behavior.

Recently, FERREIRA [1965] in a review of the emotional factors in the prenatal environment stated that one crucial issue in the problem of maternal influences is the extent to which the fetus can respond to outside agents. These agents may be maternally induced or received directly from the environment or some combination of both. The literature contains examples that direct experimental manipulation can affect fetal behavior. For example, SONTAG and WALLACE [1935a, 1936] have described the fetal response to sound stimulation which consisted of an immediate increase in heart rate and a marked increase in the level of fetal movements. There is also evidence that maternal response to stimulation (for example, to smoking) can affect the fetal heart rate and result in cardiac acceleration [SONTAG and WALLACE, 1935b]. More recently, investigators have demonstrated marked and possible long-lasting fetal cardiac changes as a result of maternal distress

Reprinted from *Human Development 12*:1–9, 1969. Copyright S. Karger,Basel.

This research was supported in part by Grants No. HD-00868, FR-00222 and FR-05537 from The National Institute of Mental Health, United States Public Health Service. Our appreciation is given to JOAN KING for her aid in data reduction and analysis.

caused by some traumatic incident [SONTAG, 1966; COPHER and HUBER, 1967; LIEBERMAN, 1963]. Thus, the fetus can be affected by stimulation either directly from the environment or through the maternal response to that stimulation as well as being affected by maternal distress or emotional state.

In most of the reported studies involving the emotional state of the mother only gross distress was explored. This brings into focus the question of the dimensions and nuances of the maternal emotional experience as it affects the developing fetus.

The purpose of the present study is an attempt to evaluate the possible physiological impact on the fetus of such common-place and non-traumatic maternal experiences as listening to music while resting quietly.

Method

Subjects. Seventeen women in the last six weeks of pregnancy volunteered to serve as subjects for this study. They were seen in the Fels Fetal Behavior Laboratory on five consecutive week-day mornings.

The average age of the fetuses was 25 days before birth. The fetuses ranged in age from two through 41 days before birth[2].[*]

Apparatus. The fetal electrocardiogram was recorded using the procedures described by WELFORD, SONTAG, PHILLIPS and PHILLIPS [1967]. This procedure utilizes four Beckman silver silver-chloride electrodes fastened to the external body wall of the maternal abdomen: one electrode over the symphisis pubis and three at the level of the fundus uteri, one midline and two lateral. This yields three separate ECG channels, each amplified by means of Tecktronix Model FM 122 preamplifiers which have been modified to yield a gain of 5000. The signal is then fed to the driver amplifier of a Grass Model 7 Polygraph. A fourth ECG channel, designed to allow clearer recording of the fetal heart wave complex (commonly referred to as the QRS complex) is derived from the three.

The maternal ECG was also obtained and the beat to beat interval (R–R interval) recorded on an IBM punch paper tape system (SETAR) for direct computer input [see WELFORD, 1962]. The polygraph and SETAR recorders were kept synchronous by means of a timer which marks both records simultaneously, every 15 sec.

[*] All the fetuses were born as normal and full-term infants.

The subject room was a quiet, pleasantly furnished room with a hospital-type bed in which the subject was able to lie in a comfortable, semi-reclining position.

Procedure. Prior to testing, the mothers were asked to indicate a favorite piece of music which was then used as the music stimulus for that particular *S*. From their selection, a 10-min passage of music was tape-recorded. Thus, for each session, *S* heard the same selection of her choice.

Subjects, upon arriving at the Institute, were given a brief description of the technique of fetal electrocardiography. The experimental procedure was explained and any questions answered before the procedure was begun. *Ss* were made comfortable in the hospital-type bed in the private subject room. Electrodes were attached by a female assistant who stayed with *S* until a readable fetal ECG had been obtained. After the fetal signal was clearly established, the assistant left the room and the base period was begun.

The initial base period lasted for 10 min and was followed by the 10 min of music. The music was presented through two AR 2a floor speakers which were placed on the floor at the foot of the bed. The music level was held relatively constant, varying

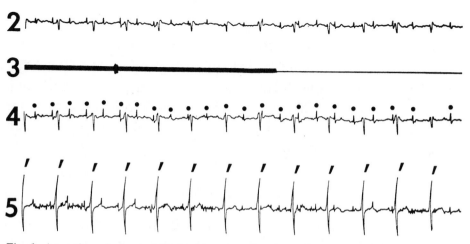

Fig. 1. A portion of a typical fetal and maternal polygraph record where the fetal QRS pattern was visible.

from 65 db to 100 db with an average of 75 db measured at the S's head. Following the offset of the music, there was a 15-min post-stimulation rest period. The ECG data was recorded continuously throughout the 35-min session.

Measurement. Figure 1 presents a 10-sec sample of a polygraph record showing each of the three ECG channels associated with the three leads discussed above. These are represented on channels 1, 2 and 5. Channel 4 presents the fourth ECG record which is derived from the other three. The derived channel was edited for fetal ECG. This is seen as dots above the R spike. The fifth channel shows the maternal R spike which, for the sake of exposition, has also been edited.

Channel 3 presents the recording of fetal movement as a thickening of the line. This was obtained by instructing the mother to record perceived fetal movement by pushing a small lever at her right hand. This activated the event pen labeled 3 in figure 1. The mark observed within the movement period is the 15-sec time marker. All 15-sec segments in which the mother reported any fetal movement were tabulated.

After editing the fetal record, each R–R interval was read, using a Benson-Lehner Oscar-E record reader. This instrument converts the distance between two beats or R–R interval into time and these readings are punched onto IBM cards for processing with an IBM 1620 Computer. The maternal R–R interval data was recorded directly onto IBM punch paper tape with the SETAR recorder.

Results

Data are reported here only for those sessions where the fetal ECG was clear and readable. There was one session per day and each lasted approximately 35 min. There are data presented here for 34 sessions from 11 mothers. The number of sessions for each subject ranges from one to five.

Cardiac Rate Changes

Observation of the data indicated that maternal and fetal responses to music were most likely to occur at stimulus onset, that is, when there is energy change. This is consistent with other studies of cardiac responsivity which also show maximum cardiac change at stimulus onset [LEWIS and SPAULDING, 1967; CHASE and GRAHAM, 1967]. Thus, only the first 2 min of stimulation are reported. The data indicate that both fetal and maternal heart rate returned to prestimulation levels soon after the first 2 min. Further, stimulus termination failed to produce any significant heart rate changes.

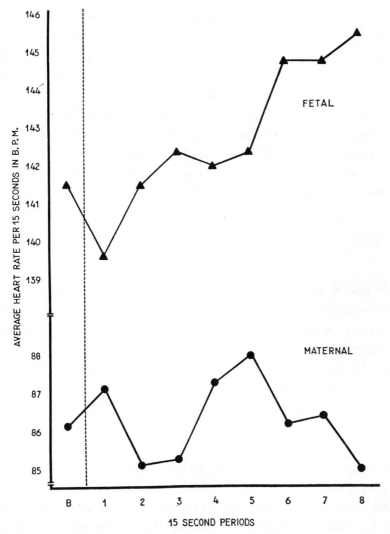

Fig. 2. Mean fetal and maternal heart rate by 15-sec intervals. The 15-sec interval prior to stimulation is presented to the left of the vertical line while the 2 min after onset is located on the right. B.P.M. = Beats per minute.

Figure 2, therefore, presents the mean group data for the average heart rate per 15 sec for the first 2 min of stimulation. For each *S* for each session, the number of beats in each 15-sec segment was recorded and converted into the corresponding average beats per minute. The group data represents the mean of each S's median data over sessions.

Fetal Response

The fetal data indicate a predominant response of cardiac acceleration during the first 2 min of the music presentation. A comparison of the five fastest beats (R–R intervals) 15 sec prior to onset to the fastest five beats during the first 2 min of stimulation indicate a significant cardiac acceleration (by Wilcoxon paired replicates, p <0.001). A second analysis compared each of the 15-sec sequences to the base period in order to determine at what time the cardiac rate increase was significantly higher than the base period. This occurred 90 sec after stimulus onset (by Wilcoxon's paired replicates, p <0.05, two-tailed).

Maternal Response

The maternal response is not as clear as the fetal response. An initial deceleration then followed by acceleration was exhibited and each of the analyses performed on the fetal data indicated a lack of significant change for the maternal response. There was, however, a trend toward a significant deceleration after 30 sec and toward a significant acceleration 75 sec after stimulation (Wilcoxon paired replicates, p <0.10, two-tailed).

Cardiac Variability

Fetal response. The measure of heart rate variability, the high-low difference, was computed by taking the mean of the six fastest beats and subtracting it from the mean of the six slowest beats in each 15-sec segment of the record. To analyze this data, a median H–L difference score for the 15 sec prior to stimulation and for the 120 sec following stimulation was obtained for each S. By use of a Wilcoxon's paired replicates test, the data revealed significant increases in cardiac variability over the first 2 min (p <0.01).

Maternal response. The maternal variability data again showed no significant effect.

Fetal movement. The mean number of 15-sec periods where any fetal movement occurs was observed for each *S*. During the pre-stimulus base period of 1 min, there was a total of 22 movement episodes. There were 17 and 30 movement episodes for minutes 1 and 2 during stimulation indicating no significant fetal activity changes as a function of stimulus onset.

Discussion

The data indicate that there is a gradual acceleration of fetal heart rate following the onset of music which reaches a peak at about 2 min after onset. While there is some variation in the mother's rate during this 2-min period, the changes are not statistically significant. What changes there are in the mother's heart rate are biphasic—an initial deceleration followed by acceleration. An important question yet to be answered concerns the mechanism of this fetal cardiac acceleration. It could be argued that the sounds, represented by the music, were transmitted through the soft tissue and amniotic fluid to the fetus resulting in a startle reflex response similar to that described by SONTAG *et al.* An alternative hypothesis is that the fetal response was mediated through the emotional reaction of the mother; that is, a physiological response resulted from her reaction to the music and mediated through her bloodstream and maternal placental interchange. German physicians [FORBES and FORBES, 1927] have reported instances of expectant mothers experiencing severe discomfort from violent fetal kicking during attendance at symphonies and opera. They were at a loss to determine whether such modified fetal behavior resulted from the fetuses' perception of the sound stimulus or whether it resulted from maternal sensory response mediated again through her endocrine humoral mechanisms.

The second hypothesis receives support from two facts. It is to be noted that there were no changes in the activity of the fetus. This suggests that the heart rate changes may have been less a result of a startle reflex and more a result of the mother's emotional response to the music. Further, in the changes in fetal heart rate to a directed stimulus as reported by SONTAG and WALLACE, it is to be noted that the change rate was almost instantaneous upon the application of the stimulus; i.e., within 10 sec there was a marked increase in cardiac rate which, by 15 sec, had reached its maximum. In contrast, the fetal cardiac acceleration which occurred in the experiment reported here, that is, to indirect stimulation, took a full 2 min to achieve its maximum, suggesting that the factor producing the acceleration was mediated through another system, namely, that of the mother. Either hypothesis, however, fails to disrupt the central thesis of this paper, namely, that relatively non-traumatic and commonplace events in the maternal environment can affect the fetal cardiac response.

The present data, as well as an earlier report from this laboratory, indicate that there are significant individual fetal differences in base heart rate and variability as well as in responsivity to environmental stimulation.

The degree of response to environmental stimulation both of the mother and fetus and its relationship to subsequent development is an intriguing question. To answer this, it appears evident that the fetal response as a consequence of the maternal response, and the fetal response as a consequence of direct stimulation, must be separated. The task for the investigator of fetal behavior is, therefore, not only to explore the effects of stimulation, but to determine the interactions between these events and the individual differences in responsivity of the mother and fetus.

Summary

A non-stressful auditory stimulus was presented to 11 mothers during their last trimester of pregnancy. Maternal and fetal heart rate and fetal activity were recorded. The data indicated significant changes in the fetal heart rate to the first 2 min of the stimulus presentation. While it was not possible to clearly determine whether the maternal response mediated the fetal change or whether the fetus responded directly to the stimulus, the data suggest that the former hypothesis was the more parsimonious.

References

CHASE, W.G. and GRAHAM, F.K.: Heart rate response to non-signal tones. Psychonom. Sci. *9:* 181–182 (1967).

COPHER, D.E. and HUBER, C.P.: Heart rate response of the human fetus to induced maternal hypoxia. Amer. J. Obstet. Gynec. *98:* 320–335 (1967).

FERREIRA, A.J.: Emotional factors in prenatal environment. J. nerv. ment. Dis. *141:* 108–118 (1965).

FORBES, H.S. and FORBES, H.B.: Fetal sense reactions: Hearing. J. comp. Psychol. *7:* 353 (1927).

LEWIS, M. and SPAULDING, S.J.: Differential cardiac response to visual and auditory stimulation in the young child. Psychophysiol. *3:* 229–237 (1967).

LIEBERMAN, M.: Early developmental stress and later behavior. Science *141:* 824–825 (1963).

SONTAG, L.W. and WALLACE, R.F.: The movement response of the human fetus to sound stimuli. Child Develop. *6:* 253–258 (1935a).

SONTAG, L.W. and WALLACE, R.F.: The effect of cigarette smoking during pregnancy upon fetal heart rate. Amer. J. Obstet. Gynec. *29:* 77–82 (1935b).

SONTAG, L.W. and WALLACE, R.F.: Changes in the rate of the human fetal heart in response to vibratory stimuli. Amer. J. Dis. Child. *51:* 583–589 (1936).

SONTAG, L.W.: Implications of fetal behavior and environment for adult personalities. Ann. N.Y. Acad. Sci. *134:* 782–786 (1966).

WELFORD, N.T.: The SETAR and its uses for recording physiological and behavioral data. IRE trans. biomed. Elect. *9:* 185–189 (1962).

WELFORD, N.T.; SONTAG, L.W.; PHILLIPS, W. and PHILLIPS, D.: Individual differences in heart rate variability in the human fetus. Amer. J. Obstet. Gynec. *98:* 56–61 (1967).

DONALD R. OTTINGER & JAMES E. SIMMONS

15   Behavior of Human Neonates and Prenatal Maternal Anxiety

Summary.—A population of obstetrical patients was administered the IPAT Anxiety Scale during each trimester of pregnancy. Nineteen women representing extreme total scores were selected to test the hypothesis that there would be a positive relationship between the mothers' anxiety scores during gestation and neonatal behavior. Body activity and crying behavior were recorded on the second, third, and fourth day of life. Body weight was recorded at birth and on each day. The data confirmed the hypothesis of a positive relationship between mothers' anxiety level and amount of neonatal crying.

There is a growing body of literature concerned with the relationship between maternal stress or emotionality levels during pregnancy and offspring behavior. Sontag (1944) reported that prolonged emotional stress during pregnancy resulted in infants who weighed less than average and had high activity levels. Thompson (1957) found a relationship between experimentally-induced "anxiety" in rat mothers and the offsprings' emotional behavior. Ottinger, Denenberg, and Stephens (1963) found a relationship between observed pre-

Reprinted with permission of author and publisher from *Psychological Reports 14*:391–394, 1964.

Appreciation is expressed to the Departments of Obstetrics and Nursing, Indiana University Center, for their help and support.

This investigation was supported in part by Research Grant M-5154 from the National Institute of Mental Health, U. S. Public Health Service.

pregnancy emotional (open-field activity) levels in rat mothers and the emotional behavior of their offspring. Highly emotional mothers produced highly emotional offspring and mothers of low emotionality produced offspring of low emotionality. Group differences in body weight of offspring were also found. In additional experiments, Ottinger, *et al.* (1963) employed a cross-fostering procedure and found that both prenatal and postnatal periods had an independent relationship with emotionality of offspring. Regardless of whether the offspring were reared by a mother of high or low emotionality, there was a significant relationship between the offspring's open-field behavior and the behavior of the natural mother.

It is this prenatal phenomenon that was the focus of the current investigation. Clinical observations and the above mentioned animal studies led to this study of the relationship between human maternal anxiety during gestation and salient aspects of the neonate's behavior. It was predicted there would be a positive relationship between human mothers' anxiety levels during gestation and their offspring's body activity and amount of crying during the first four days of life.

METHOD

Subjects.—Ss were 19 mothers and their babies. The group included both primipara and multipara. Mothers undergoing Caesarean section and those having grossly prolonged or abnormal deliveries were excluded. The infants had no gross physical deviations. All Ss were patients in an obstetrical ward.

Apparatus.—A stabilimeter was placed between the bassinet and the movable supporting cart. The stabilimeter consisted of a plywood platform, supported by three airpots. Movement by the baby depressed the airpots and caused a flow of air to activate an electrical counter. The stabilimeter did not interfere with the baby's movement in any way. The movement score was an index of the duration of motility.

A directional microphone was attached inside the bassinet. Any crying sound from the baby activated an electrical counter but the microphone was not sensitive to other babies' crying or other sounds in the nursery. The crying score was an index of the duration of crying.

Procedure.—A population of expectant mothers was administered an anxiety scale, the IPAT self analysis form, during each trimester of pregnancy. Ss were then ranked on the basis of their total scores. Approximately the upper third and lower third of the range were designated as high and low anxiety levels. Cut-off points were arbitrary but obvious. This resulted in 10 Ss with a mean group total score of 110.00 in the high group and 9 Ss with a group total mean score of 35.20 in the low group. When a baby was born the birth weight was recorded in grams. Because of hospital routine and physicians' orders it was necessary to wait 24 hr. after birth before all Ss were on a feeding schedule. The baby was then put on the stabilimeter. The motility and audio recording systems were turned on 30 min. prior to each feeding. After the feedings, the baby received a clean diaper and was replaced on the stabilimeter. The baby was not handled during the recording period. Recordings were taken again for 30 min. and independent scores were recorded for before- and after-feeding periods. Body weight was recorded each day. This procedure was followed until the baby left the hospital.

RESULTS AND DISCUSSION

The data were analyzed in a repeated-measures analysis of variance design.* The groups did not differ in body weight at birth or on any of the first four days, but the interaction between groups and days approached significance ($p = .10$). The babies of mothers in the high anxiety group tended to be the heaviest at birth but then lost weight at a faster rate than the babies of the low mothers. As expected, there was a weight loss over days for both groups that was significant beyond the .01 level.

The babies of the highly anxious mothers cried significantly more than those of the low group ($p = .01$). Group means are shown in Table 1. There was significantly more crying before feeding than after feeding for both groups ($p < .01$). There were no significant changes in crying over days, but the group by before-after interaction was significant beyond the .01 level. This is

TABLE 1

MEAN GROUP CRYING SCORES BEFORE AND AFTER FEEDING

Mother's IPAT Classification		Day 2		Day 3		Day 4	
		Before	After	Before	After	Before	After
Low	M	172.06	154.77	303.40	63.37	349.15	122.13
	SD	118.71	135.79	124.26	42.29	135.97	172.49
High	M	560.80	116.39	485.09	159.33	567.96	142.66
	SD	532.28	128.82	212.74	180.35	173.87	186.06

illustrated in Fig. 1 which shows the greatest difference between groups occurred before feeding and no significant group differences after feeding. There were no significant differences in body movement scores but the pattern of scores was similar to that for the crying data.

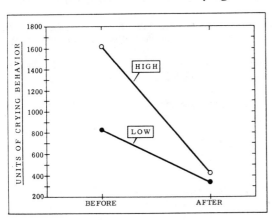

FIG. 1. Crying behavior before and after feeding for babies of low and high anxiety mothers

The body weight of the two groups did not differ significantly on any day of the study, but the babies from mothers of high anxiety were slightly heavier at birth and were somewhat lighter at three days of age. The differences in body weight appear to be

*A summary table of the analysis of variance and table of mean daily crying scores for each S have been filed with the American Documentation Service, Auxiliary Publications Project, Photoduplication Service, Library of Congress, Washington 25, D. C. Order Document No. 7867, remitting $1.25 for photocopies or 35-mm. microfilm.

a chance occurrence, but the difference in rate of loss over days for the two groups approached significance at the .10 level. The more rapid loss of weight in the initially heavier babies concurs with the expected (Stuart & Stevenson, 1954) proportionately greater weight loss in heavier babies. The post partum weight loss is primarily a loss of excess body fluids and has no clinical significance.

The babies' crying behavior was significantly related to the mothers' anxiety level during the pregnancy. The design of the study did not reveal the mechanism responsible for this phenomenon. However, it is important to note the significant group by before-after feeding interaction on the crying variable. The babies of the two maternal groups were significantly different before the feeding experience but the crying behavior did not differ after feeding. Perhaps the simplest explanation of this interaction is that the feeding experience was a powerful enough variable to override the behavioral differences. However, this interaction does support the position that the total behavioral difference was a prenatal and/or genetic phenomenon rather than a function of the differences of the mothers' handling of the infant during feeding. This position is further supported by the fact that the significant group differences were found in the first four days of life with minimal mother-child contact.

Additional research is needed to determine the significance or predictive value of neonatal crying or body activity. The data of this study are consistent with the animal data of Ottinger, et al. (1963). Whether rat mothers are treated experimentally to produce levels of emotionality or the variable is taken as an existing naturalistic phenomenon, the rat mother's emotionality level during gestation is directly related to the offspring's emotional behavior. In an analogous fashion the present study found that human mothers' anxiety levels during gestation were significantly related to demonstrable differences in neonate behavior. The predictive value of neonate behavior must be determined by longitudinal study.

REFERENCES

OTTINGER, D. R., DENENBERG, V. H., & STEPHENS, M. W.   Maternal emotionality, multiple mothering, and emotionality in maturity.   *J. comp. physiol. Psychol.*, 1963, 56, 313-317.

SONTAG, L. W.   War and fetal maternal relationship.   *Marriage & fam. Living*, 1944, 6, 1-5.   Cited by P. H. Mussen & J. J. Conger, *Child development and personality.* New York: Harper & Brothers, 1956.   Pp. 66-67.

STUART, H. C., & STEVENSON, S. S.   Physical growth and development.   In W. E. Nelson (Ed.), *Textbook of pediatrics.*   Philadelphia, Pa.: Saunders, 1954.   Pp. 1-28.

THOMPSON, W. R.   Influence of prenatal maternal anxiety on emotionality in young rats. *Science*, 1957, 125, 698-699.

BIOLOGICAL AND PHYSIOLOGICAL

DETERMINANTS

Chapter Five

SEX HORMONES

One of the exciting findings in recent years has been the discovery that the sex hormones, especially the male hormone testosterone, play a critical role during prenatal and neonatal life in determining and influencing sexual development. These hormones cause physical, physiological, and psychological changes.

We had been aware for some time that measurable amounts of sex hormones could be detected in animals in very early life, that the hormones then disappeared for a while, and that they reappeared at the time of puberty. The obvious question was whether the hormones had any function during infancy. The answer to that question is now known.

An important principle which has come from this research is that one function of the sex hormones in very early life is to *organize* the brain of the developing animal to make it either a male or a female brain, while the function of the sex hormones in later life is to *activate* an already organized brain. Putting this another way, during early development the brain has the potential to adopt either masculine or feminine patterns of sexual physiology and behavior, regardless of whether the organism is a genetic male or a genetic female. Which pattern is chosen is determined by sex hormones acting upon the developing brain. The basic pattern of the brain, however, is feminine, and it is only if the male hormone, testosterone, acts upon the brain during early development that a masculine pattern occurs.

What do the expressions "male brain" and "female brain" actually mean? They refer to certain physiological and behavioral states of the animal. The *normal male* has a certain pattern of sexual behavior that culminates in mounting the female, intromission, and ejaculation. Another standard masculine pattern, not directly related to sexual behavior, is aggression. The *normal female's* sexual physiology includes an estrous or menstrual cycle and ovulation. Her sexual behavior pattern includes receptivity to the male's advances when she is in heat. With rodents this receptivity is most easily seen in the mating posture called lordosis, in which the back is arched and the tail moved to one side to facilitate the male's clasping and entering. Another feminine characteristic is lack of aggression.

These characteristics of normal males and females differ from those of feminized males and masculinized females. The *feminized male* animal shows a reduced inclination or a failure to mount and copulate. He may display feminine sexual behavior to the extent of allowing a control male to mount him. He may be less aggressive than normal. The *masculinized female* often fails to have an estrous cycle and may fail to ovulate. She shows reduced sexual activity and mating behavior. The lordosis response may be absent, and she may vigorously resist the attempts of the male to mount her, to the point of attacking him. At times she exhibits masculine sexual behavior, as indicated by mounting a control female. She may be more aggressive than normal females. These various physiological and behavioral states are known to be under neural control, and their occurrence defines the "male brain" and the "female brain."

How do we know that this effect is at the level of brain organization rather than at a more peripheral site such as the gonad or the pituitary? This question can be answered by means of the classical transplantation experiment commonly used in endocrinology. If an intact, healthy ovary is transplanted from a female rat into a castrated male rat, the ovary stops its cycling. Since the ovary continues to cycle when transplanted to another female and does not cycle when transplanted to a male, it follows that the "maleness" or "femaleness" resides at some site other than the ovary, and it is this other site which determines cyclicity. The next step is to examine the pituitary gland, which directly influences ovarian activity. It is possible to remove male and female pituitaries and exchange them. If a male pituitary is placed into a female whose own pituitary has been removed, or vice versa, no changes occur in sexual physiology or behavior. Thus, we infer that the level of organization must be higher than the pituitary. Since the pituitary is directly connected to the brain, we conclude that the level of organization must reside somewhere within the brain. Confirming evidence for this inference is obtained by placing sex hormones directly into the brain, where they cause appropriate sexual events to occur.

The procedures used to investigate the effects of sex hormones in experimental animals are to inject either male or female sex hormones at different times during early development as a method of adding a source of hormonal substrate, or else to use a subtraction procedure of removing the animal's natural source of hormone by castration. The introduction of the exogeneous hormone by injection, or the removal of the endogeneous hormone by castration, must be done at highly specific times while the brain is developing in order to obtain this effect. There is definite evidence of a critical period here (see Chapter Two). For precocial species like the rhesus monkey and the guinea pig, it is necessary to inject hormones prenatally. For a more slowly maturing species, like the rat or mouse, the hormone must be injected within the first 5 to 10 days of life, or castration must be done within this time, to obtain the effect. If the same experiment is performed on the rat after 10 days of age, little change is found in sexual physiology or behavior of either the male or the female.

Not all animals treated with sex hormones show all the behavioral and physiological changes described above, though most show several of them. A number of critical parameters are involved, including the species of animal, the type of hormone, the dose employed, and the age when administered. Many of these points are brought out in Paper 16, which also gives a brief historical review of Young's important contributions to the field and a summary of current research activities.

Although testosterone appears to be the hormone that determines whether the organism will be masculine or feminine, the female hormone, estrogen, also has an effect. Paper 17 reports that females given one injection of estrogen at 4 days of age were less likely to mate with a male in adulthood. Since a female hormone administered in infancy resulted in less feminine behavior in adult life, it is apparent that the presence of a particular hormone during the neonatal period does not necessarily bring about the same behavior pattern as that hormone normally elicits in an adult organism.

It is important to emphasize that the effects of sex hormones are not limited exclusively to sexual physiology and behavior, but affect a host of sex-related activities. Paper 18 nicely demonstrates this by showing that male mice, which are typically aggressive, have a greatly reduced potential for aggressive behavior if they have been given estrogen in infancy; while the female, which is rarely aggressive, can become a vicious fighter if given either testosterone or estrogen in infancy. The finding that estrogen, one of the essential female hormones, has the same effect as testosterone, the male hormone, is odd, and no completely satisfactory answer is known as yet. However, we do know that very high doses of estrogen must be injected to obtain a masculinizing effect, and these doses are beyond the usual physiological limits found in the animal. Thus, this effect may be related only to pharmacological dose levels and may not reflect the animal's behavior under normal circumstances. For an extensive follow-up of this paper, see Bronson and Desjardins (1970).

The experimental findings with animals have cast light upon a number of clinical sexual aberrations in the human. While it is morally and ethically indefensible to introduce hormonal manipulation during human intrauterine development for experimental purposes, certain medical conditions may necessitate hormone administration during pregnancy and certain hormonal malfunctions may occur because of a genetic anomaly. For example, certain synthetic hormones sometimes given to prevent a threatened miscarriage have testosterone-like properties and consequently masculinize female babies. Paper 19 describes the distribution of IQ scores and the nature of psychosexual identity of 10 girls who were exposed to a testosterone-like hormone in utero. Masculinizing effects also occur in human populations because of genetic aberrations. Paper 20 describes the adrenogenital syndrome, which causes an excessive amount of androgen (the male sex hormone) to be present during fetal development. The psychosexual attitudes of 15 girls born with this disturbance are compared with those of 15 control females. In both these papers a common finding is the greatly increased "tomboyism" of the masculinized girls. However, the authors are properly cautious in their interpretation of these findings. They also point out that the human does not appear to be as adversely affected by fetal exposure to masculine hormones as are infrahuman species.

Reference

Bronson, F. H., and Desjardins, C. Neonatal androgen administration and adult aggressiveness in female mice. *Gen. Comp. Endocrinol.*, 1970, 15, 320-325.

WILLIAM C. YOUNG, ROBERT W. GOY, & CHARLES H. PHOENIX

16 Hormones and Sexual Behavior

Research on the relationships between the hormones and sexual behavior has not been pursued with the vigor justified by the biological, medical, and sociological importance of the subject. Explanation may lie in the stigma any activity associated with sexual behavior has long borne. In our experience, restraint has been requested in the use of the word *sex* in institutional records and in the title of research proposals. We vividly recollect that the propriety of presenting certain data at scientific meetings and seminars was questioned. Counteracting this deterrent is the stimulation which has come from colleagues in many disciplines to whom we have appealed for help, and the satisfaction we have felt in seeing a picture emerge as the pieces of the puzzle have been studied and fitted together.

Relationships in the Adult

Causal connections between gonadal hormones and the development of the capacity of infrahuman vertebrates to display sexual behavior have long been assumed, although the existence of such relationships in man is questioned (*1–3*). Doubt has also been expressed that a specific relationship exists between any one hormone (or class of hormones) and the behavior it facilitates in adults in general, from fish to man (*4–6*).

A number of explanations may be given for the uncertainty which exists. Human sexual activity is influenced by

Reprinted from *Science 143*:212–218, 1964. Copyright 1964 by the American Association for the Advancement of Science.

many psychologic factors, the social level, cultural background, and tradition. The many reports are not completely trustworthy. Physiological correlates with individual behavior are largely nonexistent, and controlled study in man as we know it in laboratory animals is impossible. In our opinion the many differences in behavior which in the growing child and adult are socially rather than hormonally determined have obscured the possible role of the hormones in maintaining the strength of the sexual drive. Even in lower mammals the same quantity of hormone elicits almost as many modes of response as there are individuals. This fact may have contributed to the doubt, to which we have alluded, that there is any great degree of hormonal specificity. In the human female, sexual responsiveness does not have the sharp relationship to folliculogenesis and to the functioning of the corpus luteum in the ovary that it does in most lower mammals (7). The degree to which this evolutionary change within the primates has been accompanied by an emancipation from the effects of hormonal action is not known.

The need for testicular androgen in the maintenance of sexual vigor in the male has been questioned by some students of the problem. In man (5, 8), the dog (9), the domestic cat (10), fishes (6), and birds (11), there is, in males, a persistence of sexual activity for some weeks or months after castration which has not been explained satisfactorily; a corresponding persistence is encountered rarely if at all in females below the primates. The restoration of sexual vigor by replacement therapy also requires weeks in the male and only hours or days in the female. The longer time lapse which occurs, regardless of the direction of hormonal change, suggests that the manner of hormonal action in the male is greatly different from that in the female rather than that the strength of sexual behavior is independent of the presence of testicular androgen.

Finally, in this brief consideration of the subject, there are the important studies of deviant sexual types by Hampson and Hampson (1), Money (2), and the recent report by Völkel (3). The data these clinical investigators collected led them to conclude that the establishment of gender role or psychologic sex can be independent of chromosomal sex, gonadal sex, hormonal sex, internal reproductive structures, and external genital morphology. They relate the process rather to "the many experiences of growing up, including those experiences dictated by his or her own bodily equipment" (1).

The interest of one of us (W.C.Y.) in the relationship of the hormones to sexual behavior goes back to an observation made during his graduate years at the University of Chicago when he was looking for signs that would be useful in the identification of female guinea pigs in heat. No active interest was taken, however, until more than 6 years later. During a lull at Brown University, Young, Hugh I. Myers, and Edward W. Dempsey, while waiting for what turned out to be the disapproval of an application for a small amount of money for work on the function of the epididymis, fell into a discussion of the abrupt and dramatic change that occurs in the behavior of the female guinea pig when she comes into heat. They wondered whether this change is associated with any structural change in the ovaries. Continuous day and night observation of the laboratory animals for several months was rewarded by the information Young and his co-workers were seeking. The beginning of heat was found to coincide closely with the beginning of the preovulatory growth phase of the Graafian follicle (*12*); it could be that the three investigators, none of whom had any training in psychology, had stumbled on the only spontaneously occurring macroscopic structural change associated with the alteration of a behavioral state in a mammal.

The reports that ovariectomized mice, rats, rabbits, and dogs copulated after the injection of follicular fluid or of the estrogens that were available at that time suggested that the same behavior would occur in the guinea pig. To the surprise of Young and his associates, irregular results were obtained. These led to the conclusion that a second substance must participate. With the help of Roy Hertz, who worked with the group that year, Dempsey took his cue as to the nature of this substance from the demonstration that the preovulatory growth phase in anestrous cats is stimulated by hypophyseal luteinizing hormone (*13*). Tests soon revealed that this gonadotrophin does not produce heat directly; they suggested that by stimulating preovulatory swelling, ovulation, and production of progesterone luteinizing hormone leads indirectly to the display of estrous behavior by animals previously injected with an estrogen (*14*). The progesterone as it turned out, was the second participating substance. Its synergistic action in combination with estrogens to bring latent mating behavior to expression has since been demonstrated in an impressive number of mammalian species (see *7*). Astwood (*15*) showed later that the hypophyseal gonadotrophin responsible for the production of progesterone is luteotrophin rather than luteinizing hormone.

Importance of Soma

The familiarity obtained with the behavior of the female guinea pig and later with that of the rat and male guinea pig revealed (i) that in repeated tests individual differences in behavior were remarkably consistent and reliable (*16, 17*); (ii) that in the female these differences, except perhaps for the male-like mounting behavior, are not related to the number of rupturing Graafian follicles (*18, 19*); and (iii) that in neither sex are the differences in the vigor of the behavior related to the quantity of administered hormones, provided of course a threshold has been exceeded (*17, 20*). These findings led to the realization that the nature of the latent behavior brought to expression by gonadal hormones depends largely on the character of the soma or substrate on which the hormones act (*19*). The substrate was assumed to be neural (*9*). Unknown to Young and his co-workers until 15 or 20 years later, Goodale (*21*) in 1918 had been impressed by the failure of ovaries implanted into capons to feminize their behavior and had written, "the character of sexual reactions seems to depend upon the substratum, while the gonad merely determines that it shall be given expression."

Factors Influencing Character of Soma

It follows from this principle that an investigator trying to account for the behavioral differences between individuals, instead of looking to the gonadal hormones, would do better to look to the factors which influence the character of the tissues on which these hormones act. The age of the animal was one of the first factors investigated, and data indicating that age is significant were obtained immediately. Responsiveness or reactivity of the tissues to injected gonadal hormones is lacking during early infancy and increases gradually to the level observed in the adult (22, 23).

The possibility of further changes as aging progresses has not been investigated. The thyroid was thought of as a factor influencing responsiveness, and Young and his co-workers found that female guinea pigs surgically thyroidectomized and given I[131], to suppress any accessory thyroid activity, ovariectomized, and injected with estradiol and progesterone were less responsive to the latter substances than control females (24). The many reports of the effects of thyroid hormone on the vigor of sexual behavior in the male are so contradictory (7) that prediction of the relation of this hormone to the animal's responsiveness to androgens, before adequately designed experiments have been carried out, would be unwise.

The belief that the genetic background is an influential determinant of the character of the soma was soon confirmed. Intact male and female guinea pigs of the highly inbred strains 2 and 13 exhibit significant differences in their behavior. The differences are displayed consistently after gonadectomy and injection of the same amounts of the appropriate hormones (20, 23, 25). The hereditary basis of sexual behavior was studied. For both male and female behavior a high degree of heritability was demonstrated. The inheritance is autosomal, of the sex-limited or sex-influenced type, and appears to be polygenic for most of the behavioral characteristics studied. Sexual behavior is not inherited as a unitary trait, and the elements composing the patterns of behavior show a surprising degree of independence of one another. In the male, phenotypic dominance of strain 13 was found for specific behavioral characteristics—for example, frequency of mounting. With respect to other characteristics, such as latency to ejaculation, strain 2 was dominant (26). In the female, the characteristics of frequent male-like mounting, vigorous lordosis, and responsiveness to injected estrogen appeared to have independent modes of inheritance and separate genetic bases (27).

Attention was drawn to the possibility that experiential or psychologic factors might have a role in the determination of the character of the soma by two young psychologists in the laboratory, Elliott S. Valenstein and Walter Riss, who could not accept the view that inheritance was accounting for the entire action. Again, the hunch was a good one. In a relatively short time after they directed their attention to the behavior of males raised in isolation from the day of birth, except for association with the mother, the necessity of contact with other animals for the maturation of normal patterns of sexual behavior was demonstrated (28). These males were sexually aroused to the same degree as normal males and attempted to mount frequently. However, the males that had been raised in isolation displayed an inability to properly mount and clasp a female. Presumably as a result of this inability, intromission was

rarely achieved. These behavioral deficiencies characteristic of males reared
in isolation were not overcome by injections of testosterone propionate and
therefore cannot be attributed to a hormonal deficiency. The effect of isolation
on maturation of the behavior of the
female is less pronounced, except, in-
terestingly, that isolation has an inhibiting effect on the male-like mounting
behavior displayed so commonly by
the female guinea pig (29). The guinea
pig is not alone in needing contact
with other animals for the maturation
of normal behavior. This need has been
demonstrated many times in species as
widely separated phylogenetically as
ring doves, domestic turkeys, rats, cats,
rhesus monkeys, chimpanzees, and man
(10, 30).

Special Influence of

Early Hormonal Factors

Up to this point nothing in the work
with young or adult animals had suggested that gonadal hormones serve to
organize the tissues mediating sexual behavior in the sense of differentiation, as
experimental embryologists use the
word. Conceivably the action is organizational before birth or before sexual
maturation, and activational in the
adult.

We were aware that numerous investigators have obtained a full functional
sex reversal (including breeding) in
fishes and amphibians after administering heterotypical hormones during the
embryonic and larval stages [see 31 for
a few of the many reports reviewed by
Young (32)]. More important for our
thought was the statement by Dantchakoff (33) that female guinea pigs given
testosterone prenatally had ovaries and

two sets of duct systems. Oviducts, uterus, and vagina existed along with
epididymides, ducti deferentes, seminal vesicles, prostate, Cowper's glands,
and a penis, all differentiated and developed to varying degrees. An inverse
relationship was found between penile
structure and the degree of vaginal development. After injections of testosterone, masculine behavior was displayed.
A repetition of Dantchakoff's experiment was dictated by the circumstance
that no controls seem to have been
used in her studies of this species, in
which most normal females display
male-like mounting as a part of the
estrous reactions. Once a satisfactory
method of administering the hormone
had been developed by Myron D. Ted-
ford, whose interest was mainly in the
structural changes, pseudohermaphroditic females were produced routinely. The
genital tracts were similar to those described by Dantchakoff, although probably encompassing a larger range of
variations in structure. A marked display of masculine behavior was seen,
as well as a lowered capacity to display feminine behavior (34)—an effect
not observed by the earlier workers.
Loss of the ability to come into heat
was greatest when androgen treatment
was started on day 30 of the 67- to
71-day gestation period, regardless of
the duration of treatment and the total
amount of androgen (35) (Table 1).

For us, these results produced an exciting moment. It was clear, first, that
the gonadal hormones, or at least testicular androgens, have a dual role in
the control of sexual behavior in the
guinea pig. During the fetal period the
hormones have an organizing action
on the neural tissues destined to mediate
mating behavior after the attainment

Table 1. Loss of the ability of female guinea pigs to come into heat relative to the amount of androgen (testosterone propionate) injected in the prenatal period and to the length of the period of treatment.

Period of prenatal injection of androgen (days)	Total amount of androgen injected (mg)	Percentage failing to come into heat
15 to 30	40	0
15 to 40	50	12
15 to 45	55	36
15 to 60 +	70 +	27
20 to 65	70	45
25 to 40	40	23
30 to 45	40	67
30 to 55 or 65	50 or 60	92 or 91
35 to 65	55	60
40 to 65	50	33
50 to 65	40	0

of adulthood; during adulthood their role is one of activation. In other words, during fetal morphogenesis androgens exert a fundamental influence on the organization of the soma, determining whether the sexual reactions brought to expression in the adult will be masculine or feminine in character.

Second, it was clear that the rules of hormonal action are identical with those shown by the experimental embryologists to be applicable to the genital tracts (36). During the fetal period the gonadal hormones influence the direction of differentiation. During adulthood they stimulate functioning, be it contraction of smooth muscle fiber, secretion of epithelial cells, or endometrial sensitization for implantation.

The comparison can be extended. Evidence has been presented by experimental embryologists that, as the male develops, fetal testicular hormone is responsible for differentiation of the Wolffian duct system (precursor of the male genital tract) and suppression of the Müllerian duct system (precursor of the

female genital tract). In the female and in the castrated fetal male, in both of which testicular androgen is absent, there is development of the Müllerian duct system and regression of the Wolffian duct system. In our experiments the administration of an androgen to developing female fetuses was followed by the production of individuals in which there had been a stimulating action on the tissues (presumably neural) having the potential capacity for mediating masculine behavior, and a suppressing action on the tissues destined ordinarily to mediate feminine behavior.

In order to complete the analogy it was necessary to demonstrate that genotypic males castrated before the end of the period in which the organizing action of the fetal testicular hormone ordinarily occurs would display feminine behavior as adults. For us, such an operation on the young fetal guinea pig was not feasible. The best available evidence from tests of fertility and mating behavior indicated that this organizational period in the rat, a species with a short period of gestation, is postnatal (37) rather than prenatal, and that it ends at approximately the 10th day after birth. If the analogy could be extended, male rats castrated during this short period after birth should display feminine behavior, or at least elements of feminine behavior, when injected with estrogen and progesterone as adults.

An experiment designed to test this hypothesis has just been completed by Kenneth L. Grady, a graduate student. Male rats were castrated at 1, 5, 10, 20, 30, 50, and 90 days of age, and as a criterion, females were ovariectomized at 90 days. When they were 120 days old, and from then on, all animals were tested, after injections of estradiol and progesterone, for the display of feminine behavior in response to mounting by intact males. As we had expected, the experimental males displayed feminine behavior. Those castrated on day 1 or day 5 displayed significantly more receptive behavior than those castrated as late as day 10. Castration later than day 10 did not promote the retention or development of female behavioral characteristics *(38)* (see Table 2).

Tests of masculine behavior in male rats castrated soon after birth and

Table 2. Mean copulatory quotients (lordosis/mounts) for rats gonadectomized at different ages and tested after injection of estradiol and progesterone at 120 days.

Day of gonadectomy	Quotient
Females	
90	0.619
Males	
1	0.436
5	.218
10	.014
20	.029
30	.042
50	.026
90	.019

tested as adults are currently in progress. When these tests are completed the model established by the experimental embryologists will have been duplicated for behavior. The results may be anticipated from an early study in which male rats castrated on day 1 exhibited a marked deficiency in copulatory ability as compared with those castrated on day 21 or later *(39)*. If this proves to be a representative finding, our work on the two sexes will have produced complementary pictures of the organizational influences of androgen. On the one hand, females treated with

androgen during the appropriate period show a regression or inhibition of feminine behavior and an accentuation of masculine behavioral traits. Males deprived of the principal source of endogenous androgen during a comparable period show accentuated feminine behavior and the absence of, or a greatly diminished capacity for, masculine behavior.

Extension to Sex-related Behavior

When Phoenix, Goy, Gerall, and Young *(34)* were summarizing their data on the behavior of the female pseudohermaphroditic guinea pigs, they suggested that the organizing or sex-differentiating action of fetal gonadal substances may affect behavior beyond that which is primarily sexual in the sense of being directed solely toward the attainment of sexual aims. The rhesus monkey seemed better suited than the guinea pig or rat for a test of this hypothesis, so we proceeded accordingly.

Although an androgen treatment entirely compatible with the maintenance of pregnancy has not been worked out, we have succeeded in producing three female pseudohermaphroditic subjects with conspicuous genital alterations (Fig. 1). Two have been studied in considerable detail. We based our study of the early social patterns displayed by these individuals on the model established by Leonard Rosenblum during his graduate training at the University of Wisconsin. Accordingly, the pseudohermaphroditic females were allowed unrestricted social interaction with two untreated females for 20 minutes per day, 5 days per week, in a specially designed play room.

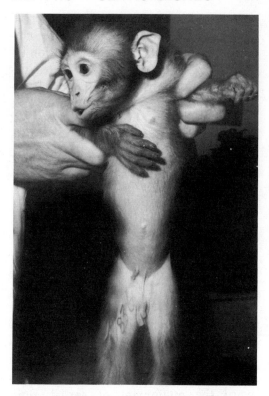

Fig. 1. Female pseudohermaphrodite produced by injecting testosterone propionate into the mother during pregnancy. The treatment involved injection of 25 mg daily from post-coital day 40 through day 50; 20 mg from day 51 through day 70; and 10 mg from day 71 through day 90. There were no injections during the balance of the 166-day period of gestation. A prominent and well-formed phallus is visible to the right of the empty scrotal fold. The surgical scar in the right inguinal region resulted from a laparotomy which showed that there was no testis.

The results from 90 such observational sessions, covering the second through the fifth months of life, have been analyzed recently. A number of social behaviors, known to be sexually dimorphic and without any immediate instrumentality relative to mating, appear to have been influenced in the masculine direction by our prenatal treatments with androgen. The social behavior of the untreated females did not differ importantly from that described for normal females by Rosenblum, but the behavior of the treated females much more closely resembled his description of that of males. The pseudohermaphroditic females threatened, initiated play, and engaged in rough-and-tumble play patterns more frequently than the controls (Figs. 2–4). Like the males studied by Rosenblum, these pseudohermaphrodites also withdrew less often from the initiations, threats, and approaches of other subjects.

Analysis of the sexual behavior displayed by these pseudohermaphroditic females, although far from complete, already shows that it is not only in their patterns of withdrawing, playing, and threatening that they display a bias toward masculinity. In special tests with pairs of females, one pseudohermaphroditic and one normal, the pseudohermaphrodites consistently displayed more frequent attempts to mount, regardless of whether the normal female was brought to the hermaphroditic female's cage or vice versa. Their attempts to mount, while infantile and poorly oriented, are beginning to be integrated with pelvic thrusting and even, on a few occasions, phallic erection.

Our work with the primates has not progressed to a point where it may be considered definitive, partly because of the limited duration of the study and partly because of the very small number of subjects. We nevertheless consider the results to be highly encouraging and supportive of the general conclusions developed in our more extensive studies with the infraprimate mammals, concerning the action of the gonadal hormones.

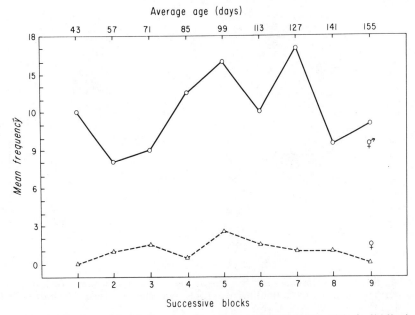

Fig. 2. Display of facial threat by female pseudohermaphroditic (solid line) and normal female (broken line) monkeys plotted relative to age. The abscissa is scaled in successive blocks of five trials.

Implications

Implied in the present discussion of data bearing on the organizing action of androgen on the neural tissues destined to mediate sexual behavior is the view that a part or parts of the central nervous system are masculine or feminine, depending on the sex of the individual. This concept is not new; it has been developing over the years in the writings of investigators whose approach has been entirely different from ours (*4, 40*). What we have found adds

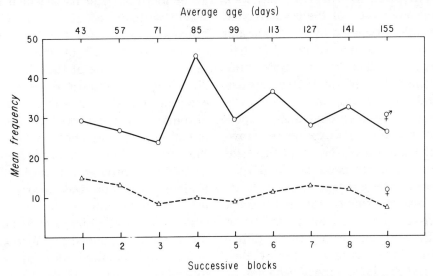

Fig. 3. Invitation to play by female pseudohermaphrodite (solid line) and normal female (broken line) monkeys, plotted relative to age. The abscissa is scaled in successive blocks of five trials.

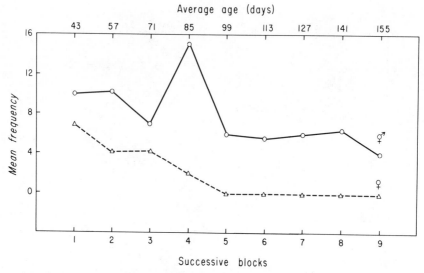

Fig. 4. Rough-and-tumble play by female pseudohermaphroditic (solid line) and normal female (broken line) monkeys, plotted relative to age. The abscissa is scaled in successive blocks of five trials.

support to this view and suggests something of the way in which masculinity or femininity is conferred on the nervous system.

An additional thought merits attention. It is that the principles of hormonal action in effecting this sexual differentiation of the developing brain provide a model to which we may look for a reexamination of the psychosexual incongruities discussed by Hampson and Hampson (*1*) and by Money (*2*) in their reviews and in their many articles published since the middle 1950's. We accept and, in our own work with lower mammals, have documented the importance of the subject's experience. However, explanation of the cases these investigators present need not lead to a rejection of the concept of a predetermined psychosexuality for the concept of a psychologic sexual neutrality at birth. If the endocrinology of the differentiation of the capacity to display masculine and feminine sexual behavior as we have worked it out for the guinea

pig and the rat is applicable to man, the incongruities in the patients these workers examined can be explained without postulating a psychosexual neutrality at birth and attributing the gender role and sexual orientation solely to the individual's life experiences while growing up. In view of what we have learned an endocrinological basis which is consistent with the concept of psychologic bisexuality exists for the interpretation of most if not all of the cases they report. This is true of their hermaphrodites with ambiguous or masculinized external genitals and with a female sex chromatin pattern (comparable with our female pseudohermaphrodites); of the cryptorchid hermaphrodites with a male sex chromatin pattern, in which testicular function was clearly subnormal; of the simulant females with a male sex chromatin pattern but with the as yet unexplained feminizing testes; and of the "females" born with gonadal dysgenesis and an XO or XY chromosome pattern (Turner's syndrome). The large group of hyperadrenocortical patients with the female sex chromosome pattern probably would fit into this picture were the circumstances such that more information about the parameters of the excessive androgen production could have been obtained.

We realize as we venture into a clincal area that a question exists regarding the extent to which what we have found in the guinea pig, rat, and monkey is applicable to man. We call attention, however, to an interesting similarity revealed by Milton Diamond during his graduate work at the University of Kansas. After noting that testosterone does not induce masculinization of the adult female guinea pig while it is pregnant, he examined the clinical literature and found an apparent comparable lack of masculinization in pregnant human beings: 27 of 31 women who received androgenic hormones or gestagens in quantities sufficient to masculinize the female fetuses were not themselves virilized (*41*).

Direction of Future Research

As we have proceeded with our analysis of the relationships of the hormones to sexual behavior and, more recently, to sex-related behavior, we have always been aware that many questions remain to be answered. At the same time a picture is emerging, and, with good fortune in the selection of materials and techniques, much more of it will be revealed in the future.

Without discounting the influence of psychologic factors, which we know is great, or the need for carefully recorded observations of behavior, we expect that, increasingly, the materials and techniques used will be those of the neurologist and the biochemist. The directions many neurologists are taking are indicated by the various reports of efforts to locate the neurological sites of hormonal action and define the pathways of stimuli for the many responses that are given (see *42*).

Few biochemists have been attracted to the problem, but it is they who must clarify the mechanisms of hormonal action in organizing the tissues of the central nervous system during development and in bringing behavior to expression in the adult. They may be helped in such a search by the circumstance that cellular elements in the genital tracts, which differentiate and are activated under the influence of these same hormones, are at present more accessible for histophysiological study than those in tissues of the central nervous system. It is to be hoped that clues will come from the work of the many investigators whose studies are described in recent reviews (*43*).

The need for studies of sexual behavior in man is great. Methods for collecting trustworthy, meaningful data and means of ascertaining whether the many behavioral states are associated with hormonal action in the developing fetus and in the adult should be worked out. The possibility that such relationships exist and that typical and deviant behaviors have a physiologic as well as a psychologic basis may no longer be excluded.

Summary

From an attempt made 30 years ago to attain a limited objective, we have proceeded with what turned out to be a long-term investigation. Evidence has accumulated indicating that the gonadal hormones have a broad role in the determination of behavior. We have long known that they act to bring sexual behavior to expression, certainly in adult vertebrates below man. We now know, in addition, that during a period of organization and differentiation which is prenatal in the guinea pig and monkey and postnatal in the rat, the hormones act according to principles which appear to be identical with those operative during the differentiation of the genital tracts, and they effect a corresponding differentiation or organization of neural tissues.

The data thus far accumulated from a study of the behavior of two female pseudohermaphroditic monkeys suggest that this early hormonal action is also responsible for the establishment of much of the sex-related behavior which is a part of the masculinity or femininity of an individual but which is not related directly to the reproductive processes.

References and Notes

1. J. L. Hampson and J. G. Hampson, in *Sex and Internal Secretions*, W. C. Young, Ed. (Williams and Wilkins, Baltimore, ed. 3, 1961), p. 1401.
2. J. Money, *ibid.*, p. 1383.
3. H. von Völkel, *Psychiat. Neurol.* **145**, 257 (1963).
4. J. T. Eayrs, *Ciba Found. Colloq. Endocrinol.* **3**, 18 (1952).
5. A. C. Kinsey, W. B. Pomeroy, C. E. Martin, P. H. Gebhard, *Sexual Behavior in the Human Female* (Saunders, Philadelphia, 1953).
6. L. R. Aronson, in *The Physiology of Fishes*, M. E. Brown, Ed. (Academic Press, New York, 1957), p. 272.
7. W. C. Young, in *Sex and Internal Secretions*, W. C. Young, Ed. (Williams and Wilkins, Baltimore, 1961), p. 1173.
8. F. A. Beach, *Hormones and Behavior* (Hoeber, New York, 1948); J. Bremer, *Asexualization, a Follow-up Study of 244 Cases* (Macmillan, New York, 1959).
9. F. A. Beach, *Ciba Found. Colloq. Endocrinol.* **3**, 3 (1952).
10. J. S. Rosenblatt and L. R. Aronson, *Behaviour* **12**, 285 (1958).
11. J. Benoit, *Arch. Zool. Exptl. Gen.* **69**, 217 (1929); C. R. Carpenter, *J. Comp. Psychol.* **16**, 25, 59 (1933); H. M. Scott and L. F. Payne, *J. Exptl. Zool.* **69**, 123 (1934); F.

Caridroit, in *Nouveau Traité de Physiologie*, G. Duma, Ed. (Alcan, Paris, 1946), vol. 3, bk. 2, p. 109.
12. H. I. Myers, W. C. Young, E. W. Dempsey, *Anat. Rec.* **65**, 381 (1936).
13. M. A. Foster and F. L. Hisaw, *ibid.* **62**, 75 (1935).
14. E. W. Dempsey, R. Hertz, W. C. Young, *Am. J. Physiol.* **116**, 201 (1936).
15. E. B. Astwood, *Endocrinology* **28**, 309 (1951).
16. W. C. Young, E. W. Dempsey, C. W. Hagquist, J. L. Boling, *J. Comp. Psychol.* **27**, 49 (1939); R. J. Blandau, J. L. Boling, W. C. Young, *Anat. Rec.* **79**, 453 (1941); W. C. Young and W. R. Fish, *Endocrinology* **36**, 181 (1945); W. C. Young, in *Roots of Behavior, Genetics, Instinct, and Socialization in Animal Behavior*, E. L. Bliss, Ed. (Hoeber-Harper, New York, 1962), p. 115.
17. J. A. Grunt and W. C. Young, *Endocrinology* **51**, 237 (1952).
18. W. C. Young, H. I. Myers, E. W. Dempsey, *Am. J. Physiol.* **105**, 393 (1933).
19. W. C. Young, E. W. Dempsey, H. I. Myers, C. W. Hagquist, *Am. J. Anat.* **63**, 457 (1938).
20. R. W. Goy and W. C. Young, *Behaviour* **10**, 340 (1957).
21. H. D. Goodale, *Genetics* **3**, 276 (1918).
22. J. G. Wilson and W. C. Young, *Endocrinology* **29**, 779 (1941).
23. W. Riss, E. S. Valenstein, J. Sinks, W. C. Young, *ibid.* **57**, 139 (1955).
24. R. M. Hoar, R. W. Goy, W. C. Young, *ibid.* **60**, 337 (1957).
25. E. S. Valenstein, W. Riss, W. C. Young, *J. Comp. Physiol. Psychol.* **47**, 162 (1954).
26. J. S. Jakway, *Animal Behaviour* **7**, 150 (1959).
27. R. W. Goy and J. S. Jakway, *ibid.*, p. 142.
28. E S. Valenstein, W. Riss, W. C. Young, *J. Comp. Physiol. Psychol.* **48**, 397 (1955); E. S. Valenstein and W. C. Young, *Endocrinology* **56**, 173 (1955); E. S. Valenstein and R. W. Goy, *J. Comp. Physiol. Psychol.* **50**, 115 (1957).
29. R. W. Goy and W. C. Young, *Psychosom. Med.* **19**, 144 (1957).
30. H. F. Harlow and M. K. Harlow, *Sci. Am.* **207**, 136 (1962); W. Craig, *J. Animal Behavior* **4**, 121 (1914); M. W. Schein and E. B. Hale, *Animal Behaviour* **7**, 189 (1959); F. A. Beach, *J. Genet. Psychol.* **60**, 121 (1942); G. Zimbardo, *J. Comp. Physiol. Psychol.* **51**, 764 (1958); J. S. Rosenblatt and L. R. Aronson, *Animal Behaviour* **6**, 171 (1958); H. W. Nissen, unpublished manuscript (available from the University of Kansas Library); J. Bowlby, *Bull. World Health Organ.* **3**, 355 (1951).
31. L. Gallien, *Bull. Biol. France Belgique* **78**, 257 (1944); ———, in *Progress in Comparative Endocrinology*, K. Takewaki, Ed. (Academic Press, New York, 1962), p. 346; R. R. Humphrey, *Am. J. Anat.* **76**, 33 (1945); W. Laskowski, *Arch. Entwicklungsmech. Organ.* **146** (1952), 137 (1953); T. O. Yamamoto, *J. Exptl. Zool.* **123**, 571 (1953); ———, *ibid.* **141**, 133 (1959); C. Y. Chang and E. Witschi, *Proc. Soc. Exptl. Biol. Med.* **89**, 150 (1955).

32. W. C. Young, in *Comparative Biochemistry*, M. Florkin and H. Mason, Eds. (Academic Press, New York, in press).

33. V. Dantchakoff, *Compt. Rend.* **206**, 945 (1938); ——, *Compt. Rend. Soc. Biol.* **127**, 1255 (1938); V. Dantchakoff, *Biol. Zentr.* **58**, 302 (1938).

34. C. H. Phoenix, R. W. Goy, A. A. Gerall, W. C. Young, *Endocrinology* **65**, 369 (1959).

35. R. W. Goy, W. E. Bridson, W. C. Young, *J. Comp. Physiol. Psychol.*, in press.

36. R. K. Burns, *Surv. Biol. Progr.* **1**, 233 (1949); ——, in *Sex and Internal Secretions*, W. C. Young, Ed. (Williams and Wilkins, Baltimore, ed. 3, 1961), p. 76; A. Jost, *Arch. Anat. Microscop. Morphol. Exptl.* **36**, 151, 242, 271 (1947); ——, *Recent Progr. Hormone Res.* **8**, 379 (1953); ——, in *Conference on Gestation: Transactions of the 3rd and 4th Conferences*, C. A. Villee, Ed. (Josiah Macy Jr. Foundation, New York, 1957), p. 129; L. J. Wells, M. W. Cavanaugh, E. L. Maxwell, *Anat. Rec.* **118**, 109 (1954); D. Price, E. Ortiz, R. Pannabecker, *Proc. Intern. Congr. Cell Biol., 10th, Paris* (1960), p. 158.

37. C. A. Barraclough, *Endocrinology* **68**, 62 (1961); R. W. Goy, C. H. Phoenix, W. C. Young, *Anat. Rec.* **142**, 307 (1962).

38. K. L. Grady and C. H. Phoenix, *Am. Zool.*, **3**, 482 (1963).

39. F. A. Beach and A. M. Holz, *J. Exptl. Zool.* **101**, 91 (1946).

40. C. A. Pfeiffer, *Am. J. Anat.* **58**, 195 (1936); J. W. Everett, C. H. Sawyer, J. E. Markee, *Endocrinology* **44**, 234 (1949); G. W. Harris, *Neural Control of the Pituitary Gland* (Arnold, London, 1955); ——, in *Frontiers in Brain Research*, J. D. French, Ed. (Columbia Univ. Press, New York, 1962), p. 191;——, *J. Reprod. Fertility* **5**, 299 (1963); G. W. Harris and S. Levine, *J. Physiol. London* **163**, 42 (1962).

41. M. Diamond and W. C. Young, *Endocrinology* **72**, 429 (1963).

42. J. L. Green, C. D. Clemente, J. de Groot, *J. Comp. Neurol.* **108**, 505 (1957); G. W. Harris, R. P. Michael, P. P. Scott, in *Ciba Foundation Symposium on the Neurological Basis of Behaviour*, G. E. W. Wolstenholms and C. M. O. O'Connor, Eds. (Little, Brown, Boston, 1958), p. 236; M. Kawakami and C. H. Sawyer, *Endocrinology* **65**, 652 (1959); ——, *ibid.*, p. 631; C. H. Sawyer and M. Kawakami, *ibid.*, p. 622; R. D. Lisk, *J. Exptl. Zool.* **145**, 197 (1960); R. D. Lisk and M. Newton, *Science* **139**, 223 (1963); C. H. Phoenix, *J. Comp. Physiol. Psychol.* **54**, 72 (1961); R. W. Goy and C. H. Phoenix, *J. Reprod. Fertility* **5**, 23 (1963); R. P. Michael, *Science* **136**, 322 (1962).

43. C. D. Kochakian, *Lab. Invest.* **8**, 538 (1959); A. Csapo, in *Cell, Organism, and Milieu*, D. Rudnick, Ed. (Ronald, New York, 1959), p. 107; P. Talalay and H. G. Williams-Ashman, *Proc. Natl. Acad. Sci. U.S.* **44**, 15 (1958); C. A. Villee, in *Sex and Internal Secreations*, W. C. Young, Ed. (William and Wilkins, Baltimore, ed. 3, 1961), p. 643; J. T. Velardo, in *The Ovary*, H. G. Grady, Ed. (Williams and Wilkins, Baltimore, 1962), p. 48; R. J. Boscott, in *The Ovary*, S. S. Zukerman *et al.*, Eds. (Academic Press, New York, 1962), vol. 2, pp. 1, 47.

44. During the years in which the investigations discussed were in progress at Brown University, the Yale Laboratories of Primate Biology, and the University of Kansas, support was provided by the National Research Council's Committee for Research in Problems of Sex, and by grants, particularly MH-00504, from the National Institute of Mental Health, Bethesda, Md. Dr. Leon H. Schmidt, who, at the time of this work was director of the Christ Hospital Institute for Medical Research, and Dr. Harry F. Harlow, director of the Wisconsin Primate Research Center, extended the use of facilities in their laboratories for the production and study of female pseudohermaphroditic monkeys. Testosterone propionate (Perandren) was generously supplied by CIBA Pharmaceutical Corporation, Summit, N.J.

RICHARD E. WHALEN & RONALD D. NADLER

17 Suppression of the Development of Female Mating Behavior by Estrogen Administered in Infancy

Abstract. *The administration of estradiol benzoate subcutaneously to 4-day-old female rats resulted in reduced mating in response to estrogen and progesterone in adulthood.*

It is reasonably clear that sexual differentiation in mammals is influenced by fetal sex hormones. Male hormones, in particular, seem to be critical for the appropriate development of the Wolffian duct system, and, ultimately, of male external genitals. Only recently has the influence, on adult sexual behavior, of hormones secreted or administered during the embryonic, fetal, and neonatal periods begun to be studied.

Phoenix *et al.* (*1*) found that the administration of testosterone to pregnant guinea pigs resulted in female offspring which, in adulthood, exhibited reduced female sexual behavior and enhanced male sexual behavior. Using the rat, Barraclough and Gorski, and Harris and Levine (*2*) have shown that the application of testosterone to the 5-day-old female leads to the failure of spontaneous mating activity at maturity. Further, treated females fail to mate if castrated and treated with exogenous estrogen and progesterone. In addition, Harris and Levine have found that comparable effects prevail if the male rat is treated with estrogen during infancy. At maturity the male fails to copulate even if administered normally adequate doses of testosterone propionate.

These studies suggest that the neural structures which determine sexual behavior may be deleteriously affected by heterotypical hormones acting during a critical stage of their development. To date, the effects of homotypical hormones administered during infancy in a single injection have not been studied. The present investigation was designed to help fill this gap.

Nineteen female rats from a locally maintained, randomly bred, pigmented strain were treated on the fourth day after birth. Fourteen of the females were injected subcutaneously with 200 μg of estradiol benzoate in 0.2 ml of mineral oil. The five control females were given 0.2 ml of mineral oil (*3*). Subjects were reared in groups until 95 days of age, when they were ovariec-

tomized and caged in pairs. Mating tests began at approximately 130 days of age.

Subjects were primed with estradiol benzoate, 50 μg at 72 hours and 25 μg at 48 hours prior to each set of mating tests. Five hours before testing they were given 1.0 mg of progesterone. This procedure has been found to reliably induce receptivity in spayed females. At the appropriate time after the final priming injection a female was placed with a male in a cylindrical glass observation cage for a 15-minute period. Each individual was tested twice, with an inter-test interval of 14 days. During each test the observer recorded, for the male, the frequency of mounts without intromissions, intromissions, and ejaculations, and for the female, the frequency of assuming the mating posture (lordosis) and the number of times the female kicked her hind legs at the male. The kicking response is an index of sexual refractoriness.

Table 1 shows the percentage of each group which exhibited the various sexual responses *at least once* during the two tests, and the frequency of the responses averaged over both tests. Males mounted all females in both groups, and with similar frequencies, but were unsuccessful in achieving intromission with the females treated with estrogen in infancy. When mounted by males, the estrogen-treated females did not show lordosis; instead, on 40 percent of the mounts the female responded by kicking the male. The reduced lordosis frequency accounts for the low intromission and ejaculation frequencies among treated females. Control females, given only oil in infancy, assumed the lordosis posture when mounted by the male and per-

Table 1. Mating responses of female rats treated with estrogen in infancy. Abbreviations: χ^2, chi-square analysis of percentage data; F, analysis of variance of frequency data; p, probability; n.s., not significant.

Sexual responses	Estrogen treated ($N = 14$)		Oil treated ($N = 5$)		χ^2	F
	% of females	Mean frequency	% of females	Mean frequency		
By male:						
Mount	100	13.0	100	9.1	*	1.4 (n.s.)
Intromission	36	0.68	100	4.6	6.1 ($p < .025$)	35.6 ($p < .001$)
Ejaculation	21	0.11	80	0.80	5.4 ($p < .05$)	*
By female:						
Lordosis	29	0.46	100	12.8	7.5 ($p < .01$)	*
Kicking	100	5.2	40	1.0	10.0 ($p < .01$)	7.2 ($p < .025$)

* Not analyzed because of nonnormality of distributions.

mitted intromission and ejaculation. Except for the frequency with which the females were mounted by males, the two groups of females differed significantly in their sexual behavior according to analysis of variance and chi-square tests. The indiscriminate mounting by the males probably reflects only the extreme vigor of these animals. The absence of intromission does not reflect estrogen-induced changes in genital morphology as the vaginae of these animals appear normal.

Thus, estrogen treatment at the appropriate dose level during the neonatal period acts, as does testosterone, to reduce the sexual responsiveness in fe-males which is normally induced by estrogen and progesterone. Although it seems likely that estrogen treatment acts to alter the responsiveness to hormones of those neural cells which determine sexual behavior, it must be admitted that the actual mode of action of the estrogen administered in infancy is obscure.

References and Notes

1. C. H. Phoenix, R. E. Goy, A. A. Gerall, W. C. Young, *Endocrinology* **65**, 369 (1959).
2. C. A. Barraclough and R. A. Gorski, *J. Endocrinol.* **25**, 175 (1962); G. W. Harris and S. Levine, *J. Physiol.* **163**, 42P (1962).
3. The hormones used were supplied by R. R. McCormick, Schering Corp., Bloomfield, N.J.

F. H. BRONSON & CLAUDE DESJARDINS

18 Aggression in Adult Mice: Modification by Neonatal Injections of Gonadal Hormones

Abstract. *Incidence of spontaneous aggression in adult male mice given a single injection of estradiol benzoate (0.4 milligram) when they were 3 days old was less than that of controls injected with oil. Aggressiveness was increased among adult females injected with either estradiol or testosterone propionate (1 milligram) at*

Reprinted from *Science* 161:705–706, 1968. Copyright 1968 by the American Association for the Advancement of Science.

the same age. The increased aggressiveness noted among females given androgen was further documented during subsequent mating tests, when these females often attacked, wounded, and, in one case, killed naive males.

The sexual differentiation of particular behavioral or neuroendocrine control systems may be influenced by the presence of gonadal hormones during infancy in rodents (*1*). For example, neonatal administration of androgens to females results in an acyclic, male-like secretion of gonadotropin during adulthood rather than in the cyclic pattern characteristic of normal adult females (*2*). Similarly, sexual behavior of female rats may be masculinized to a degree if they are given neonatal injections of androgen, or that of males may be feminized if they are castrated during infancy, provided that appropriate gonadal hormones are administered during adulthood (*1, 3*). Estrogens, depending upon the time and dose of their injection, may mimic some of these effects of androgens (*4*). We hypothesized that aggressive behavior could also be modified following treatment with androgens or estrogens during infancy. Our results demonstrate that aggressiveness was increased in adult female mice if they were given either androgen or estrogen as neonates; aggressiveness in adult males was partially suppressed if they were injected with estrogen during infancy.

Complete litters of 3-day-old C57BL/6J mice of both sexes were injected subcutaneously with 0.05 ml of corn oil containing either 1 mg of testosterone propionate, 0.4 mg of estradiol benzoate, or nothing. Mice were weaned at 21 to 25 days of age and housed singly until tested for aggressiveness at 80 to 90 days of age. Spontaneous aggression (*5*) was measured in test chambers (12 by 12 by 6 inches) with removable partitions in the middle. Single mice of the same sex and treatment were placed on either side of the partition. It was removed 20 minutes later and the mice were observed until a fight was initiated, or for a maximum of 15 minutes (Table 1). The same pair of mice was tested once

Table 1. Number of pairs (of same sex) in which fighting occurred at least once during three encounters and total number of fights occurring during all three encounters.

Neonatal treatment	Fighting at least once (No.)	Fights in three encounters (No.)
Males		
Oil	23/24	51/72
Testosterone	18/19	46/57
Estradiol	10/20	20/60
Females		
Oil	1/24	1/72
Testosterone	5/18	10/54
Estradiol	4/14	5/42

Table 2. Number of male-female pairs in which severe fighting occurred within the first hour after pairing and number in which wounding of one member occurred within 18 hours. Females had been previously tested in the primary experiment (Table 1), after which they were given progesterone daily for 8 days and then paired with naive males.

Neonatal treatment of females	Fighting (1st hour)	Wounding (18 hours)
Oil	0/20	0/20
Testosterone	12/23	5/23*
Estradiol	4/14	0/14

* One pair in which female was wounded, three pairs in which male was wounded, and one pair in which male was killed.

daily for three consecutive days, after which vaginal smears were obtained for five consecutive days from all females. All males and 12 females from each group were then autopsied to verify the expected effects of neonatal injections on reproductive tract morphology. Ovaries, uteri, and testes were weighed and examined histologically. Seminal vesicles were homogenized in water and analyzed for fructose (6).

The remaining females from each of the three groups received subcutaneous injections of progesterone (0.3 mg per mouse per day) for 8 days to induce estrous cycles (7). On the afternoon of the 8th day, they were paired with naive males in the females' home cages. Our purpose in this secondary experiment was to verify the lack of mating in females treated neonatally with testosterone or estradiol and to follow a suggestion by Barraclough that changes in aggressiveness might be more obvious in such a situation (8). Incidence of fighting was recorded for the first hour after pairing, and all pairs were inspected for wounding and presence of vaginal plugs on the following three mornings. Males used in this experiment were about 100 days old, intact, and sexually and experimentally inexperienced; each male had been housed with four or five others since weaning.

The results of the primary experiment, in which mice were given the opportunity to fight only members of the same sex and treatment group, are presented in Table 1. Spontaneous fighting occurred at least once during three encounters in all but one pair of males in each of the two groups that received injections of either oil or testosterone during infancy. Neonatal injections of estradiol reduced the inci-

dence of fighting in adult males to 50 percent ($P<.01$). Only 4 percent of the control females fought, whereas fighting among pairs that had received neonatal injections of either testosterone or estradiol increased to 28 and 29 percent, respectively ($P < .05$ in both cases).

The secondary experiment, in which females were injected with progesterone for 8 days and then paired with normal males, revealed marked aggressiveness on the part of females injected neonatally with testosterone (Table 2); fighting among such pairs was often vicious and usually initiated by the females. Females treated with estradiol also fought with males, but both the incidence and severity of fights were lower. No fighting was noted among pairs in which the female had been injected only with oil in infancy. No vaginal plugs were found in any females receiving steroid neonatally, but 55 percent of the females injected with oil had plugs during the 3 days after pairing.

The effects of neonatal injections of estradiol or testosterone on vaginal cycles and reproductive tracts were similar to previous findings (2, 4) and will be reported here only to an extent necessary for correlation with the behavioral data. Neonatal injections of estradiol in males resulted in decreased body and reproductive organ weights and relative aspermia. Injections of testosterone in infancy also decreased weights of male organs but to a lesser extent than that caused by estradiol (Table 3). All vaginal smears obtained from all females injected neonatally with either steroid contained approximately 80 percent cornified cells and 20 percent leukocytes, and ovaries of such females were polyfollicular and devoid of corpora lutea. Body and uter-

Table 3. Body weight, relative (paired) organ weights, and fructose concentrations in seminal vesicles of males treated neonatally with oil, testosterone, or estradiol; body and relative uterine weights of similarly treated females (mean ± standard error).

Neonatal treatment	Oil	Testosterone	Estradiol
		Males	
Number	48	37	40
Body weight (g)	27.8 ± 0.4	27.3 ± 0.5	24.4 ± 0.4*
Testes			
(mg/g body wt.)	7.53 ± 0.52	5.93 ± 0.20*	4.61 ± 0.41*
Seminal vesicle			
(mg/g body wt.)	2.42 ± 0.27	1.98 ± 0.08*	1.07 ± 0.15*
Seminal vesicle			
fructose (µg)	174.0 ± 6.3	137.0 ± 5.4*	48.2 ± 4.7*
		Females	
Number	12	12	12
Body weight (g)	22.6 ± 0.7	28.2 ± 1.0*	23.1 ± 0.8
Uterus			
(mg/g body wt.)	3.19 ± 0.31	5.23 ± 0.67*	2.37 ± 0.38

*Significantly different from oil controls, as determined by analysis of variance, with a probability of at least $P < .05$.

ine weights were increased among females injected neonatally with testosterone.

Androgen is a necessary prerequisite for attack behavior in inexperienced male mice (9), whereas estrogen administered during adulthood has no effect on aggressiveness of males (10). The reduction in spontaneous aggression shown by males injected with estrogen in our study was correlated with large changes in their reproductive tracts, and secretion of testicular androgen was probably considerably reduced. Weights of reproductive organs were also lower in males given neonatal injections of androgen, but they were as aggressive as control males. These facts suggest that those males injected with androgen neonatally probably had sufficient androgen in their circulation during adulthood to permit a high degree of aggressive behavior, whereas those that received estrogen did not. The amount of fructose in seminal vesicles, a good correlate of androgen titers (6), was reduced by 72 percent among males given estradiol in infancy compared to that in controls given oil (Table 3). The comparable figure for males receiving testosterone neonatally was only 21 percent and, hence, the postulate appears reasonably good on this basis.

The low incidence of spontaneous aggression found among control females agrees well with observations of other workers using mice (11). Androgen will not increase aggressiveness in either immature or mature gonadectomized females (12). However, neonatal injections of testosterone, and to a lesser extent estradiol, increase aggressiveness in females after maturity. These effects were significant in both experiments although more dramatic in the uncontrolled secondary experiment where some previously tested females were paired with naive males in the females' home cages after receiving progesterone to induce estrous cycles. Under such conditions mating did not occur, and the females usually attacked and sometimes wounded males. Wounding was sufficiently severe to cause death in one case. The reasons for the dramatic effects observed in this experiment are not readily obvious because of its uncontrolled nature and the data are presented only as an extreme example of a phenomenon observed in the primary experiment. Two investigators have reported that "masculine or aggressive responses" interfered with normal female sexual behavior when rats were treated with estrogen or testosterone in infancy (13) but not to the extent shown in the present study with mice.

A reasonable hypothesis to explain the increased aggressiveness of females treated neonatally with gonadal hormones is the alteration of a neural mechanism whose sexual differentiation is normally regulated by androgen in infancy. Such a concept parallels the conclusions of many studies dealing with either sex behavior or the hypothalamic control of gonadotropin secretion, and some degree of experimental mimicking of androgen by estrogen is well documented in this respect. It does not seem reasonable at this time, however, to suspect the hypothalamus at the expense of other neural structures because the number of brain areas known to function in aggression is relatively large (14). Furthermore, as evidenced by changes in body weight in both sexes, the effects of early administration of steroids may be widespread.

References and Notes

1. S. Levine and R. F. Mullins, *Science* **152**, 1585 (1966).
2. C. A. Barraclough, *Endocrinology* **68**, 62 (1961); R. A. Gorski, *J. Reprod. Fertil. Suppl.* **1**, 67 (1966).
3. R. E. Whalen and D. A. Edwards, *Anat. Rec.* **157**, 173 (1967).
4. G. W. Harris and S. Levine, *J. Physiol. London* **181**, 379 (1965).
5. J. P. Scott, *Amer. Zool.* **6**, 683 (1966).
6. J. S. Davis and J. E. Gander, *Anal. Biochem.* **19**, 72 (1967).
7. C. A. Barraclough, *Fed. Proc.* **15**, 9 (1956).
8. ———, personal communication.
9. E. A. Beeman, *Physiol. Zool.* **20**, 373 (1947); E. B. Sigg, C. Day, C. Colombo, *Endocrinology* **78**, 679 (1966).
10. J. E. Gustafson and G. Winokur, *J. Neuropsychiat.* **1**, 182 (1960).
11. E. Fredericson, *J. Comp. Physiol. Psychol.* **45**, 89 (1952).
12. J. V. Levy, *Proc. West Virginia Acad. Sci.* **26**, 14 (1954); J. Tollman and J. A. King, *Brit. J. Anim. Behav.* **6**, 147 (1956).
13. H. H. Feder, *Anat. Rec.* **157**, 79 (1967); A. A. Gerall, *ibid.*, p. 97.
14. J. M. R. Delgado, *Amer. Zool.* **6**, 669 (1966).
15. This investigation was supported in part by PHS grants FR-05545-05 and HD-00767.

ANKE A. EHRHARDT & JOHN MONEY

19   Progestin-Induced Hermaphroditism: IQ and Psychosexual Identity in a Study of Ten Girls

INTRODUCTION

Within the past twenty years, synthetic progestins have sometimes been given to pregnant mothers in the United States to prevent threatened miscarriages. A number of these women have given birth

Reprinted from *The Journal of Sex Research* 3(1):83–100, 1967.

Supported by Research Grants #HD-00325 and #HD-00126 and Research Career Development Award #HD-K3-18,635, The National Institute of Child Health and Human Development, The United States Public Health Service.

to a partially masculinized genetic female baby (Figure 1).[*] In 1960, seventy recorded cases of fetal masculinization of female infants associated with the oral administration of progestins to their mothers were reviewed by Wilkins. The abnormality of sex differentiation was found to be confined to partial masculinization of the external genitalia; namely, an enlarged phallus which may or may not be associated with varying degrees of fusion of the labioscrotal folds. Fetal masculinization of the external genitalia with identical anatomical findings occurs also in female hermaphroditism with congenital virilizing adrenal hyperplasia. These two types of female hermaphroditism differ in two ways: (1) the girls with the progestin-induced syndrome do not have elevated urinary 17-ketosteroids, and (2) they do not show progressive virilization with precocious growth and osseous development. At puberty, normal feminization with menstruation and ovulation occurs spontaneously. No hormonal treatment is required. Dependent on the degree of masculinization, surgical feminization of the genitalia (Figure 1) is necessary—the sooner after birth, the better. The babies should always be assigned as females since they grow to be morphologically and reproductively normal.

Wilkins, Jones, Holman and Stempfel (1958) and Wilkins (1959; 1960) discussed the probable etiologic role of the drugs administered in the masculinization of the offspring. Most of the mothers received 17-ethinyltestosterone or 19-nor-17-ethinyltestosterone which have been marketed under trade names such as Progestoral, Pranone and Norlutin. Though both compounds are synthetic steroids not formed normally in the body, they typically have progestinic effects when given orally but they may also have an androgenic effect, since the chemical structure of these compounds is closely related to 17-methyltestosterone. Wilkins (1959) stated that differences in placental permeability or fetal susceptibility could account for the fact that not all infants are affected whose mothers have been treated during gestation. It seems probable that the magnitude of the dosage of these compounds and the age of the fetus are important factors. Wilkins considered that labioscrotal fusion could occur only when the medication is given to mothers before the fourth month, but that phallic enlargement could occur at any time.

We became interested in the psychosexual identity of progestin-induced hermaphroditism as part of our long-term clinical work with hermaphroditism of all types. This interest was enhanced by findings stemming from animal studies. Phoenix, Goy, Gerall and Young

*Figure 1 has been omitted.

(in Young, Goy and Phoenix, 1965) bred hermaphroditic guinea pigs by administering testosterone to the pregnant mothers. They found in divers subsequent mating tests that the experimental animals gained scores nearer to the masculine than to the feminine control scores. The authors ventured the hypothesis that prenatal androgen had affected neurosexual organization, and thus, the organization of behavior. Preliminary primate observations by the same authors suggest that not only mating and copulatory actions are affected by prenatal androgens, but also childhood play and social interaction and eventually parental behavior. The animals studied are female rhesus monkeys rendered hermaphroditic with complete labioscrotal fusion and formation of a normal-looking penis through exogenous androgen administered to the pregnant mother.

Purpose

The purpose of this paper is to make a first psychologic report on a group of human beings whose progestin-induced hermaphroditism is the clinical counterpart of androgen-induced hermaphroditism in animals. We report on IQ and various preferences and aspects of gender role related to tomboyishness in childhood.

Sample Selection

The sample is composed of ten cases of girls whose mothers received progestin while pregnant. Nine were born with abnormal genitalia and the tenth, a sister of one of the nine, was not. The ten ranged in age from $3\%_{12}$ years to $14\%_{12}$ years at the time of testing. All patients are reared female. They come from nine white, middle-class families (two patients are sisters) and have a history of maternal intake of progestins during gestation (Table 1). Their cases were among thirty-seven studied since 1950 in the pediatric endocrine clinic of Dr. Robert Blizzard and the late Dr. Lawson Wilkins at The Johns Hopkins Hospital. They are ten of a group of twenty names originally selected for the present study on the basis of the following criteria: (1) they lived within the geographic area of Maryland, Virginia, West Virginia, Delaware, and the District of Columbia, and (2) they were above the age of three years. It was difficult to contact the patients, since there had been no need for them to keep in touch with the endocrine clinic for several years. In eight cases, the family could not be located and in two cases, the parents wished not to risk upsetting their daughters by exposing them to further follow-up. Thus, even though a sample of ten may be deemed small, it is

TABLE 1

Background Medical Data on Nine Patients with Progestin-Induced Hermaphroditism, Plus One Unaffected

Name and hospital no.	Date of birth	Mother's medication		Phallus: sizes in cm.	Patient's age when diagnosed	Age at corrective surgery
		Name of drug	Time span during pregnancy			
K.B. #959869	7-28-59	Norlutin	? Second throughout sixth month	1.5 × 1.0 Minimal partial fusion	6 weeks	Cosmetically elective
S.C. #879452	8-12-57	? Ethisterone	Second throughout seventh month	1.5 × 0.5 Minimal labiofusion	2 7/12 years	7 6/12 years
R.F. #608098	12-28-50	Pranone and ethinyltestosterone	Tenth week to term	1.5 × 0.8 Minimal fusion	1 week	Elective for coitus
F.G. #876269	10-4-59	Pranone and ethinyltestosterone	Fifth week throughout fourth month	1.5 length Minimal labioscrotal fusion	4 months	10 months
E.G. #878919	8-26-58	Unknown hormone	First trimester	1.0 × 0.5 Minimal fusion	1½ years	Timing elective
B.H. #1102785	4-6-59	Nugestoral	Fourth month to term	1.5 length No fusion	2½ years	Cosmetically elective
V.H. #630386	3-8-55	Ethinyltestosterone and progestoral	Fourth week throughout eighth month	1.8 × 0.8 Marked fusion	2 days	13 months
P.M. #1166368	11-10-55	Unknown hormone	Unknown	No abnormal genitalia	2 2/12 years	Surgery not needed
T.M. #845611	12-10-57	Pranone and ethinyltestosterone	? Second month throughout fifth month	1.3 × 0.5 Marked fusion	1 day	1 1/12 years
J.T. #1013706	9-6-61	Metalutin	? Early part of pregnancy	No clitoris enlargement Moderate amount of fusion	1 month	5 months

actually very large for the psychologic study of a rare condition which is becoming more rare now that its iatrogenic etiology is known and prevented. Table 1 summarizes the pertinent background and medical data on each of the ten subjects.

PROCEDURE

The following psychological tests and methods were employed:

(1) The Wechsler Intelligence Scale for Children (WISC). One child under five years of age received the Revised Stanford-Binet Intelligence Scale, L-M.

(2) Draw-a-Person Test. Two drawings were requested. The first instruction was simply to draw a person and when it was completed, to draw one of the other sex.

(3) The It Scale for Children (Brown, 1956).

(4) Lynn Structured Doll Play Test (David and Rosalie Lynn, 1959).

(5) Interview with the child and mother, separately, and, in two cases the father also, for a minimum of two one-hour sessions each. A standard data-schedule of topics was followed, but the interviews themselves were flexible in sequence so as to be unstilted in manner. Sections of each interview were recorded in toto or else were summarized on tape by the patient.

Eight of the ten patients had an endocrine check-up and physical examination in connection with the psychologic evaluation. The other two, sisters, were seen in a home visit only, as the mother's advanced pregnancy precluded her journeying to Baltimore. All the children were physically healthy.

IQ PHENOMENA

Findings

IQ Distribution: Full IQ

The distribution of IQs is seen in Figure 2. The mean Full IQ is 125 with a standard deviation of 11.8. It is self-evident, as compared with the mean IQ of 100 in the Wechsler standardization population, that the present mean is exceptionally high. Moreover, is is noteworthy that there is no IQ under 100 and so many as six above 130.

Verbal versus Performance IQ

The Verbal-Performance IQ comparison for the nine children

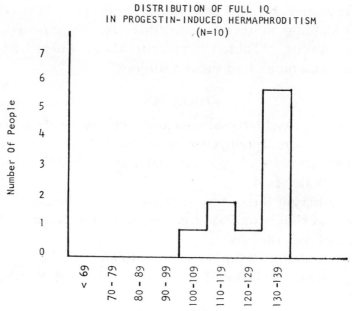

FIG. 2. Distribution of Full IQs ($N = 10$)

given the Wechsler scale is presented in Figure 3 and Table 2. The difference is obviously not significant. There were no cases in which the Verbal-Performance discrepancy was greater than nineteen points, the range being between two and nineteen. In six cases the Verbal IQ was higher (by two to nineteen points) and in three, the Performance IQ (by seven to sixteen points).

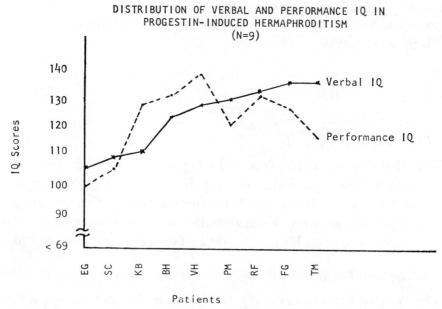

FIG. 3. Distribution of Wechsler Verbal and Performance IQs ($N = 9$)

TABLE 2
Comparison of Wechsler Verbal and Performance IQs ($N = 9$)

	Verbal IQ	Performance IQ
Mean....................	125	125
SD.......................	11.4	12.5

Parental Education and Occupation

Six of the nine families (Table 3) had at least one parent who was a college graduate; five of these had at least one parent who worked at a higher professional or business executive level. Three fathers were occupied in trades or business; both parents had no more than a high school education.

TABLE 3
Parental Education and Occupation* ($N = 9$ Families)

	Father only	Mother only	Both father and mother
Six Upper Level Families			
Higher academic degree................	3	0	1
College graduate or higher degree.......	2	0	4
Higher profession and executive..........	4	0	1
Business and lesser profession............	1	0	0
Three Lower Level Families			
High school.............................	0	3	1
Elementary school only..................	1	0	0
Skilled trades and lesser business.........	3	0	0

* Mother's occupation as housewife is not included in this table. Only one mother had a full-time career after marriage.

Table 4 shows that the IQs of the patients tend to relate to the educational and hence to the occupational level (Table 3) of the parents. There is thus a presumed relationship between child's IQ and father's intelligence as inferred from educational level.

TABLE 4
Frequency of IQ Levels by Father's Education

Father's education	IQ of child			
	100–109	110–119	120–124	130+
High school graduate or lower.....	1	2	0	0
College graduate or higher........	0	0	1	6*

* Two of these six were sisters.

Discussion of IQ

It is quite possible that all the IQs above 130 represent an unintentional bias in sampling favoring an upper socioeconomic level with high IQ. Nonetheless, it is sufficiently unusual to have 60% of IQs above 130, when only 2.2% would be expected on the basis of random sampling, that one cannot exclude the possibility that the elevation of the IQ's has some relationship to the mother's treatment with progestin, and not to sampling bias.

This hypothesis gains added credibility in view of a recent finding by Money and Lewis (1966). They tested seventy children with a diagnosis of congenital virilizing adrenal hyperplasia; in this condition the fetus is subjected to an excess of androgens which are adrenocortical in origin. The mean IQ was found to be elevated (*M* = 109.9; *SD* = 19.3) as compared with the expected IQ of 100. The elevated mean could be accounted for by an unexpectedly high shoulder on the distribution curve. Instead of the expected 25% of IQs above 110, there was an actual, observed frequency of 60%. It could not be proved that the incidence of high IQs is a function of fetal androgenization alone, rather than of a genetic factor as well, but the possibility deserves further observation and testing.

PREFERENCES AND ASPECTS OF GENDER ROLE

Findings: Tests

Draw-a-Person Test (DAP)

In our sample of ten girls between the ages of three and fourteen, seven girls drew their own sex first and three a male figure. The proportion agrees roughly with published normative findings. Weider and Noller (quoted by Harris, 1963) found that ninety per cent of primary school girls drew their own sex first. Jolles (1952) showed that eighty per cent of children, five to eight years old, drew their own sex first, when they were asked to draw a person. After age eight, the percentage of boys drawing the male first rises to as high as ninety-five per cent in some samples at the age of twelve, and the percentage of girls drawing the female first falls to as low as seventy per cent at the same age.

It Scale for Children

Daniel Brown, in 1956, published a scale of thirty-six picture cards, three by four inches, depicting various objects, figures and activities commonly associated with masculine and feminine roles. A child-figure drawing referred to as "It", unstructured as to sex, is used by having each subject make choices for "It". The scale is bipolar, ranging in its scores from zero, an exclusively feminine score, to eighty-four, an exclusively masculine score. The mean total score in our sample was found to be 48.7. According to Brown's a priori criterion of constructing the scale dichotomously, our result is close to intermediate preference between masculine and feminine roles. Unfortunately, however, studies by Brown (1956, 1957) have shown that the mean total score changes capriciously with the age of the sample. Brown also stated in his original monograph (1956) that in young children, the tendency to mixed or confused preference pattern, indicating acceptance of components of both the male and female roles, is about twice as frequent in girls as in boys.

Lynn Structured Doll Play Test (SDP)

This test consists of presenting the subject with cut-out paper dolls in a series of typical family and age-mate situations, which the subject is asked to deal with. Only one of the situations was chosen to be discussed for this paper, since it is the only one which is directly related to sex-role preference. In Situation 2A of the test, the child has to choose between a boy and a girl as a playmate. The choice in our sample was found to be six girls versus four boys; i.e., six of the children preferred a girl to a boy as a playmate. There are no normative data for children above six years of age. Our result would appear, however, in the four boy choices, to be consistent with findings (see below) on tomboyish play and recreational interests.

Findings: Interview Data

The information given under this heading was abstracted from interview records. The interview data were classified under twenty-five categories (Table 5), each composed of one to six items. Only the information contributory to the girls' gender-role and sex-role preferences is presented in the following presentation (Tables 6 through 13).

Tomboyish Energy Expenditure

Table 6 shows the high incidence of interest and participation in muscular exercise and recreation, as reported by parents and/or the patients themselves. The older ones liked to join with boys and

TABLE 5

Twenty-Five Data-Analysis Categories

1. Parents' education
2. Siblings
3. Mothers' medication
4. Degree of genital masculinization
5. Time of diagnosis
6. Surgery
7. Knowledge of uncorrected morphological defect
8. Knowledge of reproduction
9. Gender-related imagery in play and daydreams
10. Clothing and cosmetic care
11. Interest in jewelry and hairdo
12. Toy and book preferences
13. Ambitions and career
14. Boyfriends
15. Girlfriends
16. Sexual habits and practices
17. Tomboyish energy expenditure
18. Dependency and self-assertion
19. Charming and coquettish behavior
20. Labeled as a tomboy
21. Most tomboyish traits
22. Most feminine traits
23. Three wishes
24. Behavioral pathology
25. Mother's worries regarding child's abnormalities

TABLE 6

Tomboyish Energy Expenditure

Items	Frequency
Interest in organized team sports	6
Interest in informal outdoor activities	9
Liked to compete with boys in sports	9
Little need of sleep	5 + ?3
Superfluous hyperkinetic movements	0
Ability to concentrate academically	8 + ?2

compete in their sports. There were no reports of disorganized hyperkinesis, only of purposeful activities and sports. Sleep requirements were judged less than expected by the mothers in five cases, and possibly so in three others. In none of the cases was the surplus of physical energy judged to interfere with ability to focus attention and concentrate, for example at school or during the psychologic evaluation.

Anticipation of Wife and Mother Role

Nine of the girls showed a strong interest in boys' toys (Table 7). Three of these nine liked also to play with dolls occasionally. Only one of the ten clearly preferred dolls to boys' toys. She happened to be the one who did not show any sign of genital virilization in response to the mother's treatment with progestin during pregnancy.

TABLE 7

Toy and Book Interests

Items	Frequency
Dolls and other girls' toys...............................	4
Trucks, guns and other boys' toys.......................	9
Girls' books..	2
Boys' books..	2

Seven of the girls anticipated marriage and having children Table 8). Five aspired to professional careers; two of these preferred career to marriage and motherhood which they approached in a rather perfunctory way as something that might or might not happen in the future. One might have expected at least the one teenage girl to have experienced erotic imagery, even if of only kissing and hugging, but she, like all the others, disclaimed this.

With respect to participation in childhood sexual play, the girls seemed to have had no interest or experience. There were no parental

TABLE 8

Gender-Related Imagery in Play and Daydreams

Items	Frequency
Career as a professional woman........................	5
Romantic...	4
Erotic..	0
Wedding..	1
Marriage..	6
Pregnancy and motherhood............................	7

complaints of masturbation. In only two cases did the mothers report self-exploratory interest in the genitalia. Six girls had evidenced signs of romantic play, namely in the form of occasional kissing and affectionate gestures towards boys of their own age.

Clothing Choices

Table 9 shows a preference for masculine-derived styles in all cases. The girls were, in this respect, not too dissimilar from their mothers, sisters and girl friends, insofar as they did not choose or prefer attire such as shirts and pants actually marketed for boys. However, only two of them liked to wear frilly dresses when the occasion demanded. The others were more or less indifferent to dresses, if not opposed to them.

Personality Traits

A high frequency of self-assertive independence and self-reliance is noticeable in Table 10. The one atypical girl in this respect was described by her mother as defensively belligerent, but also as dependent and insecure.

On Table 11 the major factors relative to possible personality disturbance are listed. In only one case was there a symptomatic habit,

TABLE 9

Clothing Choices

Items	Frequency
Furbelows and frills	2
Simple, plain clothes	3
Masculine-derived styles	10
Boys' pants and shirts	0

TABLE 10

Dependency and Self-Assertion

Items	Frequency
Not an affectionate child	2
Reliant and not needing succor	7
Self-assertive and independent	9
Self-defending and belligerent	6
Aggressive attack in the pecking order	0

TABLE 11

Behavioral Pathology

Items	Frequency
Symptomatic habits (excluding elimination functions)	6
Bedwetting	3
Academic underachievement	1
Adequate or advanced social maturation	8

other than bed-wetting, of serious concern to the mother. This occurred in the youngest child, aged 3 9/12 years, who showed elective mutism and retardation in her speech development. Five other girls had sometime in their lives sucked their thumb or shown some nail-biting, though in no case excessively so. Three of the children had enuresis beyond the age of three years without a diagnosis of a physical component for it. Nine girls were good students according to their own and their parents' statements. One of them had initial difficulty in the first grade and was performing below expectancy relative to her high IQ. Eight of ten were regarded by parents and examiner as socially mature, perhaps even in advance of their years. They were easy to get along with, flexible, and reasonable in response to reasonable demands. Of the two rated immature, one was the child with elective mutism. The other was infantilely dependent on her mother and too defensive with other children.

Table 12 specifies whether the child was considered a tomboy. Nine were called "tomboy" by either their parents, themselves, or both. The girl who preferred dolls and showed no interest in the toys of boys also was the only one who was not described as tomboyish.

Table 13 lists quotations from the mothers' statements in reply to the question: "What is your daughter's most tomboyish trait and what is her most feminine one?" The third column on the table shows the kind of concern which was expressed by the different mothers.

Other Tomboys in Family

We did not have the opportunity to do a complete family study in all instances. It was anecdotally evident, however, that some of the sisters of index cases were tomboyish, while others were decidedly not. In one family it was possible to study the sister, a girl who had not been progestin-exposed. This sister was as tomboyish in her interests as her sister, if not more so. The mother also declared that she had been a tomboy.

TABLE 12

Label of Tomboy

Items	Frequency
Self-labeled	5
Parent-labeled	7
Peer-labeled	Not reported

TABLE 13

Quotations from Mothers' Statements

Name and hospital no.	Most tomboyish traits	Most feminine traits	Mothers' worries about abnormality
K.B. ⚥959809	"That she gets so dirty outside and that she doesn't care."	"Her interest in mother's jewelry"	"No, I was myself a tomboy."
S.C. ⚥879452	"She would rather play baseball than dolls. She comes home with all her clothes ripped up. She gets into fights. She is really rough."	"Her interest in pretty dresses and jewelry."	"She acts like a boy. It might be because of the hormones. She is the opposite from me. I was the dainty type."
R.F. ⚥608098	"Her interest in baseball. She even wanted a baseball glove."	"Her appearance."	"That she might not be normal."
F.G. ⚥876269	"She likes guns and soldiers."	"She also likes to cook."	Not worried
E.G. ⚥878919	"She was always very active. She has to go outside, even if it is raining—pouring. Her interest in boys' stuff."	"She has a soft voice."	Very worried because she is so tomboyish. Might become another Christine Jorgensen.
B.H. ⚥1102785	"Her interest in playing outside."	"She is combing her hair very much."	Worried about enlargement of clitoris; not about behavior. Mother was herself a tomboy.
V.H. ⚥630386	"She is not charming, not gracious. She has really rough manners."	"Her vanity; her interest in sewing and cooking."	Worried whether she will be physically normal, and can have children of her own.
P.M. ⚥1166368	"No, she is not a tomboy."	"She is preoccupied with her hair."	No worries; the girl has normal genitals.
T.M. ⚥845611	"She likes to play with boys."	"She is feminine when she puts on a dress; is petite and pretty."	Concern about physical development.
J.T. ⚥1013706	"That she likes to run and jump. Her interest in guns and cowboys."	"She likes combing her hair."	Concern whether speech retardation is connected with genital abnormality.

Discussion of Tomboyishness

The tomboyishness that we have found in our patients corresponds to the everyday conception of tomboyishness as a matter of athletic energy, outdoor pursuits and play with boys' toys, with minimal concern for feminine frills, doll play, baby care and household chores. So defined, tomboyishness does not preclude eventual romance, marriage, child bearing and full-time home and family care. One of the mothers was, in fact, just such a woman with a self-declared juvenile history of having been a tomboy like both of her daughters. The fact that one of these two girls was not exposed to progestin raises the question of whether tomboyishness may not be a frequent characteristic in the development of middle-class suburban and rural girls who have both the space and the tradition of the outdoor life.

This suggestion is somewhat corroborated by Rabban (1950). He asked children, age three to eight, from two diverse social groups (middle and working class) to select the toys they liked the best. The choices of lower-class boys and girls conformed more closely to traditional sex-typed standards than the choices of middle-class children. Moreover, the difference in sex-typing between the classes is greatest for girls. This finding agrees with the fact that lower-class mothers encourage divergent sex typing of behavior more consistently than do middle-class mothers (Kohn, 1959).

An alternative explanation, so far as our present sample is concerned, may be sought in terms of a fetal masculinizing effect on that part of the central nervous system that mediates energy-expending, gender-linked behavior, analogous to that found in animal studies (Money, 1965). One is reminded of the preliminary findings on induced hermaphroditism in rhesus monkeys, already referred to (Phoenix, 1966). The hermaphroditic rhesus females made scores resembling those of control males, not control females, on such sex-differentiated behavioral items as: initiating play, social threat, pursuit play, avoidance play, rough-and-tumble play, sexual play, including mounting and thrusting, and masturbation.

These experimental animals are still under five years of age. Two are already pubertal and menstruating. They have not been surgically feminized and have not been mating-tested with normal males. Nor have they been given androgen as a prerequisite for an effective copulatory test with a normal female. Their efficacy in parental behavior remains also to be ascertained.

Similarly with our girls—we must wait to ascertain their teenage and adult patterns of eroticism. The oldest girl is only fourteen. She menstruates cyclically. She appeared reticent rather than precocious in romance and boyfriends. Yet she did not give any particular impression or evidence of Lesbian tendencies. She was conservative in her expectancies as a wife and mother, as compared with her career ambitions, but she accepted womanly functions as consistent with her self-conception.

It will require more than ten cases and better control of at least the socioeconomic variable before one can answer with confidence the question of the extent to which prenatal hormones can affect subsequent behavior. Meantime, it is clear that the cyclic adolescent functioning of the pituitary-gonadal hormonal axis may be normal, since the oldest girl in our sample already menstruates. It is clear also that psychosexual identity is not reversed. Their tomboyishness notwithstanding, the girls do not conceive of themselves, as do transvestite transsexuals, as having been placed by nature in the wrong body. Whatever the role of prenatal hormones on the sex-typing of behavior, it is clear in these human subjects that the effect is not stereotyped or fixed in specific patterns, as it may be in infrahuman species.

SUMMARY

Ten girls (age three to fourteen years) with a history of maternal intake of progestins during the patients' embryologic developments were studied psychologically. Nine of them had progestin-induced hermaphroditism and one was genitally unaffected. All patients were given a standardized intelligence test, various sex-role preference tests and interviews. Parents were interviewed also. Six patients had an IQ above 130. The mean Full IQ was 125, S.D. 11.8. There was no significant difference between Verbal and Performance IQ. From the sex-role preference tests and the interview-material nine of the ten girls were tomboys. The criteria were play with boys' toys; athletic energy; outdoor pursuits; and minimal concern for feminine frills, doll play, baby care and household chores. However, tomboyishness so defined did not exclude conceptions of eventual romance, marriage, child-bearing and full-time home and family care.

ACKNOWLEDGEMENT

The clinical diagnosis and management of all patients were under the supervision of Robert Blizzard, M.D., and the late Lawson Wilkins, M.D. We appreciate their clinical cooperation and the availability of their files.

References

BROWN, D. G. Sex-role preference in young children. *Psychological Monographs.* 70, *14:* 1–19, 1956.

BROWN, D. G. Masculinity-feminity development in children. *J. Consult. Psychol.* 21: 197–202, 1957.

HARRIS, D. B. *Children's Drawings as Measures of Intellectual Maturity.* New York: Harcourt, Brace and World, 1963.

JOLLES, I. A study of the validity of some hypotheses for the qualitative interpretation of the H-T-P for children of elementary school age: I. Sexual identification. *J. Clin. Psychol., 8:* 113–118, 1952.

KOHN, M. L. Social class and parental values. *Am. J. Sociol. 64:* 337–351, 1959.

LYNN, D. B. AND LYNN, R. The Structured Doll Play Test as a projective technique for use with children. *J. Projective Techniques, 23:* 335–344, 1959.

MONEY, J. Influence of hormones on sexual behavior. *Annual Review of Medicine* (A.C. Degraff, Ed.), Vol. 16. Palo Alto, Annual Reviews, Inc. 1965, pp. 67–82.

MONEY, J. AND LEWIS, V. IQ, genetics and accelerated growth: adrenogenital syndrome. *Bull. Johns Hopkins Hosp. 118:* 365–373, 1966.

PHOENIX, C. *Psychosexual organization in nonhuman primates.* Paper delivered at the Conference on Endocrine and Neural Control of Sex and Related Behavior (Foundations Fund for Research in Psychiatry), Dorado Beach, Puerto Rico, May, 1966.

RABBAN, M. E. Sex-role identification in young children in two diverse social groups. *Genetic Psychology Monographs, 42:* 81–158, 1950.

WILKINS, L. Masculinization of the female fetus due to the use of certain synthetic oral progestins during pregnancy. *Archives d'Anatomie Microscopique et de Morphologie expérimentale. 48:* 313–330, 1959.

WILKINS, L. Masculinization of female fetus due to use of orally given progestins. *J. A. M. A., 172:* 1028–1032, 1960.

WILKINS, L., JONES, H. W., HOLMAN, G. H. AND STEMPFEL, R. S. JR. Masculinization of the female fetus associated with administration of oral and intramuscular progestins during gestation: Non-adrenal female pseudohermaphrodism. *J. Clin. Endocrinol. and Metab., 18:* 559–585, 1958.

YOUNG, W. C., GOY, R. W. AND PHOENIX, C. H. Hormones and sexual behavior. In *Sex Research: New Developments* (J. Money, ed.). New York, Holt, Rinehart and Winston, 1965.

ANKE A. EHRHARDT, RALPH EPSTEIN, & JOHN MONEY

20   Fetal Androgens and Female Gender Identity in the Early-Treated Adrenogenital Syndrome

INTRODUCTION

The present paper is one in a series of studies being done in the psychohormonal research

Reprinted from *The Johns Hopkins Medical Journal 122*:160–167, 1968. © The Johns Hopkins Press.

Supported by Grants 2-K3-HD-18653 and 5-RD1-HD-00325, United States Public Health Service, and by grants from the Erickson Educational Foundation and the Stiles E. Tuttle Trust.

unit of The Johns Hopkins Hospital on the possible effects of exposure to excess fetal androgen on subsequent behavior and gender identity in certain clinical populations. The rationale behind these clinical investigations relates to the experimental animal findings of the Oregon Regional Primate Group (1). They produce their psychohormonal research populations by experimental design as, for example, by injecting androgens into pregnant rhesus mon-

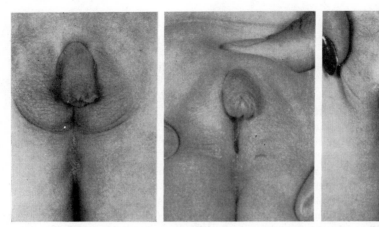

Fɪɢ 1. Two degrees of masculinization of the external genitals in the female adrenogenital syndrome and (right) the result of surgical correction.

keys. The female experimental offspring have masculinized hermaphroditic external genitalia and closely resemble the male in frequency of exhibiting certain aspects of sexual and other play behavior in the juvenile years. This same experimental design cannot, of course, be ethically duplicated on human beings. There are, however, clinical counterparts to these androgenized monkeys, namely patients with the adrenogenital syndrome and those with progestin-induced hermaphroditism (see below). By contrast, there are two clinical populations that illustrate the other end of the spectrum, namely, nonandrogenizing fetal hormone exposure. These populations are girls with Turner's syndrome and those with the androgen-insensitivity (testicular feminizing) syndrome. Patients with the former disorder have no gonads, and are, therefore, not exposed to any of their own gonadal hormones in utero. They differentiate morphologically as females. Patients with the latter syndrome are, at the cellular level, totally unresponsive to the androgens made by their testes and consequently develop, in external genitalia, as females. Both Turner's syndrome and the androgen-insensitivity syndrome will be reported in the future. The progestin-induced hermaphroditic syndrome is the subject of a report by Ehrhardt and Money (2). The adrenogenital syndrome, which is the subject of the present paper, is a genetically recessive inborn error of metabolism. An enzymatic defect in the biosynthesis of cortisone results in the production of excess fetal androgen which in turn causes masculinization of the external genitalia (Fig 1) and subsequent precocious virilizing puberty in the female. In the male, it induces precocious puberty without abnormality of the external genitalia. Treat-

ment of this syndrome with cortisone has been available only since 1950; thus, the maximum possible age of patients eligible for this present study is 16 years old.

PURPOSE

The purpose of the present paper is to report on some sexually dimorphic behavioral characteristics of fifteen early-treated genetic females with the adrenogenital syndrome and to compare them with fifteen matched controls. These characteristics are grouped under three major headings: interest in reproduction and genital morphology; romance, marriage and maternalism; cosmetic interests, physical energy and tomboyism.

SAMPLE SELECTION AND DESCRIPTION

The criteria for being included in this sample were threefold: first, the diagnosis was adrenogenital syndrome in a genetic female; second, the sex of rearing was female; and third, cortisone treatment was instituted from infancy on. One patient had been treated since age two and a half and one since age one and a half; all others had been treated within the first year of life. At birth, seven of the patients had been thought to be hypospadiac males with cryptorchidism. They all, however, were correctly diagnosed and reassigned as females within the first seven months of life. For two years following the outset of this study (1965), all patients entering the pediatric clinic of The Johns Hopkins Hospital for follow-up visits, or as new patients, who met the above criteria were included in the sample until the total number reached 15.

Since 1952, there have been approximately 140 patients with the adrenogenital syndrome seen in the pediatric endocrine clinic of The

Johns Hopkins Hospital. Of these 140, 105 have also been seen in the psychohormonal research unit; 78 of these patients are genetic females and have been reared as females, and of these 78, only 39 have been treated from early childhood. Thus, although our sample includes only 15 patients, it represents about 38% of the available cases.

After the data were compiled on the patient group, a matched control group was assembled from two large Baltimore City public schools with an enrollment of 1,564 and 924 students, respectively. The criteria of matching were sex, race (14 white and one Negro), age, IQ and parents' socioeconomic level.

The controls were chosen on a first-come first-served basis, ie, as a person was found who matched one of the patients on all criteria, that person was included in the sample. If, for some reason, the person was not cooperative about coming to the hospital for an interview, she was excluded and replaced with the next person found to fit the same criteria. In all, 18 controls were chosen, three of whom were uncooperative, before the necessary 15 were obtained.

The ages of the patients and controls were matched to within one year. At the time of the primary interview, the ages of the patients ranged from 5 yr, 2 mo to 16 yr, 1 mo with a mean of 10 yr, 8 mo and a median of 9 yr, 11 mo. The mean age of the matched control group was 10 yr, 6 mo with a range of 5 yr, 9 mo to 15 yr, 2 mo and a median of 9 yr, 11 mo.

Each patient and her respective control was matched to within plus or minus 15 IQ points, with the exception of one case in which the closest possible match was 18 IQ points. Of the 15 girls in the patient group, 14 were given a Wechsler Intelligence Scale for Children and one a Wechsler Preschool and Primary Scale of Intelligence. The intelligence scales used for the control group were those given routinely by the school. Either a Kuhlmann-Anderson intelligence test (sixth and seventh editions), or an Otis Quick Scoring Mental Abilities test (alpha, beta or gamma editions), or the Revised Stanford-Binet Intelligence Scale (third revision), or the SRA Primary Mental Abilities Test had been used. If no school IQ had been obtained, the child, already matched according to all other criteria, was given an appropriate Wechsler Intelligence Scale at the hospital before the final matching decision was made. For the patient group, the mean IQ was 111.53 with a standard deviation of 13.54, while for the control group, the mean IQ was 110.53 with a standard deviation of 11.44.

In regard to socioeconomic level, controls and patients were matched as closely as possible according to the occupational level of their fathers. Although the majority of the patients and controls fell into the upper middle class with fathers who were, according to the classification of Hollingshead (3), predominantly business managers, proprietors of medium-sized businesses and lesser professionals, all possible classes were represented, from unskilled laborers to higher executives and major professionals.

PROCEDURE

At least one interview with each patient and her mother was conducted following a standard data schedule of topics. The interviews were quite flexible, however, so as to be unstilted in manner. Some patients were seen over a period of years and others only once or twice. Each interview lasted at least two hours and was either completely recorded on tape or summarized on tape by the interviewer and patient at the end of the interview. Interviews with each control and her mother were conducted according to the same data schedule of topics used for the experimental group. Interviewing, in all cases, was done in the hospital.

In this first paper, we will report only on the information derived from the interviews with mother and daughter. Various tests that were also administered will be reported in a subsequent paper.

FINDINGS

1. Interest in Reproduction and Genital Morphology

Interview data for the first group of sexually dimorphic behavioral characteristics are presented in Table I. Examination of Part A of this Table indicates that the control and experimental group have approximately the same amount of knowledge about sex. The sources, however, are rather different. The chief source of information for the control group was the home. The patient group also got home instruction, but they were probably more accurately informed about sex and at an earlier age than the controls, since all but two of the patients were given information by us, here in the hospital. For both the patients and controls, sex education in the home tended to be more edited than that received in the hospital— which means chiefly that parents were inhibited in telling about copulation and, to a lesser degree, about delivery.

The program of sex education at the hospital was integral to the program of giving the patients information pertaining to their condi-

TABLE I

Interest in Reproduction and Genital Morphology

	P	C		P	C
A. *VERBAL CURIOSITY*			B. *INVESTIGATIVE CURIOSITY*		
1. *Sex education at home*			1. *Masturbation*		
a. open exchange	3	6	a. never recorded	13	15
b. edited exchange	6	6	b. rarely	1	0
c. no exchange	6	3	c. frequently	1	0
2. *Amount of knowledge*			2. *Shared genital inspection and play*		
a. none	2	2	a. yes (boys, girls or both)	3	2
b. menstruation and pregnancy	1	4	b. no	12	13
c. menstruation, pregnancy and delivery	2	3	3. *Attention to genital morphology*		
			a. yes (boys, girls or both)	2	2
d. menstruation, pregnancy, delivery and coitus	9	2	b. no	12	13
			c. no information	1	0
e. menstruation, pregnancy, delivery, coitus and birth control	1	4			
3. *Chief source of knowledge*					
a. home	0	7			
b. peer group	0	0			
c. school or hospital	13	6			
d. none	2	2			

* P = patient group N = 15; C = control group N = 15.

tion. Of the 15 patients, eight were found to have an adequate knowledge at the time of the study, three had a partial knowledge, three were uninformed and one was evasive and used the mechanism of denial of illness. This one girl is noteworthy in that she was the only one of the sample who had not adjusted to her condition and had severe symptoms, such as hermit-like self-isolation, withdrawing from school, and rejecting signs of femininity. She was psychosexually confused about her status as a female, though not masculine. Once, at age thirteen, she made a suicide attempt. She became grossly obese and failed to begin menstruating.

Part B of Table I shows that, according to what the mothers were able to disclose, the patients did not show more childhood investigative curiosity about sex than their matched counterparts. The frequency of masturbation and genital play was at about the same low level in both groups. One might have thought that the patients would be more inclined to investigate their genitals because of their frequent hospital examinations. The enlargement of the clitoris was not as important a stimulus to sexual play as it might have been. Each patient had had a clitorectomy within the first

few years of life with the latest one being done at age three and a half. It is noteworthy that this patient with the latest clitorectomy is the same patient who is neurotic and confused about her femininity.

2. *Romance, Marriage and Maternalism*

Table II contains the responses given by the patients and controls to questions pertaining to romance, marriage and maternalism. This group of categories reveals some striking differences between the two groups. The frequency of romance in childhood play and activity is about the same in both groups, though the controls do seem to be more advanced in dating than the more conservative patients. The small number of adolescents (four) in the sample groups rather prohibits making any strong generalizations. Only one of the adolescent patients had gone on a date and she reported no kissing or necking. In contrast, all four adolescent controls had gone on dates and three had engaged in kissing and some petting. In neither group was there ever any evidence of romantic interests in other females.

With respect to wedding and marriage, only 9 of the 15 patients had such fantasies, while

TABLE II

Romance, Marriage and Maternalism

	P	C		P	C
A. ROMANTIC INTEREST IN BOYFRIENDS			**C. MATERNALISM**		
1. *Romanticism in play and day-dreams during childhood*			1. *Daydreams and fantasies of pregnancy and motherhood*		
a. yes	8	9	a. yes	8	5
b. no	6	6	b. no	6	9
c. no information	1	0	c. no information	1	1
2. *Adolescent daydreams and relationships with boys (N = 4)*			2. *Rehearsal of mother role in play and toy preference*		
a. none	1	0	a. plays with dolls only	2	8
b. daydreams only	2	0	b. dolls preferred with boys' toys occasionally	1	6
c. daydreams and dating	1	1	c. dolls occasionally, with boys' toys preferred	8	1
d. daydreams, dating and love play	0	3	d. no interest in dolls, and interest in boys' toys only	4	0
B. WEDDING AND MARRIAGE			3. *Interest in infant care*		
1. *Anticipation in imagery and fantasy*			a. aversion	1	0
a. yes	9	15	b. indifference	9	0
b. no	5	0	c. moderate interest	4	8
c. no information	1	0	d. great interest	1	7
2. *Priority of marriage vs career*					
a. marriage preferred	1	10			
b. career preferred	5	1			
c. marriage and career equal	8	4			
d. no information	1	0			

* P = patient group N = 15; C = control group N = 15.

all of the controls had them at one time or another. The patients were also much more interested in careers than the controls, as is evidenced by both groups' responses in the category of priority of marriage versus career. Ten of the controls preferred marriage to a career, while only one of the patients wanted to become a full-time wife and homemaker.

Only a small number of patients reported an interest in infant care and doll play; that is, there was only a minimum of rehearsal of the wife and mother roles in the adrenogenital girls as in contrast to the control girls. In fact, there were two patients who, in games of "house," preferred to play the role of the father rather than the mother.

3. Cosmetic Interests, Physical Energy and Tomboyism

In contrast to the control group, the patients showed a marked interest in masculine derived styles (Table III) and boys' toys and play (Table II). Only one of the patients liked dresses exclusively and those she wore were very plain and unattractive. The majority of the patients preferred slacks, shorts and shirts to dresses. However, they would wear dresses when they were going out, and upon the insistence of their mothers. The main desire for most of the patients was to wear practical clothes which were comfortable and easy to take care of. The same attitude applied to their interest in fashionable hairdos. They accepted what their mothers chose for them, only so long as it was casual and practical for play and sport. They did not spontaneously request or insist on a boys' haircut.

Examination of Part B of Table III shows that the patients were much more interested in athletics and engaged in outdoor activity more often than the control group. The patients' mothers often described them as being very rough and competitive with boys.

We asked each of the patients and their

TABLE III

Cosmetic Interests, Physical Energy and Tomboyism

	*				*	
	P	C			P	C
A. *INTEREST IN PHYSICAL AP-PEARANCE*			2. *Behavior in childhood fights*			
1. *Clothing preference*			a. never fights and withdraws when attacked	1	3	
a. boys' clothes only preferred	0	0	b. fights only when attacked	7	11	
b. slacks, shirts and shorts strongly preferred and dresses occasionally	9	0	c. starts fights with others	1	1	
			d. no record	6	0	
c. dresses preferred and slacks, shirts and shorts only occasionally	5	11	C. *TOMBOYISM*			
			1. *Known to self and mother as a tomboy*			
d. dresses only, frills and ruffles	1	4	a. never	3	11	
			b. passing episode	1	4	
2. *Jewelry, perfume and stylish hairdos*			c. always	11	0	
			2. *Satisfaction with sex role*			
a. no interest	5	2	a. content or prefers to be a girl	7	14	
b. moderate interest	8	7	b. ambivalent	5	0	
c. strong interest	2	6	c. desires expressly to be a boy	3	1	
B. *PHYSICAL ENERGY EXPENDI-TURE*						
1. *Athletic interests and skills*						
a. intense outdoor activities	11	5				
b. periodic outdoor activities	4	9				
c. little outdoor activity	0	1				

* P = patient group N = 15; C = control group N = 15.

mothers what the word "tomboy" meant to them. The reply we received most often was that it was a girl who played with boys' toys, liked to wear boys' clothes, climbed trees, ran around outside and loved to play football and baseball. Thus, when a girl was labelled a tomboy, it implied that she had a high energy level and showed only a minimum of interest in doll play, dresses and girls' activities. The incidence of tomboyism in the two groups differed significantly. While there was no girl in the control group who was labelled a tomboy for most of her life, eleven of the patients were described as tomboys by themselves and their mothers throughout all of their childhood. In four cases of the controls, an episode of tomboyism, not lasting longer than two or three years in childhood, was reported—quite different in degree and duration from the patients.

There was also a difference in attitude toward the positive sides of the female sex role in the two groups. While only one of the controls would rather have been a boy than a girl, eight of the patients were ambivalent about the advantages or disadvantages of being a female.

However, in only one case was this ambivalence felt to be of serious psychopathological concern.

A Chi Square test showed that the difference between the control and patient groups, with respect to the incidence of being labelled a tomboy and satisfaction with sex role is statistically significant at beyond the .02 level.

DISCUSSION

The findings of Tables I, II and III show that the patients with the adrenogenital syndrome differ in certain manifestations of gender role as compared with their matched controls. The patients identified themselves, by and large, as tomboys, and the controls did not. The other differences add up to a type of behavior commonly called tomboyism. Specifically, it consists of extensive outdoor activity in the expenditure of physical energy and great interest in male-associated clothing, play toys and career preference, versus a minimal interest in female associated frills and dolls and in the anticipation of motherhood and homemaking as the primary occupation of adulthood. This tomboyism in the adrenogenital girls did not, however, extend to erotic interests or sexual play. The two groups did not differ in matters of sex knowledge, except that the patients learned more from hospital contacts than did the controls. The patients did not repudiate the future possibility of romance and marriage, even though it was for the most part subservient to career plans. Their tomboyism did not include implications of homosexuality or future lesbianism, or a belief of having been assigned to the wrong sex.

The incidence of tomboyism has been related to socioeconomic class (4), the higher incidence being attributed to the higher socioeconomic levels. There may be a simple issue of definition here, since it is possible that the type of behavior that qualifies as tomboyish is behavior for which only upper socioeconomic children have the necessary opportunity, environment and the materials. The corresponding manifestation in lower-class children may, by force of necessity, be different. Be that as it may, the issue is irrelevant here, because the patients were matched for socioeconomic status with the controls and do, indeed, exceed them in incidence of tomboyism.

The incidence of tomboyism has also been related to IQ (5), the higher incidence being attributed to the higher IQ levels. Maccoby quoted studies by Sontag and coworkers at the Fels Research Institute (6) to indicate that children whose IQ shows a progressive increase were competitive, self-assertive, independent and dominant in interaction with other children—not very feminine characteristics according to the traditional stereotype. One of the Fels workers summarized the issue by saying that the simplest way to describe the developmental history necessary to make a girl into an intellectual person is that "she must have been a tomboy at some point in her childhood." As with socioeconomic level, the issue of IQ is irrelevant here, because the patients were matched for IQ with the controls.

It would appear, therefore that tomboyism in girls with the adrenogenital syndrome has something to do with the syndrome itself. The responsible factor could be a genetic one, since the syndrome is known to be genetically recessive in etiology. Or, it could be a fetal adrenocortical androgenic effect—a postnatal androgenic effect is ruled out by reason of the history of successful cortisone regulation of excessive androgen—in each case on the hypothalamus or a related area of the brain.

Support for the fetal androgen hypothesis is found in the animal experiments already briefly mentioned in the introduction of this paper and by various other animal experiments (7, 8).

Further support for the hypothesis is also found in the study of human beings born with progestin-induced hermaphroditism whose mothers had been given oral progestin during pregnancy. These patients are exposed to an excess of fetal androgen as are the adrenogenital patients, but from an external source. The progestin, being an analogue of testosterone, caused masculinization of the external genitalia of these patients, surgically correctable at birth. Subsequently, the girls manifested definite tomboyish behavior (2).

The findings of this present study suggest that certain aspects of gender dimorphic behavior can be modified by fetal androgens in the human female. These modifications do not necessarily reverse the personal sense of gender identity as a female, but add a special quality to it. Even though some of the girls thought it preferable to be a boy, their preference did not actually include the thought of a sex-reassignment. Moreover, some of the girls were less tomboyish than others, and a few not very tomboyish at all. Even a strong degree of tomboyism did not preclude the possibilities of future marriage, childbearing and family life, if one judges by the evidence of a group of older, late-treated adrenogenital female hermaphrodites (unpublished data). These older people had had more erotic experience than those in the younger group. Their tomboyish traits included, in some cases, homosexual fantasies and dreams and, in some few cases, frank bisexualism. None believed she had been erroneously assigned as a female and should change. Some were married in what appeared to be quite satisfactory marriages and had borne their own children.

It is not possible to estimate on the basis of present data, whether individual differences in degrees of tomboyism may have reflected differences in parental attitude. Each parent knew of the child's genital masculinization at birth. This knowledge may have insidiously influenced their expectancies and reactions regarding the child's behavioral development and interests, but in a way not the same from parent to parent. Whereas one parent might accept, or even reward tomboyism and justify its appearance, another might try to suppress it. Attempted suppression might itself intensify the behavior it tries to abolish, should it elicit a reaction-formation and determination not to relinquish tomboyism.

Whatever the interplay between a fetal androgenic effect versus social conditioning, it is clear that, in the adrenogenital syndrome, the masculinization of behavior is not always of the same magnitude. Moreover, fetal androgenization is not inevitably incompatible with the differentiation of a fairly typical feminine gender identity role.

SUMMARY

A sample of 15 early-treated girls with the adrenogenital syndrome and a sample of 15 controls matched to the patients according to age, sex, IQ and father's occupational level, were interviewed according to a standard data schedule. The mothers were also interviewed. The topics in this schedule included behavior which is usually believed sexually dimorphic, namely, toy preference, athletic energy, outdoor pursuits, interest in infant care, clothing, cosmetics and boyfriends. The patients in comparison with the controls, showed a much higher incidence of interest in masculine-associated clothing and toy preference and very little interest in infant care and feminine-associated clothing and toys. In general, the patients considered themselves and were considered tomboys. Their tomboyism however, did not exclude conceptions of eventual romance, marriage and motherhood. It is possible that the tomboyish traits are a product of androgenization in utero of the hypothalamus or related areas of the brain.

ACKNOWLEDGMENTS

The clinical diagnosis and management of all patients were under the supervision of Robert Blizzard, M.D. and the late Lawson Wilkins, M.D. We appreciate their clinical cooperation and the availability of their files.

For their cooperation in assembling the control group, we wish to thank Dr. Sonia Osler, Miss Edith Walker, Assistant Superintendent of Elementary Education of Baltimore City, and the principals and vice principals of the two Baltimore City public schools, Dr. W. T. Kinn, Mr. L. Coles, Mr. E. Cohen and Mrs. I. Riefle.

We would also like to thank Mrs. Maria Luisa V. de Parra for her assistance in the testing of the patients and controls.

REFERENCES

1. PHOENIX, C.: Psychosexual organization in non-human primates. Paper delivered at the Conference on Endocrine and Neural Control of Sex and Related Behavior (Foundations Fund for Research in Psychiatry), Dorado Beach, Puerto Rico, May 1966.
2. EHRHARDT, A. A. AND MONEY, J.: Progestin-induced hermaphroditism: IQ and psychosexual identity in a study of ten girls. J. Sex Res., 3: 83, 1967.
3. HOLLINGSHEAD, A. B.: Two factor index of social position. Yale University, privately circulated, 1965.
4. RABBAN, M. E.: Sex role identification in young children in two diverse social groups. Genet. Psychol. Monogr., 42: 81, 1950.
5. MACCOBY, E. E.: Woman's intellect. In *The Potential of Woman.* (S. M. Farber and R. Wilson, eds.) McGraw-Hill Book Co., Inc., New York, 1963.
6. SONTAG, I. W., BAKER, C. T. AND NELSON, V. A.: Mental growth and personality development: a longitudinal study. Monogr. Soc. Res. Child Develop., 23: No. 68, 1958.
7. YOUNG, W. C., GOY, R. W. AND PHOENIX, C. H.: Hormones and sexual behavior. In *Sex Research: New Developments.* (J. Money, ed.). Holt, Rinehart and Winston, Inc., New York, 1965.
8. NEUMANN, F. AND ELGER, W.: Proof of the activity of androgenic agents on the differentiation of the external genitalia, the mammary gland and the hypothalamic-pituitary system in rats. Excerpta Medica, International Congress Series No. 101: Androgens in Normal and Pathological Conditions. Pp. 169–185, 1965.

Chapter Six

NUTRITION

The state of nutrition of the mother during pregnancy and while nursing strongly influences the growth and development of her offspring. We now know that nutritional deficits are highly likely to affect the development of the central nervous system, including the brain, and thus to affect the behavioral capacities of the young. For all this, researchers in the United States interested in central nervous system processes and their behavioral consequences have generally paid little attention to nutritional variables during early development. The pioneering work in this field has been carried out in some of the central European countries, in Mexico, and in South America. In these countries, malnutrition is a very real human affliction, and researchers have been concerned to understand the factors involved in malnutrition as well as its consequences. Only recently have researchers in the United States been cognizant of the effects of early malnutrition, and they have now begun to manipulate nutritional parameters in studies with experimental animals.

One of the difficulties in research of this kind lies in isolating causal factors. When an experimenter varies the quantitative or qualitative nature of food given to an experimental female, the differences observed in the progeny may be a direct result of the change in diet or an indirect result, produced through a shift in the mother's behavior toward her young because of the change in her diet. Also important are the time during development (e.g., during intrauterine life or during early postnatal development) at which nutritional deficits have an effect and whether they have different effects at different times in development. For a good discussion of many of these problems see Eichenwald and Fry (1969).

The papers presented here address themselves to certain facets of the problem of malnutrition. Cowley and Griesel (Paper 21) were concerned with the long-term consequences of malnourishment through two generations. They examined the weight, development, and behavior of rats reared on a low-protein diet whose mothers had also been reared on a low-protein diet throughout their lives. The experimental animals weighed less and showed marked retardation in development; after adulthood, the deprived male rats did less well than the controls in a problem-solving test of "intelligence." However, there was no evidence that the second-generation animals were more adversely affected than those from the first generation. That is, there was no evidence of an accumulated deficit over generations.

Ottinger and Tanabe (Paper 22) also found problem-solving deficits among their malnourished animals, and by use of a cross-fostering procedure, they demonstrated that this was due to malnourishment between the times of birth and of weaning. This does not mean that malnutrition before birth does not affect the developing fetus. Ottinger and Tanabe introduced food restriction just after pregnancy, and thus the female's reserve stores of nutrients were available to the developing young. In order to simulate a real-life situation, it would be necessary to keep the adult female on a deprived feeding schedule for some time before she became pregnant, thus depleting her reserves. This procedure was followed by Cowley and Griesel.

The finding of behavioral deficits on a measure of problem solving implicates the central nervous system. This was confirmed by Zamenhof *et al.* (Paper 23), who found less DNA and less protein in the brains of newborn rats whose mothers had been reared on a protein-deficient diet. Less DNA at birth means that the animals from protein-deficient mothers were born with fewer brain cells than those from mothers on an adequate protein diet. The authors indicate that a reduction in brain cells implies a permanent deficit in brain neurons which may affect subsequent behavior. These results do not mean that the biological deficits are the causes of the behavioral differences found in the prior studies, but they do offer an important lead for further experimentation.

At times one finds a human study in which the findings so closely parallel those of animal research as to be startling. Such is Paper 24. Winick and Rosso compared the brains of 10 well-nourished Chilean children who had died accidentally with the brains of 9 other children who had died from malnutrition. They examined the DNA and protein content of these brains — exactly what Zamenhof *et al.* had measured in their rats. The results are identical. The children who died from malnutrition had a decrease in DNA, indicating a reduced number of brain cells. Here is convincing evidence of the power of animal models to generate find-

ings predictive of the human situation. Winick and Rosso also noted that DNA content of the brains increases during the first 6 months of life and then essentially stops. Therefore, it is likely that a sensitive period for the effects of malnutrition is present during prenatal development and up through the first 6 months of life (see Chapter Two).

Paper 25 offers independent support for the idea that there is a sensitive or critical period during the first 6 months with respect to nutrition. From their clinical cases, Cravioto and Robles extracted three groups of children who suffered from malnutrition (1) before 6 months of age, (2) between 6 and 30 months, and (3) after 30 months. When these children were first admitted to the hospital, Gesell Developmental Quotients were obtained in the areas of motor, adaptive, language, and personality-social development; height and weight were also measured. The same information was obtained periodically throughout the children's stay in the hospital while undergoing treatment. The evidence strongly suggests that malnutrition during the first 6 months of life may have more severe consequences than malnourishment in later life.

Reference

Eichenwald, H. F., and Fry, P. C. Nutrition and learning. *Science,* 1969, 163, 644-648.

J. J. COWLEY & R. D. GRIESEL

21 The Development of Second-Generation Low-Protein Rats

A. PURPOSE

For some time this unit[1] has been investigating the effects of a low-protein diet on the behaviour of successive generations of white rats. The results have indicated that the low-protein diet has little effect on the parent

Reprinted from *The Journal of Genetic Psychology 103*:233–242, 1963.

[1] Developmental Research Unit, National Institute for Personnel Research, C.S.I.R., at the University of Natal.

generation, but that the first filial-generation rats are retarded in intelligence (2, 3) and that they are more emotional (4) than rats retained on a normal laboratory diet.

The present report describes the effects of a low-protein diet on the growth, development and the emergence of certain response patterns in a second filial generation of low-protein rats. The report also describes the results obtained on testing the rats on the Hebb-Williams test of animal intelligence.

B. Method

1. *The Sample*

First-filial-generation low-protein rats were mated at 120 days of age with normal male laboratory rats. The offspring constitute a second filial generation of low-protein rats, and form the sample used in the present study.

After they had been mated with the normal male rats from the laboratory colony, 15 low-protein rats and eight comparable control rats were kept in individual wire cages measuring 30 × 21 × 21 cm. The temperature of the breeding room varied between 21°–26° C, with a mean temperature of 24° C.

Table 1 shows the number of pups and litters born, and the mean number of pups in each litter in the low-protein and the control groups.

The pups were weaned at 35 days of age, the low-protein pups being retained on the low-protein diet. In the control group 2.4 per cent of the pups died before weaning, and in the low-protein group 20.2 per cent died. The

TABLE 1
COMPOSITION OF THE LOW-PROTEIN AND THE CONTROL GROUPS

	No. of litters	No. of pups born	Mean no. of pups per litter	No. of pups dying	% of pups dying
Control	4	42	10.5	1	2.4
Low-protein	12	89	7.4	18	20.2

number of pups used in the developmental testing ranged between 71–89 in the low-protein group and between 41–42 in the control group.

At 104 days of age, 14 male rats from the control group and 14 male rats from the low-protein group were randomly selected for testing on the Hebb-Williams Test of Intelligence. The testing procedure was the same as that described by Rabinovitch and Rosvold (12). Twelve female rats from the low-protein group and 11 female rats from the control group were also tested on the Hebb-Williams test at 170 days of age.

2. *Developmental Testing*

The rats were examined once each day, the time of the examination being kept constant.

a. Growth curves. From the second day after birth until the eighth day the litters were weighed daily. At weaning, when the ears were clipped and the sexes separated, the pups were weighed individually.

b. Motor coordination. Each rat was placed for two minutes on a porcelain tile, which had been marked off from the centre in one-inch and therafter half-inch concentric circles. The circles were numbered from the centre of the tile to the periphery.

The number of segments over which the pup moved on the tile was recorded, together with the presence or absence of head and limb movements. The pups were placed in the centre of the field and facing in the same direction. The procedure was repeated each day from the second day after birth until the tenth day.

c. Unfolding of the external ear flap. The number of days after birth elapsing before the upper flap of the ear unfolded, was recorded.

d. Reaction to sound. From the 10th day to the 15th day, the pups were placed individually in a small enclosure measuring approximately six inches square, and their response to a sharp sound was recorded. The sound was produced by allowing the bob of a pendulum to fall freely from the horizontal position, through an angle of 90°, to strike the tin sheeting of the side of the field. The thread of the pendulum was 127 centimeters long and the brass bob weighed 18.1 grams. The presence or absence of the startle response to the sound was recorded.

e. Upper incisors. The number of days after birth before the upper incisors broke through the gums was recorded. A blunt metal probe was moved gently across the gums in order to ascertain whether the incisors had broken through the gums.

f. Opening of the eyes. The age at which the eyes of the rats opened was noted.

g. Suckling of the pups. From the second day after birth until weaning, recordings were made three times a day as to whether the rat litters were suckling from their mothers. The times chosen for making the observations were selected at random from hourly intervals between 8 a.m. and 5 p.m. A litter was regarded as suckling if the majority of pups was feeding from the mother.

3. *The Diet*

The diet used in the investigation was similar to that previously described (2). The protein composition of the control diet has been observed to vary between 20.1–21.5 (mean 21.3) per cent, and that of the low-protein diet between 12.97–15.60 (mean 14.49) per cent. The fluctuation in the protein composition of the diets may well be accounted for by seasonal changes in local foodstuffs and more particularly in the quality of the fish meal used.

The mineral and vitamin mixtures used in the low-protein diet were supplied by the National Nutrition Research Institute (6). The composition of the low-protein and the control diets is shown in Table 2.

The composition of the low-protein diet was based on the work of Miller and Platt (10), who, on the basis of their analysis of a diet in a rural area of the Gambia, compounded a diet in which the foodstuffs, though of European origin, closely corresponded in amount to the Gambian diet.

TABLE 2
COMPOSITION OF THE LOW-PROTEIN AND CONTROL DIETS

Control	%	Low-protein	%
Yellow maize meal	56	Ground whole wheat	75
Milk powder	16	Fish meal	7
Ground nuts	6	Ground cooked haricot beans	5
Brewers' yeast	5	Dextrine	5
Fish meal	8	Ground nut oil	2
Carcase meal	4	Mineral mixture	1*
Lucerne meal	3	Vitamin mixture	2**
Bone meal	1	Vitamin A & D	.007
Calcium	.5	Lucerne meal	3
Salt	.5		
Vitamin A & D_3	.1		
Percentage protein	21.3	Percentage protein	14.49

* Percentage composition: $CaCO_3$, 20.0; K_2HPO_4, 22.83; $CaHPO_4.2H_2O$, 22.57; $Na_2HPO_4.12H_2O$, 11.74; $MgSO_4.7H_2O$, 8.07; $NaCl$, 7.66; Ca-lactate, 5.05; Fe-citrate, 1.96; KI, .05; $MnSO_4.2H_2O$, .02; $CuSO_4.5H_2O$, .02; $ZnCl_2$, .02.
** Composition (parts per 100,000): Riboflavin, 30.00; thiamine hydrochloride, 25.00; niacine, 500.00; pyridoxine hydrochloride, 125.00; calcium pantothenate, 200.00; choline chloride, 5,000.00; inositol, 5,000.00; p-amino-benzoic acid, 1,500.00; biotin, 2.00; folic acid, 25.00; vitamin B_{12} ("Cytacon"), .13; vitamin K ("Kapilin"), 5.00; ascorbic acid, 500.00; dextrine to make 100,000.

C. RESULTS

1. *Growth Curves*

Mean differences in the weights of the experimental and the control group are shown in Figure 1. On the second day after birth a mean difference of .5 grams is observable between the two groups, the mean weight of the control pups being heavier than that of the low-protein pups, even though the mean number of pups per litter is larger in the control group.

The mean daily increase in weight of the control rats, over the period extending from the second until the tenth day, is significantly greater than the mean daily increase in the experimental rats (two-tailed Mann-Whitney U test, $p < .01$).

At both the 35th and 60th days after birth the mean difference in weight between the groups is significant beyond the .1 per cent level ($t = 11.023$ and $t = 5.630$).

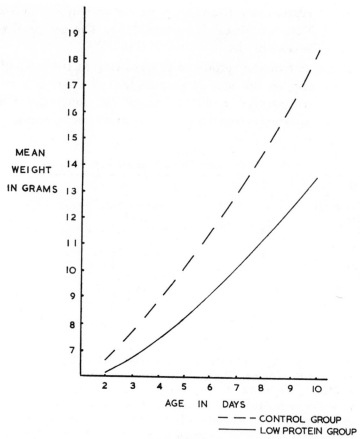

FIGURE 1

GROWTH CURVES OF THE CONTROL AND LOW-PROTEIN LITTERS

2. Motor coordination

a. Head movements. Donaldson (5) and Farris (7) have drawn attention to the characteristic searching movements of newborn rats. While the majority of the low-protein and the control rats showed head movements of this sort, a minority in both groups failed to do so.

The number of experimental rats not showing head movements was greater in the low-protein than in the control group from the third day after birth. The difference between the two groups was significant on the sixth day ($\chi^2 = 14.04$; $p < .001$), and on the seventh day ($\chi^2 = 4.93$, $p < .05$), after birth.

b. Limb movements. Paddling movements of the fore and hind limbs are observable in the majority of the control rats (83 per cent) from the fifth day, and in the low-protein rats (64 per cent) from the seventh day after birth. The chi-squared test shows the difference between the groups to be significant at less than the .1 per cent level on the fifth ($\chi^2 = 15.20$) and sixth days ($\chi^2 = 19.68$), and at less than the 1 per cent level on the seventh ($\chi^2 = 7.20$) and eighth ($\chi^2 = 9.80$) days. From the ninth day the differences between the low-protein and the control group are not significant.

c. *Coordinated movement in the field.* When placed in the field many of the rats showed movement which was restricted to the centre of the field and the first segment.

A comparison was undertaken between the number of rats entering the four outer segments of the field, and the number of rats remaining in the centre and the first segment of the field.

By the fifth day 76 per cent of the control rats and 30.7 per cent of the low-protein rats had moved beyond the periphery of the first segment ($\chi^2 = 21.95$, $p < .001$).

The difference between the number of rats in the low-protein and control groups moving beyond the first segment of the field is also significant on the sixth day ($\chi^2 = 36.96$, $p < .001$), seventh day ($\chi^2 = 19.28$, $p < .001$), eighth day ($\chi^2 = 13.48$, $p < .001$) and ninth day ($\chi^2 = 4.77$, $p < .05$) after birth.

The mean number of segments entered each day, over the nine-day observation period by the control group, was greater than the mean number of segments entered each day by the low-protein group (two-tailed Mann-Whitney U test, $p < .05$).

3. *Unfolding of the External Ear*

In the low-protein group the pinnae of the ear remained unfolded for a longer period than in the control group. In only 16 per cent of the low-protein, but in 50 per cent of the control rats, were the external pinnae unfolded by the second day after birth ($\chi^2 = 15.41$, $p < .001$). On the third day, the difference between the groups was again significant, 76 per cent of the low-protein group and 95 per cent of the control group having had the pinnae unfolded ($\chi^2 = 5.87$, $p < .02$). By the fourth day all the rat pups, with the exception of one in the low-protein group, had the pinnae unfolded.

4. *Reaction to Sound*

The control rats responded to sound at an earlier age than the low-protein rats. The earliest response that was recorded was in two control rats at 10 days after birth. On the 12th day, 93 per cent of the control rats and 30 per cent of the low-protein rats were observed to respond to the noise ($\chi^2 = 43.09$, $p < .001$). On the 13th day the difference between the groups was again marked: 98 per cent of the control rats and 57 per cent of the low-protein rats responding to the noise ($\chi^2 = 20.64$, $p < .001$). By the 14th day all the control rats and 80 per cent of the low-protein rats showed a marked startle response to the noise ($\chi^2 = 6.84$, $p < .01$), but from the 15th day the differences between the groups were not significant.

5. *Upper Incisors*

The upper incisors of 36 per cent of the control rats and 26 per cent of the low-protein rats had broken through the upper gums by the eighth day after birth ($\chi^2 = .840$, $p > .3$). On the ninth day the difference between the control group (88 per cent) and the low-protein group (69 per cent) was significant ($\chi^2 = 4.44$, $p < .05$), but by the 10th day practically all the pups of both groups had their upper incisors.

6. *Opening of the Eyes*

One of the control rats had both eyes open on the 14th day after birth. By the 15th day 60 per cent of the control rats and 22 per cent of the low-protein rats had their eyes open ($\chi^2 = 16.62$, $p < .001$). The difference between the group was also significant on the 16th day ($\chi^2 = 15.07$, $p < .001$), but not on the 17th day ($\chi^2 = 1.82$, $p > .2$) after birth.

7. *Suckling of the Pups*

The control and the low-protein mothers were ranked on the number of times they were observed suckling their pups during the preweaning period. The low-protein mothers suckled their litters more frequently than the control group (two-tailed Mann-Whitney U test, $p < .02$).

8. *Hebb-Williams Test*

The results obtained on the Hebb-Williams test are shown in Table 3.

TABLE 3

MEAN DIFFERENCE IN INTELLIGENCE BETWEEN THE LOW-PROTEIN AND THE CONTROL RATS

Group	Mean low-protein (errors)	Mean control (errors)	Standard deviation low-protein	Standard deviation control	t	p
Male	119.5	94.1	22.41	23.09	2.9512	$< .01$
Female	151.8	143.8	19.60	13.60	1.1264	$< .3$
Male & Female	134.4	116.0	26.40	31.60	2.2580	$< .05$

D. DISCUSSION

The results show clearly that in second-generation low-protein rats there is a retardation of growth and a delay in the emergence of certain early response patterns.

From the second day after birth the low-protein rats are lighter in weight than the control group and, as in first-generation rats, this difference in weight becomes greater as the rats mature (2). The mortality rate is significantly higher in the low-protein rats, but is considerably less than that which we have observed in first-filial-generation rats.

It is likely that the slightly higher protein content of the experimental diet used in the present investigation, was primarily responsible for the reduced mortality rate. It is our impression, however, that the constant handling of the rats during early infancy may also have contributed to the lower mortality rate.

Previously, we observed no difference in the frequency with which first-filial-generation low-protein rats suckled from their mothers (4). The greater frequency with which the second generation suckle may indicate that, over the two generations, the low-protein diet has had a cumulative effect on either the quantity or quality, or both quantity and quality, of the mothers' milk.

Retardation in motor development is reflected in the greater number of low-protein rats that do not show the early characteristic head movements, and the delayed appearance in this group of paddling movements of the fore and hind limbs. Further, early coordinated creeping movements are less effectively executed than by the control rats, where the criterion of effectiveness is the distance travelled in the field. Work in progress indicates that the low-protein diet my have a retarding effect on the motor development of first-filial-generation rats, though it has little effect on the temporal development of the sense organs and other anatomical features.

The eyes, and the external ear flap, open at a later age in the second-generation low-protein rats. The low-protein rats also respond at a later age than the control rats to sound, and this inclines us to the view that concurrent with the anatomical retardation there is a retardation in the functioning of the receptors.

In the present study, only the male rats show a significant difference in intelligence, though the scores of the female rats on the Hebb-Williams test are in the same direction as those of the males. The testing of the female rats at a later age than the male rats, may have contributed to the failure to obtain a significant difference in this group. Biel (1), in studying the effects of inanition on the rat, found that differences in maze learning were present at an early age, but were not permanent. In our own studies there is much that runs counter to this view. First-filial-generation low-protein female rats when tested on the Hebb-Williams test at 80 days of age, and male rats at 180 days of age, both scored a significantly greater number of errors than comparable control rats (2, 4). These results, taken in conjunction with the results of the male rats and the combined male and female scores of the second generation, indicate that the changes induced by the low-protein diet are persistent and so present in the mature rat.

Critical periods in the development of behaviour have been described, and associated with critical periods of learning. Structural changes within the nervous system, receptors and effectors presumably accompany the critical periods, and the periods would themselves be dependent on these changes (15).

The retardation in development of the low-protein rats occurs at an early age, and, if we may generalize from other species, this period may well be critical for the establishing of certain response patterns. Failure to establish such patterns, in the case of children, may lead to permanent disabilities in later life (15).

The developing brain during the foetal period and early infancy rapidly synthesises protein and lipoproteins, which Richter (13) has indicated make up 90 per cent of the dry weight of the brain. While the proteins of the brain are reported as being more resistant to depletion during starvation than other tissues, the deformation or death of the foetus may arise from a severe protein deficiency in the mother (13). A number of early studies describing structural changes in the C.N.S. following on the administration of low-protein diets are reviewed by Jackson (9).

Rose *et al.* (14) have shown that the amino acids which are necessary for the growth of the rat are also necessary for the maintenance of nitrogen equilibrium in man. The exclusion, even for a short period, of any one of the essential amino acids in man, produced changes in appetite, sensations of fatigue and marked nervous irritability.

Geber and Dean (8), in a study of African children with Kwashiorkor, a protein deficiency disease, report a retardation in development of the children when assessed on the Gesell tests. It is not known, however, whether the retardation is permanent, though Nelson (11) of this Institute has reported that the dominant E.E.G. frequencies of children with Kwashiorkor are well below those of healthy African children.

The evidence indicates that a deficiency of protein during the prenatal period, early infancy, or both, has far reaching effects on the organism. In rats, there is retardation of intelligence and an increased emotionality in the first generation, and marked retardation of development and intelligence in the second generation.

E. Summary

The effects of a low-protein diet on the growth and development of a second generation of low-protein rats are described.

The low-protein rats are retarded in growth and there is a delay in the emergence of motor activity and in the response of the rats to auditory stimulation. Frequency of suckling was more marked in the low-protein rats.

When mature, the rats were tested on the Hebb-Williams test of intelligence, where they scored a greater number of errors than a comparable control group of rats fed a laboratory diet of known composition.

The results are discussed in relation to the concept of critical periods of development, and attention is drawn to the reported effects of protein deficiency on the nervous system and on the development of African children.

References

1. Biel, W. C. The effects of early inanition on a developmental schedule in the albino rat. *J. Comp. & Physiol. Psychol.*, 1939, **28**, 1-15.
2. Cowley, J. J., & Griesel, R. D. Some effects of a low protein diet on a first filial generation of white rats. *J. Genet. Psychol.*, 1959, **95**, 187-201.

3. ————. Pre- and post-natal effects of a low protein diet on the behaviour of the white rat. *Psychol. Africana*, 1961, **9**.

4. ————. Low protein diet and emotionality in the albino rat. *J. Genet. Psychol.*, 1964, **104**, in press.

5. DONALDSON, H. H. The rat: Data and reference tables (2nd ed.) *Memoirs of The Wistar Institute of Anatomy & Biology* (Philadelphia), 1924, **6**.

6. DREYER, J. J. The relative biological value of the proteins of breads made from wheaten flour of 90 per cent extraction with or without supplements of "deodorised" fish flour. Unpublished report, South African Council for Scientific and Industrial Research, National Nutrition Research Institute, Pretoria, 1958.

7. FARRIS, E. J., *Ed.* The Care and Breeding of Laboratory Animals. New York: Wiley, 1950.

8. GEBER, M., & DEAN, R. F. A. The psychological changes accompanying Kwashiorkor. *Courrier* (International Children's Centre, Paris), 1956, **6**, 3-15.

9. JACKSON, C. M. The Effects of Inanition and Malnutrition upon Growth and Structure. London: J. A. Churchill, 1925.

10. MILLER, J., & PLATT, B. S. Chronic protein malnutrition in the rat and the effects of supplements of fish meal. Conferencia Inter-Africanade Nutricao, Secretariado General da Conferencia, Luanda, 1956.

11. NELSON, G. K. The electroencephalogram in Kwashiorkor. *E.E.G. Clin. Neurophysiol.*, 1959, **11**, 73-84.

12. RABINOVITCH, M. S., & ROSVOLD, H. E. A closed field intelligence test for rats. *Can. J. Psychol.*, 1951, **5**, 122-128.

13. RICHTER, D. Protein metabolism of the brain. *Brit. Med. J.*, 1959, **1**, 1255-1259.

14. ROSE, W. C., JOHNSON, J. E., & HAINES, W. J. The amino acid requirements of man: 1. The role of valine and methionine. *J. Biol. Chem.*, 1950, **182**, 541-556.

15. THORPE, W. H. In: Current Problems in Animals Behaviour, W. H. Thorpe & O. L. Zangwill, *Eds.* Cambridge, England: Cambridge Univ. Press, 1961.

DONALD R. OTTINGER AND GILFRED TANABE

22 Maternal Food Restriction: Effects on Offspring Behavior and Development

OTTINGER, DONALD R., and TANABE, GILFRED (1968). *Maternal Food Restriction: Effects on Offspring Behavior and Development.* DEVELOPMENTAL PSYCHOBIOLOGY, 2(1): 7–9. Pregnant rats were placed on reduced food intake or remained on adequate diet during gestation and lactation. Offspring were cross-fostered to provide for independent experiences of prenatal and/or postnatal mother malnutrition. All offspring were placed on an *ad lib* diet at time of weaning. When evaluated in adulthood, offspring whose mother was food-deprived during the lactation period showed body weight deficits and increased errors on the Hebb-Williams maze as compared to controls. There were no observed effects of the prenatal deprivation.

THE EFFECT OF INFANT nutritional deficiency on later physical development has received considerable attention in the nutrition literature (Chow & Lee, 1964), but its effects on behavioral development have received only minimal attention (Barnes, 1967). In one study that was concerned with behavioral development, Barnes, Cunnold, Zimmerman, Simmons, MacLeod, and Krook (1966) manipulated offspring nutrition by increasing the number of pups per litter during lactation and also by raising some of these pups on a low

Reprinted from *Developmental Psychobiology* 2:7–9, 1968.

protein diet postweaning. The group receiving preweaning deprivation and a low protein diet after weaning had increased error scores on a visual discrimination task in a water Y maze. Cowley and Griesel (1963, 1964) reared females on a low protein diet prior to mating and throughout gestation and lactation of their offspring. After weaning, these offspring were reared on a low protein diet. The experimental offspring were more emotional and made more errors in the Hebb-Williams maze than non-deprived controls.

Both of these experiments demonstrated that prolonged early nutritional deficiency resulted in reduced performance in a learning task. However, it is not possible to determine from these data which stages of development (i.e., prenatal, postnatal, or postweaning) are most critical in producing this phenomenon. The present report is the first study in a programmatic investigation designed to isolate the periods of development during which nutritional deficiencies have their most profound effect on later intellectual and physical development.

The purpose of the present experiment was to determine if a quantitative dietary restriction of the mother during gestation and/or lactation would differentially affect later problem-solving behavior and body weight in the offspring.

METHOD

SUBJECTS AND DIET

Preliminary research established mean daily *ad lib* food consumption for adult females during each day of gestation and lactation. Thirty-six Purdue Wistar female rats were bred at approximately 100 days of age and subsequently produced the 14 litters used in the experiment. Following 4 days of breeding, 16 females were retained on an *ad lib* diet in meal form and 20 were given 50% of the established *ad lib* diet, also in meal form. Wayne Lab-Blox was used as feed for all animals and was contained in glass feeding dishes placed within the cages. Water was available *ad lib* at all times. Later, obviously pregnant females from both groups were transferred to maternity cages containing a tray bottom partially filled with wood shavings. Cages were checked each morning for new pups, and the birth date of the litter was recorded as the previous day unless it was apparent that the litter had been born quite recently.

All litters were randomly reduced to 8 pups at birth, weighed, and litters cross-fostered both within and between the 2 prenatal groups. For example, litters from mothers restricted during gestation were given to other restricted mothers or to mothers fed *ad lib* during gestation. Once a litter had been cross-fostered, the shavings in the cage were not changed.

During lactation, mothers remained on the same diet they had received during gestation: *ad lib* or 50% of an *ad lib* diet. Thus, 4 groups of offspring were generated: (*1*) pups whose mothers were on the 50% diet during gestation and lactation, (*2*) gestation only, (*3*) lactation only, and (*4*) control pups whose mothers were fed *ad lib* throughout the experiment. All subjects were weaned, weighed, sexed, and ear punched at 21 days, placed on an *ad lib* diet, and reared thereafter in small group cages with like-sexed littermates.

PROCEDURE

Sixty subjects were randomly selected for open-field testing and body weight, and 32 offspring were tested in the Hebb-Williams maze. The open-field behavior was used as a measure of emotionality (Denenberg, in press) and the Hebb-Williams maze was used to measure intelligence (Rabinovitch & Rosvold, 1951).

Animals were weighed at weaning, 40, and 61 days of age. At 49 days of age, subjects were tested in the open field. The field consisted of a 45-in. square plywood base with walls 18 in. high. The complete unit was painted flat black except for white lines that divided the floor into 9-in. squares. Subjects were placed directly into one corner of the field and allowed to remain for 3 min during which time the number of squares entered with all 4 feet and number of boluses deposited were recorded. The subjects were tested individually once per day from days 49 to 52.

At 99 days of age, 16 rats (2 females and 2 males from each group) were tested using the Hebb-Williams maze, and similar testing was performed on the remaining 16 males and females at 130 days of age. The subject's score was the total number of errors made on the sequence of 12 test problems. The age difference was not significant and the data for all subjects were pooled for analysis.

RESULTS

Preliminary tests for litter effect indicated that litter was not a source of variation on any of the measures except body weight. Thus, the data on activity, defecation, and Hebb-Williams maze performance were classified as a $2 \times 2 \times 2$ factorial (prenatal treatment, postnatal treatment, and sex), and an analysis of variance was computed for each of these variables using subject as the experimental unit of analysis. The data on body weight were classified by pre- and postnatal conditions, sex, and age, and an analysis of variance was computed using the litter as the unit of analysis.

BODY WEIGHT

The birth weight of the offspring of the prenatally deprived mothers was significantly less ($t = 2.63$, $df = 9$, $p < .05$) than the prenatal control litters. Table 1 presents the mean body weight data for the 8 groups from weaning to 61 days. A significant effect was found for maternal dietary restriction during lactation ($F = 15.63$, $df = 1/10$, $p < .01$), but the prenatal diet variable had no measurable effect. At all ages, subjects whose mothers were fed the 50% diet during lactation weighed less than those whose mothers were fed *ad lib*. There was a significant Postnatal Diet × Sex interaction ($F=5.74$, $df=1/10$, $p<.05$): the body weight of male offspring was more affected by postnatal maternal food restriction than was the body weight of female offspring. As expected, the Sex main effect and the Sex × Age interaction were both significant.

OPEN-FIELD BEHAVIOR

No significant main effects or interactions were found for activity or defecation in the open field.

HEBB-WILLIAMS MAZE

The mean error scores for the Hebb-Williams maze are presented in Table 2. A significant effect ($F=6.73$, $df=1/24$, $p<.05$) was found for maternal dietary restriction during lactation: subjects whose mothers were given the 50% diet during lactation made significantly more errors than subjects whose mothers were fed *ad lib*. No other effect was significant.

TABLE 1. *Mean Body Weight at Three Ages*

Prenatal Deprivation	Postnatal Deprivation	Sex	21	49	61
				Days	
Yes	Yes	Male	19.88	158.42	226.19
		Female	19.18	125.56	155.75
	No	Male	60.52	238.12	304.37
		Female	56.25	123.90	160.67
No	Yes	Male	17.05	147.50	221.52
		Female	17.12	123.90	160.67
	No	Male	60.45	253.11	335.90
		Female	58.51	171.30	195.02

DISCUSSION

The purpose of this experiment was to determine if quantitative reduction of mother food intake during gestation and/or lactation would result in reduced offspring intelligence, body weight, and emotionality. The results demonstrated that maternal food restriction started during gestation did produce restricted litter birth weight, but this prenatal effect did not continue beyond birth. There were no other weight or behavioral differences due to the prenatal treatment.

Maternal food restriction during lactation affected both weight and Hebb-Williams performance of the offspring. The weight differences were present at the time of weaning, and there was no recovery even after 40 days of *ad lib* feeding.

TABLE 2. *Mean Hebb-Williams Error Scores*

Prenatal Deprivation		Postnatal Deprivation		
		Yes		No
No	Male	116.25	Male	87.50
	Female	134.25	Female	95.25
Yes	Male	102.75	Male	82.00
	Female	118.50	Female	111.00

This experiment separated the prenatal and postnatal periods and demonstrated later behavioral and body weight effects for the postnatal period, but no lasting effects for the prenatal period. Previous research has not separated these periods in a factorial design, thus making it impossible to isolate the period of development during which the treatment had its effect. Using the present program of treatment, these data clearly point to the postnatal period as critical in determining the later intellectual deficit. However, the present experiment started prenatal food restriction within the first 4 days of gestation. Recent research has found DNA levels (considered an index of brain cell number) in neonatal offspring adversely affected by maintaining female breeder rats on a low protein diet started 1 month prior to mating (Zamenhof, Marthens, & Margolis, 1968), but no behavioral correlate of this finding was determined. This suggests that in order to get a prenatal effect, it may be necessary to have pre-mating dietary restriction that would reduce maternal body reserves prior to gestation.

REFERENCES

BARNES, R. H. (1966). Experimental animal approaches to the study of early malnutrition and mental development. Paper presented at the symposium on "Relationship of nutrition to control nervous system development and function." Annual meeting of the Federation of American Societies for Experimental Biology, Atlantic City, New Jersey.

BARNES, R. H., CUNNOLD, SUSAN R., ZIMMERMAN, R. R., SIMMONS, H., MACLEOD, R. B., and KROOK, L. (1966). Influence of nutritional deprivations in early life on learning behavior of rats as measured by performance in a water maze. *J. Nutrition*, 89: 399–410.

CHOW, B. F., and LEE, C. J. (1964). Effects of dietary restriction of pregnant rats on body weight gain of offspring. *J. Nutrition*, 82: 10–18.

COWLEY, J. J., and GRIESEL, R. D. (1963). The development of second-generation low protein rats. *J. Gen. Psychol.*, 103: 233–242.

COWLEY, J. J., and GRIESEL, R. D. (1964). Low protein diet and emotionality in the albino rat. *J. Gen. Psychol.*, 104: 89–98.

DENENBERG, V. H. In press. Open-field behavior in the rat: What does it mean? *Ann. N.Y. Acad. Sci.*

RABINOVICH, M., and ROSVOLD, H. (1951). A closed-field intelligence test for rats. *Canad. J. Psychol.*, 5: 122–128.

ZAMENHOF, S., van MARTHENS, EDITH, and MARGOLIS, F. L. (1968). DNA (cell number) and protein in neonatal brain: Alternation by maternal dietary protein restriction. *Science*, 160: 322–323.

STEPHEN ZAMENHOF, EDITH VAN MARTHENS, & FRANK L. MARGOLIS

23   DNA (Cell Number) and Protein in Neonatal Brain: Alteration by Maternal Dietary Protein Restriction

Abstract. *Female rats were maintained on 8 or 27 percent protein diet by a pair-feeding schedule for 1 month before mating and throughout gestation. The brains of newborn rats from females on the 8 percent protein diet contained significantly less DNA and protein compared to the progeny of the females on the 27 percent diet. The data on DNA indicate that there are fewer cells; the protein content per cell was also lower. If, at birth, the brain cells are predominantly neurons, and their number becomes final at that time, then such dietary restriction may result in some permanent brain-neuron deficiency. This quantitative alteration in number as well as the qualitative one (protein per cell) may constitute a basis for the frequently reported impaired behavior of the offspring from protein-deprived mothers.*

The effects of malnutrition on development have been extensively studied. For brain, such studies were concerned mainly with the effects on weight or size (*1, 2*), which, however, depend on factors (such as lipids, water content) that do not reflect the number of brain cells. Winick and Noble (*3*) and Dickerson *et al.* (*4*) investigated the effect of malnutrition after birth on the DNA content of the brain. If the malnutrition occurred from birth to weaning, the animals (rats, pigs) exhibited a permanent brain DNA deficiency. The influence of malnutrition on learning behavior of rats has also been studied (*5, 6*). Many investigators have implied that protein deprivation before and after birth results in mental impairment in children (for reviews see *7*).

For the understanding of this influence of malnutrition on behavior, the study of changes in the number of brain cells is of interest. Whereas, in the rat

Reprinted from *Science 160*:322–323, 1968. Copyright 1968 by the American Association for the Advancement of Science.

the number of glial cells and the total number of brain cells increases for some time after birth (*8, 9*), the number of neurons does not increase (*8, 10, 11*), with the possible exception of short-axoned neurons (*11*). Thus, we studied the effect of maternal malnutrition before and during gestation, on the amount of brain DNA (brain cell number) in newborn animals.

Our report is a continuation of previous studies (*12, 13*) of factors influencing the amount of DNA in the brain, which reflects the number of brain cells because the DNA content of a diploid cell of a given species is constant; our eventual purpose is the elucidation of the relation between alterations in brain cell number and behavior.

We used albino rats derived from the Sprague-Dawley strain; these rats have been bred in our laboratory for at least ten generations; the females were virgin, 3 months old, and weighed 200 to 260 g. The animals were maintained (i) on powdered diets containing either 8 per-

Table 1. The effect of restriction of maternal dietary protein on weight and content of brain of newborns. Diet A, full pellet; B, full diet, containing 27 percent protein; C, restricted, containing 8 percent protein.

| Diet | Number of animals | | Offspring weights (g) | | Brain content of offspring* | |
	Mothers	Off-spring	Body	Brain*	DNA (μg)	Protein (mg)
A	5	41	5.7 ± 0.4	0.159 ± 0.071	544 ± 20	
B	4	32	6.38 ± .4	.181 ± .014	546 ± 22	9.29 ± 0.43
C	4	31	4.46 ± .22	.139 ± .081	491 ± 29	7.45 ± .57
			Decrease† (%)			
			30	23	10	19.8
			Probability			
			$P{<}.001$	$P{<}.001$	$P{<}.001$	$P{<}.001$

* Cerebral hemispheres, without cerebellum and olfactory lobes.   † Difference between 27 percent and 8 percent protein groups.

cent or 27 percent protein (*14*) by a pair-feeding schedule (intake 16 g/day); or (ii) another group was maintained on pelleted diet (*15*) as desired (16 g/day). The protein was casein. Both protein diets contained the same amounts of fats (10 percent) and salts (4 percent). In addition, the 8 percent protein diet contained 78 percent starch, and the 27 percent protein diet contained 59 percent starch. To both diets, 2.2 percent of Vitamin Diet Fortification Mixture in Dextrose (*14*) was added to a week's supply. The females were kept on these diets for 1 month before mating and throughout gestation. The restriction was such as to still permit full-term gestation (*16*) and normal number in litter.

The newborns were weighed, and then killed by decapitation, within 6 hours of delivery. The brains (cerebral hemispheres) were immediately removed without cerebellum and olfactory lobes (*13*) and weighed; they were then frozen and subsequently used for the analysis. DNA was determined by a modification of diphenylamine colorimetric method (*12, 17*), and protein was determined by

a modification of Folin colorimetric method (*18*).

The results (Table 1) show first that the rats on two different full diets exhibited differences in body and brain weights, but the total amount of DNA [and therefore total brain cell number (*19*)] was the same. Thus, cell number is a more constant indicator; the brain weight cannot be used as a measure of brain cell number.

As expected (*2, 6*), dietary protein restriction of the mother resulted in considerably (30 percent) lower body weights of the newborn offspring; however, in contrast to previous experiments (*2*), in which the dietary restriction was during gestation only, in our experiments in which the restriction was also imposed 1 month before mating, the brain weights were also considerably (23 percent) lower. This decrease is reflected in comparable percentage decrease in total protein content. All these changes are statistically significant.

The restriction also resulted in a significantly lower (10 percent) DNA content, that is, significantly lower total brain cell number. However, this difference is less pronounced than the difference in brain weight which again indicates that the latter cannot be used as a measure of the former.

Since at birth the brain cells are reported to be predominantly neurons (8), it is likely that the decrease has indeed affected the number of neurons. Since, as discussed above, the neurons essentially do not divide any more after birth, any neuron deficiency at birth may persist throughout the life of the animal. Such deficiency may contribute to the impaired behavior of the offspring of protein-deficient mothers that has been reported in the literature.

The change in protein content, twice as large as that in DNA, indicates that not only the number of cells was altered but also the cells are qualitatively different. Whether these qualitative changes are irreversible or whether they merely represent a delay in maturation is still not known. However, when evaluated at 3 months of age, the experimental animals manifested abnormalities of gait and response to environmental stimuli.

References and Notes

1. P. Gruenwald, *Biol. Neonatorum* **5**, 215 (1963); R. E. Brown, *Develop. Med. Child Neurol.* **8**, 512 (1966).
2. F. J. Zeman, *J. Nutr.* **93**, 167 (1967).
3. M. Winick and A. Noble, *ibid.* **89**, 300 (1966); **91**, 179 (1967).
4. J. W. T. Dickerson, J. Dobbing, R. A. McCance, *Proc. Roy. Soc. London, Ser. B* **166**, 396 (1967).
5. R. M. Barnes, S. R. Cunnold, R. R. Zimmerman, H. Simmons, R. B. McLeod, L. Krook, *J. Nutr.* **89**, 399 (1966).
6. D. F. Caldwell and J. A. Churchill, *J. Neurol.* **17**, 95 (1967).
7. R. Barnes, *Fed. Proc.* **26**, 144 (1967); D. Baird, *ibid.*, p. 134.
8. K. R. Brizee, J. Vogt, X. Kharetchko, *Progr. Brain Res.* **4**, 136 (1963).
9. M. Winick and A. Noble, *Develop. Biol.* **12**, 451 (1965).
10. J. B. Angevine and R. L. Sidman, *Nature* **192**, 766 (1961); M. Berry, A. W. Rogers, J. T. Eayrs, *ibid.* **203**, 591 (1964).
11. J. Altman and G. D. Das, *J. Comp. Neurol.* **126**, 337 (1966).
12. S. Zamenhof, H. Bursztyn, K. Rich, P. J. Zamenhof, *J. Neurochem.* **11**, 505 (1964).
13. S. Zamenhof, J. Mosley, E. Schuller, *Science* **152**, 1396 (1966).
14. Nutritional Biochemicals, Cleveland, Ohio.
15. Wayne Mousebreeder Block, Allied Mills, Chicago, Ill.
16. J. W. Millen, *The Nutritional Basis for Reproduction* (Thomas, Springfield, Ill., 1962).
17. F. L. Margolis, in preparation. The current absolute values of DNA are higher than those reported in reference (*13*) due to an improved extraction procedure.
18. O. H. Lowry, N. J. Rosebrough, A. L. Farr, R. J. Randall, *J. Biol. Chem.* **193**, 265 (1951).
19. From the DNA values per brain, the numbers of total brain cells could be calculated by dividing by a (constant) DNA content per cell (6×10^{-6} μg), on the basis of evidence that the cells in cerebral hemispheres are essentially diploid.
20. Supported by NIH grant HD-01909 and American Cancer Society grant E-474.

MYRON WINICK & PEDRO ROSSO

24   The Effect of Severe Early Malnutrition on Cellular Growth of Human Brain

Extract

In ten 'normal' brains, obtained from well-nourished Chilean children who died accidentally, weight, protein, and DNA and RNA content were all normal when compared with those values derived from similar children in the United States. Table I demonstrates the values obtained in these children. In

Reprinted from *Pediatric Research* 3:181–184, 1969.

nine infants who died of severe malnutrition during the first year of life, there was a proportional reduction in weight, protein, and RNA and DNA content. The actual values for these determinations are given in table II. The number of cells was reduced but the weight or protein per cell was unchanged Three infants who weighed less than 2,000 grams at birth (Infants 2, 3, and 4, table II) were the most severely affected. These data are similar to previous data in animals and demonstrate that in children, severe early malnutrition can result in curtailment of the normal increase in brain cellularity with increase in age.

Speculation

At present there is growing concern that malnutrition early in life may retard normal development. Studies conducted in Africa, in South America, in Mexico, in Guatemala, and in our own country suggest that this is true. Retarded brain growth has also been suspected in malnourished children. The decreased head circumference often noted has been cited as evidence for retardation in brain growth. Although numerous chemical changes secondary to undernutrition have been shown in brain of animals, similar studies have not been available in human brain. This study demonstrates such changes and establishes that cell division is curtailed in human brain by severe early malnutrition. The data provide yet another link in the ever lengthening chain of evidence linking malnutrition to faulty brain growth and development.

Introduction

Total content of DNA reflects cell number in any organ made up primarily of diploid cells [2]. Although some tetraploidy has been reported in brain [6], the overwhelming majority of both neurones and glia are diploid. Total brain DNA reflects the total number of brain cells, and the ratio of protein to DNA or that of RNA to DNA reflects the average amount of protein or RNA per cell.

In rats, malnutrition at a time when brain cells are actively dividing curtails cell division and results in an ultimate reduction in total brain cell number [13]. This reduction in cell number will occur if the rats are malnourished from birth or if their mothers are malnourished during pregnancy [17], and will persist even if the animals are later given an adequate diet. In contrast, 'overfeeding' rats from birth to weaning will increase the rate of cell division in brain [15]. This increase in the rate of cell division will occur even after a short period of malnutrition if rehabilitation is begun while cell division is still actively occurring [16]. It would appear that the state of nutrition from before birth to 17 days of age will influence the rate of cell division and the ultimate number of cells in rat brain.

Examination of a series of 'normal' human brains collected in the United States from therapeutic abortions and from children who died from accidents or poisonings has demonstrated that DNA content increases linearly until birth, more slowly until 6 months of age, and very little thereafter [11]. It seems probable, therefore, that if the response to malnutrition in human brain is analogous to the response in rat brain, the critical postnatal period during which cell division could be curtailed would be the first six months of life.

Table I. Control population

Age	Weight	Protein	RNA	DNA
	g		mg	
15 weeks gestation	32	1.8	28.3	22
18 weeks gestation	54	2.4	47.6	48
36 weeks gestation	280	10.8	315	520
39 weeks gestation	214	14.2	402	580
1 ¾ months	312	19.8	501	706
2 months	408	22.3	620	790
5 ¾ months	570	29.0	732	880
6 ½ months	602	31.8	924	910
8 ½ months	720	40.0	1040	920
11 ½ months	850	49.1	1306	910

Each set of values represents value for total brain of a single patient. Determinations were carried out in triplicate with less than 2 % variation in all three samples.

Materials and Methods

The studies described here were carried out in two groups of children in Santiago, Chile. In the first group, all ten children were well nourished and were within the normal height and weight curves for both Chilean [1] and American children [10]. They showed no clinical evidence of malnutrition and died acutely of accidents or poisonings. Two fetuses studied were the products of therapeutic abortions for psychiatric reasons.

In the second group, all the infants died during the first year of life and showed typical signs of severe third degree malnutrition. They were all well below the third percentile for height and weight and presented a clinical picture of severe infantile marasmus. In none of these nine cases was breast feeding practiced; the major source of food was a liquid made of flour and water.

Brains were removed within one hour of death and immediately frozen. These were homogenized *in toto* to a 20 % suspension in distilled water. DNA, RNA, and protein were separated by a modification of the Schmidt-Thannhauser procedure [8]. Incorporation and recovery studies previously performed using rat brain showed that the methods used were effective for fractionation of these components of the central nervous system. DNA was determined by Burton's modification of the diphenylamine reaction [4]. When verified by direct ultraviolet spectrophotometry, there was agreement within 5 % between the methods. RNA was determined by the orcinol reaction [5] and protein by the method of LOWRY *et al.* [7]. Complete details of these methods have been published elsewhere [11, 12, 14].

Table II. Malnourished population

Age	Weight	Protein	RNA	DNA
	g		mg	
½ month	208	10.2	345	512
1 ¾ months	136	7.4	210	380
3 ½ months	105	7.6	200	300
5 ½ months	132	7.4	160	315
6 months	400	15.8	560	700
6 ¾ months	420	18.2	595	720
7 months	386	15.6	510	680
9 months	505	20.3	660	690
11 months	557	19.0	605	510

Each set of values represents value for total brain of a single patient. Determinations were carried out in triplicate with less than 2 % variation in all three samples.

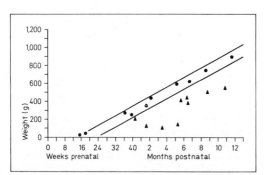

Fig. 1. Lines indicate normal range for US population [11].
● indicates normal Chilean children.
▲ indicates Chilean children who died of severe malnutrition during the first year of life.

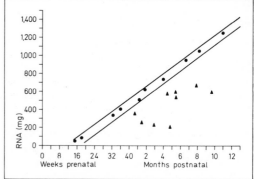

Fig. 3. Lines indicate normal range for US population [11].
● indicates normal Chilean children.
▲ indicates Chilean children who died of severe malnutrition during the first year of life.

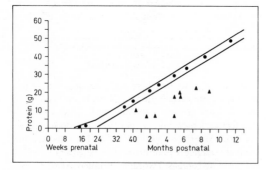

Fig. 2. Lines indicate normal range for US population [11].
● indicates normal Chilean children.
▲ indicates Chilean children who died of severe malnutrition during the first year of life.

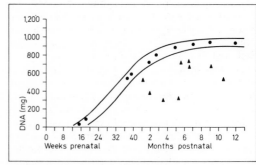

Fig. 4. Lines indicate normal range for US population [11].
● indicates normal Chilean children.
▲ indicates Chilean children who died of severe malnutrition during the first year of life.

Results

In all cases, the normally nourished infant in Santiago showed weights and amounts of protein, RNA, and DNA content in brain comparable to that of the population previously studied in the United States (figs. 1–4). The brains of the nine infants who died of severe malnutrition all showed reduced weights and reduced quantities of protein, RNA, and DNA content (figs. 1–4). In three infants (Infants 2, 3, and 4, table II), DNA content was approximately 40 % of that expected. These three infants all weighed less than 2,000 grams at birth, indicating that they were prematures or had suffered fetal growth retardation. Unfortunately, gestational age records were not available to make this distinction. The reduction in weight (fig. 1), protein (fig. 2), and RNA (fig. 3) is roughly proportional to the reduction in DNA (fig. 4) and, thus, the ratios are normal, suggesting that the average protein or RNA content per cell is normal. If the data are plotted against weight instead of age, there is no reduction in DNA content in brain, and the reduction in cell number is proportional to the reduction in the weight of these children.

Discussion

These data demonstrate that the brains of well-nourished Chilean children who died accidentally contain the same number of cells as the brains of children accidentally dying in the United States. In contrast, children who died of severe malnutrition (marasmus) during the first year of life showed a reduced DNA content in brain. The data also suggest that the younger the child when malnutrition strikes, the more marked the effects. The three children in this study who weighed less than 2,000 grams at birth had a 60 % reduction in DNA content in brain. These results imply either that the brain of a very small infant may be more sensitive to severe postnatal malnutrition or that intrauterine malnutrition had already occurred in these three infants. Better prenatal case histories will have to be collected to separate these possibilities.

The retardation in brain growth in all nine children studied can be entirely explained by the decreased number of brain cells. The protein/DNA ratio (protein per cell) remained unchanged. The retardation in brain growth, which has been inferred from measurements of head circumference [9] and demonstrated more directly by reduced brain weight [3], was a result of the curtailment of cell division. The brains of these children contained fewer cells than brains of well-nourished children of similar age.

Summary

Total brain weight and protein, RNA and DNA content were studied in children who died of severe malnutrition during the first year of life in Santiago, Chile. Brains of the well-nourished children were the same weight and contained the same quantities of DNA, RNA and protein as brains from a comparable population studied in the United States. In contrast, the brains of the infants who died of malnutrition were proportionally reduced in weight and in nucleic acid and protein content. These data indicate that severe early malnutrition retards cell division in human brain.

References and Notes

1. BARJA, I.; FUENTE, M.; BALLESTER, D.; MONCKEBERG, F. y DONOSO, G.: Peso y talle de pre-escolores Chilenos urbanos de tres niveles de vida. Rev. chil. Pediat. *36:* 525 (1965).
2. BOILVIN, A.; VENDRELY, R. et VENDRELY, C.: L'acide desoxyribonucléique du noyau cellulaire, dépositaire des caractères héréditaires; arguments d'ordre analytique. C. R. Acad. Sci. *226:* 1061 (1948).
3. BROWN, R.E.: Decreased brain weight in malnutrition and its implications. E. Afr. med. J. *42:* 584 (1965).
4. BURTON, K.: A study of the conditions and mechanisms of the diphenylamine reaction for the colorimetric estimation of desoxyribonucleic acid. Biochem. J. *62:* 315 (1956).
5. DISCHE, A.: In The nucleic acids (ed. CHARGAFF, E. and DAVIDSON, J.N.), vol. I (Academic Press, New York 1955).
6. LAPHAM, L.W.: Tetraploid DNA content of Purkinje neurons of human cerebellar cortex. Science *159:* 310 (1968).
7. LOWRY, O.H.; ROSEBROUGH, N.J.; FAAR, H.L. and RANDALL, R.J.: Protein measurement with the folin phenol reagent. J. biol. Chem. *193:* 265 (1951).
8. SCHMIDT, G. and THANNHAUSER, S.J.: A method for the determination of desoxyribonucleic acid, ribonucleic acid and phosphoproteins in animal tissues. J. biol. Chem. *161:* 83 (1945).
9. STOCH, M.B. and SMYTHE, P.M.: Does undernutrition during infancy inhibit brain growth and subsequent intellectual development? Arch. Dis. Childh. *38:* 546 (1963).
10. STUART, H.C. and MEREDITH, H.V.: Use of body measurements in the school health program. Amer. J. publ. Hlth *36:* 1365 (1946).
11. WINICK, M.: Changes in nucleic acid and protein content of the human brain during growth. Pediat. Res. *2:* 352 (1968).
12. WINICK, M. and NOBLE, A.: Quantitative changes in DNA, RNA and protein during prenatal and postnatal growth in the rat. Develop. Biol. *12:* 451 (1965).
13. WINICK, M. and NOBLE, A.: Cellular response in rat during malnutrition at various ages. J. Nutr. *89:* 3 (1966).
14. WINICK, M. and NOBLE, A.: Quantitative changes in ribonucleic acid and protein during normal growth of rat placenta. Nature, Lond. *212:* 34 (1966).

15. WINICK, M. and NOBLE, A.: Cellular response with increased feeding in neonatal rats. J. Nutr. *91:* 2 (1967).

16. WINICK, M.; Rosso, P. and FISH, I.: Cellular recovery in rat tissues after a brief period of neonatal malnutrition. J. Nutr. *95:* 623 (1968).

17. ZAMENHOF, S.; VAN MARTHENS, E. and MARGOLIS, F. L.: DNA (cell number) and protein in neonatal brain: Alteration by maternal dietary protein restriction. Science *160:* 322 (1968).

18. This research was supported by the National Foundation Grant 1270, the Nutrition Foundation Grant 357, and the New York City Health Research Council Contract U 1769.

JOAQUIN CRAVIOTO & BEATRIZ ROBLES

25   Evolution of Adaptive and Motor Behavior During Rehabilitation from Kwashiorkor

As contrasted with older patients, infants under six months old recovering from kwashiorkor did not improve their mental age calculated from their psychological test behavior. If adaptive behavior is an analogue to later intelligence, a possible loss of intellectual capacity must be seriously considered.

SINCE BROCK AND AUTRET [6] in 1952 made the scientific world conscious of the magnitude and importance of one of the most severe forms of malnutrition in children, a great amount of effort and research in countries still in the pre-industrial phase of development has been concentrated on study of severe forms. The primary objective has been to decrease the presently high mortality rate from this pathological condition. Programs for economic development, such as those presented by the Alliance for Progress, have as one of their principal aims the decrease in the mortality rate of Latin American children under five years of age to 50 per cent of the present figures. This is possible because the majority of deaths occurring in the one-to-four age group are due to the synergism between malnutrition and infection.[5] Nevertheless, it is important to bear in mind that the majority of children afflicted by malnutrition do not die. It is, therefore, necessary to know the permanent or transitory effects that can undermine the actual or potential capacity of the survivors, especially when it is considered that there are many communities in the preindustrial world where practically no adult has escaped malnutrition of some degree during childhood.

Animal experiments have shown that food deprivation, particularly early in life, produces permanent organic modifications, especially in certain para-

Reprinted from *American Journal of Orthopsychiatry* 35:449–464, 1965. Copyright ©the American Orthopsychiatric Association, Inc. Reproduced by permission.

Presented at the 1964 annual meeting of the American Orthopsychiatric Association in Chicago, Illinois. INCAP Publication I-307.

menters such as total length, length of lower limbs, dentine composition and proportion of muscular tissue present in the adult.[23, 24, 31] FIGURE 1, taken from Pratt and McCance,[13] illustrates that the femoral length in cockerels which were kept under malnourished conditions during a certain growth period does not reach the same size as that of control animals although they were fed adequate diets thereafter.

Studies on the recovery of children with advanced chronic malnutrition seem to confirm the results obtained in animals. After the child has recovered from severe malnutrition he is shorter and his skeletal development is retarded in comparison to that of individuals of the same age and ethnic group who have not suffered malnutrition.[12, 3]

In the biochemical sphere, Arroyave et al.[2] have shown that children from poor rural areas where weight and height retardation during early infancy is

FIGURE 1

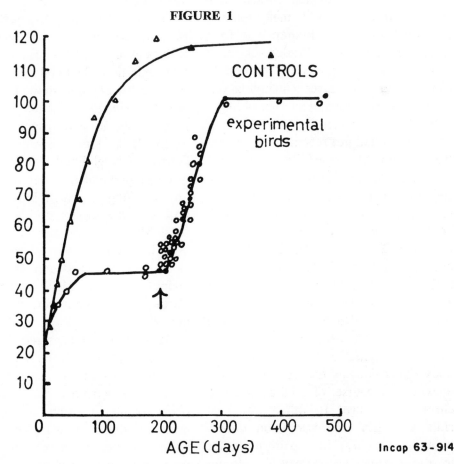

Incap 63-914

Growth in length of the femur in undernourished and rehabilitated cockerels. ●, cockerel during rehabilitation; O, undernourished and other rehabilitated birds before and after they were killed; ↑, beginning of rehabilitation; Δ, values for well-nourished Rhode Island Red controls, based on the lengths of the femur of thirteen birds of known age from the same stock.

a common phenomenon present lower creatinine excretions for their chronological age but normal for their "height age." This finding has been interpreted as indicative of a retardation in the development of muscular mass that seems to persist throughout their lives.[9]

Acheson [1] has shown that when the growth rate is temporarily reduced by some pathologic agent in the child, the subject never reaches the height corresponding to his genetic pattern. Chavarría et al.[7] have reached similar conclusions through serial measurements performed on cretin children who were receiving treatment. Prader et al.,[26] while not sharing this view, have published a series of cases (including one of anorexia nervosa and another of hypothyroidism) in which height even after many years had not reached the percentile attained before the affliction began.

When only the growth rate is considered, it is easy to recognize that during the initial periods of recovery, malnourished children present rates from two to three times greater than those in normal children of the same chronological age. Nevertheless, if observations are continued during a sufficient time, it can be proved that the speeds acquired during recovery are similar to those shown by normal children of the same body dimensions as the undernourished ones, but of course, of a much younger chronological age. In other words, a child who has recovered from undernourishment grows in a pattern similar to the normal (Waddington's Homeoresis) but with a retardation of months or years in relation to the growth rates which should have been present if he had not been chronologically malnourished.[8, 28]

Although it has been emphasized in all descriptions of malnutrition in children that psychological manifestations hold a prominent place among the clinical symptoms,[18] little attention has been given to the subsequent psychologic status, notwithstanding reports on electroencephalographic alterations in undernourished children [25] and anatomic and biochemical changes undergone by the central nervous system in animals fed diets capable of producing kwashiorkor in children.

Geber and Dean in Uganda, Africa,[14] Barrera-Moncada in Venezuela [3] and Robles et al.[30] in Mexico, have reported that undernourished children tested with the Gesell technique show a marked retardation in their language, adaptive, personal-social and psychomotor behavior. This direct association between deficits in height and weight and those in developmental quotients is of utmost interest. Similar associations have been observed in a group of children from a rural Mexican zone and another group in Guatemala, where mild forms of malnutrition (first and second degree malnutrition) are highly prevalent.[29, 11] FIGURES 2 and 3 illustrate these associations.

Because it is recognized fact that in experimental animals the magnitude and persistence of lesions caused by food deprivation depend a great deal on the period of life in which they appear, the question arises of how long the behavior alterations persist in rehabilitated children and what their presence signifies for future intellectual development. Questions such as these are fundamental. The purpose of this report is to present the results of serial measurements of ability performed after the "initial cure" on a group of severely undernourished children observed at the nutrition ward of the Hospital Infantil de Mexico.

PROCEDURE

Previous studies performed as a part of a program to establish quantitatively the influence of the factors determining the status of nutrition in Mexican rural communities (Operación Zacatepec),[10] have indicated that the evolution of weight during the first five years of life may be described by three well defined phases. The first comprises a period of four to six months after birth and is marked by weight gains similar to those presented by normal children born in highly industrialized countries. This similarity is most apparent when gains are expressed as percentages of birth weight. The second phase extends from the sixth to approximately the thirtieth month. During this phase weight gains are gradually lower and reach a minimum between the eighteenth and the twenty-fourth month, after which they

FIGURE 2

RELATION BETWEEN MOTOR (Gesell) DEVELOPMENT QUOTIENT
AND HEIGHT DEFICIT IN CAKCHIQUEL CHILDREN

"Operación Nimiquipalg"
Santa Catarina Barahona – 1962

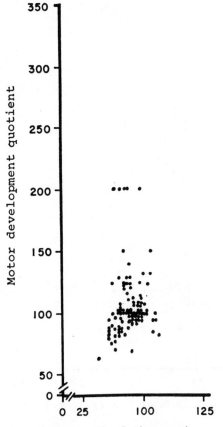

Height in % of theoretic normal for age   Incap 64-2

show a tendency to rise progressively. Finally, the third phase marks an apparent return to the normal values according to the chronological age.[27]

In view of the foregoing and taking into consideration that the animal experiments lead to the hypothesis that the greatest effect of malnutrition on ultimate size and performance of the mature individual may be produced at the period of maximum growth, it was thought necessary to assess the psycho-logical test performance of severely malnourished children at least during three different age periods: (1) below 6 months of age, (2) between 6 and 30 months and (3) after 30 months. From all the children admitted to the nutrition ward those classified as suffering from third-degree protein-calorie malnutrition were considered suitable for the study according to the criteria of Gomez et al.[17] and Bengoa's suggestion of considering all malnourished children pre-

FIGURE 3

RELATION BETWEEN ADAPTIVE (Gesell) DEVELOPMENT QUOTIENT
AND WEIGHT DEFICIT IN CAKCHIQUEL CHILDREN

"Operación Nimiquipalg"
Santa Catarina Barahona - 1962

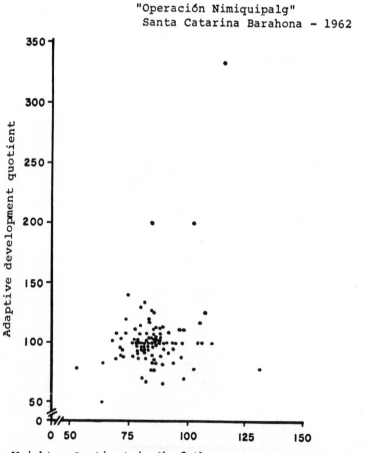

Weight = Quotient in % of theoretic normal for age

Incap 64- 1

senting edema (regardless of their weight) as belonging to the third-degree group.

Immediately after correction of any acute infectious and/or electrolyte disturbances the psychological test behavior of the children was explored through the application of the Gesell method.[16] Tests were repeated at regular intervals of two weeks during the entire period that the children were hospitalized.

At the end of one year of study it was possible to analyze serial information obtained in six infants below six months of age, nine children between 15 and 29 months and 5 children between 37 and 42 months. Certain nutritionally relevant characteristics of the children on admission to the study are shown in TABLE 1.

RESULTS

Expressing the Gesell Developmental Quotients for a given age on the basis of a scale where 100 represents the performance of healthy North American children of the same chronologic age of the child being tested, TABLE 2 shows that on the first examination the 20 children exhibited a reduction in all developmental spheres explored by the stimuli of the Gesell test. These findings confirm previous preliminary observations done in a small group of kwashiorkor chil-

TABLE 1

CERTAIN CHARACTERISTICS OF THE CHILDREN ON ADMISSION TO THE STUDY

	Chronological Age (months)	Weight (kgs)	Percentage of Mean Theoretic Weight for Age †	Height † (cms)	"Age for Height"
Sub-Group I					
No. 1	3	3.25	57	56	2
2	4	2.24	35	50	0
3	5	3.25	46	50	0
4	5	3.86	55	57	2
5	6	3.10	42	56.5	2
6	6	2.89	39	56	2
Sub-Group II					
No. 1	15	4.66	47	63	5
2	16	8.75	82	73	16
3	20	6.50	59	74	17
4	23	6.90	58	69	11
5	24	6.30	52	72	14
6	25	7.15	58	78	22
7	27	6.90	55	75	18
8	29	7.46	58	78	22
9	29	5.75	45	78	22
Sub-Group III					
No. 1	37	8.62	62	86.5	31
2	37	5.90	45	78	22
3	38	10.4	72	83	28
4	41	6.38	43	78	22
5	42	5.99	40	71	13

† Ramos-Galván, R.: Medidas convencionales de peso y talla para lactantes y pre-escolares (Conventional tables for height and weight of infants and preschool-age Mexican children). Bol. Clin. Ass. Med. Hosp. Inf. Mexico. **1:** 19, 1960.

TABLE 2

DEVELOPMENT QUOTIENTS (GESELL) AT THE INCEPTION OF STUDY OF 20 CHILDREN SUFFERING FROM SEVERE PROTEIN-CALORIE MALNUTRITION

| | Chronological Age (months) | Field of Behavior | | | |
| | | Motor | Adaptive | Language | Personal-Social |
		Developmental Quotients			
Sub-Group I					
No. 1	3	67	67	67	33
2	4	25	25	25	25
3	5	20	20	20	20
4	5	20	60	20	20
5	6	33	33	33	33
6	6	33	33	33	33
Sub-Group II					
No. 1	15	40	40	27	35
2	16	69	69	56	59
3	20	75	70	65	75
4	23	42	42	42	42
5	24	38	29	4	12
6	25	46	40	35	44
7	27	37	37	22	33
8	29	52	62	48	52
9	29	31	17	24	24
Sub-Group III					
No. 1	37	57	49	57	81
2	37	40	49	35	35
3	38	39	39	37	37
4	41	7	7	7	7
5	42	26	26	31	26

dren[30] and are in agreement with similar reports from Venezuela[3] and Africa.[14]

It is realized that the Gesell norms obtained in children of European stock are not applicable to these children because in Africa,[15] México[29] and the Cakchiquel area of Guatemala,[11] healthy infants explored by this technique showed a more advanced state of development than their European counterparts during the first three years of life. However, because the degree of advance was greater in the youngest child, the developmental quotients in TABLE 2 were calculated on the basis of the American norms in order to make the figures comparable with those of previous reports. It may be important to note that the true quotients at the beginning of the study are much lower than the values stated in the table since a normal child of these preindustrial areas has at the age of three months an adaptive or motor development equivalent to five or seven months on Gesell norms. A difference of one month between the chronological age and the age calculated as from the developmental quotient represents a reduction of approximately 80 per cent of the actual normal value, and not of 33 per cent.

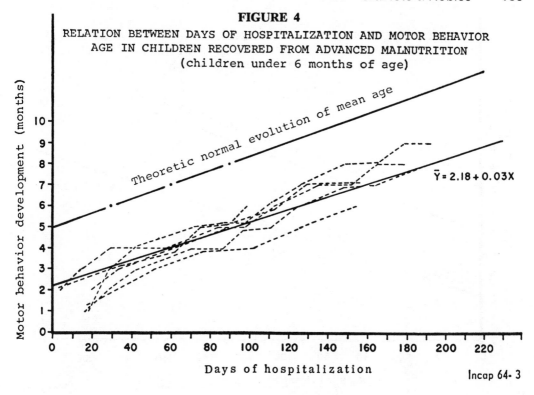

FIGURE 4

RELATION BETWEEN DAYS OF HOSPITALIZATION AND MOTOR BEHAVIOR
AGE IN CHILDREN RECOVERED FROM ADVANCED MALNUTRITION
(children under 6 months of age)

Motor behavior development (months)

Theoretic normal evolution of mean age

$\bar{Y} = 2.18 + 0.03X$

Days of hospitalization

Incap 64-3

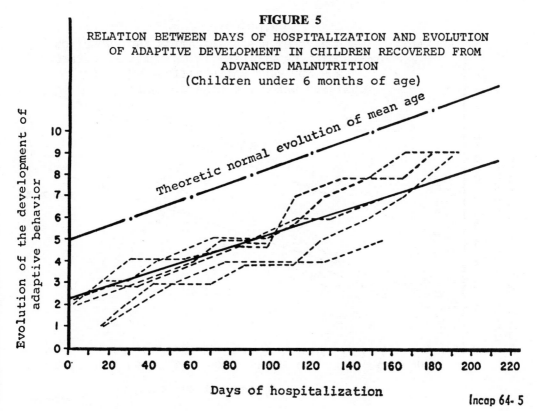

FIGURE 5

RELATION BETWEEN DAYS OF HOSPITALIZATION AND EVOLUTION
OF ADAPTIVE DEVELOPMENT IN CHILDREN RECOVERED FROM
ADVANCED MALNUTRITION
(Children under 6 months of age)

Evolution of the development of adaptive behavior

Theoretic normal evolution of mean age

Days of hospitalization

Incap 64-5

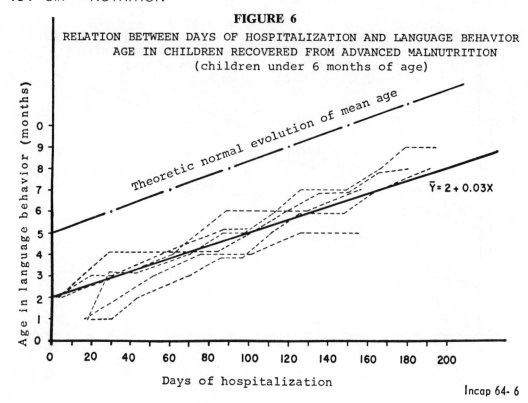

FIGURE 6

RELATION BETWEEN DAYS OF HOSPITALIZATION AND LANGUAGE BEHAVIOR
AGE IN CHILDREN RECOVERED FROM ADVANCED MALNUTRITION
(children under 6 months of age)

Age in language behavior (months)

Theoretic normal evolution of mean age

$\bar{Y} = 2 + 0.03X$

Days of hospitalization

Incap 64- 6

FIGURE 7

RELATION BETWEEN DAYS OF HOSPITALIZATION AND EVOLUTION
OF PERSONAL-SOCIAL DEVELOPMENT IN CHILDREN RECOVERED
FROM ADVANCED MALNUTRITION
(children under 6 months of age)

Evolution of the development of
personal-social behavior

Theoretic normal evolution of mean age

$\bar{Y} = 2.11 + 0.03X$

Days of hospitalization

Incap 64- 7

As recovery from malnutrition took place, developmental quotients increased in most patients and the gap between the theoretic normal and the actual performance of the child progressively diminished. Not all the fields of behavior explored with the Gesell technique exhibited the same speed of recovery. Language, which was in general the most affected sphere, also presented the lower velocity.

In order to express the improvement in performance, data for each child were plotted against days of hospitalization. The shape of the curves suggested that the findings represented a series of linear functions. Data were therefore fitted to algebraic expressions of the form $Y = a + bx$. In this equation, Y represents the performance calculated as months of specific behavior, i.e., the age at which a normal child would give the score found in the tested child; x is the number of days of treatment, and the term b is an empirical constant determined by the data. The constant b was calculated by the least-squares method for each age group and for each field of behavior. TABLE 3 presents the values of the regression equations thus obtained, and FIGURES 4 to 11 illustrate the phenomena.

The theoretical values of Y predicted by the equations when x varied from 1 to 200 were determined and compared with the mean of the empirical values. In all age groups and fields of behavior the probability (chi square test) that there was no significant difference between the observed data and that of the prediction was greater than 0.95.

From the equations and their corresponding graphs it can be seen easily that the rate of recovery from the initial deficit varies in direct relation to chronological age at admittance. The older the group the greater the value of the slope. Consequently the difference between the chronological and mental ages computed on the basis of their psychological test behavior diminished in all the children except in those younger than six months on admittance to the hospital. The increment in mental age of this group was equal to the number of months expended in the hospital ward. In other words, in the youngest group the initial deficit remained constant throughout the observation period which in some cases extended up to six and a half months.

DISCUSSION

Among the factors that contribute to the intellectual development of the child,

TABLE 3

REGRESSION EQUATIONS (form $Y = a + bx$) FOR THE RELATION BETWEEN DEVELOPMENTAL QUOTIENTS (Y) AND DAYS OF TREATMENT (X) IN THREE GROUPS RECOVERING FROM ADVANCED MALNUTRITION

Developmental Quotient (months)	Age Groups (months)					
	3–6		15–29		37–41	
	a	b	a	b	a	b
Motor	2.18	0.033	12	0.06	14	0.10
Adaptive	2.30	0.033	12	0.08	15	0.11
Language	2.0	0.033	9	0.05	15	0.07
Personal-social	2.11	0.033	10.5	0.07	16	0.11

TABLE 4

DEVELOPMENTAL QUOTIENTS OF A GROUP OF
FULL TERM BORN NEGRO CHILDREN
ACCORDING TO THE MOTHER'S
EDUCATIONAL LEVEL [21]

Maternal Level of Education	Developmental Quotient at the Age of	
	40 weeks	3 years
Less than 9 years of schooling	100	90
Between 9 and 11 years of schooling	104	102
High School graduates or more	104	105

are considered among the most influential. TABLE 4 taken from Knobloch and Pasamanick [21] shows the variation of the developmental quotients according to the level of maternal education and how this influence is progressively more manifested as the child grows older. Similar findings of direct association between the child's IQ and the parental IQ have been reported by Kagan and Moss.[19]

Although the influence of these factors has not been quantified in the case

FIGURE 8

RELATION BETWEEN DAYS OF HOSPITALIZATION AND MOTOR
DEVELOPMENT IN CHILDREN RECOVERED FROM ADVANCED
MALNUTRITION
(Group 15-29 months of age)

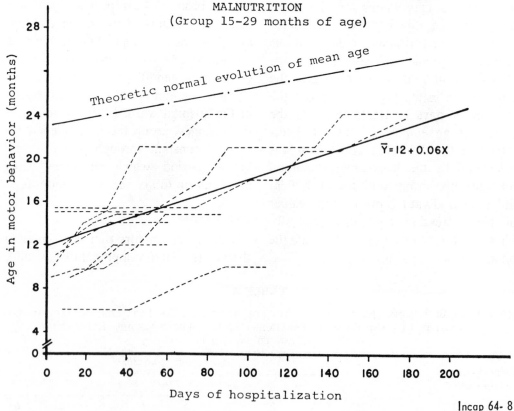

Incap 64- 8

the educational level of the parents, especially the mother, and the maternal attitude toward intellectual development of malnourished children, it is known that the great majority of these patients have parents who are either illiterate or

FIGURE 9

RELATION BETWEEN DAYS OF HOSPITALIZATION AND EVOLUTION
OF ADAPTIVE DEVELOPMENT IN CHILDREN RECOVERED FROM
ADVANCED MALNUTRITION
(Group 15-29 months of age)

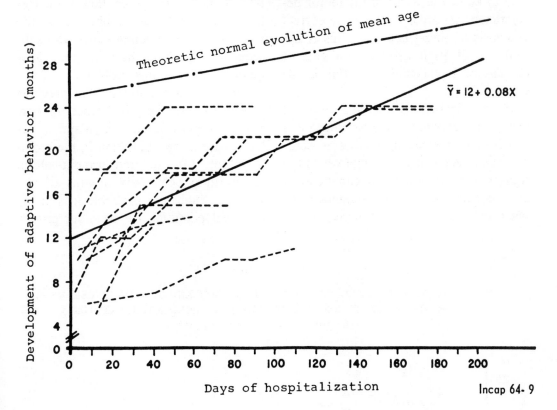

Incap 64- 9

have a very low scholastic achievement. In a study to characterize the environment in which these severely malnourished children live Martinez, De la Fuente and Ramos-Galván [22] found a great number of mothers with low intelligence quotients. Furthermore it is a recognized fact that children suffering from protein-calorie malnutrition generally come from homes where economic pressure hinders the parents from giving adequate stimulation for development.

The diagnosis of subnormal mentality seldom can be established before 16 weeks of age because the tests that can be used during this period of life bear a very poor correlation with measurements of intelligence at subsequent ages.[4] After the 16-week period the prediction of intellectual potential is more reliable, especially in those groups of individuals from whom a rich cultural environment is not expected.

Knobloch and Pasamanick,[21] in summarizing the influence of certain variables on the prediction of later intelligence conclude that it is necessary to abandon the generally accepted concept that the level of motor development is an index that will predict the future intellect of the child; accelerated motor behavior does not necessarily represent a superior intellectual potential and children with serious mental defects may have a normal motor development. Therefore, without overlooking that it is indispensable to know the status of the motor development in order to make a correct diagnosis of actual behavior, this is not sufficient by itself when an estimate of the future intellectual potential is attempted.

If intelligence is defined as the mental adjustment to new circumstances and is characterized by increasing complexity in the channels through which the subject acts on objects, it can be seen that, as Knobloch and Pasamanick have suggested, the adaptive sphere, as ex-

plored by the Gesell method, is precisely the area of behavior that can best serve as an analogue to the later intelligence since it is concerned with the organization of stimuli, the perception of interrelationships and the separation of the whole into its component parts with subsequent resynthesis in a manner adequate to solve a new problem.

Taking into account all the previous considerations, the persistence of low scores of performance in adaptive behavior during rehabilitation in the group of infants that suffered protein-calorie malnutrition before six months of age seems to indicate a probable loss in intellectual potential. In the older groups

FIGURE 10

RELATION BETWEEN DAYS OF HOSPITALIZATION AND LANGUAGE BEHAVIOR
AGE IN CHILDREN RECOVERED FROM ADVANCED MALNUTRITION
(Group 15 - 29 months of age)

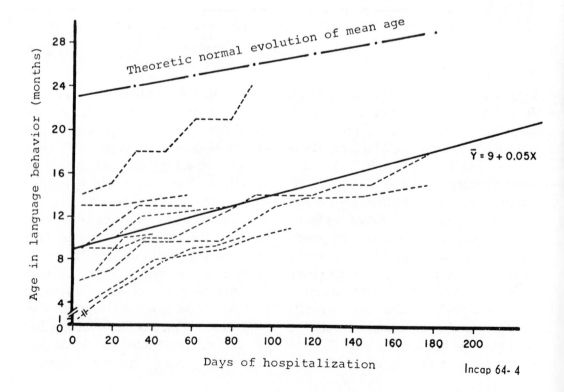

Incap 64- 4

it is possible that the initial deficit will completely disappear if other relevant factors do not interfere.

These proposals seem to be supported by the findings of Barrera-Moncada,[3] who reported that intelligence tests given agrees with the results of the present study and suggests the possibility that when malnutrition strikes at a later age, its impact on the intellectual capacity is less marked, more transitory or even nonexistent.

FIGURE 11

RELATION BETWEEN DAYS OF HOSPITALIZATION AND EVOLUTION
OF PERSONAL-SOCIAL DEVELOPMENT IN CHILDREN RECOVERED
FROM ADVANCED MALNUTRITION
(Group 15-29 months of age)

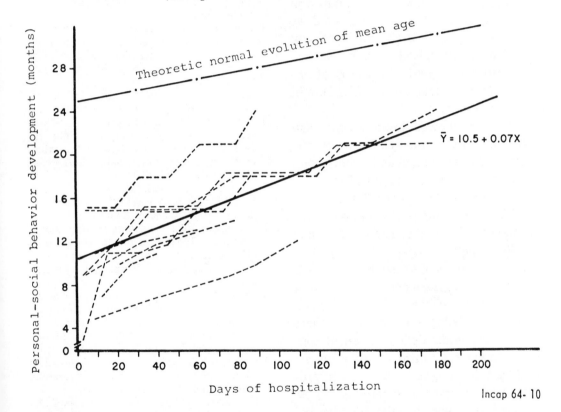

Incap 64- 10

2 years after discharge from the hospital to 20 rehabilitated cases all older than 2 years and 10 months at the time of admission to the study revealed normal intelligence quotients.

Keys et al.[20] in their classic study of malnutrition in adult volunteers found a decrease in intellectual performance but not in intellectual capacity. This also

Regarding the mental rehabilitation of the malnourished child, neither the number of children studied nor the length of the observation period guarantees any final conclusion. However, the results indicate the possibility of permanent damage and the value of using tests in the adaptive sphere of development (without discarding other tests or ignoring other factors affecting mental status). These findings demand confirmation through longitudinal studies, especially since confirmation would affect a group that constitutes in certain areas the majority of the future population.

SUMMARY

The psychological test performance during rehabilitation of a group of 20 infants and preschool children suffering from severe protein-calorie malnutrition was studied by the Gesell method as soon as they had been cured of any acute infectious episode and/or electrolyte disturbance and afterwards at intervals of two weeks during their stay in the nutrition ward.

All cases showed lower scores than those obtained from children of the same chronological age and ethnic group not affected by severe malnutrition.

As the patients recovered from malnutrition, the difference between the chronological age and the developmental age in the fields of adaptive, motor, language and personal-social behavior was found to decrease except in the group of children whose chronological age on admission was below six months. In these patients the initial deficit remained constant during the entire observation period, which in certain cases was prolonged to six and a half months.

If it is accepted that the adaptive behavior of the infant can be considered as analogous to the later intelligence of the adult, there is a high possibility that at least the children severely malnourished during the first six months of their lives, might retain a permanent mental deficit.

Testing of this hypothesis and trying to assess its significance in societies with various levels of industrialization is a major endeavor of a research unit that the Hospital Infantil de México has established for the specific purpose of studying the influence of nutrition on mental development.

REFERENCES

1. ACHESON, R. M. 1960. Effects of nutrition and disease on human growth. Symposium Soc. Hum. Biol. **31:** 73.
2. ARROYAVE, G. and D. WILSON. 1961. Urinary excretion of creatinine of children under different nutritional conditions. Am. J. Clin. Nut. **9:** 170.
3. BARRERA-MONCADA, G. 1963. Estudios sobre alteraciones del crecimiento y del desarrollo psicológico del síndrome pluricarencial (kwashiorkor). Editora Grafos, Caracas, Venezuela.
4. BAYLEY, NANCY. 1958. Value and limitations of infant testing. Children. **5:** 129.
5. BÉHAR, M., W. ASCOLI and N. S. SCRIMSHAW. 1958. An investigation into the causes of death in children in four rural communities in Guatemala. Bull. Wld. Hlth. Organ. **19:** 1093.
6. BROCK, J. F. and M. AUTRET. 1952. Kwashiorkor in Africa. WHO Monograph Series No. 8. Geneve, Switzerland.
7. CHAVARRÍA, C., S. ARMENDAREZ and J. CRAVIOTO. 1962. Crecimiento somático de niños cretinos sujetos a tratamiento sustitutivo. Bol. Med. Hosp. Inf. Mexico. **19:** 285.
8. CRAVIOTO, J. Application of newer knowledge of nutrition on psychological and mental growth and development. Meeting of the Am. Pub. Hlth. Assoc. Miami, Florida, October, 1962. Am. J. Pub. Hlth.
9. CRAVIOTO, J. 1962. Appraisal of the effect of nutrition on biochemical maturation. Am. J. Clin. Nutrition. **11:** 484.
10. CRAVIOTO, J. "Operación Zacatepec." An ecological approach to the study of malnutrition. Acta Soc. Med. Uppsala (In press).
11. CRAVIOTO, J., E. WUG and E. LICARDIE. 1964. "Operación Nimiquipalg." Las conductas adaptativa y psicomotora en niños del grupo cakchiquel. (Adaptive and Psychomotor behavior in children of the Cakchiquel linguistic group.) Guatemala Pediátrica **4:** 92.
12. DEAN, R. F. A. 1960. The effects of malnutrition on the growth of young children. Modern Problems of Pediat. **5:** 111.

13. PRATT, C. W. M. and R. A. McCANCE. **1961**. Severe undernutrition in growing and adult animals. VI. Changes in the long bones during the rehabilitation of cockerels. Brit. J. Nutr. **15**: 121.

14. GEBER, M. and R. F. A. DEAN. Gesell tests on African children. Pediatrics. **20**: 1055, 1957.

15. GEBER, M. and R. F. A. DEAN. **1957**. The state of development of newborn African children. Lancet. **1**: 1216.

16. GESELL, A. and C. AMATRUDA. **1951**. Developmental diagnosis. Normal and abnormal child development. Hoeber, N.Y.

17. GOMEZ, F., R. RAMOS-GALVÁN, S. FRENK, J. CRAVIOTO, R. CHAVEZ and J. VASQUEZ. **1956**. Mortality in second and third degree malutrition. J. Trop. Pediat. **2**: 77.

18. GOMEZ, F., J. VELAZCO, R. RAMOS-GALVÁN, J. CRAVIOTO and S. FRENK. **1954**. Estudios sobre el niño desnutrido. XVII. Manifestaciones psicológicas. Bol. Med. Hosp. Infantil. México. **11**: 631.

19. KAGAN, J. and H. A. MOSS. **1959**. Parental correlates of child's IQ and height: A cross-validation of the Berkeley Growth Study results. Child Develpm. **30**: 325.

20. KEYS, A., H. BROZEK, A. HENSCHEL, O. MICKELSEN and H. L. TAYLOR. **1950**. The biology of human starvation. Vol. II. University of Minnesota Press.

21. KNOBLOCH, H. and B. PASAMANICK. **1963**. Predicting intellectual potential in infancy. Am. J. Dis. Child. **106**: 77.

22. MARTINEZ, P. D., R. RAMOS-GALVÁN and R. DE LA FUENTE. **1951**. Los factores ambientales en la pelagra de los niños en Mexico. Bol. Med. Hosp. Infantil de México. **6**: 743.

23. McCANCE, R. A. **1960**. Severe undernutrition in growing and adult animals. Production and general effects. Brit. J. Nutr. **14**: 59.

24. McCANCE, R. A. and L. E. MOUNT. **1960**. Severe undernutrition in growing and adult animals. Metabolic rate and body temperature in the pig. Brit. J. Nutr. **14**: 509.

25. NELSON, G. K. and R. F. A. DEAN. **1959**. The electroencephalogram in African children. Bull. Wld. Hlth. Organ. **21**: 779.

26. PRADER, A., J. M. TANNER and G. A. von HARNACK. **1963**. Catch-up growth following illness or starvation. J. Pediat. **62**: 626.

27. RAMOS-GALVÁN, R., J. CRAVIOTO, G. GUTIERREZ, F. GOMEZ and S. FRENK. "Operación Zacatepec." III. **1958**. Comparación de un método indirecto y otro directo en la evaluación del estado de nutrición de los niños de una comunidad rural. Bol. Med. Hosp. Inf. Mexico. **15**: 855.

28. RAMOS-GALVÁN, J. CRAVIOTO, M. MORALES and B. ROBLES. **1961**. Requerimientos de nutrientes en lactantes menores. Bol. Med. Hosp. Inf. Mexico. **18**: 164.

29. ROBLES, B., J. CRAVIOTO, L. RIVERA, A. IVILCHES, E. SANTIBAÑEZ, L. VEGA and J. L. PÉREZ-NAVARRETE. **1959**. "Operación Zacatepec." VI. Influencia de ciertos factores ecológicos sobre la conducta del niño en el medio rural mexicano. IX. Reunión Asociación Mexicana de Investigaciones Pediátricas. A. C. Cuernavaca. México.

30. ROBLES, B., R. RAMOS-GALVÁN and J. CRAVIOTO. **1959**. Valoración de la conducta del niño con desnutrición avanzada y de sus modificaciones durante la recuperación. Bol. Med. Hosp. Inf. Mexico, **16**: 317.

31. WIDDOWSON, E. and J. W. T. DICKERSON. **1960**. The effect of growth and function on the chemical composition of soft tissue. Biochemical J. **77**: 30.

32. WIDDOWSON, E., J. W. T. DICKERSON and R. A. McCANCE. **1960**. Severe undernutrition in growing and adult animals. 4. The impact of severe undernutrition on the chemical composition of the soft tissues of the pig. Brit. J. Nutr., **14**: 457.

PROCESS VARIABLES

Additional Readings

Chapter Seven

LEARNING

Probably the most important mechanism mammals possess to help them adapt to their environment is the phenomenon we call learning. Learning is usually defined as a systematic change in performance occurring as a function of practice. The more phylogenetically advanced an animal is, the more complex is its central nervous system and, especially, its brain. The animals within the class Mammalia are superior to all other living organisms with respect to central nervous system organization and integration, and man, of course, is at the zenith of this class.

Learning ability must be closely related to central nervous system complexity, since it would be impossible to preprogram the system to respond appropriately to the vast variety of environmental situations in which the mammal, and especially the human, finds itself. This is in contrast to lower organisms (e.g., insects) in which the animal's simpler physical structure coupled with a less variable stimulus world allows a greater degree of preprogramming of the nervous system.

Along with the more complicated nervous system and greater capability of learning is found a relatively long period of infancy, and it seems reasonable to conclude that these three events are causally related. For example, there is now evidence that new neurons are formed in the brain of the mammal after birth (Altman and Das, 1965), and it is also known that the human brain continues to grow until the late teens. Thus, the long period of infancy and childhood appears to function as a buffer between the complex, booming, buzzing world of confusion and sensitive nervous tissue.

Because of the pervasiveness of learning in the human, psychologists in the United States have placed their major research emphasis upon studying learning phenomena. Even so, virtually no work was done on the topic of learning in the infant until the last decade. A few pioneers investigated learning in the newborn, but a number of these studies were reported in the Russian literature and were not available to American researchers. Several of these papers have now been translated by Brackbill, and the interested reader will find them in Brackbill and Thompson (1967).

There are several reasons why learning in the infant was a neglected area. For one thing, the use of the newborn as an experimental subject in learning studies just was not thought of until recently. In fact, one of the great advances in the 1960's was the realization that the neonate was a legitimate — indeed a necessary — subject for research studies in behavior, biology, and medicine. Among the contemporary leaders in this field, special note must be made of Hanuš Papoušek of Czechoslovakia, who carried out the first set of extensive systematic studies on conditioning in the newborn infant in the 1950's. A number of these papers are available in English, and the reader is referred to them (Papoušek, 1967a, 1967b; Papoušek and Bernstein, 1969).

A second reason for the lack of interest in infant learning is a result of the philosophy that initial development is controlled by endogenous, genetically programmed maturational processes and that learning mechanisms are not important until later in life. We no longer accept the notion of such a two-stage development, and we now know that learning may be demonstrated within a few hours to a few days after birth. See Lipsitt and Reese (1970) for a review of much of this material.

The problems of studying learning in the neonate concern the nature of the response to be learned and the type of reinforcement to be administered. If comparative learning is to be investigated, the challenge is even greater because of the extreme difficulty of comparing different learning situations across species. These difficulties can be minimized by selecting a naturally occurring response which may be compared across different species levels. In other words, the researcher should work with species-specific behavior if possible. The outstanding species-specific behavior among mammals is suckling as a method of obtaining nutrition, and milk, therefore, is an excellent reinforcing agent. The experiments reported in this chapter all used the sucking response in investigating neonatal learning.

Paper 26 is concerned with demonstrating instrumental (operant) learning and extinction in 4-month-olds as a function of milk reinforcement. It should be read in conjunction with Paper 27, by Lipsitt and Kaye, who investigated classical conditioning in 3- and 4-day-old babies who were given milk as a reinforcer. In addition to the demonstrations that the young infant is able to learn in both an instrumental and a classical framework, these studies are important because of their methodological sophistication. Note the types of controls these researchers built into their experimental designs to make certain that they measured a true learning phenomenon rather than a methodological artifact brought about by pseudoconditioning or sensitization, or an individual difference bias such as the infant's preference for turning to one side rather than to another. The mere presentation of a performance curve that changes systematically with trials is not sufficient documentation of learning unless the experimenter has eliminated or controlled possible sources of contamination in the learning paradigm, as these authors have successfully done.

The original documentation that newborn

organisms can learn was done with the human neonate. However, because of medical and ethical restrictions on research with humans, it is necessary to turn to experimentation with animals so that the investigator can introduce aversive conditioning or intervene surgically or physiologically with the growing organism. The information obtained from animal research should be of value to those concerned with developmental learning in the human. The newborn rat is usually rejected as an experimental subject for learning studies because it is so immature and fetus-like, so greatly dependent upon its mother for milk, and so small. However, Thoman and Arnold (1968a, 1968b) have developed a procedure wherein newborn rats may be successfully reared in an incubator without any maternal contact. Once the incubator technique had been worked out, an obvious question was whether the infant rats reared under these conditions differed in their learning ability from typical mother-reared rats. Thoman *et al.* (Paper 28) investigated this question and found definite evidence of earlier and more rapid learning by the incubator-raised group. They also included three control groups in their experiment to make certain that the differences could be attributed to learning factors rather than to some artifact of the experimental design. The parallel between this study and the ones reported in Papers 26 and 27 is apparent.

Puppies and kittens are convenient subjects for the investigation of neonatal learning because of their size and because they may be readily bottle-fed. Paper 29 examines appetitive and aversive conditioning in the newborn puppy. The authors were able to demonstrate that the 3-day-old puppy can learn to increase his rate of sucking on a nipple which yields milk and can learn to avoid sucking on a nipple which yields a bitter mixture of milk and quinine. This paper also carries a methodological message: a number of previous studies had been unable to demonstrate that the neonatal pup was capable of aversive conditioning, and several people had made theoretical interpretations of the meaning of this failure to learn. Stanley *et al.* demonstrated that the failure to learn was due to inappropriate techniques on the part of the researchers rather than to inability on the part of the newborn animal. The message is that one should be extremely cautious about accepting the null hypothesis as proved (in this instance the null hypothesis is that the neonatal puppy cannot learn). A second lesson, which is a corollary of the first, is that theoretical interpretations, based upon data "proving" the null hypothesis, should be relegated to the realm of speculation rather than to the realm of good theory.

Once a phenomenon has been established in science, the next step is to attempt to isolate the mechanisms involved. With respect to the sucking response, the researcher can study mechanisms at the behavioral level by determining the role of the mother in initiating and perpetuating sucking behavior, the effects of sucking deprivation, how reflexes and learning processes affect suckling, and so on. At the physiological level, he can try to isolate the neurological pathways involved in the sucking response. Kovach and Kling (Paper 30) attacked the problem of sucking in the newborn kitten at both the behavioral and the physiological levels. In a series of four experiments they were able to isolate a number of critical parameters affecting the sucking response. They first developed a technique to measure sucking by use of an artificial nipple and then studied the quantitative characteristics of this response at different ages. This revealed the presence of a reflex which acted to initiate sucking behavior. However, reflex activity alone is not sufficient to maintain sucking; a learning mechanism is necessary. Also, learning must take place within a certain time period since kittens deprived of sucking experience for 23 or more days were unable to suck when returned to their mothers. In another experiment Kovach and Kling

ablated the kitten's olfactory bulbs and found that this completely stopped the sucking from the natural mother, thus showing that the sense of smell is necessary for the activation of this behavior pattern. However, the bulbectomy did not interfere with sucking from the artificial nipple, and the authors properly point out that there are some fundamental differences between normal sucking behavior on the mother and learned sucking on the nipple. They suggest that the difference between these two types of sucking behavior may be due to different degrees of central nervous system involvement.

References

Altman, J., and Das, G. D. Postnatal origins of microneurones in the rat brain. *Nature,* 1965, 207, 953-956.

Brackbill, Y., and Thompson, G. G. (Eds.). *Behavior in Infancy and Early Childhood.* New York: Free Press, 1967.

Lipsitt, L. P., and Reese, H. W. *Experimental Child Psychology.* New York: Academic Press, 1970.

Papoušek, H. Conditioning during early postnatal development. In Y. Brackbill and G. G. Thompson (Eds.). *Behavior in Infancy and Childhood.* New York: Free Press, 1967, pp. 259-274. (a)

Papoušek, H. Experimental studies of appetitional behavior in human newborns and infants. In H. W. Stevenson, E. H. Hess, and H. L. Rheingold (Eds.). *Early Behavior: Comparative and Developmental Approaches.* New York: Wiley, 1967, pp. 249-278. (b)

Papoušek, H., and Bernstein, P. The functions of conditioning stimulation in human neonates and infants. In A. Ambrose (Ed.). *Stimulation in Early Infancy.* New York: Academic Press, 1969, pp. 229-247.

Thoman, E. B., and Arnold, W. J. Incubator rearing in infant rats without the mother: Effects on adult emotionality and learning. *Develop. Psychobiol.,* 1968, 1, 219-222. (a)

Thoman, E. B., and Arnold, W. J. Effects of incubator rearing with social deprivation on maternal behavior in rats. *J. Comp. Physiol. Psychol.,* 1968, 65, 441-446. (b)

26 Operant Conditioning of Head Turning in Four-Month Infants

Abstract

Operant conditioning of head turning in 4-mo. human infants was demonstrated. Head rotations to the right or left of a central position were selectively strengthened by experimental presentation of milk as a reinforcing stimulus. Reliable acquisition and extinction of left or right rotations were found for two experimental groups while a control group for eliciting effects of milk presentation showed no consistent changes over conditioning phases.

Introduction

The current status of operant work with children in the first year of life has been evaluated in a recent review (Lipsitt, 1963) of the experimental investigations in this area. Some of these investigators (e. g., Brackbill, 1958; Rheingold et al., 1959; Weisberg, 1963) explored the use of operant techniques with infants as young as 3 mo. old, demonstrating conditioning by using a complex reinforcing stimulus consisting of auditory, visual, and tactile components. However, further development of operant procedures with infants in their first months of life has confronted researchers with two major problems; (1) identification of responses in the infant's behavior which can be quantified and automatically recorded; and (2) identification of reinforcing stimuli which can be manipulated experimentally in a laboratory setting.

A series of recent studies by Papousek (1959, 1960), using a combination of classical and operant techniques to study the head turning response in infants, suggested the possibility of exploring this response within an operant framework. The present study represents the first of several in progress investigating the head rotation response in infants.

Method

The Ss were three groups of 10 infants, approximately 120 days old, participating in an on-going Child Development Study.[*] They were studied between 10 and 11:30 a.m., and between 1:30 and 3 p.m., from 60 to 180 min. after last feeding.

The apparatus consisted of a commercially-made infant reclining-seat on which was mounted a head cradle, constructed of light-weight plastic and lined with foam plastic. The cradle was adjustable for in-

Reprinted from *Psychonomic Science 1*:223–224, 1964.

This research was conducted while the author was a Postdoctoral Fellow of the United States Public Health Service. It was supported in part by a USPHS research grant (No. NB-04268) to Lewis P. Lipsitt, whose valuable advice during the course of this investigation is gratefully acknowledged.

*National Collaborative Project of the National Institute of Neurological Diseases and Blindness.

dividual head size and body length. A potentiometer circuit recorded changes in potential, occurring with head rotations, on a Model 5 Grass Polygraph. Sensitivity on the polygraph was set to give directional deflections of 15 mm from baseline with 45° rotations of the head cradle to the right or left from a central (neutral) position. In this study a head turn was defined as a rotation of 45° or greater to the right or left of the central position (maximum turn of 90°). A sighting device on the head cradle allowed E to discriminate rotations in excess of 45° without reference to the polygraph record. Agreement between visual discriminations of 45° turns and pen deflections of 15 mm was essentially perfect.

An experimental chamber, measuring 36 x 30 x 40 in, constructed of white enameled plywood, standing 3 ft above the floor, and open on one side, provided Ss with an environment devoid of distracting visual stimuli during conditioning procedures. The Ss were secured in the infant-seat and placed in the chamber, facing the blank white walls and ceiling, with their backs toward the open end of the box. The E and parent stood directly behind the infant's head at the open end of the chamber, outside the S's visual field. During conditioning procedures a nursing bottle could be presented by E from behind the S, and each presentation was registered on the polygraph record by an event marker activated with a foot switch.

An 8-min. conditioning procedure was used which consisted of the following: 1-min. baseline, 3-min. conditioning, 2-min. extinction, and finally a 2-min. reconditioning period. The reinforcing stimulus was the presentation of a nursing bottle containing milk to the S's mouth for a 3-sec. interval. For Group R+ the reinforcing stimulus was presented immediately following each head turn of 45° to the right. Group C provided control for the arousal and/or eliciting effect of milk presentation on head rotations. Individual control Ss were matched with experimental Ss in Group R+ on number of milk presentations over conditioning and reconditioning phases, but milk presentation was not contingent upon turning to the right. Rather, the bottle was presented according to a randomized schedule for these infants. A third group of infants, Group L+ received the nursing bottle contingent upon head rotation of 45° to the left.

Following each head turn, Ss' heads were recentered by E. For the two experimental groups, if S failed to emit a 45° turn in the specified direction over the first 30 sec. of conditioning, an attempt was made to shape the response by reinforcing turns of a smaller magnitude. However, only emitted head turns in excess of 45° were recorded as responses. Group R+ required virtually no shaping of the right turning response, while occasionally shaping of the left turn response was required for Group L+.

Results

The results for the three groups are summarized in Fig. 1. A Kruskal-Wallis one-way analysis of variance showed no significant difference between baseline response levels of right or left head turning for the three experimental groups. To test for evidence of typical acquisition and extinction effects of conditioning procedures, a series of Wilcoxon-matched-pairs signed-ranks tests were used to analyze shifts in number of head turns within each group over the conditioning phases. Group R+ demonstrated a significant increase in head turns to the right between baseline and third minute of conditioning (p < .025) and between baseline and first minute of extinction (p < .005), a decrease between first and second minutes of extinction (p < .005), and subsequently an increase in right turns between the second extinction minute and last minute of reconditioning (p < .005). Group L+ and Group C failed to show any significant shifts in right head turning over these conditioning phases. A similar analysis of shifts in number of head rotations to the left yielded no significant changes for Group R+ and Group C over these comparisons. On the other hand, Group L+ shifted significantly (p < .01) in number of left turns on each of the four comparisons.

A final analysis of the data determined whether Group R+ differed from Ss who received random presentations of a milk bottle, Group C, in number of right turns emitted during basal, conditioning, extinction and reconditioning phases of the experiment. Mann-Whitney U Tests yielded no significant differences for baseline response levels, or between response levels during the second minute of extinction, but predicted significant difference was found for the third conditioning minute (p < .001) for the first minute of extinction (p < .002), and for the last minute of the reconditioning phase (p < .002).

Discussion

In the design of this study, Group C provided a control for arousal and/or eliciting effects of milk presentation upon the head turning response. Although Ss in the control group received the same number of reinforcements as infants in Group R+, milk was presented in a random noncontingent manner. Comparisons between these two groups clearly indicate that the reliable acquisition and extinction of a right head turning response for Group R+ cannot be attributed to the arousal or eliciting effects of the reinforcing stimulus.

Furthermore, the data from this study demonstrate that direction of turning (right vs left) can be strengthened selectively through differential reinforcement. A preliminary investigation had shown consistently higher base-rate for turning right as compared with left turns across a group of 4-mo. infants. Examination of the baseline data for the three groups in Fig. 1 supports this previous finding. However, despite the relatively low base-rate for left turns in this population of 4-mo. infants, the results for Group L+ demonstrate reliable acquisition and extinction of the left turn response. Examination of the learning curve for this group reflects differentiation of left head turns from right turning as a function of reinforcing contingencies during conditioning and extinction phases.

These results show that the head turning response in 4-mo. infants can be brought under operant control when brief presentation of a standard nursing bottle is used as a reinforcing event. Under the mild deprivation conditions of this study, the experimental procedures appeared to be minimally aversive to Ss. Generally, procedures could be completed without eliciting crying or other aversive behavior. On the basis of these results, further use is being made of these techniques in studying discriminative and learning processes in the young infant.

References

BRACKBILL, YVONNE. Extinction of the smiling response in infants as a function of reinforcement schedule. *Child Developm.*, 1958, 29, 115-124.

LIPSITT, L. P. Learning in the first year of life. In L. P. Lipsitt & C. C. SPIKER (Eds.), Advances in child development and behavior. New York: Academic Press, 1963. Pp. 147-195.

PAPOUSEK, H. A method of studying conditioned food reflexes in young children up to the age of six months. *Pavlov J. higher nerv. Activ.*, 1959, 9, 136-140.

PAPOUSEK, H. Conditioned head rotation reflexes in infants in the first months of life. *Acta Pediatr.*, 1961, 50, 565-576.

RHEINGOLD, HARRIET L., GEWIRTZ, J. L., & ROSS, HELEN W. Social conditioning of vocalizations in the infant. *J. comp. physiol. Psychol.*, 1959, 52, 68-73.

WEISBERG, P. Social and nonsocial conditioning of infant vocalizations. *Child Developm.*, 1963, 34, 377-388.

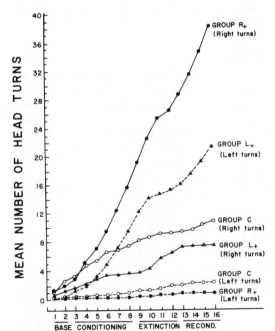

Fig. 1. Cumulative curves showing the mean response rate of right turns and left turns, for the three experimental groups, for 30-sec. periods during baseline, conditioning, extinction and reconditioning phases.

LEWIS P. LIPSITT & HERBERT KAYE

27   Conditioned Sucking in the Human Newborn

Abstract

Classical conditioning of the sucking response was demonstrated. Sucking in response to a tone was greater in infants who received paired presentations of the tone and a sucking device than in infants who received unpaired presentations of the same stimuli.

Problem

To determine whether classical conditioning is possible within the first days of human life, a tone was used as a conditioning stimulus (CS), and insertion of a nipple in the baby's mouth to elicit sucking movements constituted the unconditioned stimulus (UCS). If conditioning takes place, more sucking to the tone should occur following paired presentations of CS and UCS (experimental group, E) than following unpaired presentations (control group, C).

Method

Two groups of 10 hospital Ss in their third or fourth day were studied between 8 and 9:15 a. m., at least 3 hrs. after the previous feeding. For both groups, the CS was a low-frequency, loud (about 93 db) square-wave tone with a fundamental component of 23 cps and lasting 15 sec. For Group E, the nipple [2] was inserted in the infant's mouth 1 sec. after onset of the CS and remained to the end of the 15-sec.

Reprinted from *Psychonomic Science* 1:29–30, 1964.

[1] The writers thank Mrs. Dorothy Westlake for her assistance. This study was carried out as part of a project entitled Sensory Discrimination and Learning in Human Infants under a USPHS grant (NB-04268) to Lewis P. Lipsitt. The writers are indebted to the staff of the Providence Lying-In Hospital for their co-operation.

[2] The non-nutritive nipple used was an automatic device for the recording of sucking responses developed by Grunzke (1961) for work with monkeys. For work with humans, Levin and Kaye (1964) adapted this stainless-steel mouthpiece, shaped like a nipple and containing a small lever attached to a microswitch, by covering it with a sterile rubber nipple. As the infant sucks, the lever is depressed and released, producing digital blips on a polygraph record.

CS. For Group C, the CS and UCS were not paired; the nipple was inserted for 14 sec. approximately 30 sec. following offset of the CS.

All Ss first received 5 basal trials of CS alone. Presence and number of sucking movements to each 15-sec. tone were recorded independently by 2 Os. These trials were administered approximately 1 min. apart. Both groups then received 25 training trials, every 5th trial being a test in which sucking responses to the CS alone were recorded. For Group E, CS and UCS were paired for 14 sec. on the 20 conditioning trials. On these trials, Group C received the CS and UCS stimulations with a variable interval of 25-45 sec. (average, 30 sec.) between offset of CS and introduction of UCS. For Group E, intertrial interval was 1 min.; for Group C about 30 sec. Thus the conditioning session for Group E took approximately 31 min.; for Group C, about 38 min.

Following the conditioning period, all Ss received no less than 10 nor more than 30 extinction trials like the basal trials, these being discontinued when no responses occurred for 3 successive trials, the extinction criterion.

Results

O agreement was high for both measures, the results being essentially identical when each O's results were considered independently. Averages for both Os are plotted in Fig. 1 for the three phases of the study: 5 basal trials, 5 CS trials during conditioning, and 2 blocks of 5 extinction or test trials. The per cent measure, indicating proportions of trials in which sucking occurred during CS-alone presentations, showed an increase for Group E from beginning to end of the session, while this measure leveled off for Group C. A similar trend was present for the number-of-sucks measure. Analyses of variance for both measures yielded highly significant interactions between groups and phases [F (3, 54) = 19.4 and 12.3, p < .001, respectively], indicating increasing differences between groups over time. Individual Ss in Group E showed a significantly greater amount of change from basal to extinction periods in both per cent of response and number of sucks [t (18) = 2.14 and t (18) = 2.41, p < .05, respectively]. Finally, the trials-to-criterion measure in extinction showed that Group E gave responses on the average of 24.1 of 30 trials compared with 11.1 for Group C [t (18) = 2.42, p < .05].

Discussion

The study design attempted to control for sensitization or pseudoconditioning (Wickens & Wickens, 1940) by giving both groups identical stimulation but in different CS-UCS temporal relationships. There are two indications that this procedure did not completely eliminate such an effect: (1) Group C gave slightly (not significantly) more responses to CS than

ditioning session for the experimental Ss. Thus sucking is an efficient response for administering many paired CS-UCS presentations in a brief period.

These data agree with a much earlier experiment by Marquis (1931) and, more recently, with Papoušek (1961) that conditioning of responses involving mouth-stimulation can occur in newborns, and contrast with reservations expressed by Kessen (1963) and Scott (1963). While age-determined changes in conditioning rate apparently occur (Kantrow, 1937; Morgan and Morgan, 1944; Papoušek, 1961), failures to establish conditioning in neonates may be due as much to the use of ineffective experimental techniques as to chronological or neurophysiological deficiencies.

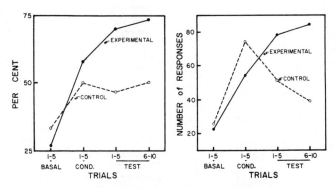

Fig. 1. Percentage and number of sucking responses to the CS (tone) in the Experimental and Control Groups.

Group E during the conditioning period, and (2) Group C responded more during the extinction phase than during the basal phase. When the individual averages from the basal trials of Group C are compared with averages from the first 10 extinction trials, the t is 2.45 for the per cent measure (df = 9, p < .05) and for the number-of-sucks measure, the t is 2.59 (p < .05). Thus the Group C treatment was itself effective in increasing response, possibly due to (1) sensitization, (2) the unlikely possibility of trace conditioning having occurred in Group C, or (3) increase in hunger or other arousing condition, 35-40 min. having elapsed between the basal and extinction periods. Regardless, it has been established that the paired stimulation administered to Group E increased response more than did the control condition.

While 20 paired presentations of CS and UCS constitute a relatively small number of trials, the frequency of sucking during presentation of the UCS is such as to produce many "pairings" within each trial. Groups E and C responded with means of 13.1 and 13.0 sucks, respectively, per nipple presentation, and they did not differ over trials in numbers of sucks made to successive UCS presentations. If each sucking response is considered independently, then an average of 260 "pairings" of CS and UCS occurred in the con-

References

Grunzke, M. E. A liquid dispenser for primates. *J. exp. Anal. Beh.*, 1961, 4, 326.

Kantrow, R. W. An investigation of conditioned feeding responses and concomitant adaptive behavior in young infants. *Univ. Ia. Stud. Child Welf.*, 1937, 13, No. 3.

Kessen, W. Research in the psychological development of children. *Merrill Palmer Quart.*, 1963, 9, 83–94.

Levin, G. R., and Kaye, H. Non-nutritive sucking by human neonates. *Child Developm.*, 1964. In press.

Marquis, D. P. Can conditioned responses be established in the newborn infant? *J. genet. Psychol.*, 1931, 39, 479–492.

Morgan, J. J. B., and Morgan, S. S. Infant learning as a developmental index. *J. genet. Psychol.*, 1944, 65, 281–289.

Papoušek, H. Conditioned head rotation reflexes in infants in the first months of life. *Acta Pediatr.*, 1961, 50, 565–576.

Scott, J. P. The process of primary socialization in canine and human infants. *Monogr. Soc. Res. Child Developm.*, 1963, 28, No. 1.

Wickens, D. D. and Wickens, C. A study of conditioning in the neonate. *J. exp. Psychol.*, 1940, 26,

28 Learning in the Neonatal Rat

The age at which animals become capable of learning has long been of interest. Conditioned responses have been reported for puppies at 10 days of age (Stanley *et al.*, 1963), for monkeys at 3 days (Mason & Harlow, 1958), and in the human infant at 4 days of age (Lipsitt & Kaye, 1964; Siqueland & Lipsitt, 1966). Volokhov (1959) presented a table which indicated that conditioning was found in the puppy and in the one-day-old guinea pig. For the rat, Caldwell & Werboff (1962) have reported conditioned leg withdrawal within 24 hr after birth. The results were statistically significant although the highest level of performance was only 32 per cent for one experimental group. Studies of early learning have generally been plagued by low, inconsistent response levels. An exception to this rule is Siqueland & Lipsitt's study (1966) of human infants, in which a head-turning response was conditioned from a base line level of probability of 0·18 to 0·73 by the end of the training. The unique demonstration of such highly reliable response elicitation suggests that immature organisms may be capable of much greater behavioural flexibility than has so far been considered possible. But whatever capacities do exist, they will be revealed only with improved procedures together with selection of the most appropriate stimuli and responses to be associated.

The present study was designed to present evidence of learning capacity of neonatal rats. Behavioural modification was achieved by manipulating suckling and generalized approach responses, which are the primary components of the response system at that young age. These responses, elicited by the mother under normal rearing conditions, were attached to neutral stimuli by means of a procedure which isolated the animals at birth, permitting substitutes for maternal stimuli.

During the first 3 days of life the isolated animals were maintained in an incubator in which, instead of physical contact with a mother rat, they were exposed to an inanimate surrogate, a warm, moist pulsating tubular object. The surrogate, like a live mother rat, reinforced approach responses with warmth and stimulation. One objective of this study was to demonstrate that such a variation in early stimulus conditions would lead to differential responding to the surrogate and to a live mother rat.

In addition to an artificial source of tactual comfort, the isolated animals were never allowed to suckle from the mother but were force-fed with a small feeding tube. Such a procedure permitted nourishment intake to be associated with mouth movements and stimulation accompanying input of the feeder tube rather than with suckling from a rat mother's nipple. The second objective of the study was to demonstrate that this variation in feeding experience would lead to modification in responding to the feeder tube and to a live mother rat.

Methods

Subjects

Sixty infant rat pups, the offspring of six Sprague-Dawley females which had been mated with Long Evans males, were used as subjects in the experiment. At birth five experimental groups or 'litters' were formed by selecting one male and one female from each of the six original litters. Hence, each of the five experimental groups contained twelve pups, two from each of six natural litters. During the first 3 days after birth these groups of twelve pups were treated in the following manners: one group of pups, *incubator*, had no further contact with a mother rat. Instead, they were maintained in an incubator from which they were removed for tube feeding every 4 hr.

A group of twelve pups, *untreated*, was placed with a foster mother and remained undisturbed until tested.

A group, *handled*, was placed with a foster mother, but each pup was handled every 4 hr for a period equivalent to that required for feeding an *incubator* pup. This group was included in order to isolate handling as a possible factor in differential responding in the test situation.

A *tube* group was also placed with a foster mother and handled every 4 hr, but they were additionally stimulated with a clean, empty feeding tube. This group was designed to provide evidence of behavioural consequences of presentation of the feeding stimuli to the pups without any nutritional reinforcement.

The remaining group of twelve pups, *quinine*, were included to test for possible conditioning of an avoidance response to an aversive stimulus. These pups were placed with a foster mother, handled and stimulated with the insertion of a

Reprinted from *Animal Behaviour 16*: 54–57, 1968.

This research was supported by NIH research grant MHO7435, NIH postdoctoral fellowship 5 F2 MH-28, 306–02, NIMH Biological Sciences Training Grant MH 08304, and NIH research career development award 5–K3–MH–19, 936.

feeding tube, but for them the tube was first dipped in a quinine solution. Thus, the stimulus conditions were equivalent to those for the feeding situation with the exception that an aversive stimulus replaced the nutritional input.

The incubator pups were kept in a temperature-controlled, water-bath type incubator. A length of dialysing tubing, with warm, moist, pulsating characteristics, served as a surrogate mother. The pups were fed through a stomach tube, inserted every 4 hr, a total of eighteen feedings or trials, during the 3 days of treatment. Details of the incubator and surrogate design, as well as the feeding formula and procedure are described elsewhere (Thoman, 1968).

Testing

On the 3rd day after birth all pups were offered in a random order from the groups to an experimentally naive judge for ratings of responses to several stimuli.

First the pups were held in the hand for 1 min and observed to determine whether or not there were body wriggling and mouth movements. A 'plus' score was given only if the wriggling was a generalized, continuous and intense overall activity.

Next, the pup's response to stimulation of the lips with a dry feeding tube was observed. Body wriggling was scored 'plus' if there was an increase in activity coincident with the presence of the tube, and vocalization was also noted.

Thirdly, responses to the actual insertion of an empty feeding tube were scored. Separate three-point rating scales were used for mouth insertion and insertion into the stomach. A 'plus' was given for mouth opening or suckling, 'zero' was recorded if there was no movement and 'minus' if there was activity but of such a nature as to force the tube out of the pup's mouth.

In addition to observations of the feeding situation a preference test for a mother rat or a surrogate tube was conducted. Two groups, incubator and untreated, which differed in this rearing experience, were compared. For this test, a lactating female, anaesthetized with Nembutal,* was placed on her side on a table top over which surgical gauze had been stretched. Three in. away, and parallel to the female, the surrogate tube was placed on the table. The distance separating the two stimulus objects was marked off into three 1-in. lanes.

The test procedure consisted of placing a pup in a central position in the middle lane, then observing the animal for a period of 3 min, recording the animal's lane position every 15 sec (twelve observations). At the same time, notes

*There is a minimal temperature loss in anaesthetized lactating rats (manuscript in preparation). During testing the rat's temperature dropped less than 1°C.

were made of contact with the mother or the surrogate and of the nature of the contact such as rooting or climbing on either stimulus object or suckling from the mother.

Results

Table I summarizes the results obtained from the judgments of responses to handling. The responsiveness of the incubator pups on both measures is distinctly different from that of any or all of the other four groups.

Table I. Responses of Pups to Being Picked up and Held in Hand

Group	No. of Pups Tested†	Per Cent of Group Showing Body Wriggling	Mouth Movements
Untreated	12	16·7	0·0
Handled	11	18·2	9·1
Tube	12	0·0	0·0
Quinine	12	16·7	0·0
Incubator	10	80·0	40·0

†Two incubator pups and a handled one died during the 3 days of treatment.

Table II summarizes the results for lip stimulation with the feeding tube; and here, the dichotomy of responsiveness of the incubator and the other four groups is almost complete. Only one out of the forty-seven pups in the latter groups responded with body wriggling

Table II. Responses of Pups to Stimulation of Lips with Feeding Tube

Group	No. of Pups Tested	Per Cent of Group Showing Body Wriggling	Squealing
Untreated	12	0·0	0·0
Handled	11	0·0	0·0
Tube	12	8·3	0·0
Quinine	12	0·0	0·0
Incubator	10	100·0	100·0

and none squealed, as against 100 per cent responsiveness of the incubator animals on both measures.

Table III summarizes the results obtained from judgments of responses to insertion of the tube into the mouth and down the oesophagus. Both tube-treated groups showed more negative responses on both measures than any of the other groups. The quinine group showed the largest number of negative responses to mouth insertion; however these differences were not found to be statistically significant using the ordered 2 × c contingency table. The difference between the incubator group and the other four groups was highly significant, $P < 0.001$, for both measures. The differences were most marked in the positive and negative categories, with the incubator group showing more postive and fewer cases of negative responses.

The results of the preference observations were inconclusive as far as preference for the mother or surrogate was concerned: of the twelve untreated pups only four moved at all, while the others remained immobile throughout the 3-min test. Of the four that did move, only one moved into an adjacent lane, and then remained quiescent. The other three moved directly to the mother, found a nipple and suckled during the remainder of the test.

On the other hand, although the behaviour of the incubator animals did not clearly indicate a preference, it was clearly distinctive from that of the untreated animals. All animals moved, the mean number of changes in lanes during the test being 5·1. They contacted both of the stimuli with equal frequency. The mean number of contacts with the lactating female was 3·5, with the surrogate, 3·4. Three pups did not contact the female at any time and three did not contact the surrogate at any time.

Learning influences were also demonstrated by the incubator animals' differential responses to the stimuli of the lactating female and the surrogate. Four of the incubator animals spent some time, 2 to 3 min, leaned on, or draped over, the surrogate, but none of the incubator animals who made contact with the lactating female responded to her in this manner. Moreover, none of the nine incubator pups which made contact with the lactating mother did any suckling although the three untreated pups which made such contact suckled at once.

Discussion

Using feeding and generalized approach responses, these results provide definite evidence for learning in neonatal rats.

After only eighteen trials, or feedings, force-fed animals responded to stimuli associated with food injection in a manner which was dramatically different from that of animals suckled by the mother.

Although there was no clear evidence of preference for a mother or mother surrogate in either group, the very high motility level of the incubator animals represented a marked modification of behaviour as the consequence of different stimulus conditions. The rearing conditions were such as to require greater mobility on the part of the incubator animals. In the normal situation it is the mother who takes the initiative in maintaining conditions at an optimum level for the young by transporting them to the nest etc., whereas the incubator animals had a surrogate which remained passive and stationary. These pups, in order to receive warmth and stimulation, had to move themselves to the surrogate and to climb on or root under it. And they did exactly that: they were continually on, under, or oriented towards the surrogate while in the incubator.

Identification of learning as a factor in very early behaviour is quite consistent with evidence for plasticity of the immature organism, provided by the numerous early experience studies, more specifically with the findings that the rat is sensitive to some stimulation effects in the first

Table III. Responses of Pups to Insertion of Clean Empty Feeding Tube

Group	No. of Pups Tested	Insertion into Mouth. Per Cent of Group Showing Mouth Response*			Insertion down Oesophagus. Per Cent of Group Showing Mouth-tongue Movement†		
		+	0	—	+	0	—
Untreated	12	16·7	50·0	33·0	0·0	25·0	75·0
Handled	11	27·3	45·5	27·3	0·0	45·5	54·5
Tube	12	16·7	41·7	41·7	0·0	8·3	91·8
Quinine	12	16·7	24·9	58·1	0·0	8·3	91·8
Incubator	10	70·0	30·0	0·0	40·0	40·0	20·0

*Mouth response definitions: + Mouth open, or suckling
      0 Mouth shut but tube could be inserted readily
      — Mouth tightly shut, pressure required to force the feeding tube into mouth was sufficient to bend it.
†Mouth-tongue movement definitions:
      + suckling
      0 No movement
      — Tongue actively moving in a manner judged to be attempted ejection of the tube.

week of life (Levine, 1962; Denenberg & Bell, 1960). Studies of early experience have been concerned with the effects of early stimulation on later behaviour, usually of the mature animal. The study of neonatal learning adds another dimension to a possible understanding of behavioural development. To the extent that response patterns can be influenced by stimulus variations, such response differences should participate in the long-run effects of early stimulation. It should not be necessary for specific stimulus-response associations to be retained throughout maturation, but only that response systems at any one stage should be a part of the total organism affected by subsequent experience.

Summary

For the first 3 days after birth, five groups of rats were differentially reared in order to vary learning opportunities. One of the groups was reared in an incubator and tube-fed. The other four groups were reared by foster mothers, and three of these groups were additionally treated with stimulus components of the artificial feeding situation.

After only eighteen feedings, or learning trials, incubator-reared pups were found to respond to being handled and to being stimulated with the feeding tube with very active wriggling, squealing and suckling movements, whereas most untreated pups either did not respond or responded negatively to the test stimuli.

In a test situation in which a pup could orient towards either a surrogate mother or a live rat mother, the untreated pups did not move to make a choice. Rather than indicating group preferences, this test revealed a striking difference between untreated and incubator-reared pups in their activity level.

REFERENCES

Caldwell, D. F. & Werboff, J. (1962). Classical conditioning in newborn rats. *Science*, **136**, 3522, 1118–1119.

Denenberg, V. H. & Bell, R. W. (1960). Critical periods for the effects of infantile experience on adult learning. *Science*, **131**, 227–228.

Levine, S. (1962). The psychophysiological effect on infantile stimulation. In *Roots of Behavior* (ed. by E. Bliss). New York: Paul Hoeber.

Lipsitt, L. P. & Kaye, H. (1964). Conditioned sucking in the human newborn. *Psychon. Sci.*, **1**, 29–30.

Mason, W. A. & Harlow, H. F. (1958). Formation of conditioned responses in infant monkeys. *J. comp. physiol. Psychol.*, **51**, 68–70.

Stanley, W. C., Cornwell, A. C., Poggiani, C. & Trattner, A. (1963). Conditioning in the neonate puppy. *J. comp. physiol. Psychol.*, **56**, 211–214.

Siqueland, E. R. & Lipsitt, L. P. (1966). Conditioned head turning in human newborne. *J. exp. Child Psychol.*, **3**, 356–376.

Thoman, Evelyn (1968). Effects of early social deprivation in maternal behavior in the rat. *J. comp. physiol. Psychol.* (in press).

Volokhov, A. A. (1959). Comparative-physiological investigation of conditioned and unconditioned reflexes during ontogeny. (USSR). *Pavlov J. higher nerv. Activ.*, **9**, 49–60.

WALTER C. STANLEY. ANNE CRISTAKE CORNWELL, CONSTANCE POGGIANI, & ALICE TRATTNER

29   Conditioning in the Neonatal Puppy

To determine whether appetitive and aversive conditioning is possible in the puppy less than 2 weeks old, 26 Shetland sheepdog and cocker spaniel puppies were divided into 3 groups and received 7 days of conditioning. They had a mean age of 3 days when training began and a mean age of 10 days when training ended. In each group the CS was a 5-sec. insertion of a manometer nipple into S's mouth. In the positive group the CS was paired with nipple-dropper-feeding of milk; in the neutral group, with reinsertion of the manometer nipple, and in the negative group, with nipple-dropper-"feeding" of a quinine solution. Sucking behavior and struggling by Ss occurred during the CS as expected from the conditions of reinforcement. It was concluded that both appetitive and aversive conditioning can occur in the neonatal puppy and that previous failures to obtain conditioning were due to inadequate conditions for learning rather than to any general unconditionability of the neonatal puppy.

Reprinted from *Journal of Comparative and Physiological Psychology 56*:211–214, 1963. Copyright 1963 by the American Psychological Association and reproduced by permission.

The purpose of this experiment was to determine whether the neonatal puppy, that is, one less than 2 weeks of age, can be appetitively and aversively conditioned. Doubt and disagreement exist concerning the existence of conditioning in the neonatal puppy. It has been concluded (Scott, 1958) on the basis of naturalistic observation (Scott & Marston, 1950) that neonatal puppies give no indication that they learn as adults do, but Volokhov (1959) presents a table in which food-reinforced conditioning is said to occur at 1 day of age. Some aversive conditioning has been found at about 2 weeks of age (Cornwell & Fuller, 1961; Volokhov, 1959), and stable appetitive and aversive conditioning has been obtained in 15-day-old puppies (Kliavina, Kobakova, Stel'makh, & Troshikhin, 1958), but, insofar as the authors are aware, no evidence has been published to show that aversive conditioning occurs in the neonatal puppy.

To maximize the probability of finding both appetitive and aversive conditioning, the present experiment: (*a*) used stimuli and measured or rated responses well within the sensorimotor abilities of the neonatal puppy; (*b*) deprived Ss of food to increase their sensitivity to tactile and liquid stimuli injected into their mouths; and (*c*) used a classical conditioning procedure which assured objectivity in *E*'s handling and stimulating Ss, but was "impure" in that it contained components of operant conditioning so that a variety of the parameters known to affect conditioned behavior could be operative.

METHOD

Subjects

The Ss were 21 Shetland sheepdog puppies and 5 cocker spaniels, the progeny of stock maintained at Hamilton Station of the Jackson Memorial Lab-

Conduct of this research and preparation of this paper were supported in part by a grant from the Ford Foundation and in part by USPHS Research Grant M-4412 from the Institute of Mental Health, United States Public Health Service. The authors wish to thank J. L. Fuller for the loan of some of the equipment used, and Thomas C. Snell and Stephen F. Schell for aid in the analysis of data. A preliminary report of the findings was presented at 1960 meetings of the Psychonomic Society, Chicago, Illinois.

oratory. Their mean age on the first day of training was 3 days, range 1 to 5 days; their mean age on the seventh and last day of training was 10 days, range 7 to 13 days.

Apparatus

The apparatus consisted of a bellows manometer with a pointer that rode over Teledeltos paper moving at a constant speed. One end of a flexible tubing was attached to the manometer. The other end had a glass tube covered with soft rubber—a simulated bitch's nipple. Soft rubber, identical in size and shape to that on the manometer tube, was put on the glass ends of two ordinary eye droppers used for injection of milk and quinine solution. The *E* timed his actions by a stop watch. A 1-cps time marker rode on the Teledeltos paper. The marker

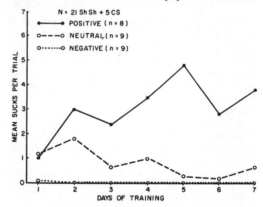

FIG. 1. Mean number of sucks per trial during CS presentation, as a function of days of training.

served as a check on *E*'s timing and also provided a base for counting individual sucks on the record.

Procedure

Twenty-four Ss were divided into eight trios, whose members were matched as to sex, breed, and litter insofar as possible. The members of each trio were then randomly assigned to one of three groups: a positive group to receive milk, a neutral group to receive no liquid, and a negative group to receive a quinine solution. The remaining two cocker spaniel Ss were randomly assigned to the neutral and the negative groups.

Each trial was conducted as follows: The *S* was picked up and held for 10 sec. Then the motor drive of the recorder was started, and 5 sec. later the manometer nipple (CS) was inserted into *S*'s mouth and kept there for 5 sec. Five seconds after removal of the manometer nipple, the *S* in the positive group was dropper-fed for 15 sec. with 0.5 cc of milk made from Esbilac (a powdered simulated bitch's milk sold by the Borden Company) and water. Thus, the US was dropper nipple plus milk in the mouth. The timing of this procedure was a classical conditioning one. But, since *S* could suck prior to the delivery of milk, the procedure, temporally, contained elements of instrumental conditioning.

The timing of events was exactly the same in all three groups. Neutral group Ss, however, received no liquid. Instead, the manometer nipple was simply reinserted in their mouths for 15 sec. Negative group Ss were dropper-"fed" for 15 sec. with 0.5 cc of quinine hydrochloride solution—500 mg/100 cc of water.

Using a nontoxic bitter-tasting substance, sucrose octa-acetate (Warren & Pfaffmann, 1959), instead of quinine hydrochloride was considered but rejected since the latencies of response both by several puppies and by Es seemed slow, being as long as 5 to 10 sec. It was assumed that the quantity of the quinine solution which might be ingested would be too small to produce any significant toxicity and, in fact, negative group Ss' weight gains were quite comparable to those of Ss in the other two groups.

On each day of training, the Ss were separated from the dam in the morning 5 to 6 hr. prior to the start of the afternoon conditioning session. The Ss received 10 trials per day, 8 paired CS-US presentations and 2 CS-alone presentations, for 7 days, with at least 10 min. between successive trials within a session. Scheduling difficulties required that occasionally less than 10 trials be given on a particular day and that up to 2 days occasionally intervene between successive training days.

Sucking behavior, as recorded on the Teledeltos paper by the manometer pointer, was the index of positive or appetitive conditioning; vigor of struggling by S as rated by E on a 0- to 3-point scale was the index of negative or aversive conditioning.

RESULTS

Positive or Appetitive Conditioning

Sucking records were examined in two ways: first, in terms of mean number of sucks per trial or CS presentation, the most sensitive measure available; second, in terms of percentage of trials during which measurable sucking behavior occurred, a less sensitive but common measure of conditioning.

Figure 1 shows mean number of sucks per trial plotted on days of training. The curves diverge as expected from the conditions of reinforcement, the positive group improving, the neutral group declining, and the negative group being markedly suppressed in performance. Friedman's nonparametric test performed on Days 2 to 7 data of the eight trios of Ss yielded a p less than .01. The p's on two-tailed Wilcoxon paired replicates tests for all the two-group comparisons were .01 or less.

A comparable and reliable divergence in performance occurred with the percentage trials measure, the positive group responding on 45% of the trials on Day 7, the neutral group on 12%, and the negative group on 0%. On Day 1 the overall percentage of responding was 16.

The most convincing evidence for learning, however, comes from an analysis of the responding during the CS Trial 1 of each session after Day 1 because such data cannot be confounded by possible arousal or suppressive effects of stimulation perseverating from one trial to the next within a session. Mean number of sucks per day were 2.0, 0.1, and 0 for the positive, neutral, and negative groups, respectively. The corresponding means for number of days on which sucking occurred were 1.8, 0.4, and 0. For mean number of sucks per trial, the Friedman p was less than .01, and the positive group is markedly superior to the other two groups, the p for each comparison being .02. For number of days on which sucking occurred, the less sensitive measure, the Friedman p was greater than .05. However, if one makes the further reasonable assumption that all that needs to be demonstrated is superiority of the positive group over the other two groups, and directly calculates Wilcoxon two-tailed p's for these two crucial comparisons, the p for the positive-neutral difference is .05, and that for the positive-negative difference is .02.

Negative or Aversive Conditioning

The ratings of vigor of struggling were examined in the same ways as were the records for sucking behavior. In terms of both measures, the negative group improved in performance, the neutral group stayed about the same, and the positive group showed increasing impairment. Friedman test p's were less than .01 for Days 2 to 7 and all two-group comparison p's were less than .02.

Mean rating of struggling per trial appears in Figure 2. Performance expressed by percentage of trials on which some struggling occurred was 99 on Day 7 for the negative group, 66 for the neutral group, and 41 for the positive group. On Day 1 the overall percentage of responding was 79. The mean rating per trial for the vigor-of-struggling data (four-point scale) for first trials only on Days 2 to 7 of training was

0.8, 1.3, and 2.1 for the positive, neutral, and negative groups, respectively. For mean rating per trial, the more sensitive measure, the Friedman p is .01, and the negative-neutral and the negative-positive differences each have a p of .01. The number of days on which struggling occurred, the less sensitive measure, was 3.8, 5.2, and 5.9 for Days 2 through 7 for the positive, neutral, and negative groups, respectively; the Friedman p is .05. The negative-positive difference p is .01; the neutral-positive difference p is .05.

DISCUSSION

The most sensitive and crucial measures of appetitive and aversive conditioning in the present experiment are mean number of

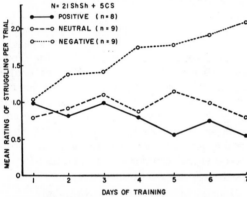

FIG. 2. Mean rating of vigor of struggling per trial during CS presentation, as a function of days of training.

sucks per trial and mean rating of vigor of struggling per trial, on first trials, Days 2 to 7. Both these measures were statistically significant for the most relevant comparisons, positive-neutral and positive-negative for sucking and negative-neutral and negative-positive for struggling. These findings plus the fact that all other group differences are as would be expected from the conditions of reinforcement and are also statistically reliable in the great majority of instances provide convincing proof that both appetitive and aversive conditioning occurs in the neonatal puppy.

The findings are obviously contrary to any contention that the neonatal puppy cannot learn and, further, mean that previous failures to obtain aversive conditioning

(Cornwell & Fuller, 1961; Fuller, Easler, & Banks, 1950; James & Cannon, 1952; Volokhov, 1959) may be attributed to the specific conditioning techniques used rather than the lack of conditionability in the neonatal puppy.

The second important feature of the data is the degree of stability of conditioned behavior which was found. Ordinarily in classical conditioning, the criterion of stability is 80 to 100% occurrence of CRs. The present findings fulfill this criterion in two ways. Sucking behavior was 100% suppressed, and near 100% struggling occurred in the negative group. Thus, not only the first occurrence of conditioning but the degree of stability of the conditioned behavior achieved at a particular age may be attributed to the specific conditioning procedure used, not necessarily to relative unconditionability of the Ss used.

How then might we interpret both the first occurrence and the attainment of a particular degree of stability of conditioned behavior at different ages when different conditioning procedures are used? We suggest that the different procedures reflect different fulfilment of the conditions required for the acquisition and the maintenance of conditioned behavior. By "conditions" we mean the temporal and quantitative properties of variables which affect conditioned behavior, as drive, modality, and intensity of stimuli, class of response required and measured, temporal and quantitative parameters of reinforcing stimuli, etc. In the present experiment, for example, drive was present because Ss were food-deprived; the specific CS, tactile stimulation of the buccal cavity, was distinctive and functional; the responses measured or rated were within the behavior repertory of the neonatal puppy; and the reinforcing stimuli, milk and quinine solution, appeared to elicit responses with a reasonably high probability in most Ss.

These variables by no means exhaust the list of variables known to affect performance during conditioning. Yet, even these were apparently neither maximally effective nor maximally adapted to our specific Ss. For example, although some hunger drive was clearly present in all Ss, it appeared markedly lower in the cocker spaniel than in the

Shetland sheepdog *S*s. The one cocker spaniel in the positive group was seldom observed to suck even when milk was injected into its mouth. Second, the specific CS, the manometer nipple, was not procedurally always equitable in the three groups. After some trials had ensued, the struggling of the negative *S*s became pronounced, and at times, the 5 sec. allowed for the insertion of the manometer nipple would terminate without such insertion being possible. This observation, in turn, suggests that the total functional stimulus pattern in our procedure probably included tactual, kinesthetic, and vestibular components correlated with picking *S* up and holding it during each trial.

Third, although the temporal aspects of procedure were classical, it is possible to interpret the findings as being largely due to operant conditioning components of the procedure. The struggling behavior of negative *S*s could avoid briefly the manometer tube, the stimulus most closely associated with aversive stimulation from quinine; hence, struggling could have been maintained by a Sidman (1953) avoidance schedule. The sucking in positive *S*s could be followed by milk injection, but since milk injection was not contingent on sucking, there would be only accidental or adventitious reinforcement of sucking by milk. It is precisely such adventitious reinforcement which can produce drifts from one class of responding to another, rather than stable maintenance of one class of response (Skinner, 1948).

In general, the present findings show that both appetitive and aversive conditioning is possible in the neonatal puppy and that the resultant behavior can be reasonably stable when conditioning procedures are specifically adapted to the neonatal puppy.

REFERENCES

CORNWELL, A. C., & FULLER, J. L. Conditioned responses in young puppies. *J. comp. physiol. Psychol.*, 1961, **54**, 13–15.

FULLER, J. L., EASLER, C. A., & BANKS, E. M. Formation of conditioned avoidance responses in young puppies. *Amer. J. Physiol.*, 1950, **160**, 462–466.

JAMES, W. T., & CANNON, D. J. Conditioned avoiding responses in puppies. *Amer. J. Physiol.*, 1952, **168**, 251–253.

KLIAVINA, M. P., KOBAKOVA, E. M., STEL'MAKH, L. N., & TROSHIKHIN, V. A. K voprosu o skorosti obrazovaniia uslovnykh refleksov u sobak v ontogeneze. *Zh. vyssh. nervn. Deiatel'.*, 1958, **8**(6), 929–936. (*Psychol. Abstr.*, 34: 838).

SCOTT, J. P. Critical periods in the development of social behavior in puppies. *Psychosom. Med.*, 1958, **20**, 42–54.

SCOTT, J. P., & MARSTON, M. V. Critical periods affecting the development of normal and maladjustive behavior of puppies. *J. genet. Psychol*, 1950, **77**, 25–60.

SIDMAN, M. Avoidance conditioning with brief shock and no exteroceptive warning signal. *Science*, 1953, **118**, 157–158.

SKINNER, B. F. "Superstition" in the pigeon. *J. exp. Psychol.*, 1948, **38**, 168–172.

VOLOKHOV, A. A. Comparative-physiological investigation of conditioned and unconditioned reflexes during ontogeny. *Pavlov J. Higher Nerv. Activ.*, 1959, **9**, 49–60.

WARREN, R. P., & PFAFFMANN, C. Early experience and taste aversion. *J. comp. physiol. Psychol.*, 1959, **52**, 263–266.

J. K. KOVACH & A. KLING

30 Mechanisms of Neonate Sucking Behaviour in the Kitten

The primacy of neonate sucking in the temporal sequence of behaviour development and its uniform presence throughout the divergent branches of mammalia make the study of sucking behaviour important for students interested in the problems of phylogenetic fixity and onto-

Reprinted from *Animal Behaviour 15*:91–101, 1967.

genetic plasticity of behaviour development. Most of the existing literature on sucking including the experiments with animals deal with motivational factors and socialization processes associated with this behaviour, and we have very little direct information on neonate sucking behaviour *per se*. The experiments to be reported here represent an inquiry into the behavioural elements, maturational and experiential factors, and CNS mechanisms associated with neonate sucking. This report will deal with: (1) the changes in the elicitability of reflex sucking at different early ages; (2) the changes in the sucking pattern resulting from experience; (3) the relationships between nutritive and non-nutritive sucking; (4) the effects of complete sucking deprivation and social isolation on the elicitability of the sucking responses; (5) the learning processes associated with neonate sucking and the maturational changes in early learning capacity; and (6) the effects of CNS lesions on sucking behaviour.

Experiment I
Sucking Patterns

This experiment was undertaken for (1) observing the elicitability of the sucking response by an artificial stimulus at progressive early age levels; (2) observing the changes in the sucking patterns resulted by experience; (3) observing the characteristic sucking patterns in well-established sucking behaviour, and (4) studying the relationship between nutritive and non-nutritive sucking.

Method and Procedure. Twelve kittens were used for recording the initial responses to an artificial nipple at birth and at 4, 10, 20, 30 and 40 days of age (N = 2 at each). Four kittens were used for recording the changes in sucking patterns while learning to suck from a feeding bottle and for recording the time spent with nutritive and non-nutritive sucking after the independent sucking habit on the bottle was established. All subjects were born in our laboratory from a breeding colony of 1 male and 7 females.

The subjects used for the recording of the initial sucking patterns were raised with the mother and had no prior experience with the feeding bottle or nipple from which the recordings were taken.

The 4 kittens used for the recording of the longitudinal changes in sucking patterns were separated from the mother at the age of 9 days and were put into isolated compartments of an incubator equipped with feeding boots and bottles (Plate II, Fig. 1). Twenty-four hr after separation from the mother they were started on a programme of learning to suck from the bottle. The training consisted of putting each subject on the bottle four times daily and keeping it in contact with the nipple until one-fourth of the daily portion of one full bottle (25 ml of milk prepared from dry Esbilac formula) was consumed. The daily amount of milk was gradually increased with the subjects' age. The training lasted until the subjects learned to approach and suck from the bottle independently. The sucking patterns were re-corded during the first daily training sessions and after the establishment of independent sucking behaviour, during the first daily encounter with the newly filled feeding bottle on the 14th, 15th, 20th, 21st, 22nd and 32nd day of age. The daily recording sessions lasted 90 min. Only one bottle of milk was given during this period. The records were marked when the milk was used up; any sucking on the empty bottle following the marked point will be referred to as 'non-nutritive sucking'.

The sucking patterns were recorded in the following manner: The free tips of two thin insulated wires were attached inside the wall and near the tip of a flexible rubber nipple (6 mm in diameter at the location of the wire tips). The wires led to the appropriate channels of a standard 8-channel dynograph. The movements of the nipple, corresponding to the oral manipulation by the subject, were recorded by the dynograph on paper moving at the speed of either 6 mm/sec or 0·6 mm/sec. In addition to the recording of the sucking patterns the experimenter kept notes of the observable behaviour changes during the training and recording sessions. The records presented below represent the characteristic patterns obtained under each of the indicated conditions.

Results. Figure 2 (Plate II) gives the characteristic initial response patterns to the artificial nipple recorded at birth and at 4, 10 and 20 days of age from subjects which had no experience with the nipple prior to the recording.

At birth (Fig. 2A) the initial insertion of the nipple into the mouth elicits an immediate regular low-amplitude sucking pattern. By the fourth day of age (Fig. 2B) there is a considerable increase in amplitude and a decrease in the regularity of the initially elicited movements. The pattern, however, is predominantly sucking. At 10 days of age (Fig. 2C) the pattern includes some irregular biting movements and attempts to expel the nipple from the mouth. The flow of milk into the mouth, initially produced by these movements, however, elicits sucking, a few bursts of which are seen on this recording. At 20 days of age (Fig. 2D) the sucking is completely absent from the initially elicited pattern, which consists of large irregular movements of the jaws and tongue aimed at expulsion of the nipple from the mouth. The flow of milk into the mouth does not elicit an immediate sucking pattern seen at 10 days of age, and it takes hours of forced practice with the nipple before the appearance of the first regular sucking pattern. Once such a pattern is elicited, however, the kitten will continue to suck from the bottle and will learn to approach it independently. The initially elicited patterns beyond 20 days of age are essentially the same as seen in Fig. 2D, but the kittens at and beyond 40 days of age

PLATE II

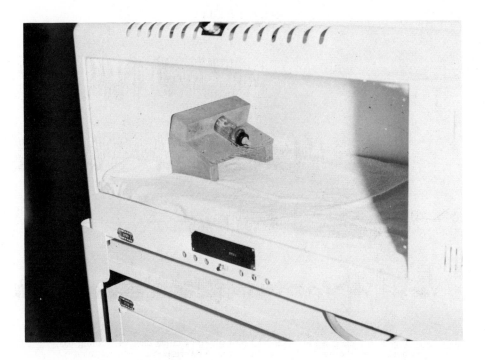

Fig. 1. The incubator with a feeding boot.

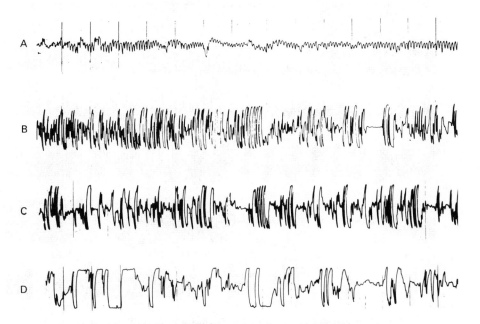

Fig. 2. Recordings of the initial sucking responses at birth (Line A), and at
the 4th (Line B), 10th (Line C), and 20th (Line D) days of age.

PLATE III

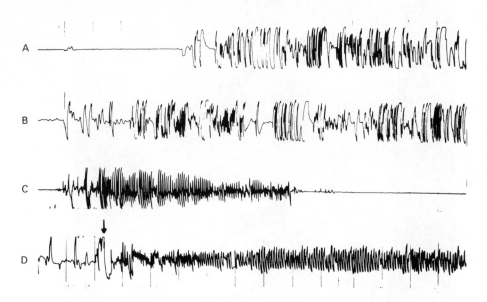

Fig. 3. Changes in the sucking pattern on consecutive days of training to
nurse from the bottle. Line A shows the initial response to the nipple on
the 1st day of training. Lines B and C, represent the recordings taken at the
1st daily forced trials on the 2nd and 3rd days. The arrow on Line D indicates the point of first independent approach of the nipple and the record
that follows shows the first independent nursing response on the 4th day of
training.

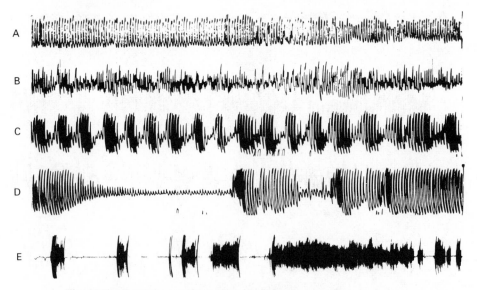

Fig. 4. Characteristic sucking patterns recorded from the kittens after the
independent nursing pattern was well established.

learned to obtain milk from the feeding bottle by chewing on the nipple and did not learn to suck (Table I, Exp. II).

Figure 3 (Plate III) shows the changes in the sucking pattern resulting from repeated forced experience with the nipple. Figure 3A shows the initial response to the nipple on the 10th day of age, at which the training started; B shows the pattern obtained on the second day of training. The two patterns A and B are essentially identical, showing irregular movements and occasional bursts of sucking which were elicited by the flow of milk into the kitten's mouth. On the third day of training the insertion of the nipple into the mouth elicited an immediate regular sucking pattern identical with the pattern recorded on the 4th day (Fig. 3D) at and after the first independent approach of the bottle.

These data, together with our direct observations, indicate that the acquisition of regular sucking pattern is sudden rather than gradual and that the regular sucking pattern appears before the kitten learns to respond to the bottle independently.

Figure 4 (Plate III) represents the characteristic sucking patterns recorded from the subjects after the independent response of approaching the feeding bottle and sucking from it was well established. Both the regular large amplitude sucking movements (Fig. 4A) and the somewhat irregular sucking (Fig. 4B), as well as the regular bursts of sucking movements (Fig. 4C) and their various mixtures, are characteristic of both nutritive and non-nutritive sucking. The regular smooth decrease in the sucking pattern (Fig. 4D) was rarely seen and it is included here, together with the common regular bursts of sucking movements seen in C, to illustrate the possible stereotypy in amplitude as well as frequency changes in sucking movements. Fig. 4E illustrates the recording taken with 0·6 mm/sec movement of the paper. This type of recording was taken for observing the changes in the time spent with nutritive and non-nutritive sucking at different age levels. The related findings are presented in Fig. 5, which shows the changes in the average amount of time spent with nutritive and non-nutritive sucking during the 90-min recording periods recorded from the 4 subjects after the establishment of independent response to the bottle. The solid line represents the total sucking time, and the broken line represents the time spent with nutritive sucking, i.e., the time spent with sucking until the bottle was emptied.

There was practically no variation in the time spent with nutritive sucking during the tested age levels. At 14 and 15 days of age all the recorded sucking was spent with nutritive sucking and the subjects did not finish the bottle of

milk during the 90-min recording period. By the 20th day of age the total amount of time spent on the bottle increased to 63 per cent of the recorded time, but only 8 per cent was required for finishing the bottle of milk. There

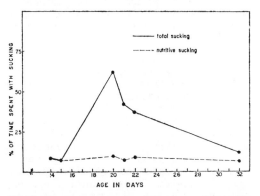

Fig. 5. The average amount of time spent with sucking and the amount of time spent with nutritive sucking during the 90-minute recording period at increasing age levels.

was a decrease in the total amount of time spent on the bottle beyond the 20th day of age, and by the 32nd day the curve almost reached the level of nutritive sucking again, indicating that there was only a negligible amount of non-nutritive sucking at this age.

The data on the immediate elicitability of a regular sucking pattern at birth (Fig. 2) suggest that the initial sucking is a reflex activity independent of learning. The complex behaviour associated with sucking on the mother however, cannot be considered as being composed of neonate reflexes alone. The early association of learning with sucking behaviour is shown by the improvement in the sucking pattern as a result of experience with an artificial nipple (Fig. 3) and by the kittens' learned response of locating and sucking from the artificial nipple. The appearance of nipple expelling movements at 10 days of age and their further development by 20 days (Fig. 2) may also be related to learning. A learned discrimination between the mother's nipple and the artificial nipple may have prevented the elicitation of reflex sucking by the artificial nipple in these subjects. However, it is also possible that the increasing delay in the elicitability of regular sucking pattern is related, at least in part, to the gradual disappearance of neonate reflex sucking with increasing age. The latter is supported by the observation that the 40-day and older kittens learned to obtain the milk from the bottle by chewing on the nipple and did not learn to suck even after prolonged training (Table I, Exp. II).

Experiment II

Changes in Learning to Suck from the Bottle at Different Early Ages

This experiment was designed for investigating the changes in the speed of learning to approach the artificial feeder and suck from it in relation to age and normal feeding pattern of the subjects.

Method and Procedure. Thirty-nine kittens were used. They were trained to approach the feeder and suck from it in a manner described in Experiment I. The training session started at birth (N = 2), and at 2 (N = 1), 4 (N = 4), 7 (N = 2), 8 (N = 11), 12 (N = 4), 20 (N = 4), 26 (N = 1), 31 (N = 3), 35 (N = 1), 40 (N = 3) and 60 (N = 3) days of ages. The kittens were raised with the mother until the beginning of the training which started 24 hr after separation from the mother. The experimenter recorded the length of time elapsed between the beginning of training and the first independent response to the feeding bottle. Upon completion of training the kittens were tested for their response to solid food (a mixture of horse meat and canned fish) presented to them in a metal bowl during a 24-hr period. They were approximately 12-hr-food deprived at the beginning of this

test and had no access to milk during the testing period.

Results. Table I shows the data obtained in this experiment. It appears that the maturational improvement in the kittens' learning capacity and sensory motor mechanisms associated with learning to approach the feeder does not occur in a smooth gradual sequence but rather in steps. There are two such improvements indicated by these findings, one at around 7 days of age, the other at 30 days.

The first improvement in the learning process may be due in part to the emergence of vision. If we adjust the length of time required for learning to the time of visual experience during the learning period, assuming that the visual experience starts with the opening of the eyes at around 7 days of age, the first improvement in the speed of learning disappears (Table I). This indicates that vision may be an important modality for the involved learning. We should note that this hypothesis of the involvement of vision in learning to approach the feeder refers only to our data and the particular conditions of this experiment. Rosenblatt *et al.* (1959) using a different feeder with more abundant tactual cues found self-feeding developing in birth-isolated kitten in a few days and before the open-

Table I. Speed of Learning to Approach and Suck from the Bottle at Different Early Ages

No. of kittens tested	Age at the beginning of training in days	The length of learning experience before the first independent response to the bottle		Average length of visual learning experience before first independent response to the bottle	Age at the 24 hr test for the response to solid food	Response to solid food
		mean	range			
2	at birth	no independent responses in 240 hr			not tested	
1	2 days	169 hr		73 hr	12 days	none
4	4	127 hr	111–157 hr	58 hr*	15 days	none
2	7	78 hr	72–84 hr	78 hr	18 days	none
11	8	83 hr	56–94 hr	83 hr	22 days	none
4	12	81 hr	68–92 hr	81 hr	26 days	none
4	20	76 hr	62–86 hr	76 hr	30 days	eating
1	26	63 hr		63 hr	35 days	eating
3	31	18 hr	6–32 hr	18 hr	35 days	eating
1	35	2 hr		2 hr	37 days	eating
3	40	8 hr	2–14 hr	8 hr†	45 days	eating
3	60	25 hr	14–38 hr	25 hr†	65 days	eating

*Subject learned to respond to the bottle before the opening of the eyes.

†Learned to obtain milk from the bottle by chewing on the nipple and while maintaining this behaviour did not learn to suck from the bottle in 4 days.

ing of the eyes. Apparently our feeder was more demanding on the visual and the motor capacity of the kittens than the feeder used in the Rosenblatt *et al.* study. One of our kittens was also able to learn to approach the bottle before the opening of its eyes, which was unusually delayed until the 12th day of age, in this subject.

The second improvement in the speed of learning took place at around 30 days of age. While the learning below this age level required an average of approximately 72 hr of visual experience, all kittens at and beyond 30 days of age learned to respond to the bottle in less than 38 hr. There was no further improvement in the learning beyond this age. The 40- and 60-days age groups learned to obtain the milk from the bottle by chewing on it instead of sucking; they did not acquire sucking habit during 4 days of experience with the feeder. All kittens beyond 30 days of age responded to solid food. Since the first mature EEG pattern in the cat appears also at around 30 days of age (Marley *et al.*, 1963) it is possible that the second and apparently final improvement in the speed of learning as well as the appearance of the response to solid food are related to the functional maturation of the cerebral cortex.

Experiment III
The Effects of Complete Sucking Deprivation on the Elicitability of Sucking Behaviour

The experiment described in this section was designed for studying the developmental changes in the ability to initiate sucking behaviour in kittens which were deprived of the opportunity to suck from birth.

Method and Procedure. Thirty-six kittens were used. Thirty-two were put into individual isolation and 4 into group isolation, all within 4 hr after birth. All of them were raised by force-feeding and none were given opportunity for nutritive sucking after the separation from the mother and until the set time limit of deprivation. The milk, prepared from dry Esbilac formula, was injected into the kittens' stomach through a thin tube ($1\frac{1}{2}$ mm in diameter) four times daily. A daily portion of 25 ml of milk was given up to the 10th day of age, and the portion was gradually increased to 75 ml by the 30th day of age. The length of isolation and complete sucking deprivation, and the number of kittens at each deprivation period are indicated on Table II. At the end of the deprivation period the kittens were returned to their mothers in exchange for their normally raised littermates, or in some instances to a foster mother in exchange for her kitten. The experimenter observed the interaction between the mother and kitten and recorded the time elapsed between the return of the kitten and the first initiation of sucking. The subjects which did

not suck on the mother during the first 12 hr period were given 10 ml of milk by force feeding, and this was repeated at the end of each successive 12 hr period during which the kitten did not suck. After the kittens made the first sucking response, or, if there was no sucking, at the end of the 4-day observation period, they were tested for their response to the nipple of the feeding bottle artificially inserted into the mouth and for their response to solid food.

Results. Our sucking deprivation procedure resulted in a very high mortality. Sixty-nine per cent of the individually isolated and force-fed kittens died before reaching the set age for return to the mother. This left us with only 10 kittens. The data collected on these subjects are presented in Table II.

The complete sucking deprivation and social isolation did not interfere with the kitten's ability to return to the mother and to initiate sucking if the deprivation lasted from birth to 19 days of age. Up to this age there was only a relatively small increase in the time elapsed between the return to the mother and the initiation of sucking. At and beyond 23 days of deprivation, however, the kittens were not able to find the nipple and did not initiate sucking during the observed 96 hr experience with the mother. The kittens tested after 23 and 26 days of deprivation occasionally approached the mother and searched for the nipple with the characteristic side movements of the head. They also showed the rooting reflex upon stimulation of the facial areas, but they were not able to locate and respond to the mother's nipple. The single kitten deprived for 35 days did not

Table II. The Effects of Complete Sucking Deprivation and Social Isolation on the Kittens' Ability to Initiate Sucking on the Mother*

No. of kittens tested	Age of return to the mother in days	Average length of time required for initiation of sucking after return to the mother
1	6	1/2 hr
2	9	1/2 hr
1	16	5 hr
2	19	3 hr
1	23	no sucking on the mother
2	24	no sucking on the mother
1	35	no sucking on the mother

*All kittens were separated from the mother within 4 hr after birth.

respond to the mother by searching movements, and the rooting reflex was also absent. The mother responded to all deprived kittens either immediately or after a short delay by licking them vigorously and by assuming the characteristic outstretched nursing position. The deficiency in the kitten's ability to nurse did not seem to relate to the lack of appropriate response from the mother. All kittens deprived for 23 days or more were seen climbing up on the mother, apparently for warmth, and occasionally falling asleep on top of her while she was in the outstretched nursing position.

On the 4th day of experience with the mother, attempts were made to orient the kitten to the mother by forcing the mother's nipple into the kitten's mouth. These attempts did not help the kitten to initiate sucking. The subjects lost the mother's nipple immediately after the experimenter released their head, and they were not seen sucking on the mother. The sucking reflex, however, was not completely absent in these kittens. At the end of 4 days experience with the mother and after repeated forced trials, the insertion of an artificial nipple into the mouth resulted in sucking. The eliciting stimulus was evidently the flow of milk into the mouth. It appears that it is not the sucking response, but the ability to locate and respond to the mother's nipple that was absent in these kittens.

Four kittens were raised by force feeding in a group from birth to the 30th day of age (Table III). All these subjects had thrived well during the deprivation period and they all initiated nursing on the mother upon return to her. The sucking deprivation of these kittens, however, was not complete. Shortly after the beginning of the deprivation period they started to suck on each other's anal and genital regions. This behaviour was maintained throughout the deprivation period and these kittens were often seen lined up in a circle, sucking on each other. Since the stimulation of the anal and genital areas in the young kitten produces elimination, it is possible that the mutual sucking was directed toward this region because of the reinforcing value of the liquid obtained by such sucking. It appears that the continuous mutual sucking practice seen in these kittens was sufficient to

enable the initiation and development of sucking on the mother.

The data of this study is not free of the common problems related to deprivation experiment. It can be argued that the individually isolated kittens were not able to return to the mother because of their general undernourished state, caused by the prolonged deprivation, and not because of any maturational disappearance of specific reflex activity related to the ability to respond to the mother's nipple. All the deprived kittens were certainly undernourished. Those raised in individual isolation weighed only 56 per cent, and the subjects in group isolation 65 per cent, of the weight of normally raised kittens by the end of the 3rd week of deprivation. They were not, however, inactive or sluggish. Whenever they were approached during the deprivation period for feeding they always reacted by vigorous vocalization and running around. They all reacted to solid food between the ages of 30–40 days and their weight gain was drastically improved once feeding on solid food began. We may safely assume, on the basis of the generally vigorous behaviour of the individually isolated subjects at the end of the deprivation period and on the basis of the intact ability for interacting with and sucking on the mother of the kitten raised in group isolation, that neither the state of undernourishment nor the lack of adequate response from the mother was the significant factor accounting for the observed absence of sucking in the individually isolated and sucking-deprived kittens. Consequently, the data seem to imply that the initiation and establishment of persistent sucking behaviour depends on the kitten's reflex response to the mother's nipple. The disappearance of this neonate reflex response at around 23 days of age renders the kitten which did not have previous sucking experience unable to initiate sucking on the mother. In other words, the initiation of the neonate sucking behaviour of the kitten seems to depend on the presence of innately given reflexes, but the maintenance of this behaviour beyond the maturational stage at which the involved neonate reflex, or reflexes, disappear depends on practice and learning. The testable implication of this interpretation is that

Table III. The Effects of Force Feeding and Isolation from the Mother in Group Situation on the Kittens' Ability to Initiate Sucking on the Mother

No. of kittens tested	Age of kittens at the time of separation from the mother	Age at return to the mother in days	Average length of time required for the initiation of sucking after return to the mother
4	within 4 hr after birth	31	12 hr

an interference with the involved reflex activities, by destroying the sense modalities that mediate them, should make the kitten unable to initiate sucking on the mother, while it may leave the learned behaviour elements associated with sucking intact. Our next experiment was designed for testing this implication. Since olfaction appeared to be the most likely sense modality involved in the mediation of at least some reflex elements of neonate sucking, we have decided to study the effects of the destruction of the olfactory bulbs on sucking from the mother and on the learned habit of sucking from the bottle.

Experiment IV

The Effects of the Removal of Olfactory Bulbs on the Reflex and Learned Components of Sucking Behaviour

Method and Procedure

A. Removal of the olfactory bulbs in kittens after various lengths of normal sucking experience with the mother

Thirteen kittens were used. They were all born in our laboratory and were raised with the mother until the age of operation. The number of subjects operated at different age levels were as follows: 2 at 2 days of age; 2 at 4 days; 2 at 5 days; 2 at 16 days; 3 at 18 days; 1 at 20 days and 1 at 26 days of age. The removal of the olfactory bulbs was done in the following manner. The subjects were anaesthetized by intraperitoneally administered Nembutal at 20 mg/kg of body weight. The craniotomies were performed under aseptic conditions through a mid-line incision. Small portions of the bone flaps were removed over the appropriate areas and openings were made through the frontal sinuses and cranium. The olfactory bulbs were taken out by suction with pipettes of small diameter. The emptied areas were stuffed with gelfoam and the incision was closed. Twenty-four hours after the operation the kittens were examined for their recovery and, if found alert and active, were returned to the mother. At the end of each 12 hr of post-operative experience with the mother the kittens which did not suck were given 10 ml of Esbilac milk by force feeding. The post-operative mother-kitten interaction was observed for 4 days and the presence or absence of sucking behaviour was noted. Following this, 4 kittens were put into training to suck from the feeding bottle independently and 6 kittens were left with the mother with continued force feeding. Attempts were made to train these kittens to suck from the mother by repeated artificial insertion of the mother's nipple into the mouth. The remaining 3 kittens were left with the mother and their force feeding was discontinued.

B. Removal of the olfactory bulbs in kittens with previously established habit of approaching the bottle and sucking from it independently

Six kittens were used. The procedure for the removal of the olfactory bulbs was the same as described above. Before the operation these subjects were trained to approach the feeding bottle and to suck from it. The training was the same as that described in the preceding sections. The ages at the beginning of the training were as follows: 7 days (N = 2); 11 days (N = 3); and 22 days (N = 1). The kittens were operated after the establishment and practice of the independent sucking habit on the bottle at the ages of 14, 22 and 28 days respectively. Twenty-four hours after the operation they were returned to their respective incubators and were observed for their responses to the feeding bottles. After determining the presence of independent sucking on the bottle they were returned to the mother in exchange for their littermates, and their interaction with the mother was observed for 2 days.

C. Control operations

Ten kittens were used. In 4 kittens the cranium was opened in the same manner as in the subjects operated for the removal of the olfactory bulbs, but the bulbs were left intact. This sham operation was made at the age of 7 days and after normal sucking experience with the mother. In 4 kittens the olfactory bulbs were left intact and extensive areas of the frontal lobes and caudate nuclei were removed instead. These subjects were operated at the age of 8 days after normal sucking experience with the mother. In 2 kittens the operation was unilateral and the olfactory bulb was removed on one side only. These subjects were operated on the 14th day of age and were trained to suck from the bottle before operation.

All kittens were sacrificed approximately 3 weeks after the completion of the post-operative testing procedures. Superficial examinations of the extent of the lesions were made on all brains and a sample of 5 brains, 2 with unilateral and 3 with bilateral olfactory bulb lesions, were sectioned and prepared for histological analysis in cresyl and weil stains.

Results

A. Histological

The superficial examination of the brains revealed the absence of olfactory bulbs in the operated sides and partial atrophy in the anterior pyriform areas, anterior portions of the amygdaloid complex and the lateral olfactory tracts. The serial microscopic examination of the brains with destroyed olfactory bulbs revealed a complete degeneration of the lateral olfactory tracts and extensive degeneration of the cells in the anterior pyriform and cortico medial amygdaloid areas of the operated sides.

B. The effect of the removal of the olfactory bulbs on the normal nursing behaviour of the kitten

None of the kittens with bilateral olfactory lesions were able to initiate sucking on the mother during the post-operative test. As can be seen on Table IV, the length of preoperative sucking experience with the mother did not alter this phenomenon. The kitten operated after 25 days of normal sucking experience with the mother was just as unable to initiate sucking post-operatively as the kitten operated after 2 days sucking experience. The 3 subjects which were left with the mother and whose force feeding was discontinued after the 4-day testing period died of starvation. The attempts to teach 6 subjects to suck from the mother by artificially inserting the mother's nipple into their mouth was unsuccessful. Although it resulted in occasional sucking movements on the mother's nipple it did not help the kittens in learning to locate the nipple and in initiating sucking on the mother. By contrast, we were successful in training 3 operated subjects to suck from the bottle independently.

It appears that the removal of the olfactory bulbs renders the kitten unable to locate and to respond to the mother's nipple. Due to this deficiency the kitten without olfactory bulbs is unable to suck from the mother and will starve to death when left with a lactating mother if not fed artificially. Both the sham operates and the subjects with parts of the frontal lobes and caudate nuclei missing as well as the kittens with unilateral olfactory bulb lesions (Table V) were able to initiate sucking within a short delay after the beginning of the post-operative test. Thus the observed post-operative deficiency in the ability to suck from the mother was specific to the bilateral removal of the olfactory bulbs.

C. The effects of the removal of the olfactory bulbs on the learned habit of sucking from the bottle

All the operated kittens retained the learned habit of sucking from the bottle (Table V). These data, when compared with the findings of the preceding section, indicate clearly that there are some fundamental differences between the normal sucking behaviour on the mother and the learned sucking habit on the bottle.

Table IV. The Effects of the Removal of Olfactory Bulbs on the Kittens' Ability to Suck

No. of kittens tested	Age at operation in days	Extirpated structure	Average length of time required to initiate sucking from mother in the post-operative test	Average length of time for learning to suck from the bottle after the post-operative test with the mother	Additional information
2	2	olf. bulbs bilaterally	no sucking from mother in 96 hr	not tested	
2	4	,,	,,	145 hr (1 only)	1 kitten died on the 6th day of training to suck from the bottle
2	5	,,	,,	not tested	
2	16	,,	,,	not tested	Both kittens died of starvation on the 4th day after the discontinuation of force feeding while with the mother.
3	18	,,	,,	104 hr (2 only)	1 kitten was left with mother and died of starvation on the 3rd day after the discontinuation of force feeding.
1	20	,,	,,	not tested	
1	26	,,	,,	not tested	
4	7	frontal areas and caudate nucleus	20 minutes	not tested	
4	8	sham	80 minutes	not tested	

Table V. Effects of Removal of the Olfactory Bulbs on the Retention of the Learned Habit of Sucking from the Bottle

No. of kittens tested	Age of kitten at the beginning of training on the bottle	Average age at the first independent response to the bottle in days	Age at operation in days	Extirpated structures	Average length of time before sucking on the bottle in the post-operative test	Response to the mother after the post-operative test on the bottle
2	7 days	11	14	olf. bulbs bilaterally	13 hr	no sucking
3	11 days	14	22	,,	8 hr	no sucking
1	22 days	24	26	,,	22 hr	no sucking
2	7 days	11	14	olf. bulbs unilaterally	26 hr	sucking in 3 hr

Discussion

The differences between sucking on the mother and the learned habit of sucking on the bottle are immediately apparent in the differences of the speed with which the sucking is initiated and established in the two situations. While the behaviour of sucking on the mother develops immediately after birth, the kittens need prolonged learning experience before they are able to suck on the bottle independently. Furthermore, the destruction of the olfactory bulbs renders the kitten unable to initiate sucking on the mother, but it does not interfere with the learned response of sucking on the artificial nipple, nor with the kitten's ability to learn to suck from the bottle.

It is an open question whether we deal here with differences in sensory functions only or with differential involvement of CNS structures responsible not only for the sensory but also for the integrative and motor functions. The extensive degeneration observed in the anterior pyriform and amygdaloid areas, brought about by the destruction of the olfactory bulbs, certainly may implicate at least some integrative functions beyond the mere transmission of sensory impulses. These functions, however, must be closely related to the sense of olfaction, since various limited bilateral lesions of the amygdala and hyppocampus, hemidecortication and complete destruction of the neocortex, with the olfactory bulbs and related structures left intact, have not been observed to interfere with the kitten's ability to suck from the mother (Kling, 1966).

The difference between the mechanisms of sucking from the mother and sucking from the bottle may well be due to the differential involvement of CNS mechanisms. While the initiation of sucking on the mother appears to be based on neonate reflexes, and may be relatively free of cortical control, the learned behaviour of sucking from the bottle may involve cortical functions. The immediate elicitability of sucking at birth, as well as the lack of ability to find the nipple in kittens deprived of the sense of olfaction and also in kittens raised with complete sucking deprivation, support the view of the involvement of specific neonate reflex activities in the initiation and maintenance of sucking on the mother. The involvement of cortical control and its functional maturity, on the other hand, may account for the initial slowness of learning to suck from the bottle and for the maturational improvements in this learning process, especially the second at around 30 days of age which coincides with the first response to solid food and with the first appearance of the mature EEG pattern.

The strongest support for the hypothesis of the necessary involvement of neonate reflex activities in the establishment of persistent sucking behaviour comes from our observation that complete sucking deprivation for 23 days or more renders the kitten unable to initiate sucking on the mother. This observation is not without parallel in the literature. Padilla (1935) reported comparable data on the domestic chicken. He found that chicks deprived of the opportunity to peck from the time of hatching to the 14th day of age (by artificial feeding in darkness) were unable to learn to peck and starved to death amidst plenty. Our deprived kittens similarly were unable to initiate feeding behaviour and would have starved to death if not fed artificially. To be sure our postulate of a maturational disappearance of the neonate reflex activities which enable the kittens to initiate sucking on the mother is not the only possible explanation for this phenomena but it is certainly the most plausible hypothesis. The learned differentiation and preference for force feeding and their interference with the initiation of feeding on the mother cannot be an adequate explanation. Apart from the social interaction with the experimenter the force-feeding procedure had no positive valence for the subjects. Without exception, their head had to be held firmly and the mouth had to be opened by force in order to insert the feeding tube and prevent aversive head movements and attempts to bite the tube.

The social experience emphasized by Rosenblatt *et al.* (1959) was an important factor in our experiments also. This is shown by the behaviour of the 4 force-fed, group-isolated kittens which were able to initiate sucking on the mother at the age of 30 days. It should be kept in mind, however, that their social interaction in great part consisted of mutual elicitation of neonate reflexes (rooting, sucking, etc.) and development of related persistent activities (mutual sucking on anal and genital areas). Consequently, this social interaction may have been essential for the initiation of sucking on the mother primarily because it provided the context for the exercise of neonate reflex activities during the period of their availability and thus enabled the development of related persistent sucking behaviour.

The presence of more or less rigid maturational schedules for the availability of neonate reflexes is an empirical fact. However, the role of these reflexes in the development of behaviour is not yet understood. Our data implicate the involvement of these reflexes in the development of persistent sucking behaviour, and, if our interpretation is correct, they also indicate the need for reformulation of the concept of 'early critical periods for socialization' in terms of 'critical periods' for the availablity of neonate reflex activities upon which the establishment of persistent behaviour patterns may be based.

Rosenblatt *et al.* (1959) in their study of the processes of early socialization in the kitten reject the concept of early critical periods and argue that 'striking behaviour changes are attributable not only to growth conditioned processes (maturation) but also to factors of experience characteristic of the existing developmental situation' and 'every age is critical for the development of normal progressive sucking pattern'. We cannot but support their view of an interlocked ontogenetic chain of maturational and experiential factors in the development of behaviour. This ontogenetic chain however should not and cannot be equated with epigenesis. Our data show specific sensory motor mechanisms and early differences in CNS functions associated with the initiation and development of neonate sucking behaviour, and we feel that the critical period concept, not as a period for early socialization but as a period for the availability of neonate reflexes on which the establishment of persistent behaviour patterns may be based, is useful, if not necessary, for identifying the separate maturational and experiential factors in the development of neonate sucking behaviour.

Summary

The mechanisms of the neonate sucking behaviour of the kitten were studied and the following observations were made: (1) while sucking on an artificial stimulus is present at birth, by the age of 20 days it is completely absent from the initial response to an artificial feeding nipple forced into the mouth. Repeated forced feeding experience with such a nipple, however, results in a regular sucking pattern up to 40 days of age. Beyond the age of 40 days the kittens learn to obtain milk from the feeding bottle by chewing on the nipple instead of by sucking. (2) With increasing age and experience there is a gradual increase and a consequent gradual decrease in the amount of time spent with non-nutritive sucking. (3) The maturational improvements in the kittens' ability to learn to suck from a bottle emerge in two steps; the first, at 7 days of age, seems to be associated with the emergence of vision, while the second, at around 30 days of age, is parallel with the newly emerged response to solid food. (4) Complete sucking deprivation and individual isolation render the kittens unable to initiate sucking from the mother if the deprivation lasts for 23 days or more. (5) Kittens raised in group isolation by force feeding learn to suck on each others' fur and genital areas; such deprivation does not interfere with the kittens' ability to initiate sucking on the mother. (6) The destruction of the olfactory bulbs renders the kittens unable to initiate sucking on the mother irrespective of the length of the sucking experience prior to the operation; it is the ability to find the mother's nipple and to respond to it that appears to be lost in these kittens. (7) The destruction of the olfactory bulbs, however, does not interfere with the kittens' ability to learn to suck from the bottle, nor does it interfere with the retention of such a preoperative habit.

These observations were discussed with particular emphasis on their possible implications for the role of neonate reflex activities in the early establishment of persistent behaviour patterns.

This research was supported by United States Public Health Service Grant HD-02277, the State of Illinois Mental Health Fund 1711, and Michael Reese Medical Research Institute Grant No. 5476.

REFERENCES

Kling, A. (1966). Behavioral and somatic development following lesions of the amygdala in the cat. *J. Psychiat. Res.* (in press).

Marley, E. & Key, J. B. (1963). Maturation of the electrocorticogram and behaviour in the kitten and guinea pig and the effect of some sympathomimetic amines. *E.E.G. Clin. Neurophysiol.*, **15**, 620–636.

Padilla, S. G. (1935). Further studies on delayed pecking in chicks. *J. comp. Psychol.*, **20**, 413–443.

Rosenblatt, J. S., Turkewitz, G. & Schneirla, T. C. (1959). Early socialization in the domestic cat as based on feeding and other relationships between female and young. In: *Determinants of Infant Behavior* (Ed. by B. M. Foss,), 51–74. New York: Wiley.

Scott, J. P. (1958). Critical periods in the development of social behavior in puppies. *Psychosom. Med.*, **20**, 42–54.

Scott, J. P. (1962). Critical periods in behavior development. *Science*, **138**, 948–957.

Chapter Eight

PERCEPTION

When the newborn opens his eyes and looks out at his world, what does he see? Is it William James' booming, buzzing world of confusion, essentially of a random nature, or is it an organized and ordered world? This problem has been debated for many decades and — as would be expected since there were few data and many ideas — theories to account for visual perception flourished. In one camp were the "nativists," who believed that we were born with the appropriate neural connections to perceive the world in an orderly fashion. Across the river were the tents of the "empiricists," who believed that we learned to perceive the world as a function of environmental inputs. Sometimes the attacks the two camps leveled at each other were quite ferocious, but none was devastating because of the lack of solid experimental data. Recently, however, observational techniques have been developed to study perceptual preference in the newborn human, and a variety of procedures have been worked out to investigate perceptual development in animals. Among the techniques available for research in animals are sensory and perceptual deprivation; electrophysiological recordings of sensory inputs to the brain; and morphological analyses of sensory organs, neural pathways, and the brain itself.

Studies using these techniques have shown that the newborn has a more complicated perceptual system than many people expected. Indeed, it seems quite likely that the newborn is able to process information, at least at a low level of organization. In addition, we know that environmental input is an absolutely necessary condition for maintenance of the integrity of the perceptual system and that these environ-

mental inputs have important, and often highly specific, effects upon the connections between the sense organ and the brain. The five papers in this chapter have been chosen to illustrate these principles in the area of visual perception.

The person who originally demonstrated that newborn infants had the capability to respond differentially to visual stimuli was Robert L. Fantz. Paper 31 is his report, showing that infants ranging in age from 10 hours to 5 days spent significantly more time looking at black-and-white patterns than at unpatterned colors of white, yellow, or red. As Fantz pointed out, these data refute the notions that the visual world of the newborn infant is random and chaotic and that the capability to perceive configurations comes about only through a learning mechanism.

Fantz' demonstration that the newborn prefers to look at black-and-white patterned stimuli rather than at colored, unpatterned stimuli suggests that the newborn has the capability for selectively responding to and processing information. The hypothesis that the newborn is capable of visual information processing was experimentally tested by Hershenson et al. (Paper 32). Working with 2- to 4-day-old infants, they found that the neonates preferred to look at random shapes which contained 10 angles than at shapes containing either 5 or 20 angles, a finding similar to results obtained with older children and with adults. Varying the number of angles of the figure is one experimental operation for varying the information content of the figure, and the finding that newborn infants prefer to look at one class of figures rather than at other classes rather clearly implies that the visual perceptual system functions in a fairly complex and coordinated manner at the time of birth.

In order to gain deeper understanding of the findings of Fantz and of Hershenson *et al.*, it is again necessary to turn to data from animal research. In the same year that Fantz published his paper, Wiesel and Hubel (1963) reported the results of experiments in which cats had been deprived of visual stimulation from birth. From their neurophysiological findings they concluded that the proper connections between the eye and the brain were present at birth and that visual deprivation brought about a disruption of these connections. In other words, visual stimulation after birth was necessary to keep intact those connections which were present at the time of birth. Paper 33 describes a later experiment by Wiesel and Hubel in which they studied the long-term effects on cats of visual deprivation during the first 3 months of life. Their procedure was to suture shut one eye of a kitten while the other eye was left undisturbed. The animals were kept under normal colony conditions of social interactions with each other and with humans. At the end of the 3-month interval the sutures were removed, and some animals were allowed to use both eyes, while in other animals the originally opened eye was sutured shut to determine how well the animal could use its deprived eye. The results showed that the cats were not able to use their originally deprived eye to perceive their visual world. Also, single-unit recordings obtained from the striate cortex revealed abnormalities, and aberrant morphological changes were found in the lateral geniculate body. These abnormalities were found as long as 1 year after the deprived eye had been opened, thus clearly indicating a long-term effect which is probably irreversible.

The Wiesel and Hubel paper showed their deprivation of visual experience led to permanent behavioral, physiological, and morphological impairments. Their previous work had shown that general visual stimulation would maintain the appropriate eye-brain connections. A question of interest was whether highly specific visual stimulation would bring about equally highly specific eye-brain connections.

This was shown to be the case by Hirsch and Spinelli (Paper 34), who kept kittens in a dark room for approximately 16 hours per day and had them wear masks during the remaining 8 hours. The masks were arranged so that one eye could see only three black vertical lines and, at the same time, the other eye could see only three black horizontal lines. These researchers then obtained electrophysiological recordings from the primary visual cortex to a stimulus of a dot which moved either in a horizontal or a vertical direction. They were able to find elongated receptive fields which were either horizontal or vertical, depending on the type of stimulation which the eye had received. Thus, Hirsch and Spinelli were able to show that eye-brain neural connections can be modified as a function of the nature of the stimulation impinging upon the eye.

The studies by Wiesel and Hubel and by Hirsch and Spinelli demonstrate that environmental stimulation is a necessary part of the self-regulatory feedback loop which the organism needs in order to be able to perceive his world correctly. What about the nature of the animal's response? Is sensory input alone sufficient, or must the animal produce movement of its own in order to close the feedback loop? In simpler words, will an animal who passively received stimulation from his environment perform as well as an animal who receives stimulation because he has active intercourse with that environment? This important theoretical issue was investigated by Held and Hein (Paper 35), who cleverly arranged an apparatus so that a young kitten explored its world visually by actively moving around a circumscribed environment while a yoked control animal was passively exposed to the identical visual world. When tested on a variety of performance measures, the active kittens were found to perform in an appropriate normal fashion, while the kittens which had received the same visual stimulation but had not been allowed to engage in any motor activity were found to be markedly deficient in their visual performance behavior. Although the study does not eliminate passive sensory input as a means of developing one's perceptual world, it does establish that active interaction with one's environment is an important, and perhaps necessary, dimension of perceptual development.

This finding of Held and Hein seems to be at variance with that of Hirsch and Spinelli, who employed an essentially passive sensory situation. However, the experiments are not comparable since the measurements were taken at different levels of central nervous system organization. Hirsch and Spinelli studied the electrophysiological response from the visual

cortex, while Held and Hein investigated visual performance. A more critical test of Held and Hein's hypothesis of the necessity of self-produced movement will occur when Hirsch and Spinelli examine the behavior of their cats.

Reference

Wiesel, D. M., and Hubel, D. H. Single-cell responses in striate cortex of kittens deprived of vision in one eye. *J. Neurophysiol.,* 1963, 26, 1003-1017.

ROBERT L. FANTZ

31   Pattern Vision in Newborn Infants

Abstract. *Human infants under 5 days of age consistently looked more at black-and-white patterns than at plain colored surfaces, which indicates the innate ability to perceive form.*

It is usually stated or implied that the infant has little or no pattern vision during the early weeks or even months, because of the need for visual learning or because of the immature state of the eye and brain, or for both reasons (*1*). This viewpoint has been challenged by the direct evidence of differential attention given to visual stimuli varying in form or pattern (*2*). This evidence has shown that during the early months of life, infants: (i) have fairly acute pattern vision (resolving 1/8-inch stripes at a 10-inch distance); (ii) show greater visual interest in patterns than in plain colors; (iii) differentiate among patterns of similar complexity; and (iv) show visual interest in a pattern similar to that of a human face.

The purpose of the present study was to determine whether it was possible to obtain similar data on newborn infants and thus further exclude visual learning or postnatal maturation as requirements for pattern vision. It is a

Reprinted from *Science 140*:296–297, 1963. Copyright 1963 by the American Association for the Advancement of Science.

repetition of a study of older infants which compared the visual responsiveness to patterned and to plainly colored surfaces (*3*). The results of the earlier study were essentially duplicated, giving further support for the above conclusions.

The subjects were 18 infants ranging from 10 hours to 5 days old. They were selected from a much larger number on the basis of their eyes remaining open long enough to be exposed to a series of six targets at least twice. The length of gaze at each target was observed through a tiny hole in the ceiling of the chamber (Fig. 1) and recorded on a timer. The fixation time started as soon as one or both eyes of the infant were directed towards the target, using as criterion the super-position over the pupil of a tiny corneal reflection of the target; it ended when the eyes turned away or closed (*4*). The six targets were presented in random order for each infant, with the sequence repeated up to eight times when possible. Only completed sequences were included in calculating the percentage of total fixation time for each target.

The targets were circular, 6 inches in diameter, and had nonglossy surfaces. Three contained black-and-white patterns — a schematic face, concentric circles, and a section of news-

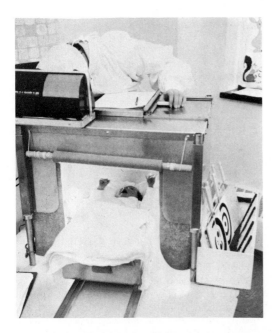

Fig. 1. Infant "looking chamber" for testing visual responsiveness to targets exposed under controlled-stimulus conditions. The patterned objects are visible in a box on the table, each with a handle for sliding it in the chamber. Observer is looking on one side of the target through the peephole, which is hidden by the timer.

paper containing print 1/16 to 1/4 inch high. The other three were unpatterned — white, fluorescent yellow, and dark red. The relative luminous reflectance was, in decreasing order: yellow, white, newsprint, face and circles, red. Squares containing the patterns or colors were placed in a flat holder which slid horizontally into a slightly recessed portion of the chamber ceiling to expose the pattern or color to the infant through a circular hole in the holder. The chamber and underside of the holder were lined with blue felt to provide a contrasting background for the stimuli, and to diffuse the illumination (between 10 and 15 ft-ca) from lights on either side of the infant's head. The subject was in a small hammock crib with head facing up directly under the targets, 1 foot away.

The results in Table 1 show about twice as much visual attention to patterns as to plainly colored surfaces. Differences in response to the six stimulus objects are significant for the infants both under and over 2 days of age; results from these groups do not differ reliably from each other, and are similar to earlier results from much older infants. The selectivity of the visual responses is brought out still more strikingly by tabulating the longest-fixated target for each newborn infant: 11 for face, 5 for concentric circles, 2 for newsprint, and 0 for white, yellow, and red. For comparison, the first choices of infants 2 to 6 months were distributed as follows: 16, 4, 5, 0, 0, 0.

Three infants under 24 hours could be tested sufficiently to indicate the individual consistency of response. Two of these showed a significant (.005 and .05) difference among the targets in successive sets of exposures, one looking longest at the face pattern in 7 of 8 exposures, the other looking longest at the "bull's-eye" in 3 of 6 exposures. The third infant 10 hours after birth looked longest at the face in 3 of 8 exposures.

It is clear that the selective visual responses were related to pattern rather than hue or reflectance, although the latter two variables are often thought to be primary visual stimuli. Specification of the prepotent configurational

Table 1. Relative duration of initial gaze of infants at six stimulus objects in successive and repeated presentations.

Mean percentage of fixation time

Age Group	N	Face	Circles	News	White	Yellow	Red	P*
Under 48 hours	8	29.5	23.5	13.1	12.3	11.5	10.1	.005
2 to 5 days	10	29.5	24.3	17.5	9.9	12.1	6.7	.001
2 to 6 months†	25	34.3	18.4	19.9	8.9	8.2	10.1	.001

*Significance level based on Friedman analysis of variance by ranks.
†From an earlier study (2).

variables is unwarranted at this time. The results do not imply "instinctive recognition" of a face or other unique significance of this pattern; it is likely there are other patterns which would elicit equal or greater attention (5). Longer fixation of the face suggests only that a pattern with certain similarities to social objects also has stimulus characteristics with considerable intrinsic interest or stimulating value; whatever the mechanism underlying this interest, it should facilitate the development of social responsiveness, since what is responded to must first be attended to.

Substantiation for the visual selection of patterned over unpatterned objects is given in an independent study of newborn infants in which more visual attention was given to a colored card with a simple figure, when held close to the infant, than to a plain card of either color (6).

The results of Table 1 demonstrate that pattern vision can be tested in newborn infants by recording differential visual attention; these and other results call for a revision of traditional views that the visual world of the infant is initially formless or chaotic and that we must learn to see configurations (7).

References and Notes

1. See, for example, Evelyn Dewey, *Behavior Development in Infants* (Columbia Univ. Press, New York, 1935); K. C. Pratt, in *Manual of Child Psychology*, L. Carmichael, Ed. (Wiley, New York, 1954); B. Spock, *Baby and Child Care* (Pocket Books, New York, 1957).

2. R. L. Fantz, J. M. Ordy, M. S. Udelf, *J. Comp. Physiol. Psychol.* 55, 907 (1962); R. L. Fantz, *Psychol. Rec.* 8, 43 (1958).

3. R. L. Fantz, *Sci. Am.* 204, No. 5, 66 (1961).

4. High reliability of a similar technique, using the same criterion of fixation, was shown with older infants (*1*). Since eye movements are less coordinated and fixations less clear-cut in newborn infants, a further check of the response measurement is desirable; I plan to do this by photographic recordings.

5. I chose the targets for their expected attention value for the older infants of the earlier study; this may be different for newborn subjects: response to the newsprint may be decreased by less acute vision (although some patterning would be visible without resolution of individual letters); "bulls-eye" elicited strong differential attention only over 2 months of age in another study (*3*); and blue is preferred to red and yellow by newborns (*5*). The face pattern might for these reasons have a relative advantage for newborns.

6. F. Stirnimann, *Ann. Paediat.* 163, 1 (1944).

7. Supported by research grant M-5284 from the National Institute of Mental Health, I am indebted to Booth Memorial Hospital for making the subjects available; to Major Purser, Caroline Holcombe, R.N., Dr. R. C. Lohrey, and other staff members for their cooperation; and to Isabel Fredericson for invaluable assistance.

MAURICE HERSHENSON, HARRY MUNSINGER, & WILLIAM KESSEN

32 Preference for Shapes of Intermediate Variability in the Newborn Human

Abstract. *Newborn humans presented with pairs of shapes, each shape differing in number of turns (angles), prefer shapes with 10 turns to shapes with 5 turns or 20 turns, as inferred from photographic recordings of eye fixations.*

Reprinted from *Science 147*:630-631, 1965. Copyright 1965 by the American Association for the Advancement of Science.

The possibility that newborn humans can perceive pattern has been suggested by recent evidence of Fantz (*1*) and Hershenson (*2*), although the results are by no means conclusive and the dimensions of pattern which presumably underlie the differential responding have not been established. One dimension on which discrimination could be established and perceptibility determined, is the number of independent turns (angles) in a figure, a dimension approximating information value (*3*). This dimension is of particular interest since it has been demonstrated to be the basis of strong preferences in adults and in children (*4*). Specifically, when presented with random shapes containing from 3 to 40 independent turns, elementary school children and adults prefer neither figures of low variability (5 or 6 independent turns) nor figures of high variability (31 or 40 turns), but show a striking preference for figures of intermediate variability (10 turns).

In our study, newborn humans were exposed to pairs of shapes, each member of a pair differing from the other in number of angles. Preference for a particular shape was estimated from the number of times it was fixated by each infant. The apparatus, procedures, and scoring techniques are described elsewhere (*2*). The study was conducted in a small room containing a table on which an experimental chamber was mounted. Babies were placed on a cushioned cradle to constrain lateral movements of the head and hips. Stimuli were projected onto two ground-glass screens which were suspended 45.7 cm above the infant's eyes, 15 degrees on either side. Eye fixations were recorded on 35-mm infrared film by means of a motion picture camera mounted above the infant. The positions of the stimulus screens were marked by infrared lamps so that eye fixations could be measured in terms of relative positions of the stimulus markers to that of the pupil itself. The film was calibrated to determine the criteria for "looking at" one or the other stimulus.

Three shapes were presented in pairs so that each shape appeared once on each side; thus six stimulus pairs were shown in all. The pairs were presented to each infant in a predetermined random order. Each pair was presented for approximately 30 seconds with a dark period of from 5 to 10 seconds between presentations. Photographs were taken at the rate of one frame per second during the entire session, which lasted approximately 5 minutes.

The shapes were constructed according to a procedure previously described by Munsinger and Kessen (*4*). Coordinates in a 100 by 100 matrix were selected and connected at random to generate a shape which was then traced on drawing paper, cut out, and photographed. The resulting negatives, when projected, produced black figures on white backgrounds. The two sets of shapes used were selected to be approximately equal in brightness and complexity (*5*).

To measure the infant's tendency to look toward one of a pair of stimuli, chi-squares were calculated, both positions of the pair—AB and BA—as well as side preference being taken into account. Z scores based on the chi-squares (*6*) were used to test the hypothesis that the number of frames in which an infant fixated one member of a pair did not differ from the number of frames in which he fixated the other member of the pair. Seventeen newborns, 2 to 4 days old, were tested in this experiment.

Figure 1 shows the pattern of scaled preferences for figures varying in number of independent turns. The figures

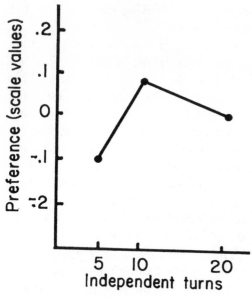

Fig. 1. Scaled preferences for figures varying in number of independent turns.

with ten angles were preferred to those with five angles ($p < .001$), indicating that newborns prefer greater variety of stimulation if given a choice between a fairly simple figure and a somewhat more variable one. This would suggest that the mediating variable had some relation to the amount of "information" in the stimuli. To be sure, the stimuli did vary minimally in complexity, but the results indicated a preference for stimuli of intermediate complexity, and the overall preferences show that the least complex stimuli were the least preferred. This is in marked contrast to the complexity-preference function for newborns previously reported by Hershenson (2) and suggests that complexity was not a contributing variable in the present study.

While the single significant preference should make one cautious in assigning the mediating role to the dimension manipulated (7), these data may be added to the accumulating evidence which now strongly suggests that the perceptual system of the newborn human is much more highly organized than previously thought. Moreover, the pattern of preferences is strikingly similar to that described by Munsinger and Kessen (4) and may be taken as partial support for the postulated limited capacity of human beings to process environmental variability.

References and Notes

1. R. L. Fantz, *Science* **140**, 296 (1963).
2. M. Hershenson, *J. Comp. Physiol. Psychol.* **58**, 270 (1964).
3. F. Attneave and M. D. Arnoult, *Psychol. Bull.* **53**, 452 (1956).
4. H. Munsinger and W. Kessen, *Psychol. Monogr.* **78**, No. 9, Whole No. 586 (1964); ———— and M. L. Kessen, *J. Exptl. Child Psychol.* **1**, 1 (1964).
5. The figures encompassed from one-quarter to one-half of the total stimulus-screen area. Relative values of complexity, defined as number of light–dark transitions in a stimulus (2), may be approximated by the perimeter: 36, 55, 68 cm for the 5-, 10-, and 20-turn figures of set 1, respectively, and 27, 40, 80 cm for those of set 2, respectively.
6. For each subject, we calculated the value of chi-square for each of the six stimulus combinations, using the respective number of frames with the infant looking at either stimulus as the observed frequencies and the relative number of frames with the infant looking at either side proportional to the overall side preference as the expected frequencies. The signed z score equivalent of the chi-squares were then averaged for the pairs of comparisons which contained the same stimuli, with sign being taken into account. Thus each subject received a signed z score for each of the three stimulus pairs. A paired-comparison scaling procedure was used for simultaneous comparisons of the stimuli.
7. M. Hershenson, W. Kessen, H. Munsinger, in *Symposium on Models for the Perception of Speech and Visual Form*, in press; W. Kessen and M. Hershenson, "Ocular Orientation in the Human Newborn Infant," paper read at meeting of American Psychological Association, Philadelphia (1963).
8. We thank A. Sameroff and P. H. Salapatek for their assistance in data collection. This research was supported in part by a grant to W.K. (M-1787) from NIH.

TORSTEN N. WIESEL & DAVID H. HUBEL

33 Extent of Recovery from the Effects of Visual Deprivation in Kittens

INTRODUCTION

IN KITTENS, deprivation of form and light over several months can lead to marked abnormalities in the visual pathway. These include behavioral blindness, morphological changes in the lateral geniculate body, and disruption of innately determined cortical connections (2, 6–8). This type of plasticity seems to be greatest in the early months of life and to decline rapidly with age; an adult cat deprived for similar periods showed no changes at all. We were naturally interested in whether the deprivation effects were permanent or whether they could be reversed by allowing normal stimuli to reach the retina again. Several kittens were therefore raised with the lids of one or both eyes sutured together for 3 months, as in previous experiments (6), and then the closed eye was reopened and the animals were allowed to live for another 3–14 months before making observations.

METHODS

Seven kittens were used, and the various procedures of deprivation and subsequent studies are summarized in Table 1. In six animals the lids of one eye were closed for the first 3 months of life. In the recovery period two of these kittens had the deprived eye opened. The other four had the deprived eye opened and the other (previously open) eye was closed. The seventh animal had both eyes closed for 3 months; the right eye was then opened. Recovery periods varied from 3 to 18 months. The animals were all kept together in a large, bright room, and were frequently played with by attendants and passersby.

Anatomical and physiological methods are described in other papers (1, 6, 8). Behavioral studies consisted mainly of observing the animal's use of vision to guide his activities. Tests of visual discrimination using operant-conditioning techniques are still being made on several animals; these will be reported elsewhere.

RESULTS

Behavior

The first kitten of this series had the right eye sutured shut from the tenth day up to 3 months of age. The lids were then separated under anesthesia. As with all the animals in this study the cornea was moist and clear; the fundus appeared normal, as were the direct and consensual pupillary light reflexes. At the outset the animal appeared to be blind in the deprived eye (7). The first signs of any recovery were noticed only after 2–3 weeks. With the good eye covered, the animal then seemed to be alerted by large objects moved in front of it, and at times would appear to follow them. These following movements showed some slight improvement with time, until after 3 months a large object was occasionally followed for several

Reprinted from *Journal of Neurophysiology* 28:1060–1072, 1965. By permission of The American Physiological Society.

This work was supported in part by Public Health Service Grants NB-02260-05 and NB 05554-01, and in part by U. S. Air Force Contracts AF-AFOSR-410-63A and AF 49(638)1443.

seconds. Even then, the animal did not always lock in on the object, but tended to lose it and go looking about wildly. Visual placing never returned. When put on the floor to roam freely, the animal would at times avoid large obstacles, but at other times would collide with them. It seldom avoided small objects such as chair legs. Placed on a chair, it would slide down, feeling its way with its forepaws. If the good eye was uncovered, the kitten would promptly jump to the floor.

Table 1. Summary of procedures performed on the seven experimental animals

Animal No.	Deprivation			Recovery			Procedure		
	Right eye	Left eye	Time, months	Right eye	Left eye	Time, months	Anatomy	Physiology	Behavior
1	Closed	Open	3	Open	Open	3	x		x
2	Closed	Open	3	Open	Open	18			x
3	Closed	Open	3	Open	Closed	3	x	x	x
4	Closed	Open	3	Open	Closed	8	x		x
5	Closed	Open	3	Open	Closed	14	x	x	x
6	Closed	Open	3	Open	Closed	18			x
7	Closed	Closed	3	Open	Closed	14	x	x	x

This behavior was typical of all animals tested. Animal *2* (Table 1) was allowed to go for 18 months after the deprived eye was opened, but it showed little if any recovery after the first 3 or 4 months.

To test the possibility that, with both eyes open, the animals might in some way be "neglecting" the previously deprived eye, we sutured closed the normal eye at the time of opening the deprived one. This was done in four kittens (no. 3–6, Table 1). Following the eye reversal these animals did just as badly as the others, indicating that they could not be forced to use the deprived eye. The change in behavior was dramatic, especially for cat *6*, which during the first 3 months had been the leader of about a dozen animals. This large, husky animal lost his prominent position in the group, became meek and cowardly, and even after 18 months is still subdued and anxious. Finally, the same kind of slow and inadequate recovery was seen in one animal (no. *7*) that was initially deprived by bilateral suture, following which one eye was opened for over a year.

Single-unit recordings

Recovery after monocular deprivation. Cortical recordings were made from 3 of the 7 animals. In kitten *3* (Table 1) the right eye had been closed for the first 3 months, after which that eye was opened and the left eye closed for another 3 months. Two penetrations were made in striate cortex, one in each hemisphere, and 54 cells were recorded. The great majority of cells (45 of 54) were still driven exclusively from the left eye. Only 9 cells could be driven from the right eye; of these 8 were abnormal, and 7 were still strongly dominated by the left eye. Two cells were exclusively driven by the right eye. The ocular-dominance distribution, given in Fig. 1, was thus still highly abnormal; indeed it was probably not significantly different from that of animals monocularly deprived for 3 months, as can be seen by comparing this

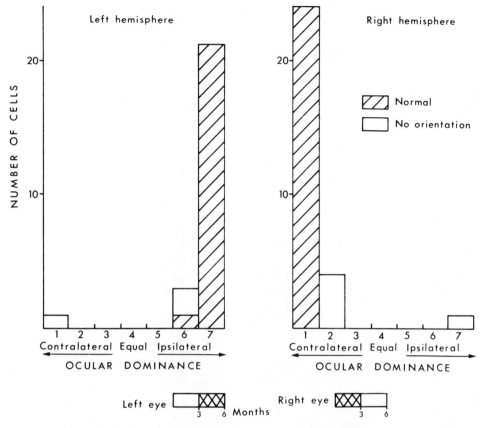

FIG. 1. Ocular-dominance distribution of 54 cells recorded from a 6-month-old cat (no. 3) in which the right eye was closed for the first 3 months of life, following which the right eye was opened and the left eye closed for the next 3 months. (Definitions of the ocular-dominance groups are as follows: cells of group 1 are driven only by the contralateral eye; for cells of group 2 there is marked dominance of the contralateral eye; for group 3, slight dominance. For cells in group 4 there is no obvious difference between the two eyes. In group 5 the ipsilateral eye dominates slightly; in group 6, markedly, and in group 7 the cells are drive only by the ipsilateral eye.)

figure with Fig. 2 in the paper on binocular deprivation (8). The 8 abnormal cells responded to a line stimulus regardless of its orientation; and showed a strong tendency to fatigue. That it was the connections between these cells and the right eye that were abnormal, rather than the cells themselves, is shown by the fact that the cells were driven in a perfectly normal manner by the left eye, having a precise receptive-field orientation and showing little tendency to fatigue. The 3 months' deprivation of the left eye immediately preceding the recording apparently had little or no effect on that eye's ability to drive cortical cells, despite the marked atrophy of the geniculate layers connected to the left eye (see below). In contrast to this, a simple closure of one eye following several months of normal vision produces a marked cortical defect (7). Taken together, these two results reinforce our conclusions from the binocular closures and strabismus experiments (8, 3) in suggesting a strong interdependence in the pathways originating from the two eyes.

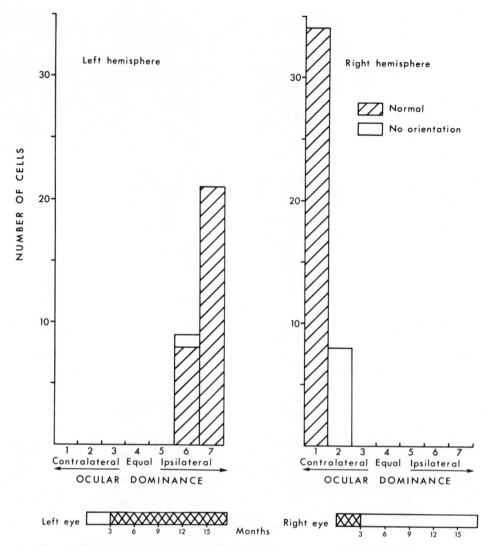

FIG. 2. Ocular dominance of 72 cells recorded from a cat (no. 5) in which the right eye was closed for the first 3 months of life, following which the right eye was opened and the left eye closed for the next 14 months.

Kitten 5 likewise had the right eye closed for the first 3 months, after which the right eye was opened and the left closed. It was then kept for over a year before recordings were made. The results of observing 72 cells in 2 penetrations are shown in Fig. 2. Again, the effects of the original deprivation to the right eye appear to have been irreversible or nearly so.

One result common to these two experiments is the absence of unresponsive cells. This contrasts with the usual monocular closure, in which some 10% of cells were not driven by either eye.

Recovery after binocular deprivation. It will be recalled that the cortical effects of depriving both eyes for the first 3 months of life are not at all what one would have predicted from the monocular deprivations (8): instead of only a very few responsive cells, 73% of the cells could be driven, and 41%

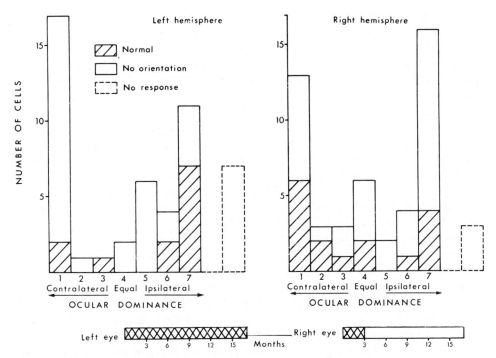

FIG. 3. Ocular-dominance distribution of 99 cells in a cat (no. 7) in which both eyes were closed for the first 3 months of life, following which the right eye was opened for the next 14 months.

responded normally. These results are summarized in the left-hand part of Table 2. In studying the cortical effects of reopening an eye one therefore begins with a totally different situation from that following monocular closure.

Cat 7 was brought up with both eyes closed for the first 3 months, at which time the right eye was opened. The animal then went for over a year with the left eye closed. Ninety-nine cells were studied in the two hemispheres, with the results shown in Fig. 3 and Table 2. The histograms show no striking predominance of the opened eye, indicating that, just as in the monocular closures, there was little tendency for recovery. On the other hand, an examination of Table 2 suggests that opening the eye did produce some changes. As in the other recovery studies, unresponsive cells were di-

Table 2. *Comparison of single-cell responses following 3-month binocular deprivation, with and without periods of recovery*

	3-Month Binocular Deprivation (8)		3-Month Binocular Deprivation Followed by 14 Months Recovery of Right Eye (cat 7)	
	Cells	Percent	Cells	Percent
Normal cells	57	41	28	30
Abnormally driven	45	32	61*	60
Unresponsive	37	27	10	10
Total cells	139	100	99	100

* Includes cells that were driven abnormally by one eye and normally by the other, as well as cells driven abnormally by both eyes.

minished, amounting to 10% of the cells instead of 27%. At the same time, cells with abnormal responses (lack of receptive-field orientation) went from 32% to 60%. The abnormal responses came mainly from the right or opened eye, which accounted for twice as many abnormal fields as the left (52 as opposed to 25). Normal cells were, if anything, slightly reduced, and fewer of these were driven by the right eye (15%) than by the left (30%).

The asymmetry in the two eyes is further illustrated by the 31 cells that were driven from both eyes. Eight of these were driven normally from the left eye and abnormally from the right, having in that eye fields that lacked any clear orientation. The reverse was not true for any of the cells. Moreover, in our study of binocularly deprived animals without recovery there were none of these asymmetric cells, normal for one eye, but abnormal for the other. Here again it is as though the number of abnormal connections from the opened eye had greatly increased.

In summary, it would seem that the recovery process had re-established connections between cortical cells and the opened eye, but that these connections were distorted ones. The fact that following recovery fewer cells were driven normally from the opened (right) eye than from the closed one is at first glance surprising. The "normal" category is, however, somewhat arbitrary and, in animals before the recovery period, it might include cells that had lost some connections and therefore responded less briskly than normal but with full specificity. If during the recovery process the lost connections were re-established, but in distorted form, one would have an increase of abnormal cells at the expense of the normal category. It does seem unlikely that opening an eye would cause abnormal connections to be established between that eye and otherwise normal cells.

Finally, this animal showed a marked increase in the proportion of cells driven only by one eye, cells of groups 1 and 7. The change resembles that seen in animals raised with squint or with alternating contact occluders (3), both conditions in which the synergic action of the two eyes is eliminated without the complication of complete disuse. Three months of binocular occlusion gave no comparable defect (8), suggesting that in the present experiment the relative increase in groups 1 and 7 must have taken place during the recovery period. Perhaps the process simply requires more time when the lack of synergy is produced by disuse, a point that could easily be settled by binocular deprivation for longer periods.

Morphology of the lateral geniculate body

Of the 5 animals whose brains have been sectioned so far, 4 were studied by examining the Nissl-stained sections and by measuring cross-sectional areas of 50 cells in each geniculate layer. The results were unanimous in failing to show the least evidence for any recovery. They are summarized in Table 3. For comparison, figures are included from an animal whose right eye was closed for the first 3 months. The average cell size of the dorsal pair of layers (A and A_1) in the normal cat at 3 months or older is about $300\mu^2$. (As discussed previously (6), cell sizes vary to some extent from one animal to the next, partly, no doubt, because of differences in fixation. We have found no evidence that cells increase significantly in size beyond 3 months of age.

Table 3. Effects of the various experimental procedures on size of cells in the two dorsal layers of the lateral geniculate body

Description of Cat	Layer	L. Side, μ^2	R. Side μ^2	Diff. Between Sides, %	Dev. From Assumed Normal of $300\mu^2$,* %	
					Left	Right
Control: simple suture R. eye closed 3 months	A	184 ± 8	279 ± 12	37 (t = 4.8)	39	
L. eye open 3 months	A_1	316 ± 14	198 ± 9	38 (t = 5.6)		34
Cat 1: simple eye opening R. eye closed 3 months, open 3 months	A	183 ± 7	254 ± 9	28 (t = 6.3)	39	
L. eye open throughout	A_1	284 ± 12	198 ± 8	30 (t = 5.7)		34
Cat 3: eye reversal R. eye closed 3 months, open 3 months	A	171 ± 8	192 ± 7	11 (t = 0.6)	43	36
L. eye open 3 months, closed 3 months	A_1	210 ± 11	158 ± 8	25 (t = 1.2)	30	47
Cat 5: eye reversal R. eye closed 3 months, open 14 months	A	160 ± 5	191 ± 10	16 (t = 2.8)	47	36
L. eye open 3 months, closed 14 months	A_1	203 ± 11	172 ± 10	15 (t = 2.1)	33	43
Cat 7: binocular R. eye closed 3 months, open 14 months	A	172 ± 7	185 ± 8		43	38
L. eye closed throughout	A_1	201 ± 7	202 ± 9		33	33

* Assumed normal based on average of 10 cats ranging in age from 3 months to $1\frac{1}{2}$ years. According to our measurements any growth in cells after 3 months is negligible.

This seems to be confirmed by comparing in Table 3 the size of normal cells in the 3-month-old control cat with the normal cell size in the 6-month-old cat *1*.)

The simplest assessment of recovery can be made for cat *1*, in which the right eye was closed for the first 3 months and was open for the next 3, the left having been open at all times. Coronal sections of the two geniculates are shown in Fig. 4. The degeneration of layers A on the left and A_1 on the right is roughly the same as in animals with one eye closed for 3 months, and no recovery period (see ref. 6, Fig. 1). Cell sizes in corresponding layers on the two sides still differ by some 30%.

The other three animals confirm this finding, and show that if growth of cells is retarded by eye suture for the first 3 months, there is little or no subsequent recovery even if the eye is reopened for over 1 year. This is particularly impressive in cat *7* in which both eyes were closed for 3 months and the right eye was then opened for 14 months. Here there was no significant difference in corresponding geniculate layers on the two sides. A coronal section through the right lateral geniculate is shown in Fig. 5, and actual cell sizes are given in Table 3.

Finally, the eye-reversal results (cats *3* and *5*) confirm our previous impression that late eye closure can produce an actual atrophy of cells (as op-

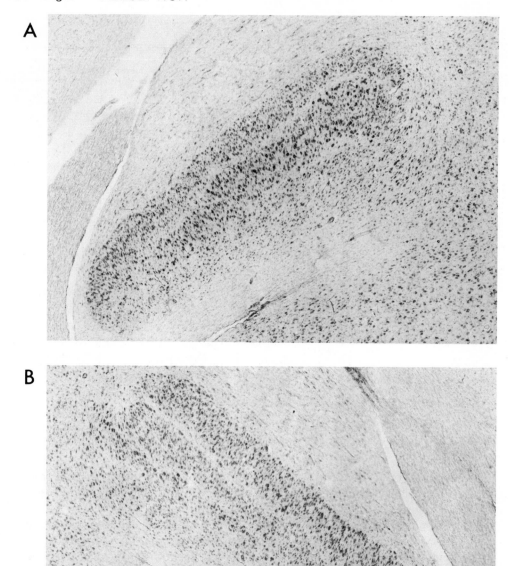

1 mm

FIG. 4. Coronal sections of left (A) and right (B) lateral geniculate bodies of a 6-month-old kitten (no. 1) in which the right eye was closed for the first 3 months of life and open for the next 3, the left being open at all times. Celloidin, cresyl violet.

posed to the failure to grow produced by closure). The shrinkage is not as pronounced as that produced by initial closure, as can be seen directly in coronal sections of the geniculates of cat 5 (Fig. 6), and also from the actual measurements of cell size given in Table 3. A comparison of the atrophy in cats 3 and 5 indicates that the main atrophic changes occur within the first 3 months of the late closure. Comparing cats 5 and 7 suggests that it makes little difference to the abnormality produced, whether an eye is closed for the first 3 months or the first 17.

DISCUSSION

The absence of any great degree of recovery in this study was surprising, since previous reports on behavioral recovery following deprivation in man (5) and in animals (4) had led us to expect some return of function, slow and perhaps incomplete, to judge from human experience, and prompt and virtually complete, to judge from the animal experiments. It is difficult to reconcile these results. The human material is particularly hard to assess, since one frequently does not know certain crucial facts such as the age of onset of cataracts, the degree of reduction of retinal illumination, and the final extent of return of vision after cataract removal. In behavioral studies in ani-

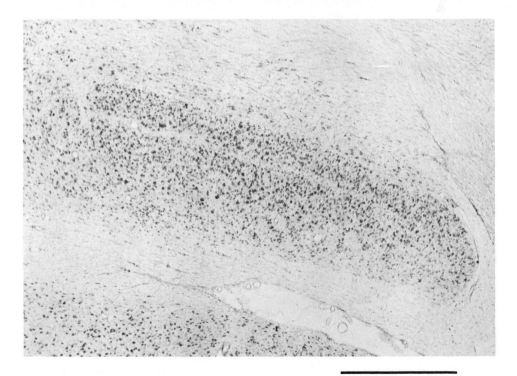

1 mm

Fig. 5. Coronal sections through right lateral geniculate body of a cat (no. 7) in which both eyes were closed for the first 3 months of life, and then the right eye was opened for the next 14 months. Note that cells in the middle layer (A₁), corresponding to the right eye, appear no different from those of the dorsal layer (A). Celloidin, cresyl violet.

A

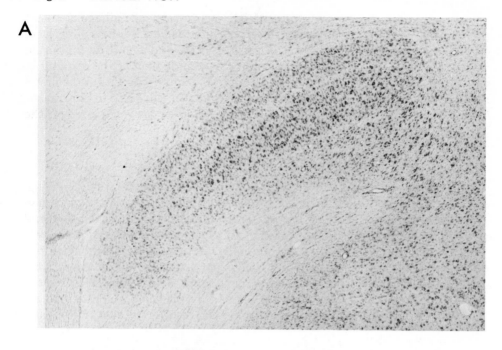

B

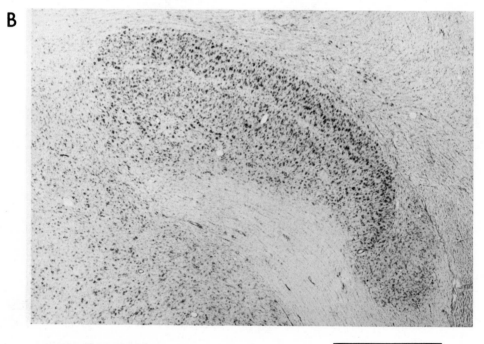

1 mm

FIG. 6. Coronal sections through left (A) and right (B) lateral geniculate bodies of a cat (no. 5) in which the right eye was closed for the first 3 months of life, following which the right eye was opened and the left eye closed for the next 14 months. Note the small size of cells in the dorsal layer of the left geniculate and the middle layer of the right, corresponding to the originally closed right eye. Celloidin, cresyl violet.

mals a direct comparison of results is not possible, since schedules of visual deprivation and testing procedures have differed from those used in the present experiments. The evaluation of visual abnormalities in animals is in any case difficult, there being no generally accepted or well-evaluated procedures for testing vision in normal animals.

All three phases of the present study—the behavioral, the physiological, and the morphological—agree in indicating only very minimal recovery from the effects of eye closure during the first 3 months of life. In the cortex such connections as did reform apparently did so in a distorted manner. There would seem to be two possible interpretations. Either connections, once lost, are incapable of properly re-establishing themselves, or the failure of recovery may simply be a matter of age—another manifestation of the decline in flexibility that occurs in the system some time between the third month and the first year. Experimentally it is difficult to know how to decide between these interpretations, since it probably requires a month or two to produce the abnormalities, by which time the period of flexibility may well be almost over.

Summary

In kittens, monocular or binocular deprivation by lid suture for the first 3 months of life leads to virtual blindness, marked morphological changes in the lateral geniculate body, and a severe deterioration of innate cortical connections. In seven kittens whose eyes had been sutured at birth for 3 months, six unilaterally and one bilaterally, an attempt was made to assess the extent of recovery by reopening an eye and allowing the animals to live for another 3–15 months. In two of the monocular closures the deprived eye was opened and the normal eye closed.

In all kittens there was some slight behavioral recovery during the first 3 months, but the animals remained severely handicapped and never learned to move freely using visual cues. There was no morphological improvement in the lateral geniculate body. Our previous impression that atrophy can develop with deprivation beginning at 3 months was confirmed. In monocularly deprived animals a few cells in the striate cortex may have recovered responses to stimulation to the originally deprived eye, but in many of these cells the responses were abnormal. In the binocularly deprived kitten there was a marked increase in the proportion of cells responding abnormally to the eye that was reopened, without any obvious increase in the total number of cells responding to that eye.

We conclude that the animals' capacity to recover from the effects of early monocular or binocular visual deprivation, whether measured behaviorally, morphologically, or in terms of single-cell cortical physiology, is severely limited, even for recovery periods of over a year.

ACKNOWLEDGMENT

We express our thanks to Jane Chen, Janet Tobie, and John Tuckerman for their technical assistance.

REFERENCES

1. Hubel, D. H. and Wiesel, T. N. Receptive fields, binocular interaction and functional architecture in the cat's visual cortex. *J. Physiol.*, 1962, *160*: 106–154.

2. HUBEL, D. H. AND WIESEL, T. N.   Receptive fields of cells in striate cortex of very young, visually inexperienced kittens. *J. Neurophysiol.*, 1963, *26*: 994–1002.

3. HUBEL, D. H. AND WIESEL, T. N.   Binocular interaction in striate cortex of kittens reared with artificial squint. *J. Neurophysiol.*, 1965, *28*: 1041–1059.

4. RIESEN, A. H.   Stimulation as requirement for growth and function in behavioral development. In: *Functions of Varied Experience*, edited by D. W. Fiske and S. R. Maddi. Homewood, Ill., Dorsey Press, 1961, pp. 57–105.

5. VON SENDEN, M.   *Raum -und Gestaltauffassung bei operierten Blindgeborenen vor und nach der Operation*, edited by J. Barth. Leipzig, 1932, English translation under the title: *Space and Sight*. Glencoe, Ill., Free Press, 1960.

6. WIESEL, T. N. AND HUBEL, D H.   Effects of visual deprivation on morphology and physiology of cells in the cat's lateral geniculate body. *J. Neurophysiol.*, 1963, *26*: 978–993.

7. WIESEL, T. N. AND HUBEL, D. H.   Single-cell responses in striate cortex of kittens deprived of vision in one eye. *J. Neurophysiol.*, 1963, *26*: 1003–1017.

8. WIESEL, T. N. AND HUBEL, D. H.   Comparison of the effects of unilateral and bilateral eye closure on cortical unit responses in kittens. *J. Neurophysiol.*, 1965, *28*: 1029–1040.

HELMUT V. B. HIRSCH & D. N. SPINELLI

34   Visual Experience Modifies Distribution of Horizontally and Vertically Oriented Receptive Fields in Cats

Abstract. *Cats were raised from birth with one eye viewing horizontal lines and one eye viewing vertical lines. Elongated receptive fields of cells in the visual cortex were horizontally or vertically oriented—no oblique fields were found. Units with horizontal fields were activated only by the eye exposed to horizontal lines; units with vertical fields only by the eye exposed to vertical lines.*

Many investigators have studied the response characteristics of single cells in the visual system in an effort to understand the neural mechanisms of perception (*1–4*). In the visual cortex of the cat and the monkey, there are units with elongated receptive fields which respond vigorously to elongated stimuli of the same orientation as the receptive field (*2–5*). It is frequently assumed that such units are important in the perception of form (*3, 6*), but no direct test of this hypothesis has been made (*7*). Ideally, one might remove all cortical units with receptive fields of a given orientation and observe the subject's visual capabilities. This would require ablation of cells on a physiological rather than an anatomical basis.

We have developed a technique for rearing kittens which results in all of the elongated receptive fields being oriented either vertically or horizontally, in contrast to the random arrangement present in normal cats (*3, 8*). Moreover, the units with horizontal fields respond only to stimulation of one eye, and the units with vertical fields respond only to stimulation of the other eye. Therefore, it should be possi-

Reprinted from *Science 168*:869–871, 1970.

ble to test the behavioral function of either class of cells by simply occluding one eye or the other.

We controlled the visual experience of kittens from birth until 10 to 12 weeks of age. Each animal's total visual experience consisted of viewing a white field containing three black vertical lines with one eye and, simultaneously viewing a field containing three horizontal lines with the other eye. The lines were 1 degree wide and their center points were 6 degrees apart. These conditions were used in order to produce discordant sensory input to the binocularly activated cortical cells.

The stimuli were mounted in a mask which provided a 50- to 60-degree field of view for each eye. Beginning at 3 weeks of age the animals wore these devices for approximately 8 hours a day. Masks were put on and removed inside a darkroom in which the animals were housed from birth whenever they were not wearing the masks. Each set of lines in the mask was positioned at the focal plane of a lens so that small changes in the position of the mask would not affect the sharpness of focus. The kittens soon became accustomed to the masks and were active and playful during the exposure periods. To insure that the animals could not pull or rub the masks off they wore a large neck ruff similar to that used by Hein and Held (9). The animals were checked repeatedly while they were wearing the masks. We estimate that slippage of the mask did not exceed 10 degrees and in most cases was less than 5 degrees; eye movements were not measured during exposure periods. It is clear from the positive results obtained that any rotations of the eyes or the mask did not interfere with the aim of the experiment.

Single unit recordings were made from the visual cortex of these animals between 10 and 12 weeks of age. We used the preparation, recording, and mapping technique developed by Spinelli (10). In brief, thiopental sodium was injected intravenously to obtain general anesthesia and a small opening was made in the skin, bone, and dura above the visual cortex in one hemisphere. Subsequently the animal was paralyzed with Flaxedil, artificially ventilated, and held in a stereotaxic instrument. All pressure points and incisions were infiltrated with a long-acting local anesthetic (Zyljectin). The cat was positioned at 57 cm from a white tangent screen; at this distance 1 cm on the screen is equal to 1 degree of arc at the eye. Contact lenses were used to correct for accommodation and to protect the cornea of the eye. The projection of the optic disk onto the screen was determined with a reversable ophthalmoscope, and the position of the area centralis was inferred (11). The estimated projections of the area centralis were centered at or near the top of the mapped region in four animals and about 5 degrees above in the remaining animal. The units were recorded from primary visual cortex between stereotaxic coordinates anterior-posterior −1.0 to +1.0 mm and medial-lateral 0.5 to 1.5 mm. In adult cats this corresponds to the region that receives projections from the area centralis (12).

The response of single units to a black spot (1 to 4 degrees in diameter) moving across the white background was recorded with tungsten microelectrodes. We used spots rather than line stimuli in mapping because this method should reveal the shape of the receptive field with the least bias (4). Elongated receptive fields of single units in the visual cortex of the cat have been mapped with stationary (3) and moving (4) spots. The responsiveness to line stimuli can be predicted from maps made with spots, at least for units which have discrete excitatory and inhibitory regions within the receptive field [(4); simple cells (3)] and perhaps for other types of units [for example, complex cells, diffuse cells (4)].

The spot was moved by a computer (Digital Equipment Corp., PDP-8) across a 25- by 25-degree field. The unit's activity was recorded at each of 2500 points within this field and presented on an oscilloscope screen as an integral contour display. In this manner the shape of the receptive field could be visualized. All units encountered during the recording were analyzed and whenever possible each was mapped at least twelve times. The mapping was first done with both eyes open and then for each eye separately. Two vertical and two horizontal maps were made for each of these conditions. During a vertical map, for example, the spot was

moved with constant speed of 10 deg/sec from bottom to top and top to bottom; 50 such scans covered the field. Data were collected separately for upward and downward motion of the spot to provide the two vertical maps. Horizontal maps were also obtained in this fashion.

Currently, a total of 50 units from five animals have been mapped in detail. Receptive fields of all units were in the lower half of the visual field. All maps were examined, but categorization of the units was based largely on the receptive field map obtained with the spot moving in the direction which elicited the strongest response from the unit (4). Units encountered during the recording were classified as either diffuse or elongated. Diffuse receptive fields have no clearly defined boundaries, and the units responded to stimulation over a wide portion of the visual field. Twenty-seven units were of this type (Fig. 1).

Receptive fields from 23 units were categorized as elongated. Their shapes ranged from somewhat elliptic to clearly edge- or bar-shaped in correspondence with elongated receptive fields described by others. Whereas normal

| Both Eyes | Horizontally Exposed Eye | Vertically Exposed Eye |
| a | b | c |

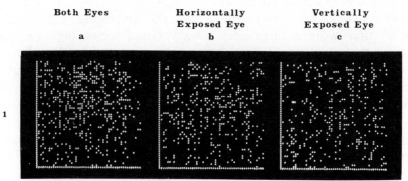

Fig. 1. Cortical unit with diffuse receptive field. Column a, Unit mapped with both eyes open; b, eye exposed by horizontal lines was left open; c, eye exposed to vertical lines was left open. The spot moved vertically during the mapping.

kittens have a full complement of receptive field orientations at birth (*13*) all of the elongated fields found in our animals were oriented either vertically or horizontally (Fig. 2). Since diagonally oriented receptive fields have been mapped in normal animals with our recording procedure [figure 7 in (*4*)], their absence here is not an artifact.

Three characteristics of these elongated receptive fields are striking when compared to elongated receptive fields found in normal cats. First, 21 of the 23 units with elongated receptive fields were predominantly or exclusively activated by only one eye, whereas normally only 10 to 20 percent of the units in the visual cortex of the cat respond to just one eye (*3, 4*). The discordant stimulation of the two eyes might have produced this loss in binocularity (*14*). The remaining two units were lost before we could determine whether they were also monocular. Second, a particular eye could activate cortical units with receptive fields of only one orientation, either vertical or horizontal, although in the normal cat receptive fields of all orientations can be activated by both eyes. Furthermore, in 20 of these 21 monocular units, the receptive field orientation corresponded to the orientation of the lines to which the eye that activated the unit had been exposed during rearing. Figure 2, rows 3 and 4, for example, shows elongated receptive fields recorded from two units found in the same cat—one unit was activated only by the eye exposed to horizontal lines, and the other only by the eye exposed to vertical lines. Third, some of the elongated receptive fields were considerably larger than those present in normal cats (*3, 4*).

The change in the distribution of orientations of cortical unit receptive fields that we found when kittens were raised with both eyes viewing different patterns demonstrates that functional neural connections can be selectively and predictably modified by environmental stimulation. Whether the discordant stimulation is a necessary condition is not known. A final aspect of our technique is that we succeeded in reviving our animals after the electrophysiological recording. Therefore, we can test the performance of these same cats in the discrimination of patterns and determine the behavioral effects of the physiological manipulation.

References and Notes

1. H. B. Barlow, R. M. Hill, W. R. Levick, *J. Physiol. London* **173**, 377 (1964); H. K. Hartline and F. Ratliff, *J. Gen. Physiol.* **41**, 1049 (1958).
2. G. Baumgartner, J. L. Brown, A. Schulz, *Neurophysiology* **28**, 1 (1965).
3. D. H. Hubel and T. N. Wiesel, *J. Physiol. London* **160**, 106 (1962).
4. D. N. Spinelli and T. W. Barrett, *Exp. Neurol.* **24**, 76 (1969).
5. D. H. Hubel and T. N. Wiesel, *J. Physiol. London* **195**, 215 (1968).
6. D. M. MacKay, in *Models for the Perception of Speech and Visual Form*, W. Walthen-Dunn, Ed. (MIT Press, Cambridge, 1967), pp. 25–43; W. R. A. Muntz, *ibid.*, pp. 126–136.
7. The following are examples of indirect tests of this hypothesis: L. Ganz and M. Fitch, *Exp. Neurol.* **22**, 638 (1968); R. W. Sekuler, E. L. Rubin, W. H. Cushman, *J. Opt. Soc. Amer.* **58**, 1146 (1968); T. N. Wiesel and D. H. Hubel, *J. Neurophysiol.* **26**, 1003 (1963); ——, *ibid.* **28**, 1029 (1965).
8. More recent data [J. D. Pettigrew. T. Nikara. P. O. Bishop, *Exp. Brain Res.* **6**, 373 (1968)] would suggest that near the visual axis vertically and horizontally oriented receptive fields may be more common than obliquely oriented receptive fields. Our observations on normal adult cats (D. N. Spinelli, unpublished data) would indicate that, whereas there is such a preference, its magnitude may be relatively small.
9. A. Hein and R. Held, *Science* **158**, 390 (1967).
10. D. N. Spinelli, *Exp. Neurol.* **19**, 291 (1967).

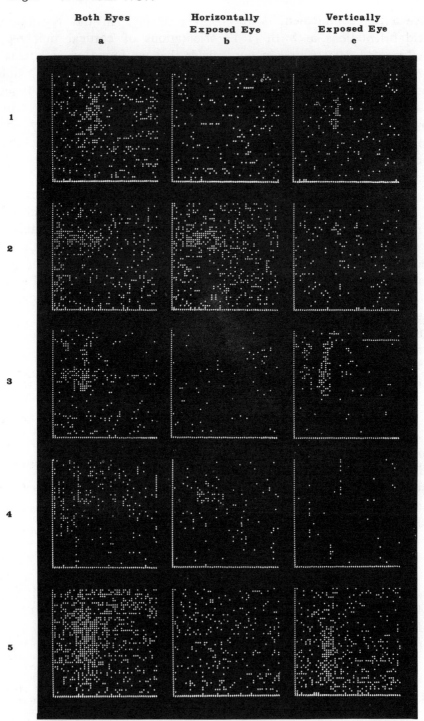

Fig. 2. Cortical units with elongated receptive fields. Rows 1 to 5 illustrate integral contour displays of receptive fields of five units. In column a, the units are mapped with both eyes open; b, units mapped with only the eye exposed to horizontal lines open; c, units mapped with only the eye exposed to vertical lines open. Rows 3 and 4 illustrate receptive fields from two units found in the same

cat. Note that all receptive fields are elongated, that the units are activated by only one eye, and that the orientation of the receptive fields is identical to the orientation of the lines to which that eye was exposed during development. The unit illustrated in row 4 has one of the most poorly defined receptive fields found when mapped with both eyes open. It should, however, be noted that the receptive field is well defined when mapped with the horizontally exposed eye open (4b) whereas it is completely absent when mapped with the vertically exposed eye open (4c). During mapping the spot moved horizontally in rows 1, 3, and 5 and vertically in rows 2 and 4.

11. G. J. Vakkur, P. O. Bishop, W. Kozak, *Vision Res.* **3**, 289 (1963).
12. R. Otsuka and R. Hassler, *Arch. Psychiat. Nervenkrankh.* **203**, 212 (1962).
13. D. H. Hubel and T. N. Wiesel, *J. Neurophysiol.* **26**, 994 (1963).
14. ———, *ibid.* **28**, 1041 (1965).

15. We thank C. R. Hamilton for help and advice as the senior author's thesis adviser. Senior author supported by NIMH predoctoral fellowship 2-F1-MH-29-103. Support provided by PHS grants NB-06501 and MH-12970. B. Bridgman and R. Phelps assisted with the electrophysiological recording.

RICHARD HELD & ALAN HEIN

35   Movement-Produced Stimulation in the Development of Visually Guided Behavior

Full and exact adaptation to sensory rearrangement in adult human Ss requires movement-produced sensory feedback. Riesen's work suggested that this factor also operates in the development of higher mammals but he proposed that sensory-sensory associations are the prerequisite. To test these alternatives, visual stimulation of the active member (A) of each of 10 pairs of neonatal kittens was allowed to vary with its locomotor movements while equivalent stimulation of the second member (P) resulted from passive motion. Subsequent tests of visually guided paw placement, discrimination on a visual cliff, and the blink response were normal for A but failing in P. When other alternative explanations are excluded, this result extends the conclusions of studies of adult rearrangement to neonatal development.

Hebb's writing (1949) has stirred interest in the effects of exposure to the environment on the development of spatial perception and coordination. The main experimental attack on the problem has used the technique of rearing animals in restricted environments (deprivation) from the time of birth or shortly thereafter. An alternative approach consists in experimentally analyzing the conditions for modifying certain sensorimotor coordinations in adults on the assumption that they are similarly plastic

Reprinted from *Journal of Comparative and Physiological Psychology* 56:872–876, 1963. Copyright 1963 by the American Psychological Association and reproduced by permission.

This research was supported by a grant from the National Science Foundation.

during the entire exposure-history of the organism (Hein & Held, 1962; Held, 1955, 1961). If this supposition is true, the analysis carried out on adults must also define the kind of contact with the environment required for development. Use of the rearrangement technique for studying plasticity in adult human Ss has yielded results which suggest its complementarity to the procedures of neonatal deprivation (Held & Bossom, 1961). This experiment demonstrates the convergence of the two approaches.

In the human adult, change in stimulation dependent upon the natural movements of S has been shown essential to the achievement of full and exact compensation for sensory rearrangements (Hein & Held,

1958; Held, 1955; Held & Bossom, 1961; Mikaelian & Held, in press). A suggestive parallel between these findings and those of deprivation studies comes from two experiments on kittens reared under different conditions of deprivation. In one experiment Ss were allowed visual experience in an illuminated and patterned environment only while they were restrained in holders which prevented them from freely moving about (Reisen & Aarons, 1959). When subsequently tested they showed deficiencies in visually guided behavior compared with their normally reared litter mates. Related deficits followed rearing in a second experiment in which Ss were allowed to move about freely in light but with diffusing hoods over their eyes (Reisen, 1961c). The exposure factor lacking under both conditions was the variation in visual stimulation produced by the full range of S's movement in normal circumstances; a result consistent with our findings.

Riesen has suggested that his deprived Ss showed deficits because they lacked sufficient opportunity for developing sensory-sensory associations in the manner proposed by Hebb (Riesen, 1961c)—even the patterned surroundings viewed by the holder-restrained Ss may not have provided sufficient variation in visual stimulation for forming the necessary associations. This interpretation agrees with ours in asserting that the variation in visual stimulation accompanying movement is essential for the development of certain coordinations but it omits our qualification that this variation can be effective only when it is concurrent with and systematically dependent upon self-produced movements (Hein & Held, 1962; Held, 1961). The alternative to our interpretation asserts that changes in stimulation irrespective of their relation to self-produced movements are sufficient. To decide between these two alternatives, we reared different sets of kittens from birth under the two implied conditions of exposure and subsequently compared their development. Under one condition stimulation varied as a result of Ss own locomotion whereas under the other it was equivalently varied by transporting Ss through an equivalent range of motion while they were restrained from locomoting.

METHOD

Subjects

Ten pairs of kittens were used; each pair from a different litter.

Exposure Apparatus and Procedure

The exposure apparatus diagramed in Figure 1 was designed to equate the visual stimulation received by each member of a pair of Ss. Stimulation varied with the locomotor movements of the active S (A in Figure 1) but varied with equivalent motion of the passive S (P). To attain this equivalence, the gross motions of A were mechanically transferred to P. These movements were restricted to rotations around three axes. The radial symmetry of the visible environment made variations in visual stimulation, contingent upon these movements, equal over time for the two Ss.

The P was placed in the gondola and held there by a neckyoke and body clamp. The lever from which the gondola was suspended was then balanced by appropriate placement of a counterweight. When attached to the opposite end of the lever by a second neckyoke and body-clamp assembly, A was free to move itself in both directions around the three axes of rotation a-a, b-b, and c-c while pulling P through the equivalent movements around a-a, b-b, and d-d by means of the mechanical linkages to the gondola. The distance between c-c and d-d was 36 in. The range of motions normally performed by Ss was somewhat reduced by the experimental apparatus. Use of ball bearings and aluminum in the construction of the apparatus reduced friction and inertia insofar as possible. The importance of these restraints is mitigated, we believe, by previous findings in re-arrangement studies which indicate that similar restraints, and constant changes in the inertia overcome by muscular movement, do not affect the adaptation process (Held & Hein, 1958; Held & Schlank, 1959). Head motion was not restricted for either A or P. This restriction seemed unnecessary since Riesen and Aarons (1959) have shown that kittens reared from birth with variation in visual stimulation consequent upon free head motions, but otherwise restricted, failed to learn a simple spatial discrimination. Because of its constraints, P could not locomote. However, its limbs were free to move and to slide along the smooth floor of the gondola. According to our observations these movements frequently occurred.

The apparatus was surrounded by a galvanized iron cylinder that was 24 in. high with a diameter of 48 in. The lever support mechanism was enclosed within a second cylinder that was 11 in. high with a diameter of 12 in. The smaller cylinder served to obscure each S's view of its mate. Patterning was provided by vertically oriented 1 in. wide stripes of black and white masking tape separated by 1 in. of bare metal. Additional texture was provided by the rough side of a piece of masonite which served as the floor. The floor was uniform throughout thus providing equivalent visual stimulation for the two Ss. Sight of the paws and other body parts was excluded by appropriate extensions of the neck stocks.

Testing Apparatus and Procedure

We used tests of visually guided behavior that minimized S's gross movements in the visible environment in order not to confound the conditions of testing with those of exposure, a confusion which past investigators have generally disregarded. For this purpose responses to stimuli were used that require no conditioning with repetition of movements but which are nonetheless contingent upon a capacity to make visual-spatial discriminations. Following the leads of earlier work, we have used three such tests:

1. Visually-guided paw placement (Riesen, 1961c). S's body was held in E's hands so that its head and forelegs were free. It was slowly carried forward and downward towards the edge of a table or some other horizontal surface. A normally-reared S shows visually-mediated anticipation of contact by extending its paws as it approaches the edge.

2. Avoidance of a visual cliff (Walk & Gibson, 1961). The visual cliff consists essentially of a narrow platform supported by vertical sides that drop a few inches to a large plate of glass. The S placed on the platform can descend to the glass on either one of two sides. Its view on the "deep" side is through the glass to a patterned surface 30 in. below. On the other side it views a similarly pat-

terned surface attached to the underside of the glass. In our apparatus, both surfaces were illuminated from below and hence the clean glass surface was practically invisible. For the vertical sides of the platform, we substituted planes inclined 35° from the vertical.

3. Blink to an approaching object (Riesen, 1958). The S was held in a standing position in a neckyoke and body clamp with a large sheet of Plexiglas positioned directly in front of its face. The E moved his hand quickly toward S, stopping just short of contact with the Plexiglas.

Several additional tests were performed to check the status of peripheral receptor and response mechanisms. These included observations of pupillary reflex to light, the tactual placing response, and visual pursuit of a moving object. The S, held in a standing position in a neckyoke and body clamp, was light-adapted in the normally illuminated laboratory prior to observation of the pupillary reflex. Change in pupillary size was then noted when a light beam from a penlight was moved across the eye from outer to inner canthus. To determine the presence of the tactual paw-placing response S was supported as in the visual paw-placing test. It was then carried to the edge of a table where the dorsa of its front paws were brought into contact with the vertical edge of the table. Observations of experimental Ss were compared with those of normals which, in response to this stimulus, place the paws on the horizontal sur-

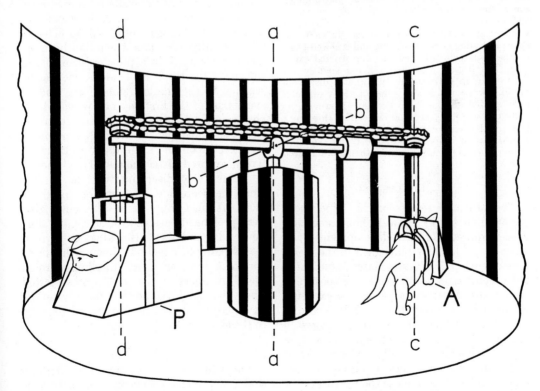

Fig. 1. Apparatus for equating motion and consequent visual feedback for an actively moving (A) and a passively moved (P) S.

face of the table. Visual pursuit was elicited by
E's hand moving slowly across S's visual field.

General Procedure

The 10 pairs of Ss were divided into two Groups,
X and Y, whose members were reared with minor
differences. Each of the eight pairs of Group X was
reared in darkness from birth until member A attained the minimal size and coordinational capacity
to move itself and its mate in the apparatus. This
age varied between 8 and 12 weeks. They then began exposure in the apparatus for 3 hr. daily. The
two pairs of Group Y received 3 hr. daily exposure,
beginning at 2 and ending at 10 weeks of age, to
the patterned interior of the laboratory while restrained in holders that allowed some head movement but prevented locomotion. They then began
exposure in the apparatus for 3 hr. daily. When not
exposed, all Ss were kept in lightless cages together
with their mothers and litter mates. We had found
in pilot studies that Ss reared in this fashion did
not show the freezing, agitation, or fear responses
reported to follow social isolation by Melzack
(1962) and Riesen (1961a).

Six repetitions of the paw-placement test were
performed after each daily exposure period for all
Ss. On the first day that one S of each pair in
Group X displayed visual paw placing, both were
tested on the visual cliff. They were retested on the
following day. For each test and retest S was required to descend from the central platform six
times. Immediately following trials on the visual
cliff on the second day, member P of each pair
was put in a continuously illuminated room for
48 hr. Retesting of visual placing and renewed trials
on the visual cliff followed this unrestricted exposure. The testing procedure differed slightly for
pairs of Group Y. On the first day that A displayed
visual paw placing, it was tested on the visual cliff
and retested on the following day. However, its
mate (P) was not placed on the cliff at this time;
instead, the passive exposure procedure was continued for 3 hr. daily for a total of 126 hr. The paw
placing and visual cliff tests were then administered
to P.

RESULTS

The principal results of this experiment
are summarized in Table 1. The amount of
time required for the development of a
visually-guided paw-placement in the members of each pair of litter mates is indicated
in the column under the heading Exposure in
Apparatus. After those periods of exposure
required by A, every P mate failed to display the response. Observations suggest a
tendency for the placing response to develop
in the livelier of the active Ss with fewer
hours of exposure than required by the
quieter ones. The blink response to an approaching hand developed concurrently with

TABLE 1
RATIO OF DESCENTS TO SHALLOW AND DEEP SIDES OF VISUAL CLIFF

Pair number	Age in weeks[a]	Exposure in apparatus (in hr.)		Ratio of descents shallow/deep	
		A	P	A	P
1X	8	33	33	12/0	6/6
2X	8	33	33	12/0	4/8
3X	8	30	30	12/0	7/5
4X	9	63	63	12/0	6/6
5X	10	33	33	12/0	7/5
6X	10	21	21	12/0	7/5
7X	12	9	9	12/0	5/7
8X	12	15	15	12/0	8/4
1Y	10	30	126	12/0	6/6
2Y	10	33	126	12/0	8/4

[a] At the beginning of exposure in the experimental apparatus.

the placing response. Pupillary reflex to
light, tactual placing response, and visual
pursuit were each noted on first elicitation,
just prior to the initial exposure in the
apparatus.

On the day that the visually-guided placing response was shown by A, he was tested
on the modified visual cliff. All As behaved
like normally reared Ss which had been observed previously in a pilot experiment. As
shown by the totals of Table 1, each A de-
scended to the shallow side of the cliff on
every trial of the first day and repeated this
performance on the trials of the following
day. The P members of Group X were tested
on the cliff on the same days as their actively exposed litter mates. They showed
no evidence of discriminating the shallow
from the deep side. Observations of the P
members of Group Y on the cliff, after
their prolonged passive exposure, gave similar results and they also failed to perform
visual paw placement. Following the 48 hr.
period of freedom in an illuminated room,
the P members of Group X were retested.
They then displayed normal visually-guided
paw-placement and performed all descents
to the shallow side of the visual cliff.

DISCUSSION

The results are consistent with our thesis
that self-produced movement with its concurrent visual feedback is necessary for the

development of visually-guided behavior. Equivalent, and even greatly increased, variation in visual stimulation produced by other means is not sufficient. However, before concluding that our thesis is valid we must consider other alternative explanations of the deficits in the behavioral development of neonates following deprivation. These alternatives assert that loss of function does not reflect deficiencies in a process of the central nervous system that depends upon exposure for its development. Instead, the capacity to perform is allegedly present but prevented from operating by either peripheral blockage or other suppressive effects of the special rearing conditions. Such negative effects fall into two categories: (*a*) anatomical or physiological deterioration and (*b*) behavioral inhibition.

Included under anatomical or physiological deterioration said to result from deprivation, are the findings of atrophy in peripheral parts of the visual nervous system, a literature reviewed by Riesen (1961b); the assumption that maturation of the retina is prevented (Walk & Gibson, 1961); and the suggestion that general debility results from lack of use of various organs (Hess, 1962). In the present experiment, the relevance of peripheral atrophy is contraindicated by the presence of pupillary and pursuit reflexes and the rapid recovery of function of the passive *S*s once given their freedom. Debility specific to the motor systems of these *S*s can be ruled out on the grounds that their tactual placing responses and other motor activities were indistinguishable from those of normals. In addition, differential losses in the periphery or differential debility could hardly be expected to result from those differences between active and passive exposures which occurred in the experimental apparatus.

Inhibition of performance attributable to the effects of shock, fright, or overactivation upon exposure to the novel and increased stimulation that follows release from the deprived state has been suggested by Sutherland (1959) and Melzack (1962). Sutherland has also suggested that habits developed during deprivation may compete with and inhibit the normal response. However, both our active and passive *S*s were raised under very similar conditions insofar as restriction was concerned and under the rather mild conditions of deprivation of this experiment we did not observe any signs of shock, excitement, or fright. Moreover, the passive *S*s were not observed performing responses that might have competed with the expected response.

These findings provide convincing evidence for a developmental process, in at least one higher mammal, which requires for its operation stimulus variation concurrent with and systematically dependent upon self-produced movement. This conclusion neither denies nor affirms that other processes, such as maturation, occur concomitantly. The results demonstrate the complementarity of studies of adult rearrangement and neonatal deprivation.

REFERENCES

HEBB, D. O. *The organization of behavior.* New York: Wiley, 1949.

HEIN, A., & HELD, R. Minimal conditions essential for complete re-learning of hand-eye coordination with prismatic distortion of vision. Paper read at Eastern Psychological Association. Philadelphia, 1958.

HEIN, A., & HELD, R. A neural model for labile sensorimotor coordinations. In E. E. Bernard & M. R. Kare (Eds.), *Biological prototypes and synthetic systems.* Vol. 1. New York: Plenum Press, 1962. Pp. 71–74.

HELD, R. Shifts in binaural localization after prolonged exposures to atypical combinations of stimuli. *Amer. J. Psychol.,* 1955, **68,** 526–548.

HELD, R. Exposure-history as a factor in maintaining stability of perception and coordination. *J. nerv. ment. Dis.,* 1961, **132,** 26–32.

HELD, R., & BOSSOM, J. Neonatal deprivation and adult rearrangement: Complementary techniques for analyzing plastic sensory-motor coordinations. *J. comp. physiol. Psychol.,* 1961, **54,** 33–37.

HELD, R., & HEIN, A. Adaptation of disarranged hand-eye coordination contingent upon reafferent stimulation. *Percept. mot. Skills,* 1958, **8,** 87–90.

HELD, R., & SCHLANK, M. Adaptation to optically-increased distance of the hand from the eye by re-afferent stimulation. *Amer. J. Psychol.,* 1959, **72,** 603–605.

HESS, E. H. Ethology: An approach toward the complete analysis of behavior. In R. Brown, E. Galanter, E. H. Hess, & G. Mandler (Eds.), *New directions in psychology.* New York: Holt, Rinehart & Winston, 1962. Pp. 159–266.

MELZACK, R. Effects of early perceptual restriction on simple visual discrimination. *Science,* 1962, **137,** 978–979.

Mikaelian, H., & Held, R. Two types of adaptation to an optically-rotated visual field. *Amer. J. Psychol.*, in press.

Riesen, A. H. Plasticity of behavior: Psychological aspects. In H. F. Harlow & C. N. Woolsey (Eds.), *Biological and biochemical bases of behavior*. Madison: Univer. Wisconsin Press, 1958, Pp. 425–450.

Riesen, A. H. Excessive arousal effects of stimulation after early sensory deprivation. In P. Solomon, P. E. Kubzansky, P. H. Leiderman, J. H. Mendelson, R. H. Trumbull, & D. Wexler (Eds.), *Sensory deprivation*. Cambridge: Harvard Univer. Press, 1961. Pp. 34–40. (a)

Riesen, A. H. Stimulation as a requirement for growth and function in behavioral development. In D. W. Fiske & S. R. Maddi (Eds.), *Functions of varied experience*. Homewood: Dorsey Press, 1961. Pp. 57–80. (b)

Riesen, A. H. Studying perceptual development using the technique of sensory deprivation. *J. nerv. ment. Dis.*, 1961, **132,** 21–25. (c)

Riesen, A. H., & Aarons, L. Visual movement and intensity discrimination in cats after early deprivation of pattern vision. *J. comp. physiol. Psychol.*, 1959, **52,** 142–149.

Sutherland, N. S. Stimulus analyzing mechanisms. In, *Mechanization of thought processes: National physical laboratory symposium No. 10*. Vol. 2. London: Her Majesty's Stationery Office, 1959. Pp. 575–609.

Walk, R. D., & Gibson, E. J. A comparative and analytical study of visual depth perception. *Psychol. Monogr.*, 1961, **75**(15, Whole No. 519).

ENVIRONMENTAL DETERMINANTS

Chapter Nine   ENVIRONMENTAL DEPRIVATION

Additional Readings

ENVIRONMENTAL DEPRIVATION

An experimental procedure useful in isolating causal variables in development is to rear animals in a deprived environment. The deprivation may take any of several forms, including sensory deprivation, social isolation, and barrenness of the physical environment. If, under deprivation conditions, an animal exhibits retarded or aberrant behavior, the investigator may conclude that the excluded experience is important in helping that particular behavior to develop. Similarly, he may conclude that if an animal reared in deprived circumstances shows normal behavior, the experiences of which it has been deprived do not affect the observed behavior pattern. Note that he should *not* conclude that the particular behavior studied will manifest itself independent of experience, for there may be an environment in which the animal could be reared that would cause a behavioral change.

One generalization which emerges from the considerable research in this field is that deprivation may result in behavioral and physiological deficits, though the particular deficits which occur are often rather surprising and at times quite dramatic. The six papers in this chapter are selected to illustrate this generalization. Paper 36 was published in 1943, well before the introduction of the field of "early experience" and before the advent of extensive interest in development as a dynamic process. Wolf clearly demonstrated that auditory or visual deprivation, introduced immediately after those senses became functional, would result in a behavioral deficit when rats were placed in competition with each other, though not when they were tested alone. The paper did not appear to have much impact when pub-

lished, perhaps because of Wolf's strong psychiatric interpretation of his data and its appearance in a psychiatric journal at a time when psychologists were interested chiefly in behaviorism.

At times experiments within the deprivation framework produce unexpected findings that open up exciting new research areas. Paper 37, by Melzack and Scott, and Paper 38, by Mason, report such experiments. Melzack and Scott reported that dogs raised in isolation from puppyhood to maturity were remarkably defective in perceiving pain and were unable to react appropriately to painful stimuli. Mason, working in Harlow's Primate Laboratory at Wisconsin, was the first to report that monkeys reared in social isolation were more aggressive than were control animals and — most dramatic — that the males were sexually incompetent. These findings were all the more surprising since Harlow (1959) had previously reported that these animals exhibited completely normal learning behavior. It was not until sexual maturity that any evidence of abnormality was noted.

One important contribution of these papers was to bring about a rethinking of notions concerning development. Since both the ability to perceive and react appropriately to pain and the ability to be sexually competent are necessary for the survival of the species, the associated behavior patterns were presumed to have a long evolutionary history and a strong genetic basis. Indeed, many people would have said that these behaviors would occur with maturation regardless of the nature of the environment (as long as it was nontoxic). However, demonstration of the lability of these behavior patterns, especially with species as advanced phylogenetically as the dog and the primate, indicated that the environment during development was not merely supportive of the growing organism, but instead, contributed dynamic properties which interacted with the developing organism to shape and define a number of vital behavioral capacities.

The relation between maturation and environmental deprivation was also investigated by Dennis. Paper 39 is a report on the behavioral development of twins which Dennis and his wife reared from 1 month of age under conditions of minimal social stimulation from the adults or from each other and only restricted opportunities for interaction with their physical environment. Such rearing practices would not be acceptable today, but Dennis did this study almost 40 years ago when there was virtually no knowledge concerning the effects of restriction upon behavior. He found that the restricted experiences did not have any marked effect upon the behavioral development of the twin girls. In view of the other data in this book, such a finding appears quite unusual. There are several possible reasons for this apparent discrepancy. Dennis chose to measure various aspects of physical development such as visual fixation, vocalization, and sitting alone. Since these behaviors are strongly related to the child's physical growth and maturation, it is unlikely that they would be adversely affected unless the general growth of the child were also impeded. If Dennis had examined other endpoints, perhaps some differences would have been found. Also, Dennis took his measurements during the course of the experiment, and we now know that the effects of early experiences may not manifest themselves until some later time in development.

From this and other work Dennis hypothesized that intrinsic maturational factors governed the child's development independent of the nature of the environment. In his own words: "The infant within the first year will 'grow up' on his own accord." For approximately 30 years he consistently advocated the position "that infant development consists largely of the maturation of a motor sequence

which is little affected by learning." However, in 1960 Dennis reported that Iranian children reared under conditions of severe restriction were greatly retarded in their motor behavior, and these data caused him to change his theoretical ideas about development. That report is Paper 40.

Paper 41, by Rheingold and Bayley, is a follow-up of an experiment done originally by Rheingold (1956). In that first experiment she had worked with 16 babies who were reared in an institution. Eight of the babies, the experimental group, received extensive care and mothering from one maternal caretaker, while the control babies were maintained on the usual institution routine. At the end of the study the experimental babies were found to be more socially responsive than the babies in the control group. These findings, important as they were, left unanswered the question whether there would be any long-term effects from the experimental mothering, and that was the objective of the investigation reported in Paper 41. Of the original 16 babies, 14 were tested a year after the experiment. No differences were found between the two groups on any of the behaviors measured. The authors offer some interesting speculations concerning the meaning of the lack of significant effects. They also properly emphasize an important positive feature of their negative findings — that these institution-reared children were intelligent, friendly, and well adjusted. A number of people had misinterpreted and overgeneralized some of the earlier reports, suggesting that institutionalization would have a detrimental effect upon the child's intellectual and emotional growth; the Rheingold and Bayley research helped restore proper perspective.

References

Harlow, H. F. The development of learning in the Rhesus monkey. *Amer. Sci.,* 1959, 47, 459-479.

Rheingold, H. L. The modification of social responsiveness in institutional babies. *Monogr. Soc. Res. Child Develop.,* 1956, 21, No. 63.

36 The Dynamics of the Selective Inhibition of Specific Functions in Neurosis

This is a preliminary report of an experiment devised to demonstrate the dynamics of the specific loss of function in neurosis. Much work has been done by other investigators to indicate that conflict in intention is followed by paralysis of effort to produce a variety of neurotic phenomena. Attempts have been made on the basis of animal experimentation and clinical analysis to explain the diverse nervous patterns that develop with inhibition of function.

M. J. Sanders (82) demonstrated experimentally in the rat that a threat to the animal's security is followed by a retreat from a more logical, recently acquired, mode of adaptation to a more primitive type of mastery. She trained five rats to run down an initial common path and then to take a detour either to the right or left. Both detours led to a final common path at the end of which they received food. Definite preferences were shown by individual rats for one or the other initial detour. Sanders assumed these preferences to be "unlearned" and "ontogenetically lower." The preference for a given route was strengthened by introducing a differential temporal delay in the final common path consisting of five seconds if the preferred path were taken, and ninety seconds if the unpreferred path were taken. The training period continued until the preferred path was chosen thirty-six out of forty trials. At this time the procedure was reversed, the long delay being introduced when the preferred path was chosen, and the short delay when the path originally unpreferred was taken. This procedure was continued until the animals chose the previously unpreferred path

Reprinted from *Psychosomatic Medicine* 5:27–38, 1943.

Aided by a grant from The John and Mary R. Markle Foundation. The author is greatly indebted to Dr. Abram Kardiner for suggestions and encouragement and to a laboratory assistant whose work made these experiments possible.

in thirty-six of forty trials. At this point each rat was shocked by an electric grill just before it reached the end of the initial common path. All the animals reverted at once to the originally preferred route, although this course was not now "adaptive by any objective standard," since it continued to involve a longer delay in the final common path.

O. H. Mowrer (73) devised an experiment in which "frustration" of one mode of adjustment (habit B) caused "regression" in one group of rats to an earlier mode of adjustment (habit A), but did not lead to "regression" in another group of rats that had not practised habit A before acquiring habit B.

D. M. Levy (54) in an experiment with dogs prevented completion of the suckling phase in the feeding act, i.e., caused an insufficiency of sucking. This was followed by excessive sucking activity. The animals showed increased licking tendencies until the sixty-fourth day of life.

J. McV. Hunt (45) reported an experiment to evaluate first, the effect of infantile experience upon adult behavior, and second, to determine the relationship between the age at which the experience occurred and its effect upon mature behavior. A group of rats twenty-four days old and another thirty-two days old were submitted to ten-minute feedings at irregular intervals for fifteen days, while their litter mate controls were allowed as much food as they could eat. Then, after five months of unlimited food for both experimental animals and controls, the number of food pellets hoarded by the animals in each group both before and after a five-day period of adult feeding frustration were compared. In the postfrustration tests, the experimental animals in the twenty-four day group hoarded more than two and a half times as many pellets as their litter mate controls, while the experimental animals of the thirty-two day group hoarded approximately the same amount as their controls and the controls of the twenty-four day group. These results offered evidence in favor of the theory that in lower animals infantile experience does affect behavior in maturity and that the earlier experience is more critical in its effect on adult behavior than the later.

Felix Deutsch (*21*) contends that a mutual interaction between emotional and physiological processes must be considered to be present permanently in every human being independently of whether total function proceeds normally or abnormally. This presupposes a continual fusion between somatic and emotional processes inherent in physiological or pathological function. If a pathological emotional process was once able to invalidate an organic function, any repetition of this process may lead to the same patho-physiological response and may be only the expression of this abnormal emotional state. This implies that the same disturbance may arise when a disturbed organ happens to be malfunctioning during an emotional conflict which would have been solved without difficulty if the physiological function were not upset at the critical moment. The aforementioned fusion, once expressed in organic dysfunction, can remain latent but may find visible renewal under various conditions. This fusion may be regarded as having a potential energy so that it will react as a unit and in a specific way whenever a part of this unit is stimulated, producing a psychosomatic complex of symptoms. The concept of organ neuroses stresses three facts: first, the specificity of the personality organization; second, the specificity of the organic symptom complex; and third, the interaction between these two factors. The organ or one of its functions *must* have been involved in the psychosomatic process at a very early time. The rigidity of the symptom depends upon this time factor, because the malfunction of the organ must have been associated with an emotional conflict at this early period; this is conducive to its formation. What is characteristic of the psychosomatic unit is the fact that there has been a transient disturbance of an organic nature

which coincided with a need for expression on the part of the "instinctual" drives.

In spite of these and a good deal more animal and clinical researches[1] into the significance and character of infantile experience in determining the nature of disturbed adaptation in maturity, it has not yet been demonstrated how the inhibition of various functions can be predetermined in neurotic maturity. It has never been indicated by animal experimentation just how these particular deprivations acquire their special character, why it is that one neurotic develops hemiparesis; another dysphagia, still another, stuttering, and so on. The theoretical base from which the experiment proceeded lay in the clinical observation that patients appear under stress to retreat to infantile patterns of adaptation losing in the process fully developed resources acquired in maturation. A man who was not weaned from the bottle until five years of age is discovered in neurotic maturity to overact under stress. Another patient who did not develop bladder continence until five years of age becomes incontinent under stress in maturity, and so on.

[1] Alexander (*1*), Alexander (*2*), Anderson and Liddell (*3*), Anderson, Parmenter, and Liddell (*4*), Baker (*5*), Barker, Dembo, and Lewin (*6*), Binger (*7*), Brunswick (*8*), Burrow (*9, 10, 11*), Cameron (*22*), Cook (*13, 14*), Curtis (*15*), Daniels (*16, 17, 18, 19, 20*), Deutsch and Kauf (*26*), Deutsch (*22, 23, 24, 25*), Diller (*27*), Dimmick, Ludlow, and Whiteman (*28*), Drabovitch and Weger (*29*), Draper (*30*), Dunbar (*31, 32, 33, 34, 35*), Dworkin (*36*), Finger (*37*), Freud (*38*), Frolov (*39*), Gantt (*40*), Goldstein (*41*), Hamilton and Krechevsky (*42*), Hovland and Sears (*43*), Humphrey and Marcuse (*44*), Hunt and Willoughby (*46*), Karn (*47, 48, 49, 50*), Karn and Patton (*51, 52*), Lehrman (*53*), Levy (*55*), Liddell (*56*), Liddell, Anderson, Kotyuka, and Hartman (*57, 58*), Liddell and Bayne (*59*), Liddell, Sutherland, Parmenter, and Bayne (*60*), Liddell, Sutherland, Parmenter, Curtis, and Anderson (*61*), Maier (*62, 63*), Maier and Glaser (*64, 65*), Maier, Glaser, and Klee (*66*), Maier and Schneirla (*67*), Martin (*68*), Maslow (*69*), Morgan (*70*), Morgan and Morgan (*71*), Morgan and Waldman (*72*), Mowrer (*74, 75, 76, 77*), Pavlov (*78, 79, 80*), Riemer (*81*), Taylor (*83*), Wells (*84, 85*), Witkin (*86, 87*).

Methods

The aim of the investigation was to demonstrate that by inhibiting particular functions in the nursing period one could predict in maturity the special forms maladjustment would take, and that these would be determined by the character of the infantile deprivation; to study the effect of inhibition of sight or hearing in the nursing period on reactions to stress in maturity. A plan was laid to deprive nurslings of the function of these special senses without doing them organic injury. An experimental approach to the problem under controlled laboratory conditions was devised. Animals were observed from birth to maturity. The albino rat was chosen as the subject of investigation because of its rapid rate of development. Maturation studies carried out at the Wistar Institute have indicated that for the albino rat, the period of infancy during which it is dependent upon the mother for nutrition lasts about twenty-five days. Both the male and the female reach sexual maturity in approximately sixty days.

Seven litters totalling forty-four animals were employed in the first experiment. Each litter was divided into three groups: two experimental and one control. On the tenth day after birth, the ears of one group of rats from each litter were sealed with cotton and paraffin under ether anaesthesia. Twelve to fifteen days after birth the eyes of the second group of rats from each litter were sealed under ether anaesthesia. The area immediately surrounding the eyes was covered with a small piece of gauze saturated with petroleum jelly to prevent injury to the eyes. The head was then encased in a paraffin cast with apertures for the ears, mouth and external nares. The eyes and ears were not sealed until one day after the particular sense organ had begun to function. The purpose of this procedure was to allow the animal some experience with the particular function before the sense organ was sealed. Had the eyes been closed, for example, before the animal had had any experience with vision, there would not have been a true deprivation of function. For the same reason, namely, to reinforce specific frustration in the dependent period, the rats were permitted to nurse undisturbed for the first ten or fifteen days of life. The third group of each litter was not interfered with in any way during infancy. The animals in this group served as controls.

Twenty-five days after birth, i.e., at the end of the nursing period, the various sealings were removed from the eyes or ears of the rats in the first two groups. In order to make certain that all social factors were constant every animal, now weaned, was separated from the mother. Each rat was placed in an individual cage and kept in this state of isolation for fourteen days. During this period, they were allowed to mature normally — that is they were not disturbed in any way.

Training Period A (Visual Stimulus). At the termination of the isolation period (the animals were now thirty-nine days old) each rat was subjected to a period of training in the apparatus described in Figure One. The animal was conditioned to stand quietly at one end of the training box (the area designated in the drawing by the letter A), until the bulbs at the other end of the box were illuminated. The floor of the waiting or reception chamber was wired with an electric grid which could be charged or discharged at the will of the experimenter. When the light stimulus was presented, the rat was required to run to the opposite end of the apparatus to a feeding chamber. Each rat was trained to associate the flashing light with the presentation of food. The animals were starved for twelve hours preceding each day's training; the food served as a reward; and they came to the experiment hungry and evidently eager to master the obstacles between them and the food. Each animal was trained singly and in isolation from the others until his response to the stimulus had an easy precision. The training period consisted of ten trials daily for ten consecutive days. The criterion of learning was errorless trials on the tenth day of training. If the animal responded before the stimulus was presented or failed to respond when the stimulus was presented, this was counted as an error. If the rat ran toward the feeding chamber without waiting for the signal, he was shocked electrically. Each response had to be made in less than five seconds after the stimulus was presented. If this level of learning was not reached by the tenth day training was continued until the time it was reached. In no case was it necessary to prolong training beyond the tenth day. By that time the animal was so conditioned that he would sit restlessly in the reception chamber watching alertly for the light signal, would immediately dash through the door to the feeding chamber when he saw the flash and eat the pellet in the feeding dish.

Competitive Period A (Visual Stimulus). Following the period of individual training, each animal whose eyes were sealed in infancy was placed in competition for a piece of food with an animal (of the same litter) whose ears were sealed in the nursing period. The two rats were placed in the apparatus used for their individual training. When the stimulus was presented (bulbs illuminated), the animals were required to run to the food chamber. The rat that reached the chamber first, received the food. Each control was placed in competition with another control of the same litter. The animals were given ten trials daily for twenty days. The competitive pairs were never changed, that is, in every trial the same two animals competed.

Training Period B (Auditory Stimulus). At the termination of competitive Period A each animal was again subjected to a period of individual training in the same apparatus. The procedure in this case was, with one exception, indentical with that of Training Period A. In this case the animals were required to respond to an auditory stimulus, namely, a buzzer. The response demanded was no different from that required in the previous training period.

Competitive Period B (Auditory Stimulus). Following Training Period B, the rats were again placed in competition. Each animal was pitted against its original competitor. A pair of rats was placed in the apparatus. When the buzzer was sounded, the animals were required to run to the food chamber. The rat reaching the chamber first, received the food. Each pair of animals was given ten trials daily for twenty days.

Every precaution was taken to treat the animals in a uniform way apart from the special character of the conditioning. All the rats were handled by one person. This technique excluded the possibility of a variable response to the approach of different experimenters.

Expectations

If inhibiting a function during the nursing period does produce a specific loss or at least a partial withdrawal of that function in maturity when the organism is experiencing any severe tension or stress under competition for food, the loss or disturbance would be exhibited in this experimental situation in the following manner:

1. When the animals compete in the visual situation, the rat that was deprived of vision in infancy should,
   a. not respond at all to the visual stimulus, or
   b. its ability to respond to the visual stimulus should be sufficiently disturbed as to make its responses poor in relation to its competitor's, that is, this particular rat should "lose" consistently.

2. On the other hand the animal deprived of hearing in infancy should have no difficulty whatsoever in the visual situation.

3. When the animals compete in the auditory situation, we should expect to find the same symptoms of disturbance (described above) in the animals that were deprived of hearing in infancy. Similarly, the rats deprived of vision in the nursing period should experience no difficulty.

4. As for the controls we should not expect to find any shift in the percent of total trials "won" by any animal when the visual situation is replaced by the auditory situation; that is, if control A consistently "wins" in the visual situation, we should expect that he will at least win more often than his competitor in the auditory situation. Similarly, we should expect a constant "loser" in the visual situation to be a consistent "loser" in the auditory situation.

Results

There follows a tabulation of the results with forty-four animals: fourteen in the "visual" group, fourteen in the "auditory" group and sixteen controls.

Visual Situation Results (Quantitative): Experimental Groups

In the following table are shown the number of trials "won" by each animal of every competing pair out of a total of 200 trials. The letter following each identification number indicates the litter of which the rat is a member.

Animals deprived of vision		Animals deprived of hearing	
Rat No.	No. of trials won	Rat No.	No. of trials won
1H	63	4H	137
2H	90	6H	110
7C	89	1C	111
3C	77	6C	123
4G	91	5G	109
1G	20	7G	180
12A	70	8A	130
2A	81	4A	119
6F	79	1F	121
7F	90	3F	110
2L	78	6L	122
3L	83	1L	117
6D	62	5D	138
2D	89	3D	111

Average no. of trials won: 75.86
Percentage of total won: 37.93

Average no. of trials won: 124.14
Percentage of total won: 62.07

Auditory Situation Results (Quantitative): Experimental Groups

In the following table are shown the number of trials "won" by each animal of each competing pair out of a total of 200 trials. The letter following each identification number indicates the litter to which the rat belongs.

The fourteen nursing animals originally deprived of vision won 37.93% of the trials in a situation in which the stimulus for competition was visual while the fourteen rats once deprived of hearing in infancy won 62.07%. When these *same* rats were placed in a setting in which the signal to compete for food was auditory, the results were reversed, that is, the animals whose eyes had originally been sealed "won" 61% of the trials; and the rats whose ears had once been plugged "won" 39%.

For purposes of control, sixteen rats thirty-nine days old previously undisturbed in any way were trained and placed in competition in pairs.

Animals deprived of vision		Animals deprived of hearing	
Rat No.	No. of trials won	Rat No.	No. of trials won
1H	117	4H	83
2H	102	6H	98
7C	141	1C	59
3C	98	6C	102
4G	123	5G	77
1G	84	7G	116
12A	102	8A	98
2A	131	4A	69
6F	131	1F	69
7F	159	3F	41
2L	146	6L	54
3L	124	1L	76
6D	103	5D	97
2D	147	3D	53

Average no. of trials won: 122.00
Percentage of total won: 61.00

Average no. of trials won: 78.00
Percentage of total won: 39.00

Visual Situation Results (Quantitative): Control Group

In the following table are shown the number of trials "won" by each animal of each competing pair out of a total of 200 trials. The letter following each identification number indicates the litter to which the rat belongs.

Rat No.	No. of trials won	Rat No.	No. of trials won
3H	154	5H	46
2C	110	5C	90
2G	137	3G	63
1A	156	5A	44
4F	119	5F	81
5L	154	4L	46
1D	129	4D	71
7D	105	8D	95

Average no. of trials won: 133
Percentage of total won: 66.50

Average no. of trials won: 67
Percentage of total won: 33.50

Auditory Situation Results (Quantitative): Control Group

In the following table are shown the number of trials won by each animal of each competing pair out of a total of 200 trials. The letter following each identification number indicates the litter to which each rat belongs.

The animals listed on the left hand of the table are those that won consistently in the visual situation.

Rat No.	No. of trials won	Rat No.	No. of trials won
3H	170	5H	30
2C	126	5C	74
2G	162	3G	38
1A	181	5A	19
4F	117	5F	83
5L	149	4L	51
1D	159	4D	41
7D	132	8D	68

Average no. of trials won: 149.50
Percentage of total won: 74.75

Average no. of trials won: 50.50
Percentage of total won: 25.25

In response to the bulb signal one group of eight animals "won" 66.50% of the total trials, and the second group "won" 33.50%. When the stimulus for competition was changed to a buzzer, there was no reversal in performance. In fact, the first group increased its percentage of trials "won" to 74.75, while the second group dropped to 25.25%. This result reinforces the significance of the altered response to light and sound among the animals functionally traumatized in the nursing period. The specific character of the inhibition is demonstrated by the inability to use a particular special sense under the stress of competition.

There follows a tabulation of the results with eighteen additional animals treated in the same way as the previous forty-four, but functionally deprived of sight or hearing at the 26th, 50th, and 75th day of life. The sealings were imposed for the same duration as with the nurslings and the same interval of time was allowed to elapse before training and competition were imposed.

More Mature Animals

		Division	
Age	No. of animals	Eyes sealed	Ears sealed
26 days old	6	3	3
50 days old	6	3	3
75 days old	6	3	3

Results in Maturity with Animals Subjected to Sealing 26 Days after Birth.

In the following table are shown the number of trials "won" by each animal of every competing pair out of a total of 200 trials.

Visual Situation

Animals Whose Eyes Were Sealed		Animals Whose Ears Were Sealed	
Rat No.	No. of trials won	Rat No.	No. of trials won
36	80	19	120
21	145	11	55
5	109	20	91

Average no. of trials won: 111.33
Percentage of total won: 55.66

Average no. of trials won: 88.67
Percentage of total won: 44.34

Auditory Situation

Animals Whose Eyes Were Sealed		Animals Whose Ears Were Sealed	
Rat No.	No. of trials won	Rat No.	No. of trials won
36	61	19	139
21	132	11	68
5	71	20	129

Average no of trials won: 88
Percentage of total won: 44

Average no. of trials won: 112
Percentage of total won: 56

Results in Maturity with Animals Subjected to Sealing 50 Days after Birth

In the following table are shown the number of trials "won" by each animal of every competing pair out of a total of 200 trials.

Visual Situation

Animals Whose Eyes Were Sealed		Animals Whose Ears Were Sealed	
Rat No.	No. of trials won	Rat No.	No. of trials won
61	90	62	110
64	81	69	119
68	100	63	100

Average no. of trials won: 90.33
Percentage of total won: 45.16

Average no. of trials won: 109.67
Percentage of total won: 54.84

Visual Situation

Animals Whose Eyes Were Sealed		Animals Whose Ears Were Sealed	
Rat No.	No. of trials won	Rat No.	No. of trials won
41	116	48	84
49	109	47	91
40	72	42	128

Average no. of trials won: 99
Percentage of total won: 49.50

Average no. of trials won: 101
Percentage of total won: 50.50

Auditory Situation

Animals Whose Eyes Were Sealed		Animals Whose Ears Were Sealed	
Rat No.	No. of trials won	Rat No.	No. of trials won
61	84	62	116
64	95	69	105
68	22	63	178

Average no. of trials won: 67
Percentage of total won: 33.50

Average no. of trials won: 133
Percentage of total won: 66.50

Auditory Situation

Animals Whose Eyes Were Sealed		Animals Whose Ears Were Sealed	
Rat No.	No. of trials won	Rat No.	No. of trials won
41	140	48	60
49	100	47	100
40	30	42	170

Average no. of trials won: 90
Percentage of total won: 45

Average no. of trials won: 110
Percentage of total won: 55

Results in Maturity with Animals Subjected to Sealing 75 Days after Birth

In the following table are shown the number of trials "won" by each animal of every competing pair out of a total of 200 trials.

The rats were chosen at these particular ages in order to compare them with the nurslings. Twenty-six day old animals have just completed the nursing period. Fifty-day old rats are just short of maturity. And seventy-five day old animals are adult. There were six rats in each group, three whose eyes were sealed and three whose ears were plugged. The duration of visual and auditory deprivation, free undisturbed interval, training and competitive periods were the same as with the original nurslings.

The three animals of the twenty-six day old group earlier deprived of vision "won" 55.66% of the trials in the situation in which the stimulus for competition was visual, while the three rats originally deprived of hearing in the same age group "won" 44.34%. When these *same* animals were placed in the setting in which the signal to compete for food was auditory, the group whose lids had once been sealed "won" 44% of the trials, and the animals whose ears had formerly been plugged "won" 56%. The percentage differences do not appear significant.

The three animals of the fifty-day old group earlier deprived of vision "won" 45.16% of the trials in the situation in which the stimulus for competition was visual, while the three rats originally deprived of hearing in the same age group "won" 54.84%. When these *same* animals were placed in the setting in which the signal to compete for food was auditory, the group whose lids had once been sealed "won" 33.50% of the trials, and the animals whose ears had formerly been plugged won 66.50%. The percentage difference in the visual situation does not appear significant. However, while the slightly higher percentage of trials won by the "ear" animals in the "visual" situation has no significance, the increase in the percentage "won" by the same group to 66.50 in the "auditory" situation does have meaning, because it indicates by contrast with the reversal in performance in the same setting of the animals traumatized as nurslings the failure of the functional deprivation imposed after the fiftieth day to affect the organism in maturity.

The three animals of the seventy-five day old group earlier deprived of vision "won" 49.50% of the trials in the situation in which the stimulus for competition was visual, while the three rats originally deprived of hearing in the same age group "won" 50.50%. When these same animals were placed in the setting in which the signal to compete for food was auditory, the group whose lids had once been sealed "won" 45% of the trials, and the animals whose ears had formerly been plugged, "won" 55%. The percentage differences do not appear significant although what was said in comment of the fifty-day old group, might hold here in much less degree. Perhaps the most revealing observations to be made are (1) the relative equality of performance of "eye" and "ear" animals regardless of the "visual" or "auditory" setting; (2) the failure to establish a reversal of performance with a change in the character of the stimulus; (3) the increase in percentage won in two instances with a change in the nature of the stimulus; (4) and the fact that there is no inhibition of sight or hearing in competition if these functions were sealed off between the twenty-fifth and seventy-fifth day of life. The fundamental significance of these findings is that if in the post-infantile stage a rat is subjected to the strain of competition, he is not handicapped in the functions of which he was deprived after the nursing period. A handicap appears only on such functions as were incompletely exercised during the suckling stage.

Discussion

It is felt that this research clarifies experimentally the relationship between early disturbances in the adaptive equipment of an organism and abnormal reaction-types in maturity; the reason for the specific character of symptoms in maladjustment; and the relatively minor role constitution plays in accounting for one organism's susceptibility to maladjustment and another's hardiness under similar stress. An assurance that the differences in performance demonstrated by the experimental animals in no way depend upon inherited characteristics lies in the predictability of the results among rats selected at random from the same laboratory stock. The possibility that a neurotic strain of animals was used and that this might have been the cause of the withdrawal of special functions was eliminated by the use of split litters, that is, each litter was divided into experimental animals and controls. The fact that the controls did not exhibit any inhibition of particular functions disposes of such a complicating possibility.

It is a common conception of modern psychology that most abnormal reaction-types in human beings have their origin in various conditionings and maladjustments in infancy and early childhood. However, there are limits to the comparison that can be made between behavior reactions of human beings and those of rats. In the latter, phylogenetic patterns play a greater role in adult behavior than they do in man. Nevertheless, there is sufficient individualization of performance in rats to permit certain broad analogies to be drawn, particularly where the disturbance in adaptive equipment is so critical. The experimental production of behavior disturbances in animals has been repeatedly described by Pavlov, Liddell, Schneirla, Maier, Cook and others. It is necessary to point out, however, that in all these instances the emphasis has been on partial reactions, the number of drops of saliva produced, the appearance or disappearance of certain conditioned reflexes, disturbances in eating reactions. At no time in these researches does there seem to be a conception of the animal as a total organism reacting to changes in its internal and external environment. It is from this larger aspect approximating insofar as possible our approach to human behavior disorders that laboratory animals are being studied.

It appears that animals who have been subjected to inhibition of function while in a state of infantile dependency adjust adequately in maturity with the full development of their resources until their security is threatened to such a degree that they seem unable to cope with new hazards in their environment with the easy appropriate behaviour necessary to attain mastery over a given problem. In these experiments the most effective barrier against this resourceful handling of a difficult reality has been to present the animal with the necessity to struggle for gratification in a rivalry situation. Confronted with this obstacle there is a tendency to retreat to the use of older infantile patterns that were once associated with gratification and mastery. These were the conditioned reflexes of the nursing period when security involved the exploitation of the mother. As the animal retreats to its earlier adaptation with the expectation of secure fulfillment, it is frustrated since its backsliding involves the loss of maturely developed skills. What determines the particular refinement of function that is lost is the degree to which the animal's resources are developed in dependency. He loses those functions in neurosis which were inhibited or incompletely refined in the infantile period. This seems to be a matter of conditioning. Failing masterful channelization of energy in maturity, the rat automatically recovers an older strategy which used to serve a gratifying end.

There is a possible alternative explanation for the type of response that was obtained in this experiment. It is conceivable instead of interpreting the "loser" as having suffered an inhibition of function that the "winner" be understood to have beaten his rival because of the greater acuteness of his sight or hearing. It might be said that when hearing was interfered with in the nursing period, sight was necessarily dependent upon and developed to compensate for the delimitation of auditory function; similarly that when vision was obstructed in infancy, hearing became exaggerated to improve orientation. This would put another light on the significance of "winning" and "losing" later on. The animal whose eyes were once sealed might have "won" in an "auditory" situation because of his greater auditory acuity, whereas the conviction so far has been that his rival "lost" because of his inability to hear. The ani-

mal whose ears were once sealed might have "won" in a "visual" situation because of compensatory visual acuity, whereas up to now it has been held that his competitor "lost" because of his inability to see. The conception that there was an exaggerated compensatory function that led to winning is untenable for at least three reasons. In the first place, the "winner" never responded more rapidly to the stimulus in competition than in isolated performance. This would indicate that there was no exaggeration of functional acuity. In the second place, while the timing of the "loser" was as fast as that of the "winner" in isolated performance, he invariably showed in competition a delayed response of five or six seconds after the stimulus was presented. He would always assume a rigid, tense position in the reception chamber and then hesitatingly follow the other animal toward the feeding chamber. There was no corresponding improved response to indicate better function in the "winners". All reactions to the stimuli whether in isolated trials or in competition were immediate except for the "losing" animal whose earlier deprivation of special sense was being tested. There is a third point to be made. In one mature rat whose eyes had been sealed in the nursing period without organic damage, there developed in rivalry for food a striking behavior that was suggestive of functional blindness. When food was presented and his competitor won it, he (the animal whose eyes had originally been sealed) would rise up on his hind limbs and spar aimlessly at space before him as if attempting defensively to ward off the other rat who was often nowhere near him; or he would stand similarly poised simply staring straight ahead, apparently unable to follow the movement of the other rat. A finger passed across his field of vision appeared to offer no stimulation since he always maintained this same impassive yet somehow alert attitude, much like that of a blind man. This curious behavior was assumed only when the animal was placed in competition for food. At other times he was obviously visually aware of his environment. On several occasions he was set in rivalry in a completely dark room. When a powerful beam of light was flashed into the eyes of the other animal, he blinked and closed his lids but the visually inhibited rat maintained a wide-eyed unresponsiveness to the same stimulus. Whenever the light was flashed on him in non-competitive situations, he blinked appropriately. No brief is held on the basis of this observation for the positive functional blindness of this animal but his behavior was certainly suggestive of neurotic visual inhibition. The burden of proof that it is possible to produce in rats an actual functional loss of sight lies in the body of the experiment. These findings would point in the direction of retreat to a prior adjustment with the inhibition of function then prevalent rather than to the improvement of special senses.

While studies of dominance in other animals indicate that weight during the nursing period is a significant factor determining which animal becomes dominant, there is no question of dominance involved in this experiment. "Winning" as a result of greater infantile weight, although a possible factor, is excluded as a serious complication by the large number of animals used, by the striking shift from "winning" to "losing" with the change in stimulus, by the absence of such a reversal among the controls, and by the fact that heavier animals "lost" just as frequently as they "won" in the type of competitive struggle to which they were subjected in this experiment. To avoid the complication of confusion with genetic conceptions and terminology, the words "recessiveness" and "dominance" were not used. "Passive" and "active", "submissive" and "aggressive" laid too much emphasis on the *competitive* aspects of the problem. The aim of the experiment was rather to clarify the dynamics of the withdrawal of particular function when a mature animal was under tension. It seemed most appropriate therefore to confine our terms simply to trials "won" or trials "lost".

When normal animals are placed in competition, the frustration resulting from not receiving food in the trials in which the competitor wins may produce inhibition or withdrawal on the part of the frustrated animal.

This may or may not have some effect upon the dominance status of the losing animal. However, in the author's experiment this is not the case, even if the reversibility of "winning" and "losing" were the only indication of the plasticity of the animal's response. Here the animals were prematurely deprived of some function. The fact that they "won" or "lost" in rivalry was a consequence of the inability under competitive stress to exercise a particular inhibited function whose use was essential to mastery in the struggle. The rivalry between the two mature rats resulted in the withdrawal of the function upon which the animal's ability to respond depended. This observation is supported by the finding that the rats originally deprived of sight "lost" in the "visual" situation and "won" in the "auditory" situation; that the animals originally deprived of hearing "lost" in the "auditory" situation and "won" in the "visual" situation. Therefore the words "dominance" and "submission" were irrelevant.

It is conceivable that under the strain of competition there is a tendency on the part of all the neurotic animals to inhibit various functions. However, only one function at a time is being examined during competition, sight or hearing, depending on whether light or sound is being used as a stimulus. The readiness with which the animals reverse from "winning" to "losing" with a change in the stimulus lays emphasis neither on dominance nor on competition but on the fact that neither animal is really permanently the other's master and that both lose particular functions in rivalry situations.

Summary

Limitations put upon particular functions during the nursing period are followed by inhibitions of those functions in maturity when the organism is under stress. The tabulated results show clearly that the animals deprived of vision in infancy experienced great difficulty in responding to a visual stimulus under the strain of adult competition. Similarly, the animals deprived of hearing in the nursing period experienced considerable difficulty in responding to an auditory stimulus under the strain of competition. However, the rats whose vision was interfered with in infancy were able to respond easily in the auditory situation, and the animals whose hearing was originally disturbed showed no difficulty in responding to the visual stimulus. By contrast, the change from the buzzer to the light as a conditioning signal produced no remarkable alteration in the responses of the control animals. The rats that reacted well to the visual stimulus continued to do so in response to the auditory stimulus.

Integrated capacity to cope with reality is maintained until a rat reaches a competitive impasse. At this point mature responses disintegrate. The animal retreats to an immature previously conditioned response which formerly secured mastery over the environment. In the process of withdrawal, it loses adult functions which were undeveloped in the nursing period. An analogy can be drawn with human neurotic behavior in which adults lose highly developed skills in retreating to out-moded but previously serviceable forms of adaptation and are left with inadequately evolved and incoordinate resources. The experiment illustrates the dynamics of the selective inhibition of particular function.

Bibliography

1. Alexander, F. G.: The influence of psychologic factors upon gastrointestinal disturbances; a symposium. Psychoanalyt. Quart. 3: 501, 1934.
2. Alexander, F.: The medical value of psychoanalysis. Norton, New York, 1936.
3. Anderson, O. D. and Liddell, H.S.: Observations on experimental neurosis in sheep. Arch. Neurol. & Psychiat., 34: 330, 1935.
4. Anderson, O. D., Parmenter, R., and Liddell, H. S.: Some cardiovascular manifestations of the experimental neurosis in sheep. Psychosom. Med., 1: 93, 1939.
5. Baker, L. E.: The pupillary response conditioned to subliminal auditory stimuli, Psychol. Monogr., 50: no. 3, 1938.
6. Barker, R., Dembo, T., and Lewin, K.: Experiments on frustration and regression in children. Psychol. Bull., 34: 754, 1937.
7. Binger, C.: The psycho-biology of breathing. Ann. Int. Med., 121: 195, 1937.
8. Brunswick, D.: The effects of emotional stimuli on the gastrointestinal tone. J. Comp. Psychol., 4: 19, 1924.
9. Burrow, T.: The law of the organism. Am. J. Sociol., 42: 814, 1937.
10. Burrow, T.: The organismic factor in disorders of behavior. J. Psychol., 4: 333, 1937.
11. Burrow, T.: Bio-physical factors in relation to functional imbalances. Human Biol., 10: 93, 1938.
12. Cameron, N.: Reasoning and regression and communication in schizophrenics. Psychol. Monogr., 1: 50, 1938.
13. Cook, S. W.: The production of experimental neurosis in the white rat. Psychosom. Med., 1: 293, 1939.
14. Cook, S. W.: A survey of methods used to produce experimental neurosis. Am. J. Psychiat., 95: 1259, 1939.
15. Curtis, Q. F.: Experimental neurosis in the pig. Psychol. Bull., 34: 723, 1937.
16. Daniels, G. E.: Neuroses associated with the gastro-intestinal tract. Am. J. Psychiat., 91: 529, 1934.
17. Daniels, G. E.: Psychic factors in gastro-intestinal disease. New York State J. Med., 36: 602, 1936.
18. Daniels, G. E.: Emotional and instinctual factors in diabetes mellitus. Am. J. Psychiat., 93: 711, 1936.
19. Daniels, G. E.: Present trends in the evaluation of psychic factors in diabetes mellitus; a critical review of experimental, general medical and psychiatric literature of the last five years. Psychosom. Med., 1: 527, 1939.
20. Daniels, G. E.: Treatment of case of ulcerative colitis associated with hysterical depression. Psychosom. Med., 2: 276, 1940.
21. Deutsch, F.: The choice of organ in organ neuroses. Internat. J. Psychoanal., 20: 252, 1939.
22. Deutsch, F.: Gehäuftes Auftreten von Morbus Basedowi. Med. Klin., 19: 678, 1923.
23. Deutsch, F.: Der Einfluss von Gemütsbewegungen and den Energiestoffwechsel. Hypnotische Experimente. Wien klin. Wchnschr., 38: 1127, 1925.
24. Deutsch, F.: The associative anamnesis. Psychoanalyt. Quart., 8: 354, 1939.
25. Deutsch, F.: The production of somatic disease by emotional disturbance, in the inter-relationships of mind and body. Williams & Wilkins Company, Baltimore, 1939.
26. Deutsch, F., and Kauf, E.: Über die Ursachen der Kreislaufstörungen bei den Herzneurosen. Ztschr. f. d. ges. exper. Med., 34: 71, 1923.
27. Diller, T.: The question of hysterical analysis and the theory of Babinski. J. Abnorm. Psychol., 15: 55, 1920.
28. Dimmick, F. L.; Ludlow, N., and Whiteman, A.: A study of "experimental neurosis" in cats. J. Comp. Psychol., 28: 39, 1939.
29. Drabovitch, W. and Weger, P.: Deux cas de

névrose expérimentale chez le chien. Compt. rend. Acad. d. sc., 204: 902, 1937.

30. Draper, G.: Disease, a psychosomatic reaction. J. A. M. A., 90: 1281, 1928.

31. Dunbar, H. F.: Physical-mental relationship in illness. Am. J. Psychiat., 91: 541, 1934.

32. Dunbar, H. F.: Psychic factors in cardiac disease. New York State J. Med., 36: 423, 1936.

33. Dunbar, H. F.: The psychic component of disease processes in cardiac, diabetes and fracture patients. Am. J. Psychiat., 93: 651, 1936.

34. Dunbar, H. F.: Emotions and bodily changes. Columbia University Press, New York, 1938, 2nd ed.

35. Dunbar, H. F.: Psychoanalytic notes relating to syndromes of asthma and hay fever. Psychoanal. Quart., 7: 25, 1938.

36. Dworkin, S.: Conditioning neuroses in cat and dog. Psychosom. Med., 1: 388, 1939.

37. Finger, F. W.: Quantitative studies in conflict. I. Variations in latency and strength of the rat's response in a discrimination-jumping situation. J. Comp. Psychol., 31: 97, 1941.

38. Freud, S.: Types of neurotic nosogenesis (1912). In his: Collected papers, London, Hogarth Press, 1933, v. 2, p. 113.

39. Frolov, Y. P.: Pavlov and his school. Oxford University Press, New York, 1937.

40. Gantt, W. H.: Extension of a conflict based upon food to other physiological systems and its reciprocal relations with sexual functions. Am. J. Physiol., 123: 73, 1938.

41. Goldstein, K.: The organism. American Book Co., New York, 1939.

42. Hamilton, J. A., and Krechevsky, I.: Studies in the effect of shock upon behavior plasticity in the rat. J. Comp. Psychol., 16: 237, 1933.

43. Hovland, C. I., and Sears, R. R.: Experiments on motor conflict. I. Types of conflict and their modes of resolution. J. Exper. Psychol., 23: 477, 1938.

44. Humphrey, G., and Marcuse, F.: A new method of obtaining neurotic behavior in rats. Am. J. Psychol., 52: 616, 1939.

45. Hunt, J. McV.: The effects of infant feeding-frustration upon adult hoarding in the albino rat. J. Abnorm. & Social Psychol., 36: 338, 1941.

46. Hunt, J. McV. and Willoughby, R. R.: The effect of frustration on hoarding in rats. Psychosom. Med., 1: 309, 1939.

47. Karn, H. W.: The behavior of cats on the double alternation problem in the temporal maze. J. Comp. Psychol., 26: 201, 1938.

48. Karn, H. W.: A case of experimentally induced neurosis in the cat. J. Exper. Psychol., 22: 589, 1938.

49. Karn, H. W.: The experimental study of neurotic behavior in the infra-human animals. J. Gen. Psychol., 22: 431, 1939.

50. Karn, H. W.: Review on Maier's "Studies of abnormal behavior in the rat." J. Gen. Psychol., 23: 225, 1940.

51. Karn, H. W. and Patton, R. A.: The transfer of double alternation behavior acquired in a temporal maze. J. Comp. Psychol., 28: 55, 1939.

52. Karn, H. W. and Patton, R. A.: Abnormal behavior in rats subjected to repeated auditory stimulation. J. Comp. Psychol., 31: 43, 1941.

53. Lehrman, P. R.: Analysis of a conversion-hysteria superimposed on an old diffuse central nervous system lesion. J. Nerv. & Ment. Dis., 54: 31, 1921.

54. Levy, D. M.: Experiments on the sucking reflex and social behavior of dogs. Am. J. Orthopsychiat., 4: 203, 1934.

55. Levy, D. M.: On instinct-satiation: an experiment on pecking behavior of chickens. J. Gen. Psychol., 18: 327, 1938.

56. Liddell, H. S.: The experimental neurosis and the problem of mental disorder. Am. J. Psychiat., 94: 1035, 1938.

57. Liddell, H. S., Anderson, O. D., Kotyuka, E., and Hartman, F. A.: Effect of extract of adrenal cortex on experimental neurosis in sheep. Arch. Neurol. & Psychiat., 34: 973, 1935.

58. Liddell, H. S., Anderson, O. D., Kotyuka, E., and Hartman, F. A.: The effect of cortin upon the experimental neurosis in sheep. Am. J. Physiol., 113: 87, 1935.

59. Liddell, H. S. and Bayne, T. L.: The development of "experimental neurasthenia" in sheep during the formation of difficult conditioned reflexes. Am. J. Physiol., 81: 494, 1927.

60. Liddell, H. S., Sutherland, G. F., Parmenter, R., and Bayne, T. L.: A study of the conditioned reflex method for producing experimental neurosis. Am. J. Physiol., 116: 95, 1936.

61. Liddell, H. S., Sutherland, G. F., Parmenter, R., Curtis, Q., and Anderson, O. D.: Further analysis of the conditioned reflex method in relation to the experimental neurosis. Am. J. Physiol., 119: 361, 1937.

62. Maier, N. R. F.: Studies of abnormal behavior in the rat. Harper, New York, 1939.

63. Maier, N. R. F.: Studies of abnormal behavior in the rat. IV. Abortive behavior and its relation to the neurotic attack. J. Exper. Psychol., 27: 369, 1927.

64. Maier, N. R. F. and Glaser, N. M.: Studies of abnormal behavior in the rat. II. A comparison of some convulsion-producing situations. Comp. Psychol. Mongr., 16: no. 1, 30, 1940.

65. Maier, N. R. F. and Glaser, N. M.: Studies of abnormal behavior in the rat. V. The inheritance of the "neurotic pattern." J. Comp. Psychol., 30: 413, 1940.

66. Maier, N. R. F., Glaser, N. M., and Klee, J. B.:

Studies of abnormal behavior in the rat. III. The development of behavior fixations through frustration. J. Exper. Psychol., 26: 521, 1940.

67. Maier, N. R. F. and Schneirla, T. C.: Principles of animal psychology. McGraw-Hill, New York, 1935.

68. Martin, R. F.: An attempt at the experimental demonstration of regression in hypotheses in the rat. M. A. thesis, University of Oregon, 1937 (unpublished).

69. Maslow, A. H.: Individual psychology and the social behavior of animals. Internat. J. Individ. Psychol., 1: 47, 1935.

70. Morgan, C. T.: Review of Maier's "Studies of abnormal behavior in the rat." J. Gen. Psychol., 23: 225, 1940.

71. Morgan, C. T. and Morgan, J. C.: Auditory induction of an abnormal pattern of behavior in rats. J. Comp. Psychol., 27: 505, 1939.

72. Morgan, C. T. and Waldman, H.: "Conflict" and audiogenic seizures. J. Comp. Psychol., 31: 1, 1941.

73. Mowrer, O. H.: An experimental analogue of "regression" with incident observations on "reaction formation." J. Abnorm. & Social Psychol., 35: 56, 1940.

74. Mowrer, O. H.: Reaction to conflict as a function of past experience. Psychol. Bull., 34: 720, 1937.

75. Mowrer, O. H.: Animal studies in the genesis of personality. Tr. New York Acad. Sc., Ser. 2, 3: no. 1.

76., Mowrer, O. H.: Authoritarian versus "self-government" in the management of children's aggressive (anti-social) reactions as a preparation for citizenship in a democracy. J. Social Psychol., 10: 121, 1939.

77. Mowrer, O. H.: Preparatory set (expectancy) — some methods of measurement. Psychol. Monogr., 52: no. 2, p. 43.

78. Pavlov, I. P.: Proceedings of the Conference on Experimental Neuroses and Allied Problems. National Research Council, Washington, 1937 (mimeographed).

79. Pavlov, I. P.: Problems of neurotic behavior. National Research Council, Washington, 1938 (mimeographed).

80. Pavlov, I. P.: Lectures on conditioned reflexes. International Publishers, New York, 1928.

81. Riemer, M. D.: Ideas of neglect and hoarding in the senile psychoses. Psychiat. Quart., 14: 285, 1940.

82. Sanders, M. J.: An experimental demonstration of regression in the rat. J. Exper. Psychol., 21: 493, 1937.

83. Taylor, W. S.: Readings in abnormal psychology and mental hygiene. Appleton-Century, New York, 1926.

84. Wells, F. L.: Mental regression: its concepts and types. Psychiat. Bull., 9: 445, 1916.

85. Wells, F. L.: Social maladjustments: adaptive regressions. In: Handbook of Social Psychology (Murchison). 1935, Chap. 18, p. 845.

86. Witkin, H. A.: Abnormal behavior in animals. Psychol. League J., 3: 75, 1939.

87. Witkin, H. A.: Behavior disturbances in the rat resulting from prolonged training upon antagonistic adjustments.

RONALD MELZACK & T. H. SCOTT

37 The Effects of Early Experience on the Response to Pain

There has recently been an increase of theoretical interest in the effects of early experience on behavior, together with an increasing number of experimental studies (1). In one area, however, there is a marked discrepancy between theoretical emphasis and amount of empirical investigation: the area of avoidance behavior and pain.

Reprinted from *Journal of Comparative and Physiological Psychology* 50:155–161, 1957. Copyright 1957 by the American Psychological Association and reproduced by permission.

Earlier clinical and theoretical formulations of the problem of early experience by Freud

Part of the results reported in this paper are contained in a thesis submitted by the senior author in partial fulfillment of the requirements of the Ph.D. degree at McGill University. The authors gratefully acknowledge the advice and guidance of Dr. D. O. Hebb throughout this study, and the technical assistance of Dr. Peter Milner. This experiment was supported by grants from the Foundations Fund for Research in Psychiatry, the Rockefeller Foundation, and a Fellowship stipend given to the senior author by the National Research Council of Canada.

and his followers (4, and others there cited) have not led to any experimental studies relevant to pain perception and response, although the importance of early experience as a determinant of adult behavior was fully recognized. More recently, Scott and his associates (12) have arrived at a new hypothesis of the effects of early experience. They maintain that during the development of the organism there are specific critical periods after which sufficient maturation has occurred for various types of experience to have lasting effects on adult behavior. Although Fuller (3) has provided evidence for a critical period in the dog for the acquisition of conditioned responses to pain, there is no direct evidence which relates early pain experience with the behavior of the mature organism.

Hebb's (5) distinction between pain perception as a neurophysiological event and the overt response to pain, such as avoidance, has important implications for any attempt to relate early experience and pain perception in the mature organism. Hebb conceives of pain as a disruption of spatially and temporally organized activity in the cerebrum, this disruption per se constituting the physiological basis of pain. Since aggregates of neurons are assumed to develop their particular spatio-temporal organization as a result of prolonged, patterned sensory stimulation in early life, the theory thus suggests that the degree of pain perceived is, in part at least, dependent on the earlier experience of the organism. Pain, then, in the context of Hebb's theory, is not an elementary sensation, but a complex perceptual process in which a major role is played by all kinds of earlier perceptual learning, including both specific and nonspecific experience involving all the senses. Furthermore, as a result of direct experience with noxious stimuli, the organism tends to repeat and thus acquire any responses which decrease the cerebral disruption (i.e., pain).

That early experience does indeed play an important role in perceiving and responding to pain is strongly suggested by the study of a chimpanzee deprived of normal somesthetic stimulation during infancy and early maturity (11). After removal from somesthetic restriction, the chimpanzee appeared to have a heightened pain threshold, since "he 'panted' as chimpanzees do when they are being tickled" (11, p. 502) when his legs or lower ventral trunk were poked with a sharp pencil point or pin. Furthermore, the animal was found to be strikingly poor in localizing sites of noxious stimulation on its body.

The method of sensory deprivation or restriction has proved successful in ascertaining the effects of early perceptual experience on adult behavior (7, 14). The present experiment, then, is an attempt to study the effects of early sensory restriction, with special emphasis on the restriction of pain experience, on the adult response to noxious stimuli.

SUBJECTS

Six litters of an inbred Scottish terrier strain were used. Each litter was randomly divided into two groups. One group, containing a total of 10 dogs, was placed in restriction cages. The 12 dogs which comprised the "free environment" or control group were raised normally as pets in private homes and in the laboratory.

Each restricted dog used in the present study was reared in isolation from puppyhood to maturity in a cage which was specially designed to prevent the dogs from seeing outside, although daylight was permitted to enter through a large air vent at the top of each cage. Each cage contained two compartments, and when the sliding partition between them was opened once a day, the dog was allowed to enter a freshly cleaned compartment. In this way the dogs were deprived of normal sensory and social experience from the time that weaning was completed at the age of four weeks until they were removed at about eight months of age. After the restricted dogs were released from their cages, they received the same opportunities for social and sensory stimulation as their normally reared littermates.

Testing of the dogs began about three to five weeks after the restricted animals were released. Two of the restricted dogs were tested a second time about two years after their release. Since the litters used in this study were born at different times over a three-year period, it was not possible to use all the dogs for all the tests.

EXPERIMENT I. RESPONSE TO ELECTRIC SHOCK

Method

Subjects. The Ss were seven restricted and nine free-environment dogs.

Apparatus. A toy car that could be maneuvered by hand through a battery and steering mechanism was connected to a variable electric shock source provided by a variac and transformer circuit. The dogs were tested with the car on a 6-ft. by 3-ft. sheet-metal floor surrounded by a 2-ft.-high wire-mesh enclosure.

Procedure. The toy car was used to pursue the dogs and deliver a 1500-v., 6 ma. shock when it hit them. Each shock was of 1-sec. duration, although the dogs could escape the full shock by moving away rapidly. The car, which had a constant speed, was kept in waiting about 2 ft. from S. If S were sitting, E moved the car directly toward S. If S were moving, however, E moved the car into S's path and pursued S up to one of the far sides of the enclosure.

The E tried to hit each dog ten times during a testing period. However, if at some time during testing, the dog made five successive avoidances of the approaching car without being hit and shocked, testing was discontinued for that period, and the total number of shocks received by the dog up to that time was recorded. A dog reached the *criterion* of successful avoidance learning when it received no shock during a testing period.

Results

The restricted dogs received a mean of 24.7 shocks (range: 10 to 40) from the toy car, while the free-environment dogs received a mean of 6 shocks (range: 2 to 11). This difference between the two groups provided a *t* value of 4.4, which is significant at the .001 level. By the end of the fourth test period all the free-environment dogs had reached criterion. Three of the seven restricted dogs, however, had not yet done so; and two of these had received the full 40 shocks and gave no sign of learning to avoid the toy car. Testing was therefore discontinued at this time. The mean number of shocks received by the restricted dogs, then, would probably be considerably higher than it is if the restricted dogs were tested until all had reached criterion.

Characteristic differences in the behavior of the two groups were striking. The normal dogs were found to show smooth, precise movements which were oriented directly toward the toy car. They often sat looking at the car, swaying from side to side as it moved toward them, and only at the last moment, when the car was inches away from them, did they jump up and trot out of the way. Although these dogs were excited at first, their behavior after the first few shocks showed little excitement, and they made only minimal, unhurried avoidance movements of a leg or the tail to avoid being hit.

This behavior stands in marked contrast with the wild, aimless activity first shown by the restricted dogs. Their typical behavior consisted of running around in a circular path with excessive, exaggerated movements of the whole body. They often avoided being hit only by virtue of the remarkable rapidity of their action. But there was no difficulty in hitting them if the car were moved into the circular path. They then ran right into it. At other times, they stood up at the side of the testing enclosure, in an attempt to climb out, and received the full ten shocks in this position.

Two years after restriction. Two restricted dogs were tested two years after they had been released from restriction and still showed the same exaggerated behavior. While one learned after 9 shocks, the other received 23 shocks before it began to avoid successfully. This gave a mean of 16 shocks, which differs significantly from the mean of 6 shocks for the normal animals at the .01 level ($t = 3.5$).

EXPERIMENT II. AVOIDANCE TRAINING

Method

Subjects. The Ss were 7 restricted and 12 free-environment dogs.

Apparatus. A 6-ft. by 3-ft. testing enclosure, bounded by wire mesh 2 ft. high, was divided lengthwise into two halves by a 3-in.-high barrier. The steel grid floor was connected to a variable electric shock source provided by a variac and transformer circuit.

Procedure. The threshold levels at which the dogs responded to electric shock in the apparatus were first determined by raising the voltage stepwise. The voltmeter reading at which an animal first showed signs of startle or slight jumping was recorded as the threshold value. The behavior of the animals to this value of shock was then observed for two test periods during which each dog received about ten shocks on both sides of the barrier.

For the avoidance training which followed, the side which was to be "hot" for a particular animal was the one to which it moved and which it seemed to "prefer" when placed in the apparatus. The first shock on the training days was given 1 min. after the dog was placed on the "hot" side, and a shock was given every 60 sec. thereafter, as long as the dog stayed on the "hot" side, until S had received a total of ten shocks. However, when a dog jumped to the safe side during avoidance training, it was placed back on the "hot" side, and E waited 60 sec. before shock was again presented. If a dog made three successive jumps from the "hot" to the safe side without receiving shock, testing was discontinued for that period for the animal, and the number of shocks received up to that time was recorded. The shock was of 1-sec. duration, and 1500 v., 6 ma., which was about three times the mean threshold value measured by the voltmeter. The *criteria* for successful avoidance learning were: (*a*) two successive days with no more than one shock on each day or (*b*) a training day on which a dog went to the safe side immediately and received no shock.

Results

No significant difference in the thresholds at which the two groups first responded to electric shock was obtained in this experiment. Furthermore, no behavioral differences between the two groups were observed with these minimal values of shock, either in degree of responsiveness or type of response made.

During avoidance training with 1500 v., however, differences in the behavior of the two groups were obvious. By the end of the third testing period, only 2 of the 12 free-environment dogs had not reached criterion; 5 of the 7 restricted dogs, however, had not reached criterion at this stage, and 3 of these 5 had received the full 30 shocks and gave no sign of learning. Because of the obvious differences between the two groups, and the clearly unpleasant nature of the electric shock used, testing was discontinued at this point. Thus no dog received more than 30 shocks during avoidance training.

While the free-environment dogs received a mean of 5 shocks (range: 1 to 22), the restricted dogs received a mean of 20.3 shocks (range: 1 to 30) during avoidance training. The t score of the difference between the means, 5.07, is significant at the .001 level.

The three dogs that received the full 30 shocks showed stereotyped forms of behavior to the shock. One dog whirled around violently in narrow circles on the "hot" side immediately after getting the first shock in the enclosure and continued to do so until it was removed after getting 10 shocks. The second dog always ran to a particular corner on the "hot" side after the first shock, and sat in a peculiar, awkward position, getting shock after shock without moving. The third dog learned a partial response to the shock, consisting of placing its forelegs on the barrier, while its hindquarters were on the "hot" side, in this way getting repeated shocks without learning the entire response.

Two years after restriction. Two dogs that

had been out of restriction for two years, and were reared normally in the laboratory during that time, nevertheless received a mean of 19 shocks during the three testing periods, which differed significantly from the free-environment dogs' mean of 5 shocks at the .02 level of significance ($t = 2.78$). One of these dogs received 25 shocks, and S still maintained the same awkward, "frozen" position in the corner that it had assumed when first tested two years previously, giving little sign of learning permanently to make the appropriate response of stepping over the 3-in. barrier to the safe side.

EXPERIMENT III. RESPONSE TO BURNING

Method

Subjects. The Ss were ten restricted and eight free-environment dogs.

Apparatus. A box of safety matches.

Procedure. Each dog was allowed to roam the testing room freely for 1 min., and the amount of time S spent near E in an area which had been demarcated previously by a chalk line was recorded. The S was then called by E to this area. A safety match was struck, and E attempted to push the flame into the dog's nose at least three times. Although the dog was held forcibly by E, S was able to avoid being burned by moving or turning its head away rapidly from the match. The dog was then allowed to move to any part of the room, and the time spent near E in the area of the source of burning was recorded during a 2-min. period. The percentages of time S spent near E before and after presentation of the flame were then compared.

Results

Of the eight free-environment dogs tested, six spent less time near E after he tried to burn them than before. Of the ten restricted dogs, however, nine spent *more* time in the area near E *after* nose-burning than before. While the restricted dogs spent 27.9 per cent of the time near E before stimulation, they spent 51.2 per cent of the time in that area following presentation of the match. The amount of time spent by the free-environment dogs near E decreased from 45.1 per cent before to 32.8 per cent after presentation of the match. The nonparametric sign test (9) provided a chi-square value of 5.40 with Yates' correction, which is significant at the .02 level of confidence.

One of the most remarkable features of the restricted dogs was their behavior during and following presentation of the flame. To the astonishment of the observers, seven of the ten restricted dogs made no attempt to get away from E *during* stimulation, and it was not even necessary to hold them. The sequence of behavior observed was almost identical for all seven dogs: they moved their noses into the flame as soon as it was presented, after which the head or whole body jerked away, as though reflexively; but then they came right back to their original position and hovered excitedly near the flame. Three of them repeatedly poked their noses into the flame and sniffed at it as long as it was present. If they snuffed it out, another match was struck, and the same sequence of events occurred. The other four did not sniff at the match, but offered no resistance nor made any attempt to get away after the first contact, and E was able to touch these dogs' noses with the flame as often as he wished. Only three of the restricted dogs squealed on making contact with the flame and tried subsequently to avoid it by moving their heads. Two of these, however, made no attempt to get away from E after stimulation had stopped.

In contrast, the normal dogs moved their heads so rapidly that it was often impossible to hit their noses with the flame. The E tried to move the match in from unexpected angles or to distract the Ss in order to hit them with the flame. But the normal dogs moved their heads slightly and usually successfully, receiving only one or two very brief contacts with the flame; and they then struggled to escape from E's grasp at their sides.

EXPERIMENT IV. RESPONSE TO PIN-PRICK

Method

Subjects. The Ss were eight restricted and nine free-environment dogs.

Apparatus. A large, sharp dissecting needle.

Procedure. The procedure in this experiment is the same as that used in Exp. III, except that the dogs were pin-pricked rather than burned. While the dog was held at the neck, a long dissecting needle was jabbed into the skin at the sides and hind thighs about three or four times.

Results

Of the eight restricted dogs, six spent more time near E after pin-pricking than before. These dogs increased the time spent in the demarcated area from 50.8 per cent before to 58.4 per cent after pin-pricking. The normal dogs, on the other hand, spent a mean of only 8.9 per cent of the time after pin-pricking near E, compared with 42.2 per cent before. Of the nine normally reared dogs, eight spent less time near E after pin-pricking than before. The sign test provided a chi-square value of 4.74, which is significant at the .05 level.

The behavior of the restricted dogs in response to pin-prick was almost identical with that observed with the flame: they appeared unaware that they were being stimulated *by something in the environment.* Four of the restricted dogs made no response whatever apart from localized reflexive twitches at the side or leg when they were pricked. The E was often able to pierce the skin of these dogs completely so that the needle was lodged in it without eliciting withdrawal or any behavioral indication that pain was being "felt" or responded to other than spasmodic, reflexive jerks. The remaining four restricted dogs pulled their bodies aside a few inches or yipped to *some* of the pin-pricks, but when released two of them stayed right next to E, who was able to repeat the procedure and jab them with the needle as often as he wished. The noxious stimulation received was apparently not "perceived" as coming from E, and their behavior subsequently was not oriented or organized in terms of the noxious stimulus in any noticeable way.

The free-environment dogs, however, provided an unmistakable index of perceived pain. They tried to jump aside to escape the pin-prick, yelped, and often struggled for release after two or three pin-pricks. They would then dash away from E's hand and take up a position in the farthest corner of the testing room.

Supplementary observations. The behavior of the restricted dogs in the four experiments just described is entirely consistent with everyday observations of their behavior. It was noted, for example, that their aimless activity resulted in some of them frequently striking their heads against water pipes that ran along the walls just above the floor of the testing rooms. One dog, by actual count, struck his head against these pipes more than 30 times in a single hour. This was never observed once in the normal dogs. Similarly, the rapid movement of the restricted dogs and their unpredictability as to direction resulted a number of times in the dogs' having a paw or the tail stepped on. Often there was no sign that the dogs "felt" pain when this happened, though the procedure would have elicited a howl from a normal dog, and the restricted S made no attempt to withdraw from the place where injury was received.

DISCUSSION

The outstanding feature of the behavior of the restricted dogs was their inability to respond adaptively and intelligently to the variety of stimuli which were presented to them. There can be little doubt that the restricted dogs "felt" electric shock: their disturbance by it was marked and unmistakable. Similarly, the behavior of at least three of the restricted dogs indicates that pin-prick and contact with fire were "felt" in some way. Nevertheless, it was obvious that the restricted dogs did not know how to make the proper avoidance responses which would have prevented further stimulation. The results permit the conclusion, then, that early experience plays an essential role in the emergence of such basic behavior as avoidance of noxious stimuli.

Sherrington has defined pain as "the psychical adjunct of an imperative protective reflex" (13, p. 286). And many psychologists since then (2, 8, 10) have interpreted pain in terms of imperative reflex responses. Such a view, however, is not consistent with the observations reported here. Most of the restricted dogs did indeed show localized reflex responses to the stimulation, yet their behavior was clearly inadequate to cope with the intense electric shocks or such grossly injurious stimuli as contact with fire or piercing of the skin. In comparison, their littermates which had been reared normally in a free environment exhibited the ability to avoid prolonged contact with injurious stimuli, and they were able to learn with great rapidity to make highly organized, abiently oriented responses to every form of noxious stimulus that was presented. However, the capacity of the restricted dogs to acquire good, adaptive behavior to noxious stimulation was notably limited after release from restriction, even with the adequate opportunity that was provided for them to gain varied, normal perceptual experience. Maladaptive behavior like freezing

and whirling also developed, and they were observed as consistent responses as long as two years after release. Thus, it appears that the requisite experience must come at the correct time in the young organism's life. During later stages of development, the experience necessary for adaptive, well-organized responses to pain may never be properly acquired.

The inability of the restricted dogs to cope intelligently with noxious stimuli, however, cannot be attributed to inadequate response mechanisms alone. Their reflexive jerks and movements during pin-prick and contact with fire suggest that they may have "felt something" during stimulation; but the *lack* of any observable emotional disturbance apart from these reflex movements in at least four of the dogs following pin-prick and in seven of them after nose-burning indicates that their *perception* of the event was highly abnormal in comparison with the behavior of the normally reared control dogs. Livingston (6) has made the observation that experience with pain in childhood is an important determinant of the manner in which the adult perceives and responds to pain; that is, the "meaning" involved in a perception such as pain, and the attitudes of the individual in situations involving pain, are largely a function of the earlier, related experiences of that individual. The results reported here are consistent with observations such as this and can be interpreted in a similar manner.

The isolation of the restricted dogs prevented them from acquiring experience early in life with severe skin-damage and fire. It is evident, then, that the flame and pin-prick could not have evoked the neural "phase sequences" (memories) acquired during earlier pain experiences (5) that might have been aroused in the normal dogs. The results strongly suggest that the restricted dogs lacked awareness of a necessary aspect of normal pain perception: the "meaning" of physical damage or at least *threat* to the physical well-being that is inherent in the normal organism's perception of pain. The observations of the restricted dogs' poking their noses into fire, or permitting E to cause bodily damage by fire and pin-prick without emotional disturbance apart from localized reflexes, indicates that an interpretation such as this is valid. Indeed, to say that these restricted dogs perceived fire and pin-prick as *threatening*, or even painful in any *normal* sense, would be anthropomorphism rather than inference from observed behavior.

The results which have been reported here then, make it difficult to treat behavior related to pain simply in terms of frequency and intensity of stimulations or in terms of imperative reflex responses alone (2, 8, 10) without regard to the earlier perceptual experience of the organism. The behavior of the restricted dogs suggests that perceiving and responding to pain, which is so fundamental to normal adult behavior and presumably so important for the survival of an individual or species, requires a background of early, prolonged, perceptual experience.

SUMMARY

1. Ten dogs were reared in isolation from puppyhood to maturity in specially constructed cages which drastically restricted their sensory experience. Twelve control littermates were raised normally as pets in private homes and in the laboratory.

2. In two tests using strong electric shock, the restricted dogs required significantly more shocks before they learned to make the proper avoidance responses than their free-environment littermates.

3. In tests using nose-burning and pin-pricking, the behavior of the restricted dogs was found to be strikingly different in capacity to perceive pain and respond to it when compared to their normal littermates.

4. It is concluded that early perceptual experience determines, in part at least, (*a*) the emergence of overt responses such as avoidance to noxious stimulation, and (*b*) the actual capacity to perceive pain normally.

REFERENCES

1. BEACH, F. A., & JAYNES, J. Effects of early experience upon the behavior of animals. *Psychol. Bull.*, 1954, **51**, 239–263.

2. ESTES, W. K. An experimental study of punishment. *Psychol. Monogr.*, 1944, **57**, No. 3 (Whole No. 263).

3. FULLER, J. L., EASLER, C. A., & BANKS, E. M. Formation of conditioned avoidance responses in young puppies. *Amer. J. Physiol.*, 1950, **160**, 462–466.

4. GREENACRE, P. The biological economy of birth. In O. Fenichel (Ed.), *The psychoanalytic study of the child*. New York: International Universities Press, 1945.

5. HEBB, D. O. *The organization of behavior*. New York: John Wiley and Sons, Inc., 1949.

6. LIVINGSTON, W. K. What is pain? *Sci. Amer.*, 1953, **188**, 59–66.

7. MELZACK, R. The genesis of emotional behavior: an experimental study of the dog. *J. comp. physiol. Psychol.*, 1954, **47**, 166–168.

8. MILLER, N. E. Learnable drives and rewards. In S. S. Stevens (Ed.), *Handbook of experimental psychology*. New York: John Wiley and Sons, Inc., 1951.

9. MOSES, L. E. Non-parametric statistics for psychological research. *Psychol. Bull.*, 1952, **49**, 122–143.

10. MOWRER, O. H. *Learning theory and personality dynamics*. New York: Ronald Press, 1950.

11. NISSEN, H. W., CHOW, K. L., & SEMMES, JOSEPHINE. Effects of restricted opportunity for tactual, kinesthetic, and manipulative experience on the behavior of a chimpanzee. *Amer. J. Psychol.*, 1951, **64**, 485–507.

12. SCOTT, J. P., FREDRICSON, E., & FULLER, J. L. Experimental exploration of the critical period hypothesis. *Personality*, 1951, **1**, 162–183.

13. SHERRINGTON, C. S. *Man on his nature*. New York: Macmillan, 1941.

14. THOMPSON, W. R., & HERON, W. The effects of restricting early experience on the problem solving capacity of dogs. *Canad. J. Psychol.*, 1954, **8**, 17–31.

WILLIAM A. MASON

38 The Effects of Social Restriction on the Behavior of Rhesus Monkeys: I. Free Social Behavior

The present researches are part of a series of experiments investigating the effects of restricted social experience on the social behavior of rhesus monkeys. The principal comparisons in these experiments are between monkeys living under free-ranging conditions until captured, and laboratory-born monkeys separated from their mothers in early infancy and raised under conditions which limited the nature and extent of early social experience.

To insure uniform and controlled living conditions and provide ready access to infant Ss for testing, early maternal separation is virtually essential to the effective conduct of a major psychological research program utilizing infant monkey Ss. Such a program has been in progress at the University of Wisconsin since 1953, and a large number of infant monkeys have been separated from their mothers and housed in individual living cages at the Primate Laboratory.

When maintained in accordance with the general recommendations of van Wagenen (1950), there is no indication that early maternal separation adversely affects the growth and viability of the infant macaque. However, the reduction in intraspecies social contacts and the routine and relatively impersonal nature of the caretaking methods employed in the laboratory create an impoverished social environment which approaches the more extreme forms of institutional environments for human children.

Investigations assessing the effects of institutionalization on human personality development and social behavior have been summarized by Bowlby (1952), and the

Reprinted from *Journal of Comparative and Physiological Psychology* 53:582–589, 1960. Copyright 1960 by the American Psychological Association and reproduced by permission.

Support for this research was provided through funds received from the Graduate School of the University of Wisconsin, Grant G6194 from the National Science Foundation, and Grant M-722 from the National Institutes of Health.

findings indicate that deprivation of normal socialization experiences in human children results in a wide range of personal and social deficiencies and aberrations including affective disorders, limited capacity for sustained and effective social relationships, and psychopathic tendencies.

Although there exist no comparable data on the effects of similar restrictions on the development of social behavior in the nonhuman primates, field workers have generally assumed that prior socialization experience is of fundamental importance in the development of orderly and efficient patterns of social interaction characteristic of nonhuman primate societies (Carpenter, 1942; Imanishi, 1957). Because of formidable practical difficulties, however, careful longitudinal studies have not been completed under field conditions, and the process of socialization in free-ranging primates has not been fully described. The available evidence indicates that under natural conditions there is ample time and opportunity for complex social learning to occur. The period of infantile dependency in Old World monkeys is relatively long, extending in most forms for approximately two years. Following this there is a period of several years during which the tie to the mother gradually weakens and the individual has the status of a juvenile which associates with other young monkeys and does not participate fully in adult functions and activities. Adult status is probably not attained by the male before its sixth year; females mature somewhat earlier.

During these early years the young monkey has considerable social mobility, providing a wide range of social contacts and many opportunities to observe and participate in a variety of activities with peers and with adults of both sexes. It is probable that basic social attachments binding the individual to the group are established and strengthened during this time and many of the essential patterns of social intercourse are developed and refined. Thus, restriction upon the nature and extent of early socialization experience might be expected to produce inadequacies in subsequent relations.

The present research investigated differences in the form and frequency of spontaneous social interactions of feral and laboratory-raised rhesus monkeys.

EXPERIMENT 1: INTRAGROUP COMPARISONS OF FERAL AND SOCIALLY RESTRICTED MONKEYS

Method

Subjects. The Ss were two groups of six adolescent monkeys. One group of three males and three females, the Restricted group, was born in the laboratory. They were separated from their mothers before the end of the first month of life and were housed in individual cages which allowed them to see and hear other young monkeys, but which prevented physical contact between them. Opportunities for more extensive intraspecies social contacts were confined to a few brief periods during the first year of life. Interspecies social experience was limited almost entirely to daily contacts with human beings in connection with routine caretaking and testing activities. At the start of the experiment three Ss were 28 months of age and three were 29 months old.

The second group of three males and three females, the Feral group, was captured in the field. Immediately following their arrival in Madison they spent approximately 3 months on a zoo monkey island with about 20 other monkeys of similar age and background and the next 3 months with the same animals in a large group living cage in the basement of the zoo's primate building. This section is not on exhibition. The entire group was shifted to the laboratory when the 6 Ss later used in this study were about 20 months old. They were housed in pairs for 8 months. At the time of separation, one month before the start of the experiment, none was caged with any other member of the group of 6. During the month before the experiment began and throughout the period covered by this research, the Ss lived in individual cages. They were selected from the larger group to match the Ss of the Restricted group in sex, weight, and dentition. It is estimated the age differences among Ss were no greater than one month.

Apparatus. The test chamber, constructed of gray plywood, measured 6 ft. by 6 ft. by 6 ft. and was illuminated from above by a 150-w. bulb. Two opposing walls contained one-way observation panels, and in each of the other walls was a large hinged door fitted with a smaller sliding door through which the Ss entered the chamber from an adjacent carrying cage. Behavior was recorded on a multiple-category keyboard which operated the pens of an Esterline-Angus recorder, giving a continuous record of the frequency, duration, and temporal patterning of social interactions. By appropriate wiring of the keyboard a total of 11 response categories were available for each member of a test pair.

TABLE 1
DEFINITIONS AND RELIABILITY OF RESPONSE CATEGORIES

1. Approach: Moves to within 6 in. of other monkey (75%).
2. Aggression: Includes intense vocalization (barks, growls), biting, pulling. Threat or bluff (Chance, 1956) was not scored as aggression. No occurrence during reliability check.
3. Groom: Systematically picks through another's fur with hands (95%).
4. Mount: Characteristically, grasps the partner's hips with hands, and feet clasp her legs (96%).
5. Play: Tumbling, mauling, wrestling, and nipping. Less vigorous and intense than aggression, is not accompanied by intense vocalization, and rarely elicits squealing or other evidence of pain in partner (79%).
6. Sexual presentation: Assumption of female mating posture. Hindquarters are elevated and turned toward the partner (60%).
7. Social facilitation of exploration: Activity of one animal with respect to some inanimate feature of the room elicits approach, observation, or display of similar behavior from another (59%).
8. Social investigation: Close visual, manual, and/or oral investigation of the partner. Particular interest toward apertures. No occurrence during reliability check.
9. Thrusting: Piston-like movements usually accompanying mounting (95%).
10. Visual orientation: Passive observation of other (66%).
11. Withdrawal: Abrupt movement away from other. Not scored during play or aggression unless it terminated interaction (65%).

Procedure. Once a day for 14 days each S was individually placed in a carrying cage at the entrance to the chamber and was allowed 3 min. in which to enter and explore the room. This was followed by seven daily 3-min. sessions in which entry was forced for all Ss not entering the room during the first few seconds of the session.

In the social testing which followed these individual adaptation sessions, Feral and Restricted monkeys were paired only with the other members of their group. Each of the 15 pairs obtainable from each group was observed in a series of 16 social test sessions each 3 min. long. To initiate a session, the sliding door on the O's right was raised and when the S had entered the room, the second sliding door was raised. When both Ss were in the chamber, the Esterline-Angus recorder was started. A timer automatically stopped the recorder at the end of the test period. The testing schedule was so arranged that all pairs were tested once every two days with the restriction that no S participated in two successive test sessions. For each pair the order of testing and the side from which the Ss entered the chamber were counterbalanced over sessions.

The behavior of each S was separately recorded by depressing the appropriate response-keys during the period of behavioral occurrence. To provide an estimate of the reliability of the method, two *O*s were present and independently recorded the social interactions of 15 pairs on a total of 90 sessions. Table 1 presents definitions of the response categories and their corresponding reliability values for frequency measures. Reliability is expressed in terms of per cent agreement:

$$\frac{\text{Frequency of agreements}}{\text{Frequency of agreements} + \text{disagreements}}$$

Results

To conserve space only the response categories of play, grooming, aggression, and sexual behavior are analyzed in detail. Among the other response measures, differences between groups in the frequency of approaches, withdrawals, and social investigation were not statistically significant. The frequency of visual orientation responses was higher among Feral *S*s, and socially facilitated exploration occurred more frequently in the Restricted group. These differences were statistically significant, *p* being .01 for each of these comparisons. Unless otherwise indicated these and all subsequent statistical comparisons were based on *t* tests performed on total individual scores.

Play. Although the form of play behavior was similar in both groups, play occurred more frequently among Restricted *S*s. The mean total incidence of play was 342.0 and 179.8 for Restricted and Feral groups, respectively. Although the difference between groups is substantial, it falls short of significance at the .05 level, principally because within each group there were large and consistent sex differences in the incidence of play. Both males and females of the Feral group had lower scores than like-sexed *S*s in the Restricted group, and all females showed less play behavior than did males. Mean play scores for females were 115.7 and 29.0 in Restricted and Feral groups, respectively, whereas corresponding values for males were 568.2 and 330.7. Play behavior did not occur in female pairs in the Feral group and occurred in female pairs of the Restricted group in only six sessions. The difference between sexes in the frequency of play for the combined groups is significant at the .001 level.

Grooming. The incidence of grooming was relatively low in both groups, occurring in three *S*s in the Restricted group in 10 sessions and in four *S*s in the Feral group in 25 sessions. Grooming was observed in seven Feral pairs and in five Restricted pairs. These differences were not statistically significant.

Grooming episodes tended to be substantially longer in Feral pairs and occasionally occupied nearly the entire test period. The mean duration of grooming behavior, determined by dividing total duration by number of occurrences, was 1.6 sec. and 25.3 sec. for Restricted and Feral groups, respectively, and this difference is significant at the .05 level.

Qualitative differences between groups were observed in the response to grooming. While being groomed members of the Feral group were characteristically passive and immobile, whereas the *S*s in the Restricted group showed no specific or consistent complementary responses.

Aggression. The mean total frequency of aggression for Restricted and Feral groups was 11.7 and 2.0, respectively, and this difference is significant at the .05 level. Eleven pairs in the Restricted group engaged in aggression in at least one session and seven pairs fought in more than one session. In the Feral group, aggression occurred in six pairs, and in only two of these pairs did fighting occur in more than one session.

Aggressive episodes tended to be longer in the Restricted group, the mean duration being 4.87 sec. for these *S*s, as compared with 1.21 sec. for Feral *S*s. This difference, however, was not statistically significant. Although there were no apparent differences between groups in the form of individual aggressive responses, it was characteristic of the *S*s in the Restricted group, particularly during the early phases of the experiment, to respond with aggression when attacked, whereas Feral *S*s generally withdrew from attack or submitted passively and without retaliation.

Sexual behavior. A striking difference was apparent between Feral and Restricted males in the frequency and integration of sexual behavior. Mean total frequencies are presented in Figure 1, and it is evident that Feral males showed more mounting and thrusting and had sexual episodes of substantially longer duration. All differences were significant at the .05 level. The incidence of mounting was negligible among females in both groups.

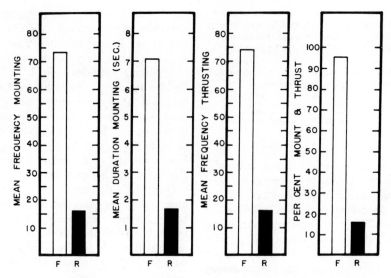

Fig. 1. Comparisons of sexual behavior of Restricted (*R*) and Feral (*F*) males.

Gross qualitative differences in the organization of the male sexual act were present. Males in the Restricted group never clasped the partner's legs with their feet during mounting and would frequently assume inappropriate postures and body orientation. Many responses by these males could not be categorized as sexual until thrusting was observed, hence mounting was not scored for 64% of the total thrusting responses. Inasmuch as the presence of thrusting presumably implies some attempt to mount, the mounting scores of the Restricted males were subsequently increased by the number of thrusting responses in which mounting was not recorded. This raised their mean total mounting score from 16.0 to 23.3. The difference between groups was still statistically significant (p = .05).

Ejaculation was not observed in either group. Menstrual cycles in the females were absent or irregular, and there was no apparent relationship between male sexual behavior and cyclic activity of the females.

With the exception of one highly dominant female in the Feral group, assumption of the female sexual posture (presentation) occurred in all *S*s. Mean total frequency of sexual presentation was 23.5 and 12.2 in Feral and Restricted groups, respectively. Males in both groups made this response less frequently than females, accounting for 28% and 10%

of total presentations in Feral and Restricted groups, respectively. Differences between groups and between sexes in the frequency of sexual presentation were not statistically significant.

Sexual presentation was notably more stereotyped for Feral animals of both sexes. In this group presentation was occasionally preceded by gazing intently at the partner while making rapid movements of the lips, and it was virtually always accompanied by postural adjustments, including flexing of the legs as the partner mounted. These behaviors were never observed among Restricted *S*s.

To provide further evidence on the nature of the differences between groups in the male sexual pattern, a second experiment was run in which the males from Feral and Restricted groups were tested with the same socially experienced females, thus eliminating differential social experiences of the sexual partner as a factor contributing to differences in male sexual performance.

Experiment 2: Behavior of Restricted and Feral Males with Socially Experienced Females

Method

Subjects. The *S*s were the three Feral and three Restricted males previously described, and three adolescent females captured in the field and without prior contact with any of the males. During the six-month period between Experiments 1 and 2, each male participated about 10 hr. in the social tests of gregarious tendencies and food competition. The males lived in individual cages throughout the period covered by the preceding experiments, and all Ss were individually housed during the present research.

Apparatus and procedure. The apparatus and the testing and recording procedures were the same as those described in Experiment 1. In the present experiment, however, only male-female pairs were tested. Following five individual 3-min. adaptation sessions for all Ss, each male was tested in ten 3-min. sessions with each female. Males participated in one test session a day and each female was used in two sessions. No female was tested in two successive sessions. The response categories used in Experiment 1 were extended and modified to provide further information on the integration of the male sexual pattern. Response categories retained from Experiment 1 without modification included aggression, approach, groom, play, sexual presentation, thrusting, and withdrawal. Measures of visual orientation and social facilitation were not obtained in the present experiment. Mounting was classified as follows: "Appropriate mounting orientation"—longitudinal axes of the bodies are aligned during mounting, with the Ss facing in the same direction. "Inappropriate mounting orientation"—all attempts

at mounting not scored as appropriate mounting. Additional categories included: "Hip clasp"—within 5 sec. before mounting the male places both hands on partner's hips. "Foot clasp"—male grasps female's legs with both feet during mounting. "Anogenital investigation"—visual, manual, and oral investigation of partner's anogenital region.

Results

Mean and individual totals for frequency of nonsexual responses in males are presented in Table 2. None of the differences is significant, although what differences there are tend to be in the same direction as in Experiment 1.

The sexual responsiveness of the Restricted males showed a striking increase relative to their performance levels in Experiment 1. In the present experiment the mean incidence of mounting per session, including both appropriately and inappropriately oriented responses, was 2.44 as compared with 0.20 in Experiment 1. Similarly, the mean frequency of thrusting increased from 0.13 per session to 1.84. These changes are significant at the .02 level as determined by t tests for correlated measures. Although the higher frequency of mounting behavior might conceivably be related to modification of scoring categories between Experiments 1 and 2, the same interpretation would not apply to measures of thrusting. A more reasonable hypothesis is that the behavior of the socially experienced female partner and/or experience gained by Restricted males in the social tests intervening between Experiments 1 and 2 contributed to this increase in sexual responsiveness.

Comparative data on the sexual performance

TABLE 2

NONSEXUAL RESPONSES OF FERAL AND RESTRICTED MALES IN EXPERIMENT 2

Response	Feral S				Restricted Ss			
	331	336	337	Mean	3	4	5	Mean
Aggression	1	1	0	0.7	0	0	0	0.0
Approach	368	293	38	233.0	641	228	358	409.0
Groom	9	14	0	7.7	0	1	0	0.3
Dur. groom (sec.)	4.8	15.4	0	6.7	0	1.0	0	0.3
Play	114	47	0	53.7	144	79	129	117.3
Withdrawal	26	7	15	16.0	14	2	21	12.3

TABLE 3

SEXUAL RESPONSES OF FERAL AND RESTRICTED MALES IN EXPERIMENT 2

Measure	Feral S				Restricted S				p
	331	336	337	Mean	3	4	5	Mean	
Approp. mount	64	53	1	39.3	25	30	18	24.3	ns
Inapprop. mount	0	0	0	0.0	60	40	47	49.0	.01
% approp. mount	100	100	100	100.0	29	43	28	33.3	.01
Mounting dur. (sec.)	4.2	5.3	10.0	6.5	2.4	2.5	2.7	2.5	ns
Thrusting	65	53	1	39.7	69	55	42	55.3	ns
% mount + thrusting	100	98	100	99.3	81	79	68	76.0	.01
Foot clasp	63	53	1	39.0	0	7	0	2.3	ns
% mount + foot clasp	98	100	100	99.3	0	10	0	3.3	.01
Hip clasp	49	47	0	32.0	24	30	14	22.7	ns
% mount + hip clasp	66	81	0	49.0	16	34	9	19.7	ns
Anogenital investig.	27	21	0	16.0	4	2	5	3.7	ns

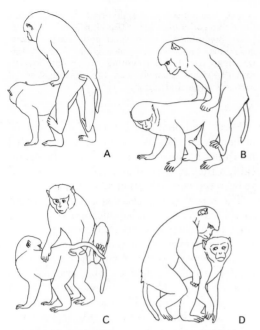

FIG. 2. Sexual behavior of Feral and Restricted males with socially experienced female partners. *A.* Rear view of Feral male in typical copulatory position. *B.* Side view of Feral male in typical copulatory position. *C.* Restricted male attempting to mount from the side. Note elevation of left foot. *D.* Sexual behavior of a Restricted male. Although mounting orientation is appropriate (as defined herein), the hands are placed high on the female's trunk and she remains sitting. The male is thrusting against the female's back. All figures were traced from moving-picture film.

of Restricted and Feral males in the present experiment are presented in Table 3. The differences between groups in the frequency of mounting and thrusting were not statistically significant. Interpretation of this outcome is complicated by the fact that Feral Male No. 337 mounted only once in this test series, as compared with 83 mounts in Experiment 1. The remaining animals in this group showed no evidence of lowered sexual responsiveness relative to their performance in Experiment 1. There is no indication, however, that these animals differed reliably from Restricted males with regard to frequency of thrusting and mounting (appropriate and inappropriate mounting orientations combined), which provides further evidence of enhanced sexual responsiveness of Restricted males in the present experiment.

In spite of more frequent sexual responses the sexual performance of the Restricted

males was poorly integrated (see Fig. 2). Only 33% of total mounts in this group were appropriately oriented, 76% of total mounts were accompanied by thrusting and only 3%, included clasping the partner's legs. Comparable values for the Feral males exceeded 98% and the differences between groups were significant at the .01 level. The duration of mounting was again substantially shorter among Restricted males, mounting was less frequently preceded by grasping the partner's hips and the incidence of anogenital investigation was lower. These differences, however, were not statistically significant. Ejaculation was not observed in either group.

The behavior of the females clearly suggested that they were not responding equivalently to the two groups of males. Females frequently failed to assume appropriate receptive postures in response to sexual advances of Restricted males (see Fig. 2D), and made fewer approaches to these animals. Furthermore, the high incidence of cowering and grimaces in the presence of Restricted males suggested that the females were afraid. This impression receives support from the finding that their withdrawal scores were higher with Restricted partners (Mean totals: Restricted, 210.7; Feral, 66.0). This difference was significant at the .01 level as determined by Wilcoxon tests performed on individual trial totals.

DISCUSSION

The results of Experiment 1 indicate that restriction of intraspecies social experience of rhesus monkeys during the first two years of life retards the development of integrated social responses and orderly patterns of social interaction. Fighting was more frequent and prolonged among Restricted monkeys. They groomed less frequently, and grooming episodes were shorter. Sexual behavior in Restricted *S*s was brief and showed gross deficiencies in organization, which were particularly evident in the behavior of males. The extent to which the performance of the Restricted monkeys was influenced by the brief social contacts provided them during the first year of life cannot be determined, but unpublished data on animals whose social experience was even more severely restricted suggest that this early social experience had some effect. Although the members of the Feral group in Experiment 1 were not strangers, the absence of any major changes in the social behavior of Feral males between Experiments 1 and 2 strongly suggests that possible pre-experimental contacts among members of the Feral group did not appreciably influence the present results.

The data on sexual behavior of Restricted males suggests that the components of the male copulatory pattern are differentially dependent upon social experience. The tendency to approach and bring the genitalia in contact with the partner was present from the first tests, as evidenced by the fact that all Restricted males attempted to mount on the first day of Experiment 1. Grasping the partner with the hands also appeared early in testing, but throughout the present experiments this response was less stereotyped and precise among Restricted males and was often accompanied by nipping, tugging, or other playful behaviors. Foot clasping was particularly deficient in Restricted males. This response was never observed among Restricted males in Experiment 1. In Experiment 2, only one of these males ever succeeded in grasping the partner's legs with both feet simultaneously, and this occurred only 7 times in 70 mounting attempts. A second male in this group occasionally raised its feet alternately as though attempting to place them, but never grasped with both feet simultaneously (see Fig. 2C). Closely related to this deficiency was the absence of efficient and appropriate postural orientation with regard to the sexual partner.

The data on sexual behavior are consistent with previous observations (Bingham, 1928; Foley, 1935; Maslow, 1936; Yerkes & Elder, 1936), and support the generalization that among nonhuman primates social experience is relatively more important to male than to female sexual behavior (Ford & Beach, 1952). Had more sensitive measures of female sexual behavior been used, however, there is little doubt that deficiencies would also have been demonstrated in the performance of Restricted females, although it is unlikely that these were sufficient to prevent effective coitus with an experienced male.

Social organization among nonhuman primates is characteristically orderly and effi-cient. Presumably, regular social relationships are dependent upon stable interindividual stimulus-response tendencies. Sexual presentation, presentation for grooming, grasping the hips preparatory to mounting, and the threat pattern are a few of the highly stereotyped responses described for rhesus monkeys which ordinarily function as social cues, eliciting appropriate reciprocal responses from other animals. These stimulus-response relationships form the basis for social coordination, communication, and social control in feral groups (Carpenter, 1942; Chance, 1956; Maslow, 1936). Insofar as the present findings bear on this problem, they suggest that among animals whose socialization has been restricted, the cue function of many basic social responses is poorly established if not absent altogether.

SUMMARY

1. Comparisons were made of the spontaneous social interactions of monkeys raised in a socially restricted laboratory environment and Feral monkeys captured in the field.

2. Pairs of Restricted monkeys showed more frequent and prolonged fighting and fewer and less prolonged grooming episodes than Feral pairs. Differences between groups were found in the frequency, duration and integration of sexual behavior, which were particularly evident in the behavior of males.

3. Restricted and Feral males were subsequently tested with the same socially experienced females, thus eliminating inadequacies in the sexual partner as a factor contributing to the differences in male sexual performance. Gross differences in the organization of the male copulatory pattern were still apparent.

4. In addition to differences between groups in the form and frequency of these basic social responses, the data suggest that responses to social cues are poorly established in monkeys with restricted socialization experience.

REFERENCES

BINGHAM, H. C. Sex development in apes. *Comp. psychol. Monogr.*, 1928, **5**, 1–165.

BOWLBY, J. *Maternal care and mental health.* Geneva: World Health Organization, 1952.

CARPENTER, C. R. Societies of monkeys and apes. *Biol. Sympos.*, 1942, **8**, 177–204.

CHANCE, M. R. A. Social structure of a colony of *Macaca mulatta. Brit. J. anim. Behav.*, 1956, **4**, 1–13.

FOLEY, J. P., JR. Second year development of a rhesus monkey (*Macaca mulatta*) reared in isolation during the first eighteen months. *J. genet. Psychol.*, 1935, **47**, 73–97.

FORD, C. S., & BEACH, F. A. *Patterns of sexual behavior.* New York: Harper, 1952.

IMANISHI, K. Social behavior in Japanese monkeys, *Macaca fuscata. Psychologia*, 1957, **1**, 47–54.

MASLOW, A. H. The role of dominance in the social and sexual behavior of infra-human primates: III. A theory of sexual behavior of infra-human primates. *J. genet. Psychol.*, 1936, **48**, 310–338.

VAN WAGENEN, G. The monkey. In E. J. Farris (Ed.), *The care and breeding of laboratory animals.* New York: Wiley, 1950. Pp. 1–42.

YERKES, R. M., & ELDER, J. H. Oestrus, receptivity, and mating in chimpanzee. *Comp. psychol. Monogr.*, 1936, **13**, 1–39.

WAYNE DENNIS

39 Infant Development under Conditions of Restricted Practice and of Minimum Social Stimulation: A Preliminary Report

This is a further report upon the development of female twins born January 19, 1932, and reared in the experimenter's home from February 22, 1932, until March 22, 1933.   Previous reports upon the outcome of this investigation have dealt with the establishment of social smiling (2), the effect of restricted practice upon reaching, sitting, and standing (3), and the laterality of function in the subjects (4).   The present report deals chiefly with the rate of development of behavior during the period when the environmental conditions of the subjects were most severely restricted, namely, the first seven lunar months (ending on day 192).   Later development is treated for the sake of completeness, but it is of less interest as it occurred under circumstances which more nearly approximated American family life.

The circumstances of the twins from the beginning of the experiment to the end of the seventh lunar month were in brief as follows: The sole care of the infants was exercised by Mrs. Dennis and myself.   They were fed on a lactic acid cow's milk formula prepared for us by the University of Virginia Hospital.   Feedings were

Reprinted from *The Journal of Genetic Psychology* 53:149–158, 1938.

This paper was read before the Infant Behavior Section of the American Psychological Association at Hanover, N. H., Sept. 2, 1936.

Acknowledgment is gratefully made to the Institute for Research in the Social Sciences at the University of Virginia for defraying the expenses of the research and to Mrs. Dennis for her invaluable coöperation and assistance.

approximately at 4-hour intervals. A daily bath was given in a small tub in the nursery and a daily sun bath was given before an open window.

The subjects were kept in individual Kiddie Koops, and were always placed in the supine position. The Kiddie Koops were separated by an opaque screen. The subjects were taken from their cribs only for feeding, bathing, cleaning, and dressing, and for a few experiments. They were taken from their nursery room only for monthly medical examinations at the nearby hospital. No one entered the nursery unless accompanied by one of the experimenters. The infants were not propped up in a semi-sitting position and no toys were given them. Only tree-tops and the sky were visible from the windows of the room, and no pictures or mirrors were hung on the walls. The nursery contained a minimum of furnishings.

We did not smile at the subjects nor did we speak to them, romp with them, or tickle them except as these actions occasionally were incorporated into routine experiments. We talked to each other when in the nursery but did not direct our remarks to the infants. We did not punish the subjects for any act on their part, and we tried to avoid rewarding them for any act, either by praise, patting, or special attentiveness. However, when either infant cried insistently, we entered the room and corrected whatever condition seemed to be the cause of the cry. We did not adhere rigidly to the feeding schedule. If either infant seemed quite hungry before the usual hour, she was fed; and on the other hand neither infant was ordinarily awakened if she was asleep at the usual hour for feeding.

Additional details with respect to the care of the infants will be found in previous reports (2, 3, 4).

Notes on the behavior of the infants were taken each time we entered the room, which we did on the average about 12 times per day.

While some of the restrictions just outlined may seem extreme, it must be borne in mind that they were applied during the first seven lunar months when infants are awake but little longer than is required for feeding, bathing, and dressing. Beyond the seven months' period, the restrictions upon motor practice and upon social stimulation were abandoned one by one. The restrictions were removed not because of any restiveness on the part of the subjects nor because any detrimental effects were apparent, but because the imposition of such conditions is a novel one in child psychology and it was felt that a prolonged experiment of this character should not be undertaken until after the effects of a short period of restriction had been demonstrated.

The stringent conditions of the first seven months were subsequently altered as follows:

On day 192, we began to speak to the subjects and occasionally to romp and play with them. The subjects' initial reactions to such behavior were of course recorded.

Beginning with day 254, the infants were often placed prone on quilted pads on the floor for periods of five to thirty minutes daily. Practice in maintaining the sitting posture was begun on days 262 and 263 as reported earlier (3). Placing the subjects in high chairs was started on day 300, and rattles, the only toys which were presented to them, were introduced on day 341. Training in standing with support first occurred on day 364 (3). During the final month of the experiment the infants were introduced to a variety of new conditions, and their environment was no longer of a decidedly restricted sort. However, even at the close of the experiment the majority of their waking hours were spent in the cribs.

Behavioral Development

Mrs. Dennis and I have recently compiled the developmental records of 40 subjects of baby biographies (6). The reader is referred to the original publication for definitions of the items of behavior, as they are too long to warrant repetition in full.

In Figure 1 the notations along the left margin are short descriptions of the behavior items. The horizontal line opposite each notation indicates the age range during which this item made its appearance in the biographies and the short vertical which cuts each horizontal line indicates the median age for the appearance of that item. The figures at the left of the chart indicate the number of reports of each item. All of the infants whose records are on this chart were described as healthy and of normal intelligence, and none was very unusual in the amount of training which was given it. Since less than 40 records, and in some cases only 10 records, are represented for each item, it is altogether likely that the ranges here represented are too narrow.

The circles and triangles show the ages at which each of our subjects first performed the items listed on the chart. The circles indicate the records of the larger twin, named Rey, and the triangles the records of Del, the smaller of the two. A few items show no

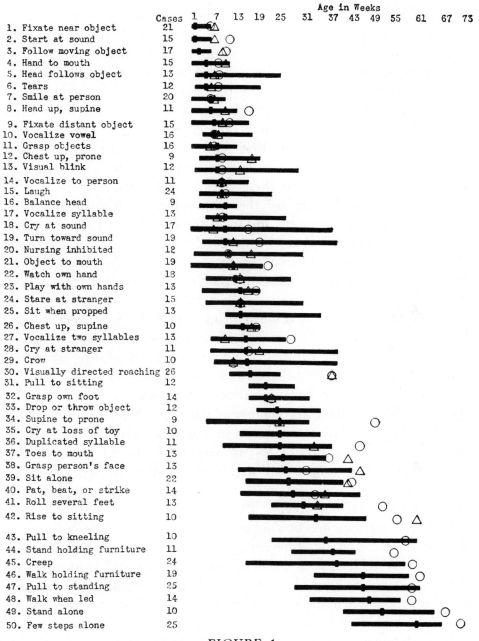

	Cases	Age in Weeks
1. Fixate near object	21	
2. Start at sound	15	
3. Follow moving object	17	
4. Hand to mouth	15	
5. Head follows object	13	
6. Tears	12	
7. Smile at person	20	
8. Head up, supine	11	
9. Fixate distant object	15	
10. Vocalize vowel	16	
11. Grasp objects	16	
12. Chest up, prone	9	
13. Visual blink	12	
14. Vocalize to person	11	
15. Laugh	24	
16. Balance head	9	
17. Vocalize syllable	13	
18. Cry at sound	17	
19. Turn toward sound	19	
20. Nursing inhibited	12	
21. Object to mouth	19	
22. Watch own hand	18	
23. Play with own hands	13	
24. Stare at stranger	15	
25. Sit when propped	13	
26. Chest up, supine	10	
27. Vocalize two syllables	13	
28. Cry at stranger	11	
29. Crow	10	
30. Visually directed reaching	26	
31. Pull to sitting	12	
32. Grasp own foot	14	
33. Drop or throw object	12	
34. Supine to prone	9	
35. Cry at loss of toy	10	
36. Duplicated syllable	11	
37. Toes to mouth	13	
38. Grasp person's face	13	
39. Sit alone	22	
40. Pat, beat, or strike	14	
41. Roll several feet	13	
42. Rise to sitting	10	
43. Pull to kneeling	10	
44. Stand holding furniture	11	
45. Creep	24	
46. Walk holding furniture	19	
47. Pull to standing	25	
48. Walk when led	14	
49. Stand alone	10	
50. Few steps alone	25	

FIGURE 1

records for our subjects because in these respects we failed to make observations comparable to the biographical reports.

By referring to the chart, it will be seen that with respect to the items whose upper limits appear within the first seven lunar months, the twin subjects with few exceptions fall within the age range of children with normal environments. In the upper half of the chart, the items in which the subjects fall beyond the range of the comparison subjects are chiefly the first three items, which occur at such an early age that it seems unlikely that the retardation of the twins was due to the experiment. It seems more likely that this may have been due to the poor nutritional condition of the infants when we received them. Aside from the first three items, the only other apparent retardations among the items which ordinarily appear within the first seven months occur in Rey's case only. They are "head up, supine," "object to mouth," and "vocalize two syllables." In none of these cases is Rey more than two weeks beyond the upper range of the biographical subjects, and since records are available in some instances for less than 20 infants, there is a strong likelihood that the ranges here shown are too narrow. It is concluded therefore that the records of our subjects within the first seven months are not distinguishable from those of the children whose records have been kept by biographers.

A similar conclusion is reached if instead of the biographical data, Shirley's recent data (7) are used for comparison. Shirley followed a number of children through the first two years of life, obtaining a longitudinal record of behavioral development. We have selected from her tables those behavior items which do not involve special tests, and hence which are comparable to our observational account of development. These are shown in Figure 2, which is constructed in the same way as Figure 1. In respect to the 14 items in this chart whose upper ranges fall within the first seven lunar months, our subjects' only retardation is a one-week delay in "startled by sound" on the part of Rey.

Such comparisons are of course not ideal, as the different sets of data were gathered by different people and in somewhat different ways. Nevertheless, it is believed that they are sufficient to show clearly that no striking abnormalities of development occurred during the period when the environment of the subjects of the experiment was highly restricted.

It is of course quite possible that had conditions been normal our subjects might have developed any one of the items at an age different from that at which it actually appeared. That slight differences in behavior may have been induced by the experiment, there is no intent to deny, and no means to prove or disprove. But it must be concluded that whatever the effects of the experiment may have been, they were not sufficient to force our subjects beyond the range of infants reared under normal conditions.

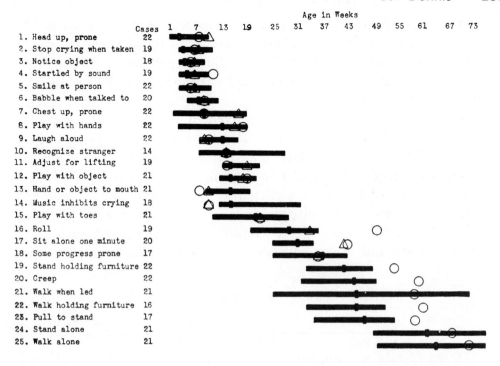

	Cases	Age in Weeks
1. Head up, prone	22	
2. Stop crying when taken	19	
3. Notice object	18	
4. Startled by sound	19	
5. Smile at person	22	
6. Babble when talked to	20	
7. Chest up, prone	22	
8. Play with hands	22	
9. Laugh aloud	22	
10. Recognize stranger	14	
11. Adjust for lifting	19	
12. Play with object	21	
13. Hand or object to mouth	21	
14. Music inhibits crying	18	
15. Play with toes	21	
16. Roll	19	
17. Sit alone one minute	20	
18. Some progress prone	17	
19. Stand holding furniture	22	
20. Creep	22	
21. Walk when led	21	
22. Walk holding furniture	16	
23. Pull to stand	17	
24. Stand alone	21	
25. Walk alone	21	

FIGURE 2

After the seventh lunar month, the subjects show some records beyond the range of the comparison cases. The responses in which retardation is greatest are visually directed reaching, sitting alone, and standing with support, and these retardations have been shown in a previous report (3) to be due probably to restricted opportunities for practice. It should be emphasized here, as it has been in the previous publication, that although these responses were absent when first tested for at ages beyond the normal limit, yet each of them was rather promptly established without example and without reward when opportunities for practice were provided. It seems reasonable to suppose therefore that the lack of instruction and of socially administered rewards was not responsible for these retardations, but rather that they were due to the lack of self-directed practice.

It is necessary to comment on the performance of each of our subjects in respect to the last eight items of Figure 1 and the corresponding items of Figure 2, all of which are locomotor in character. In all of these responses Rey is near or just beyond the upper limit of the control cases. She is so near the upper extreme, however, and the number of control cases is so small, that it is uncertain whether the combined restriction of practice and restriction of social stimulation had any effect upon these items. Any influence of the experiment upon Rey's locomotion becomes doubtful when we widen our sampling of normal children. The upper ranges of Shirley's study are slightly beyond the biographical ranges, and Rey's record is in many respects indistinguishable from the slowest of Shirley's cases, who of course were not deprived of social encouragement or practice. (This fact is not shown clearly by Figure 2 because Shirley was not able to obtain complete data for her most retarded subject.)

On the other hand, Del's locomotor performances in the items at the bottom of the chart occurred at ages considerably beyond the upper limits set by the biographical records or by other studies of normal children. They are too retarded to be presented on a chart of this width and in consequence are shown in Table 1. The last

TABLE 1
DEL'S LOCOMOTOR ITEMS

	Weeks of Age
Pull to kneeling	77
Stand holding furniture	67
Creep	never
Walk holding furniture	92
Pull to standing	81
Walk when led	81
Stand alone	111
Few steps alone	111

of these items, which is walking alone, occurred only shortly before the second birthday.

Certain considerations make it extremely doubtful that this retardation was due to the experiment. The subjects of the experiment are now slightly more than six and one-half years old. While Rey throughout her history has been essentially normal, it has become apparent during the past two years that Del has some disability of her left arm and leg. Her left arm is much more awkward than her right in all respects and is almost unused by her. Her left leg is very inferior to the right. Del has been submitted to a thorough clinical examination, and the medical report shows no anomalies of bone or muscle and gives a diagnosis of mild left hemiplegia probably referable to cortical injury at birth. This injury may also be the reason for Del's low *IQ,* which at four and one-half years was 70 while that of Rey was 107 (Stanford-Binet).

Neither the hemiplegia nor the low IQ of Del made themselves manifest at an early age. It will be seen upon examination of Figure 1 that Del was retarded in practically nothing prior to nine months of age. Extensive movie records taken in the third month reveal no disability on the left side. These facts of course agree well with the view that the cortex is very incomplete at that age, and with the recent findings that later intelligence cannot be predicted within the first year (1).

While the special facts of Del's case deserve attention in themselves, it must be kept in mind that they are relevant in the present connection only because they tend to show that the retardation which appeared following the first year was in all likelihood due not to the experiment but to some organic deficiency.

DISCUSSION

It seems to us that the experiment shows that normal behavioral development can occur in some infants when most of the first year is spent under conditions of minimum social stimulation and of very restricted practice. In other words, a large number of acts on the part of the adult which have been held by some people to be of importance may be dispensed with. Fondling is not necessary for the development of interest in, and every sign of affection for, the adult. The child does not need more than the barest materials in order to achieve the development shown by the chart. Furthermore, he need not be carefully watched for the proper administration of rewards and punishments. The infant within the first year will "grow up" of his own accord.

SUMMARY

Two infants reared under conditions of minimum social stimulation and restricted practice for the first seven lunar months of life, and under less stringent conditions during the remainder of the first year, yielded during most of the first year a record of development not distinguishable from comparison records of infants in normal environments. Retardations in the onset of certain responses are believed to have been due to specific restrictions of motor practice. No general retardation appeared in one subject. The general retardation of the other subject from 10 months of age onward is referable to an intracranial birth injury and not to the experiment.

REFERENCES

1. BAYLEY, N. Mental growth during the first three years: A developmental study of sixty-one children by repeated tests. *Genet. Psychol. Monog.*, 1933, **14**, 1-92.

2. DENNIS, W. An experimental test of two theories of social smiling in infants. *J. Soc. Psychol.*, 1935, **6**, 214-223.

3. ————. The effect of restricted practice upon the reaching, sitting and standing of two infants. *J. Genet. Psychol.*, 1935, **47**, 17-32.

4. ————. Laterality of function in early infancy under controlled developmental conditions. *Child Devel.*, 1935, **6**, 242-252.

5. ————. A psychologic interpretation of the persistence of the so-called Moro reflex. *Amer. J. Dis. Child.*, 1935, **50**, 888-893.

6. ———— & DENNIS, MARSENA G. Infant development during the first year as shown by forty biographies. *Psychol. Rec.*, 1937, **1**, 349-361.

7. SHIRLEY, M. M. The First Two Years. (3 vols.) Minneapolis: Univ. Minnesota Press, 1931-1935.

WAYNE DENNIS

40 Causes of Retardation among Institutional Children: Iran

A. INTRODUCTION

Considerable interest has recently been shown in the fact that in some institutions for children there occurs a decided retardation in behavioral development. The observations of Spitz (8, 9, 10) in particular have received much notice, chiefly because of the interpretations which Spitz has placed upon his data. In our opinion, the primary importance of these observations lies in their challenge to the theory that infant development consists largely of the maturation of a motor sequence which is little affected by learning.

Aside from the investigations of Spitz, studies of behavioral retardation among institutional children have been few in number. The scarcity of such

Reprinted from *The Journal of Genetic Psychology* 96:47–59, 1960.

This study was conducted during 1958-1959 when the author was on leave from Brooklyn College and served as a visiting professor at the American University of Beirut, Lebanon. The investigation was made possible by a grant from the Rockefeller Brothers Fund to the American University of Beirut, and by a grant to the author from the Social Science Research Council. In Tehran, the assistance of Miss Gay Currie of the U.S.P.H.S. and I.C.A. was invaluable. The institutions in Tehran participating in the study were most coöperative; they have not been named in this report but can readily be identified by persons acquainted with the local scene. Special thanks are due to Mrs. B. Azuri who served as interpreter and research assistant. The manuscript has greatly benefited from the suggestions and criticisms of colleagues at the American University of Beirut and at Brooklyn College.

studies is due in large part to the fact that institutions in which conditions comparable to those described by Spitz can be found are not numerous. In many countries institutional care has been replaced by other methods of caring for dependent children. However, institutions in which behavioral development is retarded can still be found in countries which are "under-developed" not only in regard to modern technology but also in respect to newer methods for the care of foundlings and other homeless infants.

The present paper reports studies of development in three institutions in Tehran, the capital of Iran. In two of these institutions, children are exceedingly retarded in their motor development. In the third little retardation is present. It is believed that comparisons of child care in these institutions, and of behavioral development in them, will throw considerable light upon the nature of the environmental factors which influence motor development. This paper supplements a recent report on behavioral retardation in a Lebanese institution by Dennis and Najarian (4). In the earlier report attention was directed primarily to motor development in the first year of life, whereas in the present instance the period from one year to four years of age is the one with which we are mainly concerned. Preliminary observations indicated that development during the first year in the two Iranian institutions in which retardation occurs is essentially the same as in the Lebanese institution described in the previous paper. For this reason in the present study attention is given chiefly to the age period to which little attention was directed in the earlier report.

B. Description of the Institutions

The two institutions in which marked retardation occurs, which will be called Institutions I and II, are supported chiefly by public funds; the third institution, to be labeled III, is supported by private funds. Several other children's institutions both public and private, exist in Tehran. The present report should not be taken to imply that retardation prevails in the majority of Iranian institutions.

It is worthy of note that the number of children to be found in institutions in Tehran is quite large. This number is explained by several factors. For one thing, Tehran is a large city, having approximately two million inhabitants. The recent growth of Tehran has taken place in the main through migration from villages. This has led to a considerable amount of social disorganization which has increased the number of illegitimate children, foundlings, abandoned children, orphans and half-orphans. Furthermore in Tehran at the present time, provisions for the care of dependent children, other than by institutionalization, are quite inadequate. Consequently, almost all children not living with parents or relatives are to be found in institutions.

1. *Institution I*

Institution I feels obligated to accept all foundlings and all abandoned children under three years of age who are brought to it. The population of the institution varies from day to day because of departures and admissions. During the time of the present study (September, 1958) the average daily population was about 600; of these about 275 were between birth and one year of age, 135 were between one and two years of age, and about 110 were between two and three years of age. While children above three years are generally transferred to other institutions, a few remain in Institution I beyond this age.

The excess of younger children over older children in Institution I may be due to several causes, including an increased intake rate in recent years, a higher death rate during the first year than in later years, return of older children to relatives, and transfer of older children to other institutions. The data at our disposal do not permit an assignment of relative weights to these factors.

More than nine-tenths of the children in Institution I are recorded as having been under one month of age at the time of their admission. When the actual date of birth is not known, an estimate of age at admission, based on weight, size, and appearance is made and placed in the child's record.

The mother never accompanies the child to Institution I nor sees him after admission.

In general children are placed in individual cribs, although at times, because of over-crowding, two infants temporarily occupy the same crib. In such instances, the heads of the two babies are placed at opposite ends of the bed.

A child is bathed on alternate days. Except when being bathed, the younger children spend practically their entire time in their cribs. They are given milk and other liquids while lying in bed, the bottle being supported by a small pillow. When semi-solid foods are introduced, infants are sometimes held by an attendant and sometimes fed in bed. The children are placed in bed in the supine position. They are never placed prone and seldom get themselves into this position.

The paucity of handling is due primarily to the attendant-child ratio. On the average there were eight children per attendant. In addition to feeding the children, bathing them, and changing clothing and diapers, the attendants are also responsible for changing the bed-linen and cleaning the rooms, and have some responsibilities for preparing food. Each attendant is on duty 12 hours per day. In general there are 32 children and four attendants to a room, although this varies somewhat according to the size of the room. There is no assignment of attendants to particular children. The attendants have no special training for their work and are poorly paid.

The emphasis on the part of the supervisors seems to be on neatness in the appearance of the rooms, with little attention to behavioral development.

In his crib the child is not propped up, and is given no toys. The child who can pull himself to sitting, and hence is in some danger of falling from his shallow crib, is placed, when awake, on a piece of linoleum on the composition stone floor of the room. Until he himself achieves the sitting position he remains in bed. In two rooms some of the children who can sit are seated in a row on a bench which has a bar across the front to prevent falling. Aside from these two benches and the frames for the cribs, the rooms have no children's furniture and no play equipment of any kind.

2. Institution II

This institution accepts children over three years of age. The children in this institution come mainly from Institution I. Child care practices in II are a continuation of the practices existing in I, but sanitation and cleanliness are poorer and the appearance of the children suggests that nutrition and health are poorer. However, in neither I nor II are there any records of growth in height or weight, and it was not possible for us to obtain any objective assessment of nutritional status.

3. Institution III

Institution III was established only one year prior to the present study. It was started primarily to demonstrate improved methods of institutional care. The children in III come from Institution I but are selected for transfer in the early months of life. It seems likely that those sent to Institution III are chosen from among the more retarded children. They remain in III until three years of age unless adopted before that date. The number of children per attendant is 3–4. Children are held in arms while being fed, are regularly placed prone during part of the time they are in their cribs, are propped up in a sitting position in their cribs at times and are placed in play pens on the floor daily when above four months of age. Numerous toys are provided. Attendants are coached in methods of child care, and supervisors emphasize behavioral development as well as nutrition and health.

Individual growth charts are available for each child in Institution III and show without exception that these children are much below prevailing weight norms on arrival but attain normal weight within a few months.

C. Types of Behavioral Data

Quantitative observations on the behavioral status of the groups described above were made only with regard to motor coördinations. Some general observations on social and emotional behavior will be presented after motor behavior has been discussed.

In respect to motor development, each child who was a subject of this study was classified with regard to his ability to meet each of the following behavioral criteria:

1. *Sit alone.* The child was placed in a sitting position on the floor. He was scored as sitting alone if he maintained this position for one minute. However, if a child could maintain this position at all he ordinarily could maintain it indefinitely.

2. *Creep or Scoot.* The child was placed sitting on the floor and was encouraged to locomote by having the attendant hold a cookie, or extend her arms, toward the child at a distance of about six feet. He was scored as passing the test if he covered the distance in any manner. If he locomoted, his mode of progression was recorded. The modes of locomotion will be discussed at a later point.

3. *Stand by holding.* The child was held under the arms and placed adjacent to the horizontal bars of a child's bed. It was observed whether or not he grasped the bars and maintained a standing position.

4. *Walk by holding.* The child who could stand by holding was observed for some minutes to determine whether he took steps while holding. He was urged to walk by the attendant.

5. *Walk alone.* The child who could walk by holding objects was placed standing without support and was encouraged to walk to the outstretched arms of the attendant. The child was scored as walking alone if he took at least two steps without support.

In the above tests one of the attendants with whom the child was familiar was coached to make the tests while the experimenter remained at a distance of six feet or more from the child and somewhat behind him. This procedure was followed because it was found that the child's unfamiliarity with the experimenter often inhibited the child's behavior if he was tested by the examiner himself. Communication between the attendant and the examiner was conducted via an Iranian interpreter. Tests were conducted among the children of a given room only after the experimenter and the interpreter had made several visits to the room and somewhat decreased the children's shyness. If a child failed a test, the attendant was asked whether or not he could usually perform the required response. If the answer was positive, renewed efforts were made to elicit a successful performance. The experimenter is convinced that subjects who were scored as failing a test were actually unable to perform the required task.

The numbers of children tested at each age level in each institution are shown in Table 1. In Institutions I and II the total number of children tested was 123. In selecting children to provide this sample, the children of appropriate ages were selected at random from each of several rooms, the rooms so far as we could determine not being unusual in any respect. However, we excluded from testing any child who had sensory or motor defects, who was ill or who had recently been ill. In Institution III all children between age one and three were tested. They totaled 51.

TABLE 1
PER CENT OF EACH GROUP PASSING EACH TEST

Institutions	I	I	II	III	III
N	50	40	33	20	31
Ages	1.0-1.9	2.0-2.9	3.0-3.9	1.0-1.9	2.0-2.9
Sit alone	42	95	97	90	100
Creep or Scoot	14	75	97	75	100
Stand holding	4	45	90	70	100
Walk holding	2	40	63	60	100
Walk alone	0	8	15	15	94

D. RESULTS OF TESTS

Table 1 shows the per cent of each group which passed each test. The reader is asked to direct his attention first to the retardation which is evident in Institutions I and II. Among those children in Institution I who were between 1.0–1.9 years of age, fewer than half could sit alone and none could walk alone. In normative studies, of home-reared children, such as those conducted by Jones (6), Gesell (5), Dennis and Dennis (2) and others, it has been found that by nine months of age all normal non-institutional American children can sit alone. By two years of age nearly all can walk alone. A majority of the children of Institution I cannot perform these responses at ages at which almost all home-reared children can perform them. It will be noted that even between 2.0–2.9 years of age only 8 per cent of the children in Institution I are able to walk alone and only 15 per cent of those children in Institution II who are 3.0–3.9 years of age are able to walk alone. We are not aware that any groups so retarded as Groups I and II have previously been reported.

In Institution III the picture is different. Of those children between 2.0–2.9 years of age nearly every child is able to walk unaided. While these children do not equal the performance of home-reared children, their motor behavior is much superior to that of children in Institutions I and II. In other words it is not institutionalization per se which handicaps Groups I and II since Group III children who are also institutionalized are but slightly retarded in motor development. The records of Group III also show that motor retardation is not a general characteristic of Tehran children.

Of special note is the difference in types of pre-walking locomotion between Institutions I and II on the one hand and Institution III on the other.

Of the 67 children in Institutions I and II who engaged in creeping or scooting, only 10 did so by creeping, i.e., going on hands and knees or on hands and feet. All others progressed by "scooting," i.e., their locomotion took place in the sitting position, the body being propelled forward by pushing with the arms aided by propulsion from the legs. Many children who could not walk were quite adept at scooting.

Since tests for creeping or scooting were made when the child was in a sitting position, it might seem that the frequency of scooting was due to the nature of the starting position. To test the effect of starting position, many subjects who were "scooters" were placed prone and offered a cookie at some distance, a powerful incentive for locomotion in these children. In each case the child first pushed himself to a sitting position and then scooted. Scooting was definitely the preferred mode of locomotion even when the child was placed prone. So far as we could determine, the majority of the scooters were completely unfamiliar with creeping.

In Institution III, the reverse situation prevailed. Of 15 children who were observed to creep or scoot, all progressed by creeping. No scooting whatsoever was seen in this institution, yet tests were made from the sitting position as with Groups I and II. When placed sitting and encouraged to locomote, the children leaned forward, got themselves on hands and knees, and crept.

E. Interpretative Comments on Motor Development

Let us examine now the probable reasons why the children in Institutions I and II were so severely retarded relative to home-reared children and why they were so much more retarded than children in Institution III. Several different possibilities need to be considered.

Attention should first be directed to malnutrition as a possible cause of retarded motor development. As noted earlier there can be no doubt that many of the children in Group I were much smaller and lighter than non-institutional children and children of the same age in Group III. There can be no doubt, too that malnutrition can be so severe as to interfere with motor performance and motor progress. But the question at stake is not whether malnutrition can affect motor functions but whether malnutrition was in fact a major cause of the retardation of Groups I and II.

We are inclined to think that undernourishment was not the major factor. The following considerations have led us to this interpretation: In the first place, Groups I and II were not entirely listless and inactive. In this connection we need to bring out a fact that we have not noted in earlier sections, namely that these children engaged to a considerable extent in automatisms such as head shaking and rocking back and forth. In many cases, these actions were quite vigorous. These activities tend to indicate that these children were not slow in motor development simply because of motor weakness.

The second consideration is somewhat similar to the first, namely, that the locomotor activities in which the children in Groups I and II engaged seem to require as much as or more energy than the locomotor activities which are usual at their respective ages, but in which they did not engage. For example, while few two-year-olds in Group I walked, three-fourths of them locomoted, chiefly by scooting. No physiological data are available, but it seems likely that the metabolic cost of covering a certain distance by scooting is as great as, or even greater than, the effort required to go the same distance by walking. Certainly this would be true for an adult, but of course one cannot argue from the adult to the child. At any rate the possibility exists that the reason that these children scooted was because this was the only form of locomotor skill which they had learned, not that they were too weak to walk.

This interpretation seems to be borne out by the fact that the pre-walking methods of locomotion were different in different groups. The retarded groups scooted. It is difficult to believe that malnutrition can lead to scooting rather than creeping. It is far from obvious that scooting is "easier" than creeping. If it is, why should not all children choose the easier method? In other words, the differences between groups seem to us to be due to the outcome of different learning situations rather than to differences in nutritional status.

What were the differences in the situations faced by Groups I and II and Group III which may account for the development of two different types of locomotion and different degrees of retardation? We suggest the following:

In Group III and in many homes infants are propped up in a sitting position, or held in a sitting position. In this position the child can raise his head and can partially raise his shoulders for short periods and can relax these efforts without falling. He can thus practice some elements of sitting. On the other hand, the child who remains on his back has no such opportunities to learn to sit. In some respects it is surprising that children who are never propped up or held on the lap are able to learn to sit at all. But it will be remembered that in Groups I and II some children could not sit until they were more than two years of age. Until they could sit alone, all forms of locomotion were impossible for them, because they were not placed in a position in which creeping was possible.

This is not true in Group III. In this group and in many homes, the child is frequently placed prone in bed or on the floor. In this position he can raise his head from the surface, push with his arms, raise his chest, pull his arms and legs beneath his body—in other words, he can practice acts which are employed in creeping. The child who lies on his back nearly every moment of the day is denied such practice. Thus one specific item of child care, i.e., occasionally placing the child face downward, may well contribute to the development of creeping in most children and its absence may account for the lack of creeping in Groups I and II.

The question may be raised as to why children in Institutions I and II did not get themselves into the prone position in their cribs. Repeated observations of these infants in their cribs showed that few ever attained the prone position. The probable reasons are the small size of the cribs and the softness of the beds, both of which made turning over very difficult.

It is likely that this item, i.e., absence of placement in the prone position, may lead to delayed development not only in regard to creeping but also in respect to walking. The child who can creep can go to a piece of furniture, grasp it and pull to his knees. This may lead to walking on his knees while holding furniture. Many children go from knee walking to walking by holding to furniture and thence to walking alone. In contrast to the child who creeps, the child who scoots to a piece of furniture is sitting when he arrives at his goal and can attain a higher position only by lifting his entire weight by his arms. In our opinion, the lack of creeping accounts in large measure for the retardation in walking of Groups I and II.

We are well-aware that some persons have interpreted the behavioral retardation of institutional infants to emotional factors rather than to a paucity of learning opportunities. Some have even suggested that under certain conditions institutional infants simply "waste away" from psychological, not from medical causes, a process called marasmus.

If marasmus actually exists, it has somehow been escaped by several hundred children in Iranian institutions living under conditions which are supposed to foster it. Although the prevailing emotional tone of children in Institutions I and II is dysphoric, it is difficult to conceive of mechanisms whereby their unhappiness retards their motor development and causes them to scoot rather than to creep.

There remains the necessity of relating the results of the present study to certain findings reported earlier by the present author. We refer to a study which found no apparent effect of cradling upon the motor development of Hopi children (3) and a study which indicated that infant development can proceed normally under conditions described as "minimal social stimulation" (1). On the surface these results seem contradictory to those here reported, because the former studies found that environmental deprivations had but little effect whereas the present study reports that major consequences can ensue from them. In fact, however, the studies are not contradictory but complementary. To bring the results of these studies into harmony, one needs only to examine the kinds of deprivation which were involved and their severity. Certain differences among these studies seem to us to be crucial. The Hopi children were limited in regard to learning opportunities only *while on the cradleboard.* As we pointed out in our original report, they were on the cradleboard chiefly during these sleeping hours, when in any case little learning is expected to occur. When awake they were handled, held upright against the mother, placed sitting on her lap, and placed prone. Their deprivation of learning opportunities was much less than that encountered by the children in Institution I who 24 hours per day for many months remained in a supine position.

A similar contrast exists between Rey and Del, the subjects of an experiment in environmental deprivation, and children in Institutions I and II. Rey and Del were not deprived to the same degree nor in the same manner as the institutional children described above. As the original report shows (1), Del and Rey, beginning at nine months, were regularly placed in a prone position on a pad on the floor. After it was found that they could not sit alone they were given special practice in sitting. Del and Rey were also given special training in supporting their weight when held upright. Such training was not given in Institutions I and II.

These experiences with special training given to Del and Rey suggest that the retardation of the institutional children could be fairly rapidly remedied if intensive specialized practice were given them. Unfortunately it was not possible for us to undertake such experiments while we were in Tehran. The speed with which delayed skills can be developed remains an important problem for future researches with institutional children.

So far as the permanency of motor deficiencies is concerned it should be noted that Institution II had many children between ages 6 and 15 years who presumably were as retarded at ages two and three as were the children whose behavior was described above. Yet these children were attending school, playing games, doing chores, and being trained in difficult skills, such as the weaving of Persian rugs. There was nothing in their general behavior to suggest that any permanent consequences issued from the extreme retardation in motor development during the early years. To be sure, we have no direct evidence that these children were retarded at two and three years of age, but so far as we could ascertain there has been no change in the child care offered by Institutions I and II and no reason to suppose that their early development was different from that of their counterparts in the present study.

Finally let us note that the results of the present study challenge the widely-held view that motor development consists in the emergence of a behavioral sequence based primarily upon maturation. Shirley's chart of the motor sequence is a textbook favorite. It shows sitting alone at seven months, creeping at 10 months, and walking alone at 15 months. The present study shows that these norms are met only under favorable environmental conditions. Among the children of Institution I not only was sitting alone greatly retarded but in many cases creeping did not occur. Instead, an alternate form of locomotion was employed. These facts seem to indicate clearly that experience affects not only the ages at which motor items appear but also their very form. No doubt the maturation of certain structures, which as yet cannot be identified, is necessary before certain responses can be learned, but learning also is necessary. Maturation alone is insufficient to bring about most post-natal developments in behavior. This is also the conclusion which we reached in the Del-Rey experiment, but the present study supports this position more dramatically because the limitations of learning in Institutions I and II are more drastic and more long-continued than were those in the Del-Rey study.

F. Social and Emotional Behavior

Only incidental observations were made relative to social and emotional behavior. Several of these had to do with the infants' reactions to visitors.

In the weeks preceding our tests, it appears that Institution I seldom had visitors. The children of Institution II formerly had few visitors but several weeks before our arrival a volunteer social service group, aware of the isolation of these children, began to make periodic visits to them, taking them from their beds, holding them, and carrying them about. Institution III also had several visitors, partly because of the demonstration nature of this orphanage.

Children in Institution I, probably because of their unfamiliarity with visitors, were somewhat afraid of us during our first visit. They did not smile with us and, in most cases, would cry if we picked them up. On repeated visits, however, they became more friendly, smiled at us, and before our work was completed some of them would hold out their arms to be carried.

Most of the children in Institution II were positive to visitors at the beginning of our work. Several employed attention-seeking devices before visitors and cried if other children were selected for attention. In contrast in Group III, probably because of the greater time spent with attendants and because of their familiarity with visitors, there was little fear of strangers and only limited attention seeking.

Eagerness for food appeared to be greatest in Institution II. In this institution there was much crying before meal time. Children of this group handled cups and spoons quite well. In general there was very little wasting of food on the part of these children. Cups of milk were reached for eagerly, handled carefully, and drunk rapidly. There were attempts, sometimes successful, on the part of those who had finished eating to obtain the food of others, and hitting, pinching, and biting were sometimes the outcomes of such clashes. Children who could not walk could nevertheless manage to attack others and to defend themselves with considerable skill. After feeding they became much more jovial and nearly every child could be made to smile or laugh by an adult who shook him lightly or tickled him.

G. Summary

This paper has presented data concerning behavioral development among

174 children, aged one year to four years, in three Iranian institutions. In Institutions I and II infant development was greatly retarded. The behavioral progress of children in the third institution was much less retarded. The interpretations offered for these differences in behavior among the children of different institutions are as follows: the extreme retardation in Institutions I and II was probably due to the paucity of handling, including the failure of attendants to place the children in the sitting position and the prone position. The absence of experience in these positions is believed to have retarded the children in regard to sitting alone and also in regard to the onset of locomotion. The lack of experience in the prone positions seems in most cases to have prevented children from learning to creep; instead of creeping, the majority of the children in Institutions I and II, prior to walking, locomoted by scooting. In Institution III, in which children were frequently handled, propped in the sitting position, and placed prone, motor development resembled that of most home-reared children. The retardation of subjects in Institutions I and II is believed to be due to the restriction of specific kinds of learning opportunities. This interpretation was found to be congruent with the results of other studies in environmental deprivation. In the light of these findings, the explanation of retardation as being due primarily to emotional factors is believed to be untenable. The data here reported also show that behavioral development cannot be fully accounted for in terms of the maturation hypothesis. The important contributions of experience to the development of infant behavior must be acknowledged.

REFERENCES

1. DENNIS, W. Infant development under conditions of restricted practice and of minimum social stimulation. *Genet. Psychol. Monog.,* 1941, **23**, 143-189.

2. DENNIS, W., & DENNIS, M. G. Behavioral development in the first year as shown by forty biographies. *Psychol. Rec.,* 1937, **1**, 349-361.

3. ————. The effect of cradling practices upon the onset of walking in Hopi children. *J. Genet. Psychol.,* 1940, **56**, 77-86.

4. DENNIS, W., & NAJARIAN, P. Infant development under environmental handicap. *Psychol. Monog.,* 1957, **71**, 1-13.

5. GESELL, A. Infancy and Human Growth. New York: Macmillan, 1928.

6. JONES, M. C. The development of early behavior patterns in young children. *Ped. Sem.,* 1926, **33**, 537-585.

7. SHIRLEY, M. M. The First Two Years: Vol. I. Postural and Locomotor Development. *Inst. Child Welfare Monog. Series,* No. 6. Minneapolis: Univ. Minn. Press, 1933.

8. SPITZ, R. A. Hospitalism, an inquiry into the genesis of psychiatric conditions in early childhood. *Psychoanal. Stud. Child,* 1945, **1**, 53-74.

9. SPITZ, R. A. Hospitalism: A follow-up report. *Psychoanal. Stud. Child,* 1946, **2**, 113-117.

10. SPITZ, R. A. Anaclitic depression. *Psychoanal. Stud. Child,* 1946, **2**, 313-342.

HARRIET L. RHEINGOLD & NANCY BAYLEY

41 The Later Effects of an Experimental Modification of Mothering

An extensive literature in psychology attests to the effect of early experience upon later behavior. For the human infant an important determiner of early experience is maternal care. Some of the dimensions of maternal care thought to be of consequence are amounts and kinds of care, interruptions of care, the number of persons giving care, as well as their attitudes. There is not yet, however, any considerable *experimental* literature on the effects of these variables upon the later behavior of children. The present study reports an attempt to discover the presence, a year later, of a change in behavior brought about in a group of infants by an experimental modification of maternal care (5).

Sixteen children, living in an institution for approximately the first nine months of life, were the original subjects of study. From the sixth through the eighth month of life, half of them, the experimental group, were cared for by one person alone, the experimenter, for 7½ hours a day. They thus received more attentive care than the control subjects who were completely reared under institutional routine; and of course the number of different persons from whom they received care was markedly reduced. As a result the experimental babies became more responsive to the experimenter almost at once, while with time they became more responsive to other persons as well. They did not however do reliably better than the control subjects on the Cattell Infant Intelligence Scale or on tests of postural development and cube manipulation. At the conclusion of the study the experimental subjects returned to the full-time care of the institution. Details of the institutional care, of its experimental modification, of the tests used, and of the results may be found in the report referred to above.

One by one, all but one of both the experimental and the control subjects were placed outside the institution—in their own homes, or in adoptive or boarding homes. Approximately a year after the conclusion of the study, the children, then about 18 months of age, were seen again, in an attempt to detect the effects of the earlier treatment. Since the only clear difference between the groups at the time of the study had been an increase in social responsiveness among the experimental babies, it would be here that one would expect a difference, if any, to persist. Still, the possibility existed that differences might appear later as new functions matured. On the other hand, the subsequent, and more recent, experience of several months' duration in different life situations might reduce the chance of finding a difference.

Reprinted from *Child Development* 30:363–372, 1959. ©1959 by the Society for Research in Child Development, Inc.

The effects of experimental treatment were sought in two areas of behavior, the social and the intellectual. Would the experimental subjects be more socially responsive, that is, more friendly and outgoing than the control group to two examiners who visited the home? Would the experimental subjects, in addition, be more responsive to the original experimenter than to another person? If not, the variable under test is really their responsiveness to strangers. Second, would the experimental subjects now do better on a test of developmental progress?

It was planned, in addition, to use the retest data to explore the effect of type of home placement, as well as to evaluate the performance of the whole group considered as a sample of institutionalized children.

PROCEDURE

Subjects

Fourteen of the original 16 children were located and tested; one from the experimental group and one from the control group could not be found.[1]

The mean age of the experimental group was 19.8 months (range, 17.6–22.1), of the control group, 20.1 months (range, 17.5–21.7). The experimental group had spent an average of 9.2 months in the institution before being placed in homes (range, 4.0–13.6); for the control group the mean time was 10.4 months (range, 6.5–18.1). If the control subject who was still in the institution was omitted from the calculations, the average stay for the control group became 9.2 months (range, 6.5–12.2). In respect, then, to age and to duration of stay in the institution both groups were similar.

The children left the institution at different ages. Two experimental subjects left after only three weeks of treatment. One control subject left in the sixth week of the study, another in the seventh week. All the other subjects stayed at least through the eight weeks of treatment.

The home placements were varied. Three experimental and two control subjects returned to their own homes. With one exception, the own parents of these five subjects were of foreign birth and the homes were marked by poverty. Two of the experimental and four of the control subjects were in adoptive homes which, in general, were superior to the own homes in socioeconomic status. Two experimental subjects were living in boarding homes, pending a release for adoption. And one control subject, a Negro boy, remained in the institution only because a home could not be found for him. Furthermore, there was no difference between the experimental and the control groups in the intellectual stimulation provided by the homes or in the friendliness of the mothers, according to ratings made by the Experimenter and the Examiner after each visit. In type of home placement,

---

[1] We are grateful to Father Bernard Brogan, Director of the Catholic Home Bureau of Chicago, for his generous cooperation.

therefore, there appeared to be no major difference. Rather, the difference between homes within each group appeared to be larger than any difference between the groups.

The Tests

Each child was seen in his own home. The homes were scattered widely through Chicago, its suburbs and neighboring cities, with one home in another state. Two persons, the original Experimenter and an Examiner, visited the homes together, with one exception: the child who lived out of the state was examined by the Experimenter alone. The Experimenter knew all the children but, of course, had been especially familiar with the experimental subjects. She served *only* as a stimulus person in the social tests. The Examiner had no previous acquaintance with any of the children and did not know which had been the experimental subjects. She also served as a stimulus person in the social tests, but it was she alone who recorded the children's responses to both the Experimenter and herself, and who administered the test of developmental progress.

The social test resembled those reported in the first study, but was made more suitable for older children. It was composed of three parts, each of which set up a rather natural situation between adult and child, with an easy transition between the parts. In the first part, the responses to the stimulus person in the first few minutes after her entrance into the home were recorded. During this time the stimulus person did not talk to or approach the child but sat at some distance from him and talked to the mother, occasionally smiling at the child. The Examiner recorded the child's responses to whichever stimulus person happened first to engage his attention, then to the other person. At an appropriate moment one of the persons smiled and spoke warmly to the child, saying, "Hi (child's name) come to me," accompanying her words by stretching out her arms in invitation. This constituted the second situation. In the third situation, the stimulus person actually approached the child, smiling, talking, and gesturing as in the second situation. After the child's responses had been recorded, the other stimulus person presented herself to the child similarly. The order of stimulus persons was determined by the convenience of the moment: whoever was closer to the child or was receiving more glances was the first stimulus person.

The child's responses were recorded on a checklist under these categories: *positive facial expression,* which included seven items of behavior ranging from "stares with expression" to "laughs"; *physical approach* with nine items ranging from "shows toy" through "makes physical contact" to "makes social overtures while in the stimulus person's lap"; *vocalizations* for which a child received a score of one for each part of the test in which he vocalized, whether he said discrete sounds, jargon, or words; *negative facial expression,* which included eight items ranging from "a fleeting sober expression" to "cries"; *physical retreat* with six items ranging from "hangs head" to "leaves room"; and *response to mother* (during the social test period) which included a series of six items, from "turns toward mother" to "stays in contact with mother."

Within each category, items of behavior were thus arranged in what seemed a reasonable progression in terms of duration or amplitude of response. Each item within a category was arbitrarily assigned a value of one. Because the items were arranged in ascending order, the score for any item was one plus the value of all other items below it in that category. The scores for the categories of positive facial expression, physical approach, and vocalizations were summed to yield a measure of *positive social responsiveness*. Similarly, the sum of both negative categories gave a measure of *negative social responsiveness*. The sum of these two measures was the measure of *total social responsiveness*. The category of "response to mother" was calculated separately and not included in the other measures.

After the social tests, the Cattell Infant Intelligence Scale (2) was administered by the Examiner, with the Experimenter *not* present. Lastly, the number of words in the child's vocabulary was calculated from his performance on the language items of the Cattell and from the mother's report.

RESULTS

The Effect of Treatment

Table 1 shows that both the experimental and the control subjects responded similarly to the Experimenter and to the Examiner. The close

TABLE 1

MEANS AND RANGES OF THE SOCIAL TEST

Subjects	Experimenter		Examiner		Combined Score
	Mean	*Range*	*Mean*	*Range*	*Mean*
*Experimental Group**					
Total Social Responsiveness	32.1	27–39	30.9	27–38	31.6
Positive	17.4	2–30	16.0	2–37	16.7
Negative	14.7	1–37	14.7	3–29	14.7
Response to Mother	2.3	0–16	5.7	0–19	4.0
Control Group†					
Total Social Responsiveness	28.0	14–39	28.3	22–44	28.4
Positive	19.8	5–32	20.2	4–37	20.1
Negative	8.2	3–12	8.2	2–18	8.0
Response to Mother	4.5	0–11	4.8	0–10	5.4

* *N* is 7.
† *N* is 6 for responses to Experimenter and to Examiner, but 7 for Combined Score. See text for explanation.

agreement of all means, and of the ranges, is apparent in the part, as well as in the total, scores. The only difference of any size between the two stimulus persons appeared in the experimental group's response to mother. But since only one subject of the seven gave a response to the mother when the Experimenter was the stimulus person, and only three subjects of the seven, when the Examiner was the stimulus person, this difference, as all the others, was not statistically significant. From the results we conclude that the experimental subjects did not appear to remember the Experimenter.

Furthermore, since the experimental and the control groups gave similar scores to both persons, it was assumed that they were of approximately equal stimulating value. Therefore, a combined score for each subject (the average of a subject's responses to both stimulus persons) was used in the analyses which follow. This procedure made it possible to add to the control group the subject who was seen by the Experimenter alone. If every other subject responded similarly to both stimulus persons, it may be assumed that this subject would too. (It will be seen in Table 1 that the addition of this subject to the control group made the combined means slightly different from the separate means.)

The combined scores showed that the experimental subjects were more responsive to both persons than the control subjects, but the difference was not statistically significant. The part scores, further, revealed that the control group gave more positive responses, the experimental group, more negative responses. Again, the differences were not statistically reliable. Moreover, inspection of the data revealed that the negative responses of only two of the seven experimental subjects were responsible for the difference between the groups. The findings therefore do not warrant the conclusion that the experimental subjects were either more or less responsive to the stimulus persons, positively or negatively.

Because some of the subjects made no response to their mothers during the social tests, the means for this category of behavior were not subjected to test. Only three of the seven experimental subjects and five of the control subjects made some contact with the mother during social stimulation by one or the other of the stimulus persons, a difference which permits no conclusive statement of difference.

Although vocalizations had been included in the measure of positive social responsiveness (as explained above), a measure which did not differentiate the groups, they were also analyzed separately. Inspection showed that five of the seven experimental subjects vocalized to one or the other of the stimulus persons but only one of the control subjects did. The difference was significant by the Fisher exact probability test at $p = .051$ (one-sided), a finding in agreement with the original study in which, at the end of the experimental treatment, the experimental subjects also vocalized more than the control subjects.

On the Cattell Infant Intelligence Scale the mean IQ for the experimental group was 97.4 (range, 82–110); for the control group it was 95.4 (range, 83–122). More attentive care given during a limited period in the first year of life therefore appeared to produce no difference in IQ on retest a year later.

The experimental subjects had a larger spoken vocabulary than the control subjects (17.9 and 13.7 words), but the difference was again not statistically significant.

The Effect of Home Placement

It early became clear that the adoptive homes were of a higher socioeconomic level than the own homes, and therefore it seemed desirable to look for differences in the performance of the children in these two types of home placement. The adoptive homes were also ranked higher than the own homes by the investigators on the basis of the friendliness of the mother during the visit and of the intellectual stimulation the home seemed to offer the child.

On the social test the children in adoptive homes gave more positive responses than those in own homes; the means were 21.6 and 15.6, respectively, but the difference was not statistically significant. It should be noted, however, that one subject in a boarding home and the subject still in the institution made higher positive scores than the mean of the adoptive home group.

Similarly, the mean IQ of the children living in adoptive homes was higher (98.8) than that of those living in own homes (95.4), but the difference was not reliable. The two children living in boarding homes had IQs of 95 and 102. And, while the child still in the institution obtained an IQ of only 83, two children in own homes had lower IQs, one of 79 and one of 82, and one child in an adoptive home had an IQ of 84.

Finally, the children in adoptive homes had a larger vocabulary than the children in own homes (means were 18.6 and 13.4, respectively), although again the difference was not significant.

In summary, there was no reliable evidence that the children in adoptive homes were more socially responsive or more developmentally advanced than those in own homes.

The Group as a Whole

We may now evaluate the performance of the group as a whole ($N = 14$), representing as it does a sample of children who spent approximately nine months of the first year of life in the care of an institution and who then experienced a major change in life situation.

In general, the group was marked by a friendliness which seemed warm and genuine. Eleven of the 14 Ss not only approached the stimulus persons but also allowed themselves to be picked up and held. Only two subjects, both boys, presented a different social response: they clung to their mothers and cried when the stimulus persons approached them. No comparable data are available for children who have lived all their lives in own homes, but in preliminary testing of the social test on three such children not one approached the examiners. Instead, they looked at the examiners from behind their mothers' skirts and retreated whenever the examiners moved in their direction.

On the Cattell Infant Intelligence Scale the mean IQ of the group was 96.4. At six months of age the mean IQ for these 14 children was 93.8; at eight months it was 94.3. They continue therefore to score in the normal range. Furthermore, the mean number of words in their vocabulary was 15.5, which compares favorably with Gesell's (3) norms of 10 words at 18 months and 20 words at 21 months. Certainly, the group showed no sign of mental dullness or of language retardation.

No child, furthermore, showed the marked apathy or attention-seeking behavior believed by some to characterize the behavior of children reared in institutions. Differences there were, to be sure, between the children, but none seemed to depart markedly from the normal in temperament or personality. In fact, several of the mothers spontaneously commented upon how easy these children were to handle in comparison with their other children. They mentioned, specifically, their good eating and sleeping habits and their ability to amuse themselves.

DISCUSSION

The discussion will take up three separate points: (a) the effect of the experimental treatment, (b) the effect of own home versus adoptive home placement, and (c) the characteristics of the whole group considered as a sample of institutionalized children.

On the basis of the changes in social behavior produced at the time of treatment, one might have expected that the experimental subjects on retest would have been more responsive to the Experimenter than to the Examiner. Instead, no reliable difference was found in their responses to either person. The Experimenter was not remembered. Further, we did not find, except in the vocalizing of the children, any evidence that the experimental subjects were more responsive than the control subjects. It seems, therefore, that the experiences provided by the more attentive mothering were not great enough to maintain the experimentally produced difference over a year's time, except in one class of behavior.

The findings give rise to several speculations. First, it is possible that the verbal behavior of young children is more sensitive to changes in the environment than are other classes of behavior. In this connection, the responsiveness of vocalizations to conditioning in the three-month-old infant has already been demonstrated (6). Second, differences between the experimental and control groups may well have existed but in some untested area of behavior. Third, the expected (or some other) differences may make their appearance in the future in some more complex behavior incorporating the experiences of treatment. Finally, serious limitations to the study were imposed by the small number of subjects and by the diversity of home placements within each group. Differences would have to be very large indeed to surmount these limitations.

That no difference was found between the experimental and control groups in developmental status is not surprising, considering that no difference was found at the end of treatment. Some of the speculations about the course of social responsiveness may apply here, too.

We turn now to a consideration of the effect of home placement. The adoptive homes in general were of a higher socioeconomic level, the mothers were more sociable, and the homes were judged to offer more intellectual stimulation. For these reasons we would have expected the children in adoptive homes to be more socially responsive and more advanced in developmental status. But significant differences were not found. Possible explanations are that the differences between the two groups of home may have been not as great as they seemed, or that the number of cases was too small.

Lastly, the characteristics of the group as a whole may be assessed for the effects of a life experience usually thought of as deprived. All the children had been cared for in an institution for the first half of their lives, all but one had experienced a major "separation" in going from one life situation to another, and, furthermore, three children were now living in depressed socioeconomic environments, two were in boarding homes, and one was still in the institution. Yet, as a group, the children were healthy, of normal intelligence, and they appeared to be making a satisfactory adjustment. In addition, they seemed to be more friendly to strangers than children who have lived all their lives in own homes and, according to mothers' reports, were more adaptable than their other children. In no way, then, did they resemble the emotionally disturbed and mentally retarded children described in studies of the effect of institutional or hospital life or of separation from the mother.[2] They did not show apathy or the inability to form relationships or make excessive bids for attention. Even earlier, at the beginning of the study when the infants were still in the institution, they were physically robust, mentally alert, and socially responsive.

It is true that in kind and duration of experience they resemble exactly no other group of children reported in the literature. There is a tendency

---

[2] Glaser and Eisenberg (4) present a recent review of studies on maternal deprivation.

among workers, however, to lump together studies of children who actually differ in age and experience and to generalize from them to all children who have experiences which may be similar in only one of many possible respects. It is to be hoped that as more prospective (in contrast to retrospective) studies are carried out, the dimensions of deprivation and of its effects can be clarified. Certainly, we may expect to find that the effects will depend upon the age of the child, the nature and duration of the deprivation, and the experiences prior to and subsequent to it (1). The present study of the effects of early experience, limited as it is, emphasizes the need for more precise measurement both of deprivation and of its effects.

SUMMARY

The present study reports an attempt to discover the presence, a year later, of a change in behavior brought about in a group of infants by an experimental modification of maternal care.

Sixteen babies, living in an institution for approximately the first nine months of life, were the original subjects of study. Half of them, the experimental subjects, received more attentive care by one person, the Experimenter, from the sixth through the eighth month of life. As a result they became more socially responsive than the control group who were cared for under the usual institutional routine. They did not, however, do better upon tests of developmental progress.

Subsequently all but one of the children were placed in homes. A year later, when the children were about 19 months old, 14 of the original 16 subjects were located, and tested for their social responsiveness and developmental progress.

The results did not reveal any statistically significant differences between the experimental and the control groups except that more of the experimental subjects vocalized during the social tests. It is concluded therefore that the experience provided by the more attentive mothering, while great enough to produce a difference at the time of study, was not great enough to maintain that difference over time, except in one class of behavior. It is possible that the verbal behavior of young children is more sensitive to changes in the environment than are other classes of behavior.

No statistically significant differences in social responsiveness and developmental status were found between children living in own homes and in adoptive homes, although the adoptive homes were of higher socioeconomic status.

Finally, the group as a whole was friendly, of normal intelligence, and apparently was making a satisfactory adjustment. They did not resemble the emotionally disturbed and mentally retarded children described in studies of the effects of institutional life or of separation from the mother.

REFERENCES

1. AINSWORTH, MARY D., & BOWLBY, J. Research strategy in the study of mother-child separation. *Courrier,* 1954, 4, 105-131.

2. CATTELL, PSYCHE. *The measurement of intelligence of infants and young children.* New York: Psychol. Corporation, 1940.

3. GESELL, A., & AMATRUDA, CATHERINE S. *Developmental diagnosis.* New York: Hoeber, 1941.

4. GLASER, K., & EISENBERG, L. Maternal deprivation. *Pediatrics,* 1956, 18, 626-642.

5. RHEINGOLD, HARRIET L. The modification of social responsiveness in institutional babies. *Monogr. Soc. Res. Child Develpm.,* 1956, 21, No. 2. (Serial No. 63)

6. RHEINGOLD, HARRIET L., GEWIRTZ, J. L., & ROSS, HELEN W. Social conditioning of vocalizations in the infant. *J. comp. physiol. Psychol.,* 1959, 52, 68-73.

Chapter Ten

ENVIRONMENTAL ENRICHMENT

Many of us are concerned to find ways to improve the intellectual performance of our children so that they are more adept at solving problems and at thinking clearly and deeply. We are interested in improving their cognitive capabilities. The considerable emphasis on education and the great amounts of money we invest in this enterprise are examples of this concern. Our concern is reflected at the national level by such programs as Head Start, Follow Through, and Upward Bound — all aimed at improving the educational experiences of children and, we hope, their cognitive capabilities and motivational qualities as well.

Animal researchers also have shown interest in the development of cognitive processes. This interest has not stemmed from a philosophy of education or an attempt to develop better methods of rearing or educating children. Instead, the basic motivation has been to find out how the brain develops and how this development is affected by various sorts of early experiences, including environmental enrichment (discussed in this chapter) and environmental deprivation (discussed in Chapter Nine). Even though the stimulation for the animal studies is quite different from the motivation for human research, we know from the history of science that lines of thought and experimentation which develop independently may ultimately converge for the benefit of all. It is possible that animal studies on the effects of experience upon brain development and research on procedures to improve the cognitive capabilities of underprivileged children are nearing convergence. The readings in this chapter relate to this topic.

The first series of systematic experimental investigations in the area of early experiences was concerned with the effects of early enrichment upon subsequent problem-solving and perceptual behavior. This work was initiated and stimulated by Hebb, who in 1949 published an important monograph entitled *The Organization of Behavior,* in which he suggested that neural growth and organization were significantly dependent upon the kinds of experiences the organism had during its early development. A number of researchers in the United States, as well as several students working in Hebb's laboratory at McGill University, began testing some of these ideas. Experimental reports started coming into the literature in the early 1950's and advances continue to be made in this research area.

The group at McGill made two important methodological contributions to early experience research. First is the idea of the enriched environment (called a "free environment" in some publications). This is a large enclosure into which weanling animals (usually rats) are placed. The enclosure contains a variety of "playthings," such as ramps, marbles, and small cans. In a sense it is like a nursery school for young animals. Some of the free environments are multilevel, and the young can climb up onto platforms by means of ladders or ramps. In some experiments food and water units are placed at fixed points in this environment, while in other experiments these are systematically changed at regular intervals. The basic concept here is that placing the young animal into an environment which is complex ("enriched") and allowing him to interact with that environment will enhance development of his cognitive and perceptual capabilities. Experimental tests over the last 20 years have clearly substantiated this assumption. The experiments discussed in this chapter all made use of free-environment experience for the young animal, though the nature of the apparatus is different in the various studies.

A second important methodological contribution from the McGill group is a test for measuring "intelligence" or "problem-solving behavior" in the rat. In 1946 Hebb and Williams published a paper suggesting a method for evaluating animal intelligence and differentiating intelligence from learning. In 1951 Rabinovitch and Rosvold modified the procedures of Hebb and Williams and developed an apparatus and a standardized procedure for measuring problem solving which they called "a closed-field intelligence test for rats." This test is now used by virtually all researchers interested in measuring problem solving. Since the Rabinovitch and Rosvold procedure is constantly referred to in the literature, Paper 42 is their publication describing the test. The emphasis is upon the development of the test and the procedure for administering it, though the authors do report briefly one experiment in which free-environment-reared animals were found to be better problem solvers than controls.

The enriched free environment is a relatively complex situation involving multiple dimensions of stimulation. For example, the enclosure in which the animals are reared is much larger than the usual laboratory cage, the presence of the various playthings is a form of stimulation not found under normal laboratory rearing conditions, and the visual stimulation impinging upon the young animal is much greater and more varied than is generally found in a laboratory. The objective of the experiment by Forgays and Forgays (Paper 43) was to attempt to dissect out the contribution that each of these elements made to the ability of the animal to solve problems. Both the size of the free environment and the presence of playthings were found to be important. In a second study these researchers also demonstrated that

animals reared under enriched conditions were more likely to use visual distance cues for orientation than were control animals reared under normal or restricted conditions, thus implying a qualitative difference in perceptual behavior.

A meaningful question, and one which has a number of applied implications, is whether the age at which the subject receives enriched experiences is important. This is related to the critical period hypothesis discussed in Chapter Two. According to Hebb's original formulation, as well as the theoretical positions of many others in the field, the enriched experiences should occur during early development in order to be maximally effective. Once the central nervous system has matured, these experiences would be expected to have much less effect, if any at all. Paper 44, by Forgays and Read, investigated this question by giving different groups of rats enriched experiences at different times during their development. One of the groups received this enrichment between birth and weaning, while at the other extreme the last experimental group received its experience between 88 and 109 days — by which time the rat has reached adulthood. Forgays and Read found that enrichment immediately after weaning was maximally beneficial. Enriched experiences during other times in early development also resulted in an improvement in problem solving, but enrichment after maturity had no facilitatory effect upon problem-solving behavior.

Hebb's theory assumed that the changes in the brain brought about by early enrichment would be permanent. To test such a notion, a considerable time gap must exist between the termination of the enriched experience and the ultimate test for problem solving. This hypothesis had never been rigorously tested, since in most experiments the animals were given the problem-solving test immediately or very shortly after being removed from the enriched environment. This important assumption of Hebb's was tested by Denenberg *et al.* (Paper 45). They reared rats in an enriched free environment between birth and weaning or between weaning and 50 days of age. All animals were then placed into standard laboratory cages until they were approximately a year old, at which time they were given the Rabinovitch and Rosvold problem-solving test. Almost a year after the termination of the enriched experience, the experimental groups still performed better in problem solving than did the control group. Those animals which received the enriched experience immediately after weaning performed the best, but preweaning enrichment also brought about a permanent improvement in problem solving.

Since these experiments were all carried out with rats, the validity of the findings for other species had to be investigated. In an effectively designed study (Paper 46), Wilson *et al.* investigated the performances of cats which had, as kittens, been given enriched experience, handling experience, a combination of both, or neither (the control group). The animals were given a variety of tests to measure emotional reactivity, problem solving, avoidance learning, and discrimination reversal learning. The results obtained with the cats were quite similar to findings obtained with rats. The animals handled in infancy were less "fearful" than nonhandled kittens (see Chapter Eleven for a report on similar findings with rats), and the animals reared in the free environment learned the Hebb-Williams maze better than did their controls. However, the enriched experience in early life did not aid the animals in discrimination reversal learning, which many researchers consider to be as good a measure of animal "intelligence" as the Hebb-Williams maze. Wilson *et al.* raise some thoughtful questions concerning the underlying processes measured by the Hebb-Williams maze, and they emphasize the need to measure animals on a variety of criterion tasks as well as the necessity of improving the scaling of the "impoverishment-enrichment" dimension of experience.

One thing on which all the animal studies agree is that some form of enriched experience during early development results in a subsequent improvement in behaviors involving perceptual and cognitive factors. Which experiences will be "enriching" depends upon the species involved as well as on the environmental conditions under which that species is reared. One of the human being's unique characteristics is dependence upon and facility with language. Many measures of human achievement place a high demand upon language skills. Thus, it would seem reasonable that a language-enrichment program for young disadvantaged children who are not raised in the language-rich environment of middle-class children should result in improved performance on a test which measures verbal skills. In a nicely controlled experimental study (Paper 47), Blank and Solomon showed that a special language program for socially disadvantaged young children was able to increase significantly the IQ score of these children.

In developing the rationale for their study, the authors criticize the approach of enriching the child's environment in a general fashion; they do not believe this will facilitate abstract thinking in culturally underprivileged children. Their argument is well taken. Some researchers working with humans have carried over directly to the human setting the *experimental operations* as well as the theoretical concepts used in animal studies. For the concepts to be meaningful, however, the researcher must be aware (1) that the operations which may be effective with the rat or the cat may not be effective with the human, and (2) that their effectiveness is in part dependent upon the endpoint used for assessing the environmental manipulations. Thus, the researcher must understand not only the natural behavior patterns of the species he is studying, but also the developmental history of his particular group of organisms and thus their particular developmental deficits.

The Blank and Solomon paper is noteworthy for another reason. Their children received only about 15 to 20 minutes of tutoring per day; yet this was sufficient to bring about a significant increase in IQ score. Many animal studies involving infantile stimulation or early enrichment have also shown that relatively brief periods of exposure are sufficient to bring about long-term permanent changes. This suggests that the central nervous system of the developing mammal is sufficiently labile and plastic to assimilate and integrate brief experiences and store them effectively for later utilization.

References

Hebb, D. O. *The Organization of Behavior.* New York: Wiley, 1949.

Hebb, D. O., and Williams, K. A method of rating animal intelligence. *J. Genet. Psychol.,* 1946, 34, 59-65.

M. S. RABINOVITCH & H. ENGER ROSVOLD

42 A Closed-Field Intelligence Test for Rats

IN 1946 Hebb and Williams (2) described a method of rating intelligence in the rat using a closed-field type of test apparatus. The present report describes the results of several studies which were aimed at refining and standardizing this test.

The closed-field test in its early form had been used in the psychology laboratory of McGill University, making available considerable data on the performance of rats in this type of test situation (4), (7). These data were collected and analysed to determine the discriminating value, the level of difficulty, and the reliability of each item. The results of this analysis were used to design several studies which tested the value of new items and which measured the effects of serial position on the items. The final step was to integrate all that had been learned about the test and to construct and standardize a more complete and satisfactory form of the test. The new test items were selected so as to: (i) sample a wide range of behaviour by the inclusion of a large variety of problems; (ii) obtain a series of items with a wide range of difficulty to aid in discriminating extremes of test behaviour; (iii) make the solutions independent of any particular location of the apparatus; (iv) result in a test having satisfactory reliability and discriminatory capacity.

APPARATUS

The closed-field apparatus consists of a box with an entrance alley and food compartment at opposite corners of an open field. This box is mounted on legs permitting the examiner to sit alongside the apparatus

Reprinted from *Canadian Journal of Psychology* 5:122–128, 1951.

Some of the material in this paper is from a thesis submitted by the senior author in partial fulfilment of the requirements for the degree of M.A. in the Department of Psychology, McGill University.

Fig. 1. The closed-field test apparatus.

when testing animals. The details of the apparatus are shown in Figure 1.*

The floor of the box is made of ¼″ plywood and left unpainted, or is painted white. The walls are painted black and made from stock ½″ × 4″ dressed lumber. There are thirty-six five-inch squares outlined in black on the floor of the open field. These serve to define error zones and also act as markers for placing the barriers. The barriers used to construct the problems are painted black and are made from stock ½″ × 4″ dressed

* The necessary details for construction of this apparatus are available in blue-print form from the author.

lumber. They are constructed so that, set on edge, they reach exactly from the floor of the box to the screen top. They are made to the following specifications: 3 barriers, each 5″ long; 4 barriers, each 10″ long; 3 barriers, each 15″ long; 2 barriers, each 20″ long; 2 barriers, each 25″ long.

A small piece of sheet metal, 2″ × ½″, is nailed to the bottom of each barrier as a support to keep it standing on edge. To prevent the barrier from moving once the screen is fastened down, a ¾″ brad with head cut off is put into the top of the barrier at each end so that it engages the mesh of the screen top.

TRAINING PROCEDURE

The essential in the preliminary training is to teach the rat where in the box food is to be found, to adapt him to the apparatus and to handling, and to establish the habit of eating in the food box, so that when he is put into the entrance alley he will go to the food without fear and with a minimum of exploratory behaviour, in spite of changes in the position of the barriers.

Adaptation sessions. Problem A, as illustrated in Figure 2, is set up in the first adaptation session, problem B in the second, and so on until the series A to F is completed. The series is repeated until the rats run to the food compartment immediately upon being placed in the box.

At no time is the same training problem to be used on succeeding occasions. Having been deprived of food for ten hours, the rats are placed four at a time in the box and allowed to find their way around the barriers to the food compartment where they are allowed to eat moist ground food for forty-five minutes. Thereafter they are never fed in their home cages. Each adaptation period should last about an hour and there should be two periods a day.

Preliminary runs. As soon as the animals are eating well and give the impression of being well adapted to the box, they are run individually with as much handling as possible. Time is recorded from the moment the animal enters the apparatus until he takes his first bite of food. When he reaches the food he is allowed to take a few bites and is then replaced in the entrance alley and again allowed to go to the food, being timed as previously. This process is repeated nine times, twice daily, until all the animals reach the same criterion of adaptation to the apparatus; namely, making nine runs to food in a total of sixty seconds on two consecutive occasions. When an animal is not running as fast as it should, less total food should be given, otherwise each animal is allowed to eat for fifteen to thirty minutes after completing the runs in the apparatus. It was found that it saved time to have an eating place where an animal could be placed to eat the remainder of his food while another animal was being run in the apparatus.

It should not be expected that all rats will meet these training requirements at the same time. Those that do not should be given less food, extra

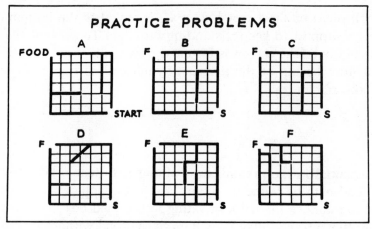

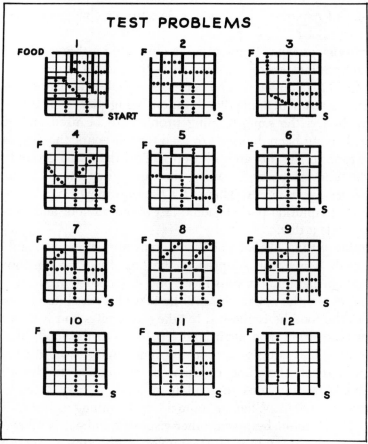

Fig. 2. Floor plan of training and test problems.

handling, and several extra runs in the apparatus each session. In a group of animals there will be some that reach the criterion of adaptation earlier than the others. These should continue in the training but should be run only three or four times each period instead of the usual nine. These extra runs do not influence subsequent scores, neither are these precocious animals more likely to do better than the others on the subsequent test problems. Seven to ten days will usually be sufficient for this adaptation and training to be accomplished.

Testing Procedure

After about ten hours of food deprivation the animals should be given eight runs in the first problem situation and then allowed to eat outside their living cages for about fifteen minutes. Approximately ten hours later the same procedure is repeated with the next problem, continuing in this way until the twelve test problems[*] as illustrated in Figure 2, numbers 1 to 12, have been completed. No days should be missed and it is desirable to keep all conditions as constant as possible.

In each test problem the animal's score is the total number of error zones entered. Time does not count. An error is scored each time an animal's two forefeet cross into an error zone. These error zones are indicated in Figure 2 by the broken lines. Where a blind alley contains two error zones (two broken lines), two errors are scored if the animal crosses the second error line, but no error is scored when he emerges from the alley through the first error zone. However, if an animal, having emerged from an error zone with both forefeet, turns about and goes back, a further error is scored. The total number of error zones entered by an animal in the twelve test items is that animal's score on the test.

Since even well-trained animals react to noises, movements in the room, and changes in the amount of lighting entering the testing room, it is suggested that these factors be controlled. It should also be noted that the animals adapt very easily to the presence of the experimenter seated at the apparatus, and probably use his figure as a cue in the problem solutions, making it inadvisable to change the experimenter's position during the testing period.

Standardization Study

This study was designed to establish the reliability and validity of the newly constructed test series.

Procedure. A group of 28 male hooded rats from the colony main-

---

[*] Item 12 is slightly different from that used in the study. Subsequent work indicated that the original item was too difficult for a test, however appropriate it might have been as a learning problem.

tained in the comparative psychology laboratory at McGill University were divided into three groups and treated as follows:

(a) Nine rats were reared uneventfully in cages measuring 9″ × 10″ × 12″, three per cage.

(b) Ten rats were reared similarly to those above except that at the age of ninety days these rats underwent cerebral cortex extirpation operations. The lesions were made in various cortical regions. None of the animals showed any gross motor or sensory defects at the time of testing.

(c) Nine rats were reared in a free environment similar to the one described by Hymovitch (3). In this environment the animals were able to move about freely in an area of approximately thirty cubic feet which contained various attempts to provide an "amusement park" for rats.

When the animals were one hundred and fifty days old they were started in the closed-field apparatus according to the above schedule of training. After eight days of preliminary training the entire group had reached the required criterion of nine runs in sixty seconds on two consecutive occasions. This amounted to thirteen exposure periods of thirty minutes each and three individual run sessions. The animals were then tested with the twelve test items, two problems being given each day about ten hours apart. No days were missed and in six days the test series was completed. The animals were returned to their cages and put on a regular feeding schedule.

For three days the rats were fed and watered in the usual fashion. On the fourth day the entire group of animals was put back on a closed-field test training schedule. This time the preliminary training took two days, two exposure periods of thirty minutes each on the first day followed by two criterion run sessions the next day. Training problems A, B, C, D were used to bring the group to the required criterion. All the rats were then tested as previously except that this time the problems were presented in their mirror-image form. This was done to counteract any direct memory of the test solutions. It is felt that this is an unnecessary precaution and that the test items in their original form would have yielded identical results.

RESULTS

That the closed-field method is useful in discriminating animals that have suffered cortical damage and also those that have been reared in "superior" environments is shown in Table I. The normals are significantly inferior to the rats exposed to superior environments but superior to those that were operated on. These findings agree with the reports of Lashley (5) and others on the effects of rat brain extirpation as well as with the results obtained by Hymovitch (3) in working with free environment rearing.

TABLE I

TEST AND RETEST MEAN SCORES OF THREE GROUPS

Group	N	Test Mean	P value of Diff.	Retest Mean	P value of Diff.
Operates	10	159.5		95.9	
Normals	9	102.2	(O-N) < 1%	66.0	(O-N) < 1%
Free Environment	9	88.0	(N-F) 10%	43.6	(N-F) < 1%

Table II indicates the test-retest reliability obtained with the closed-field test. When all animals are compared on test-retest scores the correlation (Rho) equals .84; when only the unoperated scores are considered Rho is .80. It should be noted that this reliability and the ability of the test to differentiate the experimental groups in both the test and the retest may also be an indication of validity; despite the marked degree of learning (shown in the lowered means in retesting), those animals which were poorest on the first test tend to be poorest on the second.

TABLE II

CORRELATION OF TEST-RETEST SCORES

	N	Rho
All Animals	28	.84
Normals	18	.80

DISCUSSION

The results reported in this paper regarding the closed-field intelligence test for rats indicate that it is a reliable instrument and compares very favourably with traditional measures of rat intelligence. Miles (6) in comparing the elevated and alley mazes reported reliabilities of .75 and .73 respectively. Burlingame and Stone (1) reporting on the multiple-T maze obtained a reliability of .78. These were actually odd-even reliabilities, and no one has found anything like as high a correlation between two independent learning scores in a test-retest procedure with alley or elevated maze. The study described in this paper was able to achieve a reliability of .84 for a group of twenty-eight rats, including ten that had cortical damage. The results also indicate the ability of the instrument to discriminate fine experimental variables. On inspection of the brains which were removed from the animals that had cortical damage, no extirpation seemed to exceed 10 per cent of cortical tissue and several were rather small.

It should be noted that the closed-field test described in this paper bases its quantitative score on qualitative analyses of performance on twelve different tasks. This is a deliberate attempt to evaluate rat intelligence as a more general and integrated phenomenon than has been done in the past, and in this way to accomplish the measurement of a capacity in the rat which more closely approaches our concept of intelligence in man.

SUMMARY

This paper describes the apparatus and test items of a closed-field test of rat intelligence. This method is adaptable to other animal species and has the important advantage of measuring intelligence by analysis of qualitative behaviour rather than by inference from learning scores. Data indicating the reliability and validity of the method are presented.

REFERENCES

1. BURLINGAME, M., and STONE, C. P. "Family Resemblances in Maze-Learning Ability in White Rats" (*National Society for the Study of Education, 27th Yearbook*, Part I, 1928, 89-99).

2. HEBB, D. O., and WILLIAMS, KENNETH. "A Method of Rating Animal Intelligence" (*Journal of Genetic Psychology*, 34, 1946, 59-65).

3. HYMOVITCH, W. (Unpublished Ph.D. thesis, 1949. Redpath Library, McGill University. Referred to by permission.)

4. LANSDELL, H. C. (Unpublished Ph.D. thesis, 1950. Redpath Library, McGill University. Referred to by permission.)

5. LASHLEY, K. S. *Brain Mechanisms and Intelligence* (Chicago: University of Chicago Press, 1929).

6. MILES, W. R. "The Comparative Learning of Rats on Elevated and Alley Mazes of the Same Pattern" (*Journal of Comparative Psychology*, 10, 1930, 237-61).

7. RISHIKOFF, R. J. (Unpublished M.A. thesis, 1949. Redpath Library, McGill University. Referred to by permission.)

DONALD G. FORGAYS & JANET W. FORGAYS

43 The Nature of the Effect of Free-Environmental Experience in the Rat

The problem of the effect of varied infant environments upon adult behavior has long interested the psychologist, although experimental analysis of the issue has been curiously slow in materializing. The few relevant studies in the last decade or so include research on the perception of figures by adult rats reared

Reprinted from *Journal of Comparative and Physiological Psychology* 45:322–328, 1952. Copyright 1952 by the American Psychological Association and reproduced by permission.

This work was done at the psychological laboratories of McGill University. Thanks are due to Dr. D. O. Hebb for his kind cooperation and many suggestions.

in darkness (2), on inhibition of sensory function in adult rats placed in a stressful situation after deprivation of the concerned function during the nursing period (10), on infantile food-frustration and adult hoarding in the rat (6, 7), and on infantile auditory stimulation and adult emotional stability in the mouse (1).

There has been, as yet, scanty research on the question of the intellectual capabilities of the adult after varied infant experiences. Exploratory work by Hebb (3, 4) on small groups of rats indicated that differences in problem-solving ability could be demonstrated between rats reared with and rats reared without vision, and between rats reared in ordinary small cages and rats brought up in the much wider environment of a home in which, within limits, they had the run of the house. These experiments were repeated and elaborated with much larger samples of rats and with more adequate control by Hymovitch (8). He confirmed the earlier work by finding that rats reared in a complex environment (free environment) were significantly superior in problem-solving ability, as measured by the Hebb-Williams test (5), to animals raised under conditions which severely limited their total experience (restricted rats). Hymovitch employed as the complex environment a large box containing a number of "playthings" (simple wooden and metal structures) to afford the rats a variety of experience. In addition, he also placed in this structure small mesh cages in which other rats were reared and which were moved occasionally from place to place both inside and outside the box. As adults these mesh-caged rats were unexpectedly good at problem-solving behavior; in fact, they were indistinguishable in this regard from those animals that were given free run of the box during the same period of time. Hymovitch determined that the differential effects of varied early environments on adult rats did not result from unequal opportunity for motor experience or from differential motivation of the various groups.

Would the free-environmental animals be superior to restricted rats if the playthings were not present during rearing? What are the factors which contribute to the problem-solving ability of the animals that are reared in mesh cages in the complex environment? As an attempt to answer these questions, the present study was undertaken.

PROBLEM-SOLVING

Method

In order to subject the appropriate animal groups to different specific environments within the same general environment, that is, the same section of the experimental room, a four-story structure was erected measuring 5 ft. in height, 4 ft. in width, and 2 ft. in depth. The framework was wooden and covered with ½-in. wire mesh. Each story was 1 ft. high (the bottom layer standing a foot off the laboratory floor) with plywood flooring, the ceiling being the plywood floor of the stage above. Playthings were placed in two of the stories, and two mesh cages 8 in. in diameter and 6 in. in height were set in each of the layers. A diagram of the structure, the playthings, and the mesh cages appears in Figure 1.

Male hooded rats of the McGill University strain were used. The male pups of several litters born within a day or so of each other were weaned at 26 days of age and selected randomly for each of seven experimental groups. At this time 3 rats were placed in each of the mesh cages, forming four mesh-caged groups of 6 animals each; 11 rats were placed in each of two stories of the free-environmental structure; and 8 rats were confined to small laboratory cages, 8 by 10 by 12 in. in size with three solid metal walls, a grill top,

FREE-ENVIRONMENTAL STRUCTURE

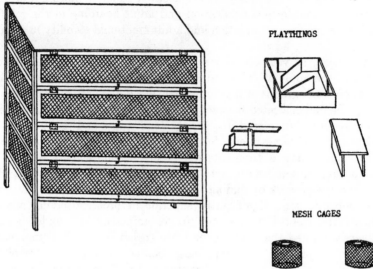

PLAYTHINGS

MESH CAGES

FIG. 1. DRAWINGS OF THE FREE-ENVIRONMENTAL STRUCTURE, PLAY-THINGS, AND THE MESH CAGES EMPLOYED DURING THE REARING PERIOD OF THE APPROPRIATE EXPERIMENTAL GROUPS

and a small mesh door. The latter group was considered a restricted group; the cages of this group were kept on top of the large structure discussed above. In the four stories of the structure, then, are found:

1. Eleven free-environmental animals; playthings; two mesh cages with three rats in each.
2. Eleven free-environmental animals; two mesh cages with three rats in each.
3. Playthings (same as above); two mesh cages with three animals in each.
4. Two mesh cages with three rats in each.

The various cages and stories of the box were cleaned weekly, necessitating handling some of the rats. To equate the groups on this factor, all the rats were handled the same amount of time on these occasions. Cleaning time afforded an opportunity to move all the rats of one stage to another. For example, the rats, mesh cages and playthings of Stage 1 would be moved to Stage 2; those in Stage 2 would be moved to Stage 3; and so on. In this way, all the rats spent about the same amount of time in each of the layers of the box. This was done as an attempt to control the possible differential visibility aspects of the various levels. When the rats in the free-environmental box and in the restricted cages were approximately 90 days of age, they were removed from their respective surroundings and placed randomly in large colony cages, 2 by 2 by 1½ ft. They were then given preliminary training on the Hebb and Williams (5) test of animal intelligence for one week and the actual test problems during the following four weeks. Two series of 12 problems each were used as test problems; they had been standardized by Rabinovitch (9) and correlate highly with each other.* The problems were completed at the rate of one per day with food deprivation preceding each testing session for about 23 hr.

Results

The mean error scores of the various groups on the 24 test problems and a statistical comparison of each group with every other group will be found in Table 1. These results indicate that the free-environmental animals that had

---

* Use of this recently designed series of closed-field test problems does not permit the direct comparison of the present results with those of Hymovitch.

TABLE 1

MEAN ERROR SCORES OF THE VARIOUS GROUPS ON THE HEBB-WILLIAMS TEST AND A STATISTICAL COMPARISON OF EACH GROUP WITH EVERY OTHER GROUP

The significance of the differences between means of small correlated samples was calculated in all cases.

GROUP	(1)	(2)	(3)	(4)	(5)	(6)
(1) Free-environmental with playthings Mean = 126.00	—					
(2) Free-environmental without playthings Mean = 162.00	$df = 20$ $t = 6.909$ $P = <0.01$					
(3) Mesh-caged in a layer with FE* animals and with playthings Mean = 189.50	$df = 15$ $t = 9.313$ $P = <0.01$	$df = 15$ $t = 3.509$ $P = <0.01$				
(4) Mesh-caged in a layer without FE animals and without playthings Mean = 191.66	$df = 15$ $t = 10.253$ $P = <0.01$	$df = 15$ $t = 3.965$ $P = <0.01$	$df = 10$ $t = 0.216$ $P = >0.8$			
(5) Mesh-caged in a layer without FE animals but with playthings Mean = 192.00	$df = 15$ $t = 9.129$ $P = <0.01$	$df = 15$ $t = 3.660$ $P = <0.01$	$df = 10$ $t = 0.227$ $P = >0.8$	$df = 10$ $t = 0.032$ $P = >0.8$		
(6) Mesh-caged in a layer with FE animals but without playthings Mean = 227.33	$df = 15$ $t = 16.033$ $P = <0.01$	$df = 15$ $t = 8.818$ $P = <0.01$	$df = 10$ $t = 3.837$ $P = <0.01$	$df = 10$ $t = 3.833$ $P = <0.01$	$df = 10$ $t = 3.393$ $P = <0.01$	
(7) Restricted animals Mean = 241.25	$df = 17$ $t = 19.915$ $P = <0.01$	$df = 17$ $t = 11.874$ $P = <0.01$	$df = 12$ $t = 5.842$ $P = <0.01$	$df = 12$ $t = 5.896$ $P = <0.01$	$df = 12$ $t = 5.291$ $P = <0.01$	$df = 12$ $t = 1.673$ $P = <0.13$

* FE = free-environmental.

playthings as part of their early experience are better problem solvers than any other group. The free-environmental rats raised without playthings, although inferior to those raised with playthings, are statistically superior to the remaining groups. There is no significant difference between one mesh group—those reared in a layer containing free-environmental animals but no playthings—and the restricted rats, and both are statistically inferior to *all* other groups. The remaining mesh groups are not statistically different from one another, but all are inferior to the two free-environmental groups and superior to the mesh group and restricted animals mentioned above. An analysis of the mean error scores of the various groups on each of the two series of 12 problems indicates that the rate of improvement on the second series is roughly the same for all groups. Within the limits of this testing program, then, the measured differences may be considered as being permanent.

ROTATION OF THE TESTING APPARATUS

Evidence had been found by Hymovitch (8) which indicated that distance cues were used in the closed-field problem-solving situation more extensively by the free-environmental than by the restricted rats. To test the employment of distance cues in the maze situation as a factor which could be used to differentiate the various experimental groups of rats of the present study, the following modifications of testing procedure were introduced.

Method

A day after the rats had completed the 24 test problems, the maze apparatus was rotated 90° counterclockwise in the experimental room. The problem area was left open, that is, no barrier problem was placed within it. All the rats were given ten runs in this situation after 23 hr. of food deprivation. On the following day, the apparatus was rotated 90° clockwise with respect to its normal position. Within the box, at this time, a barrier problem was set up, and again all rats were given ten trials after 23 hr. of food deprivation. A scoring scheme had been devised previously by the senior author and B. Hymovitch and is described by the latter in his report (8). Errors were based upon deviations from a defined "correct" route, locomotion in a direction away from the goal (food box), "sniffing" the area where the food box would have been had the testing apparatus remained in its customary position, and re-entry of the starting box. There were no obvious constant auditory distance cues in the environment. The total score is considered, then, a measure of the use an animal makes of visual distance cues in maze-running; if its total score is high, it makes much use of such cues and vice versa.

TABLE 2

MEAN ERROR SCORES OF THE VARIOUS GROUPS ON THE TWO MAZE PROBLEMS RUN AFTER
ROTATION OF THE APPARATUS

GROUP	MEAN ERROR SCORE
FE* with playthings	25.27
FE without playthings	21.27
Mesh-caged in a layer with FE animals and with playthings	17.16
Mesh-caged in a layer without FE animals and without playthings	18.83
Mesh-caged in a layer without FE animals but with playthings	15.83
Mesh-caged in a layer with FE animals but without playthings	8.83
Restricted animals	8.62

* FE = free-environmental.

Results

Table 2 reports the mean error scores of the various groups on the rotation problems. It is apparent that the free-environmental animals made many more errors than the restricted rats and the mesh-caged group reared in a layer containing free-environmental animals but no playthings. The other mesh-caged groups made error scores about midway between these extremes.

DISCUSSION

In general confirmation of the results of Hebb (3, 4) and Hymovitch (8), there seems to be little doubt that free-environmental experience in early life is reflected in the adult rat by problem-solving ability superior to that of rats reared under restricted conditions. The presence of playthings, the most obvious agent of a direct-transfer effect in the situation, apparently benefits the animal over and above the large open field. Either of these rearing environments, however, leads to superior problem-solving ability. It would appear, then, that the effect of free-environmental experience, as such, is not simple transfer.

The results of the distance-cue study indicate that the free-environmental rat uses visual distance cues to a much greater extent in the maze situation than does the restricted animal. This evidence points the way to a theoretical explanation of the present findings in terms of the amount of perceptual experience gained in the early environment. Those animals having a good opportunity for perceptual learning during rearing turn out to be better adult problem solvers than animals that do not have the same opportunity. This explanation is in essential agreement with that offered by Hymovitch (8).

The same reasoning can be used to account for the fact that one mesh-caged group was on a par with the restricted rats in regard to problem-solving ability and use of distance cues. The potential perceptual experience of this group during rearing was limited because the free-environmental animals in the same layer habitually would rest either on top of the mesh cages or about them. The free animals in the other layer usually rested in the shaded areas of the playthings. Mesh-caged animals, apparently, if reared under certain conditions in the free-environmental box, are in no more advantageous a situation in regard to opportunity for perceptual experience and learning than are the restricted rats.

The problem remains to account for the divergence of the present results from those of Hymovitch (8). He had found that his mesh-caged group, reared with free-environmental animals and playthings, was indistinguishable in problem-solving ability from the free-environmental rats; in the present study a mesh-caged group fairly comparable to his was found to be inferior in its problem-solving ability to the free-environmental rats but superior to the restricted rats. It should be pointed out that the free-environmental box used by Hymovitch was much larger than each of the layers of the box employed in the present study; this, of course, afforded a greater number of positions to which the mesh cages could be moved. Hymovitch moved the mesh cages about more frequently and to more different positions, both inside and *outside* the box, than attempted here. Moreover, in the present study three rats were reared in the same mesh cages in which Hymovitch raised only one rat. These differences in experimental procedure might have provided more opportunity for visual experience and learning in the mesh-caged group of Hymovitch's study. This was then reflected in adulthood by equality with free-environmental animals in problem-solving ability in a maze situation in which success is apparently closely related to the effective use of visual cues. It would appear that, depending upon the environmental conditions during their rearing, mesh-caged rats may be as superior in their problem-solving ability as free-environmental animals or as inferior as restricted animals.

SUMMARY

1. This experiment studied in the rat the effect of varied infant environments upon adult problem-solving ability. Young male rats were reared under different environmental conditions; some were raised in layers of a large four-story box, with and without "playthings," some in mesh cages within the layers of this box, and others in small laboratory cages. When they were mature, they were kept together in ordinary colony cages and tested in the Hebb-Williams closed-field test of rat intelligence.

2. The free-environmental rats that had playthings as part of their early environment were found to be better problem solvers than any other group.

3. Free-environmental animals reared without playthings, although inferior to those raised with playthings, were better than all remaining groups.

4. The restricted rats and the mesh-caged group reared in a layer of the box containing free-environmental animals but no playthings were statistically inferior to *all* other groups, but they were not different from each other.

5. The remaining mesh-caged groups were not statistically different from one another, but all were inferior in their problem-solving ability to the free-environmental groups, and all were superior to the restricted animals and the mesh-caged group mentioned above.

6. Visual distance-cue use in the maze situation was tested by means of two additional maze problems. The relationship between error score on the Hebb-Williams test and the employment of visual distance cues apparently is an inverse one.

7. An attempt is made to explain the present findings in terms of differential opportunity for visual experience and learning during rearing.

REFERENCES

1. HALL, C. S., AND WHITEMAN, P. H. The effects of infantile stimulation upon later emotional stability in the mouse. *J. comp. physiol. Psychol.*, 1951, **44**, 61–66.
2. HEBB, D. O. The innate organization of visual activity: I. Perception of figures by rats reared in total darkness. *J. genet. Psychol.*, 1937, **51**, 101–126.
3. HEBB, D. O. The effects of early experience on problem-solving at maturity. *Amer. Psychologist*, 1947, **2**, 306–307.
4. HEBB, D. O. *The organization of behavior.* New York: Wiley, 1949.
5. HEBB, D. O., AND WILLIAMS, K. A method of rating animal intelligence. *J. gen. Psychol.*, 1946, **34**, 59–65.
6. HUNT, J. McV. The effects of infant feeding-frustration upon adult hoarding in the albino rat. *J. abnorm. soc. Psychol.*, 1941, **36**, 338–360.
7. HUNT, J. McV., SCHLOSBERG, H., SOLOMON, R. L., AND STELLAR, E. Studies of the effects of infantile experience on adult behavior in rats. I. Effects of infantile feeding frustration on adult hoarding. *J. comp. physiol. Psychol.*, 1947, **40**, 291–304.
8. HYMOVITCH, B. The effects of experimental variations on problem solving in the rat. *J. comp. physiol. Psychol.*, 1952, **45**, 313–321.

9. RABINOVITCH, M. S. Standardization of a closed field intelligence test for rats. Unpublished Master's thesis, McGill Univer., 1949.

10. WOLF, A. The dynamics of the selective inhibition of specific functions in neurosis: A preliminary report. *Psychosom. Med.*, 1943, **5,** 27–38.

DONALD G. FORGAYS & JANET MICHELSON READ

44   Crucial Periods for Free-Environmental Experience in the Rat

Psychologists have known for some time that the type of early experience provided an animal can influence his adult performance on a variety of tasks (Beach & Jaynes, 1954). Recently, researchers (Bingham & Griffiths, 1952; Forgays & Forgays, 1952; Forgus, 1954; and others) have demonstrated that rats reared in large complex environments are superior in problem-solving ability to rats reared under more restricted conditions. In addition, Hymovitch (1952) found evidence indicating that the enriched experience must occur before maturity if it is to lead to the reported effect. In a study using form discrimination as the response measure, Forgus (1954) reported that the enriched experience must occur extremely early in the life of the rat. In this latter study, testing of the two groups of animals constituting the design was accomplished well before full maturity of the rats so that in this sense, at least, the results cannot be compared directly with those of Hymovitch.

As yet there has not been reported a systematic investigation of several quite important aspects of the early-experience issue; namely, just how much experience is necessary in these complex environments to produce a superior adult animal, and when, specifically, during early life must this experience occur, assuming that it must take place before full maturity. A still more interesting matter is the interaction of these two dimensions, that is,

Reprinted from *Journal of Comparative and Physiological Psychology* 55:816–818, 1962. Copyright 1962 by the American Psychological Association and reproduced by permission.

This study was supported in part by a research grant from the Rutgers University Research Council.

the possibility that a greater amount of experience occurring during one developmental period produces the same results in the adult animal as a smaller quantity of such experience during another period. Moreover, it would be desirable in any such studies to examine the functioning of the adult animals on a variety of intellectual, emotionality, and other measures.

The present study is an attempt to investigate in part the second of the issues raised above; that is, When, specifically, during the relatively short maturation period of the rat, must a limited amount of exposure to a complex environment occur in order to effect superior problem-solving ability in the adult animal?

METHOD

Apparatus

Exposure to the complex environment was provided by placing the animal Ss for certain periods of time during early life in a large box 49 in. long, 28 in. wide, and 11 in. high. The box had wire-mesh sides and top; in it were placed several wooden and metal objects ("playthings") which have been described elsewhere (Forgays & Forgays, 1952). This setting is referred to below as Free Environment (FE).

Subjects

This study was run in a modified replication design in two phases. In the initial phase, data on Groups 3, 4, 5, and nine animals of Group 2 were collected (see Table 1 for group descriptions). In the second phase, run several months later, data on Groups 1 and 6 and the remaining eight animals of Group 2 were collected.

In the initial phase of this study, 36 male albino rats of the Rutgers University Psychology Laboratory strain were assigned at random to four groups of 9 animals each. These animals were all members of eight litters born within a few days of each other. For the second phase of the study, 24 rats of the same strain were assigned at random to three groups of 8 each. These animals were all members of five litters born within a few days of each other.

Procedure

In the initial phase of the study, when the animals averaged 21 days of age, the first group of nine animals was placed in the FE box; the other three groups were placed in small laboratory cages in the same general location of the laboratory as the FE box. Twenty-one days later, the second group of nine animals was placed in the FE box and the first group removed to the small cages. This procedure was repeated in subsequent 3-week periods for the remaining two groups. When the fourth group was taken out of the FE box, all of these animals averaged 111 days of age; all Ss were then housed in small cages.

In the second phase of the study, the first group of eight animals was placed in the FE box within 20 hr. after birth and remained until 21 days of age. One of the mother animals, of the five available, was placed in the box with the pups to care for them during this period. When this first group averaged 21 days of age, it was removed and replaced with another group of eight animals which were 22 days of age upon entry to the FE box and 43 days old when they were removed to the small laboratory cages from which they had come. This group is a replication of one of the groups of the earlier phase. A third group of eight animals (Control) received no experience in the FE box.

All animals were weaned at 21 days of age. During rearing, the FE box and small cages were cleaned once a week; care was taken at these times to handle all animals equally. Animals of all groups were confined in the small laboratory cages in groups of four or five rats.

When the animals were approximately 114 days old, each was placed for two 5-min. trials, one per day, on an elevated Y maze, the arms of which were 30 in. long and 6 in. wide. The total amount of activity (in terms of number of 10-in. sections entered), the number of urinations, and the number of boli excreted were recorded for each animal.

When the animals were about 123 days old, they began training on the Hebb-Williams maze (Rabinovitch & Rosvold, 1951). After training for 1 week, the rats were exposed to the 12 test problems at the rate of one per day. They were food-deprived for approximately 23 hr. prior to running each problem and were fed for an hour after each.

RESULTS

The results of the two phases of this study are presented and discussed together below. Data obtained from Group 2 animals, split over the two phases, were quite comparable over the two runnings for all measures and thus are combined.

Incidence of urination and defecation on the Y maze was negligible and is not reported here; there were no group differences on the basis of few such responses. Results of the activity measure averaged for the two trials are presented in Table 1. As seen there, the differences among the six groups of this study are slight, the animals having had the earliest FE exposure demonstrating a bit more activity than the other groups. None of these means is significantly different from any other.

The mean error scores of the six groups of animals on the 12 Hebb-Williams closed-field problems are given in Table 1. As seen there, Group 2 animals, which had the FE exposure from 22 to 43 days, made the fewest errors; Group 6 animals, which had no FE exposure, made the greatest number of errors; and the remaining four groups of animals made error scores at points between these extremes.

Statistical analysis of the significance of the differences between the various mean

TABLE 1

MEAN ACTIVITY SCORES AND MEAN ERROR AND STANDARD DEVIATION SCORES OF THE SIX GROUPS OF Ss ON THE HEBB-WILLIAMS TEST AND t's OF THE VARIOUS MEAN COMPARISONS

Group	N	Time of Enriched Experience (Days of Age)	Mean Entries of Y Maze	Hebb-Williams Test		t				
				Mean Error Score	Standard Deviation	2	3	4	5	6
1	8	0–21	74.88	174.25	15.56	2.53*	1.30	1.08	0.21	2.15*
2	17	22–43	73.59	153.29	25.29		0.64	0.56	2.07*	3.70**
3	9	44–65	67.67	160.33	25.34			0.02	1.22	2.70*
4	9	66–87	63.67	160.56	31.94				1.07	2.37*
5	9	88–109	61.00	176.67	28.00					1.38
6	8	No enriched experience	69.52	195.75	25.41					

* $p < .05$.
** $p < .01$.

error scores was made by t test and the results are reported with appropriate probability statements in Table 1. As seen there, the animals which had no FE exposure (Group 6) made significantly more errors, at the .05 level of confidence or better, than all other groups of the study except the group of animals which had the FE exposure at a time when a rat could be considered a mature animal, between 88 and 109 days of age (Group 5).

As can also be seen in Table 1, Group 2, which received the FE exposure for 3 weeks immediately after weaning, made significantly fewer errors on the closed-field test than Group 1 (FE exposure during the first 3 weeks of life) and Group 5 (FE exposure at about the time of maturity), in addition to the Group 6 difference mentioned above.

DISCUSSION

While reference to Table 1 reveals reasonably large percentage differences among the activity scores of the various groups of animals tested, none of the 15 possible comparisons is significant, likely reflecting the considerable variability in the distributions of this measure. As indicated above, the incidence of urination and defecation by these animals was negligibly low; special care was taken to handle all animals equally and often in an attempt to dissipate emotionality differences among groups which may be the result of differential handling experiences. Activity, urination, and defecation measures have been used by others as indices of emotionality in the rat (Forgus, 1956; Hall, 1934). Whatever is being measured by such indices, it must be concluded that the six groups constituting the present design are equivalent on these bases.

It is difficult to compare the results of this study with those few other relevant studies available in the literature. However, the treatment accorded Group 5 in this study was quite similar to that of the group of animals in Hymovitch's study (1952) which received FE exposure at the end of the growth period; in his study this group was found to be no different in problem-solving ability from animals restricted to small cages throughout rearing (similar to Group 6 in the present study). The present results may be seen as substantiating those of Hymovitch on this specific point.

It is noteworthy that Group 1 animals were found to be adult problem-solvers superior to Group 6 animals. The eyes of the animals of Group 1 did not open until the middle of their FE exposure period, and they spent much of the total period nestled with the mother rat provided. The significant difference in mean error score found would suggest that a very brief exposure to the wider environment in early life can have rather lasting effects.

The results of this study may be viewed as generally confirming the finding of Hymovitch (1952) that FE experience, as described above, must occur before maturity if it is to result in adult rats of superior problem-solving ability, at least as measured by the Hebb-Williams test. In addition, the results are in essential agreement with the finding of Forgus (1954) that such experience must occur in early infancy. Our results show clearly that there is a "critical" period for such exposure. Within the limitations of this study, the period seems to occur long before maturity and soon after the eyes of the rat are first open. Much additional research is necessary, however, before we will have acceptably complete answers to questions concerning the interaction of time of FE exposure and amount of such experience.

SUMMARY

This experiment studies in the rat the effect upon adult problem-solving ability of exposure to a complex environment at different periods during growth. It was found that animals having had no such exposure were significantly poorer adult problem-solvers than animals having had 3 weeks of such experience at several different times before 90 days or so of age. It was also found that animals exposed immediately after weaning at 21 days of age were significantly better adult problem-solvers than animals which had the experience either earlier or later. It was concluded that there is a critical period for such exposures but that considerable additional research is required before we will know exactly how much experience is necessary to produce such effects and the specific period when it must occur.

REFERENCES

BEACH, F. A., & JAYNES, J. Effects of early experience upon the behavior of animals. *Psychol. Bull.*, 1954, **51**, 239–262.

BINGHAM, W. E., & GRIFFITHS, W. J., JR. The effect of different environments during infancy on adult behavior in the rat. *J. comp. physiol. Psychol.*, 1952, **45**, 307–312.

FORGAYS, D. G., & FORGAYS, J. W. The nature of the effect of free-environmental experience in the rat. *J. comp. physiol. Psychol.*, 1952, **45**, 322–328.

FORGUS, R. H. The effect of early perceptual learning on the behavioral organization of adult rats. *J. comp. physiol. Psychol.*, 1954, **47**, 331–336.

FORGUS, R. H. Advantage of early over late perceptual experience in improving form discrimination. *Canad. J. Physiol.*, 1956, **10**, 147–155.

HALL, C. S. Emotional behavior in the rat: I. Defecation and urination as measures of individual differences in emotionality. *J. comp. Psychol.*, 1934, **18**, 385–403.

HYMOVITCH, B. The effects of experimental variations on problem solving in the rat. *J. comp. physiol. Psychol.*, 1952, **45**, 313–321.

RABINOVITCH, M. S., & ROSVOLD, H. E. A closed-field intelligence test for rats. *Canad. J. Psychol.*, 1951, **5**, 122–128.

VICTOR H. DENENBERG, JAMES M. WOODCOCK, & KENNETH M. ROSENBERG

45 Long-Term Effects of Preweaning and Postweaning Free-Environment Experience on Rats' Problem-Solving Behavior

Between birth and 21 days of age, 38 rats were raised in maternity cages or in enriched free environments. At 21–50 days of age, half of each group were in laboratory cages and half were in free environments. Then all *S*s were kept in laboratory cages until Hebb-Williams problem-solving testing began at an average age of 371 days. Both preweaning and postweaning enriched experiences independently improved problem-solving performance. The findings offer strong support for Hebb's hypothesis that enriched experiences in early life result in permanent brain changes.

Two broad research areas in the field of early experience have been concerned with the effects of physical stimulation in infancy, i.e., between birth and weaning, and after weaning. In the first category are the studies involving such independent variables as handling, electric shock, heat, and cold. One of the major generalizations resulting from this research is that extra stimulation in infancy results in a relatively permanent reduction in emotionality (Denenberg, 1964). Different investigators have

Reprinted from *Journal of Comparative and Physiological Psychology* 66:533–535, 1968. Copyright 1968 by the American Psychological Association and reproduced by permission.

This research was supported in part by Grant HD-02068 from the National Institute of Child Health and Human Development.

Supported by United States Public Health Service Fellowship 1-F1-MH-30,916-01A1 (MTLH) from the National Institute of Mental Health.

Supported by Training Grant 1 T1 MH-10267 from the National Institute of Mental Health.

tested rats at various ages 180–544 days and have found that those *S*s stimulated in infancy were still significantly less emotional than nonstimulated controls (see review by Denenberg, 1966).

The second broad category of early experience research involves manipulating the early perceptual environment in an attempt to alter *S*'s subsequent perceptual and problem-solving behavior. Such studies have resulted primarily from Hebb's (1949) theory that enriched experiences early in life lead to permanent brain changes which enhance *S*'s problem-solving capability. Virtually all studies which have tested this theory have found that exposure to an enriched environment after weaning increased *S*'s problem-solving and perceptual abilities. However, in most experiments *S*s were tested immediately or very soon after being removed from the enriched environment. Thus, these studies are not a valid test of that portion of Hebb's theory which states that the changes brought about by early enrichment are relatively permanent. In only one instance has there been any appreciable time gap between the termination of enriched experiences and the initiation of problem-solving testing. Forgays and Read (1962) gave five independent groups free-environment experiences in 3-wk. blocks at 0–109 days of age and studied Hebb-Williams performance at about 123 days; their data supported Hebb's position.

The purpose of the present study was to make a more stringent evaluation of Hebb's (1949) theory by testing the animals when they were about 1 yr. old. By then an interval of approximately 330–360 days had intervened since early enrichment. In addition, Ss received enriched experience either before or after weaning in a 2 × 2 factorial design so that the impact of the enrichment at different stages in ontogeny could be evaluated.

METHOD

Preweaning Experience

The Ss were female Purdue-Wistar rats born of mothers which had been handled during their own infancy. Pregnant females were placed either into maternity cages or into free-environment boxes. The 15 × 10 × 7½ in. stainless-steel maternity cages contained a tray floor covered with shavings and a food hopper and water bottle were attached to the outside of the front door of the cage.

The free environments were triangular-shaped compartments formed by placing a diagonal insert into a 34-in.-sq. box with 16-in.-high walls. The walls and insert were of unpainted Masonite and the floor was wire mesh. During the preweaning interval the floor was covered with sheet metal (so that the pups would not fall through) and topped with shavings. Food was scattered on the floor and water was supplied by an externally mounted bottle. "Toys" (a wooden block, a tin can, a ramp, and a running disc) were placed in each free environment.

The cages and boxes were inspected each morning for births. All litters were cut back to eight Ss consisting of at least four females.

Postweaning Experience

On Day 21 Ss were weaned and ear punched. The males were discarded and the females from each litter were randomly split, half going into a 11 × 8¼ × 7½ in. stainless-steel laboratory cage with mesh floor and half into a free-environment box with diagonal partition and sheet-metal floor covering removed. Two to three Ss were placed into each laboratory cage while 10–12 Ss shared each free environment. On Day 50 the females were removed from the free environments and placed into laboratory cages.

Adult Testing

The Ss were tested on the Hebb-Williams problem-solving maze following the procedure of Rabinovitch and Rosvold (1951). They were adapted to the apparatus and the 23-hr. food deprivation schedule and then were given two practice problems a day for 3 days. At an average age of 370.7 days (the age range of the mid-90% of Ss was 331–402 days), testing began on the sequence of 12 test problems described by Rabinovitch and Rosvold. One test problem was given per day with 10 trials on each problem. The S's score was the total number of errors made during the testing period.

When two Ss from the same litter were available, one of which had been reared in the free environment after weaning while the other had been reared in a laboratory cage, they were tested as a pair. Otherwise, single Ss from different litters were tested.

RESULTS

Table 1 summarizes the mean number of errors per S over all 12 problems. The statistical analysis was carried out on the data from litter mates using a split-plot unweighted means analysis of the 2 × 2 factorial design (Winer, 1962).

The preweaning experience and postweaning experience main effects were both significant ($Fs = 10.07$ and 74.01, respectively, $df = 1/12$, $p < .01$) and the interaction was significant ($F = 5.76$, $p < .05$). Free-environment experience either before or after weaning acted to reduce errors on the problem-solving maze. The significant interaction was primarily brought about by the markedly poorer performance of the group which received no free-environment experience at all; in addition, the group which received free-environment experience both before and after weaning had a significantly smaller error score than the group which had free-environment experience only before weaning.

TABLE 1

MEAN HEBB-WILLIAMS ERROR SCORES FOR EXPERIMENTAL Ss

Preweaning experience (Days 0–21)	Postweaning experience (Days 21–50)					
	Single Ss			Litter-mate pairs[a]		
	n	Laboratory cage	n	Free environment	n	Laboratory cage	Free environment
Maternity cage	10	238.0	10	157.4	6	234.8	157.7
Free environment	9	170.4	9	127.1	8	170.9	127.4

[a] Between litters: $MS = 1497.71$, $df = 12$; Litters × Postweaning Environment interaction: $MS = 337.37$, $df = 12$.

DISCUSSION

The Ss were tested when approximately 1 yr. old, roughly 330–360 days after the termination of free-environment experience. Since by this age the rat has covered one-third to one-half of its total life span, we may conclude that enrichment during infancy or immediately after weaning has a long-term effect upon problem-solving behavior. These findings strongly support Hebb's (1949) hypothesis concerning permanent brain changes as a function of enriched experiences.

An examination of the means in Table 1 shows that free-environment experience after weaning had a greater impact upon S's later problem-solving behavior than did free-environment experience during infancy. This is consistent with our knowledge of the rat's sensory and neurological development. In a sense, the surprising finding is that preweaning enriched experience had such a positive effect. These results are consistent with those of Forgays and Read (1962), but are in disagreement with Denenberg's (1966) suggestion that learning probably plays only a minor role in preweaning stimulation. Because of the extreme immaturity of the rat at birth, it is likely that enrichment during infancy only has an effect upon the rat during the last week to 10 days of the preweaning period, i.e., after S has developed proficiency in locomotion and after the eyes have opened.

We should consider two alternative hypotheses to our conclusion that these results reflect permanent brain changes. The first is that early enriched experiences reduce fear of novel complex environments, which is the reason for the better performance of the experimental groups on the Hebb-Williams maze. There are two points against this hypothesis. First, the adaptation and pretraining procedures on the Hebb-Williams maze tended to eliminate individual differences in emotional reactivity. Second, preweaning experience would be expected to have a greater effect than postweaning experience if the differences were due to emotionality, since it is during the period of infancy that one finds the greatest effect of stimulation upon subsequent emotional reactivity (Denenberg, 1966). The second hypothesis is that there is some specific transfer of training from the enriched environment to the adult test situation. In the adult test situation S was required to go around barriers to obtain food at an already-learned goal box. However, during early life Ss had food scattered on the floor at all times and never had to learn to go to a specific place to obtain it, and no barriers were present in the free environment. We conclude that the hypothesis that early enrichment brings about permanent brain changes appears to describe these data more adequately.

REFERENCES

DENENBERG, V. H. Critical periods, stimulus input, and emotional reactivity: A theory of infantile stimulation. *Psychol. Rev.*, 1964, **71**, 335–351.

DENENBERG, V. H. Animal studies on developmental determinants of behavioral adaptability. In O. J. Harvey (Ed.), *Experience, structure and adaptability*. New York: Springer, 1966.

FORGAYS, D. G., & READ, J. M. Crucial periods for free-environmental experience in the rat. *J. comp. physiol. Psychol.*, 1962, **55**, 816–818.

HEBB, D. O. *The organization of behavior*. New York: Wiley, 1949.

RABINOVITCH, M. S., & ROSVOLD, H. E. A closed-field intelligence test for rats. *Canad. J. Psychol.*, 1951, **5**, 122–128.

WINER, B. J. *Statistical principles in experimental design*. New York: McGraw-Hill, 1962.

MARGARET WILSON, J. M. WARREN, & LYNN ABBOTT

46 Infantile Stimulation, Activity, and Learning by Cats

Groups of kittens were handled for 5 min. per day from birth through 45 days, placed in a complex free environment for 5 hr. a day from 46 to 90 days of age, or subjected to both or neither of these treatments. Kittens

Reprinted from *Child Development* 36:843–853, 1965. ©1965 by the Society for Research in Child Development, Inc.

This research was supported by grant M-4726 from the National Institute of Mental Health, U. S. Public Health Service.

handled in infancy approached strange toys and humans more readily and required more trials to learn an active avoidance response than kittens that were not handled. Subjects that were exposed to the complex environment made significantly fewer errors in the Hebb-Williams maze and were more active in initial testing in an open field. No significant differences among the groups were observed on 15 of 16 measures of activity nor in discrimination or reversal learning. The results from cats appeared to be generally similar to those obtained from rats subjected to similar treatments. Some difficulties were discussed that were encountered in attempting to generalize the results of experiments on infantile stimulation across species and treatments.

Infantile stimulation generally reduces emotional reactivity in rats. Rats that have been shocked or handled in infancy are more active and defecate less frequently than unstimulated controls in open field tests, and stimulated rats are less severely distressed than controls in avoidance-learning situations (Denenberg, 1964).

Directly contradictory results have been obtained from mice. Inbred mice of several strains (C57/BL/1, C3H/Bi, DBA/8, JK) subjected to intense auditory stimulation during the first postpartum week are more emotionally reactive (Lindzey, Winston, & Manosevitz, 1963) and less competent in maze learning (Winston, 1963) than control mice. The discrepancy between the results with rats summarized by Denenberg and the findings obtained in the experiments with mice are impossible to interpret unequivocally, since differences in species and the type of infantile stimulation employed are confounded. The mere fact that inconsistent results have been obtained from rats and mice, however, emphasizes the need for investigating more broadly the effects of differential early experience upon the behavior of other species of mammals to determine the generality of the relationships observed in experiments with rats.

This experiment was designed, therefore, to answer three questions concerning the effects of infantile stimulation on the later behavior of cats: (1) Does handling before weaning reduce emotional reactivity in cats as it does in rats? (2) Does exposure to a complex environment after weaning facilitate problem-solving in cats as it does in rats? (3) Are there interactions between the effects of pre- and postweaning experience on the subsequent behavior of cats?

METHOD

Subjects

Forty-one kittens were assigned at birth to one of the following four groups:

Control (C).—These kittens received only the minimum amount of handling compatible with survival during the first 90 days.

Handled (H).—The cats in this group were taken from their cages and petted 5 min./day from birth through the forty-fifth day. All of the kittens vocalized most of the time they were out of the living cage and resisted handling until they were about 20 days old; handling was apparently an unpleasant form of stimulation during this period. The handled group were treated in exactly the same fashion as the controls from days 46 to 96.

Playroom (P).—The kittens in this group were minimally stimulated during the first 45 days. On days 46 through 90 they were placed for 5 hr. per day in a large playroom (15 × 9½ ft.) containing kittens from other litters, toys, boxes, a scratching post, stairs, etc.

Handled plus playroom (HP).—This group was exposed to both experimental treatments, handling from birth to 45 days and the playroom on days 46 through 90.

There were 11 cats in the control group and 10 in each of the other three groups. The split-litter technique was used to the extent possible with variation in litter size about the mean of 4. It should be emphasized that all of the kittens remained with their mothers and litter mates in large (25 × 25 × 29 in.) cages until the age of 90 days. The kittens had an unobstructed view of a busy colony room and ample space for social play. Thus the controls were not subjected to any severe social or perceptual deprivation and may best be described as having been reared under relatively normal laboratory conditions. The three groups of experimental kittens differed from the controls in that they received additional stimulation—preweaning handling, postweaning exposure to a complex environment, or both these treatments—so that the experiment is obviously one concerned with the effects of environmental "enrichment" rather than "impoverishment."

Procedure

From the fourth through the seventh month, all the Ss were observed on four tests, open field, the Hebb-Williams maze, reversal learning, and avoidance conditioning, administered in the same sequence and under identical conditions.

1. *Open field.*—Subjects were released from a start box into a 12 × 12-ft. enclosure with 2-ft. squares ruled on the floor. On every session, two Es recorded the number of squares entered during a 5-min. observation period and starting latency, the time that elapsed between raising the door of the start box and S's exit from the box.

The test was given for 5 days under each of three stimulus conditions: (*a*) with the field empty; (*b*) with toys, different from those used in the playroom, present in the center of the field; and (*c*) with a human, seated on a chair in the center of the enclosure, who gently stroked Ss that approached within easy reach. Under the last two conditions, Es recorded latency to contact with the toys or person present in the field, and the number of 30-sec. periods during which the kitten contacted the stimulus object or approached it within 2 ft. These counts yielded "contact frequency" and "proximity" scores, respectively. The maximum possible values of these scores was 10.

2. Hebb-Williams maze.—The apparatus was a kitten-sized version of the maze for rats standardized by Rabinovitch and Rosvold (1951), a 6 × 6-ft. enclosure with fixed start and goal boxes in diagonally opposite corners. The 18-in. walls and floor of the maze were black; contrasting white barriers, 18-in. high and 1 to 3-ft. long, were arranged in 12 set patterns to constitute the problems illustrated in Rabinovitch and Rosvold (1951).

The Ss were tested under 23 hr. of food deprivation and reinforced with slices of pork kidney. Initial adaptation consisted of training the kittens for 20 trials per day until they were running directly from start to goal within 5 sec. or less on all 20 trials given in a single session. Since this test was given in a room different from those used to provide the playroom experience and to test for activity in the open field, three additional measures of locomotor activity in an unfamiliar environment were obtained during the adaptation period: (*a*) trials to the adaptation criterion, (*b*) median starting latency on the first day of adaptation, and (*c*) median running time on the 20 trials tested on the first day of adaptation. The kittens were then trained on 8 practice and 12 test problems according to the procedures described by Rabinovitch and Rosvold (1951).

3. Reversal learning.—The apparatus consisted of a grey start box, 9-in. wide and 18-in. long, that opened into a grey choice area, 10-in. deep, beyond which were two compartments separated by an opaque wall. The compartment on the right was black, and the one on the left, white; both were 12-in. square.

Subjects were tested 23 hr. after their last feeding and were reinforced with ¼-in. cubes of pork kidney. On the day before discrimination training was begun, each kitten was tested 20 trials with responses to either side rewarded to determine its initial position preference. Training with differential reinforcement began the following day, and S was required to respond to the originally nonpreferred side; 20 trials were given daily until a criterion of 10 consecutive correct responses was attained on the original discrimination and on 10 serial reversals of the positional discrimination habit. The noncorrection method was used throughout.

4. Avoidance conditioning.—The apparatus was a two-compartment shuttle box with a floor made of ⅜-in. round aluminum bars spaced ½ in. apart; the box was painted grey throughout except for glass panels in the sides to facilitate observation. Each compartment was 18 × 24 × 22 in., and a 3-in. barrier, covered with sheet aluminum, and a guillotine door separated the compartments. The shock source, a Model 250 Applegate Constant Current Stimulator, was connected to the grid bars through a shock scrambler and provided a 3.0-ma. shock on every trial.

The Conditioned Stimulus was a door buzzer which was sounded when the door between compartments was raised. Elevation of the door also activated a Hunter interval timer connected to the shock source. If S ran into the other compartment before 5 sec. elapsed he avoided shock. If S failed to respond within 5 sec., shock came on and continued until he escaped to the other compartment or 2 min. had elapsed.

The kittens were tested 20 trials per day, with a balanced irregular sequence of 60-, 90-, 120-, 150-, and 180-sec. intertrial intervals. The criterion was 9 avoidance responses in 10 consecutive trials. The number of spontaneous crossings between the two compartments made by each kitten during a 5-min. period preceding the introduction of shock reinforcement was observed to provide still another measure of spontaneous locomotor activity.

Experimental Design

The scores obtained on all measures of performance in the four testing situations were evaluated by analyses of variance. For handling (Groups C and P *vs.* Groups H and HP), playroom experience (Groups C and H *vs.* Groups P and HP), and the H P interaction, *F*'s were computed with the within-groups mean square as the error term.

RESULTS

The results of analyses on 16 measures of activity and on four measures of learning are summarized in Table 1, which shows the significant prob-

TABLE 1

SUMMARY OF ANALYSES OF VARIANCE

	SOURCE		
DEPENDENT VARIABLE	Handling	Playroom	H × P
Open field:			
Activity	....	.01	....
Starting latency	....	....	....
Open field with toys:			
Activity	....	....	....
Starting latency	....	....	....
Contact latency	....	....	....
Contact frequency	.01	....	....
Proximity	.01	....	....
Open field with human:			
Activity	....	....	....
Starting latency	....	....	....
Contact latency	.01	....	....
Contact frequency	.01	....	....
Proximity	....	....	....
Hebb-Williams maze:			
Starting latency: day 1	....	....	....
Trial time: day 1	....	....	....
Trials in adaption	....	....	....
Total errors	....	.01	....
Discrimination reversal:			
Errors in discrimination learning	....	....	....
Errors in reversal learning	....	....	....
Avoidance:			
Spontaneous crossings	....	....	....
Trials to criterion	.01	....	....

ability values obtained; ellipses indicate that F was not significant at even the 5 per cent level. It is immediately apparent that none of the 20 interactions was significant. Thus, the two forms of stimulation studied in this experiment were statistically independent in regard to their influence on the behaviors measured by our sample of tests.

The statistically significant results are summarized in Figures 1 through 5. Figure 1 shows that kittens handled in infancy (Groups H and HP) spent more time in close proximity to unfamiliar toys and contacted them more frequently than kittens that were not handled in infancy (Groups C and P). Figure 2 shows that the handled groups established contact with humans and spent more time in contact with humans in the open field than the nonhandled groups. The results summarized in Figure 3 indicate that the handled kittens required significantly more trials to learn

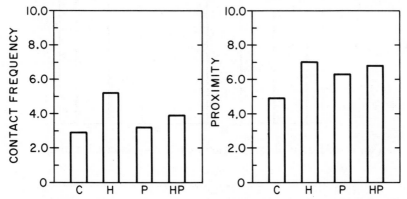

Fig. 1.—Mean contact frequency and proximity scores in the open field with toys.

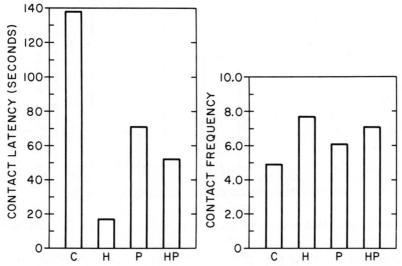

Fig. 2.—Mean contact latency and contact frequency scores in the open field with a human present.

an active avoidance response than the nonhandled kittens. All of these findings suggest that the kittens that were handled before weaning were less "fearful" in later life than the kittens that were not handled before weaning.

The only significant difference between groups in activity was obtained on the first 5 days of testing in the open field. As may be seen in Figure 4, the groups (P and HP) exposed to the playroom after weaning were more active than the groups (C and H) that did not have this experience. It is

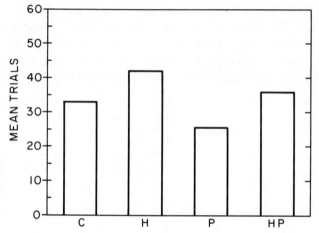

FIG. 3.—Mean trials to criterion in active avoidance learning.

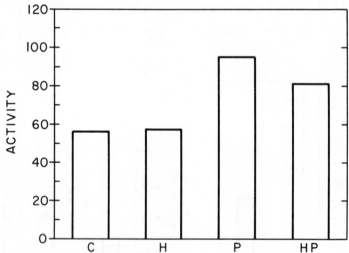

FIG. 4.—Mean activity scores in empty open field.

important to note that under *no* conditions of testing were the cats handled in infancy more active than those that were not handled in infancy.

Mean errors for the four groups of kittens on the Hebb-Williams maze problems are graphed in Figure 5, which shows that the kittens given the playroom experience made approximately 34 per cent fewer errors than the

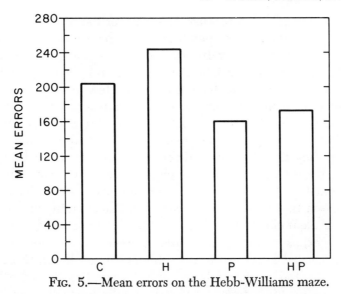

Fig. 5.—Mean errors on the Hebb-Williams maze.

animals that had not been in the playroom, the means being 166 and 223 for the combined groups P and HP and for C and H, respectively.

DISCUSSION

In many respects the findings obtained in this experiment with cats are compatible with observations on rats. Kittens handled daily during infancy were less "fearful" than nonhandled kittens, in that they approached strange toys and humans more readily and required significantly more trials to learn on active avoidance response than unstimulated controls. Early handling often retards avoidance learning by rats (Levine & Wetzel, 1963). Infantile handling does not facilitate performance in the Hebb-Williams maze by rats (Denenberg & Morton, 1964), nor were the handled kittens superior to nonhandled controls on this task.

Kittens that were exposed to a complex free environment after weaning were superior to Ss that had not had this experience in learning the Hebb-Williams maze problems. Comparable results have been obtained in at least six experiments with different strains of rats (Cooper & Zubek, 1958; Denenberg & Morton, 1962; Forgays & Forgays, 1952; Forgays & Read, 1962; Hebb, 1947; Hymovitch, 1952). In addition, cats, like rats (Denenberg & Morton, 1962), that have been in a complex free environment after weaning are more active than controls in an open field.

The results obtained from cats, however, differ from those obtained from rats in two respects. First, handling in infancy does not affect subsequent activity by cats in an open field as it seems to do very consistently in rats (Denenberg, 1964). This difference is of importance chiefly because it illustrates the points that indexes of emotional arousal are often species specific and that a measure which is useful in work with one species may be of no value in research with another. It was never thought for a moment that frequency of defecation in an open field would be a practical index of emotionality in cats. Over the past 10 yr., hundreds of cats have been observed in open-field situations in this laboratory. Never has one defecated. Cats are active predatory animals and have been subjected to little or no selection favoring immobility and huddling in corners as responses to novel environments. Consequently, the fact that kittens that were and were not handled in infancy fail to differ in gross locomotor activity is no more surprising than the fact that they fail to differ in defecation rates. It seems likely that approaching and contacting unfamiliar objects are more valid indexes of the absence of emotional disturbance than simple locomotor activity in cats. It is for this reason that we tentatively conclude that infantile handling has apparently equivalent effects upon later emotionality in cats and rats.

Second, exposure to environmental complexity did not facilitate discrimination reversal learning by cats, although rats (Krech, Rosenzweig, & Bennett, 1962) and dogs (Melzack, 1962) reared in "enriched" environments are superior to controls reared individually in small cages in learning reversals of a brightness discrimination. Our failure to obtain comparable results with cats can not be explained in unequivocal terms. The cats were trained on an easier problem with confounded positional and brightness cues, while the rats and dogs were trained on a nonspatial discrimination task. It seems more probable, however, that the discrepancy reflects the fact that the control groups of kittens were not subjected to nearly as severe social and perceptual deprivation as the deprived rats and dogs. This inference is supported by the absence of emotional abnormalities in our cats compared to the striking disturbances seen in Melzack's dogs (Melzack & Burns, 1963).

Thus the results from cats and rats can be harmonized, at least superficially, but a more general question remains to be considered: What do the studies with animal Ss tell us about the role of early experience in the development of intelligence?

It has often been shown that exposure to environmental complexity facilitates performance on the Hebb-Williams maze problems, but what does this mean with respect to problem-solving ability in general? Is the Hebb-Williams maze a good general measure of "animal intelligence"?

The problems of defining and measuring intelligence in animals have received far too little critical attention, but probably it would be generally agreed that a good test is one that is sensitive to phyletic and ontogenetic differences, a task on which lower vertebrates do less well than higher forms and immature animals less well than older animals. The Hebb-Williams maze must be judged deficient in both these respects. The performance of cats and rhesus monkeys does not improve as a function of chronological age in either species, nor is the performance of the monkeys superior to that of the cats. (Warren, 1965b). Recent research has shown, however, that the ability to improve in performance over a series of reversals of a single discrimination habit is positively correlated with both phyletic status and developmental status within species (Warren, 1965a). Thus, the results of the present experiment with respect to learning are somewhat paradoxical. Exposure to the playroom facilitated performance on the Hebb-Williams maze, which is insensitive to phyletic and maturational variables, but playroom experience did not affect performance on discrimination reversal, a task that is sensitive to differences in taxonomic and maturational status.

Assuming that discrimination reversal is a more generally valid measure of problem-solving capacity, the results of this experiment indicate that kittens that grow up under typical laboratory conditions, without being subjected to unusual social or sensory deprivation, develop essentially normal learning ability. Experience in the playroom is apparently necessary for optimum performance on tests, such as the Hebb-Williams maze, that require precise spatial orientation in similar complex environments but is not necessary for adequate performance in situations like the discrimination box.

This interpretation implies that the amount and variety of stimulation required for the development of normal proficiency in learning by animals varies as a function of the criterion task used. It will be important in future research on the development of intelligence in animals to study a wider variety of learned behaviors and to develop more adequate means for scaling the "impoverishment-enrichment" dimension(s). Only then will students of animal behavior be able to provide a maximally useful comparative perspective on the development of intelligent behavior.

It is necessary to end on a note of caution regarding some of the limitations of this research. Infantile handling appears to produce somewhat similar effects on emotional reactivity in cats and rats, but this finding cannot be generalized to other species and other forms of stimulation at this time. The discrepancy between the results obtained in many experiments with rats (Denenberg, 1964) and the studies of the effects of intense auditory stimulation on the subsequent behavior of baby mice (Lindzey et al., 1963) discussed earlier still exists. The preceding paragraphs indicate the necessity for continued caution in interpreting the effects of exposure to environmental complexity until a wider variety of species is studied under more favorable conditions with respect to the specification of independent variables and to the measurement and analysis of dependent variables.

REFERENCES

Cooper, R. M., & Zubek, J. P. Effects of enriched and restricted early environments on the learning ability of bright and dull rats. *Canad. J. Psychol.*, 1958, **12**, 159–164.

Denenberg, V. H. Critical periods, stimulus input, and emotional reactivity: a theory of infantile stimulation. *Psychol. Rev.*, 1964, **71**, 335–351.

Denenberg, V. H., & Morton, J. R. C. Effects of preweaning and postweaning manipulations upon problem-solving behavior. *J. comp. physiol. Psychol.*, 1962, **55**, 1096–1098.

Denenberg, V. H., & Morton, J. R. C. Infantile stimulation, prepubertal sexual-social interaction, and emotionality. *Animal Behav.*, 1964, **12**, 11–13.

Forgays, D. G., and Forgays, J. W. The nature of the effect of free-environmental experience in the rat. *J. comp. physiol. Psychol.*, 1952, **45**, 322–328.

Forgays, D. G., & Read, J. M. Crucial periods for free-environmental experience in the rat. *J. comp. physiol. Psychol.,* 1962, **55,** 816–818.

Hebb, D. O. The effects of early experience on problem-solving at maturity. *Amer. Psychologist,* 1947, **2,** 306–307. (Abstract)

Hymovitch, B. The effects of experimental variations on problem solving in the rat. *J. comp. physiol. Psychol.,* 1952, **45,** 313–321.

Krech, D., Rosenzweig, M. R., & Bennett, E. L. Relations between brain chemistry and problem solving among rats raised in enriched and impoverished environments. *J. comp. physiol. Psychol.,* 1962, **55,** 801–807.

Levine, S., & Wetzel, A. Infantile experiences, strain differences and avoidance learning. *J. comp. physiol. Psychol.,* 1963, **56,** 879–881.

Lindzey, G., Winston, H. D., & Manosevitz, M. Early experience, genotype and temperament in *Mus musculus. J. comp. physiol., Psychol.,* 1963, **56,** 622-629.

Melzack, R. Effects of early perceptual restriction on simple visual discrimination. *Science,* 1962, **137,** 978–979.

Melzack, R., & Burns, S. K. Neuropsychological effects of early sensory restriction. *Bol. Inst. Estud. Med. Biol. Méx,* 1963, **21,** 407–425.

Rabinovitch, M. S., & Rosvold, H. E. A closed-field intelligence test for rats. *Canad. J. Psychol.,* 1951, **5,** 122-128.

Warren, J. M. The comparative psychology of learning. *Ann. Rev. Psychol.,* 1965, **16,** 95–118. (a)

Warren, J. M. Primate learning in comparative perspective. In A. M. Schrier, H. F. Harlow, & F. Stolnitz (Eds.), *Behavior of nonhuman primates: modern research trends.* New York: Academic Pr., 1965. Pp. 349–382. (b)

Winston, H. D. Influence of genotype and infantile trauma on adult learning in the mouse. *J. comp. physiol. Psychol.,* 1963, **56,** 630–635.

MARION BLANK & FRANCES SOLOMON

47   A Tutorial Language Program To Develop Abstract Thinking in Socially Disadvantaged Preschool Children

A specialized language program was developed to facilitate abstract thinking in young deprived children through short, individual tutoring sessions on a daily basis. The role of individual attention in the experiment was controlled through the use of a comparison group which had daily in-

Reprinted from *Child Development 39*:379–389, 1968. ©1968 by the Society for Research in Child Development, Inc.

This research was supported by U. S. Public Health Service grant K3-MH-10, 749. The authors wish to thank the Bronx River Day Care Center and Miss E. Johnson for their cooperation and participation in this research. A preliminary version of this paper was presented at the meetings of the Society for Research in Child Development, New York, March, 1967.

dividual sessions without the specialized tutoring. A second comparison group was included which consisted of children who received their usual training in the regular nursery school program. The results show a marked gain in IQ for the groups who received the specialized tutoring and no significant gains for the control groups.

Widespread deficiencies ranging across the cognitive, affective, motivational, and social areas have been found in deprived children. Compensatory programs have therefore aimed at exposing the children to a different and wider range of almost every type of stimulus deemed to be beneficial (e.g., better equipment, parent participation, trips, perceptual training). In essence, this approach assumes that all factors contribute an equal amount to the alleviation of the deficits found in the deprived child.

This paper outlines an approach which offers an alternative to the philosophy of total enrichment. The premise of this approach is that, while total enrichment is not without value, it does not diagnose the key deficits of the deprived child. The usual concept of enrichment is also limited by the idea that exposure to the previously absent stimuli is sufficient for learning.

We feel that exposure to an infinite number of ostensibly enriching stimuli does not necessarily overcome the deficits. Presentation alone does not insure that the child will partake of newly available material. If learning is to occur, the child must involve himself actively with the stimuli so as to comprehend their significance. Active involvement refers, not to motor activity, but rather to the internal mental manipulation of experience. The latter applies to skills involving the ability to organize thoughts, to reflect upon situations, to comprehend the meaning of events, and to structure behavior so as to be able to choose among alternatives.

These skills coincide with many of the characteristics defining the abstract attitude (Goldstein, 1959). Research by the senior author (Blank & Bridger, 1964, 1966, 1967) has led us to postulate that the failure to develop this abstract attitude represents the most glaring deficiency of deprived children. *Their behavior reflects the lack of a symbolic system by which to organize the plentiful stimulation surrounding them.*

The problem then arises of what is the most effective means for developing abstract thinking. We feel that an internal symbolic system can best be achieved through the development of abstract language (Vygotsky, 1962). Certain types of language, such as labeling clear, circumscribed objects (e.g., bottle, table, ball), can be grasped easily through illustration and/or imitation. Therefore, no great effort is required to learn these words. By contrast, words referring to properties which are not immediately evident require much elaboration for understanding. For example, a word such as "top" is much more abstract than a word such as "book." The word "top" can refer to such physically different things as the "top" of one's head, the "top" of one's desk, and the "top" of a building. The word unites these instances only when there is an understanding that "top" refers to the highest point on anything, regardless of how different the "anythings" look. Other examples requiring a similar level of abstraction are time (before, after), direction (underneath, between), and relative judgments (warmer, heavier). It is here that an articulate person, be it mother, teacher, or sibling, is required to offer the necessary corroboration or negation of the child's emerging ideas.

This type of feedback is readily available in the middle-class home, but it is rare in the lower-class home (see Freeberg & Payne, 1967). We therefore propose that this lack of an ongoing, elaborated dialogue is the major experiential deficit of the deprived child (Bernstein, 1960).

Previous attempts to transmit this aspect of learning to disadvantaged children have relied on using the group situation (Bereiter & Engelmann, 1966; Deutsch, 1964; Gray & Klaus, 1965). A serious question arises of whether early language skills can be fostered in a group situation or whether we must in some way mirror the middle-class one-to-one situation. For example, if given a direction to "place the red block on top of the blue one," a child in the group setting can wait to see what the other children do and simply *imitate* their action. Of course, the child *might* listen to the language and associate it with the key features of the performance he just imitated. However, this method relies on the hope that the child will avail himself of this opportunity to learn. Nothing inherent in the situation requires him either to heed or to understand the language in order to fulfil the demands placed upon him.

In the latter example, the child at least had to make a response; in many classroom situations, no overt response is required. It is assumed that, when the teacher instructs, the child makes the appropriate inner response even though he is not required to answer overtly. If the inner response is lacking, he cannot follow the dialogue, and the teaching, no matter how well organized, is lost. By contrast, the one-to-one situation can be easily designed so that the child is required to use his language skills, and then he cannot function on a level lower than the goals set by the teacher. In addition, since goals set in individual instruction are designed for the child's specific capabilities, they are more likely to be appropriate.

Although most educators acknowledge that ideal teaching would be a one-to-one relation, this has been deemed impractical because of the costs involved. The conclusion of excessive costs is based on the implicit assumption that individual teaching would or should occupy most of the teaching day. Little consideration has been given to the possible effectiveness of short periods of daily individual instruction, even though such instruction is widely and effectively used in the initial teaching of language to other language-deficient groups, such as deaf children (Blank, 1965). In addition, the limited attention spans of young children suggest that relatively brief sessions involving frequent reinforcement of new (language) skills would theoretically be the most effective means of teaching.

In summary, our assumptions were:

1. Deprived preschool children do not have a firm language base for thinking. They will develop one only if they are given consistent guidance.

This leads to the further assumption that the most effective teaching is based on individual tutoring.

2. Language acquisition, like any new complex skill, may be met with some resistance. To prevent resistance from becoming established, the child should not be permitted to leave a task unfinished. If necessary, the task can be simplified, but the child should still be required to fulfil the demands set by the teacher. Once these initial difficulties have been conquered, the child is able to experience great pleasure both in using this new tool and in knowing that he has this tool to use.

3. Young children have short attention spans and therefore need relatively brief but frequent reinforcement of new skills (i.e., 5 days a week for 15–20 minutes each day, resulting in a total of about 1½ hours of tutoring per week).

4. The new command of language will allow the child to cope more effectively with an otherwise debilitating environment. Therefore, marked improvements in many aspects of maladaptive behavior should occur.

Based on these considerations, an exploratory program was developed which involved brief daily teaching of language skills for abstract thinking. The central hypothesis was that intervention limited to the development of language for reflection would play such a vital role in cognition that it would facilitate not only language but many other aspects of thinking.

METHOD

Teaching Techniques

Even though we are stressing abstract language, we are not deceived into thinking that the young child is capable of the highest level of concept formation. His concepts must still be bound to direct referents because he needs some tangible evidence of the idea being demonstrated. Nevertheless, the young child can be taught to bring to his level of conceptualization the processes of thinking vital to the development of abstraction.

The first goal of the teaching was to have the child recognize that information relevant to his world was not immediately evident but could be and *had* to be sought from his previous experience. Thus he was taught to question, to probe, to investigate. For example, the teacher put on her coat at the end of a session. The child said, "Why are you going home?" The teacher replied, "How do you know I am going home?" to which the child said, "You're not going home?" This response meant that the child had dropped any attempt at reasoning; he had interpreted the teacher's query to mean that he must negate his earlier inference. To encourage the child to pursue the matter, the teacher said "I *am* going home, but what makes you think I am going home? When you get ready to go home, what do you do?" The child said, "I get my coat." A discussion then followed to solidify the significance of these observations. Thus Socratic dialogue was employed instead of didactic teaching.

Various teaching methods were devised to achieve these goals. A common denominator of all the methods was that the child was confronted with situations in which the teacher used no gestures; to accomplish the task correctly, the child had to understand and/or use language. Another consistent factor was that the child was led to produce an independent response relevant to a situation created by the teacher and to extend the situation set forth by her. This extension focused on having the child discuss situations which did not exist in front of him at the moment but which were relevant to the present situations (e.g., past, future, alternative courses of action, giving explanations of events). By structuring the teaching time in this way, the teacher made maximum use of every opportunity to aid the child in developing his budding ability to think and to reflect. Some of the major techniques used are described below. As the work progresses, we hope to expand and refine this list. It should be noted that each technique is specifically geared to overcome a particular deficiency. This is in contrast to the concept of an enriched environment where the aim is to give a massive dosage that will somehow hit the individual deficiencies. Specifically, the method attempted to develop the following:

a) Selective attention.—The young child has few guidelines to assist him in discriminating selectively from the plethora of stimuli which surround him. He tends to be drawn to stimuli which may not be of great cognitive importance but which have potent perceptual qualities (e.g., blast of a horn, a whirling disk). The aim of this technique was to teach the child to recognize essential elements by requiring him to compare objects and make choices among them (e.g., if given a group of different-colored blocks, he was asked to take "two red blocks and one green block"). In this example, the higher-level concept of number helps the child restrain his impulse to respond primitively to the sensory impact of color alone.

b) Categories of exclusion.—When the adult gives specific instructions (e.g., "get a crayon"), the child does not need to reflect upon the characteristics of a particular category; he merely responds to direct commands. When the adult gives no direction, the child works aimlessly. When the child can work within the confines of exclusion, however, it means that he has understood the teacher's frame of reference and can independently make appropriate responses. To develop this skill, the child may be asked to make decisions within the confines set by the teacher. For example, the child may be asked to draw something, and he may draw a circle. To encourage the development of exclusion, he would then be asked to draw something "other than a circle."

c) Imagery of future events.—The young child can easily describe existing objects and situations. Difficulty arises when he must perceive the meaning of this information relevant to a particular context (see John, 1963). To increase this capacity, the child was required to think through the results of realistically possible but not present courses of action. The child might be first asked to locate a doll that was on the table. After the child completed this correctly, the doll would remain on the table, and the child might be asked, "Where would the doll be if it fell from the table?"

d) Relevant inner verbalization.—We have found that many deprived children will use language to direct their problem-solving only when asked to; they will not spontaneously use language when these external requirements are not imposed. Thus it is not a matter of not having the words but rather a matter of not voluntarily using these words without specific demands. This technique attempts to train the children to develop inner verbalization by retaining words as substitutes for objects. In this method, the child must use language silently and then express it upon request. He might be asked to look at a picture, say the name to himself, and then after the picture has been removed tell the name to the teacher.

e) Separation of the word from its referent.—Young children tend to respond to language automatically without fully recognizing that the word exists independently of the object or action represented. If this separation is not achieved, the child will not generalize the meaning of words beyond the particular contexts in which he hears them. To encourage the ability to reflect upon meaning, the child might be given a command which he must repeat aloud *before* acting out the command—for example, "Jump up two times," "Walk to the door and open it."

f) Models for cause-and-effect reasonings.—Our research (Blank & Bridger, 1966, 1967) has indicated that the perceptual powers of deprived children are intact; they need help, however, in organizing their observations so as to comprehend their significance. To achieve this comprehension, the child can be led to observe common but not frequently noted phenomena (e.g., "What is the weather outside today?" "Can we go out and play today?"). He can then be asked to draw upon his previous experience to determine the reasons underlying these observations (e.g., "Why can't we go out and play?" "Where is the rain coming from?").

g) Ability to categorize.—The place of categorization in thinking has been well documented, and its importance was recognized in this project. To aid the children in this sphere, elementary categories such as food, clothing, transportation, and job functions were taught. Thus, after feeding a doll an imaginary apple, the child was asked to name some other fruits that the doll might eat. Then, utilizing the process of exclusion (*b* above), the child might be asked to name some foods that were *not* fruits.

h) Awareness of possessing language.—Frequently young children are only passive recipients of instruction. This deficiency means that they are unaware that they can independently invoke language to help order their world. This weakness can be overcome by techniques such as asking the child to give commands to the teacher. The teacher might say to the child, "What shall I do with these pencils?" "Now *you* ask *me* to draw something," "Now tell me what the doll should do this afternoon."

i) Sustained sequential thinking.—Just as musical notes attain their full meaning only when heard within a melody, words attain their full potential only when imbedded in context. This is true even at the elementary level of a simple sentence, and it becomes increasingly important as chains of events extending into time and space must be understood. To be able to see objects, events, and words as located within their appropriate framework, the child has to be taught to maintain concentration and to determine all the possibilities of a course of action. For example, in discussing ways in which material can be altered, the discussion might begin with vegetable dyes (their function, their appearance, etc.). The issue can then be raised as to what can happen to these dyes under various conditions (diluting them with water, leaving them in concentrated form, etc.). In each case, the child is required to apply the necessary change (e.g., add the water) so that he can directly and immediately experience the phenomenon being discussed.

These techniques for achieving higher mental processes are in contrast to the language programs stressing concepts as an end in themselves. In our view, concepts were seen as the necessary preliminary tools for thinking; accordingly, they occupied only a segment of the program. The type of concept taught could not be illustrated by simple direct examples or simple labeling. For example, to call an object a "book" may facilitate communication, but it does not serve to abstract anything more of the object than does a gesture. In addition, the child who can label glibly is often deceptive, since his facile use of words gives the false appearance of understanding. Concepts such as number, speed, direction, temperature, and emotions are suitable for stressing the more abstract functions of language. Techniques for teaching these concepts have been well documented by Bereiter and Englemann (1966).

Common inexpensive objects readily available in the child's environment were the only ones used in the teaching, (e.g., papers, crayons, blocks, toy cars, simple books). The materials were used only as points of departure from which the child could discuss increasingly abstract (non-presently-existing) situations which were relevant to the materials. The same materials, when used alone by the child without supervision, might prove useless in terms of the aims of the study—namely, the avoidance of aimless, scattered, stimulus-bound activity.

Subjects and Procedure

The subjects were selected from a nursery school in a socioeconomically deprived area in New York City. All 22 children from the youngest classes were tested on the Stanford-Binet Intelligence Test (S-B Test) and the Leiter Scale. The children ranged in age from 3 years, 3 months to 4 years, 7 months. Based on these test results, the children were divided into four groups, two tutored and two untutored, matched as closely as possible for IQ, age, and sex. Each child in the first tutored group received individual teaching for 15–20 minutes daily, five times per week; each child in the second tutored group received the same training only three times a week. This tutoring involved taking the child for this short period from his classroom to a familiar room in the school. Each child in one untutored group had daily individual sessions with the same teacher, but no attempt was made to tutor the child. During this time, the child was exposed to the identical materials and was permitted to engage in any activity of his choice. While the teacher was warm and responsive to the child's questions and comments, she did not initiate or extend any cognitive interchange. This group was included to control for the possible role of individual attention alone in facilitating intellectual performance. Another untutored group of seven children remained in the regular nursery school program with no additional attention.

All the tutoring was conducted by a professional nursery school teacher who was trained in the techniques outlined above. The experiment took place over a 4-month period, after which the children were retested. Both the pre- and posttesting were conducted by two research assistants who did not know to which of the groups the children had been assigned and who had had no contact with the children other than at the time of testing.

RESULTS

The pre- and posttest results on the S-B Test are shown in Table 1. Mean IQ increases in tutored groups 1 and 2 were 14.5 and 7.0 points, respectively; in untutored groups 1 and 2, the changes were 2.0 and 1.3 points, respectively. A Kruskal-Wallis analysis of variance indicated that the changes in the four groups were significantly different ($p < .05$). A Mann-Whitney Test indicated that the rise in the tutored groups was significantly greater than the rise in the untutored groups ($p < .02$). Although the difference was not significant, the gain by the group tutored five times a week was greater than that of the group tutored three times a week. This suggests that improvements in performance may be directly correlated to the amount of tutoring per week. The lack of a clear difference in gain between the two untutored groups indicates that the element of individual attention from an adult without specialized tutoring was not sufficient to achieve the rise in IQ scores.

The results on the Leiter Scale, though somewhat less marked, are in accord with those on the S-B Test. Thus, tutored groups 1 and 2 showed mean increases of 4.5 and 9.5, respectively, while untutored groups 1 and 2 showed 5.0 and 1.9, respectively. The lower overall gains on the Leiter Scale may also be a reflection of the fact that this test does not require verbal abilities, while the teaching techniques emphasized verbal development. The Leiter scores, however, showed erratic variations. For example, untutored children who remained in the classroom showed spontaneous losses and gains of up to 20 points. This result leads us to believe that the Leiter performance is not a reliable indicator of functioning at this age range.

These IQ changes must also be evaluated in conjunction with the dramatic behavioral changes that accompanied these rises. For example, three of the children were so excessively withdrawn that they had not ut-

TABLE 1

PRE- AND POSTTEST STANFORD-BINET SCORES

			IQ		
SEX	AGE[a]	TOTAL HOURS TUTORED	Pre	Post	Change
Tutored group 1 (5 times/wk.):					
F1..................	3.8	11	70	98	+28
F2..................	3.11	11	100	109	+9
F3..................	3.4	13	104	115	+11
M1..................	3.3	12	111	127	+16
M2..................	3.11	14	90	109	+19
M3..................	3.7	14	111	115	+4
Mean.............			97.7	112.2	+14.5
Tutored group 2 (3 times/wk.):					
F4..................	3.9	8	89	105	+16
F5..................	4.7	6	86	98	+12
F6..................	4.5	7	103	103	0
F7..................	3.3	6	79[b]	96	+17
M4..................	3.11	9	94	93	−1
M5..................	4.0	5	107	105	−2
Mean.............			93.0	100.0	+7.0
Untutored group 1 (5 times/wk.):					
F8..................	4.1	13	107	111	+4
M6..................	4.4	10	101	99	−2
M7..................	4.2	11	80	84	+4
Mean.............			96.0	98.0	+2.0
Untutored group 2 (classroom):					
F9..................	4.6	...	97	99	+2
F10.................	3.5	...	105	107	+2
F11.................	3.11	...	105	103	−2
F12.................	4.2	...	117	114	−3
M8..................	4.2	...	115	124	+9
M9..................	4.2	...	88	88	0
M10.................	3.5	...	93	94	+1
Mean.............			102.8	104.1	+1.3

[a] Age at beginning of study.
[b] No basal score was achieved; a basal MA of 2 years was assumed for the calculations, thus overestimating the score.

tered any coherent verbalizations during their entire time in school. They also exhibited other severe symptoms, such as drooling, "ramlike" head-butting, and bizarre physical coordination. Within 1 month after the program was started, all three were speaking clearly, coherently, and appropriately, and there was a diminution of all symptomatology. No comparable changes were noted in the two children from the control groups who exhibited similar symptomatology.

Even among the children who were relatively well functioning, striking improvements were found. For example, on the S-B Test the pretest response of one girl in describing a picture was "a lady, a horse"; the posttest response was, "The mother is trying to catch the dog with the clothes, the dog takes the clothes, and the mother was trying to get it." This response illustrates the growth from simple labeling to a coordinated, sequential story construction.

The most striking gains in the program were the apparent joy in learning and the feeling of mastery which the children displayed as the tutoring progressed. The untutored children, even those who received individual attention, showed none of these attitudes. This result is extremely important in that it strongly suggests that exposure to materials, a school-like situation, and an interested adult is not sufficient for learning. Both mastery and enthusiasm for learning will come only when the child can be shown how to become actively involved in the learning process.

DISCUSSION

The program outlined above is offered as a means of teaching those language skills necessary for developing abstract thinking in disadvantaged preschool children. We feel that most enrichment programs, and indeed most nursery school programs, are remiss in this area. It is generally assumed that abstract thinking will evolve naturally by school age from having an enriched environment available in the early years. This expectation is often met in the case of middle-class children, because the skills not taught by the nursery school are learned in the verbally rich home environment. In the case of the lower-class child, these experiences are not available.

Although the disadvantaged child has not been given the necessary tools for thinking, there are implicit expectations when he enters school that he has a well-formulated abstract attitude. For example, multiple-choice questions are common in reading-readiness tests. Aside from the content, this type of question assumes that the child can evaluate a series sequentially, can refocus attention selectively, and can realize that he must make a definitive choice between alternatives. How is this abstract attitude to emerge? Our research indicates that high-level language skills are central to the development of this kind of thinking. Even at the preschool level, there are tasks for which abstract language is the only means of solution (Blank & Bridger, 1964). Therefore, it is risky to hope that the "fallout" from a perceptually enriched environment will encourage the formation of what is the central core of intelligence.

Even where the language deficits of the deprived preschooler are recognized, they are treated through enlarging the vocabulary, since vocabulary is seen as the basic unit of language. Implicit in this approach is that, as in perceptual training, mere exposure to the basic units will "lubricate" the entire language system. It is our thesis that these children do not simply need more and better words; rather, they need to use the language they already have, as well as any new words they learn, to structure and guide their thinking.

Although this approach benefited the children in this study, its full potential needs further exploration. In addition, it is believed that the program would have to be maintained for a considerable period of time, probably for about 2–3 years, for the gain to be maintained independently thereafter by the child. Reasoning is still difficult for these children, and they need continuing guidance for it to become firmly established. However, considering the amount of time (approximately 60–90 minutes per week per child), the low cost of the materials, and the rapid gains in performance, it seems worthwhile to pursue this program as a technique for facilitating cognitive growth in young children from deprived backgrounds.

REFERENCES

Bereiter, C., & Engelmann, S. *Teaching disadvantaged children in the preschool.* Englewood Cliffs, N.J.: Prentice Hall, 1966.

Bernstein, B. Language and social class. *British Journal of Sociology,* 1960, **2**, 271–276.

Blank, M. Use of the deaf in language studies: a reply to Furth. *Psychological Bulletin,* 1965, **63**, 442–444.

Blank, M., & Bridger, W. H. Cross-modal transfer in nursery school children. *Journal of Comparative and Physiological Psychology,* 1964, **58**, 277–282.

Blank, M., & Bridger, W. H. Deficiencies in verbal labeling in retarded readers. *American Journal of Orthopsychiatry,* 1966, **36**, 840–847.

Blank, M., & Bridger, W. H. Perceptual abilities and conceptual deficiencies in retarded readers. In J. Zubin (Ed.), *Psychopathology of Mental Development.* New York: Grune & Stratton, 1967, 401–412.

Deutsch, M. Facilitating development in the preschool child: social and psychological perspectives. *Merrill-Palmer Quarterly,* 1964, **10**, 249–263.

Freeburg, N. E., & Payne, D. T. Parental influence on cognitive development in early childhood: a review. *Child Development,* 1967, **38**, 65–87.

Goldstein, K. Functional disturbances in brain damage. In S. Arieti (Ed.), *American Handbook of Psychiatry.* Vol. 1. New York: Basic Books, 1959, 770–794.

Gray, S. W., & Klaus, R. A. An experimental preschool program for culturally deprived children. *Child Development,* 1965, **36**, 887–898.

John, V. P. The intellectual development of slum children: some preliminary findings. *American Journal of Orthopsychiatry,* 1963, **33**, 813–822.

Vygotsky, L. S. *Thought and language.* New York: Wiley, 1962.

Chapter Eleven

INFANTILE STIMULATION

One of the most surprising findings emerging from the research on early experiences is that experimental manipulations which appear innocuous can have powerful and long-lasting effects upon the developing organism. This is probably most clearly illustrated by the procedure called "handling," which is used as a method of stimulating animals, primarily rodents, between birth and weaning. Handling consists of removing the newborn young from the nest box — generally the mother is left in the cage, but in some experimental procedures she is removed beforehand — and placing them into containers where they remain for 3 minutes. At the end of this time the young are gathered together and returned to the nest box. This procedure is generally repeated daily until the animals are weaned — usually at 21 days, sometimes as late as 30 days. This procedure seems so trivial that the initial reports on the effects of handling which appeared in the middle and late 1950's were greeted with some degree of skepticism. However, the broad principle that handling in infancy has major effects upon a variety of behavioral and biological capacities of the organism was soon verified by a number of reports from different laboratories.

Another interesting report published at the same time indicated that electric shock, when administered to young animals between birth and weaning, also modified the animal's subsequent behavior and biology. In fact, electric shock and handling in many instances were found to yield the same results. This was unexpected, since eletric shock is such an apparently traumatic event, at least to the eyes and ears of the human observer, while handling appears to be such a neutral event. Still more surprising was the finding that electric shock administered to animals between birth and weaning generally resulted in an *improvement* in the animal's biobehavioral characteristics. This was unexpected because many researchers have been influenced by Freudian theory and the general notion that trauma in infancy is inherently bad for the developing organism. The expectation, therefore, was that animals shocked in infancy would be less able to adapt to circumstances of later life, and the finding of contrary results brought into question some of the psychoanalytical tenets. It should be emphasized that handling or electric shock must occur between birth and weaning to produce these results. If done after weaning, it may produce no effects or diametrically opposite effects. For a review of much of this literature, see Denenberg (1969).

Because handling and electric shock had similar effects, many researchers concluded that handling must be "stressful" because electric shock was stressful. This assumption was not verified until recently when Denenberg *et al.* (1967) found that handling the 2-day-old rat resulted in secretion of the hormone corticosterone from the adrenal cortex of the neonatal animal. This hormone is released as a response to novel or noxious stimuli and is part of the homeostatic control mechanism involved in the alarm reaction.

Why does handling have such extensive effects, and how can we place this laboratory manipulation into the context of the naturally developing animal? We will consider the second question first. Operationally the procedure of handling requires that the pups and mother be disturbed. The pups are removed and placed into an environment different from their nest (some of these differences include a lower temperature, more lighting, and new odors) and are then returned to their mother, who picks them up, carries them about, and replaces them in the nest. There are two consequences of all this: (1) the pups are exposed to a wider range of stimulation and to greater stimulus variability when they are removed from the nest, and (2) the young receive extra maternal attention and stimulation when they are returned to the nest. But note that the stimulus changes brought about by handling the pups are the kinds of changes which may also occur when the mother interacts with her litter. That is, at times she herself disturbs the litter and scatters the young around, thus exposing them to changes in temperature, brightness, and so on; and she then retrieves the young, grooms them, nurses them, and places them back into the nest. Thus, handling may be thought of as a simulator of certain aspects of the mother's behavior toward her pups.

The first question — why does handling have such extensive effects? — is more difficult to answer. We indicated earlier that handling in infancy causes the release of the hormone corticosterone from the adrenal cortex. Other forms of stimulation, such as heat and electric shock, also cause a corticosterone release (Haltmeyer et al., 1966). More recently Zarrow et al. (1968), using radioactive corticosterone, showed that this hormone goes into the brain after release from the adrenal gland, with particular concentration in the hypothalamus. Denenberg and Zarrow (1971) and Levine (1969) have hypothesized that corticosterone acts upon the developing brain to change many of the animal's behavioral and physiological activities, usually in an adaptive manner. Further discussion of this topic is beyond the scope of this book, and the interested reader is referred to the papers by Denenberg and Zarrow and by Levine.

Several generalities have emerged from the research on infantile stimulation. One is that infantile stimulation leads to more rapid maturation of several biological processes. Paper 48 illustrates this point by demonstrating that handling results in precocious sexual development in the rat.

A second generalization is that the handled animal is more curious and exploratory than one who has not received such stimulation in infancy. Paper 49 documents this by showing that the stimulated animal seeks out stimulation, while the nonhandled control avoids excess stimulation.

Another broad generalization is that animals receiving stimulation in infancy are less emotionally reactive than nonstimulated controls. Papers 50 and 51 are concerned with that principle. Levine et al. obtained both behavioral and physiological measures of emotional reactivity from their handled and nonhandled animals and showed that the handled animals were less reactive behaviorally (measured by activity and defecation in the open field) and physiologically (measured by the amount of corticosterone in the blood). Levine (Paper 51) described both a handled and a shocked group which could be compared with each other as well as with a nonhandled control group. He found that both the shocked group and the group receiving extra stimulation without shock (i.e., the handled group, which is called NS for "not shocked" in this paper) were less emotional as measured by a consummatory behavior index. Special note should be taken of the procedure and rationale for measuring consummatory behavior. Rats are deprived of water for some time and the amount they ingest when the water bottle is replaced on the cage is recorded. The rationale is that thirst is a novel internal stimulus which engenders a state of emotional upset. The animal which is least emotional would be expected to recover most rapidly when the bottle is replaced and should drink the greatest amount of water. An important methodological point is that this behavior can be measured without handling the rats in adulthood. Since Levine obtained significant effects, the argument that there is some specific carry-over or transfer from handling in infancy to handling in the adult test situation is eliminated. In addition to the behavioral results, Levine found that the handled rats weighed more in adulthood than did the controls.

This finding of a body-weight difference is another generality that has emerged from research on infantile stimulation and it formed the basis of a study by Landauer and Whiting (Paper 52) which attempted to test one of the principles of infantile stimulation at the human level. They tested the principle that stress during early infancy would result in greater physical growth. Landauer and Whiting approached this problem on a cross-cultural basis by using the Human Relations Area Files at Harvard to classify a number of primitive tribes according to whether they engaged in stressful infant care practices (such as piercing or molding) during the first 2 years of life. The height of the adult male was found to be approximately 2.5 inches greater in tribes which did engage in such practices than in tribes where the infant was not exposed to stress. These findings were confirmed in a second independent replication. In addition to being intrinsically interesting, the Landauer and Whiting paper is important in showing how principles derived from research at the animal level can be cleverly tested at the human level. One caution: The fact that they were able to obtain similar findings in their study does not mean that the principle tested has been proved at the human level; it does add substance to the generality.

It was indicated earlier that handling results in a considerable increase in the range and variability of stimuli to which the young animal is exposed and that handled animals generally benefit from such stimulation both physiologically and behaviorally. It would therefore be expected that lack of stimulation and stimulus variability would be detrimental to the growth and development of the young organism. One way to achieve such a lack is to rear the neonate under sensory deprivation (see Chapter Nine). However, it is not necessary to employ a sensorily deprived environment; a sensorily *constant* environment is almost as deleterious because the newborn habituates to the constant sensory input. Unless there is *variation* in stimu-

lation, the organism reacts as though there is no stimulation.

Such a sensorily constant environment is found in the incubator used for the premature baby. The baby is maintained under constant temperature, constant light, and constant noise from the air pump, and is disturbed by the nursing staff only when necessary for feeding and diaper changing. One would expect that the introduction of stimulus variation into this monotonous environment would be beneficial to the premature baby, and that is the hypothesis which Solkoff *et al.* investigated in the experiment reported in Paper 53. To stimulate their experimental infants they used a procedure which they called "handling." While their procedure differs considerably from that used with rodents, both techniques are similar in giving stimulus variation to the newborn.

Their handled babies were more active, regained their birth weight faster, and were physically healthier than the nonstimulated controls — findings consistent with the data from the animal literature on handling. We must repeat the caution applied to Paper 52: obtaining similar findings with humans in one study does not mean that the principle derived from extensive animal research has been validated at the human level; it merely adds substance to the generality of that principle. In addition, Solkoff *et al.* studied only a small number of babies and were therefore unable to apply standard statistical analyses to the data (see the editor's note at the end of the paper). In spite of these limitations the paper is important because it shows how an investigator can integrate findings and principles from animal research with human clinical observations to attack an important practical problem, i.e., what is the best environment in which to rear the premature baby.

References

Denenberg, V. H. The effects of early experience. In E. S. E. Hafez (Ed.). *The Behaviour of Domestic Animals,* 2nd ed. London, Balliere, 1969, pp. 95-130.

Denenberg, V. H. Brumaghim, J. T., Haltmeyer, G. C., and Zarrow, M. X. Increased adrenocortical activity in the neonatal rat following handling. *Endocrinology,* 1967, 81, 1047-1052.

Denenberg, V. H., and Zarrow, M. X. Effects of handling in infancy upon adult behavior and adrenocortical activity: Suggestions for a neuro-endocrine mechanism. In D. N. Walcher and D. L. Peters (Eds.). *Early Childhood: The Development of Self-Regulating Mechanisms.* New York: Academic Press, 1971, pp. 39-64.

Haltmeyer, G. C., Denenberg, V. H., Thatcher, J., and

Zarrow, M. X. Response of the adrenal cortex of the neonatal rat after subjection to stress. *Nature,* 1966, 212, 1371-1373.

Levine, S. An endocrine theory of infantile stimulation. In A. Ambrose (Ed.). *Stimulation in Early Infancy.* New York: Academic Press, 1969, pp. 45-55.

Zarrow, M. X., Philpott, J. E., Denenberg, V. H., and O'Connor, W. B. Localiation of ^{14}C-4-corticosterone in the 2 day old rat and a consideration of the mechanism involved in early handling. *Nature,* 1968, 218, 1264-1265.

JOHN R. C. MORTON, VICTOR H. DENENBERG, & M. X. ZARROW

48 Modification of Sexual Development Through Stimulation in Infancy

THE PRESENTATION of extrinsic stimulation during infancy to rats and mice has been shown to result in marked behavioral and physiologic changes in adulthood. The two techniques most commonly used to introduce extrinsic stimulation have been a procedure called handling (defined below) and electric shock. Usually, though not always, animals stimulated in infancy have been found to do better on simple learning tasks, to be more active and to defecate less in a strange and noxious environment, to weigh more, and to be more resistant to a variety of stressors. See Denenberg (1) for a general review of the literature.

In a series of experiments, Levine (2) has reported that stimulation in infancy can lead to earlier physiologic growth and development. For example, rats handled in infancy show a significant depletion of adrenal ascorbic acid at 12

Reprinted from *Endocrinology* 72:439–442, 1963.

This research was supported, in part, by a grant from the Purdue Research Foundation and by Research Grant M-1753 from the National Institute of Mental Health, National Institutes of Health, USPHS.

ABSTRACT. Newborn rat pups were either handled for 3 min/day for the first 24 days of life or else they were not disturbed during this interval. After weaning at 25 days, females were raised either in groups or individually. Rupturing of the vaginal membrane and onset of estrus occurred significantly earlier for females which were handled in infancy and group-reared after weaning.

Males were sacrificed at 35, 41 or 47 days; the testes, prostates and seminal vesicles were excised and weighed. The seminal vesicles and prostates of handled rats were found to be significantly heavier than those of unhandled controls. No differences were found for testes weight.

days of age, while controls do not show such a response until 16 days (3). In another study, Levine and Alpert (4) found that rats handled for the first 11 days of life had a significantly greater amount of brain cholesterol present at 12 days of age than nonstimulated controls.

No research has been done relating preweaning stimulation to sexual development, though observations have suggested that handling in infancy resulted in a more rapid onset of sexual maturity. The purpose of the present experiments was to study systematically the effects of infantile stimulation upon sexual development in the male and the female rat.

Materials and Methods

Subjects

Pregnant Purdue-Wistar rats were placed into 9 in. ×9 in. ×15 in. maternity cages containing a tray bottom partially filled with shavings. A food hopper and water bottle were attached to the outside of the wire mesh front door. Cages were inspected each morning and the date of birth was recorded as the previous day unless it was apparent that the young had just been born. All litters were reduced to 8 pups when first found. After the litter was born, the shavings in the cage were not changed until weaning at 25 days.

Complete litters were randomly assigned to the undisturbed control condition or the experimental handling condition. Handling consisted of removing the tray containing the young, leaving the mother in the cage, and placing each pup into a one gallon container partially filled with shavings. The young were left in the containers for 3 min and then returned to the home cage. This was done once daily from day 1 through day 24. The control litters were never disturbed until weaning. In all, there were 61 handled females, 71 unhandled females, 50 handled males and 41 unhandled males.

All animals were weaned at 25 days and assigned to the experimental conditions described below.

Postweaning Experience: Females

Individual Rearing. Twelve handled and 11 unhandled females were put into Wahmann activity wheels at 25 days of age, while 9 handled and 12 unhandled females were placed individually into cages. Starting at 30 days, all animals were checked daily for vaginal membrane rupturing and for onset of estrus as determined by cornification of the vaginal smear.

Group Rearing. After weaning, 6 handled females were placed into a large group cage and 5 handled females into a second group cage. There were 3 cages of unhandled females containing 6, 6 and 5 animals. Starting at 30 days, the animals were checked daily for vaginal opening and appearance of first estrus.

Twenty-nine handled and 31 unhandled females were housed 5 to a cage except for one cage which contained 4 unhandled females and another cage with 6 unhandled females. At 30 days of age, 2 experienced male breeders were placed into each cage nightly and removed in the morning. Females were inspected for vaginal membrane rupture, and smears were taken to determine when estrus occurred and when sperm was first deposited.

Postweaning Experience: Males

Males were housed 3 to a cage until killed at 35, 41 or 47 days. Testes, prostate and seminal vesicles were excised, stripped free of excess tissue, and weighed on a torsion balance.

Results

Females

Table 1 summarizes the mean age of vaginal membrane rupture for the eight treatment groups. Vaginal opening oc-

TABLE 1. Means and standard deviations for age of vaginal opening in rats

Preweaning Handling	Postweaning Environment Conditions			
	Group Reared		Individually Reared	
	Without Males	With Males	Cages	Activity Wheels
Handled				
Mean	39.09	38.93	40.22	39.58
SD	2.30	3.72	4.33	4.17
N	11	29	9	12
Not Handled				
Mean	44.71	41.84	41.83	38.18
SD	3.12	4.85	3.01	5.08
N	17	31	12	11
t Ratio	6.93	2.45	1.02	.233
P	< .01	< 05	> .10	> .10

TABLE 2. Mean and standard deviations for age of first estrus in rats

| | Group Reared | | Individually Reared | |
	Without Males	With Males	Cages	Activity Wheels
Handled				
Mean	40.88	39.38	40.22	40.67
SD	3.18	3.08	4.32	3.23
N	8*	29	9	12
Not Handled				
Mean	51.00	43.42	44.16	41.09
SD	4.05	6.66	5.69	4.53
N	10†	31	12	11
t Ratio	5.77	3.00	1.81	.068
P	<.01	<.01	<.10	>.10

* Three of 11 animals did not show an estrus smear.
† Seven of 17 animals did not show an estrus smear.

curred significantly earlier for animals handled in infancy and group-reared after weaning. There were no significant differences among the groups which were raised in isolation after weaning.

The time of occurrence of first estrus (Table 2) parallels the data on vaginal opening. Cornified smears were obtained significantly earlier for those females which received infantile handling and were group-reared after weaning. There is also some evidence that this phenomenon is present when the rats are individually reared in cages, since the mean difference approaches significance (*P* <.10).

No significant difference was found between handled and unhandled rats with respect to age of deposition of first sperm (mean age for handled females =41.79 days; mean age for unhandled females =44.74 days; *t*=1.22; *P*>.10). This failure to find a significant difference may be artifactual. Observations indicated that a full-grown male breeder had difficulty in mounting the young females and thus achieving intromission and ejaculation. The size factor appears important, because the handled females seemed to be more docile and receptive toward the approaches of the males than the unhandled controls.

The handled females ran more in the activity wheels than did the controls (mean number of revolutions per day =3,521 *vs.* 2,245), but this difference was

TABLE 3. Mean organ weights and standard deviations in mg/100 g of body weight at three ages for rats handled or not disturbed in infancy

Treatment	N	Age in Days		Testes	Seminal Vesicles	Prostate
Control	14	35	Mean	726.6	20.0	51.9
			SD	184.8	4.3	14.4
Handled	14	35	Mean	759.8	29.7	73.7
			SD	120.3	6.2	16.0
Control	14	41	Mean	943.4	25.5	65.7
			SD	131.4	4.2	11.4
Handled	16	41	Mean	964.9	26.3	64.1
			SD	15.0	3.9	11.9
Control	13	47	Mean	1,051.3	39.8	68.0
			SD	237.9	12.7	12.6
Handled	20	47	Mean	1,123.3	46.1	66.7
			SD	142.0	10.3	10.7

not significant because of the great variation within each of the groups.

Males

Table 3 summarizes the findings on the testes, seminal vesicles and prostates. All weights were converted to mg/100 g of body weight and then evaluated by use of the analysis of variance. No significant difference was found between the testicle weights of handled and unhandled males. A significant difference ($P < .01$) between males handled in infancy and controls was found for the seminal vesicle weight throughout the age range studied. The prostate of handled males was found to be significantly heavier than that of controls ($P < .01$) at 35 days of age; no significant differences were found at the other two ages.

Discussion

The data indicate that stimulation in infancy results in earlier sexual development of males and females. In addition, the variable of social grouping must be considered, at least in the female. When the females were group-reared after weaning, the rats handled in infancy had earlier vaginal membrane rupture and an earlier onset of estrus than nonhandled controls; no significant differences were obtained when both groups were individually reared. This suggests that postweaning social experience accentuates the effects of stimulation in infancy.

The present results add another type of environmental stimulus to the number already described that influence reproductive physiology. It has already been well documented that light (5), sound (6) and smell (7) influence some aspects of reproductive activity. To this may now be added stimulation in infancy.

References

1. Denenberg, V. H.: *In* Hafez, E. S. E. (ed.): The Behavior of Domestic Animals, Baillière, Tindall and Cox, London, 1962.
2. Lavine, S.: *In* Bliss, E. L. (ed.): Roots of Behavior, Harper, New York, 1962.
3. Levine, S., M. Alpert and G. W. Lewis, *J. Comp. Physiol. Psychol.* **51**: 774, 1958.
4. Levine, S. and M. Alpert, *A.M.A. Arch. Gen. Phychiat.* **1**: 403, 1959.
5. Fiske, V. M., *Endocrinology* **29**: 187, 1941.
6. Zondek, B. and I. Tamari, *Amer. J. Obstet. Gynec.* **80**: 1041, 1960.
7. Parkes, A. S. and H. M. Bruce, *Science* **134**: 1049, 1961.

GARLAND Y. DeNELSKY & VICTOR H. DENENBERG

49 Infantile Stimulation and Adult Exploratory Behavior: Effects of Handling upon Tactual Variation Seeking

40 experimental rats were handled daily between birth and weaning; 40 controls were not disturbed during this interval. In adulthood they were tested for tactual exploratory behavior in a Greek cross apparatus in which 4 degrees of tactual stimulus variation had been created by the use of smooth Masonite and sandpaper of differing degrees of coarseness. As the degree of stimulus variation increased, the exploratory behavior of handled Ss increased while the exploratory behavior of the controls was depressed (p < .01). In addition, control Ss defecated more than handled rats (p < .05).

Reprinted from *Journal of Comparative and Physiological Psychology 63*:309–312, 1967. Copyright 1967 by the American Psychological Association and reproduced by permission.

This research was supported in part by Grant MH-07381 and by Grant HD-02068 from the National Institutes of Health.

The past 15 years have produced a great deal of research directed at studying a class of behaviors which come under the labels of curiosity, novelty seeking, and exploration (Fowler, 1965). However, only a few of these studies have attempted to relate the relative strength of these behaviors to S's early life experiences. Those studies which have focused in this direction have often produced conflicting results. For example, some studies have shown that rearing rats in enriched environments increased their exploratory behavior compared with controls which were raised in more typical laboratory environments (Luchins & Forgus, 1955); other studies have obtained the opposite result (Zimbardo & Montgomery, 1957); while still other experiments have found no relationship between rearing conditions and adult exploration (Montgomery & Zimbardo, 1957).

Few studies have been directed towards determining whether variables other than rearing in an enriched or restricted environment affect adult exploration or variation-seeking behavior. Denenberg and Grota (1964) found that Ss which were handled daily from birth until weaning spent more time as adults in chambers of a test apparatus providing social contact and novelty than did nonhandled controls. In a similar vein, Meyers (1962) reported that merely carrying infant rats in a tray without actually handling them resulted in an increase in two measures of exploratory behavior in adulthood. These findings indicate that stimulation in infancy may affect exploratory behavior as well as emotional reactivity. Evidence supporting this view has been reported by Whimbey and Denenberg (1966), who factor analyzed a number of behavioral measures obtained on rats which had received different forms of early experience; they found "exploration" and "emotional reactivity" to be independent factors which could be influenced to different degrees by early experiences.

Even though these several studies strongly imply that infantile stimulation affects exploratory behavior independently of changes in emotional reactivity, no one has designed an experiment specifically to investigate this question. That was the purpose of this experiment. To carry out the study it was necessary to devise a testing situation in which gross activity and defecation (commonly used as measures of emotional reactivity in the open-field test) could be experimentally separated from activity induced by S's exploratory behavior. A five-chambered Greek cross apparatus was used for this purpose. The stimulus characteristics of the chambers were varied, thus changing the degree of stimulus variation along an ordinal scale. Since curiosity and exploration may be broadly defined as behaviors that have the function of altering the stimuli impinging upon an organism (Fowler, 1965), Ss which explore more in the Greek cross apparatus may be viewed as those which seek a greater amount of stimulus change, or variation, than do less exploratory Ss.

METHOD

Subjects

The 80 male Ss used in this study came from 20 litters of Purdue-Wistar rats. Pregnant females were placed in $7 \times 10 \times 15$ in. stainless steel maternity cages which were enclosed at the back, sides, and top. Each cage contained a removable tray floor partially filled with wood shavings; a water bottle and a food hopper were attached to the outside of the door of the cage.

The cages were inspected each morning to determine whether young had been born. Unless it was obvious from the condition of the pups that they had just been born, the date of birth was recorded as the previous day. All litters of more than eight were reduced to eight by randomly removing the extras after determining that at least four males were present in each litter. Litters with fewer than eight, and with fewer than four males, were not used in this experiment.

Infantile Experience

At birth a complete litter was randomly assigned to one of two infantile-experience conditions: handled or nonhandled controls. Daily handling from Day 1 through Day 20 of life consisted of removing the tray containing the pups from the home cage, leaving the mother in the cage; each pup was placed individually into a 1-gal. tin can partially filled with shavings and left there for 3 min. before being returned to its cage. During this same interval, cages of the control Ss were not disturbed or opened. Shavings were not changed for any litters from birth until weaning.

At 21 days of age the Ss were weaned, sexed, ear punched, and placed with like-sexed littermates in wire colony cages. Two males were housed in each cage from weaning until testing.

Apparatus

A diagram of the test apparatus is shown in Figure 1. The unit, constructed in the shape of a Greek cross, was built from unpainted Masonite; the walls were 15 in. high; the four outer chambers and the center compartment were each 9 in. square. The walls were joined in a single unit and could be easily removed and fitted to each of four floors, also constructed of Masonite.

The four floors were constructed so that they could be rank-ordered along a dimension of tactual stimulus variation. One floor was smooth Masonite (Stimulus Condition 1) and another was completely covered with a sandpaper of intermediate coarseness (Stimulus Condition 2); these provided minimal tactual stimulation variation as S moved from one compartment to another. A third floor contained sandpaper of intermediate coarseness in the four outer chambers with the center left uncovered so that the rat in crossing from one outer chamber to another had to cross from sandpaper, to smooth Masonite, to sandpaper (Stimulus Condition 3). The fourth floor, providing maximum variation, was like the third floor in that it contained sandpaper only in the outer chambers with the center left smooth, but it contained four different grades of sandpaper in the four outer chambers ranging from quite smooth to quite coarse (Stimulus Condition 4). The sandpaper was attached to the floors with rubber cement, a procedure that permitted the sandpaper to be readily changed when it became soiled. In Stimulus Conditions 2 and 3, D weight 80 production paper was used; in Stimulus Condition 4 the four different grades were A weight 220, D weight 80, D weight 50, and D weight 36 production paper.

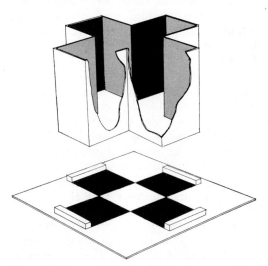

Fig. 1. Diagram of the Greek cross test apparatus.

All four types of sandpaper were produced by the Minnesota Mining and Manufacturing Company.

Thin white lines were painted on all four floors to demarcate the four outer chambers from the center compartment. Illumination was furnished by overhead fluorescent fixtures which provided approximately 14 ftc. of illumination on the floor where the apparatus was placed.

Adult Testing

A split-litter procedure was used at the time of adult testing. The four males in a litter were randomly assigned to each of the four stimulus conditions and were tested for 4 consecutive days in the same condition at roughly the same time each day. Approximately the same number of handled Ss as nonhandled Ss were tested at any given time of day. The age of the handled Ss was 86–92 days at the first day of testing, with a mean of 89.1 days, while the age of the nonhandled controls was 82–90 days, with a mean of 86.6 days.

Testing was performed in the same room in which Ss were housed. The S was removed from its cage and placed in the center compartment of the apparatus corresponding to the stimulus condition to which it had been assigned. A record was kept of the number of compartments, including the center compartment, which S entered in a 5-min. period. An S was considered to have entered a compartment when its head and front paws were across the white line which divided each outer compartment from the center compartment. The number of boluses defecated by S during each testing session was also recorded.

RESULTS

The basic experimental design was a 2 × 4 × 4 factorial composed of the two infantile treatments, the four stimulus conditions, and the 4 days of testing. The daily mean activity and mean defecation score for each stimulus condition for the handled and nonhandled Ss is given in Table 1. See DeNelsky (1966) for the raw data and for the analyses of variance.

Activity Data

Handled animals entered significantly more compartments than did the nonhandled controls ($F = 33.69$, $df = 1/18$, $p < .01$). In addition, the Handling × Stimulus Condition interaction was significant ($F = 9.22$, $df = 3/54$, $p < .01$). This interaction is illustrated in Figure 2. While there were differences between handled Ss and nonhandled controls in those conditions offering lesser amounts of potential tactual variation (Stimulus Conditions 1

TABLE 1

Mean Number of Compartments Entered and Mean Number of Boluses for Handled and Nonhandled Ss in Each Stimulus Condition

Variable	Stimulus condition			
	1	2	3	4
Handled Ss				
Entries	19.50	21.38	26.72	31.75
Boluses	0.78	1.12	1.62	1.52
Control Ss				
Entries	17.75	16.60	8.75	6.12
Boluses	2.00	2.35	2.78	1.75

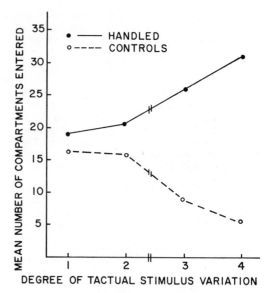

Fig. 2. Mean number of compartments entered as a function of degree of tactual stimulus variation for handled and nonhandled Ss.

and 2), these differences became much greater in those conditions offering greater amounts of potential variation (Stimulus Conditions 3 and 4). As the amount of stimulus variation increased, the exploratory behavior of handled Ss increased while the exploratory behavior of the controls was depressed.

The main effect of Days was significant ($F = 41.23$, $df = 3/54$, $p < .01$). Activity decreased in a negatively accelerated manner over the 4 test days. A trend analysis using orthogonal polynomials indicated that both the linear and quadratic components were significant at the .01 level ($F = 91.61$, $df = 1/54$ for linear; $F = 31.85$, $df = 1/54$ for quadratic).

Defecation Data

The only significant finding in the analysis of the defecation data was that the nonhandled controls defecated more than handled Ss ($F = 4.54$, $df = 1/18$, $p < .05$).

Discussion

In this experiment it was possible to separate, experimentally, behavior related to the construct of emotional reactivity from behavior related to the construct of exploration. Summed over all stimulus conditions, handled Ss were more active and defecated less than nonhandled controls. These findings may be taken to mean that the handled Ss were less emotional (Den-

enberg, 1964). Independently of the above, as the degree of potential stimulus variation increased, Ss handled in infancy increased their activity while nonhandled controls decreased theirs. Thus, infantile handling resulted in Ss which were more exploratory, or curious, than nonhandled controls. This experimental separation of the effects of infantile handling upon exploration and emotionality complements the Whimbey and Denenberg (1966) factor analysis study which also revealed that infantile stimulation independently affected these same two behavioral dimensions.

The interaction of infantile experience and stimulus variation raises an interesting point. It is possible that providing a stimulus situation which offers a minimum of potential variation, or which is extremely familiar to the animal, would result in a greater amount of exploratory activity by nonhandled than by handled animals. This would support the view that the amount of actual exploration observed in any situation is a function of both the stimulus complexity and the individual's "complexity," a concept similar to one proposed by Dember and Earl (1957).

REFERENCES

DEMBER, W. N., & EARL, R. W. Analysis of explor-atory, manipulative, and curiosity behaviors. *Psychol. Rev.*, 1957, **64**, 91–96.

DENELSKY, G. Y. The influence of early experience upon adult exploratory behavior. Unpublished doctoral dissertation, Purdue University, 1966.

DENENBERG, V. H. Critical periods, stimulus input, and emotional reactivity: A theory of infantile stimulation. *Psychol. Rev.*, 1964, **71**, 335–351.

DENENBERG, V. H., & GROTA, L. J. Social-seeking and novelty-seeking behavior as a function of differential rearing histories. *J. abnorm. soc. Psychol.*, 1964, **69**, 453–456.

FOWLER, H. *Curiosity and exploratory behavior.* New York: Macmillan, 1965.

LUCHINS, A. S., & FORGUS, R. H. The effect of dif-ferential postweaning environment on the rigidity of animal's behavior. *J. genet. Psychol.*, 1955, **86**, 51–58.

MEYERS, W. J. Critical period for the facilitation of exploratory behavior. *J. comp. physiol. Psychol.*, 1962, **55**, 1099–1101.

MONTGOMERY, K. C., & ZIMBARDO, P. G. Effect of sensory and behavioral deprivation upon ex-ploratory behavior in the rat. *Percept. mot. Skills*, 1957, **7**, 223–229.

WHIMBEY, A. E., & DENENBERG, V. H. Programming life histories: Creating individual differences by the experimental control of early experi-ences. *Multivar. behav. Res.*, 1966, **1**, 279–286.

ZIMBARDO, P. G., & MONTGOMERY, K. C. Effects of "free environment" rearing upon exploratory behavior. *Psychol. Rep.*, 1957, **3**, 589–594.

SEYMOUR LEVINE, GARY C. HALTMEYER, GEORGE G. KARAS, & VICTOR H. DENENBERG

50 Physiological and Behavioral Effects of Infantile Stimulation

LEVINE, S., G. C. HALTMEYER, G. G. KARAS AND V. H. DENENBERG. *Physiological and behavioral effects of infantile stimulation.* PHYSIOL. BEHAV. 2 (1) 55–59, 1967.—Male Purdue–Wistar rats were handled for 20 days in infancy or were not disturbed (total *N* = 312). In adulthood these animals were subdivided and tested in the open field for 1, 2, 3, or 4 days. Activity and defecation in the field were recorded. Following the termination of testing the animals were killed immedi-ately, 5 min afterwards, or 15 min afterwards; and the free plasma corticosterone was assayed. Animals handled in infancy were more active in the open field on the last three test days, defecated less in the field on all four test days, and had a lesser corticosterone response on all four test days. These data allow one to draw the general conclusion that stimulation in infancy results in an animal which is less responsive to novel stimuli (i.e., is less emotional) as measured both at the behavioral and physiological level. In addition, the corticosterone response was found to increase as a function of time between removing from the open field and killing; and to decrease as a function of number of days of open field testing.

THAT INFANTILE experience affects many aspects of the organism's subsequent behavior has been well documented [2, 3, 7, 13, 18]. In most instances in which differences have been obtained between neonatally stimulated and non-stimulated animals, the testing situation has included stimuli of an affective-emotional nature [3]. One such testing situation is the open field, and a well established phenomenon concerning infantile stimulation is that rats manipulated in infancy will generally be more active and will defecate less when tested in an open field in adulthood. Since the open field is a novel stimulus situation which has been shown to measure emotional reactivity, the general conclusion is that infantile stimulation results in animals which are less emo-tionally responsive in adulthood [4].

It has now been demonstrated by a number of investi-gators that exposure to novel stimuli results in an increase in circulating adrenal steroids [5, 16]. It might be expected, therefore, that animals which are less emotional, as defined by the behavioral criterion of the open field, should show a reduced physiological response following exposure to the

same situation. Thus, the major purpose of this study was to determine the relationship between open-field behavior and changes in adrenal corticoid levels for two groups of animals: those which had been stimulated in infancy and nonhandled controls.

Typically, when animals are repeatedly exposed to a stimulus or stimulus-complex, an habituation phenomenon is noted. Classical examples of this are the fading out of the orienting reponses [19] and reduction in the startle response following repeated presentations of a loud noise [1]. Within the context of early experience research there are two classes of studies which are directly relevant to the question of habituation. When animals are repeatedly tested in the open field, there is observed a general increase in activity and, in addition, stimulated animals increased at a faster rate than controls [15, 17]. When consummatory behavior is investi-gated, water consumption is found to increase significantly following repeated testing under conditions of water depriva-tion, with different rates of change for stimulated and non-stimulated animals [10, 11]. Therefore, a second purpose of this experiment was to study the phenomenon of habituation to the open field both at a behavioral and a physiological level, for stimulated and nonstimulated animals.

Reprinted from *Physiology and Behavior* 255–59, 1967.

This research was supported, in part, by Research Grants MH 07435, MH 07381, and HD 02068 from the National Institutes of Health, and in part, by a grant from the Purdue Research Foundation.

With regard to the detection of changes in adrenal corticoids following exposure to stimulation, temporal factors are particularly critical. Characteristically, the steroid response is a sluggish one, usually involving minimally 3–5 min before barely detectable increases are demonstrable. The steroid response has been shown to be more rapid and more vigorous for infantile stimulated animals following exposure to an acute and intensely noxious electric shock [12]. The third purpose of this experiment was to compare the steroid response of stimulated and nonstimulated animals over time following exposure to novel stimuli.

METHOD

Subjects

Pregnant Purdue–Wistar rats were placed into stainless steel maternity cages containing shavings on the tray floor. At birth litters were sexed and reduced to 8 pups with a minimum of 4 males. Litters were randomly assigned to one of two infantile treatment conditions: nonhandled controls or handled on Days 1–20. Handling consisted of removing the pups from their mothers and placing them in individual cans partly filled with shavings. After 3 min the pups were returned to their home cage. This procedure was repeated daily from Day 1 through Day 20. Nonhandled controls were not disturbed between the time of litter reduction and weaning.

The offspring were sexed, weighed, earpunched, and weaned at 21 days of age. Four males were randomly selected from each litter and housed by pairs in suspended stainless steel cages. The animals were kept in a quiet room, and an effort was made to reduce all extraneous stimulation to a minimum.

Testing

Adulthood testing was initiated at 80 days of age for 288 rats and consisted of open-field tests for 1, 2, 3, or 4 days. Testing started at 5.30 a.m. and usually finished prior to 10.00 a.m. The open field consisted of a 45-in. square plywood base with walls 18 in. high. The unit was painted flat black except for thin white lines which divided the floor into 9-in. squares. The field was approximately evenly lighted throughout by overhead fluorescent lights. The rat was placed onto one corner of the field and observed for 3 min. Total number of squares entered and total number of boluses dropped were recorded. After the 3-min test the rat was either returned to the colony room or taken into surgery to await decapitation. The interval between open-field testing and decapitation was spent in cages identical to the home cage. The animal was alone in the cage during this interval. The rats were decapitated at intervals of 0, 5, or 15 min after the final open-field test. Additional group of handled and nonhandled controls ($N = 12$ per group) were removed from their home cages and decapitated at once to determine corticosterone resting levels.

Plasma samples were obtained from each animal and the concentration of corticosterone determined by the microfluorimetric method reported by Glick, Redlich, and Levine [6]. All steroid assays were carried out blind.

RESULTS

Table 1 summarizes the open-field activity and defecation data. The corticoid means are presented in Table 2.

Behavioral Data

Because of the decreasing N on successive days, separate analyses for activity and defecation were computed for each day. On the first day of testing control animals were more

TABLE 1

OPEN-FIELD ACTIVITY AND DEFECATION DATA

Treatment in infancy	Day 1	Day 2	Day 3	Day 4
Nonhandled				
Mean activity	12.36	4.90	4.10	5.75
Per cent defecation	52.08	50.93	61.11	61.11
N	144	108	72	36
Handled				
Mean activity	8.69	8.81	11.92	16.03
Per cent defecation	38.89	31.48	27.78	36.11
N	144	108	72	36
$t$activity	1.94*	2.37†	3.87‡	3.36‡
χ^2defecation	4.54†	7.64‡	14.88‡	3.56*

*$p < 0.10$
†$p < 0.05$
‡$p < 0.01$

TABLE 2

PLASMA LEVELS OF CORTICOSTERONE IN μg/100 ml FOR ALL EXPERIMENTAL CONDITIONS

Treatment in infancy	Time	Day 1	Day 2	Day 3	Day 4
Nonhandled	0 min	18.1	15.8	10.4	11.7
Handled	0 min	13.3	11.5	9.2	10.5
Nonhandled	5 min	24.7	25.9	25.8	21.9
Handled	5 min	20.6	18.7	19.6	22.3
Nonhandled	15 min	36.1	26.9	35.2	35.6
Handled	15 min	29.4	24.8	26.5	30.7

Resting Levels
  Nonhandled Controls $= 9.7$
  Handled $= 9.9$
$MS_{error} = 76.94$, $df = 264$
SE_{mean} (for $N = 12$) $= 2.53$

active than handled animals though the difference was not significant ($p < 0.10$). On Days 2 through 4 the animals handled in infancy were significantly more active.

Because a large number of animals did not defecate at all in the open field, these data were evaluated by means of the chi-square test (corrected for discontinuity). On all four test days nonhandled controls had a greater incidence of defecation than did handled animals. This difference is significant on the first three days, but drops to the 0.10 level on Day 4. This drop in significance is due to the loss of statistical power because of the reduced N on Day 4.

Physiological Data

The steroid data consisted of handled or nonhandled animals which were tested for 1, 2, 3, or 4 days in the open field and were decapitated 0, 5, or 15 min after being removed from the field. There were 12 animals per cell. These data were analysed in a $2 \times 4 \times 3$ factorial design. The handling variable was highly significant ($F = 17.03$, $df = 1/264$, $p < 0.01$) with animals stimulated in infancy having a lower plasma corticoid level than nonhandled controls. The time interval involved in decapitation was also significant ($F = 94.61$, $df = 2/264$, $p < 0.01$); rats killed immediately had the lowest steroid values while those killed after 15 min had the greatest values. In addition, the interaction between number of test days and the temporal factor was significant at the 0.01 level ($F = 2.92$; $df = 6/264$). This interaction was apparently brought about by a confounding in the experimental design which is discussed below. No other main effect or interaction was significant.

In addition to this overall analysis, two separate analyses of variance were computed to answer questions of special relevance to this study. The first analysis concerned the steroid response for the animals tested and killed on Day 1. These data represent a straightforward evaluation of steroid levels of handled and nonhandled animals to a novel stimulus with no involvement with subsequent testing. At each time interval the handled animals had a significantly lower steroid response to the novel open-field stimulus than did non-handled controls (F = 6.44, $df = 1/264$, $p < 0.05$). Fig. 1 presents these data.

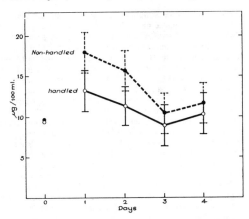

FIG. 2. Plasma corticoid levels for handled (solid line) and non-handled (dashed line) rats over days following 3 min in the open field. The points represent the mean value and bars represent the standard error of the mean. The two points at 0 days are the base levels of corticosteroids for handled (open circle) and nonhandled (closed circle) rats.

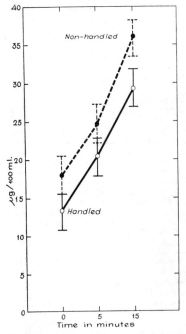

FIG. 1. Plasma corticosteroid levels over time for handled (solid line) and nonhandled (dashed line) rats. Each point represents the mean value and bars represent the standard error of the mean.

The second analysis was concerned only with those animals which were removed from the open field and decapitated immediately thereafter on each of the four test days. The curves for the handled and nonhandled animals are shown in Fig. 2. The major question of concern in this analysis involved the phenomenon of habituation. Analysis of the Days effect found that there was, overall, a significant linear decrease in plasma steroid output as a function of number of days of testing (F = 5.06, $df = 1/264$, $p < 0.05$). Though the handled animals have a lower adrenal response than non-stimulated controls, this difference is only at the 0.10 level in this analysis (two-tailed test).

The 5- and 15-min steroid values of animals on Days 2, 3 and 4 are somewhat confounded. In addition to open-field exposure, which might have induced habituation, these animals were subjected to the additional novel experience of being placed into a holding cage in isolation for either a 5- or 15-min period. Thus, it is impossible to evaluate whether the increase in steroid values following Day 1 is a function of the exposure to the open field, the additional novel experience, or some combination thereof. It is for this reason that it is impossible to interpret the significant interaction between test days and the temporal factors. However, the data are entirely consistent with the proposition that

handled animals are less responsive than nonhandled controls in terms of changes in adrenal corticoids to novel stimuli.

DISCUSSION

Animals handled in infancy were found to have a smaller incidence of open-field defecation on all four test days. In addition, handled animals were more active than controls on the last three days of testing. The pattern of high activity and low defecation is commonly interpreted as indicative of low emotionality [4]. However, the reversal in activity on Day 1 might appear to invalidate this conclusion. Such reversals in Day 1 activity have been commonly observed in our laboratories, and it is for this reason that animals are given four days of open-field testing. We have recently quantified this observation by showing that activity on Day 1 is positively correlated with defecation scores while the activity-defecation correlations are negative thereafter; and we further found, in a factor analysis, that high Day 1 activity is indicative of high-emotional reactivity while high activity on Days 2, 3, and 4 reflects low emotionality [20]. The present findings are completely consistent with the Whimbey data and permit us to conclude, at a behavioral level, that animals handled in infancy are less emotional than animals which did not receive any infantile stimulation.

Further, the data on corticoid levels in response to the open field are consistent with the interpretation that neonatally stimulated animals are less responsive to the open-field situation (i.e., are less emotional) than their control non-stimulated counterparts. Therefore, we may draw the general conclusion that stimulation in infancy results in an animal which is less responsive to novel stimuli (i.e., is less emotional) as measured both at the behavioral and at the physiological level.

With the exception of Day 1, the activity data indicate differential habituation for the two groups, with infantile handled animals increasing in their activity rate during the last three days, while the curve for the nonhandled controls shows essentially no change (See Table 1). The steroid data, however, do not reveal any evidence of differential habituation (Fig. 2). This, however, may be a function of the time interval between the onset of stimulation and the obtaining of the blood samples. Three minutes is at the borderline where elevations of steroids are detectable. It is entirely possible that, if the animals were permitted a longer time in the open field before decapitation, differences in habituation to the steroid response might have been obtained.

Finally, regardless of whether the animals are decapitated 0, 5, or 15 min. after removal from the open field, the non-handled animals show an overall greater, and constant, increase in plasma corticoids as compared to animals stimulated in infancy (Fig. 1). The lack of differential rates of response between handled and nonhandled animals is in contrast to previously reported data in which electric shock was used as the stressor in adulthood [12]. In the Levine study the animals stimulated in infancy showed a more rapid elevation of adrenal steroids following electric shock; this elevation persisted over the 15-min test period. Recently Haltmeyer, Denenberg, and Zarrow [9] have obtained essentially similar findings of different rates of steroid response over time when animals receive shock stimulation during adult testing. Thus, it appears that both the rate and the magnitude of the steroid response in adulthood is dependent upon an interaction between early experience and the adult test situation.

The hypothesis has been advanced that one of the consequences in infantile stimulation is to impart to the organism the capacity for making finer discriminations concerning the relevance of environmental stimuli [13]. Thus, in situations where distinctly noxious stimuli are involved, the handled animal seems to be more reactive in terms of its adrenal-cortical response. However, in the present experiment where the test situation does not involve intense, noxious stimulation, the steroid response of the handled animals is of smaller magnitude. The nonhandled animal, however, appears to have much less discrimination with regard to the test situation and reacts with a large corticosterone response regardless of the specific aspects of the test situation. At this time it is too early to speculate concerning the mechanisms whereby animals handled in infancy develop the capability to make these finer discriminations concerning the nature of their environment. However, some recent evidence concerning adrenal development indicates that adrenal-cortical mechanisms in infancy may in some way be implicated in this process [8, 14, 21].

REFERENCES

1. Brown, J. S., H. I. Kalish and I. E. Farber. Conditioned fear as revealed by magnitude of startle response to an auditory stimulus. *J. Exp. Psychol.* 41: 317–328, 1951.
2. Denenberg, V. H. The effects of early experience. In: *The behaviour of domestic animals*, edited by E. S. E. Hafez. London: Bailliere, Tindall and Cox, 1962.
3. Denenberg, V. H. Animal studies of developmental determinants of behavioral adaptability. In: *Flexibility, adaptability, and creativity: Nature and developmental determinants*, edited by O. J. Harvey. New York: Springer, 1966, in press.
4. Denenberg, V. H. Stimulation in infancy, emotional reactivity, and exploratory behavior. In: *Biology and behavior: Neurophysiology and emotion*, edited by D. C. Glass. New York: Russell Sage Foundation, 1966, in press.
5. Fortier, C. Sensitivity of the plasma free corticosteroid response to environmental change in the rat. *Archs. Int. Physiol. Biochem.* 66: 672–673, 1958.
6. Glick, D., D. V. Redlich and S. Levine. Fluorometric determination of corticosterone and cortisol in 0.02–0.05 milliliters of plasma or submilligram samples of adrenal tissue. *Endocrinology* 74: 653–655, 1964.
7. Haltmeyer, G. C. Effects of early experience upon behavior and physiology of rats. Ph.D. dissertation, Purdue University, 1966.
8. Haltmeyer, G. C., V. H. Denenberg, J. Thatcher and M. X. Zarrow. Response of the adrenal cortex of the neonatal rat following stress. *Nature, Lond.* 1966, in press.
9. Haltmeyer, G. C., V. H. Denenberg and M. X. Zarrow. Modification of the plasma corticosterone response as a function of infantile stimulation and electric shock parameters. *Physiol. Behav.* 2: 61–63, 1967.
10. Levine, S. Infantile experience and consummatory behavior in adulthood. *J. Comp. Physiol. Psychol.* 50: 609–612, 1957.
11. Levine, S. Noxious stimulation in infant and adult rats and consummatory behavior. *J. Comp. Physiol. Psychol.* 51: 230–233, 1958.
12. Levine, S. Plasma-free corticosteroid response to electric shock in rats stimulated in infancy. *Science* 135: 795–796, 1962.
13. Levine, S. The effects of infantile experience on adult behavior. In: *Experimental foundations of clinical psychology*, edited by A. J. Backrach. New York: Basic Books, 1962.
14. Levine, S. Maturation of the neuroendocrine response to stress. *Excerpta Med., Int. Congr. Ser.* 99: E103, 1965.
15. Levine, S. and P. L. Broadhurst. Genetic and ontogenetic determinants of adult behavior in the rat. *J. Comp. Physiol. Psychol.* 56: 423–428, 1963.
16. Mason, J. W., J. V. Brady and M. Sidman. Plasma 17-hydroxycorticosteroid levels and conditioned behavior in the rhesus monkey. *Endocrinology* 60: 741–752, 1957.
17. Morton, J. R. C. The interactive effects of preweaning and postweaning environments upon adult behavior. Ph.D. dissertation, Purdue University, 1962.
18. Newton, G. and S. Levine (Eds.) *Early experience and behavior.* Springfield, Thomas, 1966, in press.
19. Sokolov, E. N. Neuronal models and the orienting reflex. In: *The central nervous system and behavior*, edited by M. A. B. Brazier, New York: Josiah Macy Foundation, 1960.
20. Whimbey, A. E. The factor structure underlying the experimentally created individual differences studied in "early experience" research. Ph.D. dissertation, Purdue University, 1965.
21. Zarrow, M. X., G. C. Haltmeyer, V. H. Denenberg and J. Thatcher. Response of the infantile rat to stress. *Endocrinology* 1966, in press.

SEYMOUR LEVINE

51 Infantile Experience and Consummatory Behavior in Adulthood

Recent experiments by Levine, Chevalier, and Korchin (6) and Levine (5) have shown that rats which were either handled or shocked prior to weaning were significantly superior

Reprinted from *Journal of Comparative and Physiological Psychology* 50:609–612, 1957. Copyright 1957 by the American Psychological Association and reproduced by permission.

in avoidance learning when tested as adults than Ss which received no handling prior to weaning. These studies further indicated that non-handled Ss were significantly more "*emotionally*" unstable as defined by greater defecation, more freezing, and lowered activity. To account for these results the following general hypothesis was presented: "restriction of experience results in an increase in the animals' susceptibility to emotional disturbance. Thus when the non-handled *S* is presented with novel and/or traumatic stimuli, the resulting high degree of emotional disturbance is sufficiently intense to interfere with subsequent adaptive behavior" (5, p. 77).

It should be noted that in the earlier studies it was necessary to handle the non-handled *S*s prior to adult testing. It seems clear that no handling results in greater susceptibility to emotional disturbance. It is difficult, however, to determine whether this is a generalized emotional response to any novel or traumatic stimulus or whether these effects are attributable to the initial handling prior to testing. In order to test the hypothesis that lack of handling experience predisposes *S*s to emotionality in general, it is necessary to show disturbance of behavior in situations that do not involve handling as a component of the adult testing.

A series of recent studies (1, 2, 8) has revealed that emotional disturbance can affect consummatory behavior such as drinking after a period of deprivation. Within the limits that drinking is affected by emotionality, and that drinking following a period of deprivation can be measured without handling, the use of this response is one method by which the proposition of the general emotionality of the non-handled *S*s can be tested.

The purpose of this study was to determine the effects of infantile experience upon consummatory behavior before and after water deprivation. It is hypothesized that since deprivation constitutes a novel internal stimulus complex for non-handled *S*s, the novelty should result in greater emotional disturbance and produce reduced water consumption following a period of deprivation.

METHOD

Subjects

The 42 *S*s used in this study came from six litters bred from stock Sprague-Dawley (Holtzman) rats. The three experimental treatments were randomly

This investigation was supported by a research grant PHS M-1051 from the National Institute of Mental Health of the National Institutes of Health, Public Health Service. The study was conducted while the author was at the Institute for Psychosomatic and Psychiatric Research and Training, Michael Reese Hospital.

assigned to complete litters. All *S*s within each litter received the same treatment. Each group (*N* = 14; 7 males, 7 females) was composed of *S*s from two different litters.

Apparatus

The grid for shocking the infant *S*s was an adaptation of an alley runway described by Campbell and Kraeling (4). The device is essentially a small metal box with two narrow shelves for a floor; the shelves are too narrow to permit the *S* to maintain its balance on a single shelf. At least one foot must be placed on each shelf, insuring the continued flow of current. Current was supplied by a 110-v. a.c. source. Three alternative resistors (1.1, 0.5, and 0.3 megohms) were wired in series with the *S*. Three grid units were used in the experiment.

Procedure

The plan of the experiment can be presented conveniently in two sections, one dealing with the infantile treatments and the other the adult testing. The three groups consisted of *S*s shocked in infancy (S), non-shocked *S*s (NS), and non-handled *S*s (NH).

Infantile treatment. The experimental treatment was started on the day following birth. Two of the three conditions, S and NS, required that the pups be removed from the nest for treatment. In the third condition, NH, the *S*s were neither removed from the nest nor handled in any way from birth until weaning.

For the S and NS groups which required handling the following procedure was followed. Half a litter of pups were removed from the mother. Each *S* was placed on the grid for 3 min. For the S group the shock was turned on as soon as the *S* was placed on the grid, kept on for 3 min., and turned off just before the *S* was removed. The NS *S*s received identical handling, but were not given shock.

All *S*s were given one treatment per day. For the S group the 1.1-megohm resistor was used in the shock circuit for days 1 through 5. From days 6 through 15 the 0.5-megohm resistor was used, and for the remaining days 16 through 20 the 0.3-megohm resistor was used. This procedure was used in an attempt to maintain an equivalent level of shock, taking into account the increasing resistance of the *S*.

All *S*s received their last treatment on day 20. On day 21 the *S*s were weaned, marked, and the sexes separated. They were then placed in group cages (6 to 8 per cage) and not handled in any way until the time of adult testing, at 65 days of age. Food and water were always available throughout this period.

Adult testing. Testing was started on day 65. At this time all *S*s were removed from the group cages, weighed, and placed in individual cages. The dimensions of the individual cage were 6 in. by 6 in. by 9 in. For the first seven days *S*s were given food and water ad lib. The water bottles were removed and weighed at 24-hr. intervals. At the end of this period the *S*s were put on the following schedule: 5 P.M., water removed from cage; 11 A.M., water replaced in cage for 10 min.; 11:10 A.M., water removed from cage and weighed; 11:15 A.M., water replaced for 30 min.; 11:45 A.M., water removed and weighed; 3:30 P.M., water replaced in cage for

1½ hr. Thus, the level of the thirst drive was based on 18 hr. of water deprivation. This regimen was maintained for four days.

RESULTS

The results of this study revealed significant weight differences between the handled Ss (S and NS) and the NH group. The mean weight at 65 days for group S was 221.81 gm., group NS 226.40 gm., and group NH 209.42. The difference between NH Ss and the two other groups was significant beyond the .01 level.

In view of the significant weight differences between groups, water intake was cal-

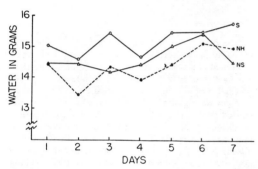

FIG. 1. Mean 24-hr. water intake for the period prior to deprivation.

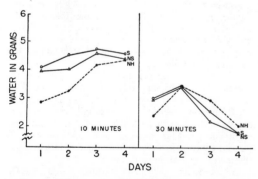

FIG. 2. Mean water intake for 10- and 30-min. periods following 18 hr. of deprivation.

culated in terms of amount consumed per 100 gm. of body weight. This procedure was used to control the effects of size differences on intake. This adjustment of water intake tends to reduce the differences. The unadjusted scores yield even larger differences between groups.

Figure 1 presents the 24-hr. water intake for the seven-day predeprivation adult test period. An analysis of variance for repeated measures yielded a between-group F of .44 and a between-days F of 2.09. Neither of these F ratios was significant. There was, however, a significant difference during the 10-min. drinking period following deprivation.

Figure 2 presents the water intake for the 10- and 30-min. drinking periods. The analysis of variance for these periods are presented in Tables 1 and 2. It is important to note that although the over-all difference in water intake during the 10-min. drinking period is statistically significant ($p = .05$), this difference mainly reflects Ss' intake for the first two days. The NH group consumed significantly less water during the first two days following deprivation (S vs. NH, $p = .02$) NS vs. NH, $p = .05$; S vs. NS, $p = .10$; There were no significant differences on days 3 and 4, nor were there any significant differences present during the 30-min. drinking period.

Rate of drinking. A study by Stellar and Hill (9) showed that Ss consume a maximum of their intake during the first 10 min. of drinking. Insofar as the relationship between the 10- and 30-min. drinking periods indicates crudely the rate of drinking, the present data are consistent with the findings of Stellar and Hill. All groups consumed significantly more water during the 10-min. period than the 30-min. period (S: $p = .001$; NS: $p = .001$; NH: $p = .02$). There appears to be an inverse relationship between the two drinking periods. The between-days difference (see Table 1 and 2) is significant beyond the .01 level, indicating that as more water was consumed during the 10-min. periods, less water was consumed during the 30-min. periods.

DISCUSSION

The results found in this experiment continue to support the interpretation that the absence of extrinsic stimulation in infancy results in an increase in the S's susceptibility to emotional disturbance. Thus, when the non-handled S is confronted with a novel stimulus complex, the resulting emotional disturbance is sufficiently intense to interfere with subsequent adaptive behavior. It seems clear that even in the absence of handling in adulthood, a change in the environmental stimuli, in this case the experience of a novel drive stimulus, differentially affects the be-

TABLE 1

Analysis of Variance for 10-min. Drinking Period

Source	df	Mean Square	F
Independent observations between infantile treatments	2	10.156	3.692*
Between Ss	39	2.751	—
Correlated observations between days	3	8.274	10.227**
Days × treatment	6	1.219	1.507
Pooled Ss × days	117	0.808	
Total	167		

* p = <.05.
** p = <.01.

TABLE 2

Analysis of Variance for 30-min. Drinking Period

Source	df	Mean Square	F
Independent observations between infantile treatments	2	0.215	0.248
Between Ss	39	0.864	
Correlated observations between days	3	16.889	4.795*
Days × treatment	6	1.198	0.340
Pooled Ss × days	117	3.552	
Total	167		

* p = <.01.

havior of non-handled Ss. This argument gives emphasis to the interaction between novel stimuli and emotionality and postulates that a S who is susceptible to emotional disturbance is made *emotional* by the "strangeness" of the stimuli, regardless of whether the novel stimuli are external or internal.

There is, however, another explanation consistent with the concept of a lowered threshold for emotional disturbance in non-handled Ss. Mowrer (7) has postulated that fear accompanies any strong, persistent primary drive. It has been shown previously (5) that non-handled Ss react differently to fear-producing stimuli (shock), showing much more crouching and freezing behavior. If a strong primary drive creates fear, then it is possible that fear caused by deprivation can result in the same freezing and crouching behavior which would interfere with the drinking response.

It appears, however, that there is relatively

rapid extinction of this disturbance created by deprivation. Drinking is inhibited only on the first two days following deprivation. The decrement in drinking is reflected *only* during the 10-min. periods. Whether this represents an adaption to the novelty of the drive stimuli or an extinction of the fear response associated with the primary drive is an open question. The intensity of the fear created by the primary drive manipulation may be moderate. More intense fear, created by a stronger drive or noxious stimuli, may result in a more persistent effect upon consummatory behavior.

A secondary finding in this study was that Ss who were handled in infancy (S and NS) were significantly heavier than NH Ss. This finding is similar to the findings of several other studies (3, 10). However, there are two important differences between this study and the previous experiments which have revealed weight differences. First, the Ss in this experiment were handled during the first 20 days of life, whereas in other studies the handling or "gentling" (10) started after the Ss were 21 days of age. Second, the Ss in previous experiments were handled for 10 min. per day, whereas the Ss in this experiment had minimum contact with the E. The total amount of actual contact was approximately 12 sec. per day. It is difficult to see how rats given merely a few seconds of handling per day could be considered "gentled." It is more difficult to conceive of Ss shocked in infancy as being "gentled." Since these procedures yield superior growth, we may assume there is something in common between the stimuli involved in "gentling" and those involved in shocking. It has been proposed (5) that handling is a noxious stimulus complex for the infant S, and the early experience with noxious stimuli (particularly during the nursing period) leads to a superior organism both physiologically and psychologically. The specific effects of handling or shocking on physiological development still remain to be clearly determined.

SUMMARY

Forty-two albino rats were given various treatments in infancy to determine the effect of infantile experience on consummatory behavior in adulthood. The two experimental groups consisted of Ss that were shocked in infancy and Ss that were given the same treatment without shock. A control group received no handling. At 65 days of age water consumption was measured before and after 18 hr. of water deprivation.

The results revealed that there were no significant differences in water intake for the period prior to deprivation. However, the non-handled control group drank significantly less following deprivation.

The results were interpreted as consistent with the hypothesis that the absence of extrinsic stimulation in infancy renders these animals more susceptible to emotional disturbance when they are presented with novel stimuli and that this disturbance produces responses that interfere with drinking behavior.

REFERENCES

1. AMSEL, A. The effect upon level of consummatory response of the addition of anxiety to a motivational complex. *J. exp. Psychol.*, 1950, **40**, 709–715.

2. AMSEL, A., & MALTZMAN, I. The effect upon generalized drive strength of emotionality as inferred from the level of consummatory response. *J. exp. Psychol.*, 1950, **40**, 563–569.
3. BERNSTEIN, L. A note on Christie's "Experimental naïvete and experiental naïvete". *Psychol. Bull.*, 1952, **49**, 38–40.
4. CAMPBELL, B. A., & KRAELING, DORIS. Response strength as a function of drive level and amount of drive reduction. *J. exp. Psychol.*, 1953, **54**, 97–101.
5. LEVINE, S. A further study of infantile handling and adult avoidance learning. *J. Pers.*, 1956, **25**, 70–80.
6. LEVINE, S., CHEVALIER, J. A., & KORCHIN, S. J. The effects of shock and handling in infancy on later avoidance learning. *J. Pers.*, 1956, **24**, 475–493.
7. MOWRER, O. H. Two factor learning theory reconsidered, with special reference to secondary reinforcement and the concept of habit. *Psychol. Rev.*, 1956, **63**, 114–128.
8. SIEGEL, P. S., & SIEGEL, H. S. The effect of emotionality on the water intake of the rat. *J. comp. physiol. Psychol.*, 1949, **42**, 12–16.
9. STELLAR, E., & HILL, J. H. The rat's rate of drinking as a function of water depriation. *J. comp. physiol. Psychol.*, 1952, **45**, 96–102.
10. WEININGER, O. The effects of early experience on behavior and growth characteristics. *J. comp. physiol. Psychol.*, 1956, **49**, 1–9.

THOMAS E. LANDAUER & JOHN W. M. WHITING

52 Infantile Stimulation and Adult Stature of Human Males

RECENT experimental research has shown that extraordinary stimulation of animals (particularly rats) during infancy has profound and enduring physiological effects. One of the more persistent and striking of these effects, an increase in rate of growth and size attained at adulthood, is of particular relevance to this paper. It has been summarized by Levine (1960:85), one of the leading researchers in the field, as follows: "In all respects, in fact, the manipulated infants exhibit a more rapid rate of development. They open their eyes earlier and achieve motor coordination sooner. Their body hair grows faster, and they tend to be significantly heavier at weaning. They continue to gain weight more rapidly than the nonstimulated animals even after the course of stimulation has been completed at three weeks of age. Their more vigorous growth does not seem to be related to food intake but to better utilization of the food consumed and probably to a higher output of the

Reproduced by permission of the American Anthropological Association from *American Anthropologist* 66(6):1007–1028, 1964.

somatotrophic (growth) hormone from the pituitary." As will be discussed below, it seems reasonable to interpret these unusual early experiences as stressful to the immature animals.

Although the exact mechanism underlying the stimulating effects of these early experiences upon growth has not been established, it is known that a lasting change in the endocrine system does occur. Since growth is presumably inhibited by corticosteroid stress response hormones, one might hypothesize that animals stressed in infancy are in some manner less responsive to stress following this early experience, since this would lead to a lower average level of circulating corticosteroids and allow more uninterrupted growth. There is some experimental evidence suggesting that this may indeed be the case. When adult rats are placed on an enclosed table top, those stressed in infancy show significantly *less* defecation, urination, crouching, and wall seeking behavior than non-stimulated controls. Furthermore, infant-stressed rats taken from a colony and wheeled down on a cart to a laboratory showed a significantly lower leukocyte count than stressed controls (Levine and Lewis: 1962). Since both of the above types of response indicate the action of growth-inhibiting stress hormones, a mechanism for the effect of infant stress upon growth is suggested.

It should be pointed out, however, that the experimental animals when subjected to electric shock show a more rapid increase in circulating corticosteroids as well as a higher concentration of them at the end of a 15-minute interval (Levine and Lewis: 1962). This seems to be evidence against the above interpretation. Levine suggests, however, that "it is possible that the non-stimulated subjects, although slower in their initial responses, may show higher sustained levels." He concludes that animals stressed in infancy "are more reactive to distinctly noxious and threatening situations, but that the nonstimulated (in infancy) animal appears to react to a greater variety of environmental changes. The nonstimulated subject seems to require less extreme changes in the environment to elicit a physiological stress response, and in this sense they are hyperreactors."

METHOD AND MEASURES

Most of the animal studies showing the effect of infant stress upon growth have used body weight as a measure (for example, Reugamer and Silverman 1956; McClelland 1956; Denenberg and Karas, 1959). One study (Weininger 1956), however, showed that the animals in the experimental group that had been removed from their cages and stroked each day for three weeks following weaning had significantly longer skeletons ($p<.001$) and longer tails ($p<.01$) upon reaching adulthood than the unstimulated control group. Furthermore, since there was no indication that the greater weight reported in the other studies was due to obesity, these studies also suggest that greater skeletal length is a consistent effect of infant stimulation.

This assumption allowed us to use height as the dependent variable to investigate the possible relation between infant stress and human growth, quantitative data on adult human male stature being available for a considerably larger number of societies than any other index of growth.

The choice of apparently "stressful" infant care practices as the independent variable requires more explanation. In early rat studies (Hammett 1922;

Greenman and Dehring 1931; Weininger 1956) the experimental treatment generally consisted of taking the rat pups from their cages and gently stroking them for ten minutes or so each day for several weeks. Many of these studies explicitly referred to Freudian theory and interpreted this treatment as "tender loving care." Weininger (1956), for example, refers to the effects of maternal neglect reported by Spitz (1946), Goldfarb (1943, 1949), and Levy (1934) implying that the rat pups left with their mother were more "neglected" than those petted by the experimenter.

More recent studies, however, indicate that "petting" probably has a frightening or stressful effect. In these studies (Levine, Chevalier, and Korchin, 1956; Levine 1957; Levine 1958; Levine and Lewis 1959; Werboff and Havlena 1963), it has been shown that a mild electric shock, drug-induced febrile convulsion, jiggling in an oscillating cage, or separation from the mother by removal from the nest for 3 minutes a day, has an effect very similar to "petting." The behavior and/or growth of rat pups treated in these ways differs significantly from the control animals that are simply left in the home cages. This led to a reexamination of the effect of the "petting" procedure and it was observed that rat pups while being so treated often showed signs of disturbance such as defecating, urinating, and squealing. Thus, more recent experimenters have interpreted the petting procedure as stressful. We, therefore, decided to look for customs of infant care in humans that were unusually stimulating or stressful rather than those which indicated the degree of "tender loving care."

Our method of attacking the problem was, therefore, to study cross-culturally the relation between apparently stressful infant care practices and the stature of adult males. A few words must be said about the assumptions underlying our use of the cross-cultural method for the purpose of testing this hypothesis. In many cases the stature data and the data on infant experiences of a given society had to be obtained from different sources, and had been collected at different times. Even when the same source provided both kinds of data, the descriptions of infant care pertained to a different generation than did the measurements of height. However, if we assume that customs pertaining to treatment of infants probably do not often change radically during one of a few generations, then it is reasonable to assume that the adults whose heights were reported were treated as infants in much the same manner as infants described in contemporaneous ethnographies.

We first obtained as much data as possible on 80 societies about which appropriate information was readily available. Data were taken from societies in the Human Relations Area Files with a few supplementary cases. Each society in the sample was treated as a separate case. The customary ways of treating infants in a given society was one variable. The mean adult stature of males was the other. Thus, the sample of 80 societies actually represented data from a much larger number of individuals.

Sampling of societies was primarily determined by the availability of information, but the sample included a fairly representative cross-section of the world's geographical areas, racial stocks, and cultural groupings.

To begin with, quantitative data on adult male stature were obtained. Next, a person who did not know the hypothesis to be tested and had not seen the height data, abstracted information on infant care from ethnographic reports on each of the societies. From examination of these abstracts we made a list of discrete practices which we thought might be stressful, or unusually stimulating in some manner, and which occurred sometime in early infancy. These were as follows:

1. Piercing, e.g., piercing the nose, lips, or ear to receive an ornament; circumcision, innoculation, scarification, or cauterization.
2. Molding, e.g., stretching the arms or legs, or shaping the head (usually for cosmetic purposes).
3. Extreme Heat—hot baths or exposure to fire or intense sunlight.
4. Extreme Cold—cold baths or exposure to snow or cold air.
5. Internal Stressors—administration of emetics, irritants, or enemas.
6. Abrasions—rubbing with sand, or scraping with a shell or other sharp object.
7. Unusually intense sensory stimulation—massaging, rubbing, annointing, painting, or exposing to loud noises.
8. Binding—swaddling tight enough to be judged painful or other severe restrictions of movement.

For a first rough index a society was given one point for each occurrence of any one of these practices if we judged it to be only slightly stressful; two points for each occurrence which we judged to be severely stressful. These intensity scores were then multiplied by the number of times during the first two weeks of the infant's life they were reported to occur. The judgments were made independently by two judges whose total scores correlated with each other approximately .80. Total scores obtained by simply adding up these ratings for each society were then correlated with mean adult male height. The product moment correlation coefficient was .33, which would be expected on the basis of chance alone less than one time in 100.

The next step was to redo the analysis in a less crude way. First, it seemed reasonable to distinguish between piercing and all other types of stress on the grounds that if the skin was broken as in ear or nose piercing or circumcision, this should put the organism under continued stress until the wound healed. The painful after-effects of these operations are often reported in the ethnographic literature. We decided therefore to consider piercing as stressful if it occurrred but once, but to consider other types as stressful practices only if they were performed daily for at least two weeks. On the basis of this assumption the only types of stress that occurred in enough societies to obtain a reasonable estimate of their effect were piercing, molding, cold, and binding. Only three or less societies of our sample reported the daily occurrence for two weeks of any of the other types of stress. Furthermore, with the above restricted definition, only piercing and molding showed the predicted relation to stature. Both binding and cold stress showed a slightly (insignificant) negative relation. For these reasons further investigation was limited to only two classes of stressors—piercing and molding. A test of the effects of other types of stress must be carried out in some other manner.[2]

In our initial study, early infancy was arbitrarily defined as the first two weeks of life (primarily because it made sampling and data collection more convenient). It would seem more appropriate to choose a period corresponding to the observed "critical period" for beneficial effects of stress in lower organisms. Unfortunately, however, there is no adequate way to extrapolate from animal studies to determine what the analogous period might be in humans. If there is such a critical period in humans, its duration will have to be determined empirically (and we will present a small amount of suggestive evidence concerning this question below). Nonetheless, the animal studies make it abundantly clear that the effects of early stress can be very different, in some instances opposite, from those of later stress. It was therefore essential to delimit the time period to be considered in *some* (hopefully reasonable) way. The one to three week period for beneficial effects of stress in rats and mice appears to correspond very roughly with the usual time of weaning. Since the average time for weaning for humans, cross-culturally speaking, is approximately two years (Whiting and Child 1953) we decided to change our age criterion for infant stress from the first two weeks to the first two years, in the hope that this criterion would prove more biologically meaningful.

A review of the initial study revealed a further weakness. There were a number of societies for which the data on stature was at best suspicious because only a handful of people had been measured or because we had accepted an undocumented assertion by an ethnographer. To correct this weakness, we omitted all societies for which we did not have a report of actual measurement on at least 25 individuals. This reduced the size of our original sample from 80 to 36.

RESULTS

Reduced Original Sample

Results of reanalysis of the reduced original sample are given in Table 1. Societies which stressed infants produced males who were over two inches taller in adulthood than societies in which such practices were absent. The difference is statistically reliable at the .002 level.

TABLE I. REDUCED ORIGINAL SAMPLE

	Piercing or molding during first 24 months of life	
Mean adult male stature—in.	Present (n=17) 65.18	Absent (n=18) 62.69

t=3.72, p<.002

New Sample

Since we had chosen piercing and molding stressors, and the two year age criterion for the analysis of the reduced original sample at least partly on the basis of results from the full original sample, we might have been capitalizing on chance to an unknown degree. It was obviously desirable, therefore, to retest the hypothesis on a completely new and independent sample. For this purpose another 30 societies with appropriate information were obtained and rated in exactly the same manner.[3]

The results for the new sample are shown in Table 2. Again societies which practice molding or piercing had significantly taller adult males than those which practice neither. The difference in average height was again over two inches and highly reliable (*p*<.001).

Combined Sample

Since the two samples yielded such similar results, it seems safe enough to combine them. Table 3 shows the association of each of the two classes of

TABLE 2. RETEST SAMPLE

	Piercing or molding during first 24 months of life	
Mean adult male stature—in.	Present (n=19) 66.05	Absent (n=11) 63.41

t=4.68, p<.001

stressors, shaping and molding, separately for the combined sample. Societies practicing one or the other or both had significantly taller males than societies practicing neither. (Mean difference, 2.5 in. *p*<.001). The average heights associated with piercing alone, molding alone, or both together were approximately the same, which suggests some sort of threshold effect in which any sufficient stress will produce the maximum effect.

Critical Period

As has been suggested above, the animal studies indicate that there is a "critical period" for the effects of stress. For example, Denenberg and Karas (1959) showed that both rats and mice handled during the first ten days of life were significantly heavier as adults than those not handled during this time (i.e. a control group not handled at all and a second experimental group handled between the eleventh and twentieth day). Our data provide some information on this problem with respect to humans. Apparently, because molding and shaping are more effective when the bones are soft, this practice is invariably begun almost immediately after birth. There is, however, considerable variation in the age at which an infant is circumcised, scarified, or pierced for ornaments. Although the age estimates are rough and the number of cases at some of the intervals is small, Table 4 suggests that the first two years could indeed be the critical period for humans.

Tests of Alternative Explanations

It remains to determine whether the association between infant stress and adult stature may be interpreted as the result of a causal relation. Since the observation is purely correlational, cause cannot be determined with any certainty. The problem is that there may be some third variable which occurs by chance in association with stressful infant care practices that is the real cause of variation in stature; or, alternatively, that there is some characteristic of certain groups of people that makes them tall and at the same time likely to stress their children. Thus, if there is any factor that occurs in the same societies of our sample as do the stressful infant care practices, serious doubt would be cast on our findings if this factor can reasonably be interpreted as promoting growth. We therefore tried to discover whether any of the factors known or commonly thought to influence height could be producing the observed correlation.

By obtaining data on our sample relevant to several such factors—genetic stock, sunlight, and diet—we adduced evidence that tends to reject some of the more obvious alternative explanations of the stress-height correlation.

In order to control genetic variables to some degree at least, we broke our sample down into the five major regions of the world—Africa, Eurasia, Insular Pacific, North and South America.[4] If the relation holds true for each of these regions, then it would be difficult to argue that our findings were due to

TABLE 3. COMBINED SAMPLE
Type of Stressor

Mean Adult Male Stature in Inches	Piercing: Absent Molding: Absent	Absent Present	Present Absent	Present Present
70			x	
69			x	
68				
		x	xxx	
67		x	xx	x
	x		xxx	
66	x	x	xx	x
		x	xxxx	x
65	x		x	x
	xxxx	xx		x
64	xxx	x	xx	x
	xxxxx			
63	xxx		x	x
	xx		x	
62	xx		x	
	xxx			
61				
60	xx			
	x			
59				
	x			
58				
Mean	62.9	65.6	65.8	65.0

Significance level	Absent Absent	Absent Present	Present Absent	
Absent Present	$p < .02$			
Present Absent	$p < .001$	$p > .10$		
Present Present	$p < .10$	$p > .10$	$p > .10$	

Each "X" represents a society on which the mean adult stature was available for at least 25 individuals. For the difference between the absence of both types of stressor and the presence of one and/or the other, $p < .001$. All significance levels were obtained by Scheffé's (1959) method of multiple comparisons.

genetics. As can be seen from Table 5, even though the mean for stature differs from region to region, a similar effect of infant stress appears in each region of the world.

TABLE 4. AGE AT FIRST STRESS

Stature	Under 2 weeks	2 weeks to 2 years	2 to 6 years	6 to 15 years	Not before 15
>67"		69.5 34 Shilluk B; 68.5 724 Yankee I; 68.0 70 Dutch I			
67"	67.5 893 Bambara S; 67.5 39 Lau M; 67.0 422 Somali B; 67.0 384 Maori M; 67.0 79 Marquesans M	67.5 385 Tuareg S; 67.0 94 Mossi S			
66"	66.5 1095 Navaho E; 66.0 1130 Yoruba SCM; 66.0 623 Azande M	66.5 292 Serbians I; 66.5 82 Toda E; 66.0 331 Arabs (Pal.) C; 66.0 529 Riffians C			66.5 712 Ganda; 66.0 91 Comanche
65"	65.5 583 Iranians C; 65.5 30 Klamath M; 65.5 44 Ojibwa EM; 65.5 166 Hausa S; 65.0 624 Ibo CM	65.5 579 Poles I; 65.5 5179 Bulgarians I; 65.0 50 Telugu C	65.0 597 Kurd C		
64"	64.5 1051 Kazak M; 64.5 57 Javanese M; 64.5 82 Eskimo (Cop.) M; 64.0 31 Araucanians M; 64.0 453 Aranda B	64.0 199 Chukchee E; 64.0 408 Zuni E	64.5 39 Kikuyu E; 64.5 40 Kuwait C; 64.0 50 Ulithi E; 64.0 42 Marshallese E; 64.0 473 Bhil B	64.5 39 Hadramaut C	64.5 47 Ashanti; 64.0 100 Gond
63"	63.0 276 Hopi E; 63.0 187 Mosquito M		63.5 250 Oraon E; 63.5 73 Nama EB; 63.5 270 Rwala C; 63.0 32 Bontoc C	63.0 946 Lesu CE; 63.0 178 Malayans C	63.5 145 Tarascans
62"		62.5 81 Orokaiva EN; 62.0 213 Khasi E	62.0 622 Ainu E; 62.0 67 Yaghan S		62.5 197 Koryak; 62.5 56 Aymara
61"				61.5 74 Kung S	61.5 57 Lepcha; 61.5 68 Carib
<61"				59.5 257 Semang N; 58.5 438 Andamans T	60.0 41 Cuna; 60.0 300 Kapauku
Number of societies:	20	16	12	6	11
Number of individuals:	8249	9250	2555	1932	1814
Mean Stature:	65.4	65.9	63.6	61.7	63.0

At the left of each society is entered the mean adult male stature and the number of individuals upon which it was based. At the right, the type of stress is indicated by the following code: B = Burning, E = Ear piercing, C = Circumcision, I = Innoculation, L = Lip piercing, N = Nose piercing, S = Scarification, M = Molding.

Sunlight (one of the main sources of vitamin D) was studied by using an estimate of the number of sunny days in a year. This estimate was derived from ethnographic reports supplemented by maps showing annual variations in climate (Goode's Atlas 1957; 14–15). Mean annual rainfall was the best inverse index of sunlight available. Obviously, this measure should be taken as only a rough index of sunshine and hence of the growth-stimulating vitamin D.

The results of this attempt to estimate the effect of this variable upon stature are presented in Table 6. It will be seen from this table that males growing up in sunny climates average 1.9 inches taller than males growing up where it rains frequently. This is in itself an interesting and perhaps surprising finding. For the purposes of this paper, however, it is more important to note

TABLE 5. GEOGRAPHICAL-GENETIC REGION

Mean Adult Male Stature in Inches / Infant Stress	Africa Absent	Africa Present	Eurasia Absent	Eurasia Present	Insular Pacific Absent	Insular Pacific Present	North and South America Absent	North and South America Present
70		x						
69				x				
68		xx		x		x		
67	x	xx				xx		
66		xxx		xx			x	x
65		x	x	xxx				xx
		x		x				
64	xx		xx	x	xx	x		x
63	x		xx		xx		x	xx
			x		xx	x		xx
62			x	x		x	x	
61	x		x				x	
60					x		x	
59			x					
58			x					
Mean	64.1	66.7	62.8	65.6	62.8	65.4	62.6	64.5
Difference	2.6		2.8		2.6		1.9	
p	<.01		<.001		<.01		<.05	

Each "X" represents a society for which the mean adult male stature was available for at least 25 individuals. Significance levels are based on t tests.

that stress has some effect upon stature in both sunny and rainy climates, particularly in the latter. Our findings therefore cannot reasonably be attributed to an effect of climate.

Controlling for the effect of diet upon stature was difficult since we could find no index of diet that, in our sample at least, correlated with adult stature. Although Marjorie Whiting (1958) in a cross-cultural study reported that both the caloric value and the percentage of protein in the average adult diet were positively correlated with adult male stature, these relations did not hold for our sample. An estimate of relative availability of protein based upon the staple crop (Whiting 1963) again showed no relation to adult stature. This failure to find a relation between diet and stature may be due to an inadequate

TABLE 6. MEAN ANNUAL RAINFALL

Infant Stress:	Equal or greater than 60 inches		Less than 60 inches	
Mean Adult Male Stature in Inches	Absent	Present	Absent	Present
70				x
69				x
68				x
		xx		x
67		xx		x
			x	xxxx
66		x	x	xxx
				xxxxxx
65		x	x	x
			xxxx	xx
64	x	x	xx	xxx
		x	xxxx	
63	xxxx			x
	x	x	x	
62		x	xx	
	xx	x	x	
61				
60	xx			
	x			
59				
	x			
58				
Mean	61.6	64.9	63.9	65.9
Difference	3.3		2.0	
p	<.001		<.001	
Mean	63.2		65.0	
Difference		1.8		
p		<.001		

Each "X" represents a society on which the mean adult male stature was available for at least 25 individuals. Significance levels are based on t tests.

estimate of diet. We think that it is also possible, however, that the relation between diet and growth is not as simple as it has sometimes been presumed. A review of the literature indicates that much of the evidence linking diet with stature is an inference from the frequently observed positive correlation between stature and socio-economic class (Tanner, 1962:137 ff.). Clearly, there are many consistent differences other than diet that distinguish the upper from the lower classes (perhaps, even including differences in stressful infant care practices). It may well be unwarranted to assume that the amount of calories or protein in the diet is the crucial factor.

A final alternative which we cannot at present adequately rule out is that these stressful infant care practices actually tend to kill infants who would otherwise grow up to be short. Much more elaborate data are required to deal with this problem adequately. However, we have seen no reports of deaths resulting from piercing or molding in our sources—the native theory in most cases regards the practices as beneficial to health and strength. Furthermore, the mortality of rats is decreased rather than increased by the analogous procedures (Levine 1962).

DISCUSSION

The dangers inherent in inferring causation from correlation have been well advertised and need not be belabored here. Certainly, we would be the last to claim that our data give conclusive evidence that infantile stress enhances growth. There are a large number of possible contaminating variables which might account for our findings and which we have not been able to investigate. To mention but a few, it is possible that parents who stress infants in the ways we have studied also rear them in some way which promotes growth, for example by providing them with better medical care, more sunshine, vitamins, etc., or have a higher value on size which they implement by selective mating or in some other way. Conversely, it is possible that only societies which have strong, fast-growing children can afford the otherwise dangerous luxury of decorating them with scars and deformations. (This is related to the possibility, discussed above, that infant stress is itself a selective factor which spares primarily those who will grow tall.) Or, it may be that children stressed in infancy acquire a mediating characteristic which induces them to engage in some activity which in turn results in increased stature in the population. For example, men stressed in infancy might be more pugnacious with the result that only the large survive, or they might have an acquired sexual preference for large mates (perhaps produced by some Freudian mechanism involving the interaction of the stressor trauma and the period of infantile sexuality in which it occurred.) None of these possibilities (or the many, many more which the fertile imagination can provide) can be ruled out a priori. This is the problem of correlational research.

However, evidence from the present study has two advantageous features, not ordinarily associated with correlational investigations, which make it somewhat more reasonable than usual to entertain the possibility of a causal relation. The first is that the extensive study of human growth has produced a very limited number of demonstrated correlates of stature and it has been possible, in the present study, to rule some of these out by statistical analysis.

Second, and more importantly, the correlation observed in the present study for humans corresponds to an experimentally demonstrated effect in laboratory mammals, and the type of phenomenon—endocrine control of growth—is one in which interspecies generality is common. Therefore, it seems to us that the inference from our data of a causal relation between infant experience and human growth is sufficiently plausible to warrant serious consideration.

SUMMARY

In summary, we have reviewed some recent studies that have shown that rats and mice stimulated during an early period of life attain greater size at adulthood. We have indicated that there are plausible explanations for this effect involving changes in functioning of the adrenal-pituitary system. In exploring whether these results could be generalized to humans, we found that for two independent cross-cultural samples, in societies where the heads or limbs of infants were repeatedly molded or stretched, or where their ears, noses, or lips were pierced, where they were circumcised, vaccinated, innoculated, or had tribal marks cut or burned in their skin, the mean adult male stature was over two inches greater than in societies where these customs were not practiced. The effects of these practices appear to be independent of several other factors known to be associated with increased stature.

NOTES

[1] This paper in an abbreviated form was read at the American Anthropological Association meeting in November 1962 at Chicago. We thank J. Merrill Carlsmith, and Emily H. McFarlin for assistance in data collection.

[2] While we can speculate that the piercing and molding practices correlate with height while the others do not because they intuitively seem more severe and "stressful" than the others, there are really no solid grounds on which to judge what was and was not stressful for the infants involved in the study. Consequently, our interpretation of piercing and molding (laceration and deformation) as special cases of "stressful" treatment in general is open to some question, and must be regarded as tentative.

[3] In our search for these societies we were greatly aided by Dr. Edward E. Hunt, Jr. whose knowledge of the literature on world anthropometry was invaluable.

[4] We decided that since there has been so much controversy recently as to what constitutes a race, the regional division was a safer procedure. It should be noted that we counted only aborigines of the new world. Yankees were classed with the Eurasians. If Coon's classification of races is used instead of the regional classification shown in Table 5, the effects of stress are significant at better than the .01 level for Caucasoids and Mongoloids, but, although the differences are in the same direction and of the same magnitude for the Australoids and Congoids, the number of societies representing these races was too small for the differences to reach statistical significance. Since there are only two Capoid societies in our sample and neither are stressed, no test is possible for this group.

REFERENCES CITED

DENENBERG, V and G. G. KARAS
    1959   Effects of differential infantile handling upon weight gain and mortality in rat and mouse. Science 130:629.

GOLDFARB, W.
    1943   The effects of early institutional care on adolescent personality. Journal of Experimental Education 12:106–129.
    1949   Rorschach test differences between family-reared, institution-reared and schizophrenic children. American Journal of Orthopsychiatry 19:624–633.

GOODE, J. PAUL
    1957   Goode's World Atlas. Tenth Edition. Rand McNally.

GREENMAN, M. J. and DEHRING, F. L.
  1931 Breeding and care of the albino rat for research purposes. Philadelphia, The Wister Institute of Anatomy and Biology. Second Edition.
HAMMETT, M. S.
  1922 Studies of the thyroid apparatus. Endocrinology 4:221–229.
LEVINE, SEYMOUR J.
  1957 Infantile experience and resistance to physiological stress. Science 126:405.
  1958 Noxious stimulation in infant and adult rats and consumatory behavior. Journal of Comparative and Physiological Psychology 51:230.
  1960 Stimulation in infancy. Scientific American 202:80–86.
  1962 Psychophysiological effects of infantile stimulation. *In* Roots of behavior, E. L. Bliss, ed. New York, Paul B. Hoeber.
LEVINE, SEYMOUR J., J. A. CHEVALIER, and S. O. KORCHIN
  1956 The effects of early shock and handling in infancy on later avoidance learning. Journal of Personality 24:475–493.
LEVINE, SEYMOUR J. and G. W. LEWIS
  1959 The relative importance of experimenter contact in an effect produced by extra-stimulation in infancy. Journal of Comparative and Physiological Psychology 52:368–370.
LEVY, D. M.
  1934 Experiments on the sucking reflex and social behavior in dogs. American Journal of Orthopsychiatry 4:202–224.
McCLELLAND, W. J.
  1956 Differential handling and weight gain in the rat. Canadian Journal of Psychology 10:19–22
REUGAMER, W. R. and F. T. SILVERMAN.
  1956 Influence of gentling on physiology of the rat. New York, Proceedings of the Society for Experimental Biology 92:170–172.
SHEFFÉ, H.
  1959 The analysis of variance. New York, Wiley
SPITZ, RENE A.
  1946 Hospitalism: a follow-up report. *In* Anna Freud et al (eds.) Psychoanalytic study of the child. New York, International University Press 2:113–117.
TANNER, J. M.
  1962 Growth at adolescence. Springfield, Ill., Charles C Thomas, Second edition.
WEININGER, O.
  1956 The effects of early experience on behavior and growth characteristics. Journal of Comparative and Physiological Psychology 49:1–9.
WERBOFF, JACK and JOAN HAVLENA.
  1963 Febrile convulsions in infant rats, and later behavior. Science 142:684–685.
WHITING, MARJORIE G.
  1958 A cross-cultural nutrition survey of 118 societies representing the major cultural and geographic areas of the world. Unpublished D.Sc. thesis, Harvard School of Public Health.
WHITING, JOHN W. M.
  1963 Effects of climate upon certain cultural practices. Unpublished manuscript.
WHITING, JOHN W. M. and IRVIN L. CHILD.
  1963 Child training and personality. Yale University Press.

ETHNOGRAPHIC BIBLIOGRAPHY
AINU
  BACHELOR, JOHN
    1927 Ainu life and lore: echoes of a departing race. Tokyo. Kyobunkwan.
  KOYA, Y et al.
    1937 Rassenkunde der Aino. Tokyo, Japanische Gesellschaft zur Förderung der Wissenschaftlichen Forschengen.
  LANDOR, ARNOLD H. S.
    1893 Alone with the hairy Ainu: 3,800 miles on a pack saddle in Yezo and a cruise to the Kurile Islands. London, John Murray.

ANDAMANS

MAN, EDWARD H.
1932 On the aboriginal inhabitants of the Andaman Islands. London, The Royal Anthropological Institute of Great Britain and Ireland.

RADCLIFFE-BROWN, A. R.
1922 The Andaman Islanders: a study in social anthropology. Cambridge, England, Cambridge University Press.

TEMPLE, RICHARD C.
1903 The Andaman and Nicobar Islands. Census of India, 1901 3:1–137. Calcutta, Office of the Superintendent of Government Printing.

ARANDA

BASEDOW, HERBERT
1925 The Australian aboriginal. Adelaide, F. W. Preece and Sons.

CAMPBELL, T. D. and C. J. HACKETT
1927 Adelaide University Field Anthropology: Central Australia No. 1. Introduction: descriptive and anthropometric observations. Transactions and Proceedings of the Royal Society of South Australia, 51:65–75.

SPENCER, WALTER B. and F. J. GILLEN
1927 The Arunta: a study of a Stone Age people, London, Macmillan and Co., Ltd.

ARAUCANIANS

HILGER, M. INEZ
1957 Araucanian child life and its cultural background. Smithsonian Miscellaneous Collections, Vol. 133. Washington, Smithsonian Institution.

LATCHAM, R. E.
1904 Notes on the physical characteristics of the Araucans. Journal of the Royal Anthropological Institute 34:170–180.

TITIEV, MISCHA
1951 Araucanian culture in transition. Occasional Contributions from the Museum of Anthropology of the University of Michigan, No. 16. Ann Arbor, University of Michigan Press.

ASHANTI

RATTRAY, R. S.
1923 Ashanti. Oxford, Clarendon Press.
1927 Religion and art in Ashanti. Oxford, Clarendon Press.

AYMARA

ROUMA, GEORGES
1933 Quitchouas et Aymaras. Etude des populations autochtones des Andes Bolivien-nes. Bulletin Societe Royal Belge d'Anthropologie et de Prehistorie. Bruxelles, Vol. 48:30–296.

TSCHOPIK, HARRY, JR.
1946 The Aymara. Bureau of American Ethnology Bulletin, No. 143, Vol. 2: 501–573. Washington, Smithsonian Institution.

1951 The Aymara of Chucuito, Peru: 1. Magic. Anthropological Papers of the American Museum of Natural History, Vol. 44: 133–308. New York.

AZANDE

LAGAE, C. R.
1926 Les Azande ou Niam-Niam: L'organization Zande, croyances religieuses et magiquis, coutumes familiales. Bibliotheque-Congo, Vol. 18, Bruxelles, Vromant and Co.

LARKEN, P. M.
1926-7 An account of the Zande. Sudan Notes and Records, 9:1–55, 10:85–134. Khartoum, McCorquodale and Co., Ltd.

SELIGMAN, CHARLES G. and BRENDA, Z. SELIGMAN
1932 Pagan tribes of the Nilotic Sudan. London, George Routledge and Sons, Ltd.

BAMBARA

DIETERLEN, GERMAINE
1951 Essai sur la religion Bambara. Paris, Presses Universitaires de France.

MONTELL, CHARLES
 1924 Les Bambara du Segou et du Kaarta: etude historique, ethnographique et lit-
 teraire d'une peuplade du Soudan Francaise. Paris, Emile Larose.

PAQUES, VIVIANA
 1954 Les Bambara. International African Institute, Ethnographic Survey of Africa,
 Western Africa, French Series, Part I. Paris, Presses Universitaires de France.

BHIL

NAIK, T. B.
 1956 The Bhils: a study. Delhi, Bharatiya Adimjati Sevak Sengh.

RISLEY, HERBERT
 1915 The people of India. (Second Edition) Calcutta-London, W. Crooke.

BONTOC

JENKS, ALBERT E.
 1905 The Bontoc Igorot, Department of the Interior Ethnological Publications,
 Vol. 1. Manila, Bureau of Public Printing.

BULGARIANS

SANDERS, IRWIN T.
 1949 Balkan village. Lexington, University of Kentucky, Press.

VATEV, S.
 1904 Contributiona l'etude anthropologique des Bulgares. Bull. et Mem. Soc. Anthrop.
 de Paris, 437–458.

CARIB

GILLIN, JOHN
 1936 The Barama River Caribs of British Guiana. Papers of the Peabody Museum
 of American Archaeology and Ethnology, Vol. 14, No. 2.

CHUKCHEE

BOGORAZ-TAN, VLADIMIR G.
 1904, 1907 and 1909 The Chukchee: Parts 1–3, Memoirs of the American Museum of
 Natural History, Vol. 11. Leiden, E. J. Brill, Ltd. New York, G. E. Stechert
 and Co.

DEBETS, G. F.
 1949 Anthropological research on Kamchatka: a preliminary report. Kratdie Soob-
 shcheniia, Instituta etnografii, Vol. 5:3–18. Moskova and Leningrad, Akademiia
 Nauk S.S.S.R.

COMANCHE

BOAS, F.
 1895 Zur anthropologie der nordamerikanischen Indianer. Zeitschrift für Ethnologie
 27:366–416.

WALLACE, ERNEST and E. ADAMSON HOEBEL
 1957 The Comanches: lords of the South Plains. Norman, University of Oklahoma
 Press.

COPPER ESKIMO

JENNESS, DIAMOND
 1922 The life of the Copper Eskimos. Report of the Canadian Arctic Expedition,
 1913–1918, Vol. 12, Part a. Ottawa, F. A. Acland.

CUNA

HARRIS, R. G.
 1926 The San Blas Indians. American Journal of Physical Anthropology, 9, 1.

HRDLICKA, ALES
 1926 The Indians of Panama and their physical relation to the Mayas. American
 Journal of Physical Anthropology, 9:1.

INGLRDISD, MARVEL ELYA and CHRISTINNE H. MORAN
 1939 From the cradle to the grave: the story of the typical San Blas Indian maiden.
 Cristobal.

STOUT, DAVID B.
 1947 San Blas Cuna acculturation: an introduction. Viking Fund Publication in
 Anthropology, No. 9. New York

WAFER, LIONEL
    1934 A new voyage and description of the isthmus of America. Oxford, The Hakluyt
          Society, Series 2, No. 73.

DUTCH
    COON, C. S.
        1939 Races of Europe. New York, Macmillan and Co.
    KEUR, JOHN Y. and DOROTHY L. KEUR
        1955 The deeply rooted: a study of the Drents community in the Netherlands. Mono-
              graphs of the American Ethnological Society, 25. Assen, Netherlands, at the
              Royal VanGorcum Ltd.

GANDA
    MAIR, LUCY P.
        1934 An African people in the twentieth century. London, George Routledge and Sons.
    ROSCOE, JOGHN
        1911 The Baganda. London, Macmillan and Co.

GOND (Hill Maria)
    GRIGSON, WILFRID V.
        1949 The Maria Gonds of Bastar. Introduction by J. H. Hutton. Reissued in 1949
              (first published in 1938) with a supplement containing 80 pages of additional
              matter and 39 illustrations by the author and Verrier Elwin. London, Oxford
              University Press.

HADRAMAUT
    THOMAS, BERTRAM
        1932 Anthropological observations in South Arabia. Journal of the Royal Anthropo-
              logical Institute of Great Britain and Ireland 62:83–103.

HAUSA
    SMITH, MARY F.
        1954 Baba of Karo: a woman of the Muslim Hausa. London, Faber and Faber Ltd.
    TALBOT, P. A. and H. MULHALL
        1962 The physical anthropology of Southern Nigeria: a biometric study in statistical
              method. Occasional Publications of the Cambridge University Museum of
              Archaeology and Ethnology. Cambridge, The University Press.

HOPI
    HRDLICKA, ALES
        1935 The pueblos, with comparative data on the bulk of the tribes of the southwest and
              northern Mexico. American Journal of Physical Anthropology, 30:235–460.
    MURDOCK, GEORGE P.
        1934 The Hopi of Arizona. *In* Our primitive contemporaries, 324–358. New York,
              Macmillan Co.
    SIMMONS, LEO W.
        1942 Sun Chief: the autobiography of a Hopi Indian. Published for the Institute of
              Human Relations. New Haven, Yale University Press.

IBO
    FORDE, C. D. and G. I. JONES
        1950 The Ibo and Ibibio speaking peoples of southeastern Nigeria. Ethnographic Sur-
              vey of Africa, Western Africa, Part III. London, International African Institute.
    TALBOT, P. A. and H. MULHALL
        1962 The physical anthropology of southern Nigeria: a biometric study in statistical
              method. Occasional Publications of the Cambridge University Museum of
              Archaeology and Ethnology. Cambridge, The University Press.

IRANIANS
    DONALDSON, BESS ALLEN
        1938 The wild rue: a study of Muhammadam magic and folklore in Iran. London,
              Luzac and Co.
    FIELD, HENRY
        1939 Contributions to the anthropology of Iran. Publications of the field Museum of
              Natural History, Anthropological Series, Vol. 29. Chicago.

MASSE, HENRI
> 1938 Croyances et coutumes Persanes. Paris, Librairie Orientale et Americaine.

JAVANESE

GEERTZ, HILDRED
> 1961 The Javanese family a study of kinship and socialization. New York, The Free Press of Glencoe, Inc.

KOHLBRUGGE, J. H. F.
> 1901 Longeur et poids du corps chez les habitants de Java. L'Anthropologie, 12:277–282.

KAPAUKU

BIJLMER, H. J. T.
> 1939 Tapiro Pygmies and Pania Mountain Papuans. Results of the Anthropological Mimika Expedition in New Guinea 1935–1939. Nova Guinea, Vol. 3:113–184. Leiden.

POSPISIL, LEOPOLD
> 1958 Kapauku Papuans and their law. Yale University Publications in Anthropology, No. 54. New Haven, Yale University Press.

KAZAK

FIELD, HENRY
> 1948 Contributions to the anthropology of the Soviet Union. Smithsonian Miscellaneous Collections, Vol. 110, No. 3:1–244. Washington, Smithsonian Institution.

GRODEKOV, N. I.
> 1889 Kirgizy i Karakirgizy Syr Dar'inskoi Oblasti. Vol. I, Juridical Life. Tashkent, The Typolithyography of S. I. Lakhtin.

KHASI

GUHA, B. S.
> 1931 The racial affinities of the people of India. Census of India, Vol. I, Part III, Simla, Government of India Press.

GURDEN, P. R. T.
> 1907 The Khasis. London, David Nutt.
> 1904 Note on the Khasis, Syntengs, and allied tribes inhabiting Khasi and Janital Hills district in Assam. Journal of the Asiatic Society of Bengal, Vol. 73, Part 3, No. 4:57–75.

KIKUYU

BRIGGS, L. CABOT
> 1958 The living races of the Sahara Desert. Papers of the Peabody Museum of Archaeology and Ethnology. Vol. 28, No. 2.

KENYATTA, JOMO
> 1953 Facing Mount Kenya: the tribal life of the Gikuyu. London, Secker and Warburg.

ROUTLEDGE, W. S. and KATHERINE ROUTLEDGE
> 1910 With a prehistoric people: the Akikuyu of British East Africa. London, Edward Arnold.

KLAMATH

BOAZ, FRANZ
> 1895 Zun Anthropologie der nordamerikanischen Indianer. Zeitschrift für Ethnologie 28:391.

SPIER, LESLIE
> 1930 Klamath ethnography. University of California Publications in American Archaeology and Ethnology, Vol. 30. Berkeley, University of California Press.

KORYAK

JOCHELSON, WALDEMAR
> 1905–1908 The Koryak: Part I, religion and myths of the Koryak. Part 2, Material culture and social organization of the Koryak. Jessup North Pacific Expedition Publication, Vol. 6 (American Museum of Natural History Memoirs, Vol. 10)

KUNG BUSHMEN

BLEEK, D. F.
> 1928 Bushmen of Central Angola. Bantu Studies, Vol. III, No. 2.

MARSHAL, LORNA
    1959   Marriage among the Kung Bushmen. Africa 29:335–364.
THOMAS ELIZABETH MARSHALL
    1959   The harmless people. New York, Alfred A. Knopf.

KURD
  FIELD, HENRY
    1961   Ancient and modern man in southwestern Asia: II. Coral Gables, Florida, University of Miami Press.
  MASTERS, WILLIAM M.
    1953   Rowanduz: a Kurdish administrative and mercantile center. Unpublished Ph.D. thesis, University of Michigan.

KUWAIT ARABS
  DICKSON, H. R. P.
    1951   The Arab of the desert: a glimpse into Badawin life in Kuwait and Saudi Arabia. London, George Allen and Unwin, Ltd.
  FIELD, HENRY
    1961   Ancient and modern man in southwestern Asia: II. Coral Gables, Florida, University of Miami Press.

LAU
  HOCART, ARTHUR M.
    1929   Lau Islands, Fiji. Bernice P. Bishop Museum, Bulletin 62. Honolulu.
  THOMPSON, LAURA
    1940   Fijian frontier. Studies of the Pacific, No. 4. San Francisco, Institute of Pacific Relations.
    1940   Southern Lau Fiji: an ethnography. Bernice P. Bishop Museum Bulletin 162. Honolulu.

LEPCHA
  GORER, GEOFFREY
    1938   Himalayan village: an account of the Lepchas of Sikkim. London, Michael Joseph Ltd.
  MORRIS, JOHN
    1938   Living with Lepchas: a book about the Sikkim Himalayas. London, William Heinemann, Ltd.
  RISLEY, H. H.
    1891   The tribes and castes of Bengal. Anthropometric Data, Vol. 1. Calcutta, Bengal Secretariat Press.

LESU
  POWDERMAKER, HORTENSE
    1933   Life in Lesu, the study of a Melanesian society in New Ireland. New York, W. W. Norton and Co., Inc.
  SCHLAGINHAUFIN, O.
    1914   Anthropometrische Untersuchungen an Eingeborenen in Deutsch-Neuguinen. Abhandl. und Besichte des Museums Dresden, 14.

MALAYS
  FIRTH, ROSMARY
    1943   Housekeeping among Malay peasants. Monographs on Social Anthropology No. 7. London, London School of Economics and Political Science.
  HEBERER, G. and W. LEHMANN
    1950   Die Inland-Malaien von Lombok und Sumbawa. Gottingen, Muster-Schmidt.
  LEHMANN, W.
    1934   Anthropologische Beobachtungen auf den kleinen Sunda-Inseln. Zeitschrift für Ethnologie 66:268–276.
  WILKINSON, R. J.
    1920   Papers on Malay subjects. Life and customs, Part I. The incidents of Malay Life. Singapore, Kelly and Walsh.

MAORI

Buck, Peter (Te Rangi Hiroa).
    1949   The coming of the Maori. Wellington, Maori Purposes Fund Board, Whitcombe and Tombs, Ltd.

Ritchie, Jane
    1957   Childhood in Rakau: the first five years of life. Victoria University Publications in Psychology, No. 10 (Monographs on Maori Social Life and Personality, No. 3) Wellington, Victoria University College.

MARQUESANS

Handy, E. S. Craighill
    1923   The native culture in the Marquesas. Bernice P. Bishop Museum Bulletin No. 9. Honolulu.

Linton, Ralph
    1939   Marquesan culture. *In* The individual and his society: the psychodynamics of primitive social organization, Abram Kardiner. New York, Columbia University Press.

Sullivan, Louis R.
    1923   Marquesan somotology with comparative notes on Samoa and Tonga. Memoirs of the Bernice P. Bishop Museum, Vol. 9:139–249. Honolulu.

MARSHALLESE

Kramer, Augustin and Hans Nevermann
    1938   Ralik-Ratak. Ergebnisse der Südsee-Expedition 1908–1910, II. Ethnographie: Mikronesian, Vol. II. Hamburg, Friederichsen, De Gruyter and Co.

Wedgewood, Camilla H.
    1942   Notes on the Marshall Islands. Oceania 13:1–23.

MOSQUITO

Conzemius, Eduard
    1932   Ethnographical survey of the Miskito and Sumu Indians of Hondruas and Nicaragua. Smithsonian Institution.

Kirchoff, Paul
    1948   The Caribbean lowland tribes: the Mosquito, Sumo, Paya, and Jicaque. Smithsonian Institution, Bureau of American Ethnology. Bulletin No. 143, 4:219–229. Washington, Smithsonian Institution.

Pijoan, Michel
    1946   The health and customs of the Miskito Indians of North Nicaragua: interrelationships in a medical program. Mexico, Instituto Indigenista Interamericano.

MOSSI

Mangin, Eugene
    1921   Les Mossi, essai sur les us et coutumes du peuple Mossi a Soudan occidental. Paris, Augustin Challamel.

Tauxier, L.
    1917   Le noir du Yatenga: Mossis, Niconicsses, Simos, Yarses, Silmi, Mossis, Peuls, 225–273. Paris, Emile Larose.

NAMA HOTTENTOTS

Schapera, Isaac
    1930   The Khoisan peoples of South Africa: Bushmen and Hottentots. London, George Routledge and Sons.

Schultze, L.
    1907   Aus Namaland und Kalahari. Jena, Gustav Fischer.
    1928   Zur Kenntnis des Körpers der Hottentotten und Buschmänner. Zoologische und anthropologische ergebnisse einer Forschungsreise im westlichen und zentralen Südfrika, 5:145–227.

NAVAHO

Kluckhohn, Clyde
    1947   Some aspects of Navaho infancy and early childhood. Psychoanalysis and the Social Sciences 1:37–86. New York, International Universities Press.

KLUCKHOHN, CLYDE and DOROTHEA LEIGHTON
    1946   The Navaho. Cambridge, Harvard University Press.
LEIGHTON, DOROTHEA and CLYDE KLUCKHOHN
    1946   Children of the people. Cambridge, Harvard University Press.

OJIBWA (Chippewa)
DENSMORE, FRANCES
    1929   Chippewa customs. Bureau of American Ethnology, Bulletin No. 86. Washing-
          ton, Government Printing Office.
GRANT, J. C. B.
    1930   Anthropometry of the Chipewyan and Cree Indians of the neighborhood of Lake
          Athabaska. Ottawa, National Museum of Canada, Bulletin No. 64, Anthropological
          Series No. 14.
HILGER, M. INEZ
    1951   Chippewa child life and its cultural background. Smithsonian Institution, Bureau
          of American Ethnology, Bulletin 146. Washington, Smithsonian Institution.

ORAONS
ROR, S. C.
    1915   The Oraons. "Man in India" Office, Church Road Ranchi, India.

OROKAIVA
REAY, MARIE
    1953   Social control among the Orokaiva. Oceania 24:110–118.
WILLIAMS, FRANCIS E.
    1930   Orokaiva society. London, Oxford University Press.

PALESTINE ARABS
FIELD, HENRY
    1961   Ancient and modern man in southwestern Asia: II. Coral Gables, University of
          Miami Press.
GRANQUIST, HILMA N.
    1947   Birth and childhood among the Arabs: studies in Muhammadan village in
          Palestine. Helsingfors, Finland, Söderström and Co.

POLES
BENET, SULA
    1951   Song, dance, and customs of peasant Poland. New York, Roy Publishers.
COON, C. S.
    1939   Races of Europe. New York, Macmillan Co.

RIFFIANS
BRIGGS, L. CABOT
    1958   The living races of the Sahara desert. Papers of the Peabody Museum of Archae-
          ology and Ethnology, 28, No. 2.
COON C. S.
    1901   Tribes of the Rif. Harvard African Studies, No. 9. Cambridge, Peabody Museum,
          Harvard University.
WESTERMARCK, EDWARD
    1926   Ritual and belief in Morocco. London, Macmillan and Co.

RWALA
BRIGGS, L. CABOT
    1958   The living races of the Sahara Desert. Papers of the Peabody Museum of Archae-
          ology and Ethnology. Vol. 28, No. 2.
MUSIL, ALOIS
    1928   The manners and customs of the Rwala Bedouins. New York, The American
          Geographical Society, Oriental Explorations and Studies, No. 6.
RASWAN, CARL R.
    1947   Black tents of Arabia. New York, Creative Age Press.

SEMANG
EVANS, IVOR H. N.
    1937   The Negritos of Malaya. Cambridge, The University Press.

SCHEBESTA, PAUL
  1927   Among the forest dwarfs of Malaya. London, Hutchinson and Co.
SKEAT, W. W. and C. O. BLAGDEN
  1906   Pagan races of the Malay peninsula. New York, Macmillan and Co.

SERBS
  COON, CARLETON S.
    1949   Racial history. *In* Yugoslavia, Robert J. Kerner, ed. Berkeley, University of California Press.
  HALPERN, JOEL M.
    1956   Social and cultural change in a Serbian village. New Haven, Human Relations Area Files.

SHILLUK
  RIAD, MOHAMED
    1955   Some observations of a fieldtrip among the Shilluk. Wiener Völkerkundliche Mitteilungen, Vol. 3:70–78. Wien, Völkerkundliche Arbeitgemeinschaft in der Anthropologischen Gesellschaft in Wien.
  SELIGMAN, CHARLES G. and BRENDA Z. SELIGMAN
    1932   Pagan tribes of the Nilotic Sudan. London, George Routledge and Sons, Ltd.

SOMALI
  BRIGGS, L. CABOT
    1958   The living races of the Sahara desert. Papers of the Peabody Museum of Archaeology and Ethnology, Vol. 28, No. 2.
  LEWIS, I. M.
    1955   Peoples of the horn of Africa. Ethnographic Survey of Africa, North Eastern Africa, Part I, London, International African Institute.
  PAULITSCHKE, PHILIPP
    1888   Beiträge zue Ethnographie und Anthropologie der Soma, Galla, und Harari. Leipzig, Eduard Baldamus.

TARASCANS
  BEALS, RALPH L.
    1948   Cheran: a Sierra Tarascan village. Institute of Social Anthropology Publication No. 2. Washington, Smithsonian Institution.
  LASKER, GABRIEL W.
    1953   Ethnic identification in an Indian Mestize community: II. Racial characteristics. Phylon 14: 187–190.

TELUGU
  DUBE, S. C.
    1955   Indian village. Ithaca, Cornell University Press.
  GUHA, B. S.
    1931   The racial affinities of the people of India. Census of India, Vol. I, Part III. Simla, Government of India Press.

ZUNI
  PARSONS, ELSIE CLEWS
    1919   Mothers and children at Zuni, New Mexico. Man 19:168–173. (Article 86)
  STEVENSON, MATILDA C.
    1904   The Zuni Indians: their mythology, esoteric fraternities, and ceremonies. 23rd Annual Report of the Bureau of American Ethnology to the secretary of the Smithsonian Institution, 1901–02, 1–634. Washington, Government Printing Office.

NORMAN SOLKOFF, SUMNER YAFFE, DAVID WEINTRAUB
& BARBARA BLASE

53   Effects of Handling on the Subsequent Developments of Premature Infants

The immediate and subsequent effects of handling on the behavioral and physical development of 10 low birth weight infants were studied. The 5 experimental infants were stroked in their isolettes 5 minutes every hour of the day, for 10 days, while the 5 controls were provided with routine nursery care. The handled infants were more active, regained initial birth weights faster and were described as physically healthier in terms of growth and motor development than the controls. Home ratings of intensity and variety of stimulation were also higher for the handled infants at between 7 and 8 months of age.

A variety of anomalies has been found to be associated with low birth weight or prematurity. Among the sequelae enumerated have been such deficiencies as intellectual impairment, even at ages ranging into adolescence. (Harper, Fischer, & Rider, 1959; Wiener, Rider, Oppel, & Harper, 1968), slow learning (Harmeling & Jones, 1968), lack of concentration (Drillien, 1961), confusion, hyperactivity and disorganization (Rogers, Lilienfeld, & Pasamanick, 1955), linguistic immaturity, especially as reflected in oral language and lack of reading readiness (DeHirsch, Jansky, & Langford, 1964), visual disorders (Dann, Levine, & New, 1958, 1964), motor retardation (DeHirsch, Jansky, & Langford, 1966; Rabinovitch, Bibace, & Caplan, 1961), and neurological abnormalities (Knobloch & Pasamanick, 1966).

Most investigators have emphasized neurological defect or minimal brain damage as explanatory hypotheses for these undesirable sequelae and have suggested numerous environmental factors presumed to underlie both the prematurity and associated neurological involvement.

One factor insufficiently considered in pre-

Reprinted from *Developmental Psychology* 1:765–768, 1969. Copyright 1969 by the American Psychological Association and reproduced by permission.

This study was supported by General Research Support No. 18, State University of New York at Buffalo.

vious research has been the possible role of sensory deprivation in producing some of the impairments associated with low birth weight. There are considerable clinical and experimental animal data to suggest that a dearth of early environmental stimulation may deleteriously and irreversibly affect a wide range of behaviors (Denenberg, 1959; Levine, 1957; Levine & Otis, 1958; Spitz, 1945, 1946). In view of the nature of the immediate postuterine environment of the premature infant, it therefore becomes reasonable to explore the possible adverse effects of life in the well-controlled, monotonous environment of an isolette where the infant receives minimal emotional, sensory, or tactual stimulation for several weeks. Specifically, the problem posed by the present research is: What are the immediate and subsequent effects of one form of stimulation, handling, on the behavioral and physical development of premature infants?

In one of two studies on early stimulation of premature infants, Hasselmeyer (1964) found that infants who received increased sensory, tactile, and kinesthetic stimulation were made significantly more quiescent, especially before feeding; while a low-handled group exhibited more crying behavior before feedings. There were no significant differences between the groups in morbidity, weight gain, number of defecations, or in response to an interruption of the feeding process. In the second study, Freedman, Boverman, and Freedman (1966) found that among five co-twin control cases, the rocked twin (rocked twice daily for 30 minutes 7–10 days after an upward weight trend was established) gained weight at a greater rate per day than did the control twin in every instance, although the advantage of the rocked group was only a temporary one.

Method

Subjects

The subjects in the present study were to consist of 20 white premature infants, 10 boys and 10 girls, with birth weights between 1,190 (2 pounds 8 ounces) and 1,590 grams (3 pounds 8 ounces). However, because of a variety of personnel problems and an unexpected reduction in the number of premature births in the Buffalo area, the sample for this pilot study was reduced to a total of 10 infants, 4 boys and 1 girl in the experimental group, with the same number and sex distribution in the control group. The mean birth weight for the experimental group was 3.00 pounds and for the control group, 3.02 pounds.

Procedure

Within 12 hours after delivery, each infant was examined by a physician and those ascertained to be functioning within "normal" limits were randomly assigned to either an experimental or control group. The subjects in the control group were treated in the manner customarily employed in the care of premature infants at the nursery. Handling of these infants took place at 3-hour intervals in association with the feeding process, and was mainly confined to rubbing the infant's back until a burp had been produced. Aside from handling associated with diaper change, stimulation produced by spontaneous movements, and the usual environmental stimuli in the nursery, these infants experienced no additional stimulation for a period of 10 days.

In addition to the stimulation received by the control subjects, each infant in the experimental group was handled in his isolette 5 minutes each hour, for 24 hours, for a period of 10 days. Handling was accomplished in the following way: As close as possible to the beginning of each hour, and while awake, the infant's neck, back, and arms were gently rubbed by a nurse or aide. Although it was impossible to ensure equal handling pressures, a fair degree of similarity was achieved through training. After the 10-day experimental period, and until discharge from the nursery, the experimental infants were treated in the same manner as were the controls.

Dependent Variables

Activity. To provide continuous activity recording, each infant rested on a stabilimeter (Lipsitt

& DeLucia, 1960) which was placed in his isolette. During each of the 10 experimental days, polygraph readings, from a Honeywell recorder, were taken at the following times: (*a*) every 4 hours, (*b*) 5 minutes before each feeding, (*c*) 5 minutes after each feeding, (*d*) 5 minutes after handling, and (*e*) during three crying periods.

Weight. From the time of delivery until leaving the nursery, each infant was weighed once a day, at about the same time.

Temperature. Six times each day, for the 10-day experimental period, each infant's axillary temperature was taken for 1 minute.

Startle responses. Once a day, the magnitude of the startle response to a constant, sudden noise was recorded on the stabilimeter.

Crying. Six 10-minute observations by two independent observers (Sophomore medical students) were made of the intensity of crying and vigor of accompanying bodily movements.

Frequency of urination and defecation. The infants' diapers were loosely attached so that hourly checks could be made as to whether the infant urinated or defecated.

Physical development. After a period of time varying from 6 to 9 months, each infant was examined by the same pediatrician who knew nothing of the nature of the experiment.

Results

Immediate Effects of Handling

Because of the small size of the sample no formal statistical procedures were applied to the data, and all findings must, therefore, be considered tentative.

Two measures seemed to be affected by the experimental conditions: The handled infants were more active and they regained their initial birth weights faster than did the control infants. The control group regained its birth weight in 15.4 days while for the experimental group it was 10.8 days. However, by the time the infants were 6 weeks old, the initial advantage of the experimental group was lost. There was also some indication that the experimental infants cried less than did the controls.

In relation to the finding on activity, it was interesting to note some of the nurses' observations. They seemed to feel that after several handling experiences, the infants began to act as though they anticipated additional handling. They based this conclusion on the observation that the infants gradually became more active immediately prior to each subsequent stimulation period. The possibility of temporal conditioning having occurred will have to be studied under more carefully controlled conditions with an additional sample of infants.

Follow-Up Effects

Somewhere between 7 and 8 months after the infants were discharged from the premature nursery, the Bayley Test of Mental and Motor Development (Bayley, 1965) and a complete physical examination were administered to each infant by a pediatrician who was unaware of the nature of the study. In addition, a home visit to obtain a history of the child's physical and behavioral progress and to assess the home environment was made by a second-year medical student who was also in the dark as to the experimental or control status of a given infant.

Generally, the handled infants fared better than their nonhandled controls. All of the handled babies were described as active and physically healthy. Of the five nonhandled infants, three were rated as more than two standard deviations below the growth mean for their age and one was at the lower limit of normal. Two of these four children were also rated as suspicious for cerebral palsy. Thus, only one child in the nonhandled group was considered to be developing normally.

Whereas only one of the handled babies showed poor gross and fine motor development, four of the nonhandled infants were below the mean for their age in motor development.

Assessments of the home environment were made in a rather subjective fashion and consisted of interviews with the mother and observations of certain physical arrangements in the home. In general, the homes of the handled infants were found to offer the child more stimulation (e.g., more toys, greater mother-infant interaction, etc.) than was the case in the homes of the nonhandled babies. It is tantalizing to speculate whether the handling procedures may have more positively affected the infants' behavior, thereby resulting in a more positive attitude on the part of the mother toward her infant.

Discussion

In contrast to the opinions of some pediatricians and nurses, there were no deleterious effects of the handling procedures on any of the infants.

On the basis of these pilot data, suggestive differences do appear between handled and nonhandled prematures in respect to both activity level and the speed with which initial birth weight is regained.

In view of the small size of the present sample, some of the differences reported may be due entirely to chance. For example, the two infants diagnosed as suspicious for cerebral palsy may have unfavorably biased the results for the nonhandled group. It is therefore imperative that subsequent studies of this nature very carefully match control and experimental infants.

In subsequent research, the present study will be replicated, differences in conditionability as a function of handling will be studied, and the behavioral effects of other types of early stimulation, for example, visual, auditory, will be evaluated.

REFERENCES

Bayley, N. Comparisons of mental and motor test scores for ages 1–15 months by sex, birth order, race, geographic location, and education of parents. *Child Development*, 1965, **36,** 379–411.

Dann, M., Levine, S. Z., & New, E. V. The development of prematurely born children with birthweights or minimal postnatal weights of 1000 grams or less. *Pediatrics*, 1958, **22,** 1037–1053.

Dann, M., Levine, S. Z., & New, E. V. A long-term follow-up study of small premature infants. *Pediatrics*, 1964, **33,** 945–960.

De Hirsch, K., Jansky, J. J., & Langford. W. S. The oral language performance of premature children and controls. *Journal of Speech and Hearing Disorders*, 1964, **29,** 60–69.

De Hirsch, K., Jansky, J., & Langford. W. S. Comparisons between prematurely and maturely born children at three age levels. *American Journal of Orthopsychiatry*, 1966, **36,** 616–628.

Denenberg, V. H. Effects of differential handling upon weight gain and mortality in the rat and mouse. *Science*, 1959, **130,** 629–630.

Drillien, C. M. The incidence of mental and physical handicaps in school-age children of very low birthweight. *Pediatrics,* 1961, **27,** 452–464.

Freedman, D. G., Boverman, H., & Freedman, N. Effects of kinesthetic stimulation on weight gain and on smiling in premature infants. Paper presented at the meeting of the American Orthopsychiatric Association. San Francisco, April 1966.

Harmeling, J. D., & Jones, M. B. Birthweights

of high school dropouts. *American Journal of Orthopsychiatry*, 1968, **38**, 63–66.

HARPER, P. A., FISCHER, L. K., & RIDER, R. V. Neurological and intellectual status of prematures at three to five years of age. *Journal of Pediatrics*, 1959, **55**, 679–690.

HASSELMEYER, E. G. The premature neonate's response to handling. *American Nurses' Association*, 1964, **11**, 15–24.

KNOBLOCH, H., & PASAMANICK, B. Prospective studies on the epidemiology of reproductive casualty: Methods, findings and some implications. *Merrill-Palmer Quarterly of Behavior and Development*, 1966, **12**, 27–43.

LEVINE, S. Infantile experience and resistance to physiological stress. *Science*, 1957, **126**, 405.

LEVINE, S., & OTIS, L. S. The effects of handling before and after weaning on the resistance of albino rats to later deprivation. *Canadian Journal of Psychology*, 1958, **12**, 103–108.

LIPSITT, L. P., & DeLUCIA, C. A. An apparatus for the measurement of specific response and general activity of the human neonate. *American Journal of Psychology*, 1960, **73**, 630–632.

RABINOVITCH, M. S., BIBACE, R., & CAPLAN, H. Sequelae of prematurity: Psychological test findings. *Canadian Medical Association Journal*, 1961, **84**, 822–824.

ROGERS, M. E., LILIENFELD, A. M., & PASAMANICK, B. *Prenatal and paranatal factors in the development of childhood behavior disorders.* Copenhagan: Munksgaard, 1955.

SPITZ, R. A. Hospitalism: An inquiry into the genesis of psychiatric conditions in early childhood. *Psychoanalytic Studies of the Child*, 1945, **1**, 53–74.

SPITZ, R. A. Hospitalism: An inquiry into the genesis of psychiatric conditions in early childhood. *Psychoanalytic Studies of the Child*, 1946, **2**, 113–117.

WIENER, G., RIDER, R. V., OPPEL, W. C., & HARPER, P. A. Correlates of low birthweight: Psychological status at eight to ten years of age. *Pediatric Research*, 1968, **2**, 110–118.

Editor's note: This article by Solkoff, Yaffe, Weintraub, and Blase has been published with its small *N* and absence of conventional statistical treatment of data because of its important implications for the health and later welfare of prematurely born infants. Additionally, it is very relevant to the growing theory and literature about early organism stimulation. The authors clearly recognize and frankly state its deficiencies as a finished piece of research, but join the Editor in believing that it is useful to publish it at this time.

SOCIAL DETERMINANTS

Chapter Thirteen   SOCIAL FACTORS

Chapter Twelve

MATERNAL INFLUENCES

The fact that the mammalian mother is a source of warmth, nurturance, and stimulation to her offspring is immediately apparent. Though it is intuitively obvious that the mother plays a critically important role in shaping the future destiny of her offspring, it has been difficult to verify this empirically, to determine the extent of her influence, and to isolate the mechanism involved. One reason for this has been the psychiatric, especially psychoanalytical, bias of a number of older investigators, which led them to assume the critical importance of the mother and to interpret their findings as proof of this assumption rather than attempting to test the validity of the assumption. Other reasons have been their failure to pay adequate attention to the need for appropriate controls and to consider alternative hypotheses to account for their data.

Despite the limitations of their findings, these early researchers stimulated further research and brought about changes in medical practices. One such pioneer was John Bowlby, whose World Health Organization monograph in 1951 on maternal deprivation focused attention upon the deleterious consequences of separating an infant or young child from its mother when the child had to be hospitalized. Bowlby did not present a solid scientific case for his thesis, but the sum total of his argument was convincing enough to persuade many hospitals to change their rules and allow the mother to stay with her child during his hospitalization.

Another central figure of this era was Rene Spitz, who reported that children reared in orphanages had severe emotional and physical disturbances, to the point of wasting away and dying (Spitz, 1945, 1946a, 1946b, 1951; Spitz

and Wolf, 1951). No one questioned that Spitz was reporting on a population of very sick infants and children, but his claim that the *cause* of these distresses was lack of adequate mothering was never documented. Since Spitz refused to reveal the locations of the children and would not allow others to examine his raw data, his reports cannot be considered part of the body of scientific knowledge — which demands independent investigation and verification — but are better thought of as the considered clinical judgment of an experienced physician. For a detailed critique and dissection of Spitz' reports, see Pinneau (1955a). The reader should also examine Spitz' (1955) reply to Pinneau, and the latter's rejoinder (Pinneau, 1955b).

Thus, the physicians to whom rich clinical populations were available for study and analysis never presented convincing scientific documentation of the effects of maternal influence upon the offspring's behavior. No one questioned the clinical judgment of these physicians, and indeed, virtually everybody held the same basic belief, but science does not advance by belief alone. Hard facts are needed to allow researchers to describe the phenomena under investigation and see cause-effect relationships which will ultimately lead to the understanding of mechanisms. The arguments of the psychiatrist, based upon very soft data, were inadequate.

In addition to clinical observations of human populations, another source of information is animal experimentation. Although some noteworthy individuals were interested in the problems of maternal influence, there was no concentrated effort from any laboratory on this problem. When research on infantile experiences did become a major activity in a number of laboratories in the 1950's, the emphasis was not on maternal influence but on experimenter-mediated stimulation, such as handling or electric shock (see Chapter Eleven). Experimenter-mediated stimulation was chosen because it allowed the researcher control over the parameters he was manipulating (e.g., amount of time away from mother, intensity of electric shock, temperature to which the animal was exposed while out of the nest box) — a control he could not maintain over the behavior of the mother.

However, after several years of research with experimenter-mediated variables, a number of workers involved in this type of experimentation had obtained sufficient data to realize that they could not fully account for their findings with the variables they were manipulating. Also, observations of infant animals returned to the nest box showed clearly that the mothers acted differently toward these young than did the mothers of nondisturbed controls. Thus, a number of researchers began to turn their attention to investigating maternal variables. As more and more research data were gathered concerning maternal variables, much of the mystique of motherhood began to disappear. It is clear that "the mother" is a highly complex multidimensional stimulus who interacts with her infant in a reciprocal fashion. One of her characteristics is supplying stimulation and stimulus variation (see Chapter Eleven), so the lack of a mother may have the same consequences as other forms of environmental deprivation (see Chapter Nine). Other characteristics include acting as a social stimulus, as a reinforcer, and as a model to be emulated. Some of these features are brought out by the readings in this chapter.

These papers are all concerned with affective endpoints. These include emotional reactivity, the responsivity of the adrenal cortex, aggression, sexual and maternal behaviors, fear and preferences, and reactions to strangers. In all instances maternal variables have been shown to be of prime importance. Oddly enough, neither those people working with animals nor those investigating humans have extensively studied cognitive, intellectual, or perceptual endpoints, and so the relationship between maternal influence and subsequent behaviors involving higher cortical processes is not as well known as is the relationship between maternal influence and subsequent affective behaviors.

Ottinger *et al.* (Paper 54) used rats to test two clinical hypotheses derived from human observations and research. These hypotheses were that (1) there would be a positive relationship between the level of maternal emotionality and the emotionality of the offspring, and (2) offspring reared under a multiple mothering situation, where there was less consistency and predictability of the mother's behavior, would exhibit greater emotional upset than would animals raised under single mothering conditions. This paper illustrates the kind of experiment in which the animal is used as a "model" or a simulator of the human. The assumption here is that the same principles which apply at the human level also apply at the animal level. Since the animal has a simpler nervous system which develops at a much more rapid rate, since its experiences can be deliberately controlled and programmed, and since experimental manipulations are permissible with animals which cannot be justified with humans, testing the animal is often more convenient and more appropriate than testing a human. This generalization from one phylogenetic level to another without benefit of a comparative series of experiments is not unique to behavioral research. In molecular biology, for example, genetic principles and the nature of the DNA molecule have been worked out with bacteria and viruses and have been assumed to apply to all living matter.

A different use of animal material is seen in Paper 55, by Southwick, who investigated the role of the mother in affecting aggressive behavior in mice by the procedure of cross-fostering newborn pups from one mouse strain to another. Unlike Ottinger *et al.*, who attempted to test two general propositions derived from human research, Southwick was concerned with ascertaining whether the mother influences a species-specific behavior pattern — namely, aggression. The ultimate aim of this type of research is to isolate the mechanisms by which the mother modifies the offspring's subsequent aggression, rather than to establish a general phylogenetic principle. In this sense then, Southwick's work concerns animal behavior. Southwick found that pups born of a docile strain of mice became much more aggressive when reared by a female from an aggressive strain. However, the opposite was not found to be true; mice from a genetically aggressive strain did not become less aggressive if they were reared by a nonaggressive foster mother.

The Southwick findings should not be interpreted to mean that aggression can only be increased, not decreased. Previously, other researchers had shown that the species-specific aggressive behavior in the mouse could be markedly reduced, and in some instances virtually eliminated, if the mice were fostered to a lactating rat mother (Denenberg *et al.,* 1964; Hudgens *et al.,* 1968). A concern of these researchers, and one shared by Southwick, was whether the behavioral differences in aggression were a function of the foster mother's behavior toward her young (whether the foster mother was a rat or a mouse), or whether the observed differences were brought about by hormonal or biochemical factors in the milk of the different mothers. This was the problem to which Denenberg *et al.* addressed themselves in the work reported in Paper 56. Instead of having a rat mother rear young mice from birth, they introduced a rat "aunt" into a cage containing a mouse mother and her litter of pups. The rat aunt exhibited essentially the same maternal behavior pattern toward the mouse pups as did a rat mother except that she did not nurse them. These researchers found that the presence of the rat aunt modified the reactivity of the mice's adrenal cortex and also reduced their open-field activity — findings virtually the same as those obtained in a previous study in which rat mothers had reared the mouse pups. Since the milk factor had been eliminated through the use of the rat aunt, this study strongly implied that the mouse pups' behavioral and physiological changes were mediated through a behavioral mechanism involved in the mother-young or aunt-young interactions during the nursing period.

Another way to study the functions of the mother's influence on her offspring's behavior is to rear the young animal without its mother. This can be done with the rat (Thoman and Arnold, 1968a, 1968b; also see Paper 28), but because this animal is very immature at birth and must be handled frequently in order to be fed, the effects of maternal deprivation are difficult to separate from the effects of extra handling stimulation. It is more convenient to use a precocial animal which, though normally raised by its mother, is well enough developed physically and physiologically so that it can live alone if given a source of food and maintained in a competent environment. The rhesus monkey meets these specifications, and Paper 57 is a delightful report by Harlow on the development and expression of sexual behavior in this animal. The initial portion of the paper is concerned with a description of the development of male and female behavior patterns in monkeys normally reared with their mothers or else reared with surrogate mothers made of wire or cloth (see Harlow and Zimmerman, 1959). Up until puberty the surrogate-reared animals appeared to be as normal as controls, but after this Harlow found gross incompetence in both sexual and maternal behaviors. An important point derived from these findings is that the effects of early experiences may not express themselves until much later in development, and thus it is dangerous to conclude that certain forms of infantile stimulation or early experience are without effect until the animals have been studied well into maturity. Further analysis by Harlow indicated that the lack of competent sexual behavior appears to be more related to the lack of peer group interactions than to the lack of mother-young interactions. This finding should not be overgeneralized since the nervous system of the rhesus monkey is much better developed at birth than the human's nervous system, making comparisons between these two primate species difficult.

Harlow's study found gross social incompetence in adulthood as a function of maternal and peer deprivation. Green and Gordon (Paper

58) were interested in determining some of the effects of maternal deprivation during early development on the visual preferences of the young. Monkeys raised normally by their own mothers showed a strong initial preference for looking at adult females in a two-choice preference test. However, this interest declined over the 30-week testing interval, while their interest in looking at age peers increased. The results for the group of monkeys reared without mothers were very different: these animals were uniformly uninterested in looking at any stimuli. The authors indicate that this lack of interest was probably due to the exaggerated fear and inappropriate behavior of the experimental animals when placed into the test situation. Thus, part of the contribution which a monkey mother makes to her young's development is aid in reducing fear and in helping to establish a preference hierarchy toward social stimuli.

The difficulties involved in trying to determine the role of maternal influence at the human level are obvious. The nice experimental manipulations in which animal researchers can engage are not permissible, and so the researcher has to look for a "natural experiment" or depend on correlational techniques to study the relationships between maternal variables and subsequent infant behavior. A good example of the latter procedure is reported in Paper 59. These investigators correlated the amount of time a mother and her infant looked at each other (gazing or mutual visual regard) during the first and third months of the infant's life with (1) the amount of time the infant looked at a stranger at 8 months and at 9.5 months of age, (2) the infant's fear of strangers, and (3) his social approach to strangers. They found that the more time the mother and infant spent looking at each other during the first several months of life, the less fearful of strangers was the infant later on and the more often he looked at the stranger. Since these are correlational data, interpretation within a causal framework must be cautious. One interpretation is that the mother's action in looking at her baby during early infancy was instrumental in reducing the baby's fear of strangers and increasing his social approaches toward the

stranger. However, as the authors point out, gazing is a reciprocal relationship, and part of the behavioral differences observed with the strangers may be a function of the infant's visual behavior rather than the visual activity of the mother. Nevertheless, since gazing is reciprocal, the role of the mother as part of this two-way system is established.

Paper 60 illustrates the "natural experiment" approach to studying the influence of maternal behavior in humans. It is a preliminary report which offers the potential for some exciting research with newborns. These researchers were aware of animal studies showing the importance of mother-young interaction for the well-being of both members of the pair and the deleterious effects of separation. A "natural" situation where the human mother-infant bond is broken occurs when a premature baby is kept in an incubator for 3 to 13 weeks. This results in a form of deprivation for both the mother and infant, though the nature of the deprivational experience obviously differs for each member of the pair. In their pilot study Barnett *et al.* investigated the effects upon the mother of allowing her to visit the premature nursery and touch and handle her infant from as early as the second day of life. Those mothers who had this experience were found to be more committed to their infants, to have greater self-confidence in their ability to mother the infant, and to be more adept at caretaking activities. Although no follow-up data were available at the time this paper was written, it is reasonable to assume that these changes in maternal behavior would influence the infant's development.

References

Bowlby, J. *Maternal Care and Mental Health.* Geneva: World Health Organization, 1951.

Denenberg, V. H., Hudgens, G. A., and Zarrow, M. X. Mice reared with rats: Modification of behavior by early experience with another species. *Science,* 1964, 143, 380-381.

Harlow, H. F., and Zimmermann, R. R. Affectional responses in the infant monkey. *Science,* 1959, 136, 421-431.

Hudgens, G. A., Denenberg, V. H., and Zarrow, M. X. Mice reared with rats: Effects of preweaning and postweaning social interactions upon adult behaviour. *Behaviour,* 1968, 30, 259-274.

Pinneau, S. R. The infantile disorders of hospitalism and anaclitic depression. *Psychol. Bull.,* 1955, 52, 429-452. (A)

Pinneau, S. R. Reply to Dr. Spitz. *Psychol. Bull.,* 1955, 52, 459-462. (b)

Spitz, R. A. Hospitalism: An inquiry into the genesis of psychiatric conditions in early childhood. *Psychoanal. Stud. Child,* 1945, 1, 53-74.

Spitz, R. A. Anaclitic depression. *Psychoanal. Stud. Child,* 1946, 2, 313-342. (a)

Spitz, R. A. Hospitalism: A follow-up report. *Psychoanal. Stud. Child,* 1946, 2, 113-117. (b)

Spitz, R. A. The psychogenic diseases of infancy: An attempt at their etiologic classification. *Psychoanal. Stud. Child,* 1951, 6, 255-275.

Spitz, R. A. Reply to Dr. Pinneau. *Psychol. Bull.,* 1955, 52, 453-458.

Spitz, R. A., and Wolf, K. M. Autoerotism: Some empirical findings and hypotheses on three of its manifestations in the first year of life. *Psychoanal. Stud. Child,* 1951, 3/4, 85-120.

Thoman, E. B., and Arnold, W. J. Incubator rearing in infant rats without the mother: Effects on adult emotionality and learning. *Develop. Psychobiol.,* 1968, 1, 219-222. (a)

Thoman, E. B., and Arnold, W. J. Effects of incubator rearing with social deprivation on maternal behavior in rats. *J. Comp. Physiol. Psychol.,* 1968, 65, 441-446. (b)

DONALD R. OTTINGER, VICTOR H. DENENBERG, & MARK W. STEPHENS

54 Maternal Emotionality, Multiple Mothering, and Emotionality in Maturity

3 experiments were conducted to test the hypotheses that offspring emotionality is positively associated with mother's level of emotionality (rated from prepregnancy open-field behavior) and that offspring experiencing multiple mothering (mother rotated between her own litter and one foster litter every 24 hr.) are more emotional in adulthood than offspring reared by a single mother. Ss were 269 Purdue-Wistar rats from 36 litters. Experiment 1 employed a 3 × 2 factorial design. Offspring were weighed at 21, 50, and 62 days and tested in the open field daily on Days 50–53. Open-field emotionality data confirmed both hypotheses. Experiments 2 and 3 established that offspring emotionality is independently related to both prenatal and postnatal emotionality of mother.

A prior study by Denenberg, Ottinger, and Stephens (1962) found that offspring emotionality in rats could be increased, and body weight affected, by experimentally increasing maternal "anxiety," or emotionality, *post*natally; and that offspring emotionality and body weight were similarly affected by "multiple mothering." The three

Reprinted from *Journal of Comparative and Physiological Psychology* 56:313–317, 1963. Copyright 1963 by the American Psychological Association and reproduced by permission.

This investigation was supported in part by Research Grant M-1753 from the National Institute of Mental Health of the National Institutes of Health, United States Public Health Service.

studies reported herein are extensions of that experiment, with additional controls. One important difference in procedure was that rather than experimentally inducing maternal emotionality by shock as in the first study, variance in maternal emotionality in these studies was defined by previously *observed* differences in emotionality among the mothers used.

From two common clinical assumptions it was predicted that offspring emotionality would be positively associated with the mother's level of emotionality and that offspring experiencing multiple mothering would be more emotional in adulthood than offspring reared by a single mother.

METHOD

Subjects

For all three experiments combined 269 Purdue-Wistar rats (previously called Harvard-Wistar) from 36 litters were used.

Open-Field Emotionality Testing

The open field consisted of a 45 in. square plywood base with walls 18 in. high. The complete unit was painted flat black except for thin white lines which divided the floor into 9 in. squares. The field was approximately evenly lighted throughout by overhead fluorescent lights. Entrance into the field was by means of a hole 6 in. in diameter cut in one side of the box and placed ½ in. from the baseboard. This hole could be uncovered by a sliding metal door. The S was carried from its home cage to the box in a 1-gal. circular container which would be attached to the side of the box over the hole. The raising of the metal door permitted S to enter the field. S was given 2 min. to enter the field. If it had not done so by then, it was gently forced out by means of a "plunger" inside the circular container, and the door was closed behind S. The S was left in the field for 2 min. Latency to emerge from the can, total number of squares entered with all four feet, number of center (i.e., nonwall) squares entered, and number of boluses were recorded.

Emotionality Classification of Mothers

The classification of adult females into low-, medium-, or high-emotionality levels was done by testing all females in the colony in the open field as described above. The Ss were then ranked on each of the three measures, and these ranks were divided into thirds representing low, medium, or high emotionality. The Ss were placed in one of these classifications by first using unanimous agreement in rank grouping on the three measures. When these cases were exhausted, the activity measure was used as the principal criterion; Ss could deviate somewhat on either of the other two measures. Finally, the latency to emerge score was used as the major criterion. The Ss were then placed into standard breeding cages and, when obviously pregnant, each S was placed in an individual maternity cage.

Infantile Rearing Conditions

The litters were born and reared in cages measuring $9 \times 9 \times 15$ in. with the tray bottom partially filled with wood shavings. The back, sides, and top of the cage were covered with a metal hood. A food hopper and water bottle were attached to the outside of the wire mesh front door. All litters were randomly reduced to eight pups when first found. Once a litter was born, the shavings were never changed.

EXPERIMENT 1

Procedure

The two independent variables in this study were the emotionality classification of the mothers and the presence or absence of multiple mothering. A 3×2 factorial design was employed. Multiple mothering was achieved by rotating a mother between her own litter and *one* other foster litter. Rotation was always done between litters born on the same day and with mothers of equivalent emotionality level (i.e., two high-emotional mothers, or medium- or low-emotional mothers). Starting on the day after birth, the rotated mothers were removed from their own litter and placed with the other litter in the rotation pair. The rotated mothers were returned to their own litters 24 hr. later. This procedure of rotating mothers between their own litter and a single foster litter was continued on a daily basis until the pups were weaned at 21 days. As a control for the effects of handling the mothers, the nonrotated mothers were removed from their cages each day and then returned to their own litter. At *no* time from birth to weaning were the pups handled or touched in any manner by E.

At 21 days the pups were weaned, weighed, ear-punched, and placed in small group cages with like-sexed litter mates. Food and water were available ad lib. The Ss were never disturbed until adult testing started at 50 days. They were tested in the open field once daily from Day 50 through Day 53. The Ss were weighed on Day 50 after their open-field testing and were weighed again on Day 62.

The sample consisted of 25 mothers and their 191 offspring. There were 4 litters each in 5 of the 6 cells of the 3×2 factorial design and 5 litters in the medium emotionality, nonrotated cell.

Results

Because of known differences between males and females in body weight and open-field behavior, the dimension of sex was included in all analyses. This resulted in unequal Ns and an unweighted means analysis of variance was used (Walker & Lev, 1953). To obtain the error MSs, the pooled Ss-within-cells error term was divided by the harmonic mean of the cell frequencies. The square root of this value equals the standard error of the mean.

Open-field behavior. Analysis of the total number of squares entered revealed that the variables of Rotation ($F = 10.17$, $df = 1/179$), Maternal Emotionality ($F = 21.96$, $df = 2/179$), and Sex ($F = 22.79$, $df = 1/179$) were all significant beyond the .01 level. In addition, each of these variables

TABLE 1

MEAN NUMBER OF SQUARES ENTERED IN OPEN FIELD ON EACH TRIAL AS A FUNCTION OF ROTATION AND MATERNAL EMOTIONALITY VARIABLES

Experimental Treatment		N	Trial			
			1	2	3	4
Rotation	No	100	15.92	21.34	25.77	28.37
	Yes	91	15.62	15.53	19.80	18.95
Maternal emotionality	Low	63	20.94	25.20	30.40	34.37
	Medium	67	13.37	16.21	22.01	20.40
	High	61	13.00	13.89	15.94	16.21

$MS_{Ss} = 33.20, df = 179.$
$MS_{Ss} \times \text{Trials} = 7.60, df = 537.$

interacted significantly with Trials ($p < .01$ in all three instances). Table 1 summarizes the Rotation and Emotionality main effects and interactions. Offspring whose mothers had not been rotated were significantly more active than offspring reared by rotated females and, in addition, their rate of increase of activity over the 4 days was significantly greater. Table 1 demonstrates the relationship between maternal emotionality and offspring activity: the less emotional the mother, as defined by prepregnancy open-field behavior, the more active the offspring. There is a corresponding increase in the rate of change of activity over the four trials: offspring of low-emotionality mothers had the greatest rate of change, while offspring from high-emotionality mothers showed the least change. Females were found to be more active than males and to increase their activity at a faster rate than the males.

The latency, center square, and bolus data were markedly nonnormal. These variables were analyzed by assigning a score to each S based on the number of days upon which a particular behavior occurred. Analysis of the center square measure revealed that Rotation ($F = 8.96, df = 1/179$), Emotionality ($F = 7.26, df = 2/179$), and Sex ($F = 9.65, df = 1/179$) were all significant beyond the .01 level. The latency results yielded the same findings except that the Rotation variable was significant at the .05 level. The only variable found signifi-

TABLE 2

MEAN BODY WEIGHT IN GRAMS AT 21 DAYS OF Ss REARED BY ROTATED OR NONROTATED MOTHERS OF DIFFERENT EMOTIONALITY LEVELS

	Maternal Emotionality Level		
	Low	Medium	High
Rotated	44.21	34.72	37.56
Nonrotated	39.20	38.68	39.90

$MS_{Ss} = 2.27, df = 179.$

cant for the bolus measure was Sex ($F = 27.42, df = 1/179, p < .01$). Since the direction of differences for those three measures was the same as with the total activity scores only the latter measure will be discussed hereafter.

Body weight. Analysis of the body weight at 21 days revealed that Maternal Emotionality ($F = 11.16, df = 2/179$) and the Emotionality Rotation interaction ($F = 10.07, df = 2/179$) were significant beyond the .01 level. Table 2 summarizes these data. Overall, the offspring of low-emotionality females weighed significantly more than offspring from medium- or high-emotional mothers. However, this difference was primarily due to the body weight of the offspring reared by low emotional-nonrotated mothers.

Analyses of the body weight at 50 days found a significant difference as a function of Maternal Emotionality ($F = 5.97, df = 2/179, p < .01$) and Sex ($F = 136.52, df = 1/179, p < .01$). The same findings were obtained at 62 days except that the Emotionality variable was significant beyond the .05 level. Table 3 summarizes these data. Unlike the findings at 21 days, the body

TABLE 3

MEAN BODY WEIGHT IN GRAMS AT 50 AND 62 DAYS FOR Ss REARED BY MOTHERS OF DIFFERENT EMOTIONALITY LEVELS

Age (Days)	Maternal Emotionality Level			Individual Variability	
	Low	Medium	High	MS_{Ss}	df
50	165.78	152.43	162.95	33.14	179
62	210.54	199.94	214.90	55.48	179

weight differences in adulthood were brought about by the Ss of medium-emotionality mothers. These Ss weighed significantly less than Ss reared by either high- or low-emotionality females while the latter two groups did not differ significantly from each other.

EXPERIMENT 2

Procedure

In Experiment 1 rotation took place *within* a maternal emotionality level, that is, the rotated mothers for a given litter were of equivalent emotionality level. Significant differences in offspring open-field behavior as a function of maternal emotionality could have been brought about either (*a*) by genetic or prenatal factors associated with the selection of the mothers on an individual difference basis, or (*b*) by the behavior of the mother toward the young after birth. The objective of Experiments 2 and 3 was to separate these two factors.

The sample for Experiment 2 consisted of 4 mothers and their 28 offspring. Two of the mothers were classified as high emotional and the other two as low. The multiple mothering rotation procedure was the same as in Experiment 1 except that there was one high- and one low-emotional mother in each rotation pair. The procedure was identical to that in Experiment 1 in all other respects.

Results

Open-field activity. The mean open-field activity scores of Ss born of high-emotional mothers was 148.58 squares entered ($N = 14$) while the activity of Ss born of low-emotional mothers was 146.38 squares ($N = 14$). These means did not differ significantly. The failure to find significant differences is evidence against the hypothesis that the relationship between the mother's emotionality level and offspring open-field behavior was brought about solely by prenatal or genetic factors. These two means were then pooled and compared with the means from Experiment 1 of offspring reared by rotated high-emotional mothers $\bar{X} = 97.12$, $N = 31$) and by rotated low-emotional mothers ($\bar{X} = 190.30$, $N = 31$). The open-field activity of the high-low reared S is almost at the mean of the high-high reared and low-low reared S. These data strongly suggest that the relationship between maternal emotionality level and offspring open-field activity is a function of postnatal maternal behavior.

Body weight. The Ss born of low-emotional mothers did not differ significantly in

TABLE 4

OFFSPRING OPEN-FIELD ACTIVITY AS A FUNCTION OF PRENATAL AND POSTNATAL MATERNAL EMOTIONALITY

Maternal Emotionality Level		N	Total No. of Squares Entered
Prenatal	Postnatal		
High	High	13	61.27
	Low	8	87.67
Low	High	14	96.12
	Low	15	106.31

Note.—$MS_{Ss} = 29.77$, $df = 42$.

body weight from the Ss born of high-emotional mothers at 21, 50, or 62 days of age. Comparison of the pooled mean of these Ss against the mean of the low-low reared Ss and the high-high reared Ss also failed to reveal any significant differences at any of the three ages. These data are consistent with the findings of Experiment 1 since the rotated groups did not differ among themselves at 21 days (Table 2) while the offspring of high-emotional mothers and low-emotional mothers did not differ significantly at 50 or 62 days (Table 3).

EXPERIMENT 3

Procedure

To further separate the effects of the prenatal environment (including possible genetic factors) from those of the postnatal environment, a cross-fostering experiment was carried out in Experiment 3. High- and low-emotionality females were bred. When a high- and a low-emotional mother gave birth on the same day, each mother was removed and placed with the other's litter. Care was taken not to disturb the young when the mothers were moved. Other high- and low-emotionality mothers reared their own young. Other than switching the mothers and reducing all litters to 8 pups when first discovered, neither the mothers nor the young were disturbed in any way until weaning. This procedure resulted in a 2 x 2 factorial design: the natural mothers of the Ss were either high or low in emotionality, and the Ss were reared by either a high- or a low-emotional mother. Initially there were 8 litters in the experiment, 2 per condition. However, one litter born of a high-emotional mother and reared by a low-emotional female died, leaving only one litter for that treatment cell. The final N consisted of 7 females and their 50 offspring.

The open field used in this experiment had the same dimensions as in the prior studies but did not have the entrance can. The Ss were placed directly into the field (in a corner square) and observed for 3 min.

Results

Table 4 presents the 50-day activity scores of the four groups. (Since the open-field apparatus and testing differed somewhat from that of the prior two experiments, the means of this study cannot be directly compared to those of the other two studies.) The analysis of variance revealed that Ss born of low-emotional mothers were significantly more active than Ss whose natural mothers were highly emotional ($F = 12.01$, $df = 1/42$, $p < .01$). In addition, Ss reared by low-emotional mothers were significantly more active than Ss reared by high-emotional mothers ($F = 5.62$, $df = 1/42$, $p < .05$). The interaction between prenatal and postnatal maternal factors was not significant.

DISCUSSION

Early experience research to date has concerned almost exclusively the effects of E-mediated stimulation (e.g., shocking, handling, gentling). The concern of the present experiments, as of the earlier one by Denenberg et al. (1962), was another source of infantile stimulation: what might be termed mother-mediated stimulation. That mother-mediated stimulation may be critical in the development of the offspring is suggested from at least two sources. First, mother-mediated stimulation can be assumed to be a significant part of the total stimulus complex impinging upon most infant animals; variation in this aspect of the infant's environment might be suspected, then, to be important in the same way that variation in other stimulus parameters has been found to be. Second, one of the most common assumptions in clinical practice is that it is specifically the "early experiences" with maternal (and paternal) figures which are critical to human behavioral development. Experimentally, Harlow's research (1962) is strongly suggestive of the importance of mother-mediated stimulation.

Since the offspring of these experiments were never touched by E until weaning at 21 days, all behavioral and weight effects were mediated through the mother. Thus,

the behavioral data support both hypotheses—and the more general assumption of the importance of mother-mediated stimulation. Multiple-mothered offspring were significantly more emotional in the open field than were single-mothered young. Further, a direct relationship was found between the emotionality level of the mother and the emotionality level of her offspring.

The results of Experiment 3 indicate that there is both a prenatal and a postnatal (or experiential) basis for the influence of maternal emotionality on offspring emotionality. Both of these periods will require further research to indicate the means by which these effects are transmitted to the young.

Some measures of maternal behavior adapted from Seitz (1954, 1958) were obtained during Experiment 1. These measures failed to demonstrate any systematic differences among high-, medium-, or low-emotionality mothers in the infant-care behaviors rated, or between rotated and non-rotated mothers. The scales did not offer any conclusive data to indicate why the offspring emotionality differences occurred, but they did indicate that none of the mothers obviously neglected their foster litters. These data are further discussed by Ottinger (1961).

The findings of the present experiments are in marked disagreement with some recent data of Broadhurst (1961). He found no significant maternal effect when offspring of high- and low-emotional mothers were cross-fostered at birth and later tested for emotional behavior. Since Broadhurst's high- and low-emotional Ss had been obtained through genetic selection, it is likely that strain differences are part of the reason for the discrepancies in results.

The following conclusions are suggested by these studies:

1. Mother-mediated, as well as E-mediated, postnatal stimulation of infant animals is an important variable in the behavioral and physical development of rats.

2. Offspring emotionality is directly related to both prenatal and postnatal emotionality of the mothers.

3. Multiple mothering significantly increases offspring emotionality.

4. The significance of the postnatal ma-

ternal emotionality factor is of considerable methodological importance in studies exploring genetic and other prenatal factors related to emotionality.

REFERENCES

BROADHURST, P. L. Analysis of maternal effects in the inheritance of behaviour. *Anim. Behav.*, 1961, **9**, 129–141.

DENENBERG, V. H., OTTINGER, D. R., & STEPHENS, M. W. Effects of maternal factors upon growth and behavior of the rat. *Child Developm.*, 1962, **33**, 65–71.

HARLOW, H. F. The heterosexual affectional system. *Amer. Psychologists*, 1962, **17**, 1–9.

OTTINGER, D. R. Some effects of maternal inconsistency and emotionality level upon offspring behavior and development. Unpublished doctoral dissertation, Purdue University, 1961.

SEITZ, P. F. D. The effect of infantile experiences upon adult behavior in animal subjects: I. Effects of litter size during infancy upon adult behavior in the rat. *Amer. J. Psychiat.*, 1954, **110**, 916–927.

SEITZ, P. F. D. The maternal instinct in animal subjects: I. *Psychosom. Med.*, 1958, **20**, 215–226.

WALKER, H. M., & LEV, J. *Statistical inference.* New York: Holt, 1953.

CHARLES H. SOUTHWICK

55 Effect of Maternal Environment on Aggressive Behavior of Inbred Mice

Abstract

The aggressive behavior of young adult mice of a passive strain (A/J) was significantly increased by fostering at birth to females of a more aggressive strain (CFW). The chase-attack-fight score increased 83 to 87 percent over non-fostered controls and 52 percent over in-fostered controls. Attack score alone more than doubled. The aggressive score and attack latency of CFW males were not altered by fostering at birth to females of the A/J strain. Cross-breeding also produced results suggestive of maternal influences. The mechanism by which the maternal environment influences the ontogeny of aggressive behavior in mice is unknown.

Introduction

Several investigators have demonstrated

Reprinted from *Communications in Behavioral Biology 1:* 129–132, 1968.

Supported by USPHS Grant 5 R01 HD 00365-03 from the National Institute of Child Health and Human Development.

I am indebted to Linda H. Clark for technical assistance, and to A. J. Reading, J. A. King and J. H. Bruell for critical reading of the paper.

maternal influences on strain specific patterns of behavior in inbred mice. Reading (1966a) has shown that cross-fostering between C57Bl/6 and Balb/C produced significant changes in activity, exploratory latency and defecation patterns compared to controls reared by foster mothers of the same strain. These behavioral effects were not simply due to differences in growth and maturation. Ressler (1963, 1966) showed that both within-strain and cross-strain fostering produced significant changes in operant response rates. Within-strain fostering raised the response rates of Balb/C's and lowered those of C57Bl/6's. Ressler's data also showed a significant grandparental effect. Both strains responded at a higher rate if their parents had been reared by Balb/C rather than by C57Bl/6 foster parents.

Other investigators have not found that maternal environments altered strain specific behavior patterns (Broadhurst, 1961; Collins, 1964). Collins found no evidence of maternal influences affecting strain specific patterns of avoidance conditioning in inbred mice, though he indicated that this required more thorough testing with cross-fostering techniques. Broadhurst found that maternal environment had little or no influence on the emotionality of inbred rats.

Most studies of maternal influences on behavioral development have involved analyses of growth, endocrine responsiveness, and/or individual behavior traits such as exploratory and locomotory activity, defecation patterns, operant rates, etc. (Denenberg, 1963; Levine, 1962). There has been relatively little study of maternal influences on aggressive behavior in mice, and the few studies that have been done tend to show no effects. Ginsburg and Allee (1942) reported that cross-fostering had no effect on differences in social dominance between C57Bl, C3H and Balb/C strains. Fredericson (1952) measured competitive fighting over food in immature C57Bl/10 and Balb/C mice which had been cross-fostered at birth, and found that strain specific patterns of aggression were independent of the strain of the foster mother. Thus there has been no direct evidence that maternal environment has a significant influence on strain specific aggressive behavior in mice.

Methods and Materials

The present study utilized 180 male mice of the A/J strain, 170 males of the CFW strain and 80 males of the F1 hybrid generation. The A/J's were selected as a nonaggressive strain and the CFW's as an aggressive strain in comparison with 12 other inbred strains in tests of noncompetitive within-strain aggressive behavior (Southwick and Clark, 1966, 1968). Mice of each strain were placed into four groups – (A) controls normally reared within our own laboratory, (B) controls obtained directly from the suppliers at 3 weeks of age, (C) in-fostered experimentals (mice fostered to females of the same strain), (D) cross-fostered experimentals (mice fostered to females of the opposite strain).

For groups A, C and D, all young were normally born in our laboratory with the females individually isolated in small plastic cages (12 X 12 X 28 cm). The bottom of the cages were filled with wood chips (changed twice weekly), and food and water were supplied ad lib. The animal rooms were maintained between 76 degrees and 84 degrees F, and were kept on a 12 hour daylight schedule.

Within 24 hours of birth the following treatments were given – (A) normal controls were handled, weighed and returned to their own mother, (B) in-fostered mice were handled, weighed and returned to another female of the same strain who had given birth within 24 hours, and whose own young had been removed a few minutes earlier (usually these involved reciprocal within-strain crosses), and (C) cross-fostered mice were handled, weighed and returned to a female of the other strain who had given birth within 24 hours, and whose own young had been removed a few minutes earlier (also reciprocal crosses in most cases). All litters used were six mice or were reduced to six, and all litters were handled equally.

At 22 days of age, all mice were weaned, weighed and the males were isolated in individual cages of the same size (12 X 12 X 28 cm). All cages were visually isolated by cardboard dividers. The mice were kept in individual isolation for 21 days.

At 43 days of age, the males were weighed and grouped together in groups of 4 in larger cages (16 X 26 X 44 cm). Mice from a minimum of three litters and usually from four litters were placed together to reduce or eliminate sibling effects. Identities of the mice were coded so that mice of the same treatment group were placed together, but the treatment group was unknown to the test observer. The mice were then observed for one hour during which tallies were made on all aspects of aggressive behavior (threat, chase, attack and fights), and on other kinds of social interaction (huddling, social grooming, etc.). The mice were retained in these groups for 7 days throughout which observations were made on social behavior, physical condition and spatial patterns of the mice. At the end of 7 days the mice were weighed and checked for wounds.

The controls from Bar Harbor and Carworth Farms were obtained at 21 days of age from the suppliers and were placed in individual isolation one day after arrival in our laboratory. Subsequent treatment and testing was identical to lab-born controls.

Results and Discussion

The best measure of aggressive behavior was the combined chase-attack-fight frequency (C-A-F score) during the first hour of social grouping (Table 1). The strains differed significantly in this score, with the control CFW averaging C-A-F scores of 66.4 and 67.6 and the control A/J averaging 14.2 and 14.5.

The in-fostered A/J mice showed a small but nonsignificant increase in C-A-F score to 17.5, a 20.7 percent increase over Bar Harbor controls and a 23.2 percent increase over lab controls.

The cross-fostered A/J mice showed significant increases in C-A-F score to 26.6, a 52.0 percent increase over the in-fostered mice, an 83.4 percent increase over Bar Harbor controls, and an 87.3 percent increase over laboratory controls. The attack score alone, which was one of the most discrete single measures of aggressive behavior in mice, showed an even greater change in response to maternal environment. The cross-fostered A/J attack score (11.6 plus or minus 3.8/hr) was more than twice as great as that of the A/J controls (4.6 plus or minus 1.8/hr) and A/J in-fostered mice (5.5 plus or minus 1.9/hr).

Increased aggressive behavior in cross-fostered A/J mice was also reflected in the decreased attack latency from 35 minutes to 13.4 minutes, and in the percent of wounded mice after seven days of grouping (Table 1). The cross-fostered A/J group showed significantly more wounded mice (17.5 percent) than either the controls or in-fostered group (0-4.1

percent). Thus the cross-fostering treatment of the passive strain to the aggressive strain significantly increased the aggressive behavior of the passive mice above that attributable to the fostering process per se.

Fostering did not produce significant changes in the aggressive behavior of the CFW strain, and there were no differences in the percent wounded of the control and fostered groups within the CFW strain (Table 1).

These results indicate, therefore, that the aggressive behavior of a passive strain was increased by providing the maternal environment of an aggressive strain, but the reciprocal did not prevail, that is, the aggressive behavior of an aggressive strain was not lessened by providing the maternal environment of a passive strain.

Cross-breeding studies also produced results suggestive of maternal influences. The F1 hybrids of the CFW and A/J parental strains were significantly different from parental strains and from each other, dependent upon the direction of the cross. The hybrids from an A/J female and a CFW male had a C-A-F score of 41.3 plus or minus 5.2, intermediate between the parental scores. The hybrids from a CFW female and an A/J male had a C-A-F score of 107.8 plus or minus 9.4, significantly greater than either parental scores. Each of the above hybrid means are based on sample sizes of 40 mice.

There are several theoretical explanations for these differences in the F1 hybrids. The highly aggressive F1 hybrids from the CFW maternal parent could result from X-linked genetic

TABLE 1. AGGRESSIVE SCORE (CHASE-ATTACK-FIGHT FREQUENCY), ATTACK LATENCY, AND PERCENT WOUNDING IN GROUPS OF 4 MALES

Strain	Treatment	N	C-A-F Score/Hr	Attack Latency	Percent Wounded
A/J	Lab Control	36	14.2 ± 4.8	33.4 min.	2.8
A/J	Bar Harbor Control	72	14.5 ± 3.9	35.4	4.1
A/J	In-Fostered	32	17.5 ± 4.9	35.3	0
A/J	Cross-Fostered	40	26.6 ± 4.7*	13.4**	17.5**
CFW	Lab Control	28	67.6 ± 9.1	2.3	64.3
CFW	Carworth Control	72	66.4 ± 5.9	4.4	72.1
CFW	In-Fostered	16	68.0 ± 12.8	1.2	68.7
CFW	Cross-Fostered	44	65.1 ± 7.4	1.7	68.7

*Significantly different from in-fostered and control groups, P less than 0.05 by x^2
**Significantly different from in-fostered and control groups, P less than 0.01

factors in the CFW strain which contribute to aggressiveness, but which are expressed only in the presence of male hormone. This mechanism would require either a maternal influence or a heterotic effect to elevate the F1 aggression score above the CFW parental score. The intermediate aggressiveness of the F1 hybrids from the A/J maternal parent could result from a lack of the CFW maternal influence or from some unknown genetic mechanism such as X-linked suppressors of aggressive behavior in the A/J strain.

Theoretically, maternal influences could result from maternal behavior, such as patterns of nest attendance, grooming, punitive action, etc., or from hormonal or biochemical mechanisms in milk. We do not have adequate data as yet on differences in maternal care between these two strains, and we have no data on pertinent biochemical differences. Preliminary observations on the maternal behavior of three females of each strain indicate differences in nest attendance. Mothers of the two strains seem to spend different amounts of time on their litters. Within the first two days after birth no significant differences were seen, but by the fourth day after birth, the A/J females spent two to three times more time on the litter than the CFW females. This influences both the ambient temperature in which the young develop and the feeding pattern of the young. Interstrain differences in parental handling between the C57Bl/10 and the Balb/C strains are known to exist from the work of Ressler (1962), so we feel that this is a distinct possibility in the case of CFW and A/J strains. The topic requires further study, however. It is also known that minor differences in ambient temperature influence growth patterns of mice, and therefore potentially behavior patterns.

The demonstration of maternal effects in this study, in contrast to their absence in previous studies of aggressive behavior, may be related to three things. (A) According to our previous work on 14 strains (Southwick and Clark, 1966, 1968), the differential in aggressive behavior between the CFW and A/J strains is much greater than that between the C57Bl/6 and Balb/C strains used in previous studies. (B) One of the previous studies (Fredericson, 1952) tested mice at 30 days of age, prior to sexual maturity and full maturation of social behavior. (C) The present study measured noncompetitive aggression, whereas former studies worked primarily with competitive aggression, especially over food. Noncompetitive aggression may be a more basic social trait less modified by temporal, experimental and situational variables such as hunger and previous food-getting experience.

Bibliography

Broadhurst, P. L. Analysis of maternal effects in the inheritance of behavior. *Animal Behaviour, 9:* 129-141, 1961.

Collins, R. L. Inheritance of avoidance conditioning in mice — a diallel study. *Science, 143:* 1188-1190, 1964.

Denenberg, V. H. Early experience and emotional development. *Scientific Americann, 208*(6): 138-146, 1963.

Fredericson, E. Reciprocal fostering of two inbred mouse strains and its effect on the modification of aggressive behavior. *American Psychologist 7:* 241-242, 1952.

Ginsburg, B. E., and W. C. Allee. Some effects of conditioning on social dominance and subordination in inbred strains of mice. *Physiological Zoology 15:* 485-506, 1942.

Levine, S. Psychophysiological effects of infantile stimulation. In E. L. Bliss (Ed.). *Roots of Behavior* New York, Harper, 1962, pp. 246-253.

Reading, A. J. Effect of maternal environment on the behavior of inbred mice. *J. Comp.Physiol. Psychol. 62:* 437-440, 1966a.

Reading, A. J. Influence of room temperature on the growth of house mice. *J. Mammal. 47:* 694-697, 1966b.

Ressler, R. H. Parental handling of two strains of mice reared by foster parents. *Science 137:* 129-130, 1962.

Ressler, R. H. Genotype-correlated parental influences in two strains of mice. *J. Comp. Physiol. Psychol. 56:* 882-886, 1963.

Ressler, R. H. Inherited environmental influences on the operant behavior of mice. *J. Comp. Physiol. Psychol. 61:* 264-267, 1966.

Southwick, C. H. and L. H. Clark. Aggressive behavior and exploratory activity in fourteen mouse strains. *American Zoologist 6:* 559, 1966.

Southwick, C. H., and L. H. Clark. Interstrain differences in aggressive behavior and exploratory activity of inbred mice. *Comm. Behav. Biol. 1,* 1968.

VICTOR H. DENENBERG, KENNETH M. ROSENBERG,
RICHARD PASCHKE, & M. X. ZARROW

56   Mice Reared with Rat Aunts: Effects on Plasma Corticosterone and Open Field Activity

In recent experiments newborn C57Bl/10 mice were fostered to lactating rat mothers; in some cases rat peers were also present before or after weaning.[1-4] Mice reared in such conditions were markedly less aggressive, less active in an open field, and preferred a rat to a mouse in a two choice social preference test. Further experiments established that one of the principal variables involved in these shifts in behaviour was the rat mother.

More recently, Swiss-Albino mice were fostered to rat mothers to study the relationship between open field activity and corticosterone from the adrenal gland.[5] At weaning, blood was collected for the assay of corticosterone by killing immediately or after exposure to a novel stimulus, while other mice were tested in the open field. The rat-reared mice gave a lesser corticosterone response to the novel stimulus than mouse-reared mice, and rat-reared mice were also less active than control mice.

The rat mother could be influencing the mouse offspring either (a) through her behavioural interaction with the pups between birth and weaning, or (b) through biochemical factors present in her milk. To bypass the problem of rat milk influencing the mouse offspring we put nonlactating adult female rats ("aunts") together with pregnant female mice in the expectation that the rat would engage in many of the usual maternal caretaking activities while the mouse would supply the milk for the young. This expectation was based on the work of Rosenblatt,[6] who showed that non-pregnant female rats performed a variety of maternal behaviours including nest building, retrieving and hovering over the young. A pilot study established that the rat aunts did behave maternally toward the mouse offspring, while the mouse mothers maintained sufficient contact with

Reprinted from *Nature* 221:73–74, 1969.

their pups for adequate nursing. In addition, post-mortem examination of the rats' mammary glands revealed no evidence of milk. This report describes our first two experiments on the rat-aunt preparation.

In the first experiment, Purdue-Wistar female rats to be used as aunts were "primed" before being placed with mouse litters by placing the non-lactating female into a cage containing a rat mother and her pups. The aunt was left there for 6 days and was then placed in a large plastic cage (9 inches × 18 inches × 6 inches) with a Swiss-Albino mouse mother and her 4-day-old pups. The aunt remained with the litter until weaning at 21 days. Control pups were reared in smaller plastic cages (6.5 inches × 11 inches × 5 inches) until weaning. All mouse litters were reduced to eight pups maximizing the number of males.

At weaning, two mice from a litter were killed immediately and their blood was pooled to obtain resting concentrations of corticosterone.[7] Two others were isolated in cans containing shavings; 30 min later they were removed and blood was collected. The bodies of all dead mice were then weighed to the nearest 0.1 g.

Two other mice were placed in a black open field divided into sixty-four squares (4 inches on a side) by thin white lines. The number of squares entered in 3 min was recorded.

In the first experiment the procedure of priming rat aunts required elaborate scheduling to assure that they had received 6 days of experience with a rat litter before being placed with a 4-day-old mouse litter. Therefore, in the second experiment nine non-lactating Purdue-Wistar female rats were placed with pregnant Swiss-Albino mice approximately 3 days before expected parturition, while nine other pregnant mice were randomly assigned to the control group. The same sized cages were used here as in the first experiment but in this case litter size was not kept constant.

At weaning, the survival percentage for each litter and the body weight of the survivors were recorded. The males were then group housed until they were 200 days old. At that time each mouse was given a 3 min open field test in the same apparatus as used in the first experiment; blood was collected immediately afterwards. Approximately 5 min had elapsed from the time that the animals were removed from the colony room until they were killed.

The results are summarized in Table 1. For each endpoint (except survival percentage) the between litter mean square was tested against the subjects within litter mean square to determine the appropriate error term. In all cases there was no significant between litter variance, and so the individual animal was used as the unit of analysis.

The presence of the rat aunt did not interfere with adequate rearing of the mouse litter as indexed by the survival percentage (the mean survival percentages in Table 1 are given in arc

sin values) and body weights at weaning. This was true even though the rat aunt preparations differed in the two experiments.

In the first experiment the mice tended by aunts had a significantly lower corticosterone response to the novel stimulus of being isolated for 30 min ($P < 0.05$). In addition the aunt group was less active in the open field than the control group; the difference was not significant although it was in the expected direction.

In the second experiment testing was approximately 6 months after weaning. Again a significant corticosterone difference was obtained with the group tended by aunts yielding a lower value than the controls ($P < 0.01$). As in the first experiment the aunt group had lower activity than the controls, but not significantly so.

We have previously found that Swiss-Albino mice reared by rat mothers and tested at weaning give a lesser corticosterone response to a novel stimulus and are less active in the open field.[5] In the first experiment we then reproduced the significant corticosterone difference

TABLE 1. SUMMARY OF RESULTS OF THE TWO EXPERIMENTS

	No. of litters	No. of subjects	Control mean	No. of litters	No. of subjects	Experimental mean	F	df
First experiment								
Percent survival								
(arc sin)	15	116/120*	85.24	15	114/120	82.48	<1.0	1/28
Body weight (g)	15	60	12.59	15	60	12.92	<1.0	1/28
Corticosterone (μg/100 ml.)								
Resting concentration	15	30	4.85	15	30	5.39	<1.0	1/28
Experimental concentration	15	30	32.97	15	30	26.72	5.85†	1/28
Activity	15	30	180.90	15	30	160.27	2.51	1/58
Second experiment								
Weaning data								
Percent survival								
(arc sin)	9	75/80	83.20	9	64/89	65.77	4.04	1/16
Body weight (g)	8	61	12.74	8	60	11.53	<1.0	1/119
200-day data								
Corticosterone (μg/100 ml.)								
Activity	6	21	10.40	4	13	7.49	7.71‡	1/32
	6	21	141.67	4	13	115.46	1.89	1/32

*Numerator: No. alive at weaning; denominator: No. alive at birth. † $P < 0.05$. ‡ $P < 0.01$.

at weaning using the rat aunt, and in the second experiment[5] we showed that this is a long-term relatively permanent effect, for it persisted until mice were 200 days old. We also found that the groups tended by aunts were less active in the open field in both experiments, although neither difference was significant. In five previous studies using rat mothers the mouse reared by a rat was less active;[1-5] this difference was significant in four of the experiments. Thus the rat aunt preparation has the same qualitative effect on open field activity as the rat mother preparation but to a somewhat lesser degree. We can conclude from these data that the changes in adrenocortical activity and open field behaviour in these and in our previous studies have been brought about through behavioural mechanisms involved in interactions between mothers and young, rather than through biochemical differences in the milk of rat and mouse mothers. We also conclude that these changes persist into adulthood.

This work was supported in part by a grant from the National Institute of Child Health and Human Development, US Public Health Service.

(The word preparation is used here in the biological sense of a specially prepared organism.)

Acknowledgements

1. Denenberg, V. H., Hudgens, G. A., and Zarrow, M. X., *Science,* 143, 380 (1964).
2. Denenberg, V. H., Hudgens, G. A., and Zarrow, M. X., *Psychol. Rep.,* 18, 451 (1966).
3. Hudgens, G. A., Denenberg, V. H., and Zarrow, M. X., *J. Comp. Physiol. Psychol.,* 63, 304 (1967).
4. Hudgens, G. A., Denenberg, V. H., and Zarrow, M. X., *Behaviour,* 30, 17 (1968).
5. Denenberg, V. H., Rosenberg, K. M., Paschke, R. E., Hess, J. L., Zarrow, M. X., and Levine, S., *Endocrinology,* 83, 900 (1968).
6. Rosenblatt, J., *Science,* 156, 1512 (1967).
7. Silber, R. H., Busch, R. D., and Oslapas, R., *Clin. Chem.,* 4, 278 (1958).

HARRY F. HARLOW

57   The Heterosexual Affectional System in Monkeys

THE inspiration for this address came from observational data obtained from seven guinea pigs—two males and three females in a colony and two females brought in temporarily. Observations were provided by my ten-year-old daughter Pamela. These observations were made with love and endearment, and the behavior observed was endearment and love. Furthermore, these observations were made at a level of objectivity difficult for an adult to attain in this field.

Male and female guinea pigs are very fond of each other. They stare blissfully into the limpid pink or ruby or midnight-blue pools of each other's eyes. They nuzzle and they cuddle and the end

Reprinted from *American Psychologist 17*:1–9, 1962. Copyright 1962 by the American Psychological Association and reproduced by permission.

This research was supported by funds received from the Graduate School of the University of Wisconsin, from the Ford Foundation, and from Grant M-4528, National Institutes of Health.

production is not characterized by rush or rape. After all, one does not have to hurry if there is no hurry to be had. This, Pamela has witnessed several times. A caged, virgin adult female was brought by a friend for mating. Twirp, Pamela's large, black, gentle male, was put into the cage with the new female. He purred, nuzzled her, brushed up against her, smelled and licked her, and gradually conquered the frightened animal. A half-hour later they were snuggled up next to each other, peaceful and content, and they lived in bliss for several weeks until another friend brought in her female and Twirp repeated his patient, gentle approach. Twirp has convinced me that some male guinea pigs, at least, are endowed with an innate sense of decency, and I am happy to say that this is the way most male monkeys behave. I presume that there are some men who have as deep a depth of dignity as guinea pigs.

The guest stands, unfortunately, ended peaceful coexistence in the colony. For many months the five adult guinea pigs had lived amiably in one large cage, with Twirp in command and the second male playing second fiddle. While Twirp was host to the visiting females, White Patch commanded the permanent harem. When Twirp was reintroduced to the colony cage, it took but ten seconds to discover that he would not be tolerated. White Patch bared his teeth and lunged at Twirp, and to save the males, a new cage was acquired.

This led to various divisions of the females and led Pamela to discover particular male guinea pigs like particular female guinea pigs, and they squeal piteously when separated, even when the female is so bulging with babies that she can offer the male nothing in terms of drive reduction. Particular female guinea pigs like particular male guinea pigs. Tastes seem fairly stable, for even after weeks of peaceful residence with the unfavored male, the female will still attempt to get to her favorite male, and after weeks of quiet residence with unfavored females, the male will still try to get to his favorite female.

The females, like the males, defend their rights. In the happy one-cage days two females were separated from the group to care for their litters. White Thrush, in an advanced stage of pregnancy, lived alone with the males. When Chirp was returned to the colony cage after three weeks of maternal chores, both males approached enthusiastically, making friendly gestures. But Hell hath no fury like a female guinea pig spurned, and White Thrush would not tolerate infidelity. She hissed at Chirp, and lunged, and as Chirp fled from the cage, White Thrush pursued, teeth bared. The males also pursued, clucking and purring in anticipation. The males won, and White Thrush sulked the rest of the day. Guinea pigs apparently have a well-developed heterosexual affectional system.

Sex behavior in the guinea pig has been intensively investigated, and there are exhaustive studies on what has been called the sex drive, but I know of no previous mention of or allusion to the guinea pig's heterosexual affectional system. No doubt this stems from the paradigm which has been established for research in this area.

In a typical experiment a male guinea pig and a female guinea pig in estrus are taken from their individual cages, dropped into a barren chamber, and observed for 15 minutes. In such a situation there is a high probability that something is going to happen and that it will happen rapidly and repeatedly. The thing that happens will be reliable and valid, and all that one needs to do to score it is to count. It is my suggestion that from this time onward it be known as the "flesh count." Some-

times I wonder how men and women would behave if they were dropped naked into a barren chamber with full realization that they had only fifteen minutes to take advantage of the opportunities offered them. No doubt there would be individual differences, but we would obtain little information on the human heterosexual affectional system from such an experiment.

Sex is not an adventitious act. It is not here today and gone tomorrow. It starts with the cradle, and as a part of the human tragedy it wanes before the grave. We have traced and are tracing the development of the heterosexual affectional system in monkeys.

We believe that the heterosexual affectional system in the rhesus monkey, like all the other affectional systems, goes through a series of developmental stages—an infantile heterosexual stage, a preadolescent stage, and an adolescent and mature heterosexual stage. Although these stages are in considerable part overlapping and cannot be sharply differentiated in time, we would think of the infantile stage as lasting throughout the first year and being characterized by inadequate and often inappropriate sexual play and posturing. The preadolescent stage, beginning in the second year

FIG. 1. Initial response to female sexual-present posture. The male subsequently accepted the invitation.

and ending in the third year in the female and the fourth year in the male, is characterized by adequate and appropriate sexual play and posturing, but incompleteness. The adolescent and adult stage is characterized by behaviors which are similar in form but give rise to productive outcomes which are also reproductive.

Since in this paper sex is an unavoidable issue, we present illustrations of normal adult macaque monkey sex behavior. Sexual invitation may be initiated by the female, as in Figure 1, by a present

FIG. 2. Initial response to male sexual-present posture. The female (No. 48) subsequently approached and groomed the male.

pattern with buttocks oriented toward the male, tail elevated, and the female looking backward with a fear-grimace (not threat) pattern involving flattened ears and lip smacking. As you can see, this pattern need not involve rape nor even rush on the part of the male. The male may also solicit, as in the case of the animal in the foreground of Figure 2; this animal has assumed a posture soliciting either grooming or more intimate favors. These patterns seldom elicit violent, uncontrolled, reflex behaviors. Normal male and female overt sex behavior is shown in Figure 3, the male having assumed the complex sex posture involving ankle clasp, dorsoventral mounting, and clasp of the female's buttocks. The partner demonstrates the complete female sexual pattern of elevating the buttocks, lowering the head, and looking backward. There have been millions of rhesus monkeys for millions of years, and there will be more in the future.

FIG. 3. Normal male and female sexual positioning.

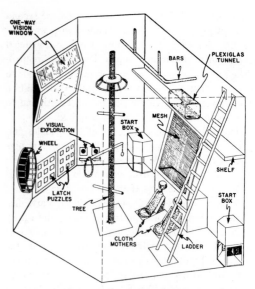

FIG. 4. Playroom test situation.

We have traced the development of the infantile heterosexual stage during the first year of life in two test situations using observational techniques. One is our playroom, illustrated in Figure 4, which consists of a room 8 ft. high with 36 feet of floor space. In this room are a platform, ladder, revolving wheel, and flying rings to encourage the infants' adaptation to a three-dimensional world, and there is an assortment of puzzles and toys for quieter activities. Two groups of four infants each, half of each group male and half female, have been observed in the playroom daily over many months. The second apparatus is shown in Figure 5. This is the playpen situation, and it consists of four large living cages and adjoining pens. Each living cage houses a mother and infant, and a three-inch by five-inch opening in the wall between cage and playpen units enables the infants to leave the home cage at any time but restrains the mothers. The playpen units are separated by wire-mesh panels which are removed one or two hours a day to allow

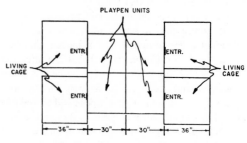

FIG. 5. Playpen test situation.

the infants to interact in pairs during the first 180 days and both in pairs and in groups of four during the next half-year of life. Again, we are referring to data gathered from two playpen setups, each housing four infants and their real or surrogate mothers. Insofar as the infantile heterosexual stage is concerned, it makes little or no difference from which situation we take our data.

The outstanding finding in both the playroom and playpen is that male and female infants show differences in sex behavior from the second month of life onward. The males show earlier and more frequent sex behavior than do females, and there are differences in the patterns displayed by the sexes. The males almost never assume the female sex-posture patterns, even in the earliest months. The females, on the other hand, sometimes display the male pattern of sex posturing, but this is infrequent after ten months of age. Predominantly, females show the female pattern and exceptional instances are to other females, not males. Frequency of sex behavior for both males and females increases progressively with age. There is no latency period—except when the monkeys are very tired.

The early infantile sexual behaviors are fragmentary, transient, and involve little more than passivity by the female and disoriented grasping and thrusting by the male. Thus, the male may thrust at the companion's head in a completely disoriented manner or laterally across the midline of the body, as in Figure 6. However, it is our opinion that these behaviors are more polymorphous than perverse.

Thus, as soon as the sexual responses can be observed and measured, male and female sexual behaviors differ in form. Furthermore, there are

many other behaviors which differ between males and females as soon as they can be observed and measured. Figure 7 shows the development of threat responses by males and females in the playroom, and these differences are not only statistically significant, but they also have face validity. Analysis of this behavior shows that males threaten other males and females but that females are innately blessed with better manners; in particular, little girl monkeys do not threaten little boy monkeys.

The withdrawal pattern—retreat when confronted by another monkey—is graphed for the playroom in Figure 8, and the significance is obvious. Females evince a much higher incidence

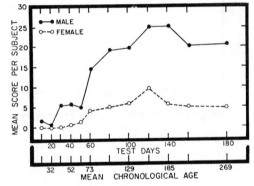

FIG. 7. Frequency of threat responses by males and females in the playroom.

of passive responses, which are characterized by immobility with buttocks oriented toward the male and head averted, and a similar pattern, rigidity, in which the body is stiffened and fixed.

In all probability the withdrawal and passivity behavior of the female and the forceful behavior of the male gradually lead to the development of normal sex behaviors. The tendency for the female to orient away from the male and for the male to

FIG. 6. Immature male and female sexual posturing, playroom observation.

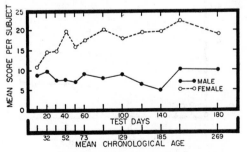

FIG. 8. Frequency of withdrawal responses by males and females in the playroom.

clasp and tussle at the female's buttocks predisposes the consorts to assume the proper positions. The development of the dorsally oriented male sex-behavior pattern as observed in the playroom situation is shown in Figure 9 and may be described as a composite yearning and learning curve.

Infant male and female monkeys show clear-cut differences in behavior of far greater social significance than neonatal and infantile sex responses.

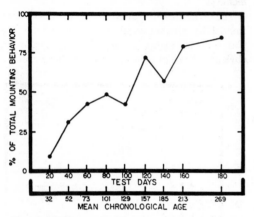

FIG. 9. Percentage of all male mounts (immature and mature) in the playroom that shows dorsal orientation (mature pattern).

Grooming patterns, which are basic to macaque socialization, show late maturation, but as is seen in Figure 10, when they appear, they sharply differentiate the two sexes. Caressing is both a property

and prerogative of the females. Basic to normal macaque socialization is the infant-infant or peer-peer affectional system, and this arises out of and is dependent upon the play patterns which we have described elsewhere and only mention here. As is shown in the solid lines of Figure 11, play behavior in the playroom is typically initiated by males, seldom by females. However, let us not belittle the female, for they also serve who only stand and

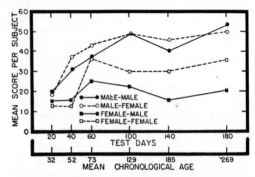

FIG. 11. Frequency of play-initiations by males and females to monkeys of the same (male-male, female-female) and other sex (male-female, female-male). Observations are from the playroom.

wait. Contact play is far more frequent among the males than the females and is almost invariably initiated by the males. Playpen data graphed in Figure 12 show that real rough-and-tumble play is strictly for the boys.

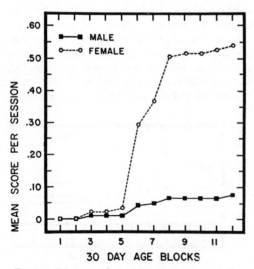

FIG. 10. Frequency of grooming responses made by males and females in the playroom.

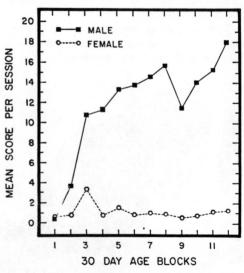

FIG. 12. Frequency of occurrence of "rough-and-tumble" play for two males and two females in the playroom through the first year of life.

I am convinced that these data have almost total generality to man. Several months ago I was present at a school picnic attended by 25 second-graders and their parents. While the parents sat and the girls stood around or skipped about hand in hand, 13 boys tackled and wrestled, chased and retreated. No little girl chased any little boy, but some little boys chased some little girls. Human beings have been here for two million years, and they'll probably be here two million more.

These secondary sex-behavior differences probably exist throughout the primate order, and, moreover, they are innately determined biological differences regardless of any cultural overlap. Because of their nature they tend automatically to produce sexual segregation during middle and later childhood, but fortunately this separation is neither complete nor permanent. Behavioral differences may very well make it easy through cultural means to impose a sexual latency period in the human being from childhood to puberty. We emphasize the fact that the latency period is not a biological stage in which primary sex behavior is suppressed, but a cultural stage built upon secondary behavioral differences.

We believe that our data offer convincing evidence that sex behaviors differ in large part because of genetic factors. However, we claim no originality for the discovery of intersex behavioral differences. In 1759 Laurence Sterne in his book *Tristram Shandy* described male and female differences at the most critical period in Tristram Shandy's development; indeed, it would not be possible to conceive of a more critical period.

"Pray, my dear, quoth my mother, *have you not forgot to wind up the clock?——— Good G——!* cried my father, making an exclamation, but taking care to moderate his voice at the same time——— *Did ever woman, since the creation of the world, interrupt a man with such a silly question?"* *

Men and women have differed in the past and they will differ in the future.

It is possible that the listener has been dismayed by the frequent reference to sex and the relatively infrequent reference to affection. Out of these infantile behavior patterns, both sexual and nonsexual, develop the affectional bonds and the social ordering that appear to be important or even essential to the full development of the heterosexual affectional system of macaques. Traumatic affec-

* Sterne, Laurence. *The life and opinions of Tristram Shandy, Gentleman.* J. A. Work (Ed.), New York: The Odyssey Press, 1940, p. 5.

tional errors, both transient and prolonged, may have devastating effects upon subsequent social and sexual behaviors.

For some years we have been attempting to establish experimental neuroses in infant monkeys by having them live on unfriendly and inconsistent mother surrogates. One preparation was a rejecting mother that on schedule or demand separated her baby when a wire frame embedded in her spun-nylon covering was displaced violently upward and backward. The baby was disturbed, but as soon as the frame was returned to its resting position, the baby returned to cling to its surrogate mother as tightly as ever. Next we developed an air-blast mother with a series of nozzles down the entire center of her body which released compressed air under high pressure—an extremely noxious stimulus to monkeys. The blasted baby never even left the mother, but in its moments of agony and duress, clung more and more tightly to the unworthy mother. Where else can a baby get protection? Apparently our infant had never read Neal Miller's theory that avoidance gradients are precipitous and approach gradients gradual and tenuous, for love conquered all.

We next devised a shaking mother, which on schedule or demand shook her infant with unconscionable violence until its teeth chattered. The infant endured its tribulations by clinging more and more tightly. At the present time we believe we may be on the threshold of success through Jay Mowbray's creation of the porcupine mother, which extrudes brass spikes all over its ventral surface. Preliminary studies on two infants suggest that they are emotionally disturbed. Whether or not we eventually succeed, the fact remains that babies are reluctant to develop experimental neuroses, and at one time we even wondered if this were possible.

During the time that we were producing these evil mothers, we observed the monkeys which we had separated from their mothers at birth and raised under various mothered and nonmothered conditions. The first 47 baby monkeys were raised during the first year of life in wire cages so arranged that the infants could see and hear and call to other infants but not contact them. Now they are five to seven years old and sexually mature. As month after month and year after year have passed, these monkeys have appeared to be less and less normal. We have seen them sitting in their cages strangely mute, staring fixedly into space, relatively indifferent to people and other monkeys. Some clutch their heads in both hands and rock back and forth—the autistic behavior pattern that we have seen in babies raised on wire surrogates. Others, when approached or even left alone, go into violent frenzies of rage, grasping and tearing at their legs with such fury that they sometimes require medical care.

Eventually we realized that we had a laboratory full of neurotic monkeys. We had failed to produce neurotic monkeys by thoughtful planning and creative research, but we had succeeded in producing neurotic monkeys through misadventure. To err is human.

Because of housing pressures some of these monkeys and many of our surrogate-raised monkeys lived in pairs for several years while growing to sexual maturity, but we have seldom seen normal sex behavior, and we certainly have not had the validating criterion of newborn baby monkeys. Instead, these monkeys treat each other like brother and sister, proving that two can live in complete propinquity with perfect propriety as long as no one cares.

Their reason for being, as we saw it, was to produce babies for our researches, and so at this point we deliberately initiated a breeding program which was frighteningly unsuccessful. When the older, wire-cage-raised males were paired with the females at the peak of estrus, the introduction led only to fighting, so violent and vicious that separation was essential to survival. In no case was there any indication of normal sex behavior. Frequently the females were the aggressors; even the normal praying mantis waits until the sex act is completed.

Pairing such cloth-surrogate-raised monkeys as were sexually mature gave little better end results. Violent aggression was not the rule, and there was attempted sex behavior, but it was unreproductive since both the male and female behaviors were of the infantile type we have already described.

At this point we took the 17 oldest of our cage-raised animals, females showing consistent estrous cycles and males obviously mature, and engaged in an intensive re-education program, pairing the females with our most experienced, patient, and gentle males, and the males with our most eager, amiable, and successful breeding females. When the laboratory-bred females were smaller than the sophisticated males, the girls would back away and sit down facing the males, looking appealingly at these would-be consorts. Their hearts were in the right place, but nothing else was. When the females were larger than the males, we can only hope that they misunderstood the males' intentions,

for after a brief period of courtship, they would attack and maul the ill-fated male. Females show no respect for a male they can dominate.

The training program for the males was equally unsatisfactory. They approached the females with a blind enthusiasm, but it was a misdirected enthusiasm. Frequently the males would grasp the females by the side of the body and thrust laterally, leaving them working at cross purposes with reality. Even the most persistent attempts by these females to set the boys straight came to naught. Finally, these females either stared at the males with complete contempt or attacked them in utter frustration. It became obvious that they, like their human counterpart, prefer maturer men. We realized then that we had established, not a program of breeding, but a program of brooding.

We had in fact been warned. Our first seven laboratory-born babies were raised in individual cages while being trained on a learning test battery. William Mason planned to test their social behaviors subsequently, and great care had been taken to keep the babies socially isolated and to prevent any physical contacts. Neonatal baby monkeys require 24-hour-a-day care, and infant monkeys need ministrations beyond a 40-hour week. We had assigned the evening care to Kathy, a maternal bit of fluff who had worked for several years as a monkey tester while studying to become an elementary school teacher.

Checking on his wards one night near 10 P.M., Mason found Kathy sitting on the floor surrounded by seven baby monkeys, all eight of the primates playing happily together. Before the horrified scientist could express his outrage, Kathy had risen to her full height of five feet two. Already anticipating the carping criticisms which he was formulating, she shook her finger in his face and spoke with conviction: "Dr. Mason, I'm an education student and I know that it is improper and immoral to blight the social development of little children. I am right and you are wrong!"

Although we were angry with Kathy, we did think there was a certain humor in the situation and we did not worry about our monkeys. We simply transferred Kathy to an office job. Alas, she could not have been more right and we could not have been more wrong! We have already described the social-sexual life of these 7 monkeys and the next 40 to come.

Two years later we had more than theoretical reasons to be disturbed because Mason tested a group of these isolation-raised monkeys, then between 2.5 and 3.5 years of age, and found evidence of severe social abnormalities, which might be described as a sociopathic syndrome. He matched the laboratory-raised monkeys on the basis of weight and dentition patterns with monkeys that had been born and raised in the wild for the first 12 to 18 months, then captured and subjected to various kinds of housing and caging treatments for the next year or two. In the test situations the laboratory-raised monkeys, as compared with feral monkeys, showed infantile sexual behavior, absence of grooming, exaggerated aggression, and absence of affectional interaction as measured by cooperation.

We are now quite certain that this sociopathic syndrome does not stem from the fact that the baby monkeys were raised in the laboratory but from *how* they were raised in the laboratory. Our infants raised in the laboratory by real monkey mothers and permitted opportunity for the development of normal infant-infant affection demonstrate normal male and female sexual behavior when they enter the second year of life. Furthermore, our playroom and playpen studies show that infant monkeys raised on cloth mothers but given the opportunity to form normal infant-infant affectional patterns, also develop normal sexual responses.

In a desperate attempt to assist a group of 18 three- to four-year-old cloth-surrogate-raised monkeys, half of them males and half females, we engaged in a group-psychotherapy program, placing these animals for two months on the monkey island in the Madison Zoo, as shown in Figure 13. Their summer vacation on the enchanted island was not without avail, and social grooming responses rapidly developed and were frequent in occurrence. After a few days of misunderstanding, patterns of social ordering developed, and a number of males and females developed friendship patterns. Unfortunately, sexual behavior was infrequent, and the behavior that was observed was completely inadequate—at least from our point of view. In desperation we finally introduced our most experienced, most patient, and most kindly breeding male, Smiley (the male in Figures 1 and 2), and he rapidly established himself as king of the island and prepared to take full advantage of the wealth of opportunity which surrounded him. Fortunately, the traumatic experiences he encountered with unreceptive females have left no apparent permanent emotional scars, and now that he has been returned to our laboratory breeding colony, he is again making an important contribution to our research program. If normal sexual

FIG. 13. Group of cloth-surrogate-raised monkeys on the monkey island in the Madison Zoo.

behavior occurred, no member of our observational team ever saw it, and had a female become pregnant, we would have believed in parthenogenesis.

But let us return to the monkeys that we left on the island and the older ones that we left in their cages. A year has passed, and the frustrations that both we and our monkeys experienced are in some small part nothing but a memory. We constructed larger and more comfortable breeding

FIG. 14. Typical behavior of unmothered mother toward her infant. Mother is looking upward while crushing her baby against the cage floor.

cages, and we designed a very large experimental breeding room 8 feet by 8 feet by 8 feet in size with appropriate platforms and a six-foot tree. Apparently we designed successful seraglios for I can report that not all love's labors have been lost. It does appear that the males are completely expendable unless they can be used in a program of artificial insemination. Certainly we can find no evidence that there is a destiny that shapes their ends unless some Skinnerite can help us with the shaping process. We have, however, had better success with some of the females, particularly the females raised on cloth surrogates.

Even so, one of the wire-cage-raised females is a mother and another is pregnant. Three cloth-surrogate females are mothers and four or five are expectant. We give all the credit to three breeding males. One, Smiley, does not take "no" for an answer. Smiley has a way with females. Patient, gentle, and persuasive, he has overcome more than one planned program of passive resistance. One female did not become pregnant until the fifth successive month of training. Month after month

she has changed, and now she is mad about the boy. Male No. 342 behaves very much like Smiley. Even when females threaten him, he does not harm them. Given time, he has been able to overcome more than one reluctant dragon, and he is a master of the power of positive suggestion.

Breeding male No. 496 has helped us greatly, particularly with the younger, cloth-surrogate-raised females. His approach differs from that of Smiley and No. 342. His technique transcends seduction, and in contract bridge terms it may be described as an approach-forcing system.

Combining our human and male-monkey talents, we are winning the good fight and imparting to naive and even resistant female monkeys the priceless gift of motherhood. Possibly it is a Pyrrhic victory. As every scientist knows, the solution of one scientific problem inevitably leads to another, and this is our fate (Figure 14). Month after month female monkeys that never knew a real mother, themselves become mothers—helpless, hopeless, heartless mothers devoid, or almost devoid, of any maternal feeling.

PHILLIP C. GREEN & MICHAEL GORDON

58   Maternal Deprivation: Its Influence on Visual Exploration in Infant Monkeys

Abstract. Visual exploration was studied in maternally reared and maternally deprived monkeys. When an animal pressed a bar an opaque screen was raised providing a brief view of either of a pair of stimuli. Subjects reared by their mothers pressed more to see animate than inanimate objects. With increasing age, the number of bar-pressing responses decreased for an adult female stimulus, increased for an age peer and for food, and remained low for geometric forms and an empty chamber. Maternally deprived subjects established uniformly low response levels to all stimuli.

Butler (*1*) has shown that adult monkeys, placed inside a small dimly lighted chamber, will persistently open a hinged wall-panel for no incentive other than the opportunity to observe

Reprinted from *Science 145*:292–294, 1964. Copyright 1964 by the American Association for the Advancement of Science.

briefly various objects placed outside the chamber. It has been demonstrated further by Harlow (*2*) that young monkeys, separated from their mothers at birth and reared on mother surrogates, will learn to press a bar so that the artificial mother can be seen. However, little is known concerning the early visual preferences of infant primates entirely deprived of their mothers during development. In this study we attempted to investigate the relative influence of maternal rearing as opposed to maternal deprivation on visual exploratory behavior in the infant macaque.

Nine infant monkeys were randomly assigned at birth to one of two groups. Group 1 consisted of four infants reared by their mothers, and group 2 consisted of five maternally deprived animals. Shortly after birth, each infant in group 1 was taken away for a physical examination, but was immediately afterward returned to its mother which was collared and chained to the cage so that the infant could be retrieved for testing. Each infant in group 2, however, was separated permanently from its mother, housed in an individual cage, and handled only for purposes of feeding and examination.

The test apparatus was a modified version of a unit designed at the University of Wisconsin (1) and consisted of an enclosed chamber containing two large distinctively painted bars, each located on opposite interior walls. Each press of the bar by the subject constituted a response which caused a motor-driven panel located directly above its respective bar to be raised for 10 seconds permitting a view of, but no manual contact with, the contents of a small booth adjoining each door.

Stimuli were presented in pairs as follows: (i) both stimulus booths empty (control conditions, EE); (ii) empty versus food (EF); (iii) empty versus age peer (EP); (iv) empty versus adult female "mother" (EM); (v) empty versus plastic geometric forms (EPl); (vi) food versus geometric forms (FPl); and (vii) adult female (mother) versus age peer (MP).

The stimulus presentation schedule was designed so that the subjects received all paired combinations during the test period according to a prearranged schedule. After a 3-day adaptation period in the test chamber for all subjects (bars removed), each pair of stimuli was presented once during a series of consecutive 3-week periods. Ten presentations were made for each condition described above so that the period of development during the test schedule covered approximately the first 8 months of life. Although the location of the stimulus-viewing panels was such that there was no clearly definable "right" or "left" side, preliminary data indicated small nonsignificant preferences in almost all animals for one bar over the other in the initial control (EE) condition. Consequently, for all stimulus presentations, objects from each pair were varied randomly from side to side, with the provision that each booth location was sampled half the time.

The preference data for the seven stimulus-pair conditions, averaged over the 30-week test period, are presented in Fig. 1 (3). Differences in response rates between groups 1 and 2 were highly significant ($p = .005$, Mann-Whitney U test) on all stimulus pair comparisons. For the control condition (EE), both groups pressed the bars at relatively low but equal rates. For the remaining pairs of stimuli, however, the animals in group 1 maintained high response rates and demonstrated clear preferences, with food being preferred to the empty booth ($p = .02$), age peer to empty ($p = .01$), adult female to empty ($p = .01$), and adult female to age peer ($p = .05$). The preference for food, when paired with geometric forms, fell just short of significance and suggested that these stimuli were about equally attractive.

Response rates in group 2 were uniformly low for all stimulus combinations. The moderate rates seen in this group on the EP, EM, EPl, and MP pairings are misleading since the average number of responses for these pairings increased only toward the end of the experimental series when the animals were somewhat older; responses were virtually absent during the earlier period of testing. With the possible exception of condition EM, whose difference lacked significance, this group showed little evidence for stimulus preferences among the various conditions.

It was also of interest to trace performance changes to the individual stimulus conditions as a function of age. Although the data for the maternally separated group could not be eval-

uated statistically because of the low response rates, these trends are presented for the maternally separated group in Fig. 2. To minimize the effect on the data of a competing stimulus, only those conditions were chosen in which the paired stimulus for "mother," "peer," "geometric forms," and "food" was the empty condition.

The results indicated that standard deviations were proportional to the means. Accordingly, all data were subjected to a logarithmic transform and best fitting linear functions were determined for each pair of stimuli over the ten test sessions. The responses to adult female and peer stimuli showed opposite trends, namely, with increasing age maternally reared subjects showed an apparent decrease in interest for the adult female and a corresponding increase for the age peer. Geometric forms and food reflected generally lower response levels, with levels for the former showing little change, while those for the latter showed an increase corresponding to a normal transition from liquid to solid food at about 2 months of age. The empty booths, as expected, attracted the least attention. The means of the

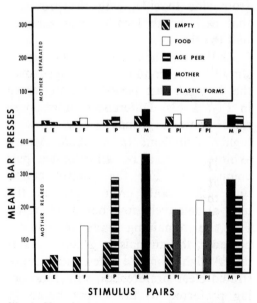

Fig. 1. Mean bar-press responses of group 1 (mother reared) and group 2 (mother separated) during ten 1-hour test sessions for each stimulus-pair condition.

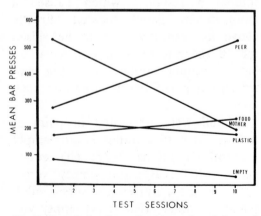

Fig. 2. Best fitting linear functions plotted for each stimulus condition over test sessions (group 1, mother reared, only).

first five test sessions were compared with those of the last five test sessions by *T*-tests, which indicated significant differences on the "peer" and "mother" conditions ($p \leqq .04$). None of the other stimuli showed significant changes.

It is clear that early in development maternally reared infant monkeys establish a hierarchy of visual preferences for a variety of stimulus objects. Of those used in this study, the adult female was the most attractive to all infants in group 1, particularly during the early stages of development. Although none of the subjects possessed sufficient neuromuscular development to press the bars effectively before the 3rd week of life, this response was well established after the 5th week. The intensity of preferences changed considerably with increasing maturation and followed a trend toward progressively fewer responses to the adult female, more responses to the age peer, and relatively fewer responses to the inanimate objects.

Maternally deprived monkeys showed few responses to any stimulus compared with maternally reared animals, despite a comparable number of adaptation trials. These animals showed evidence of exaggerated fear and general inappropriateness of response throughout testing. In a typical trial, after several minutes in the experimental chamber, a deprived animal would visually sample each stimulus booth, retreat to a corner of the test chamber, and crouch almost continuously, exhibiting repetitive stereotyped movements such as rocking, hair-pulling, clasping, and "fear" vocalization. These nonadaptive responses emphasize the importance of mothering during the development of adaptive modes of behavior.

It is recognized that the variable of maternal deprivation is a complex one. The relative contributions of maturation, learning, and motivational variables to development of visual responses in the infant monkey must remain conjectural until more experimental evidence is available.

References and Notes

1. R. A. Butler, *J. Comp. Physiol. Psychol.* **47**, 358 (1954).
2. H. F. Harlow, *Am. Psychol.* **13**, 673 (1958).
3. Amygdala lesions were created surgically in two animals in group 1 and three animals in group 2. These lesions appeared to have no influence on the response rates or object preferences of either group and the data for all the animals in each group were accordingly combined for analysis.
4. This research was supported by grant USPHS HD 00356 from the National Institutes of Health and grant 1711 from the State of Illinois.

KENNETH S. ROBSON, FRANK A. PEDERSEN, & HOWARD A. MOSS

59 Development Observations of Diadic Gazing in Relation to the Fear of Strangers and Social Approach Behavior

This report describes relations among maternal attitudes assessed during pregnancy, the frequency of mother-infant gazing assessed at 1 and 3 months of age, and 3 measures of approach-avoidance behavior, including

Reprinted from *Child Development* 40:619–627, 1969. ©1969 by the Society for Research in Child Development, Inc.

infant-stranger gazing, assessed at 8 and 9½ months in 45 infants. For males, mother-infant gazing correlates positively with infant-stranger gazing and another social approach variable. The latter 2 variables and mother-infant gazing, again for males, correlate positively with antecedent maternal attitudes. For both sexes, stranger-infant gazing is intercorrelated with the other approach-avoidance variables. The possible significance of these relations is discussed.

In previous publications we have suggested that mutual visual regard, between mother and infant, is a form of social interchange that has important developmental consequences (Moss & Robson, 1968; Robson, 1967). From longitudinal observations on a sample of primiparous mothers and infants, we have shown that the frequency of mother-infant gazing, assessed in home observations during the first 3 months of life, correlates for both sexes with antecedent maternal attitudes and for female infants with subsequent visual fixation times to two-dimensional facial stimuli. We have now followed our sample into the latter part of the first year of life and can report on further relations between early mutual visual regard and later social behaviors in infants.

Hutt and Ounsted (1966) note that looking at another person indicates a "readiness to interact." Conversely, they view gaze aversion as a means of avoiding social contact. In many animal species, looking away serves as a "cut-off" act which permits an organism to modulate its flight or aggressive responses while maintaining physical proximity to a conspecific (Chance, 1962). To the extent that these tendencies to look at or away from another person are subject to environmental modification, it seems reasonable to hypothesize that an infant's early diadic gaze experiences with his mother may contribute to the manner in which he will subsequently interact with strangers. The aims of this paper are twofold: to assess the predictive value of early mutual visual regard between mother and infant in relation to the fear of strangers and social approach behavior measured several months later; and to describe the extent to which an infant's gaze behavior with a stranger is a useful measure of his overall readiness to approach or withdraw from social objects.

METHOD

Subjects

The sample for the early observations consisted of 54 primiparous mothers and their infants, half males and half females. The mothers were between 18 and 34 years of age, and their education ranged from the completion of tenth grade to the possession of a professional degree. Their mean age was 24.5 years, and their mean education was 2.7 years of college. At the time of our follow-up visits the sample was reduced to 45 mother-infant pairs, 20 males and 25 females. This decrease was accounted for by nine subjects having moved out of the greater Washington, D.C., area.

Procedure

Pregnancy interview.—These women were first seen during the last trimester of pregnancy when they were administered a standard interview schedule. The interviews averaged 1½ hours in length and dealt with the expectant mother's feelings and thoughts about the pregnancy and her functioning in the maternal role. From these interviews ratings were made on a nine-point scale for several variables. Two of the authors divided the interviewing and made the ratings for the cases they interviewed. One of the variables, Interest in Affectionate Contact with Infants (IAC), assessed the extent of a mother's investment in and expected pleasure from affectionate physical contact with her baby. The interrater reliability coefficient for this variable was .75. IAC, which was previously found to be positively correlated with the frequency of mother-infant gazing, will be included in the present analysis.

Mother-infant observations.—Three naturalistic observations, each 6 hours long, were conducted in the home after the birth of the infant. Two of these observations occurred at the end of the first month of life and one at the end of the third month. The cases were divided equally among three observers, with each observer studying nine male and nine female infants. Throughout the data collection, the observers worked together in pairs observing mothers and infants not included in the core sample, for the purpose of obtaining interrater reliabilities. The reliability observations were 3 hours long, and three observations were made in each of 10 homes so that all observer combinations were used for each reliability case.

A modified time-sampling technique was used for coding the observational data. The time-sample units were 1 minute in length, and the observer, using a printed form, placed a number opposite the appropriate behavior to indicate its respective order of occurrence. Since each variable could be coded only once for each observational unit, a score of 360 was the maximum for one 6-hour observation. The time-sampled variables included a number of maternal and infant behaviors. For the present analysis we will only deal with mutual visual regard (VVM), which was defined as the frequency with which mother and infant simultaneously looked at one another's faces. One score for this variable (VVM$_1$) was obtained by averaging the two early observations and a second score (VVM$_3$) was obtained from the 3-month observation. The interrater reliability coefficients for VVM, for each combination of raters, were .91, .89, and .78.

Stranger-infant observations.—Two of the authors, one of whom had had no previous contacts with the sample, conducted these observations. Each mother-infant pair was visited in their home at 8 months and again at 9½ months. A brief telephone follow-up was made at 11 months. These ages were selected as the time of peak intensity of the fear of strangers (Schaffer & Emerson, 1964; Tennes & Lampl, 1964). The observation sessions lasted approximately 50 minutes and were made at a time during the day when the infant had been recently fed and was ordinarily awake.

Both sessions consisted of a structured interview with the mother and a number of behavioral observations of mother and infant.

Upon entering the home, both observers seated themselves across the room from the mother. After 2 minutes of introduction, during which the infant was not restrained, the mother placed him on her lap and the first fear-of-strangers assessment began. One observer approached the infant slowly and steadily, picked him up, and held him for approximately 1 minute while looking at the eye area of his face. He was then returned to his mother's lap. This procedure was repeated again at the end of the interview. Otherwise the infants were not restrained. During these assessments the experimenter was silent and maintained a pleasant but non-smiling demeanor. Throughout each session, until the second fear-of-strangers procedure was completed, neither observer made social overtures toward the infant.

Parenthetically, during the first visit every mother was asked whether her infant's behavior when approached and held by the experimenter was characteristic of how he currently reacted to strange adults. Of the sample, 24 per cent felt that their babies exhibited more avoidance, 19 per cent felt that there was less avoidance than was usual, and 57 per cent could detect no difference. Thus, the formal and somewhat stressful manner which we used in our experimental design seemed to yield a moderately true-to-life picture of these infants in their natural state.

Behavioral ratings were made of the infant's fear of strangers (FS), of his gaze behavior in relation to the experimenter carrying out the fear-of-strangers interventions (VVS), and of his unsolicited social approaches toward the observers during unstructured portions of the session (SAS).

The FS rating was based on a modification of the scale designed by Tennes and Lampl (1964; Katherine Tennes, personal communication). This 13-point scale described a continuum of behaviors ranging from active avoidance accompanied by crying and refusal to be held to active approach with smiling, vocalizing, and seeking physical contact with the observer. A total of four FS ratings, two during each home visit, were made for every infant. The interrater reliabilities for the four FS scores averaged .89. Using the means of both observers' ratings, at 8 and 9½ months, respectively, the intrasession FS scores were intercorrelated .70 and .60. The mean 8-month FS score correlated .69 with the 9½-month score. The mean values of FS, both within and between sessions, were not significantly different from one another.

VVS was defined as the frequency and duration of the infant's looking at the experimenter's face during the FS procedure. As was the case in our earlier assessments of maternal-infant mutual visual regard, we attempted to rate the baby's gazing only when he was scrutinizing the eye area of the experimenter's face. VVS was rated on a seven-point scale ranging from total avoidance of the experimenter's face to frequent and sustained periods of face-to-face gazing throughout the FS procedure. The interrater reliabilities for the four VVS ratings averaged 0.85. The intrasession VVS correlations for both observations were .39. The correlation between the mean VVS scores at each point in time was .45.

SAS measured the amount of approach behavior the infant *initiated* toward both observers while unrestrained, and was rated on a 13-point scale which ranged from more or less constant smiling at, vocalizing to, and seeking of physical contact with the experimenters (other than during the FS procedure) to total avoidance and lack of interest in them. The interrater reliabilities for the SAS scores for each session were .69 and .86. Though the mean value of SAS at 9½ months was higher than at 8 months, this difference did not reach significance. The intersession SAS correlation coefficient was .67.

Single scores for FS, VVS, and SAS were derived by combining both observers' ratings and taking the mean of all assessments for each variable.

RESULTS

Previous findings on this sample included sex differences. Tennes and Lampl (1964) described sex differences in the intensity of fear of strangers. Hence, all data analyses to follow will be made separately for males and females.

The Course of Fear of Strangers

Before exploring the longitudinal and cross-sectional relations among our variables, it was important to know whether there were sex differences in the age at onset and maximum intensity of the fear of strangers. The age at onset of the fear of strangers was defined as the month in which the first episode of a clear-cut avoidance response to an unfamiliar adult was reported. These data were derived from the 8- and 9-month interviews and the 11-month telephone follow-ups. The mean age at onset for the females was 6.7 months and for the males was 9.1 months; this difference was significant ($t = 3.4$, $p < .01$). Furthermore, the females had a higher, though not significantly different, mean FS rating than the males. The mean SAS score for the males was higher than that of the females. Overall, these data suggest that within our sample the fear of strangers in females described an earlier course than in the males.

Longitudinal Findings

The relations among all of our variables have been summarized in Table 1. As reported elsewhere (Moss & Robson, 1968), maternal IAC was positively and significantly related to the frequency of mother-infant gazing at 1 month (VVM_1) for both sexes (males, $r = .45$, $p < .01$; females, $r = .34$, $p < .05$) and to the frequency of mother-infant gazing at 3 months (VVM_3) for females alone ($r = .43$, $p < .05$). The frequency of VVM at 3 months was almost twice that of the 1-month observation, but at both points in time these scores were comparable for the sexes.

TABLE 1

Intercorrelations among Approach-Avoidance Variables, Early Mother-Infant Gazing, and Pregnancy Ratings for Males and Females Separately

Variable	VVS	FS	SAS	VVM$_1$	VVM$_3$	IAC
VVS........	...	$N = 25$ $-.70^{***}$	$N = 25$ $.28$	$N = 25$ $-.20$	$N = 25$ $-.19$	$N = 25$ $-.16$
FS........	$N = 19$ $-.57^{***}$	...	$N = 25$ $-.57^{***}$	$N = 25$ $-.03$	$N = 25$ $.28$	$N = 25$ $.09$
SAS........	$N = 19$ $.66^{***}$	$N = 19$ $-.65^{***}$	...	$N = 25$ $.34^*$	$N = 25$ $.08$	$N = 25$ $-.05$
VVM$_1$......	$N = 19$ $.57^{***}$	$N = 20$ $-.38^*$	$N = 19$ 66^{***}	...	$N = 27$ $.24$	$N = 27$ $.34$
VVM$_3$......	$N = 19$ $.31$	$N = 20$ $-.23$	$N = 19$ $.40^*$	$N = 27$ $.59^{***}$	...	$N = 27$ $.43^*$
IAC........	$N = 19$ $.39^*$	$N = 20$ $-.06$	$N = 19$ $.43^*$	$N = 27$ $.45^{**}$	$N = 27$ $.31$	...

Note.—The correlations for males are presented below the diagonal rows of dots and for females above the diagonal rows of dots.
* $p < .05$; one-tailed test.
** $p < .01$; one-tailed test.
*** $p < .005$; one-tailed test.

We can now examine the relations among the frequency of mother-infant mutual visual regard and FS, VVS, and SAS. As can be seen in Table 1 there is, for males, a low but significant negative correlation between FS and VVM$_1$ ($r = -.38$, $p < .05$) but not VVM$_3$. For females, neither correlation is significant.

There is a stronger association for the males between diadic gazing at 1 month and the extent to which these infants looked at the experimenter. VVS and VVM$_1$ bear a positive and highly significant relation to one another ($r = .57$, $p < .005$). The correlation between VVM$_3$ and VVS, though in the same direction, does not reach significance ($r = .31$). For females, however, neither the 1- nor 3-month VVM score correlates with VVS. Thus, for males, the frequency of mother-infant mutual visual regard at 1 month of age is predictive of gaze behavior with a stranger when measured 7–8½ months later.

Again for males, SAS is positively and significantly correlated with both VVM$_1$ ($r = .66$, $p < .005$) and VVM$_3$ ($r = .40$, $p < .05$). VVM$_1$ does correlate with SAS for females ($r = .34$, $p < .05$), but by 3 months this association is no longer significant. Hence, primarily for boys, the frequency of diadic gazing in early infancy is predictive of spontaneous social behavior with strangers assessed several months later.

Finally, are there any associations between maternal IAC and our approach-avoidance variables? FS, VVS, and SAS for females are not significantly related to IAC. Yet for males both VVS ($r = .39$, $p < .05$) and SAS ($r = .43$, $p < .05$) are positively and significantly correlated with the pregnancy measure. These relations suggest that antenatal maternal attitudes in the mothers of males contribute both to the frequency of early mutual gazing with the infant and to his later approach and avoidance behaviors in relation to strangers.

Cross-sectional Findings

Since we were interested in the extent to which an infant's gaze behavior reflected his social orientation toward strangers, we can now consider the relations among VVS, FS, and SAS. These, too, can be seen in Table 1. FS and VVS were negatively and significantly correlated for both males and females (males, $r = -.57$, $p < .005$; females, $r = -.70$, $p < .005$). The more an infant looked at the experimenter, the less fearful he seemed to be. Since these two variables were rated simultaneously, they are not independent measures. The most parsimonious explanation of these intercorrelations is that the infants' gaze behavior was a major component of our FS rating.

FS and SAS were also negatively and significantly correlated for both sexes (males, $r = -.65$, $p < .005$; females, $r = -.57$, $p < .005$). The extent of an infant's approach or avoidance behavior in the FS procedures tended to be predictve of his unsolicited social behavior during the remainder of the session.

Although FS and VVS were strongly intercorrelated for both sexes, the relation between VVS and SAS was different for males and females. For the boys VVS and SAS were positively and significantly correlated ($r = .66$, $p < .005$). But for the girls this correlation did not reach significance ($r = .28$). Since the difference between these correlations was not significant, and since the correlation for the pooled sample was significant ($r = .48$, $p < .005$), this finding should not be overemphasized. Nevertheless, looking away in females (both children and adults) carries a different social valence than in males. The little girl who averts her gaze is coy, coquettish, or even seductive, while the boy is usually labeled shy or fearful. Such sex-role sterotypes could reflect fundamental differences in social behavior between the sexes. In general, these cross-sectional data suggest that an infant's interpersonal gazing is a useful behavioral measure of his sociabilty.

To summarize our findings, the extent to which an 8–9½-month-old infant of either sex looks at a stranger is negatively related to his fearfulness of that stranger and, for males, is positively related to his unsolicited approaches toward him when unrestrained. Furthermore, primarily for male infants, the frequency of mother-infant mutual visual regard during the first 3 months of life is positively correlated with both gazing at and social approaches toward strangers. Finally, maternal interest in affectionate contact with infants, assessed during pregnancy, is positively related to early mother-infant gazing for both sexes, and to looking at and social responsiveness toward strangers for males alone.

DISCUSSION

Although mainly for males, our data support the hypothesis that the frequency of mutual visual regard between mother and infant should be associated with later social behaviors. These findings raise two questions: What are the possible meanings of our longitudinal correlations? What factors could account for the sex differences? We shall consider these questions in order.

It is while a mother looks at her infant *en face,* during the early months of life, that she simultaneously smiles at and talks to him (Robson, 1967; Watson, 1965). Whether the gaze itself has reinforcing properties has yet to be demonstrated. Learning theory would predict that the amount of early social reinforcement an infant receives from his primary caretakers should generalize to his response expectancies from and behavioral output toward other adults. This point of view provides a reasonable explanation for the positive correlations between VVM_1, VVM_3, and our later measures of social behavior. The associations of maternal IAC with VVS and SAS lend further support to this interpretation.

We must stress, however, that the gaze interchange is diadic and that the infant as well as the mother contributed to our VVM scores. Hence, it is possible that infant differences may have contributed to a substantial portion of the variance in the correlations of early mutual visual regard both with IAC and our later measures.

We can now turn to the sex differences in our longitudinal relations. It seems plausible that the paucity of correlations for the females could lie in the timing of our interventions. Previous observations on this sample and the work of Kagan and his co-workers (Kagan, Henker, Hen-Tov, Levine & Lewis 1966; Kagan & Lewis, 1965) support the idea that female infants are more developmentally advanced than males. The fact that the age at onset for the fear of strangers in this sample was substantially earlier for females than for males lends further support to this point of view. Thus, earlier experimental intervention might have brought out longitudinal relations more clearly for the females.

Another factor that could relate to our sex differences is the fact that we used male experimenters exclusively. Morgan and Ricciuti (1969) noted that there was a tendency for infants of both sexes to display more approach behavior toward a female observer. Since the behavior of both males and females was altered in the same direction, it seems improbable that the sex of the experimenter would contribute significantly to the lack of longitudinal correlations for the females in our sample.

The cross-sectional data from this study are also of interest. The fact that an infant's interpersonal gazing tends to index his social behavior suggests that the gaze system may be a profitable framework within which to study further development. For example, there is as yet no information about the extent to which the fear of strangers is predictive of interpersonal behavior at an older age. Although the more overt manifestations of this fear tend to disappear during the second year of life, we have no reason to assume that the response tendency is no longer present. With increasing age a child develops more subtle ways to deal with social discomfort. It may be that his interpersonal gaze behavior continues to reflect earlier approach-avoidance tendencies. An understanding of the constitutional and environmental factors that control the development of interpersonal gazing may contribute to our knowledge of human social behavior.

REFERENCES

Chance, M. R. A. An interpretation of some agonistic postures; the role of "cut-off" acts and postures. *Symposia of the Zoological Society of London*, 1962, 8, 71–89.

Hutt, C., & Ounsted, C. The biological significance of gaze aversion with particular reference to the syndrome of infantile autism. *Behavioral Science*, 1966, 11, 346–356.

Kagan, J., Henker, B. A., Hen-Tov, A., Levine, J., & Lewis, M. Infants' reactions to familiar & distorted faces. *Child Development*, 1966, 37, 519–532.

Kagan, J., & Lewis, M. Studies of attention in the human infant. *Merrill-Palmer Quarterly*, 1965, 11, 95–127.

Morgan, G. A., & Ricciuti, H. N. Infants' responses to strangers during the first year. In B. Foss (Ed.), *Determinants of infant behaviour* Vol. 4. London: Methuen, 1969.

Moss, H. A., & Robson, K. S. Maternal influences in early social-visual behavior. *Child Development*, 1968, 39, 401–408.

Robson, K. S. The role of eye-to-eye contact in maternal-infant attachment. *Journal of Child Psychology and Psychiatry*, 1967, 8, 13–25.

Schaffer, H. R., & Emerson, P. E. The development of social attachments in infancy. *Monographs of the Society for Research in Child Development*, 1964, 29, (3, Serial No. 94).

Tennes, K. H., & Lampl, E. E. Stranger and separation anxiety in infancy. *Journal of Nervous and Mental Disease*, 1964, 139, 247–254.

Watson, J. S. Orientation-specific age changes in responsiveness to the face stimulus in young infants. Paper presented at the annual meeting of the American Psychological Association, Chicago, 1965.

CLIFFORD R. BARNETT, P. HERBERT LEIDERMAN, ROSE GROBSTEIN, & MARSHALL KLAUS

60   Neonatal Separation: The Maternal Side of Interactional Deprivation

ABSTRACT. Studies of maternal behavior in non-human mammals have suggested that the degree of interaction permitted between mother and infant in the postpartum period will influence later maternal attachment and infant development. The hypotheses raised by these studies can be explored with human mothers and infants through manipulation of care procedures of mothers and newborns in the immediate postpartum period.

A pilot study was conducted to determine the feasibility of changing premature care procedures in order to study the effects of interactional deprivation in the neonatal period on maternal attitudes and behavior. Forty-one mothers were permitted to enter the nursery and touch or handle their premature infants in incubators as early as the second

Reprinted from *Pediatrics* 45:197–205, 1970.

day after birth. The feasibility of admitting mothers to the premature nursery without increasing the risk or occurrence of infection, or disrupting the organization of the care of the infants, was demonstrated.

We are now conducting a long-term study based on this pilot model to delineate the differences in commitment, feelings of competence, and behavior in the two differentially treated groups of mothers and to relate their behavior to the motor and mental development of the infants.

S TUDIES of maternal-infant separation in humans have focussed upon the consequences of separation for the infant, rather than the mother.[1-3] Under most study conditions infants separated from their mothers early in the postpartum period (1 day to 3 months after birth) have been institutionalized, and the absent mother has not been available for assessment of her reactions to the infant during and following the separation.

It is extremely difficult to manipulate the human condition so as to experimentally separate a human mother from her infant in the immediate postpartum period and then reunite the pair and observe her subsequent behavior. We have found it is possible to approximate this study design by modification of the hospital procedures for the care of premature infants. The usual care routine for a premature infant requires that the mother be separated from her infant immediately after birth for a period of time ranging from 3 to 12 weeks, depending upon the weight and health of the infant. By experimentally permitting some mothers to have physical contact with their premature infants and other mothers to experience the usual separation, we are studying the effects of separation on maternal attitudes and behavior.

The purposes of this paper are: (1) to present some of the theoretical issues regarding the effects of separation in the neonatal period which can be answered through experimental manipulation of care procedures for the newborn, and (2) to describe our findings regarding the feasibility of so modifying care in a premature nursery.

THE SIGNIFICANCE OF NEONATAL SEPARATION

From the earliest and sometimes apocryphal reports of "wolf children"[4,5] to the contemporary work of Spitz,[6] Bowlby and coworkers,[7] and Ainsworth,[8] studies of maternal-infant separation have described the effects of long-term maternal separation on the infant in terms of its detrimental effects on his motor, mental, and affective development. While there has been a theoretical recognition that separation involves both the mother and the infant,[9,10] little attention has been paid to its effects on the mother.

This one-sided focus on the infant is particularly unfortunate in the light of the many mammalian studies of maternal behavior which emphasize the importance of the young in stimulating maternal behavior. These studies suggest that the timing and duration of the animal mother's earliest contact with her young are crucial in determining her later behavior toward her infant. If contact with her young is delayed by separating the animal mother from her infant for a period of time immediately or shortly after birth, she may exhibit maladaptive maternal behavior when contact is permitted.[11-14]

The components of mother-infant interaction most affected by separation in the early postpartum period are: (1) the timing and duration of contact, (2) the sensory modalities of interaction, and (3) the caretaking nature of the interaction. With reference to the significance of the timing of interactional deprivation, Yarrow[15] has summarized the evidence for the human infant: "The most sensitive time may be the period during which the infant is in the process of establishing stable affectional relationships, approximately between six months and two years." Bronfenbrenner's[16] later review of the literature confirms this finding.

There are no comparable data, however, regarding what might be the most "sensitive time" for the human mother to undergo separation from her infant. Research on animals has demonstrated that separation of a mother from her young, even for an hour in some species, produces a disturbance in the mother-infant relationship that is often irreversible.[12] Considering the cultural expectancies built up in the human mother, and the physiological changes she has undergone in preparation for establishing a relationship with her infant, it is reasonable to hypothesize that the immediate postpartum period may be a time of maximum sensitivity for the mother. Separation from her infant in the neonatal period may not permit the mother to develop an attachment to her infant at the time when she is most sensitized to be responsive to him.

The sensory modalities involved in the interaction between mother and infant throw some light on the mechanisms of maternal attachment with which separation interferes. Harlow and his associates[17] have demonstrated, for example, that rhesus mothers who were allowed to see or hear their infants, but not to touch them, rapidly decreased the time spent viewing their infants after 2 weeks of tactile deprivation. Whether this deprivation leads to the same results for humans as well as animals is as yet unknown. Certainly, the visual eye-to-eye contact between mother and infant which Robson[18] has suggested is important for the development of infant-mother attachment, is greatly impeded for the mother of a premature infant who must view her infant from afar. If, as the animal studies suggest, the mother responds to the presence of the infant by behaving in a maternal fashion, the different modes, as well as the quantity, of stimulation provided by the infant to the mother may produce different responses from the mother toward the infant. Bell's[19] review of the literature

on the effect of the child on parental behavior points in this direction.

The third component of mother-infant interaction is the caretaking element of the mother's interaction with her infant. We refer here to our clinical experiences with mothers of premature infants who report that they first felt "close" to their babies when they were able to feed them or do something for them. As one mother of a premature infant commented to us: "Love is a two-way street. It requires the infant to be totally dependent for all of his needs on the mother before she can take care of him in a loving way." Researchers who have studied mothers in the Israeli kibbutz system, where full care is provided for the infants by trained personnel, report that kibbutzim mothers have demanded that they be permitted greater involvement in the care of their infants.[20,21] As Spiro has summed up the situation: "It seems that many mothers need *to do* something for their children."[22]

LEVELS AND SOURCES OF INTERACTIONAL DEPRIVATION

Manipulation of the three components of interaction produces different levels of interactional deprivation on the day of birth (Table I). The mother of a full-term infant who gives birth in a hospital, for example, experiences moderate interactional deprivation (Level III). She may have some contact with her infant involving all sensory modalities when he is placed on her abdomen in the delivery room and when he is

TABLE I

LEVELS OF INTERACTIONAL DEPRIVATION
AND COMPONENT VARIABLES

Levels of Deprivation	Duration of Interaction	Sensory Modalities of Interaction	Caretaking Nature of Interaction
I, no deprivation	Full time	All senses	Complete
II, partial deprivation	Part time	All senses	Partial
III, moderate deprivation	Part time	All senses	None
IV, severe deprivation	Part time	Visual only	None
V, complete deprivation	None	None	None

brought to her for a short time during the day. She will not be permitted, however, to spend long intervals with him, nor will she be allowed to feed him for the first 24 hours. In contrast to the deprivation built into the usual hospital situation, the 2% of mothers who give birth at home in the United States[23] may undergo almost no separation from their infants and consequently almost no deprivation (Level I).

The timing and duration of mother-infant separation (and consequent deprivation) past the first day of birth also are determined by the birth situation which is under the control of pediatricians, obstetricians, hospital administrators, and state laws (Table II). By postpartum day 1, only the full-term mother in a rooming-in situation[24] or the mother who has given birth at home experiences no interactional deprivation. This progression, from partial deprivation to no deprivation within the first 3 days of birth, is a timing sequence more typical of nonwestern societies where home births are more common and breast feeding is the only available method of providing nutriments to the infant.

The mother of a premature infant is subject to a much longer period of deprivation. On the day of birth she is completely deprived of contact with her infant. Late in the first postpartum day, she may be wheeled to the nursery only to view her infant in the incubator from behind protective panes of glass. She is subject to this type of severe deprivation until about the third to twelfth week postpartum when the infant reaches 2,100 gm and is taken out of the incubator and placed in the discharge nursery. The mother may then be allowed to hold her infant for the first time and will be taught how to feed and bathe him. This situation, which produces partial deprivation, is not relieved until the infant is sent home with his mother, usually a week after he has been placed in the discharge nursery.

With reference to premature infants, Table II illustrates how a slight change in care procedures may radically alter the nature and sequencing of interactional deprivation. If the mother of a premature infant were allowed into the nursery on postpartum day 3 to touch her infant while he was in an incubator, she would be subject to moderate rather than severe deprivation.

TABLE II

DEPRIVATION LEVELS OVER TIME, RELATED TO BIRTH SITUATION

Birth Situation	Deprivation Levels, Days and Weeks Postpartum					
	Day 0	Day 1	Day 3	Day 7	Week 8	Week 9
Home, full term	II, partial deprivation	I, no deprivation	I, no deprivation	I, no deprivation	I, no deprivation	I, no deprivation
Hospital, full term, rooming-in	III, moderate deprivation	I, no deprivation	I, no deprivation	I, no deprivation	I, no deprivation	I, no deprivation
Hospital, full term, regular care	III, moderate deprivation	II, partial deprivation	II, partial deprivation	I, no deprivation	I, no deprivation	I, no deprivation
Premature, mother allowed into nursery	V, complete deprivation	IV, severe deprivation	III, moderate deprivation	II, partial deprivation	II, partial deprivation (discharge nursery)	I, no deprivation (home)
Premature, regular care (separated)	V, complete deprivation	IV, severe deprivation	IV, severe deprivation	IV, severe deprivation	II, partial deprivation (discharge nursery)	I, no deprivation (home)
Unwed mother, refuses contact	V, complete deprivation	V, complete deprivation	V, complete deprivation	V, complete deprivation	V, complete deprivation	V, complete deprivation

She might not assume any caretaking duties but could have tactile and some aural contact with her infant. By postpartum day 7, the infant may be off gavage feeding and the mother may then, under the nurse's supervision, bottle-feed the infant and change his diapers. For the 3 to 12 weeks the infant is in the incubator, this mother would then experience a form of partial deprivation, rather than the severe deprivation to which mothers are subject under the more usual pattern of care.

We hypothesize that the mother who is deprived of tactile and caretaking contact with her premature infant in the postpartum period will be less responsive to the infant than the mother who is allowed to handle her infant in the incubator.[18,25] The mother who is not attached to her infant because of her separation from him shortly after birth may, in turn, deprive her infant of adequate stimulation when she becomes largely responsible for his care.[26]

EXPERIMENTAL MODIFICATION OF PREMATURE CARE

Design

In order to determine the feasibility of testing these hypotheses with an experimental design, we modified the care procedures of the Stanford Premature Research Center Nursery at specified times beginning in December 1964 to permit some mothers to have tactile contact with their premature infants shortly after birth. These mothers were permitted to handle and to care for their infants while they were in incubators. This procedure changed the timing and reduced the duration of separation after parturition commonly experienced by mothers of premature infants; it also provided them with kinesthetic and caretaking experience as well as the usual stimulation of seeing their infants.

Over a 2-year period, 41 mothers were allowed first to handle and later to feed their infants. Of this group, 13 mothers were randomly selected for observation and interview during the time their infants were in the unit and after discharge. A comparison group of 16 mothers, who were not allowed to enter the nursery, were followed in similar fashion.

Feasibility

Although there is some precedent for permitting mothers to have contact with their premature infants,[27] it never has been systematically part of modern American pediatric practice. Thus, the initial question in this pilot study was the practicality of allowing parents to enter the nursery. Mothers were told they could come in at any time of the day or night to handle their infants. Before being allowed to enter the nursery, they were instructed by nurses in handwashing procedures and they were masked and gowned. The nurses accompanied the mothers and stood by while they put their hands through the portholes of the incubator. Once the infant could be fed easily and successfully, the mother was permitted to feed him. After the initial period of instruction, the mother was left alone with her infant with the nurse on call to answer questions or help if the need arose.

INFECTION: Weekly surveillance cultures continued during the entire time mothers were permitted in the nursery. Cultures were taken from the umbilicus, skin, and nares of each infant as well as from the incubator gaskets, water reservoirs, oxygen masks, suction bottles and sink handles. The culture results for 3 years are summarized in Table III. During 1964, which may be taken as a base year, only two mothers were permitted to handle their infants in incubators. All other mothers first came into contact with their infants when they were in bassinets in the separate room of the discharge nursery. Twenty-seven mothers were permitted into the incubator nursery in 1965, and 12 were permitted to enter in

TABLE III

CULTURE RESULTS OF INFANTS AND EQUIPMENT, BY YEARS

Nursery Population	1964	1965	1966
Number of infants in unit	38	48	49
Number and percent of mothers allowed to handle infants in incubators	2 (5%)	27 (56%)	12 (25%)
Infant data			
total cultures of nares and umbilicus	680	718	694
number of potential pathogens isolated and percent of positive cultures*	146 (21%)	102 (14%)	119 (17%)
Equipment data			
total cultures of equipment†	390	420	489
number of potential pathogens isolated and percent of positive cultures*	44 (11%)	20 (5%)	24 (5%)

* Includes coagulase positive staphylococci, Beta hemolytic streptococci, pseudomonas, proteus, pneumococcus, yeast, clostridia perf.

† Weekly cultures of incubator gaskets, water reservoirs, oxygen masks, suction bottles, and sink handles.

1966.* Between 1964 and 1965, the number of cultures with potentially pathogenic organisms isolated from the infants and the equipment actually declined. In 1966, there was a slight but not significant rise in the number of potential pathogens found over 1965, even though a smaller number and proportion of mothers entered the unit. A chart review showed no occurrence of staphylococcal, hemolytic streptococcal, or upper respiratory viral disease in the infants during the time when mothers went into the nursery. From these data, it would appear that the presence of mothers in the nursery did not increase the risk or the occurrence of infection.

It is not clear why an overall decline occurred in the number of potential pathogens between 1964 and the succeeding 2 years. It cannot be attributed to a conscious change in surveillance methods, since collecting and culturing techniques remained the same over the entire period, 1964–1966.

It may simply reflect the range of variation common in many nurseries, or the reinforcement of aseptic practices secondary to teaching them many times over to the mothers entering the nursery for the first time.

REACTIONS OF THE STAFF: The introduction of mothers into the nursery was preceded by a series of orientation meetings with the Premature Research Center staff and was followed by bi-weekly group meetings with the study staff which included psychiatric and behavioral science consultants. The initial reaction of the nurses, which varied from mild skepticism to guarded enthusiasm, rapidly shifted to one of wholehearted enthusiasm. We observed that the nurses readily included the mothers in caretaking procedures.

The reaction of the house staff to the presence of the mothers was more mixed. Orientation programs were continued, but the high turnover rate of the resident staff due to the rotation system did not permit sufficient time for them to adjust to the presence of mothers in the unit. The continuing medical staff of faculty and visiting pediatricians, however, was enthusiastic about the program.

---

* The decline in the number of mothers in the nursery in 1966 was due to the ending of the pilot phase of the study and the beginning of a systematic longitudinal study which commenced with a return to separating mothers from their infants, March-September 1966.

Reactions of the Mothers

Mothers in both groups were interviewed while their infants were in the nursery and following discharge. These interviews served the dual purpose of allowing us to monitor any untoward reactions in the mothers allowed into the nursery and to begin the development of interview schedules, attitude scales, and self-rating instruments. It appeared that separation might produce differences between the two groups of mothers in three areas: (1) in commitment or attachment to the infant, (2) in development of a sense of confidence in her mothering abilities, and (3) in her ability to establish an efficient caretaking regimen. All of these areas are also affected by many other variables in addition to separation, such as the desire to have the child, the parity of the mother, the sex of the child, and his birth weight and prognosis. Given the large number of variables affecting the mother and the small number of subjects used to determine the feasibility of modifying care procedures in the premature nursery, no rigorous statement of outcome for the mothers as related to separation or non-separation could be expected from analysis of the pilot cases. Certain general observations can be reported at this time, however, along with a number of new questions which were raised and incorporated into the subsequent study design.

All but two of the 13 mothers we observed who were invited into the nursery reacted positively to the opportunity to handle their infants in the incubators. After her introduction to the baby in the incubator by the nurse, a mother typically touched and explored all aspects of the infant's body many times. The mother also spontaneously talked to her infant or cooed to him, despite the plastic barrier between them. During later visits, the exploratory behavior decreased somewhat as the mother was permitted to feed and diaper her infant.

In the two cases where our invitation to enter the nursery was refused, the concern of the parents focused upon the initially poor prognosis given them for their infants. They delayed a month in naming the babies and went through a period of mourning in anticipation of the death of the infants, which lasted well beyond the time the infants were declared to be out of danger.[29] These mothers recognized implicitly that increased contact with the infant would produce attachment. As one of these mothers commented: "I don't want to get that close. I don't want to touch her. . . . She isn't really a part of our family, but she will be when she comes home."

The responses of the mothers who refused to handle their infants made clear to us that no single approach to maternal care of premature infants will be appropriate for all mothers. With regard to the specific circumstances of the two refusal cases, however, there is little systematic data available to determine whether it is psychologically better for a mother to grieve over a "baby" that exists in her fantasy or over one with which she has had some interaction and to which she has developed some real attachment. A study design incorporating variations in the mother-infant contact for premature and other high-risk infants should supply answers to this question.

The pilot experience also raised the possibility that alterations in the level of interactional deprivation obtaining between mother and infant might affect the father's attachment to the infant. For all of our cases, the father was the parent who first saw the infant while his wife was still recovering from the birth. Initially, he was the intermediary between his wife and the infant in the nursery. Under conditions of severe interactional deprivation, a mother was denied all but visual contact with her infant while he was in the incubator. Both the mother and father could do little but view their infant, and their roles *vis-a-vis* the infant were equivalent. This role equivalence appeared to carry over to the time the infant was at home, so that the husbands of the separated mothers tended to be more involved with the care of their infants than fathers whose wives were allowed to interact with their infants while they were in the incubators.

In a small number of instances mothers of premature infants who were deprived of, or refused interaction with, their infants tended to resume responsibilities and interests they had prior to giving birth during the 3 to 12 weeks of separation from their newborn infants. When the infant was taken home, he appeared to enter the family as an individual and had to compete for the mother's time and attention. The pilot study thus raised the question of whether a mother who has been deprived of interaction with her newborn infant will provide the same type and amount of stimulation to the infant at home as will a mother who has not undergone severe interactional deprivation. This question is now being studied experimentally by monitoring the growth and development of the infant, pre- and post-discharge, as well as the interaction of the mother with her infant at home.

SUMMARY

The interactional framework presented here emphasizes the need to study the mother as well as the infant during and after they experience varying conditions of interactional deprivation.

The behavioral components of interaction between mothers and infants (timing and duration, sensory modalities, and care-taking) can all be studied experimentally in human beings by taking advantage of situations familiar to pediatricians and obstetricians. The manipulation of deprivation conditions surrounding the immediate postpartum period can be truly experimental (such as changing care conditions in a premature nursery) or they can be manipulated by judiciously choosing contrasting natural situations (rooming-in versus routine newborn care). The pilot phase of our research

in this area has demonstrated that it is possible to introduce mothers into the premature nursery without clinically endangering the infant or disrupting the organization of care.

On a case basis, differences between those mothers who were allowed into the nursery and experienced only partial interactional deprivation and those who were not allowed in and thus underwent a longer period of severe deprivation appeared to center in three areas: commitment to the infant, self-confidence in the ability to mother the infant, and behavior toward the infant (e.g., stimulation and skill in care-taking). The latter area raised the question of whether separation might also produce effects upon the infant to the extent that the mother's stimulation of the infant at home may be affected by the prior separation experience.

The framework of interactional deprivation suggested here could also include investigations of a number of superficially diverse areas such as the effects of rooming-in, bottle feeding and breast feeding in relation to maternal attachment, and the effects of infant contact on both unwed mothers who plan to give up their infants and on mothers whose infants are at high risk. Such researches should no longer be viewed as segmental studies of particular situations. Rather, they can be considered as studies which will throw light upon fundamental questions concerning the effects of different levels of mother-infant interaction in the early postpartum period upon maternal attachment and infant development.

REFERENCES

1. Bowlby, J.: Maternal Care and Mental Health. WHO Monogr. Ser., No. 2, 1951.
2. Casler, L.: Maternal Deprivation: A Critical Review of the Literature. Mongr. Soc. Res. Child Develop., 26:1, 1961.
3. Spitz, R. A.: Hospitalism: An inquiry into the genesis of psychiatric conditions in early childhood. Psychoanal. Stud. Child, 1:53, 1945.

4. Singh, J. A. L., and Zingg, R. M.: Wolf Children and Feral Man. New York: Harper and Brothers, 1942.

5. Davis, K.: Final note on a case of extreme isolation. Amer. J. Sociol., 52:432, 1947.

6. Spitz, R. A.: Unhappy and fatal outcomes of emotional deprivation and stress in infancy. *In* Galdston, I., ed.: Beyond the Germ Theory. New York: Health Education Council, pp. 120–131, 1954.

7. Bowlby, J., Ainsworth, M., Boston, M., and Rosenbluth, D.: The effects of mother-child separation: A follow-up study. Brit. J. Med. Psychol., 29:211, 1956.

8. Ainsworth, M.: The effects of maternal deprivation: A review of findings and controversy in the context of research strategy. *In* Deprivation of Maternal Care: A Reassessment of Its Effects. Geneva: WHO Public Health Paper No. 14:97–165, 1962.

9. Sears, R. R.: A theoretical framework for personality and social behavior. Amer. Psychol., 6:476, 1951.

10. Yarrow, L. J.: Maternal deprivation: Toward an empirical and conceptual re-evaluation. Psychol. Bull., 58:459, 1961.

11. Noirot, E.: Changes in responsiveness to young in the adult mouse: the effect of external stimuli. J. Comp. Physiol. Psychol., 57:97, 1964.

12. Moore, A. U.: Effects of modified maternal care in the sheep and goat. *In* Newton, G., and Levine, S., ed.: Early Experience and Behavior. Springfield, Illinois: Charles C Thomas, pp. 481–529, 1968.

13. Klopfer, P. H., Adams, D. K., and Klopfer, M. S.: Maternal "imprinting" in goats. Proc. Nat. Acad. Sci., 52:911, 1964.

14. Rosenblatt, J. S., and Lehrman, D. S.: Maternal behavior of the laboratory rat. *In* Rheingold, H.: Maternal Behavior in Mammals. New York: John Wiley and Sons, pp. 8–57, 1963.

15. Yarrow, L. J.: Separation from parents during early childhood. *In* Hoffman, M. L., and Hoffman, L. W.: Review of Child Development Research, Vol. 1. New York: Russell Sage Foundation, p. 122, 1964.

16. Bronfenbrenner, U.: Early deprivation in mammals: A cross-species analysis. *In* Newton, G., and Levine, S., ed.: Early Experience and Behavior. Springfield, Illinois: Charles C Thomas, 627–764, 1968.

17. Harlow, H. F., Harlow, M. K., and Hansen, E. W. The maternal affectional system of rhesus monkeys. *In* Rheingold, H. L., ed.: Maternal Behavior in Mammals. New York: John Wiley and Sons, pp. 254–281, 1963.

18. Robson, K. S.: The role of eye-to-eye contact in maternal-infant attachment. J. Child Psychol. Psychiat., 8:13, 1967.

19. Bell, R. Q.: A reinterpretation of the direction of effects in studies of socialization. Psychol. Rev., 75:81, 1968.

20. Spiro, M. E.: Children of the Kibbutz. Cambridge, Massachusetts: Harvard University Press, 1958.

21. Rabin, A. I.: Kibbutz mothers view "collective education." Amer. J. Orthopsychiat., 34:140, 1964.

22. Spiro, M. E.: Children of the Kibbutz. Cambridge, Massachusetts: Harvard University Press, p. 53, 1958.

23. Vital Statistics of the U.S., 1966, Vol. 1, Natality. Washington, D.C.: U.S. Department of Health, Education and Welfare, pp. 1–21, 1968.

24. McBryde, A.: Compulsory rooming-in in the ward and private newborn service at Duke Hospital. J.A.M.A., 145:625, 1951.

25. Moss, H. A.: Sex, age and state as determinants of mother-infant interaction. Merrill-Palmer Quart. Behav. Develop., 13:19, 1967.

26. Rubenstein, J.: Maternal attentiveness and subsequent exploratory behavior in the infant. Child Develop., 38:1089, 1967.

27. Kahn, E., Wayburne, S., and Fouche, M.: The Bagawanath premature baby unit—an analysis of the case records of 1,000 consecutive admissions. S. Afr. Med. J., 28:453, 1954.

28. Wortis, H.: *In* discussion of Kaplan, D. M., and Mason, E. A.: Maternal reactions to premature birth viewed as an acute emotional disorder. Amer. J. Orthopsychiat., 30:549, 1960.

29. Lindemann, E.: Symptomatology and management of acute grief. Amer. J. Psychiat., 101:141, 1944.

Acknowledgment

This research was made possible through the cooperation of the Premature Infant Research Center, which is supported by the National Institutes of Health, grant number FR-00081 to the Department of Pediatrics, Stanford University School of Medicine. Continuing research based upon the pilot experience is supported by grants from the Grant Foundation, New York, New York, and the National Institutes of Health, grant number HD-02636. Appreciation is expressed to Marjorie Seashore, Ph.D., Philip Sunshine, M.D., Norman Kretchmer, M.D., and the nurses of the Premature Infant Research Center for help in various facets of this research.

Chapter Thirteen

SOCIAL FACTORS

The previous chapter was concerned with how maternal factors influence the offspring's development and behavior. Although in a sense, mother-young interactions may be thought of as a kind of social behavior, they are considered separately because they involve a number of features not found in any other social relationship. In this chapter we will consider how various other social factors may influence later behavior.

Social processes in development constitute one of the least studied fields in the general area of early experiences, and the use of animal models in their investigation has been rare. This is probably because of certain assumptions concerning the mechanisms underlying the development of social processes. For many years researchers in the behavioral and social sciences assumed that social behavior was purely psychological and determined by the individual's interaction with the group or by one group's interaction with another. They believed that the components of these interactions could be understood only from a psychological or sociological point of view. Furthermore, the subject was so complex that researchers automatically took a human-centered approach in interpreting their findings. Certainly no one gave much credence to the idea that a biological framework would aid understanding of human social interactions.

Today, the validity of the purely psychological approach to the study of social behavior is open to serious question. There is massive evidence for a biological basis for social behavior in animal populations. Consider the ritualized fighting among males, the courtship and mating patterns of various species, the manner in which

a group of animals lives and moves together, the way in which the mature males guard the others from attack, how leadership of a group changes as the alpha animal becomes too old to continue his domination. All these behavior patterns may be interpreted as adaptive to the survival of the species, and thus a biological substrate must underlie them (See Ginsburg (1949) for a detailed elaboration of this position). And yet, when the subject is social patterns of humans, there is still a strong tendency to dismiss all knowledge of social behavior in animals and to state dogmatically that human social behavior is purely a product of upbringing and experiences, unrelated to the biology of the individual.

An example may illustrate the inadequacy of a purely psychosocial approach. One need only glance at the headlines of any newspaper any day of the week to be convinced that problems involving social behavior are among the most crucial ones facing us today. In all likelihood, these headlines will reveal evidence of aggression of one person toward another, or of one group toward another. It is extremely unlikely — if not impossible — that a purely psychological or sociological theory can account adequately for aggressiveness and offer appropriate suggestions for modifying man's aggressive nature. It is almost certainly necessary to study social behaviors in animal groups in order to acquire better understanding of our own social behaviors and their determinants.

The five papers in this chapter are concerned with aggression, competition, and social choice as affected by the social conditions under which an organism is reared. Recently there has been a surge of interest in the biological basis of aggression, in part because of the work of ethologists and other students of animal behavior during the past 10 years. However, this problem has been under study for a long time, and the author of Paper 61, Kuo, was one of the pioneers in the investigation of early experience and aggression. Kuo raised kittens and rats together in the same cage and later studied the kittens' rat-killing behavior. Kuo found that the early social interaction markedly reduced the killing response of the kittens, though he also found that killing would occur under certain conditions. In another experiment Kuo raised kittens and sparrows together from early life and again showed that this early social experience reduced or eliminated the kittens' subsequent bird-killing behavior.

Another example of interspecies aggression in nature is the mouse killing done by adult rats. This was the subject of Myer's experiment (Paper 62), which showed that rats raised in early life in the presence of mice were much less likely than control animals to kill mice in adulthood. In both Kuo's and Myer's studies the experimental animals, after initial exposure to interspecies social mates, were separated from them and reared with others of their own species for several months. They were then retested to determine whether they would "revert to kind" after living in an environment populated only with their own species. In both studies the researchers still found reduced killing, indicating that these early social experiences had long-term, relatively permanent effects.

The Kuo and Myer studies indicate that the social response of animals toward prey can be shifted from negative to either neutral or positive as a function of early social interactions. This suggests that an attachment may occur, and the development of social attachment between dog and rabbit was the concern of Cairns and Werboff (Paper 63). They reared dogs (1) in isolation; (2) in a situation where they could see, hear, and smell but not have contact with rabbits; or (3) in a situation where there was complete physical interaction between the rabbit and the dog. These researchers found that in the situation of complete physical interaction

social attachment was formed extremely rapidly, and that dogs would learn a simple maze pattern for the reward of ending up in the same chamber as their rabbit cohabitant. They also found that nonphysical interaction was more conducive than no interaction to the formation of social attachment, but was clearly much less so than complete physical interaction.

The analysis of social attachment is also the topic of Paper 64, by Pratt and Sackett, who worked with rhesus monkeys. These workers raised some animals in total isolation, another group in a situation where they could see and hear monkeys but could not contact them, and a third group under conditions of social interaction. Then each animal was given social interaction experiences with an animal from his own group as well as animals from the other two groups. After this each animal was placed in a situation where he could choose to approach an animal from his own group or from one of the other groups. They found that each animal approached another who had been reared under the same conditions as he. In other words, like preferred like. This was true even when the two monkeys were complete strangers. Thus it is apparent that social preferences are influenced by the conditions under which animals are reared, and that an animal can discriminate animals who have been reared in conditions similar to his from animals who have been reared in different conditions.

The four animal studies clearly show that the social milieu in which an animal grows up markedly affects his aggressive behavior and social preference. An analogous set of findings is seen in Paper 65, by Shapira and Madsen, who studied the cooperative and competitive behavior of Israeli children brought up in two different social milieux – the kibbutz and an urban middle-class community. The authors have pointed out that children growing up in a kibbutz are encouraged to cooperate and work together as part of communal living, while urban middle-class children may use competition as an acceptable means of achieving their goals. When the two groups of children were given a social test in which cooperation was necessary to succeed, both groups did equally well. When the rules of the game were changed so that the children competed with each other, the performance of the children from the urban community dropped markedly while the children from the kibbutzim performed slightly less well than before but tended to maintain their over-all high level of performance. Equally as important as the quantitative data are the qualitative observations reported by Shapira and Madsen. The kibbutz children were able to work out methods of cooperating among themselves even in the competitive situation, while the urban children failed to develop any such behavior.

Reference

Ginsburg, B. E. Genetics and social behavior: A theoretical synthesis. *Lectures on Genetics, Cancer, Growth, and Social Behavior.* Roscoe B. Jackson Memorial Laboratory Twentieth Anniversary Commemorative Lecture, July 26, 1949, pp. 101-124.

ZING YANG KUO

61 Further Study on the Behavior of the Cat Toward the Rat

Introduction

In a previous communication which was published in this Journal some years ago (Kuo, '30), the results of a series of experiments to determine the effects of different environmental conditions on the behavior of the kitten toward rats and mice were reported. The results showed, among other things, that if a kitten was raised in the same cage with a rat since it was very young, it, when grown up, became tolerant of rats; not only it would never attack a rat, but it adopted the rat as its "mate," played with it, and even became attached to it. Even frequent observation of killing and eating of rats by other cats could not induce such a kitten to change the type of reaction toward the rat which it had acquired in its early postnatal life.

In the experiment which is to be reported below, the condition was modified so that the new born kitten lived not only with rats in the same cage but also with two or three other kittens. The purpose was to find out whether the kitten, living under such changed conditions,

would behave toward its rat mates differently from the type of responses found in the kitten which was raised alone in the same cage with a single rat as reported in the previous article.

In addition, we shall include in this report the result of another experiment in which kittens were kept in the same cage with sparrows since they were young.

Experiment I

Methods

This experiment deals with the behavior of kittens raised in the same cage with rats. There were 17 kittens used in this experiment. They were divided into four groups, three groups having four kittens each, and one having five. Kittens in each group were of the same litter. Soon after the kittens were born, they were kept together (without their mother) in a cage in which a pair of albino rats, one male and one female, were living. At the time the kittens were introduced into the rats' cage, the latter were about one month old. Neither gray mice nor dancing mice were used in this experiment. Other conditions of the experiment were the same as those reported in the former paper.

The kittens were separated from the rats after nine months. One month after separation, each kitten was tested for its reaction to the adult albino rat. The test was made once a month for four months. The rats used for such tests were the kitten's original cage mates. But in some cases in which the original mates had been killed or died, substitutes of approximately the same size and same age were employed.

Four and a half months after separation those cats which were still indifferent to the presence of the albino rat were tested for imitation of rat killing response. The procedure of the imitation test will be described in its proper place.

Results

The results of this experiment may be briefly stated as follows:

1. During those nine months stay with two rats in the same cage all the kittens were indifferent and tolerant with reference to the rats. They let the rats run about in the cage, climb over their back or head and eat with them in the same dish. Many of the kittens would let the rats pull a piece of meat or fish away from their mouth. Seven kittens of seventeen made attempts to play with the rats.

2. None of the kittens were attached to a rat as it was the case in the previous experiment in which only one kitten was kept in the same cage with a single rat. The separation of the rats from the cage at any period and for any length of time did not cause any "seeking" or "restless" movements. Nor did the returning of the rats to the cage change the behavior of the kittens. Not a single kitten ever showed any response which might be regarded as protection for the rat. All such reactions are quite a contrast to those found in the kitten which was kept alone in the same cage with only one rat. In the latter case the kitten was generally attached to the rat. To quote from the former report, "After the cage-mate — the rat — was taken from the cage, the kitten began to mew continuously, became restless and search from corner to corner until the rat was returned to the cage." The kittens of the present experiment never exhibited such kind of responses with reference to the rat.

However, every kitten was attached to its own sisters and brothers in the cage; they played, ate, and slept together. If one of the kittens was left alone in the cage, it became restless and mewed until at least one of them was returned. The presence of the two albino rats in the cage did not alter the restless movements of the kitten, "seeking" for its missing sisters and brothers.

3. The behavior of the rats in the cage toward the kittens was also a sort of indifference. They played with each other, ran about, performed sex act, built nests, gave birth to young rats, and nursed them, as if the kittens were not present in the cage. They ate together with the kittens from the same dish and would sometimes try to pull a piece of meat or fish from the mouth of a kitten, as has been stated before. When some of the female rats were pregnant or nursing the young, they became very spirited and would attack kittens if they came near their nest. The kitten then became afraid of these rats and would not dare approach their nests.

4. The behavior of the kittens towards the new born rats in the cage was striking. Twelve out of the seventeen kittens killed and ate new born rats whenever they happened to come to the rats' nest. This was always done in the absence of the mother rat from the nest. If the mother was in the nest, the kittens kept away from it. The young rats were stolen from the nest and killed and eaten in some other place in the cage. In many cases the mother rat saw the kittens eat her young in a corner of the cage without making any effort to interfere with them as long as they were not near her .nest. Some of the mother rats would, however, carry the dead bodies of the young rats back to the nests after they were killed and left alone without being eaten by the kittens. Others would join the kittens and share with them the meat of their own young.

The kittens began to steal and eat new born rats when they were from two to four months old. Once they tasted the meat of young rats, they would repeat the same act each time the mother rat gave birth to a new litter. One group ate as many as five litters during their nine months stay with the rats. The behavior of the kittens toward the adult rats remained the same as before even after they had eaten several litters of their offspring.

5. In view of the fact that the kittens killed and ate new born rats without changing their original behavior toward the adult rats, tests were made to find out whether their reactions to the rats not living together with them in the same cage would be the same as those to the young rats. As the kittens always killed and ate young rats before hair grew out on their body, the test rats were divided into two groups: in one the fur was completely shaved, while in the other the hair of the rat was kept intact. The ages of the test rats in the two groups were the same: one day old, one week, two weeks, one month, two months, and three months old. The tests were made when the kittens were about five months old. The kittens were tested separately. One test was given every other day. In each test one shaved and one unshaved rat were used. They were of the same age. The unshaved rat was introduced to the kitten first. The shaved rat was put in after the unshaved one was taken out.

The result is noteworthy. Eleven of the twelve kittens which killed new born rats before invariably killed and ate hairless or shaved rats, regardless of the differences in the age of the test rats. But their reactions to the unshaved rats were the same as those to the adult rats living in the same cage with them.

Only one of those five kittens which did not kill new born rats killed two shaved rats, one of which was one month old and the other two months old.

6. The result of the tests of the kittens' behavior toward their former cage-mates – the adult rats – from whom the kittens had been separated for from one to four months was negative for sixteen cats. Throughout the four tests made during the four months of separation these kittens remained indifferent to the presence of the rats although they continued to kill and eat new born and shaved rats.

The only exception was found in one cat which killed one male rat – its original cage-mate – in the fourth test, that is, the test four months after the separation.

7. After these sixteen cats were found to still remain indifferent to the adult white rats even after four and a half months of separation, tests for imitation were initiated. The tests consisted of letting each of these cats see through, in the same cage, the performance of killing and eating rats by another cat. The rat was first put before the cat in the cage under test. If it failed to attack the rat, a rat-killing cat was added to the cage. After the killing act was performed, the killer was taken out and another rat of approximately the same size was put before the would-be imitator whose reactions to the rat were recorded. This procedure was repeated every day for two weeks or until the act of imitation was observed.

The result of the imitation test was also striking. Of the sixteen cats tested, six attempted, after several times seeing killing and eating of rats by other cats, to attack rats which were their former cage-mates. But only three of these six cats succeeded in killing rats. The other three would not dare to approach a rat again after they were once bitten back by the rat in their first attempt to attack it. These three cats, however, would carry in their mouths a dead rat killed by some other cat, and growl, hiss and play with it. But the dead rat was finally given up without being eaten. All the six cats mentioned in this paragraph killed and ate new born and shaved rats before they were separated from the adult rats with which they lived together for nine months.

Experiment II

Methods

In this experiment the purpose was to test the reaction of young kittens to sparrows which were kept in the same cage. Nine kittens from three litters were used. They were divided into three groups. Before their eyes were open each group of kittens were placed in a cage in which four to five adult sparrows had been kept. At first the sparrows were frightened by the introduction of the kittens into the cage, but after from one to three days all of them became adapted to the new situation. In this way the kittens and sparrows were kept together for six months. The behavior of the kittens in the same cage, especially with reference to the sparrows, was observed and recorded from day to day.

Results

The results of this experiment may be summarized as follows:

All of the nine kittens paid no attention to the sparrows in the cage for the first two months. Their behavior toward the sparrow is almost the same as that of the kittens toward white rats in experiment I. But when they were a little over two months old, five of the kittens began to follow the sparrows in their flight in the cage. As soon as the flight ceased, the pursuit of the kittens subsided. But some of the sparrows became frightened by the pursuit of the kittens and flew in panic. This made the pursuit of the kittens more active and zealous. Three kittens on different occasions happened to each catch one sparrow during flight. One of these kittens (No. 6) later developed a habit of capturing sparrows in flight and playing with them without any attempt to kill them. The other two (Nos. 4 and 7) did exactly the same for the first five to ten days, but later on they killed and devoured the sparrow soon after it was caught in flight. It must be noted in passing that other kittens did not "imitate" the actions of kittens 4, 6, and 7.

After six months all the nine kittens were separated from their birdmates and set free but their reactions to sparrows and other small birds were watched in the garden and elsewhere for two months. Except Nos. 4, 6, and 7, none of the kittens was ever observed to pay attention to sparrows or other small birds. But No. 6 often made attempts to capture sparrows or small birds without success. After five days its "interest" in sparrows and other small birds seemed to have waned. On the other hand, Nos. 4 and 7 continued to capture and eat sparrows and other small birds as they did when they were kept in the cage. These two kittens were seen also to catch and eat frogs and wild mice.

Discussion

The results of these two experiments seem to further demonstrate the view held by the writer many years ago, that other things being equal the behavior of the animal is determined by its early environment in which it is raised. Kittens raised in a "rat-killing environment" are most likely to be "rat-killers"; raised in isolation, the probability of rat-killing is almost fifty-fifty (Kuo, '30). But when one kitten is raised *alone* with one rat in the same cage, it became attached to the rat, and would never attack it, even after having seen through many times the act of killing rats by other cats (Kuo, '30). On the other hand, if more than one kitten is raised in the same cage with the rat, it develops no attachment to the rat. Instead, its attachment is for its brother or sister kittens. Furthermore, there is a high possibility that after long separation from the rats, these kittens may develop a habit of killing rats either spontaneously or through imitation, as we have seen in experiment I. Such a possibility is almost nil in the case in which only one new born kitten is raised in the same cage with one rat.

Again, while the writer is not as yet able to ascertain the factors which influence the kittens to eat the newly born rats, the fact that they kill and eat shaved rats and pay no attention to unshaved ones points to the same conclusion, namely, that the action of eating shaved rats is a carryover from their early behavior in eating new born rats. The results of experiment II also demonstrate the effects of early behavior which is a direct result of environmental conditions, and its carryover and transfer in later life.

In the case of the chick, the writer has given numerous evidences to show the effects of embryonic behavior upon its life after hatch (Kuo, '32). It cannot be overemphasized that ontogeny, or the developmental study of behavior is one of the most important channels through which causal factors of behavior may be discovered.

References

1. Kuo, Z. Y. 1930. The genesis of the cat's behavior toward the rat. *Jour. Comp. Psychol.*, 11, 1-35.
2. Kuo, Z. Y. 1932. Ontogeny of embryonic behavior in aves. IV. The influence of prenatal behavior upon postnatal life. *Jour. Comp. Psychol.*, 14, 109-121.
3. Kuo, Z. Y. 1937. Prolegomena to Praxiology. *Jour. Psychol.*, 4, 1-22.
4. Rogers, W. W. 1932. Controlled observation on the behavior of kittens toward the rat from birth to five months of age. *Jour. Comp. Psychol.*, 13, 107-125.

The experiments were performed at the National University of Chekiang, Hangchow, China.

JAMES S. MYER

62 Early Experience and the Development of Mouse Killing by Rats

Rats reared in social isolation after weaning and litter-mate controls reared in groups of four were tested for mouse killing when 4 mo. old. Although isolated rats were somewhat awkward and poorly coordinated in their attacks, the proportions of killers in the two groups did not differ significantly. In a second experiment, rats were repeatedly exposed to mice from weaning until they were 5 mo. Litter-mate controls were not exposed to mice. At 5 mo., both groups were isolated for 10 days, then tested for killing. 54% of the controls and 9% of the experimental group were killers. After testing, the rats were returned to their rearing cages for 2 mo., during which neither group was exposed to mice. They were then retested. Killing was exhibited by 73% of the controls and only 14% of the experimental group.

Some Norway rats attack and kill the first mouse they ever encounter, and consistently kill mice thereafter, whereas other rats never kill mice, even if provided frequent opportunities to do so. Various aspects of the killing behavior of rats have been studied, but little is known of the factors responsible for its development. Karli (1961) reported that adult nonkillers that were housed with killers and observed killing did not become killers, and that killing is exhibited by some rats whose parents did not kill mice but who had killers in their ancestry. These observations led Karli to conclude that killing is "innate."

Other investigators have attempted to demonstrate the importance of experience in the development of killing. Heimstra and Newton (1961) subjected mature rats

Reprinted from *Journal of Comparative and Physiological Psychology* 67:46–49, 1969. Copyright 1969 by the American Psychological Association and reproduced by permission.

This research was supported by Grant GB5570 from the National Science Foundation.

to a cyclic food-deprivation schedule and placed them in pairs in a food-competition situation daily for 15 days. After this training, the rats were given food for 24 hr. and then tested for killing. Fifty-five percent of the rats killed mice, whereas no mice were killed by a control group which was neither food deprived nor given competition training. Heimstra and Newton concluded that competitive experience is important in the development of killing. Whalen and Fehr (1964) repeated the Heimstra and Newton experiment, with the addition of a control group subjected to cyclic food deprivation but not given competition training. They found a greater frequency of killing in the deprived but untrained group than in the group which was both food deprived and given competition training. Heimstra (1965) obtained the opposite result in a similar experiment, and reiterated his conclusion that competitive experience is a major determinant of the development of killing.

The present experiments were conducted

to explore further the role of experience in the development of mouse killing by rats and the development of the inhibition of killing of rat pups typically exhibited by rats that kill mice (Myer, 1964). In one experiment, rats were reared in social isolation from weaning until they were tested with mice and rat pups in adulthood. In a second experiment, the killing behavior of rats reared with mice from weaning to adulthood was studied.

EXPERIMENT 1

Method

The subjects were hooded rats of the Long-Evans strain from a colony maintained by the author. When 19–22 days old, 64 male rat pups were weaned and individually caged, and 32 littermate controls were caged in groups of 4. Care was taken to assure that the rats had continuous access to food and water throughout the study. When 4 mo. old the group-reared rats were moved to individual cages, and after a 10-day adaptation period, all 96 rats were tested with mice. Each rat was presented one 20–30-gm. albino mouse each day. The bodies of killed mice were immediately removed, and mice that were not killed were removed after 2 hr. Testing continued for each rat until it reached a criterion of either killing or failing to kill on 10 successive tests. Testing was then discontinued for 10 days, after which a retest identical to the initial test was conducted. Immediately after each rat reached criterion on the retest, a series of tests to determine the reaction to rat pups began. In this test series hooded rat pups, which weighed 20–30 gm., were presented on alternate days for a 10-day period, and mice were presented on the intervening days.

Results

Rearing in social isolation did not prevent the development of mouse killing. Twenty of the 32 controls and 37 of the 64 isolated rats reached the killing criterion on the initial test. Although the isolated and the group-reared rats did not differ significantly in the percentage of rats which exhibited killing, there were interesting qualitative differences in their reaction to mice. The group-reared killers displayed a smooth, rapid, and well-integrated attack response, whereas the isolated rats were poorly coordinated in their attacks. The group-reared rats were also more consistent in their reaction to mice on early tests. Thirteen of the group-reared rats killed

the first 10 mice presented, and 5 others failed to kill on early trials, then reversed their reaction and began killing consistently. Only two rats in the control group that ultimately reached the killing criterion displayed reversals of reaction after the first kill, and only one control rat that reached the nonkilling criterion killed any mice. The maximum number of trials required to reach the killing criterion in the control group, including the criterion trials, was 14. By contrast, eight of the isolated killers displayed reversals of reaction after the first kill, and six of the isolated nonkillers killed some mice before failing to kill on 10 successive days. Nine of the isolated killers required 15 or more trials to reach criterion, and one of them required 69 trials.

When retested after a 10-day interruption, all of the group-reared rats and all but three of the isolated rats responded consistently, reaching the previously achieved criterion in 10 trials. One isolate that killed the first 10 mice presented during initial testing killed 2 mice during retesting, then failed to kill on 10 successive trials. Two other isolates which were killers in initial testing again reached the killing criterion, but failed to kill some of the mice presented.

Rearing in social isolation did not interfere with the development of the inhibition of killing rat pups which is typically displayed by mouse-killing rats. Only one control killer and two isolated killers killed all five of the rat pups presented, and one isolate killed one rat pup. The remaining killers continued killing mice during the final test period, but did not kill rat pups.

EXPERIMENT 2

Method

Fifty male rat pups were weaned when 17–21 days old, and equal numbers of pups from each litter were assigned to an experimental and a control group. The rats were housed in groups of five, with continuous access to food and water. One week after the pups were weaned, two adult mice were placed in each of the five cages housing the experimental group. Five days later the mice were removed, and 2 days thereafter two different mice were placed in each cage. For the experimental group this procedure of alternating 5-day periods with mice and 2-day periods without mice continued until the rats were 150 days old. The control group was not exposed to mice during this period. When 150 days old, the rats in both groups were individually caged and after a 10-day adaptation period they were tested for mouse killing, using the testing procedure employed in the initial test in Experiment 1. When all 5 rats from a given rearing cage reached the criterion of consistent reaction, either killing or failing to kill on 10 successive days, they were returned to their original rearing cage. Eight weeks after the beginning of initial testing, the rats again were isolated and tested for killing. Immediately after reaching criterion on this retest, each rat underwent a test series with rat pups, identical to that employed in Experiment 1. Neither group was exposed to mice during the period between the initial test and the retest. Three rats in each group died before the initial test, reducing the number of subjects in each group to 22.

Results

Prolonged exposure to mice from weaning to maturity did interfere with the development of killing. On the initial test, 12 of the 22 rats in the control group were killers, whereas only 3 of the rats in the experimental group killed any mice, and only 2 reached the killing criterion. One began killing on Day 7 and one on Day 10 of testing, and both killed consistently thereafter. The third rat killed mice on Day 7 and Day 16 of testing, then failed to kill on 10 successive trials. The difference in the proportions of rats which reached the killing criterion in the experimental and control groups on the initial test was statistically significant ($\chi^2 = 10.48, p < .01$).

The interfering effect of rearing with mice was also evidenced on the retest conducted after several weeks without exposure to mice. The 12 control rats which reached the killing criterion on the initial test killed the first 10 mice presented on retest, and 4 others began killing. The two rats in the experimental group that reached the killing criterion during the initial test killed the first 10 mice presented, and an additional rat that did not kill during the initial test began killing during retesting, reaching the killing criterion on Day 20. The experimental rat which killed two mice during the initial test killed one mouse on Trial 8 of retesting, and failed to

kill thereafter. None of the remaining 18 rats in the experimental group killed any mice. The difference in the proportions of killers in the two groups on retest was statistically significant ($\chi^2 = 15.66, p < .001$).

During the final series of tests 1 rat, a killer in the control group, killed all 5 rat pups presented. The other killers continued to kill mice, but displayed the usual inhibition of killing when presented rat pups. None of the nonkillers in either group killed any mice or rat pups.

In an attempt to identify factors associated with the occurrence of killing, comparisons were made of the litter size, body weight at weaning, and body weight at the beginning of testing of the killers and nonkillers in the control group on the initial test in Experiment 2. Mann-Whitney U tests, used to test the significance of the differences between the killers and nonkillers, failed to reveal statistically significant differences on any of the three attributes.

DISCUSSION

Previous discussions of the development of mouse killing by rats have emphasized the search for some unique experiential or genetic factor which produces the killing response in some rats. The results of this study suggest that it might be more fruitful to assume that the propensity to attack and kill mice is present in all rats, and that experience during development plays an important role in suppressing or inhibiting the behavior. Experiment 1 showed that neither a history of cyclic deprivation nor experience in competition with other rats after weaning is necessary for the development of killing, and the failure in Experiment 2 to find any relationship between killing and litter size or weaning weight suggests that competition for food before weaning is not an important determinant of the behavior. Experiment 2 showed that rearing rats in the presence of mice from weaning to adulthood not only interferes with the development of mouse killing during that period, but also that the inhibitory effect of such rearing persists at least for a period of several weeks after exposure to mice is discontinued.

The view that all rats possess the propensity to kill mice is also supported by (a) the observation that destruction of the anterior portion of the brain releases killing in adult rats that were nonkillers preoperatively (Karli, 1956) and (b) the finding that the failure of most mouse-killing rats to kill rat pups is due to an inhibition of killing, rather than to a failure of the pups to provide the stimuli which elicit attack (Myer, 1964). Although unexplained discrepancies in their results make interpretation difficult, the demonstrations of Whalen and Fehr (1964) and Heimstra (1965) that cyclic food deprivation and/or food competition induce killing might also be attributed to disinhibition of the behavior, rather than the induction of killing by such treatments.

A number of investigations of attack behavior in other animals can also be interpreted in terms of experience interfering with the expression of a behavior which would otherwise be universally exhibited in the species. The classic experiments of Kuo (1930, 1938) showed that rearing in social isolation does not prevent the development of killing behavior in cats, whereas cats reared with rats did not later kill rats. More recently, Kuo (1960, 1967) reported that dogs and cats reared in social isolation were more aggressive toward other animals of their own and other species than were dogs and cats reared with their own kind, whereas dogs and cats that were exposed to potential objects of attack during development seldom displayed aggressive or predatory behavior. King and Gurney (1954) found that rearing in social isolation from weaning to maturity resulted in increased attack latencies, but did not prevent the development of fighting behavior

in mice. Several investigators (Roberts & Kiess, 1964; Wasman & Flynn, 1962) have shown that cats that do not attack and kill mice and rats can be induced to do so by stimulation of subcortical brain structures, indicating that even though the animals do not exhibit the behavior, the underlying mechanisms are present.

REFERENCES

HEIMSTRA, N. W. A further investigation of the development of mouse-killing in rats. *Psychonomic Science,* 1965, **2**, 179–180.

HEIMSTRA, N. W., & NEWTON, G. Effects of prior food competition on the rat's killing response to the white mouse. *Behaviour,* 1961, **17**, 95–102.

KARLI, P. The Norway rat's killing response to the white mouse. *Behaviour,* 1956, **10**, 81–103.

KARLI, P. Nouvelles données experimentales sur le comporttement d'agression interspécifique Rat-Souris. *Journal de Physiologie (Paris),* 1961, **53**, 383–384.

KING, J. A., & GURNEY, N. L. Effect of early social experience on adult aggressive behavior in C57BL/10 mice. *Journal of Comparative and Physiological Psychology,* 1954, **57**, 326–330.

KUO, Z. Y. The genesis of the cat's response toward the rat. *Journal of Comparative Psychology,* 1930, **11**, 1–35.

KUO, Z. Y. Further study on the behavior of the cat towards the rat. *Journal of Comparative Psychology,* 1938, **25**, 1–8.

KUO, Z. Y. Studies on the basic factors in animal fighting: VII. Inter-species coexistence in mammals. *Journal of Genetic Psychology,* 1960, **97**, 211–225.

KUO, Z. Y. *The dynamics of behavior development.* New York: Random House, 1967.

MYER, J. S. Stimulus control of mouse-killing rats. *Journal of Comparative and Physiological Psychology,* 1964, **58**, 112–117.

ROBERTS, W. W., & KIESS, H. O. Motivational properties of hypothalamic aggression in cats. *Journal of Comparative and Physiological Psychology,* 1964, **58**, 187–193.

WASMAN, M., & FLYNN, J. P. Directed attack elicited from hypothalamus. *Archives of Neurology,* 1962, **6**, 220–227.

WHALEN, R. E., & FEHR, H. The development of the mouse-killing response in rats. *Psychonomic Science,* 1964, **1**, 77–78.

ROBERT B. CAIRNS & JACK WERBOFF

63 Behavior Development in the Dog: An Interspecific Analysis

Abstract. *Young dogs were main-tained in isolation from other dogs and under varying degrees of exposure to an alien species (mature rabbits). Parametric observations indicate that an interspecific social attachment de-velops during the initial hours of co-habitation. The later social interaction patterns of the dogs were influenced, but not irrevocably fixed, by the early cross-specific rearing experience.*

Immature animals that have been iso-lated from their own kind and reared with another species generally demon-strate a strong affinity for the "alien" animals (1). Despite the relevance of this curious phenomenon for the proc-esses of species-identification and at-tachment behavior, it has been infre-quently studied under laboratory con-ditions (2). Virtually no information is available with respect to the time-course of the process in mammals, or the extent to which the effects of early exposure to an alien species are endur-ing. To obtain parametric data on these issues, we reared young canines under various conditions of interaction with mature lagomorphs. We found that in-terspecific attachments develop with great rapidity in young dogs, an out-come which is in accord with the stimulus pattern theory of mammalian attachment behavior (2)

In our first experiment, 30 purebred dogs from the Jackson Laboratory were

placed at 29 ± 2 days of age in indi-vidual compartments (1.2 by 0.8 by 1.2 m high) enclosed on four sides by opaque walls and open at the top. The rearing conditions permitted nei-ther physical nor visual contact with other dogs. Ten animals were assigned to each of three conditions: (i) inter-action, in which a dog was permitted continuous physical contact with a rab-bit cohabitant; (ii) noninteraction, in which a dog and rabbit were separated by a double wire fence (2.5 by 5.1 cm interstices) down the midline of the compartment, which permitted visual and olfactory stimulation but no physi-cal contact; and (iii) isolation, in which a dog was reared alone. The rearing conditions were comparable for all conditions save the varying degree of contact permitted with the alien co-habitant. Five pure breeds of dogs were used: basenjis ($N = 7$), beagles ($N = 4$), cocker spaniels ($N = 2$), Shetland sheepdogs ($N = 8$), and Telomians ($N = 9$). Within each sex-breed cate-gory, animals were assigned at random to the three experimental conditions. The cohabitants were mature rabbits obtained from the stocks of the Jack-son Laboratory.

At the start of the experiment, the pups were placed alone in the com-partment for 2 hours, after which the rabbit cohabitant was introduced. To investigate the development of attach-ment formation, a series of cohabi-tant removal-replacement tests was conducted. Each test ran for 18 minutes and involved six alternating periods in which the rabbit cohabitant was in the compartment for 3 minutes and then removed for 3 minutes. The indices of disturbance recorded were the number of vocalizations emitted by the young dog and the amount of locomotion shown by the dog in the cohabitant-absent periods relative to the cohabitant-present periods. For dogs reared alone in the isolation condition, these indices were recorded during the same time periods with no removal-replacement introduced. Removal-replacement tests were conducted with every animal after 0, 1, 2, 4, 8, 24, 48, 96, and 168 hours, and thereafter at weekly intervals.

The vocalization results over the first week of cohabitation are given in Fig. 1. By the end of the first day, animals in the interaction condition whined and yelped at high rates during those occasions when the rabbit was removed. Vocalization was accompanied frequently by the dogs' moving about the compartment and scratching at its walls. Similarly, a significant but less pronounced effect was observed after 1 week of experimental confinement for dogs in the noninteraction condition. Subsequent weekly tests indicated decreasing levels of vocal and motor disruption during the absence of the rabbit cohabitant, a finding which is consistent with the report of Elliot and Scott (3). However, the interaction group after 8 weeks of cohabitation continued to vocalize at a significantly elevated rate indicating a lack of habituation to this separation. Comparable results in terms of curve form and levels of statistical significance were obtained in the analysis of general activity (that is, locomotion). The results

obtained in the noninteraction condition indicated that physical contact facilitates, but is not necessary for, the separation-disruption phenomena (4).

After 5 weeks of cohabitation, the dogs' "social" preferences were assessed in a series of learning trials in a Y maze with a noncorrective procedure. In this apparatus, the dogs could learn to choose either their rabbit cohabitant (or, in the case of dogs assigned to the isolation condition, a rabbit which had cohabited with another pup) or an empty goal area. Tests were conducted over a 5-day period, with two sets of three trials each day. For a given dog, the placement of his rabbit cohabitant was constant and he was required to learn a position response. If the dog did not enter one of the two goal areas within 6 minutes of the first day or within 3 minutes of succeeding days, he was placed in either the right or the left goal area. In all instances, the animals were permitted to remain in the goal

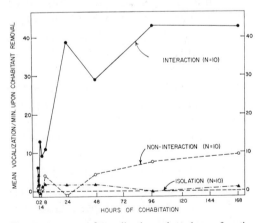

Fig. 1. Amount of vocalization, plotted as a function of number of hours of cohabitation for the three experimental conditions. These data represent the mean vocalization difference scores (vocalization when rabbit was removed minus vocalization when rabbit was present). Analysis by the L test (13) indicates that both the interaction ($P < 001$) and noninteraction ($P < .01$) conditions show increase in discriminative vocalization during the first week of cohabitation.

area for 60 seconds prior to the beginning of the next trial. The index of preference obtained was the number of trials that the dog freely selected the rabbit minus the number of trials that he ran to the empty goal compartment.

No dog (0/10) in the interaction condition, 20 percent (2/10) in the noninteraction condition, and 60 percent (6/10) in the isolation condition selected the empty compartment more frequently than the compartment containing the rabbit. Furthermore, the amount of behavioral disruption (as assessed by amount of vocalization) observed among dogs in the interaction condition during the 5th-week removal-replacement test provided a remarkably reliable gauge of the pups' choice behavior. Thus the more disrupted the dog was by rabbit-cohabitant separation, the greater was the likelihood that he would approach the rabbit (ρ = .81, P < .01). A significant correlation was found only for the dogs in the interaction condition.

A final test series was conducted after 8 weeks of cohabitation. Over four test trials given daily, the dogs were permitted to approach a rabbit in a neutral 1.8 by 1.8m test chamber. On two trials, the test animal was the dog's cohabitant, or, in the case of isolated dogs, a rabbit that had cohabited with another pup. In the remaining trials, the test animal was a rabbit which had not been maintained in interspecific cohabitation. The latency recorded was the time elapsed from the dog's entry into the compartment to the point at which it made physical contact with the test animal. If the dog did not approach the test animal within 5 minutes, the test was terminated. Again, the groups differed markedly in their approach behavior. Median la-

Table 1. Median latency (in seconds) for dogs to approach cohabitant and noncohabitant rabbits. Separate analyses of variance upon the scores obtained in a logarithmic transformation of the prime data indicate that the three groups of dogs differed in their latency in approaching both the familiar (F = 6.61, df = 2/27, P < .01) and unfamiliar (F = 6.21, df = 2/27, P < .01) test animals.

Condition	Test animal	
	Cohabitant	Noncohabitant
Interaction	4.0	9.0
Noninteraction	8.0	52.5
Isolation	128.0	193.0

tencies are presented in Table 1. Animals in the interaction condition had the shortest latencies, while animals in the isolation condition had the longest latencies, with the latter dogs frequently failing to contact the test rabbit in the entire 5-minute period (5). Apparently the essential phenomenon is trans-situational, and not restricted to a given test arrangement or limited to the particular rabbit with which the pup had cohabited.

These data are consistent in showing that interspecific rearing conditions have a pervasive influence on the young dog's response to another species to which it has been exposed. One of the more remarkable features of these results was the rapidity of formation of the interspecific attachment. Subsequent experiments confirmed that the phenomenon was not an artifact of the test procedures adopted nor of the response index employed. Independent removal-replacement results were obtained from a new group of 31 dogs maintained in an interaction condition similar to that of the first experiment, but tested only after 88 hours of cohabitation (6). These results, which were free of the influence of repeated testing, were not significantly different from those obtained after 96 hours of interaction-cohabitation in the first experiment. Nor were the effects restricted to the vocalization-disruption measure. After 4 days in the interaction condition, a significant shift was obtained in the preference of the experimental dogs for the rabbits. These data strongly suggest that significant changes in social preference occur over relatively short periods. A recently completed study by Fleener (7) indicates that human infants share this capacity for the rapid establishment of social preferences.

Observations of the animals in the first week of cohabitation yielded data which were consistent with the quantitative results. After an initial period of mutual avoidance, a considerable portion of the young dog's time was spent in grooming, lying upon, and gnawing at the extremities of his cohabitant. Such behavior continued throughout the duration of the experiment. As the dogs grew older and more capable of inflicting physical damage through grooming and "play" activities, the outcomes became increasingly more noxious to the rabbit cohabitant. By the 8th week of cohabitation, six of the ten rabbits in the interaction condition were severely injured and the pairings were discontinued. Contrary to the earlier reports of Kuo (8), continued cohabitation is not necessarily associated with the development and maintenance of peaceful relationships between species.

Preliminary information was obtained on the post-experimental sexual adaptation of dogs that had cohabitated with rabbits. A follow-up study of the subgroup of six female beagles used in the two experiments indicated that alien cohabitation does not necessarily inhibit the development of species-appropriate reproductive activities. Of the six animals observed in maturity, four were successfully mated and produced litters in their first heat. Parallel data on male dogs unfortunately were not obtained.

Our results clearly indicate that the young dog's experience prior to the 3rd week of life does not preclude the rapid establishment of a "new" social bond with respect to a member of another species. Moreover, early exposure to an animal of another species does not insure against the subsequent development of antagonistic patterns of interaction with that species.

The present findings thus are consistent with recent reports which emphasize the role of contemporary events, both endogenous and exogenous, in the control of the social behavior (9). Specifically, studies of the post-emergence behavior of dogs reared in complete isolation have demonstrated that the intensity of the treatment effects can be greatly modified by varying the conditions of emergence (10). Similarly, our previous work indicates that the primary effects of interspecific rearing in sheep can be reversed (11). While some long-term effects of early experience on social and sexual behavior patterns cannot be gainsaid (12), our data indicate that a critical examination of the conditions required for the persistence of such effects is in order.

References and Notes

1. V. H. Denenberg, G. A. Hudgens, M. X. Zarrow, *Science* **143**, 380 (1964); L. Hersher, J. B. Richmond, A. U. Moore, *Behaviour* **20**, 311 (1963); Z. Y. Kuo, *J. Comp. Physiol. Psychol.* **11**, 1 (1930); G. J. Romanes, *Nature* **12**, 553 (1875).
2. R. B. Cairns, *Psychol. Rev.* **73**, 409 (1966).
3. O. Elliot and J. P. Scott, *J. Genet. Psychol.* **99**, 3 (1961).
4. See also C. L. Pratt and G. P. Sackett, *Science* **155**, 1133 (1967); R. B. Cairns, *J. Comp. Physiol. Psychol.* **62**, 298 (1966).

5. It should also be noted that dogs maintained in isolation tended to approach rabbits which had previously cohabited with other dogs more rapidly than they approached rabbits that had not so cohabited (first and second columns, Table 1). This trend, of borderline significance (.10 > P > .05), suggests that the cohabitation experience modified the be-behavior of the rabbits as well as of the pups.
6. R. B. Cairns and J. Werboff, in preparation.
7. D. E. Fleener, thesis, Indiana University (1967).
8. Z. Y. Kuo, J. Genet. Psychol. **97**, 211 (1960). In this report Kuo indicated that attempts were made to inhibit fighting among dogs assigned to the experimental groups.
9. J. P. Scott, Ann. Rev. Psychol. **18**, 65 (1967).
10. J. L. Fuller and L. D. Clark, J. Comp. Physiol. Psychol. **61**, 251, 258 (1966).

11. R. B. Cairns, *ibid.* **62**, 298 (1966); R. B. Cairns and D. L. Johnson, Psychon. Sci. **2**, 337 (1965).
12. Including those effects related to the development of social preferences [see, for example, D. G. Freedman, J. A. King, O. Elliot, Science **133**, 1016 (1961)] and the sexual behaviors of dogs reared in isolation [see, for example, F. A. Beach in Social Behavior and Organization among Vertebrates, W. Etkin, Ed. (Univ. of Chicago Press, Chicago, 1964), p. 117].
13. E. B. Page, J. Amer. Statist. Ass. **58**, 216 (1963).
14. These experiments were conducted at the Jackson Laboratory while R.B.C. was on leave from Indiana University (PHS special fellowship 1-F3-NH-30, 205-10) and were supported in part by PHS research grants HD-01082 and GRS FR-05545-03-05 from NIH.

CHARLES L. PRATT & GENE P. SACKETT

64 Selection of Social Partners as a Function of Peer Contact During Rearing

Abstract. *Three groups of monkeys were raised with different degrees of contact with their peers. The first group was allowed no contact, the second only visual and auditory contact, and the third was allowed complete and normal contact with their peers. Animals of all three groups were allowed to interact socially; they were then tested for their preference for monkeys raised under the same conditions or for monkeys raised under different conditions. Monkeys raised under the same conditions preferred each other, even if the stimulus animals were completely strange to the test monkey.*

The early experiences of primates often have profound consequences on later behavior. In rhesus monkeys exploratory, maternal, sexual, and social behaviors appear extremely vulnerable to early social and sensory restriction (1). Monkeys reared in isolation tend to withdraw from other animals and huddle by themselves in social situations prefer each other to monkeys interact with more normal monkeys,

Reprinted from *Science* 155:1133–1135, 1967. Copyright 1967 by the American Association for the Advancement of Science.

they may not be effectively exposed to the stimuli which might lead to some degree of social adjustment. The fact that socially normal monkeys may avoid contact with monkeys reared in isolation further retards rehabilitation. We varied the amount of peer contact during rearing and investigated its effect on physical approach to a social partner, in order to determine whether monkeys reared under identical conditions prefer each other to monkeys reared under different conditions.

Three groups of rhesus monkeys were

reared from birth in the laboratory without mothers. Each group contained four males and four females. Sets of three animals were matched across groups for age, sex, and test experiences after rearing was complete. The first group (A) was reared from birth to 9 months in individual closed cages. On the first 5 to 7 days they experienced physical, but minimal visual, contact with a human during feeding. No other physical or visual contact with humans or live monkeys occurred during rearing. Changing visual experiences throughout rearing were limited to presentation of pictures of monkeys engaged in various behaviors and pictures of people and inanimate objects (2). From months 9 through 18 the monkeys in group A were housed individually in bare wire cages from which they could see and hear other isolates and humans, but physical contacts were unavailable.

Subjects in the second group (B) were reared individually in a large nursery room in bare wire cages from birth to 9 months. Other monkeys and humans could be seen and heard, but physical contact was not available. From month 9 through 18 the monkeys in group B were housed in the same room as the monkeys in group A; they were in wire cages where they could see and hear, but not touch, one another.

The third group (C) lived in wire cages in peer groups of varying sizes during the first 18 months of life. Rearing conditions and social behavior tests provided physical peer contact during this period. In summary, group A had no early contact with live peers, group B had visual and auditory but no physical contact with peers, and

group C had complete peer contact during the rearing period.

When they were 18 months old, sets of monkeys from all groups interacted during social behavior tests in a large playroom (3). Each animal was tested weekly for 12 weeks in three 30-minute sessions. In one weekly session a constant set of one group A, one group B, and one group C monkey of the same sex interacted together; the same animals were always tested together. On the two other weekly sessions constant pairs of groups A and B, A and C, and B and C subjects interacted in groups of four monkeys. After social testing, each subject had received equal playroom exposure to one monkey from its own rearing condition and to two monkeys from each of the other rearing conditions. After playroom testing was completed, the monkeys were tested for their preference for other monkeys reared under the same conditions or for those reared under different conditions.

Testing was done in the "selection circus" (Fig. 1), which consists of a central start compartment that bounds the entrances to six adjoining choice compartments. Wire-mesh cages for the stimulus animals were attached to the outside of appropriate choice compartments. The front walls of the stimulus cages, the outside walls of the choice compartments, and the guillotine doors separating choice compartments from the start compartment were all made of clear plexiglas.

For the testing, the subject was placed in the center start compartment with the plexiglas guillotine doors down for a 5-minute exposure period. The subject could see and hear the stimulus animals, but could not enter the choice

TOP VIEW OF SELF-SELECTION CIRCUS

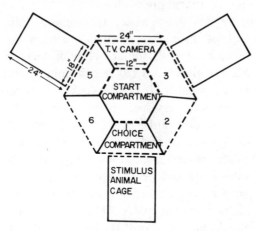

Fig. 1. Scheme of the "circus" which is constructed of aluminum channels containing plexiglas walls (dotted line), plywood walls (solid line), and plexiglas guillotine doors (wavy line). Wire-mesh stimulus cages with a single plexiglas wall are attached outside choice compartments. In testing, the subject is first placed in the start compartment. It can look into and through the choice compartments, but cannot enter them until the plexiglas guillotine doors are raised by a vacuum lift. Plywood walls block physical and visual access to choice compartments that are not used in the experiment.

compartments near them. Unused choice compartments were blocked off by plywood walls inserted in place of the plexiglas guillotine doors. After the exposure period, a 10-minute choice trial was given. The plexiglas guillotine doors were raised by a vacuum system; this procedure allowed the subject to enter and reenter choice compartments or to remain in the start compartment. The total time spent in each choice compartment during the test trial was recorded over a closed-circuit TV system.

The monkey's entry into different choice compartments served as our index of social preference. This measure of preference involves visual orientation, but, more importantly, it also involves locomotion toward a specific social object. It may be argued that a measure of viewing time, such as that used by Butler (4) in which monkeys inspected various objects through a small window, is not a proper index of social preference. Although actual physical contact was not available to our subjects, a great deal of nontactile social interaction was possible. Thus, our measure of preference based on physical approach toward a social object seems to be more analogous to an actual social situation than would be a simple viewing response.

Two types of trials were given. In the first, the stranger trial, one stimulus animal from each of the rearing groups was randomly positioned in a stimulus animal cage outside choice compartments 1, 3, or 5. These stimulus animals had received no previous social contact with the test subject but they were the same age and the same sex. A second test was identical with the stranger trial except that the three stimulus animals had received extensive social experience with the test subject during the playroom tests. Before the start of these tests, all 24 subjects had been adapted to the circus during nonsocial exploration tests. The order of serving first as a stimulus animal or as a test subject was randomized across groups.

Analysis of variance of the total time spent in the choice compartment had rearing condition as an uncorrelated variable, and type of stimulus animal and degree of familiarity as correlated variables. Familiarity did not have a significant main effect, and it did not interact with the other variables (all $P > .20$). Rearing condition had a significant effect ($P < .001$), which indicated that total choice time in all compartments differed as a function of early peer contact. Group A subjects

Table 1. Mean number of seconds spent with each type of stimulus animal for each rearing condition, averaged over the two test trials.

Rearing condition of experimental animal	Rearing condition of stimulus animal		
	A (totally deprived)	B (partially deprived)	C (peer-raised)
A (totally deprived)	156	35	29
B (partially deprived)	104	214	103
C (peer-raised)	94	114	260

spent half as much time (average = 220 seconds) in choice compartments as either group B (average = 422 seconds) or group C (average = 468 seconds) monkeys.

The interaction of rearing condition with type of stimulus animal was also significant ($P < .001$). Table 1 shows this effect, with choice times averaged over the trials with strange and familiar stimuli. These data show that like prefers like—each rearing condition produced maximum choice time for the type of stimulus animal reared under that condition. The data for individual subjects supports this averaged effect. In the group A, two of the eight monkeys did not enter choice compartments. Of the six remaining monkeys, five spent more time in the group A choice compartment than in the other two compartments (two-tailed binomial, $P = .038$, with $p = 1/3$, $q = 2/3$). In the groups B and C all subjects en-

tered choice compartments, and seven out of eight in each group spent more time with the animal reared like themselves than with the other animals (both $P = .0038$, two-tailed binomial).

The data indicate that social preferences are influenced by rearing conditions. In playroom testing the group C monkeys were the most active and socially advanced groups studied. Therefore, it was not surprising that they discriminated and showed large preferences for both strange and familiar group C animals. The group A monkeys, however, were highly retarded in their playroom behavior, and they did not show much progress over the 12 weeks of social interaction. As expected, these animals did exhibit a low degree of choice time in this study. We also thought that group A monkeys would be least likely to show preferences for a particular type of animal. It was, therefore, surprising to find that they did prefer each other to animals reared under other conditions. The group B animals, which were intermediate in social adequacy in playroom testing, also preferred each other. This result seems to strengthen the idea that animals of equal social capability, whether or not they are familiar with each other, can discriminate themselves from others, and not only discriminate but approach each other.

These results have important implications for studies designed to rehabilitate primates from the devastating effects of social isolation. The fact that socially abnormal monkeys prefer each other poses difficulties in the design of social environments which contain experiences appropriate for the development of normal social responses. Further, the finding that socially normal monkeys do not choose to approach more abnormal ones compounds the problem of providing therapy for abnormal animals.

These data also have implications for attachment behavior in mammals. Cairnes (5) suggests a learning theory approach to the formation of attachments in which the subject will approach a social object as a function of having made many previous responses while the social object was part of the general stimulus situation. Thus, indices of social attachment toward an object are expected to be higher with increases in the probability that this object occurs as part of the stimulus field in the subject's overall repertoire of responses. Although this seems a reasonable approach, the present data present some difficulties for this view. During rearing, the monkeys in group A did not have the same opportunity to learn the characteristics of other monkeys as did the monkeys in groups B and C. Yet, the monkeys in group A did prefer each other to the alternative choices available. Thus, it is possible that the preference shown by group A monkeys was not based on the conditioning of approach behavior to specific social cues, as is suggested by the stimulus-sampling theory of attachment. It is possible that the behavior of group A was motivated by avoidance of cues contained in the social behavior or countenance of the other two types of monkeys. Thus, there may be at least two distinct kinds of processes in the choice of a social stimulus. The conditioning of specific social cues to the response systems of an animal may be one factor, and the avoidance of nonconditioned cues may be a second important factor in the formation of social attachments.

The specific cues used by the monkeys studied here are not known. Neither do we yet know how our animals differentiated between the stimuli. The discrimination may be based solely on differences in the gross activity of the stimulus animals, or on more subtle and specific social cues. Analysis of the specific stimulus components operating in this situation may clarify the nature of the social cues involved. The important question to be answered is whether the types of cues used in selecting a partner are qualitatively different for different rearing conditions, or whether the same aspects of stimulation are simply weighted differently as a function of an animal's rearing history.

References and Notes

1. H. F. Harlow and M. K. Harlow, *Sci. Amer.* **207**, 136 (1962); G. P. Sackett, *Child Develop.* **36**, 855 (1965).
2. The rearing conditions are described fully by G. P. Sackett, *Science* **154**, 1468 (1966).
3. The playroom situation is described by H. F. Harlow, G. L. Rowland, G. A. Griffin, *Psychiat. Res. Rep.* **19**, 116 (1964).
4. R. A. Butler, *J. Comp. Physiol. Psychol.* **50**, 177 (1957).
5. R. B. Cairns, *Psychol. Rev.* **73**, 409 (1966).
6. Supported by NIMH grant MH-11894.

ARIELLA SHAPIRA & MILLARD C. MADSEN

65 Cooperative and Competitive Behavior of Kibbutz and Urban Children in Israel

Israeli children raised in either kibbutz or urban settings participated in 2 experiments which were designed to assess the degree of cooperative versus competitive behavior of these groups. In the first experiment both groups cooperated adaptively under group reward. With a change from group to individual reward, however, urban children began to compete in a nonadaptive manner, while kibbutz children continued to cooperate. A second experiment, in which competitive responding was more adaptive than in the first, also showed kibbutz children to be less competitive than urban children, but at a marginal level of significance.

Several researchers have attempted to determine the extent of subcultural differences in the cooperative and competitive behavior of children in the United States. McKee and Leader (1955) found preschool children of low socioeconomic level to be more competitive than children of middle-class families. Goodman (1952) found Negro children (age 4) to be more competitive than white children, while Sampson and Kardush (1965) found the opposite to be true with older children (age 7–11). Nelson and Madsen (in press) found no differences in cooperation and competition between Negro and white lower-class and white middle-class 4-year-olds. There are many methodological differences between the above studies, as well as differences of time and place. It is also probably true that subcultural groups in the United States cannot be as rigidly differentiated, with respect to social values and child-rearing practices that give rise to differential interdependent behavior, then is possible in other settings.

In an experimental study of subcultural differences in competitive and cooperative behavior, Madsen (1967) found that both rural and urban poor children in Mexico were dramatically more cooperative than Mexican urban middle-class children. An attempt was made to account for these differences in performance on experimental tasks by reference to the environmental milieu in which the different subcultural groups had developed. The study reported here was carried out in Israel and used the same techniques to compare two other subcultural groups: children from agri-

Reprinted from *Child Development* 40:609–617, 1969. ©1969 by the Society for Research in Child Development, Inc.

The authors are indebted to many Israeli officials and teachers who were, in all cases, very helpful in making subjects and facilities available for the study. The authors are also indebted to Dr. Carolyn Stern for her assistance on all phases of the study. The project was supported, in part, by Office of Economic Opportunity contract No. IED 1-66-12.

cultural social communes (kibbutzim) and those from an urban environment.

Children in an Israeli urban middle-class community are encouraged by parents and teachers to achieve and succeed. Competition is an acceptable means of arriving at this goal. In the kibbutz, on the other hand, children are prepared from an early age to cooperate and work as a group, in keeping with the objectives of communal living. Spiro (1965) found, through questionnaires given to parents in the kibbutz, that generosity and cooperation were the most frequently rewarded behaviors, while selfishness and failure to cooperate were among the behaviors most frequently punished.

The formal teaching methods in the kibbutz are also noted for their minimal emphasis on competitive goals and techniques. Grades and examinations are viewed as unnecessary or even undesirable. Competition, with all its punitive aspects, is far less intense in the classroom of the kibbutz than in that of the city. Not only do the agents of socialization avoid inducing a favorable set toward competition, but also the children themselves develop an attitude against competition. Spiro found that only one out of 28 students saw himself or his peers as being competitively motivated. By far the majority of the students said that their desire was primarily to become equal to their peers or, as Rabin (1965) observed, to raise the achievement level of their group as a whole. Generally, kibbutz children do not accept competition as a socially desirable norm and dislike those who try to excel over members of their own group. This anti-competition attitude is so strong that, according to some teachers, students are ashamed of being consistently at the top of the class. Spiro also found that these cooperative attitudes and behaviors increase with age concomitant with a decrease in competitive motivation.

In line with these basic differences in child-rearing practices and values, it was hypothesized that kibbutz children would be more cooperative than urban middle-class children when playing a social interaction game with their peers.

METHOD

Subjects

The kibbutz sample included 40 children, 20 boys and 20 girls, ages ranging from 6 to 10 years, with a mean age of 8 years. Children from three different kibbutzim were included: Beit Zerah (in the Jordan valley), Beit Hashita (in the Yisrael valley), and Ein Hahoresh (in the Sharon). Both Ein Hahoresh and Beit Zerah belong to the Hashomer Hatzair, a radical socialist movement which is ideologically the most puritanical of all kibbutz movements in Israel. Beit Hashita belongs to Hakibbutz Hameuhad, a relatively more moderate ideological movement. All of the kibbutz children who played the experimental game knew the children with whom they participated. They were usually from the same *kvutza,* a group within a kibbutz comprised of children who spend almost all their time together.

The city sample consisted of 40 children, 20 boys and 20 girls, ages ranging from 6 to 10 years, with a mean age of 8 years. These children were from Mount Carmel, an upper-middle-class community in which most people have a relatively high income. The children, who were spending their vacation at a summer day camp, had already been together for several weeks and therefore knew each other quite well. This particular group of urban children was chosen because they were quite similar to kibbutz children in intelligence and opportunities for development.

In both samples, by far the majority of the children had been born in Israel.

Apparatus

The Madsen Cooperation Board was used. This board is 18 inches square with an eyelet fastened to each of the four corners. Strings strung through each eyelet are connected to a metal weight which serves as a holder for a ball-point pen filler. A sheet of paper is placed on the board for each trial, thus recording the movement of the pen as Ss pull their strings. Because the string passes through the eyelets, any individual child can pull the pen only toward himself. In order to draw a line through the circles, the children must work together. The essential features of the apparatus and position of circles to be crossed can be seen in Figure 1.

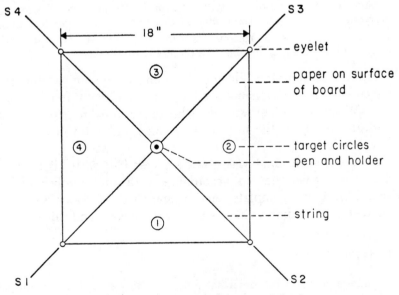

Fig. 1.—Madsen cooperation board

EXPERIMENT I

The purpose of this experiment was to train the Ss in playing the game in a cooperative manner so the children would know how to play cooperatively under the individual reward condition, if motivated to do so. It would also reveal whether there was any pre-existing tendency to behave competitively or cooperatively.

Procedure

Two treatment conditions, Group Reward (GR) and Individual Reward (IR), were compared over three trials. In trials 1–3 (GR), all four children received a prize as soon as the group was able to draw a line through the four circles within the time allowed. In trials 4–6 (IR), each of the four players had his own circle and would receive a prize only when his circle was crossed.

Four children of the same sex and approximately the same age were taken from the group (either kibbutz or city) into a separate room. The experimental board was set on a low table. The four children were seated at the four corners of the board and told that they were going to play a game. The children were instructed to hold on to the handles, one in each hand, and to listen to the instructions of the game.

Instructions for Trials 1–3

As you can see, when we pull the strings, the pen draws lines. In this game we are going to pull the strings and draw lines, but in a special way. The aim of the game is for you to draw a line over the four circles within 1 minute. If you succeed in doing this, each one of you will get a prize. If you cover the four circles twice, everyone will get two prizes, and so on. But if you cover less than four circles no one will get a prize. You may talk to each other but are not allowed to touch another child's string or handle. Are there any questions?

While the children were playing the game, E announced the number of circles crossed and also announced when a round of four circles was completed. When 1 minute was up, the children were stopped and E announced and recorded the number of rounds and extra circles the children had crossed.

At this point each child was given a paper bag with his name on it, and prizes were given out in accordance with the number of rounds completed. Trial 1 was completed and a new sheet of paper was attached to the board. The procedure was repeated for the second and third trials.

Instructions for Trials 4–6

Now the game is going to be somewhat different. Now every one of you gets his own circle. This is David's circle [E writes name on a circle to the right of

David]. This is Ron's circle [etc.]. Now, when the pen draws a line across one of the circles, the child whose name is in the circle gets a prize. When it crosses David's circle, David gets a prize; when it crosses Ron's circle, Ron gets a prize, and so on. You will have 1 minute to play before I stop you. Are there any questions?

During this trial, E announced every time a circle was crossed. When the trial was over, E announced and recorded, for each child, the number of times his circle had been crossed. Prizes were given out accordingly. Trials 5 and 6 followed the same procedure as trial 4.

Results

Figure 2 shows the mean number of circles crossed by the two subcultural samples under the group and individual reward conditions. It was indicated by t tests that there were no significant differences between city and kibbutz groups for any of the three GR trials or for the three trials combined. Similar tests indicated significant differences between these groups after the introduction of individual reward (trial 4, $p < .01$; trials 5 and 6, $p < .05$). Both groups crossed fewer circles on trial 4 than on trial 3. While the average drop from trial 3 to trial 4 for city groups was 10.1 circles, the average drop in the kibbutz was 5.6 circles. This difference in the amount of decrease was significant at the .05 level (t test).

Observation indicated that this lowered performance occurred for different reasons. On trial 4, most city groups began competing, thus reducing drastically the number of circles crossed. The kibbutz groups, on the other hand, simply slowed down. The reason for this could have been either because they made an effort to avoid competition or because they were adjusting to the new rules as if it were a different game. It can also be seen from Figure 2 that the kibbutz groups recovered on trials 5 and 6, whereas the city groups never regained the level of performance attained under the GR condition.

The same pattern of results occurred for both sexes. The mean circles crossed by boys and girls under GR within both groups was nearly identical. However, the difference between kibbutz and city groups under the IR condition was greater for the boys. The mean circles crossed by urban boys was 30.6 fewer than by kibbutz boys, whereas the urban girls crossed a mean of 12.8 fewer circles than the kibbutz girls (trials and Ss collapsed).

EXPERIMENT II

The purpose of this experiment was to compare the behavior of kibbutz and city children in a situation where competition is an adaptive behavior. Since in this situation the circles were at the corners of the page, it was possible for a competitive child to win more prizes than the others

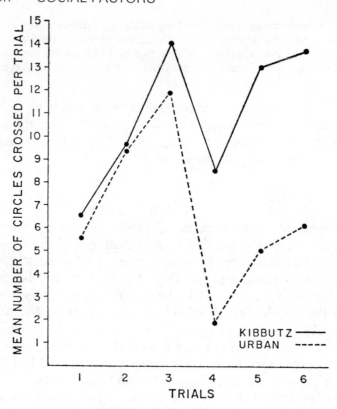

Fɪɢ. 2.—Mean number of circles crossed per trial by kibbutz and urban children.

by pulling the string sharply toward himself and drawing a line through his own circle.

Procedure

The circles were drawn at the corners of the page so that each child had a circle directly in front of him. The following instructions were given:

As you see, the circles are now at the corners of the page. This time the game is somewhat different so listen carefully. Again everyone has his own circle. [*E* writes each child's name in the circle closest to him.] Now, when the pen draws a line across the circle of one of the children, that child will get a prize. At this point, we shall stop the game and return the pen to the center of the page and begin again. We will do this four times without changing the page. Are there any questions?

When a line was drawn across one of the circles, *E* stopped the game and recorded the time of the trial and the order. The child whose circle was crossed received a prize. The same procedure was carried out for trials 2, 3, and 4. If no circle was crossed within a minute, *E* stopped the game and began a new trial.

When the experiment was over, E gave prizes to those children who had not won many during the game, so that all children received about the same number of prizes. Although the prizes were of little value (candy, gum, and small plastic charms) they were effective reinforcers, as demonstrated by the children's eagerness to work for them.

Results

Any line which passed through an individual circle without deviating more than 1 inch from the direct path from the center starting point to the circle, and which did not reverse directions within those limits, was considered a noncompetitive response. Lines which violated these criteria were considered competitive in that they indicated that children were pulling against each other.

Table 1 gives the mean number of noncompetitive responses for four trials for the two groups, by sex.

Kibbutz groups had more noncompetitive responses than urban groups (mean 2.6 vs. 1.4, respectively), but this difference only approaches significance ($t = 1.70\ p < .05 < .10$).

Most of the differences between kibbutz and city groups can be attributed to the fact that the city boys were more competitive than city girls as well as both boys and girls from the kibbutzim.

DISCUSSION

The hypothesis that kibbutz children would show more cooperative behavior than city children in Israel was confirmed. Under the individual reward condition in Experiment I, the kibbutz children showed performance superior to that of the city children. Since both groups had learned the task equally well, as evidenced by their similar performances under the group reward condition, differences in performance under the individual reward condition can be attributed to different types of motivational stress in urban and kibbutz environments. Thus, changes in instructions produced different behaviors in city children but not in kibbutz children. The slight improvement in performance for kibbutz groups under the individual reward condition probably reflects the effect of practice as the children continue to follow the cooperative techniques adopted under the group reward condition. Once reward was given out on an individual basis,

TABLE 1

MEAN NONCOMPETITIVE RESPONSES FOR KIBBUTZ AND URBAN CHILDREN BY SEX

Group	Female	Male
Kibbutz...........	2.8	2.4
Urban............	2.2	0.6

city children changed the tactics they had used to obtain group rewards and began pulling toward themselves. Even though they obviously realized, after trials 4 and 5, that these competitive procedures were not paying off for any of them, they were unable to stop their irrational competition.

Perhaps of greater interest is the fact that the children themselves did not enjoy the competition and wanted to change the rules. A number of children kept asking E not to write names on the circles, evidently realizing that as long as there were names on the circles they would continue to compete.

At times a child would suggest that they take turns, or help each other, but usually the other children refused. In some isolated cases, the children agreed to cooperate, but the instant one child pulled a little harder, cooperation broke down completely and they all started pulling toward themselves.

Among the kibbutz groups the picture was entirely different. When individual reward instructions were introduced, the first response of most of the groups was to set up rules for cooperation. Some examples of these responses were: "OK gang, let's go in turns," or "Let's help each other," or "We'll start here, then here," etc. Some groups asked E if they were allowed to help each other or whether they could go in rounds like before. When E said they could do as they wished, they always decided upon cooperation. These children were very organized in their performance. They usually had decided the order before the trial began. During the game they were also very active in directing one another.

The kibbutz children were very eager to do well as a group and tried their best to improve their performance on every subsequent trial. Some of the groups asked to compare their results with other groups and wanted to know what the best score had ever been. Such responses indicate that a desire to achieve and to do well characterizes these children, who do compete with other groups on the kibbutz but not within their group. At the group level, they cooperate and work together as a team.

In most of the kibbutz groups there was a great concern about equality in prizes ("Every one should get the same"). They were so concerned about this that, in many cases, they rotated the starting point so that if they were stopped before a round was completed a different child would get the extra prize on each trial. When, in some isolated cases, one of the children tried to compete against the others, the group usually restrained him.

In general, the results and observations indicate that, when cooperative behavior was adaptive, children of the kibbutz were generally able to cooperate successfully for maximum performance, whereas urban children were usually not able to do so.

Many aspects of kibbutz life and collective education are potentially competitive. The children of the kibbutz, more than those of the city, must compete for the nurses' attention and affection, must compete for the toys they play with, etc. It is possible that because of this, the development of cooperative tendencies is so instrumental to proper functioning of the group and that, without such a development, conflict would be exceptionally severe.

REFERENCES

Goodman, M. E. *Race awareness in young children.* Cambridge, Mass.: Addison-Wesley, 1952.

McKee, J. P., & Leader, F. The relationship of socioeconomic status and aggression to the competitive behavior of preschool children. *Child Development,* 1955, **26,** 175–182.

Madsen, M. C. Cooperative and competitive motivation of children in three Mexican subcultures. *Psychological Reports,* 1967, **20,** 1307–1320.

Nelson, L., & Madsen, M. C. Cooperation and competition in four-year-olds as a function of availability of reward and subculture. *Developmental Psychology,* in press.

Rabin, A. I. *Growing up in the kibbutz.* New York: Springer, 1965.

Sampson, E. E., & Kardush, M. Age, sex, class, and race differences in response to a two-person non-zero-sum game. *Journal of Conflict Resolution,* 1965, **9,** 212–220.

Spiro, M. E. *Children of the kibbutz.* Cambridge, Mass.: Harvard University Press, 1965.

INDEX

A

Abstract thinking: development of, 344-54

Acidosis: in diabetic children, 42-43, 45

Ack, Marvin, 22

Acoustic priming: for audiogenic seizures in mice, 26-27

Adoptive homes: effect on institutionalized children, 307

Adrenal cortex response, infantile: maternal influence on, 400

Adrenogenital syndrome: effect on behavior of human females, 149-56

Affective behavior: maternal influence on, 400

Age: chronological, 7-8
  and development, 20
  ontogenetic, 8-9
  and responsiveness to gonadal hormones, 118
  See also Critical periods

Aggression: effect of early experience on, 277
  effect of gonadal (sex) hormones on, 113-14, 129-33
  maternal influence on, 400-01, 403-11
  social factors affecting, 442-43

Alarm reaction, 355-56

Amino acids: necessity in diet, 166

Androgen-insensitivity syndrome, 150

Androgens: effect on sexual behavior, 116, 118-20, 130-33, 149-56

Animals: comparison with humans, 1-7
  measures of intelligence of, 313, 315-22, 342-43

Anomalies, genetic: and study of human development, 51-52

Anxiety, maternal: effect on offspring, 85-89, 107-10
  See also Emotionality

Appetitive (positive) conditioning: in puppies, 207

Approach behavior: correlation with gazing, in human infants, 425-33

Auditory deprivation: effects of, 254, 258-66

Auditory stimulus: cardiac response of fetuses to, 99-106

Audiogenic seizures: susceptibility of mice to, 21-22, 25-27, 98

Aversive (negative) conditioning: in puppies, 207-08

Avoidance learning: effect of handling on, 28-30

B

Babies. *See* Infants

Bayley, Nancy, 255

Behavior: genetic factors affecting, 48-84
  psychological, 5-6
  sex differences in, 417-19
  sexual. *See* Sexual behavior
  social factors affecting, 442-44
  species-specific, 4-5

Biobehavioral factors: in development, 1-14

Blank, Marion, 314

Body weight: effect of infantile stimulation on, 357, 371, 393-95
  effect of maternal emotionality on, 405-06

Bowlby, John, 399

Brain, development of: effect of enriched environment on, 312-15
  effect of prenatal malnutrition on, 170-75
  effect of sex hormones on, 113-14
  visual cortex of, modification by visual stimuli, 240-45
  See also Nervous system

Breeds (of dogs), differential responses of:
  to neonatal conditioning, 205, 208-09
  to training, 51, 66-68